Cancún, Cozumel & the Yucatán

Greg Benchwick

LEGEND

	Tollway
	Freeway
	Primary Road
	Secondary Road
	Tertiary Road
	Unsealed Road

0 ——— 100 km
0 ——— 60 miles

ELEVATION

3200m
2400m
1600m
800m
400m
200m
Sea Level

MÉRIDA (p149)
Stroll the colonial-era
streets of the peninsula's
cultural capital

CAMPECHE (p203)
Wander the cobblestone
streets of this immaculately
preserved colonial masterpiece

EDZNÁ (p214)
Get up early to visit the
2600-year-old House of the Itzáes
and a handful of neighboring ruins

**LAGUNA DE
TÉRMINOS (p219)**
Kayak through the mangrove swamps
of this vast coastal estuary, spotting
birds and turtles on your way

CALAKMUL (p222)
Explore this mysterious Maya
complex ensconced in Mexico's
largest wildlife reserve

PALENQUE (p238)
Discover the architectural
marvels of the ancient jungle
realm of King Pakal

**SAN CRISTÓBAL DE
LAS CASAS (p231)**
Witness the modern Maya
work and worship in this
resplendent cultural crossroads

Gulf of Mexico

Progres

Reserva de la
Biósfera Ría Sisal   Dzibilchal
Celestún

MÉRIDA

MEX
281   Umán

Celestún

MEX
261

Bécal

Uxmal

Ruta
Puuc

MEX
180

Bolonchén
de Rejón

CAMPECHE

Hopelchén

Dzibilnocac

Edzná Dzibalchén

Champotón   Hoch

MEX
180

Campeche

MEX
261

Puerto
Real

Ciudad del
Carmen

Laguna de
Términos   Escárcega

MEX
186   Beca

Reserva de
Biósfera
Candelaria   Calakmul

Comalcalco   Calak

Comalcalco

La Venta   Tabasco   Río Candelaria

MEX
180   La Venta

Cárdenas   Candelaria

Reforma   MEX
186
VILLAHERMOSA

Emiliano Zapata
Pichucalco   Teapa

Catazajá

Palenque   Palenque   Tenosique

Veracruz   MEX
195

MEXICO   Agua
Azul   MEX
199

Tikal

Río Grijalva   Lago
de Petén
Cañón del   Soyaló   Yaxchilán   Itzá
Ocozocoautla Sumidero   Ocosingo   Frontera Corozal Flores
Oaxaca   San Cristóbal Toniná   Bethel   Santa Elena
Juiquipilas   de Las Casas
TUXTLA   Bonampak
GUTIÉRREZ Chiapa   Amatenango   Reserva de la
de Corzo   del Valle   Biósfera Montes   Sayaxché
MEX   Azules
190   MEXICO
MEX
195   Comitán
Chiapas
Arriaga   Lagos de
Montebello
Tonalá   Fray Bartol
de Las Cas
Presa la   MEX
Puerto Arista   Angostura   190
GUATEMALA
MEX
Boca del   200   Parque Nacional
Cielo   Pijijiapan   Cordillera de los Cuchumatanes Laguna Lachuá
Cobán
PACIFIC OCEAN   5

Mapastepec   Río Polochic
El Soconusco Escuintla   Sierra de
Tacaná
(4110m)   El Progreso
Huixtla Tuxtla   Sololá   (Guastatoya) Chiquimu
Chico
Izapa   Lago de
Tapachula   Quetzaltenango   Atitlán
Ciudad Hidalgo Maza-
tenango   GUATEMALA
CITY

IZAMAL (p185)
Visit Maya pyramids, 16th-century convents and local artisan workshops in the Yellow City

RÍO LAGARTOS (p198)
Flamingos, river crocs, herons and more, easily reached from a laid-back fishing village far off the tourist track

ISLA MUJERES (p88)
Gleaming coral beaches arch into azure seas in this low-fi tropical paradise

PLAYA DEL CARMEN (p102)
The Riviera Maya's toniest Caribbean outpost offers amazing day trips to crystalline cenotes, spectacular diving and an 800-year-old ruin or two

CHICHÉN ITZÁ (p186)
A towering nine-tiered Maya-Totec pyramid presides over this modern wonder of the world

RESERVA DE LA BIÓSFERA SIAN KA'AN (p133)
Create your own adventure in this dreadlocked wilderness of mangroves, salt, sea and sun

XCALAK (p137)
Desolate, remote beaches and world-class bird-watching ensure a bit of solitude in Yucatán's most visited state

KOHUNLICH (p146)
Beat your own path to this massive Maya complex famous for its masks (Indiana Jones would be proud)

Río Lagartos
Isla Holbox
Isla Contoy
Reserva de la Biósfera Ría Lagartos
Chiquilá
Isla Mujeres
Tizimín
Cancún
Isla Mujeres
MEX 180
Punta Cancún
Izamal
Kantunil
Puerto Morelos
nceh
Cuzamá
Chichén Itzá
MEX 180D
Valladolid
Playa del Carmen
ayapán
MEX 180
Cobá
Isla Cozumel
Yucatán
Tulum
San Miguel de Cozumel
MEX 295
Tulum
Santa Rosa
Laguna Chichancanab
Palancar Reef
Bahía de la Ascensión
Felipe Carrillo Puerto
MEX 307
Bahía del Espíritu Santo
naben
Quintana Roo
Laguna Ohlec
Nohbec
Laguna Bacalar
Reserva de la Biósfera Sian Ka'an
MEXICO
Mahahual
nil
Dzibanché
CHETUMAL
Banco Chinchorro
CARIBBEAN SEA
ujil
Río Bec
Kohunlich
Corozal
Xcalak
Orange Walk
San Pedro
BELIZE
Belize River
Belize City
Turneffe Islands
BELMOPAN
Melchor de Mencos
Dangriga
Mountain Pine Ridge
Maya Mountains
Hopkins
BELIZE
Placencia
stún
a Izobel
Punta Gorda
Glover's Reef
Puerto Cortés
Lívingston
Puerto Barrios
Golfo de Honduras
Río Dulce
El Golfete
Lago de Izabal
Río Motagua
9
San Pedro Sula
Río Ulúa
Yoro
HONDURAS
Lago de Yojoa
uipulas

On the Road

GREG BENCHWICK

Fighting off the heavy-duty headache from a night of partying in Playa del Carmen, I headed over to Cristalino Cenote (see boxed text, p119) with my girlfriend, Alejandra. Cenotes (limestone sinkholes) are a remarkable geological oddity you won't see in many other places in the world, and nearly every stop on my research trip included an excursion to a cenote. By the way, yes, this is as tan as it gets.

MY FAVORITE TRIP

I kick off my favorite trip from the tony, affluent suburbs of Mérida (p149) – my girlfriend, Alejandra, was raised here, so I get to stay with her

really cool friends for free when I pass through town. Ale's friend Laura even penned a short feature (see boxed text, p161) on her favorite restaurants in town. I spend a day or two be-bopping around Mérida's colonial center (trying to time my trip right to be here on Sunday when they close the downtown streets, giving performers, artisans and food vendors reign over the Plaza Grande). Then I head out early to the low-lying ruins along the Ruta Puuc (p172). While the massive pyramid and ornate architecture of Uxmal (p167) is quite impressive, I normally skip it, instead heading out into the Maya countryside to visit villages not listed in the guidebook. Here, beyond the 'Lonely Planet Trail' (see boxed text, p175), you catch glimpses of contemporary Maya life (see boxed text, p178). They are a proud, elusive and resilient people – and honestly, they are still a mystery to me. Maybe I'll gain some more insight on my next trip.

See full author bios, page 293

HIDDEN TREASURES OF THE YUCATÁN PENINSULA

Caught between the relentless beat of progress and the echoes of tradition, the Yucatán Peninsula stands at a crossroads. On one side you have the brawny, glitzy megaresorts, on the other are the proud, steadfast traditions of the Maya; the shadows and mystery of the pyramids and ceremonial centers created by their ancestors; and the old-world allure of colonial masterpieces like Mérida and Campeche. And in between – on every peroxide-blonde beach and every patch of jungle still echoing with the roars of howler monkeys – beats the heart of Ixchel, the earth goddess, as she marvels at her remarkable creation.

From the Deep Blue Depths

From the deep blue rises the Mesoamerican Reef, the second-largest barrier reef in the world, making the Caribbean coast a diving and snorkeling destination par excellence. But you don't need to head out on a boat to revel in the whirlwind of marine life that calls the reef home: several ocean-front lagoons and cenotes offer spectacular swimming and diving accessible straight from terra firma.

Author Tip

Skip all the gear, and head out for a morning swim anywhere on the Caribbean coast: you'll be amazed at what you find. And the salt water makes treading water a snap, even for consummate doggie-paddlers like yours truly.

❶ Punta Sur

Alice in Wonderland coral formations, eagle rays, moray eels, lobsters and the Devil's Throat glide past on one of Cozumel's top dives, Punta Sur (see boxed text, p113).

❷ Laguna Yal-Kú

A chic snorkeling spot complete with a tasteful sculpture garden, Akumal's Laguna Yal-Kú (p120) is home to parrot fish, barracuda and an array of darting triggers.

❸ Cenote Angelita

Soar like an angel as you descend through Cenote Angelita's (p123) otherworldly hydrogen sulfide fogs. It's the closèst you'll ever get to flying (especially 50m underground!).

❹ Banco Chinchorro

Hurricane Dean may have pummeled the offshore atoll of Banco Chinchorro (p137) to a pulp. Or, there may be early growth on the once resplendent landward reef. Be the first in your PADI class to find out.

❺ Valladolid's Cenotes

There's a handful of lovely underground cenotes (p194) found within biking distance of Valladolid. Head out for a picnic lunch and a swim.

Natural Wonders

Despite overzealous development, the natural beauty of the chalkboard-flat Yucatán Peninsula abides. The ethereal coo of the mot-mot still reverberates overhead, while below continue to writhe the insects and creepy-crawlies that keep this scrub-jungle land renewed year after year. And deep below, in the realm of Ah Puch (god of the underworld), gurgle freshwater rivers that pull their way through massive limestone caverns all the way to the pitch-perfect waters of the Caribbean and the Gulf.

① Parque Nacional Isla Contoy

A stone's throw from the megaresorts of Cancún, the island preserve of Parque Nacional Isla Contoy (p96) gives shelter to more than 100 birds of a feather, including olive cormorants and brown boobies.

② Reserva de la Biósfera Sian Ka'an

A remote wilderness reserve on the Caribbean coast, Reserva de la Biósfera Sian Ka'an (p133) is a vast mangrove-clogged lagoon home to an amazing diversity of avian species. The amazing desolate beaches on the way there aren't bad either.

③ Reserva de la Biósfera Calakmul

Mexico's largest ecological preserve, Reserva de la Biósfera Calakmul (p222) offers the best chance in the country of seeing a jaguar. Get up early and you're sure to spot a handful of toucans and maybe a gobbling ocellated turkey.

④ Selva Lacandona

With 4300 plant species, 450 distinct butterfly species, 340 different birds and 163 mammals, the remote area of Selva Lacandona (Lacandon Jungle; see boxed text, p242) in

Chiapas is a biodiversity powerhouse. Logging and prospecting are taking their toll. See what you can do to turn the tide.

⑤ Reserva de la Biósfera Ría Celestún

Flamingos congregate in a riot of pink (oh yes, Molly Ringwald is green with envy) in the ancient mangrove forest of the Reserva de la Biósfera Ría Celestún (p180).

⑥ Cenotes de Cuzamá

You can't really enjoy the natural beauty of the peninsula without a dip in an aqua-blue limestone sinkhole. And the series of three cenotes at Cenotes de Cuzamá (p175) reached by horse-drawn rail cart are some of the most beautiful around.

⑦ Reserva de la Biósfera Ría Lagartos

Glimpse harpy eagles, river crocs and more flamingos than anywhere else in Mexico in the Gulf Coast estuary of Reserva de la Biósfera Ría Lagartos (p198).

⑧ Isla Mujeres' Playa Norte

Wait for mañana to dawn on the coral beach of Playa Norte (p90). The Caribbean waters are so warm and welcoming, you'll feel like you're swimming in Bacchus' goblet.

A Foodie's Delight

The Maya are said to be made from corn. And it's only fitting that their major staple is, in fact, maize. They grind it for tortillas, and prod it into tamales. They put it in drinks and stews, and send it to the gods at *ch'a chaak* planting ceremonies. They even offer it, with a bit of honey for good favor, to the *aluxes* (forest gnomes) that are said to roam the countryside. While much of the regional cuisine finds its base in other parts of Mexico, Yucatán will always have its corn.

Author Tip
Got the desire to whip up a feast with local produce? You can save big bucks by self-catering. There's a market in every town, a cultural crossroads of sorts that makes a great spot for people-watching.

❶ Catch of the Day
There's terrific seafood in every corner of the peninsula. Fry it, batter it, drench it in garlic or eat it raw – no matter the preparation, the end result remains the same: gastronomical bliss.

❷ I'll Take that Pibil
Yucatecans are famous for their chicken and pork *pibiles*. Wrapped in banana leaves and cooked underground for what seems an eternity, this traditional dish will melt away like butter.

❸ Nectar of the Gods
The Maya have always been proud of their honey. And throughout the countryside you'll come across little roadside stands selling the sweetest, goldest, lip-smackinest nectar this side of the Río Grande.

❹ Got Taco, Will Travel
In the large towns there's a taco stand on every corner. If you have a delicate constitution, you may wish to skip them, but if your insides are forged from iron, then you can't go wrong with an M$8 meal.

❺ Dos Cervezas, Por Favor
You really don't need much more Spanish than this. Of course, it doesn't hurt. In the countryside be bold, ask for a *balché* brew, a fermented treat made from tree bark and honey.

La Vita Activa

While the Yucatán is certainly known for its Poseidon adventures, there's plenty to do both on land and sea for folks that don't know the difference between PADI and PETA. The thick jungle makes long treks a Promethean endeavor: but hell, the conquistadors did it, didn't they? And the numerous coastal lagoons make great spots for sea-kayaking adventures. Heavy winds beat the north coast each year, making for amazing kiteboarding and windsurfing (all you'll need to do is find a board!).

'Yucatán is known for its Poseidon adventures'

Author Tip
Put this book down for a day (hell, even a week)
and see where your adventurous spirit takes you. I
know it sounds like I'm writing myself out of a job,
but we love to see people push beyond these pages
and blaze their own paths.

① Swim with Whale Sharks off Isla Holbox

Sure the Gulf waters are a bit cloudy, but
Isla Holbox (see boxed text, p97) offers the
unique opportunity to swim with whale
sharks, the largest fish in the ocean.

② Kayak Through the Misty Dawn near Xcalak

You're likely to see parakeets, kingfishers,
peccaries, storks and more as you quietly
glide through the mangrove lagoon near
Xcalak (p137). Head out later in the day for
a beachcombing expedition along an amazing arc of brown-sugar beach.

③ Camp on the Shore of Laguna Bacalar

The sun blazes above you as you camp out
along the shores of the 60km-long freshwater Laguna Bacalar (p139). The white-sand
bottom creates amazing visibility and makes
for good afternoon swims.

④ Simply Arrive at Río Bec

Test your mettle as you try to find the remote
Maya ruin of Rio Bec (see boxed text, p226)
in the backwoods of southern Campeche.
The rewards are simple: you'll probably be
the only one there.

⑤ Cycle Cozumel

Lean into the wind as you circumnavigate
the Caribbean Isla Cozumel (p108) in a day,
stopping at Maya ruins, fantasy lagoon water
parks and even a Rasta bar.

⑥ Kiteboard Progreso

You may need to bring your own gear, but
the consistent winds at Progreso (p183) off
the Gulf Coast are enough to push you to
25 knots.

14

Whispers from the Past

Around here, the past is the present and the present is the past: the two intermingle, toil and tangle eternally like brawling brothers. You'll witness it in the towering temples of the Maya, Toltec and Itza, in the coiling cobblestone streets of colonial centers, and in the sagacious smiles of southern Mexico's native sons and daughters, the Maya.

Author Tip

It's really easy to take day trips to mega archaeological sites like Chichén Itzá, Uxmal and Edzná, but by staying in the local communities near the sites you are more likely to have a positive impact on the local economy, and thus create a more sustainable model for tourism in the region.

❶ Cobá's Nohoch Mul

The towering big mound or great pyramid of Cobá (p130) is well worth the ascent. As you look out, just imagine that this city-state once covered some 50 sq km and held around 40,000 Maya.

❷ Tulum's Seafront Views

Although the city was of little historic importance, Tulum (p122; pictured on p16) is worth a visit for its sea-swept views and picturesque palace.

❸ The Talking Cross of Felipe Carrillo Puerto

There's little to do in the quiet Maya town of Felipe Carrillo Puerto (p135), but see the talking cross that kicked off the War of the Castes (see boxed text, p37). Some folks in the region still believe the war can be won.

❹ Palenque's Jungle Kingdom

Ascend to the jungle-and-mist-shrouded ruins of Palenque (p240). The superlative Templo de las Inscripciones was built in the late 7th century, and still stands, relatively intact, today.

❺ Pirate Tales of Campeche

Walk along the ramparts of the walled colonial city of Campeche (p207), imagining the wave of terror reigned down by the likes of Hawkins, Barbillas and Pegleg himself.

❻ Worship the Sun at Dzibilchaltún

The sun aligns perfectly with the doorway of the Templo de las Siete Muñecas (p182) in Dzibilchaltún on the spring and fall equinoxes.

❼ Fight the Crowds at Chichén Itzá

The feathered serpent, Kulkulcán, reveals himself on the side of the massive pyramid El Castillo (p188) at Chichén Itzá on the equinoxes. Get there a few days before or after to avoid the crowds and still enjoy the show.

❽ Discover History's Present

Head out into the Maya hinterlands outside Ticul (p176) to discover the simple and rather profound lifestyle of the modern Maya.

The Mayan ruins at Tulum (p122) enjoy a postcard-perfect Caribbean backdrop

Contents

Regional Map Contents

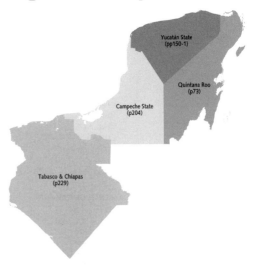

Yucatán State
(pp150-1)

Quintana Roo
(p73)

Campeche State
(p204)

Tabasco & Chiapas
(p229)

Destination Yucatán

Natural disasters have been wreaking havoc throughout Yucatán, Tabasco and Chiapas in recent years. It's not a new story – after all, this is Hurricane Alley – but it's a sad and noteworthy one.

Massive storms along the Gulf Coast caused nearly 80% of Tabasco to flood in late 2007 (see boxed text, p228). Hundreds of thousands of people were displaced, a large, 11,700-barrel oil spill contaminated portions of the Bay of Campeche, and landslides wiped out villages and roads in both Tabasco and Chiapas. If that wasn't bad enough, just months earlier Hurricane Dean romped into town, literally obliterating the southern Quintana Roo town of Mahahual (see boxed text, p133). The state capital of Chetumal also suffered damage at the muscular, sinewy hands of Dean.

The real-estate developers seem to be taking this all in their stride, using the broken infrastructure (Hurricane Wilma tromped through just a few years back, laying waste to much of the Riviera Maya) as an excuse to build bigger. Throughout the peninsula you see massive tourist development, condos are being built faster than they can be sold along the Caribbean and northern Gulf Coasts, and several plans are in place to create new cruise-ship docks along the Quintana Roo coast. But tourism development isn't all bad: it brings in much-needed revenue lost after the recent natural disasters. And some grass-roots organizations are starting to develop low-impact cultural tourism (see boxed text, p99) in the small Maya communities that dot the peninsula.

The country's presidential elections of 2006 were highly contested, with just-right-of-center Felipe Calderón Hinojosa taking over the reins from Vicente Fox. The election kicked off protests nationwide, with the opposition candidate, Andrés Manuel López Obrador, going as far as setting up an alternative government in protest against the close-call election. But things have simmered down since then. Folks seem ready to let the matter fade into history, focusing on the other problems still facing the region.

One of the biggest issues of the day is drug trafficking. Cancún has seen an explosive growth in violence tied to the drug trade. According to news reports, the city is being used as a *puente* (bridge) to bring cocaine from South America into the US. While the violence has yet to affect tourists (honestly, drug runners would rather not draw attention to themselves), it has become a serious problem here and elsewhere in Mexico. There seem to be more drug checkpoints throughout the region than there were just a few years ago, with Presidente Calderón mobilizing the military to take the fight to the traffickers.

Immigration and poverty are also hot-button topics being discussed across the peninsula. It's not just immigration to the US or the fast-growing *maquiladora* (low-paying, export-only factories) industry being talked about, it's also about immigrants coming here from Central America seeking work and perhaps a safe haven from the growing gang violence and rampant poverty plaguing the northern states of the isthmus. There have even been a few rafts turning up in Isla Mujeres from Cuba. There have also been a few shocking reports of child trafficking, primarily for sexual purposes, in the region.

But all news isn't bad news. In Chiapas, the revolutionary Zapatistas (see boxed text, p234) have quieted and pacified in recent years, making travel to this remote highland region a possibility even for mainstream tourists. Chichén Itzá, the massive Maya-Toltec site in eastern Yucatán state, was voted one of the 'Seven Modern Wonders of the World,' and the first Yucatec-Maya-language Hollywood film, *Apocalypto,* hit the silver screen in 2006, bringing both fame and infamy to the region.

FAST FACTS

Population: 3.7 million (peninsular states only)

Annual population growth: 4.7% Quintana Roo, 1.6% Campeche & Yucatán states (national 1.1%)

Area: 148,961 sq km

Percentage of national territory: 7.1%

Length of coastline: 1764km

GDP per person: M$12,218 Yucatán, M$22,159 Quintana Roo, M$24,838 Campeche (national M$15,243)

Number of foreign tourists in 2005: 5.8 million (Quintana Roo 5.2 million)

Adult literacy: 91.6%

Percentage of national oil production: 60%

Remittances from US employment: approx US$150 million

Getting Started

A journey to the Yucatán Peninsula, Tabasco or Chiapas doesn't necessarily require much advance planning. Apart from the peak periods mentioned below, just check flight times, grab your passport and you're on your way. Outside the limited peak seasons, there's little competition for accommodations, and transportation around the peninsula is cheap and frequent. Perhaps your best pretrip preparation would be to learn some Spanish – every word you know will make your trip that little bit easier and more enjoyable. See p54 and p282 for some words and phrases.

For the most part, Yucatán is no more dangerous than any major Western city. Stay street savvy, don't wear expensive jewelry, and keep in mind that the locals (especially in Chiapas) are not on display (see Traveling Responsibly, p22).

WHEN TO GO

See Climate Charts (p251) for more information.

Any time is a good time to visit the Yucatán, though perhaps the best time is during November and early December, as there are fewer tourists and prices are relatively low. September and October can be equally low-key unless a hurricane decides to pass through (see below). May to September are the months with the highest rainfall and highest temperatures, with May and June being the hottest, muggiest months. The highlands of Chiapas can get downright cold at night.

The occasional *norte* (storm bringing wind and rain from the north) can cool things off considerably for brief spells between November and February. This makes for more pleasant ruins exploration but may delay plans for snorkeling or beachcombing. Birding and wildlife-watching are good year-round, and mid-May through mid-September is the time to come to glimpse whale sharks (see boxed text, p97).

July and August are peak holiday months for both Mexicans and foreigners, as is mid-December to early January. A week either side of Easter is also a peak holiday period for Mexicans. At these times the coastal resorts attract big crowds, room prices go up in popular places, and rooms and public transportation can be heavily booked, so advance reservations are advisable. In addition, Cancún is swamped with reveling young US college students during spring break (late February to early March).

If a full-blown hurricane is predicted for the region you are in, go somewhere else – fast! At the very least go inland, far from the dangerous sea swell that invariably accompanies hurricanes. The **National Hurricane Center** (www .nhc.noaa.gov) has up-to-date info.

COSTS & MONEY

With the exception of the resort areas of the Caribbean coast (often referred to as the Riviera Maya), travel in Yucatán is still fairly inexpensive. Things get even cheaper in Chiapas, though Tabasco, with its fancy oil money, can be a bit pricey. Midrange travelers can live well in most parts of the peninsula for M$600 to M$1000 per person per day. Two people can usually find a clean, comfortable room with private bathroom and fan or air-conditioning for M$400 to M$600, and use the rest to pay for food (a full lunch or dinner in a typical decent restaurant costs around M$100 to M$150), admission fees, transport and incidentals. Budget travelers should allot M$250 to M$500 each per day for accommodations and two meals a day in cheap restaurants. Add in other costs (like contracting a guide or taking a snorkeling trip) and you'll spend more like M$500 to M$700.

Rates in the Riviera Maya can easily cost twice as much as this. Cancún is the most expensive town in Mexico, and Playa del Carmen and Cozumel are not far behind. In those places, a pair of travelers can expect to pay M$600 to M$1000 for a decent room – way more during high season.

Car-rental costs (including the mandatory third-party insurance) start around M$300 to M$500 per day, plus fuel (book ahead over the internet to save a bundle). Extra expenses, such as internal airfares, tours and shopping, will of course push your expenses up, but if there are two or more of you, overall costs per person drop considerably. Double rooms often cost only a few dollars more than singles, and triple or family rooms only a few dollars more than doubles. Children aged under 13 pay reduced prices on many buses and flights, and at some sights and attractions.

Top-end hotels and resorts run a wide spectrum of prices, often charging upwards of M$2000 for a room. Restaurants in the same class can charge M$500 per person, and are largely targeted at the tourist trade. In most cases you're better off eating at locals' joints.

TRAVEL LITERATURE

Incidents of Travel in Central America, Chiapas & Yucatan and *Incidents of Travel in Yucatan,* by John L Stephens, are fascinating accounts of adventure and discovery by the enthusiastic 19th-century amateur archaeologist. Both books contain superb illustrations by architect Frederick Catherwood, who accompanied Stephens in 1839 and 1841 as he explored a large part of the Maya region.

Aldous Huxley traveled through Mexico, too; *Beyond the Mexique Bay,* first published in 1934, has interesting observations on the Maya. Also interesting is Graham Greene's *The Lawless Roads,* chronicling the writer's travels through Chiapas and Tabasco in 1938.

Time Among the Maya: Travels in Belize, Guatemala, and Mexico, by Ronald Wright, is a thoughtful account of numerous journeys made among the descendants of the ancient Maya and will certainly help you to get a feel for Maya culture as you travel the region.

Most of the Maya codices were destroyed during the conquest (only four exist today), but *The Books of Chilam Balam,* written by a Maya prophet

---

LONELY PLANET INDEX

1L petrol M$6.70

1L bottle of water M$10

Bottle of beer M$20

Souvenir T-shirt M$80-100

Street taco M$8-10

HOW MUCH?

One-person hammock M$200

1kg freshly made tortillas M$7

Small rental car per day M$300-500

Internet per hour M$10

Major museum or archaeological site M$34

DON'T LEAVE HOME WITHOUT...

- Checking your foreign ministry's Mexico travel information (p252)
- All the necessary paperwork if you're driving into Mexico (p269)
- Clothes to cope with Yucatán's air-conditioned rooms (and buses) or the occasional cool, windy evening in *norte* (storm bringing wind and rain from the north) season (opposite)
- Any necessary immunizations or medications you require, including contraceptives (p276)
- A flashlight (torch) for some of those not-so-well-lit streets, stairways, caves or pyramid chambers – and for power outages
- An inconspicuous container for money and valuables, such as a small, slim wallet or an under-the-clothes pouch or money belt (p252)
- Your favorite sunglasses
- A small padlock
- A small Spanish dictionary and/or phrasebook
- Adequate travel insurance (p276)
- Mosquito repellent and a mosquito net if you plan to do any outdoor sleeping

during the late 15th century, chronicles much of the oral traditions and legends of the Yucatec Maya. It's a rather obscure read, and you're better off checking out the Guatemalan Quiche Maya sacred text known as the *Popol Vuh*. Michael Coe's *The Maya* is the definitive history text of these people.

TRAVELING RESPONSIBLY

Traveling sustainably is all the rage these days. But how sustainable can you actually get? After all you'll probably fly here, putting a bunch of harmful carbon dioxide into the atmosphere, and tourism creates all sorts of nasty side effects, like the homogenization of cultures, the loss of language and the degradation of the environment. But traveling can still be a good thing, right? Of course it can: it's a revenue generator, a valuable cultural interchange, an awareness builder that can often serve to protect the environment and, above all, it's fun! This book has a handy GreenDex (p309), which will lead you to some sustainable choices. Also check out 'Small Footprints, Large Impact' (p63).

Getting There & Around

While carbon offsets for your flight will not save the world, they are a good first step. There are a ton of companies out there. Lonely Planet offsets its travel through www.climatecare.org. Consider targeting your trip to lower your environmental footprint. You don't have to see all of the peninsula in one visit.

Accommodations & Food

One of the quickest ways to create a more sustainable future for tourism is by avoiding the big chain hotels and restaurants. Most of the profit gets siphoned out of the country. Also consider staying in the smaller towns that you normally would have visited on a day trip. The added revenue serves as an incentive for folks to stay in their native village, maintain their language and customs, and skip out on that job in the big city. The Maya culture has long been an insular one, but folks living in the countryside are now realizing that tourism may be key to maintaining their traditions. With this is mind, many small communities are now welcoming tourists. It's a great way to create a positive impact, and it also puts you on the edge of experiential travel.

Respect 'til the End

According to leading Mayanologist Michael Coe, the single largest threat to the Maya culture and language is tourism. So how can we as travelers help protect cultures and environments at risk of extinction? It's all about respect. Respect the locals, try to learn some of their language, respect the environment and its sanctity. And, above all, respect your mother!

Internet Resources

- **Blue Flag** (www.blueflag.org) An ecocreditation program that focuses on marinas and beaches.
- **Caribbean Sustainable Tourism Alliance** (www.cha-cast.com) Focuses mainly on the Caribbean, but also has some good reef ecology info.
- **Coral Reef Alliance** (www.coral.org) Has reef protection guidelines.
- **Green Globe** (www.greenglobe.org) For general information.
- **International Ecotourism Society** (www.ecotourism.org) Lists ecofriendly businesses that have jumped through the hoops to gain accreditation.
- **Mexican Adventure & Ecotourism Association** (www.amtave.org) Lists some of the region's ecotourism operators.
- **Mexiconservacion** (www.mexiconservacion.org) Has a green guide to the Yucatán.
- **Puerte Verde** (www.puertaverde.com.mx, in Spanish) Developing agro-tourism in Quintana Roo.
- **Responsibletravel.com** (www.responsibletravel.com) For general information.

TOP 10

FIESTAS

Consider planning your itinerary around one or more of these colorful festivals.

1 Día de los Reyes Magos (Three Kings' Day; p254), best experienced in Tizimín. First week of January.

2 Carnaval (Carnival), celebrated most wildly in Mérida (p158), Campeche (p208), Chetumal (p140) and Ciudad del Carmen (p220). Late February or early March.

3 Vernal Equinox, Chichén Itzá (p186) and Dzibilchaltún (p182). March 20 to 21.

4 Semana Santa (Holy Week), particularly colorful in Mérida (p158) and San Cristóbal de Las Casas (p235). Palm Sunday to Easter Sunday.

5 Feria de Santiago, Río Lagartos (see boxed text, p199). Second Saturday in July.

6 Festival de Nuestra Señora de Carmen, Ciudad del Carmen (p220). July 16.

7 Feria de San Román, Campeche (p208). September 14.

8 Festival Cervantino Barroco, San Cristóbal de las Casas (p235). Late October to early November.

9 Toh Festival de Aves de Yucatán (Birds Festival), Mérida and other points on the peninsula (p59). Last week of November.

10 Día de Nuestra Señora de Guadalupe (Day of Our Lady of Guadalupe), Campeche (p208). December 12.

WILDLIFE-WATCHING SPOTS

1 Reserva de la Biósfera Ría Celestún (p180) Prime destination for birders.

2 Laguna de Términos (p219) Huge freshwater lagoon where birds flock and marine turtles nest.

3 Reserva de la Biósfera Calakmul (p222) Jaguars, eagles and simians roam the tropical forest and archaeological zone.

4 Cozumel (p108) Jumping-off point for the Great Maya Barrier Reef, with astoundingly varied marine life.

5 Reserva de la Biósfera Sian Ka'an (p133) Vast wildlife habitat encompassing tropical forest and coral reefs.

6 Punta Laguna (p132) Secluded lake frequented by spider and howler monkeys.

7 Reserva de la Biósfera Ría Lagartos (p198) Wetlands haven for thousands of flamingos and a few crocodiles.

8 Parque Nacional Isla Contoy (p96) Island seabird sanctuary.

9 Chiapas' Selva Lacandón (see boxed text, p242) Megadiverse, though endangered, section of jungle.

10 Reserva de la Biósfera Pantanos de Centla (p230) Manatees, monkeys and mangroves.

MAYA RUINS

1 Chichén Itzá (p186) Modern 'Wonder of the World,' with amazing architecture and perhaps the world's largest calendar.

2 Uxmal (p167) The Puuc region's crown jewel.

3 Palenque (p240) Showcase of Maya art and architecture in wonderful jungle setting.

4 Cobá (p129) Explore a largely unexcavated city.

5 Calakmul (p222) Tikal's archrival, deep in the tropical forest.

6 Tulum (p122) Majestic temple overlooking the Caribbean.

7 Becán (p224) Moated military compound with beautiful examples of Río Bec architecture.

8 Dzibilchaltún (p182) Comes to fiery life during the equinox.

9 Edzná (p214) Totally as cool as Uxmal with about half the visitors.

10 Ek' Balam (p196) Restored and unrestored ruins with well-preserved stucco paintings.

INTERNET RESOURCES

Campeche Travel (www.campechetravel.com) Campeche State Tourism Board site.

Lonely Planet (www.lonelyplanet.com)

Maya Yucatán (www.mayayucatan.com.mx) Yucatán State Tourism Board site.

Riviera Maya (www.rivieramaya.com) Has info on the Riviera Maya's sights and activities. There's also a handy calendar on the home page.

Yucatán Today (www.yucatantoday.com) Online version of free monthly magazine covering Yucatán and Campeche states.

The other introductory chapters in this book contain more online possibilities.

Itineraries
CLASSIC ROUTES

CANCÚN & THE RIVIERA MAYA   Five to 12 Days

With just a few days in **Cancún** (p72), start off at the suicidal-blonde beaches of the **Zona Hotelera** (p76). Take a trip to **Isla Mujeres** (p88) for some fine snorkeling or diving. Then try something different: a cenote (limestone sinkhole), such as **Siete Bocas** (p100) near Puerto Morelos. You'll definitely want to visit a Maya ruin; **Cobá** (p129), **Chichén Itzá** (p186) or **Tulum** (p122) make easy day trips. Then slip over to **Isla Holbox** (p96), where you can lie back in a hammock or snorkel with whale sharks.

With another week you can cover a lot of ground or take it slow. Either way, head south to **Puerto Morelos** (p99) for a peek at its artisans market, then to uberchic **Playa del Carmen** (p102), which makes a great base camp for day trips to **Isla Cozumel** (p108), where you'll enjoy amazing diving and snorkeling. Then head south to **Tulum** (p122), where you can recharge on one of the most perfect beaches and visit the ruins.

This easy 150km to 300km trip stays close to Cancún and the Riviera Maya coastline, letting you duck out to beaches, go shopping, visit cenotes and Maya ruins, and simply relax.

ONCE UPON A TIME IN THE YUCATÁN
Two to Three Weeks

This trip is a mix of Caribbean coast, natural wonders, antique Maya artistry and culturally vibrant cities. **Cancún** (p72) is the region's gateway, but those in search of less glitzy pleasures should push on. Get in some snorkeling at the beach-fringed island of **Isla Mujeres** (p88). Then hug the coast to the more low-key resort of **Playa del Carmen** (p102), which provides easy access to **Isla Cozumel** (p108) and adjacent Great Maya Barrier Reef. Further south you reach **Tulum** (p122), with its stunning Maya temple facing the Caribbean.

When you've had your fill of sun and sea, strike inland. Visit the major Maya ceremonial center of **Cobá** (p129) on the way to **Valladolid** (p193), a relaxed colonial town in an area speckled with azure cenotes. From there, it's a brief hop to world-renowned **Chichén Itzá** (p186), where the plumed serpent of the Toltec civilization reigns supreme. Stop in the small Maya villages along the way as you head to **Mérida** (p149), where you'll enjoy traditional music and dance in the plazas, shop for embroidered clothing and dine on classic cuisine. Mérida makes a good base for trips to magnificent **Uxmal** (p167) and other Maya sites along the **Ruta Puuc** (p172), the colonial city of **Izamal** (p185) to the east and the laid-back Gulf resort of **Progreso** (p183). From Mérida, many travelers head to the walled colonial city of **Campeche** (p203) on their way to the jungles of Chiapas to admire the ruins of **Palenque** (p240), ending their trip in the contemporary Maya enclave of **San Cristóbal de Las Casas** (p231).

The 940km grand tour follows the Caribbean coast, then traverses the temple-studded heartland to Mérida, the peninsular capital, before heading off into the jungles of Chiapas and the extraordinary ruins at Palenque.

ROADS LESS TRAVELED

INCIDENTS OF TRAVEL IN CAMPECHE   Two Weeks

While tourists crowd the coastal resorts of Quintana Roo, Campeche state remains wide open to exploration. From **Chetumal** (p140) follow the highway into Campeche, a green corridor passing some of the peninsula's most fascinating, remote ruins. Base yourself in **Xpujil** (p224) – or better, **Zoh-Laguna** (p225), a lagoon community north of the highway – to survey these marvels, much as travelers Stephens and Catherwood did in the mid-19th century. Take a day to visit **Calakmul** (p222), a sprawling site ensconced within the Reserva de Biósfera de la Calakmul, and another day for the secluded ruins of **Río Bec** (see boxed text, p226), whose secrets are still being uncovered.

The road north from Xpujil traverses a landscape of corn and beehives with a string of tranquil villages alongside Maya ruins, such as **Dzibilnocac** (p217) and **Hochob** (p217). Stay in **Hopelchén** (p216) to better appreciate these eerie marvels as well as some extensive caves, the **Grutas de Xtacumbilxuna'an** (p217). Travel westward to **Campeche** (p203), the historically rich state capital, then follow the Gulf Coast southwest. Spend some time in **Sabancuy** (p219), a delightful fishing village on an estuary with easy access to deserted Gulf beaches. Proceed along the protected wetlands and bird sanctuary that make up **Laguna de Términos** (p219) to **Ciudad del Carmen** (p220), an island city known for its seafood and midsummer festival. To the west stretches the **Atasta Peninsula** (p221), a lush tropical strip that's a jumping-off point for boat trips around the wildlife-rich mangrove islets.

Phantasmagoric Maya monuments, pristine tropical forest, birder-friendly coastal wetlands and the magnificently restored colonial state capital highlight this fascinating 600km journey through 'the other Yucatán.'

TAILORED TRIPS

WHERE THE WILD THINGS ROAM

The peninsula has some amazing wildlife-watching opportunities, and most of these are found well off the beaten path. What's better, you pass through some really cool Maya towns along the way.

Leave Cancún as soon as possible, heading out for a day trip to the bird sanctuary of **Isla Contoy** (p96). From here it's off to the wilds. Swing up to the Gulf fishing towns of **Río Lagartos** (p198) and **San Felipe** (p200), a staging point to visit the **Reserva de la Biósfera Ría Lagartos** (p198), where you'll spot thousands of pink flamingos, crocs, herons and more. The bold can consider some DIY camping on the coast here.

Skip the major highways as you travel the backloads across Yucatán state to the **Reserva de la Biósfera Ría Celestún** (p180), staying in the super-chill town of **Celestún** (p179). After recharging your batteries for a day or two, taking the time to visit the mangrove swamps easily reachable from town, head down toward Campeche state through the **Ruined Haciendas Route** (p182).

With a few more weeks, you can head down through the **Chenes Ruins** (p217) to Mexico's largest wildlife preserve, **Reserva de la Biósfera Calakmul** (p222). Spend a few days camping out, visiting the ruins and exploring the wild, dreadlocked jungle before you spin eastward toward Quintana Roo.

As you head north through Quintana Roo, stop in the massive inland **Laguna Bacalar** (p139), a great off-track spot for camping and kayaking. Then it's up to **Punta Allen** (p134) for a few days of kayaking, fishing or mangrove trips through the remote **Reserva de la Biósfera Sian Ka'an** (p133). Once again, skip the major roads as you head back to Cancún, opting instead to visit **Punta Laguna** (p132) and the other **forgotten Maya villages** (see 'Off the Map –Alternative Tourism on the Rise in Quintana Roo,' p99) of the region.

MOSTLY MAYA

The architectural and artistic achievements of the Classic Maya period are dotted across the peninsula. Though the ancient cities are long abandoned, the Maya people and their traditions are still very much with us.

For background, visit the **Museo de la Arquitectura Maya** (p205) in Campeche or the **Museo de la Cultura Maya** (p141) in Chetumal. Near Campeche is **Edzná** (p214), a formidable Maya site with a five-story temple. Further east are the Chenes sites of **Dzibilnocac** (p217) and **Hochob** (p217), which have temples displaying macabre masks. Maya is widely spoken here, and you can witness the ancient arts of beekeeping and herbal medicine in **Hopelchén** (p216). To the north, the Puuc hills lend their name to an architectural style, magnificently represented by **Uxmal** (p167)! A route then leads through the villages of **Ticul** (p176),

Oxkutzcab (p178) and **Tekax** (p179), offering glimpses of traditional Maya life. Toward Valladolid is the must-see Unesco World Heritage site of **Chichén Itzá** (p186). In **Tihosuco** (p179), a museum outlines the Yucatán's definitive conflict, the War of the Castes. On the Caribbean coast, the Maya city of **Tulum** (p122) provides a mysterious backdrop for modern sun devotees.

The peninsula's south harbors numerous fascinating but scarcely visited remnants of Classic Maya civilization ensconced in the vast **Reserva de la Biósfera Calakmul** (p222). Serious Maya buffs will want to extend their explorations to the ruins of **Palenque** (p240) and the contemporary Maya domain of **San Cristóbal de Las Casas** (p231).

SUN WORSHIPPERS

Soak up rays in **Cancún** (p72), be it poolside or on a sandy, white, wave-washed beach. Then take a ferry to **Isla Mujeres** (p88) and soak up some more. Head south to **Puerto Morelos** (p99) if you like quiet, or to **Playa del Carmen** (p102) if you don't. At **Tulum** (p122) you get the best of both sun-worshipping worlds: coral-sand beaches, azure water and Maya ruins overlooking it all. When you're happy with your tan, leave the coast and check out **Cobá** (p129) and **Ek' Balam** (p196). Plan your trip for an equinox to really do full justice to **Chichén Itzá** (p186) and **Dzibilchaltún** (p182), both of which have curious solar displays. **Celestún** (p179) brings you back to the beach. From there, hit **Uxmal** (p167) and the **Ruta Puuc** (p172) for awe-inspiring insights into the Maya mind, then 'sunspire' yourself again at **Isla Aguada** (p219) and **Puerto Ceiba** (see boxed text, p231). Take a few days to visit **Palenque** (p238) and its spectacular tower, El Palacio, where Maya royals watched the sun fall onto the Templo de los Inscripciones, or head back east through **Becán** (p224), **Calakmul** (p222), **Kohunlich** (p146) and **Dzibanché** (p145).

DIVER'S & SNORKELER'S DREAM

Diving and snorkeling along the Yucatán Peninsula is probably as addictive as some of the substances you get offered from shifty guys lurking in a Cancún alleyway. Snorkelers can tag along to many of the following spots, as even after Hurricanes Wilma and Dean, many shallow spots are still spectacular. Divers must – yes, *must* – head to **Isla Cozumel** (p108) for a peek at one of the wonders Cousteau brought to the world's attention. The Santa Rosa Wall (p113) is Cozumel's most famous dive – you'll only see one-third of the wall's amazing sights with one tank. Snorkelers and novice divers should head to the Colombia shallows (p113) for great visibility and some of the area's most spectacular coral formations. If you tire of diving the reefs and walls there (you won't), cross to the mainland for a cenote dive at **Angelita** (p123) or **Dos Ojos** (p121). It's an otherworldly experience. A good place to organize a trip to the cenotes (and do some snorkeling) is **Tulum** (p122). Then head south to **Mahahual** (p136) or the remoter **Xcalak** (p137) for trips out to **Banco Chinchorro** (p137).

History

In the Yucatán, history is never kept in the past. It ebbs and flows through every aspect of modern life, like a thousand-limbed juggernaut hell-bent on its own preservation. From the beginning, it's been a tale of inequality, predation and subjugation; intellectual and spiritual triumph; independence, fame and famine. And, of course, like just about everywhere else in the world, it's mostly been a tale of greed.

While Europe was sliding into the Dark Ages, the people of the Yucatán had already reached what is arguably the pinnacle of New World civilization. The conquest and eventual subjugation of the Maya created vast riches for the landed elite as the region continued to develop independently from the rest of Mexico – though it could not help but be influenced by its powerful neighbor. More recently it has faced a different sort of cultural revolution with mass tourism taking deep root along the coast. Still, beyond Cancún's glitzy façade beats the syncopated pulse of an ancient culture charting its delicate course through the tendriled pathways of history.

For a concise but pretty complete account of the ancient cultures of southern Mexico and Guatemala, read The Maya, by Michael D Coe.

EARLY AMERICANS

Conventional wisdom holds that humans arrived in the Americas from Siberia around 40,000 years ago, via a land bridge across the Bering Strait that connected present-day Alaska with Asia. Recent evidence dates human presence in Mexico's central plateau to roughly 13,000 years ago, and the Yucatán was probably populated a few millennia later. By 5700 BC people were planting maize (corn) in the Tehuacán valley in what is now Puebla state.

By 2000 BC many Mesoamericans (peoples between present-day central Mexico and Nicaragua) were cultivating corn, squash, avocados and beans, and raising chickens, turkeys and dogs. They continued to hunt and fish as they had for generations, but they became dependent upon crops.

The jaguar motifs first used by the Olmecs were adopted by successive civilizations throughout Mesoamerica.

Mexico's ancestral civilization arose near the Gulf Coast, in the humid lowlands of southern Veracruz and neighboring Tabasco. These were the Olmecs, who invented a hieroglyphic writing system and erected ceremonial centers for the practice of religious rituals. Best known for the colossal heads they carved from basalt slabs, the Olmecs developed an artistic style, highlighted by jaguar motifs.

Even after their demise, aspects of Olmec culture lived on among their neighbors, paving the way for the later accomplishments of Maya art, architecture and science. Borrowing significantly from the Olmecs, the Zapotec culture arose in the highlands of Oaxaca at Monte Albán, and subsequent civilizations at Teotihuacán (near current-day Mexico City) and at El Tajín in northern Veracruz also show Olmec influence.

TIMELINE

up to 10,000 BC	3114 BC	2400 BC
The first humans arrive in the Yucatán region. The numbers of grassland animals dwindle as temperatures significantly increase over the next 2000 years, leading indigenous populations to begin larger-scale agriculture.	Our current universe is created – at least according to Maya mythology. Archaeologists have even been able to pin down a specific date for the creation: August 13, 3114 BC.	Maya-speaking farmers arrive in the Yucatán Peninsula, while elsewhere in Mexico more developed 'civilization' is beginning to take root. The Olmec culture creates a system of writing. Olmec culture later influences the Zapotec culture.

YUCATÁN'S DINOSAUR-KILLING METEORITE

For the past two decades there has been growing scientific agreement that a meteorite slammed into the Yucatán 65 million years ago, kicking up enough debris to block out the sun for a decade, which either triggered a global freeze or made the air so unbreathable that two-thirds of the earth's species became extinct.

In 1980 scientists theorized that the extinction of the dinosaurs had been caused by an 'impact event,' such as a meteor crash. Using seismic monitoring equipment, scientists found evidence for the existence of such an enormous crater off the northern coast of Yucatán near the port of Chicxulub.

ENTER THE MAYA

Archaeologists believe Maya-speaking people first appeared in the highlands of Guatemala as early as 2500 BC, and in the following century groups of Maya relocated to the lowlands of the Yucatán Peninsula.

Agriculture played an increasingly important role in Maya life. Watching the skies and noting the movements of the planets and stars, the Maya were able to correlate their astronomical observations with the rains and agricultural cycles. As the Maya improved their agricultural skills, their society stratified into various classes and occupations. Villages sprang up beneath the jungle canopy and temples were constructed from the abundant limestone. An easily carved substance, limestone allowed the builders to demonstrate a high degree of artistic expression. The material could also be made into plaster, upon which artists painted murals to chronicle events.

Local potentates were buried beneath these elaborate temples. As each successive leader had to have a bigger temple, larger platforms were placed upon earlier ones, forming gigantic step pyramids with a thatched shelter on top. Often these temple-pyramids were decorated with huge stylized masks. More and more pyramids were built around large plazas, much as the common people clustered their thatched houses facing a common open space. This heralded the flourishing of the Classic Maya civilization.

> Mundo Maya online (www.mayadiscovery.com) features articles on Maya cosmology, navigation and agriculture, among other aspects of this incredible ancient civilization.

The Golden Age

Over the six centuries of the Classic Maya period (AD 250 to 925), the Maya made spectacular intellectual and artistic strides, a legacy that can still be admired today throughout the peninsula. The great ceremonial centers at Copán, Tikal, Yaxchilán (p243), Palenque (p238), and especially Kaminaljuyú (near present-day Guatemala City), flourished during the early phase of this period. Around AD 400 armies from Teotihuacán invaded the Maya highlands, imposing their rule and their culture for a time, though they were finally absorbed into the daily life of the Maya, a marriage that engendered the so-called Esperanza culture.

> The elite of the Classic Maya often received enemas of a sweet mead name balché. They also thought being cross-eyed was particularly beautiful.

1000 BC–AD 250	AD 250–925	925–1530
The Pre-Classic period. The earliest Maya villages begin to form in Yucatán, Chiapas and Guatemala. The Maya have become adept farmers and astronomers. The Izapan civilization creates a calendar and writing system and massive pyramids are built.	The Classic period. It's a time of high society, marked by the invasion of the Teotihuacán, the rise of the Puuc, and the eventual collapse of the Classic Maya and the ascendancy of the Toltec.	The Post-Classic period. The bellicose Toltecs of central Mexico establish their domain at Chichén Itzá, then the Itzáes form the League of Mayapán, which dominates politics in northern Yucatán for a couple hundred years.

Chronicle of the Maya Kings and Queens, by Simon Martin and Nikolai Grube, tells in superbly illustrated detail the histories of 11 of the most important Maya city-states and their rulers.

After AD 600, at the height of the Late Classic period, the Maya lands were ruled not as an empire but as a collection of independent, but also inter-dependent, city-states. Each of these had its noble house, headed by a king who was the social, political and religious focus of the city's life. This ruler propitiated the gods by shedding his blood in ceremonies where he pierced his tongue or penis with a sharp instrument, and led his soldiers into battle against rival cities, capturing prisoners for use in human sacrifices.

Toward the end of the Classic period, the focus of Maya civilization shifted northward to Yucatán, where new nuclei developed at what is now called Chichén Itzá (p186), Uxmal (p167) and Calakmul (p222), giving us the artistic styles known as Puuc, Chenes and Río Bec.

POST-CLASSIC PERIOD
The Toltecs

The collapse of Classic Maya civilization is as surprising as it was sudden. It seems as though the upper classes demanded ever more servants, acolytes and laborers, and though the Maya population was growing rapidly, it did not furnish enough farmers to feed everyone. Thus weakened, the Maya were prey to the next wave of invaders from central Mexico.

In the wake of Teotihuacán's demise, the Toltec people emerged as Mexico's new boss, establishing their capital at Tula (north of present-day Mexico City). According to most historians, a Toltec faction, led by a fair-haired, bearded king named Topiltzin – the self-proclaimed heir to the title of Quetzalcóatl (Plumed Serpent) – was forced to leave its native land by hostile warrior clans. Quetzalcóatl and his followers retreated to the Gulf Coast and sailed eastward to Yucatán, establishing their new base at Uucil-abnal – the land that would be Chichén Itzá. The culture at this Toltec-dominated center flourished after the late 10th century, when all of the great buildings were constructed, but by 1200 the city was abandoned. Many Mexicans believed, however, that the Plumed Serpent king would someday return from the direction of the rising sun to reclaim his domain at Tula.

The Itzáes

Check www.sacred-texts .com for good translations of two sacred Maya books, the *Popul Vuh* and *Chilam Balam of Chumayel.*

Forced by invaders to leave their traditional homeland on the Yucatán's Gulf Coast, a group called the Itzáes headed southeast into northeastern Guatemala. Some continued to Belize, later making their way north along the coast and into northern Yucatán, where they settled at the abandoned Uucil-abnal around AD 1220. The Itzá leader styled himself Kukulcán (the Maya name for Quetzalcóatl), as had the city's Toltec founder, and recycled lots of other Toltec lore as well. The Itzáes strengthened the belief in the sacred nature of cenotes (the natural limestone sinkholes that provided

late 15th century	1492	1519–21
The beginning of the end of the Post-Classic period. The decline of the Maya hits full tilt, as fractious city-states replace Mayapán rule. Until the coming of the conquistadors, northern Yucatán is riddled with battles and power struggles.	Spanish arrive in the Caribbean, settling momentarily on His-pañola and Cuba, but it will be several hundred years before they truly 'conquer' the region. European diseases will eventually kill 90% of Native American inhabitants.	Hernán Cortés, first landing on Isla Cozumel, begins making his way along the Gulf Coast toward central Mexico, home of the Aztec empire. He captures the Aztec ruler Moctezuma II and conquers Tenochtitlán.

the Maya with their water supply), and they even named their new home Chichén Itzá (Mouth of the Well of the Itzáes).

From Chichén Itzá, the ruling Itzáes traveled westwards and founded a new capital city at Mayapán, which dominated the political life of northern Yucatán for several hundred years. (For more on the rise of Mayapán, see boxed text, p174.) From Mayapán, the Cocom lineage of the Itzáes ruled a fractious collection of Yucatecan city-states until the mid-15th century, when a subject people from Uxmal, the Xiú, overthrew Cocom power. Mayapán was pillaged, ruined and never repopulated. For the next century, until the coming of the conquistadors, northern Yucatán was alive with battles and power struggles among its city-states.

Back in the 1500s traveling Maya merchants would burn incense nightly on their journeys as an offering for safe passage to the god Ek-chuah.

THE NEW WORLD ORDER

Led by Christopher Columbus, the Spanish arrived in the Caribbean in 1492 and proceeded to seek a westward passage to Asia. They staged exploratory expeditions to the Yucatán in 1517 and 1518, but hostile natives fiercely resisted their attempts to penetrate Mexico's Gulf Coast.

Then Diego Velázquez, the governor of Cuba, asked his ambitious young personal secretary, Hernán Cortés, to lead a new expedition westward. Even though Velázquez subsequently tried to cancel the voyage, Cortés set sail on February 15, 1519, with 11 ships, 550 men and 16 horses.

Landing first at the isle of Cozumel off the Yucatán, the Spaniards were joined by Jerónimo de Aguilar, a Spanish priest who had been shipwrecked there several years earlier. With Aguilar acting as translator and guide, Cortés' force moved west along the coast to Tabasco. After defeating the inhabitants there, the expedition headed inland, winning more battles and some converts to Christianity as it went.

More than 66.5 million Native Americans died within 150 years of the arrival of Columbus, according to some estimates.

Central Mexico was then dominated by the Aztec empire from its capital of Tenochtitlán (now Mexico City). The Aztecs, like many other cultures in the area, believed that Quetzalcóatl would one day return from the east, according to most historians, and – conveniently for him – Cortés' arrival coincided with their prophecies of the Plumed Serpent's return. The Aztecs allowed the small Spanish force into the capital, perhaps fearful of angering these strangers who might be gods.

By this time thousands of members of the Aztecs' subject peoples had allied with Cortés, eager to throw off the harsh rule imposed by their overlords. Many Aztecs died of smallpox introduced by the Spanish, and by the time they resolved to make war against Cortés and their subjects, they found themselves outnumbered and were defeated, though not without putting up a tremendous fight.

Legend has it that the peninsula got its name when the Spanish conquistadors asked the natives what they called their land. The response was 'Yucatán' – Maya for 'We don't understand you.'

Cortés then conquered central Mexico, after which he turned his attentions to the Yucatán.

1527	1530–1821	1542
Francisco de Montejo and his son (the Younger) land in Cozumel and then in Xel-Há with the idea of conquering the region. Eventually they return to Mexico City in defeat.	The *encomienda* system is put in place, basically enslaving the native populations, and friars begin to convert the population in earnest. The Maya blend Christian teachings with their own beliefs, creating a unique belief system.	Francisco de Montejo (the Younger) and his cousin (also a Francisco de Montejo) avenges his father's legacy, establishing the colonial capital at Mérida upon the ruins of the Maya city of T'ho.

CONQUEST & THE COLONIAL PERIOD (1530–1821)
Francisco de Montejo Sr & Jr

Despite political infighting among the Yucatecan Maya, conquest by the Spaniards was not easy. The Spanish monarch commissioned Francisco de Montejo (El Adelantado, or the Pioneer) with the task, and he set out from Spain in 1527 accompanied by his son, also named Francisco de Montejo (El Mozo, or the Lad) and a band of men. Landing first at Cozumel, then at Xel-Há on the mainland, the Montejos discovered that the local people wanted nothing to do with them.

The father-and-son team then sailed around the peninsula, conquered Tabasco (1530) and established their base near Campeche, which could easily be supplied with provisions, arms and troops from central Mexico. They pushed inland to conquer, but after four long, difficult years they were forced to return to Mexico City in defeat.

The younger Montejo took up the cause again, with his father's support, and in 1540 returned to Campeche with his cousin named…Francisco de Montejo. The two Montejos pressed inland with speed and success, allying themselves with the Xiú against the Cocomes, defeating the Cocomes and converting the Xiú to Christianity.

The Montejos founded Mérida in 1542 and within four years subjugated almost all of Yucatán to Spanish rule. The once proud and independent Maya became peons, working for Spanish masters without hope of deliverance except in heaven. The conquerors' attitude toward the indigenous peoples is graphically depicted in the reliefs on the façade of the Montejo mansion in Mérida: in one scene, armor-clad conquistadors are shown with their feet holding down ugly, hairy, club-wielding savages.

The Maya lands were divided into large fiefdoms of sorts, called *encomiendas,* and the Maya living on the lands were mercilessly exploited by the landowning *encomenderos.* 'They inflicted outrageous cruelty on the Indians, cutting off their noses, arms and legs; they cut the breasts off the women and threw them into deep lagoons with gourds tied to their feet,' wrote Friar Diego de Landa in *An Account of the Things of Yucatán.* 'They wounded children with spearthrusts because they could not walk as fast as their mothers.'

With the coming of Dominican Friar Bartolomé de Las Casas and groups of Franciscan and Augustinian friars, things improved a little for the Maya. In many cases the clergymen were able to protect the local people from the worst abuses, but exploitation was still the general rule.

INDEPENDENCE FOR SOME

During the colonial period Spain's New World was a highly stratified society. Native Spaniards were at the very top; next were the criollos, people born in the New World of Spanish stock; below them were the mestizos or *ladinos,*

When the indigenous Xiú leader was baptized, he was made to take a Christian name, so he chose what must have appeared to him to be the most popular name of the entire 16th century – and became Francisco de Montejo Xiú.

1562	1810–21	1847–48
Franciscan Friar Diego de Landa orders the destruction of 27 codices and more than 5000 idols in Maní, essentially cutting the historic record of the Maya by the root.	The beginning of the War of Independence from Spain. The state of Yucatán joins the newly independent Mexican republic. The Maya remain a subjugated people. Yucatán will declare independence from Mexico in 1841.	The War of the Castes erupts. The Maya are whipped pretty solidly at first, retreating to Quintana Roo. They will continue to revolt for another 100 years, though an official surrender is signed in 1936.

FRIAR DIEGO DE LANDA

The Maya recorded information about their history, customs and ceremonies in beautifully painted picture books made of beaten-bark paper coated with fine lime plaster. These codices, as they are known, must have numbered in the hundreds when the conquistadors and missionary friars first arrived in the Maya lands. But because the ancient rites of the Maya were seen as a threat to the adoption and retention of Christianity, the priceless books were set aflame upon the orders of the Franciscans. Only four of the painted books survive today, but these provide much insight into ancient Maya life.

Among those Franciscans directly responsible for the burning of the Maya books was the inquisitor Friar Diego de Landa, who, in July of 1562 at Maní (near present-day Ticul), ordered the destruction of 27 'hieroglyphic rolls' and 5000 idols. He also had a few Maya burned to death for good measure.

Though despised by the Maya for destroying their cultural records, it was Friar de Landa who wrote the most important existing book on Maya customs and practices – the source for much of what we know about the Maya. Recalled to Spain for displaying a degree of zeal that even the clerical authorities found unwarranted, he was put on trial for his excesses. He was ordered to jot down everything he knew about the Maya. These scribblings resulted in a book, *Relación de las Cosas de Yucatán* (An Account of the Things of Yucatán), which covers virtually every aspect of Maya life as it was in the 1560s, from Maya houses, food, drink, and wedding and funeral customs, to the calendar and the counting system.

people of mixed Spanish and indigenous blood; and at the bottom were the pure-race indigenous people and blacks. Only the native Spaniards had real power – a fact deeply resented by the criollos.

The harshness of Spanish rule resulted in frequent revolts, none of them successful for long. In 1810 the disgruntled criollo priest Miguel Hidalgo y Costilla delivered his legendary *grito de Dolores*, a cry for independence, from his church near Guanajuato, inciting his parishioners to revolt. With his lieutenant, a mestizo priest named José María Morelos, he brought large areas of central Mexico under his control. But this rebellion, like earlier ones, failed. The power of Spain was too great.

When Napoleon deposed Spain's King Ferdinand VII and put his brother Joseph Bonaparte on the throne of Spain in 1808, criollos in many New World colonies took the opportunity to rise in revolt. By 1821 both Mexico and Guatemala had proclaimed their independence. The state of Yucatán, which at that time encompassed the entire peninsula, joined the Mexican union that same year.

Though independence brought new prosperity to the criollos, it worsened the lot of the Maya. The end of Spanish rule meant that the Crown's few liberal safeguards, which had afforded the Maya minimal protection from the most extreme forms of exploitation, were abandoned. Maya

Of the illustrated Maya books called codices, only four survive to the present day: the Dresden Codex, Madrid Codex, Paris Codex and Grolier Codex.

1850–93	1876–1911	1901
An independent Maya republic is established with its capital at Chan Santa Cruz. The war wages on, with the Maya (getting arms from the British) winning key victories. Britain stops arming the Indians in 1893.	The porfiriato – the name given to the era of Porfirio Díaz' 35-year rule as president-dictator, preceding the Mexican Revolution. Under Díaz, the country is brought into the industrial age.	The Mexican army under Porfirio Díaz recaptures the Maya-controlled territory, executing many Maya leaders and destroying the shrine of the talking cross in Chan Santa Cruz. Guerrilla raids continue for more than 20 years.

claims to ancestral lands were largely ignored and huge plantations were created for the cultivation of tobacco, sugarcane and henequen (a plant yielding rope fiber). The Maya, though legally free, were enslaved by peonage to the great landowners.

The Caste War of Yucatán, by Nelson Reed, is a page-turning account of the modern Maya's insurrection against the criollo elite and the establishment of an independent state.

WAR OF THE CASTES
Beginnings

Just 20 years after independence Yucatán's local government voted to break away from the union. Mexican president Santa Anna sent in troops in 1843 but Yucatán's forces managed to stave them off. Economic isolation proved to be a more powerful incentive to return to the fold, however, and a treaty was signed with Mexico that same year. But, charging that Mexico had failed to honor promised treaty concessions, Yucatán again declared independence in 1846.

For the Yucatec Maya, independence from Mexico made little difference – they remained subordinate to a white elite – and insurrection was never far off. In January 1847 indigenous rebels attacked Valladolid, rampaging through the city in an orgy of killing and looting. Now alerted, the Hispanic authorities caught a Maya *batab* (community leader) with a letter detailing a plot to attack the town of Tihosuco (in present-day Quintana Roo). He was shot at Valladolid. Undaunted, the plotters attacked the town of Tepich, south of Tihosuco, killing several criollo families. Thus began the War of the Castes, which the rebels next took to Tihosuco. Supplied with arms and ammunition by the British through Belize, they spread relentlessly across the Yucatán, and in March 1848 the rebels took Valladolid.

In little more than a year, the Maya revolutionaries had driven their oppressors from every part of the Yucatán except Mérida and the walled city of Campeche. But then the rebels suddenly abandoned the attack and went home to plant the corn they would need to carry on the fight. This gave the criollos and mestizos time to regroup. Yucatán's governor appealed to England, Spain and the USA for protection from the indigenous rebels in exchange for annexation to any of those countries. Finally Yucatán rejoined the Mexican union, receiving aid from its former adversary and regaining the upper hand against the insurgents.

One of the forgotten victims of the Caste War is the Maya calendar: shamans were too busy with war to keep track of the days, thus losing count. Luckily, priests in the Guatemalan highlands still maintain an accurate Maya calendar.

REVOLUTION, ROPE & REFORM

Porfirio Díaz, who definitively reclaimed current-day Quintana Roo for Mexico, ruled the country from 1876 to 1911 as a dictator, banning political opposition and free press. During this period, known as the *porfiriato*, Díaz brought the country into the industrial age, and passed laws that created an even larger class of landless peasants and concentrated wealth in the hands of an ever-smaller elite.

1910–20	1970s	1994
Almost two million people die and the economy is shattered during the Mexican Revolution. Eventual agrarian reform gives much of the Yucatán back to peasant cooperatives called *ejidos*.	Mexico experiences an oil boom, and widespread extraction and exploration begins in the Gulf, while environmental problems go widely unchecked. Over in Quintana Roo another boom is taking hold, with the development of Cancún.	The North American Free Trade Agreement comes into effect, and the cultural map of the Yucatán begins to shift. Lured by jobs in *maquiladoras* (for-export factories) and tourist towns like Cancún, peasants begin an exodus from the countryside.

THE TALKING CROSS & THE WAR OF THE CASTES

After criollo forces managed to get the upper hand against Maya rebels, the counterattack against the Maya was without quarter and vicious in the extreme. Between 1848 and 1855 the indigenous population of Yucatán was halved. Some Maya combatants sought refuge in the jungles of what is now southern Quintana Roo. There, they were inspired to continue fighting by a religious leader working with a ventriloquist, who, in 1850 at Chan Santa Cruz, made a sacred cross 'talk' (the cross was an important Maya religious symbol long before the coming of Christianity). The talking cross convinced the Maya that their gods had made them invincible, and they continued to fight, overwhelming the Mexican garrison in Bacalar's San Felipe fortress in 1858. By about 1866 the governments in Mexico City and Mérida gave up on the area and the British in Belize recognized the independent Maya republic.

Toward the end of the 19th century, Mexican president Porfirio Díaz launched an assault, sending troops with modern weapons to fight the rebels, who stood in the way of his plans to exploit the region's chicle and hardwoods, and to cultivate sugarcane. In June 1901 the last of the rebel chiefs were taken prisoner in Muyil and executed by firing squad in Xcán. The shrine of the talking cross at Chan Santa Cruz was destroyed, and the town was renamed Felipe Carrillo Puerto. But the local Maya continued to harass and interdict the Mexicans guerrilla-style for decades. An official, negotiated surrender was signed in 1936, but even then many refused to recognize the document signed by representatives they considered traitors. Incidents of resistance, though very few, continued into the 1950s. Today, if you visit Felipe Carrillo Puerto, you can visit the restored shrine of the talking cross (p136) above a dried-up cenote in what is now a city park, though the local Maya are very protective of it.

In the Yucatán, enormous fortunes were made by the owners of haciendas producing henequen, then a lucrative plant for making into rope, twine and other products. (For a description of this spiky plant and its cultivation, see boxed text, p181.)

Díaz was brought down by the Mexican Revolution, which erupted in 1910 and plunged the country into chaos for the next 10 years. In the decades following the revolution, agrarian reforms redistributed much of the peninsula's agricultural land, including many of the haciendas, into the hands of peasant cooperatives called *ejidos*.

THE OIL BOOM & BUST AND RECENT TRENDS

In the 1970s an Organization of Petroleum Exporting Countries (OPEC) embargo sent world oil prices soaring, around the same time that vast oil reserves were discovered in the Gulf of Mexico. Suddenly, Mexico became the darling of international investors who loaned the country billions of dollars to fuel an economic boom. With its newly borrowed wealth, the country invested heavily in infrastructure, including the installation of the

1994	**2000–1**	**2005**
The Zapatista uprising starts in Chiapas when the rebels take over San Cristobal de Las Casas. They later retreat, but continue to fight, declaring their aim of overturning the oligarchy's centuries-old hold on land, resources and power.	Vicente Fox of the Partido de Acción Nacional (PAN) party is elected president of Mexico, ending seven decades of autocratic rule by the Partido Revolucionario Institucional (PRI). Yucatán follows suit, electing PAN governor Patricio Patrón.	Hurricane Wilma, the largest Atlantic hurricane on record, blows into town. It does wide-scale damage to the tourist centers of Cancún, Cozumel, Isla Mujeres and Isla Holbox, causing M$20 billion in damage to Cancún alone.

The website of the Foundation for the Advancement of Mesoamerican Studies (www.famsi.org) contains numerous resources for broadening your understanding of Maya history.

Cantarell complex in the Bay of Campeche, which by 1981 was producing over a million barrels of crude a day.

But just as suddenly a world oil glut caused prices to drop in 1982, leading to a serious debt crisis. As a result, the government restructured the legal framework of the *ejido* system to allow outside investment as well as privatization and sales of cooperative land.

During the 1970s window of prosperity, investment also poured into Quintana Roo for the development of a resort at Cancún, igniting the peninsula's tourism industry and radically transforming the economic panorama. As tourism grew, many of the region's Maya left their villages to find work in Cancún, Cozumel, Playa del Carmen and other tourist haunts, usually as service personnel or in construction. The rise of tourism is thought by many scholars to be the single greatest threat to the culture and language of the Maya.

2006	2007	2012
The PAN party's Felipe Calderón Hinojosa holds off leftist Manuel López Obrador in the 2006 election. The much-disputed results kick off widespread protests, with Obrador going as far as setting up an alternative government.	Hurricane Dean rolls over the peninsula, leveling the Quintana Roo town of Mahahual and causing heavy damage in Chetumal. Over in Tabasco and Chiapas another storm rumbles through, flooding nearly 80% of Tabasco.	The end of the universe. On December 23, 2012, the Maya long-count reaches completion, signaling the end of this universe, according to Maya cosmology.

The Culture

REGIONAL IDENTITY

Culture is an ever-evolving monster, and the regional identity of the Yucatán is arguably changing faster today than it ever has in its history. The erosion of Maya culture, migration to large cities and tourist draws by the landed elite and destitutely poor alike, and the ever-pervasive influence of Mexico's neighbors to the north are morphing and distorting the cultural zeitgeist, creating a new paradigm for a region with a growing identity crisis.

Travelers often comment on the open, gentle and gregarious nature of the people of the Yucatán, especially the Yucatecan Maya. Here more than elsewhere in Mexico, it seems, you find a willingness to converse, a genuine interest in outsiders, while the obsequious attitude often encountered elsewhere in the country is absent. This openness is all the more remarkable when you consider that the people of the Yucatán Peninsula have fended off domination by outsiders for so long – a situation that persists today. The best land is owned or purchased by gringos, *chilangos* (natives of Mexico City) or criollos (people of Spanish descent) and, with few exceptions, those filling the desirable jobs and making infrastructure decisions are not Maya.

And with the tourist industry fast becoming the king-maker in the region, Maya culture seems to evaporate faster and faster as the Maya people abandon their language and traditions (highly rooted in an agrarian way of life) and head to Cancún or Playa del Carmen to work as busboys and waiters, maids and construction workers. But survival has always been at a premium here, and the Maya (and the rest of the region's poor) are finding ways to survive, be it by moving to the US to work, or by simply moving to Mérida to work in the *maquiladoras* (export-only factories paying workers around M$40 per day) during the week, only making it home to family (the true heart and soul of Mexican culture) on the weekends. This increased isolation from the essential and fundamental Mexican element *la familia* (the family) is leading to increases in modern-day ailments like the dreaded 'Ds': divorce and depression (and maybe even desolation, if we must continue this nasty alliteration).

But beyond this distinct history, and the modern-day challenges facing the region, the people of the Yucatán seem to share many cultural traits with other Mexicans. That is to say, despite the winds of progress and modernization, many of the age-old traditions still remain. Like their compatriots in Oaxaca, Chihuahua or Mexico City, they highly value family bonds, and are only truly themselves within the context of the family. Though they are hard-working people, the people of the region still like to enjoy leisure pursuits to the fullest, and there's never a shortage of fiestas and fun. Yucatecans are also deeply religious, though their faith is a mélange of pre-Hispanic beliefs and Catholicism. As elsewhere, traditional gender roles may seem exaggerated to the outsider, though the level of machismo on the peninsula is somewhat less pronounced.

In *The Modern Maya: A Culture in Transition,* Macduff Everton documents this period among the Yucatecan Maya with superb black-and-white photos, while reflecting on the impact of modern influences on this resilient culture.

To learn more about the culture and attractions of Chiapas, head to www .travelchiapas.com.

MIND YOUR MANNERS

Some indigenous people adopt a cool attitude toward visitors: they have come to mistrust outsiders after five centuries of rough treatment. They don't like being gawked at by tourists and can be very sensitive about cameras. Ask first if you have any doubt at all about whether it's OK to take a photo.

LIFESTYLE

Perhaps more than elsewhere in Mexico, ancient rhythms and customs form part of everyday life in the Yucatán. In rural areas this is apparent on the surface level. Women wear colorfully embroidered, loose-fitting *huipiles* (woven tunics) as they slap out tortillas in the yard; people live in traditional oval thatched houses, rest in hammocks after a day's work, and consume a diet of corn, beans and chilies. See 'Understanding the Modern Maya' (p178) and 'Indigenous Peoples of Chiapas' (p244) for more details on the modern indigenous lifestyle.

Mesoweb (www.meso web.com), Maya Explo- ration Center (www .mayaexploration.org) and goMaya (www .gomaya.com) are all fabulous resources on the Maya, past and present.

Various forms of Maya are widely spoken, pre-Hispanic religious rituals are still observed and forms of social organization followed. In some parts of the region, Maya languages prevail over Spanish, or Spanish may not be spoken at all. More than 30 Maya dialects exist, spoken by up to three million people in southern Mexico and northern Central America. Yucatecan Maya is the dialect spoken on the Yucatán Peninsula; some words and phrases appear on p288. Eight Maya languages are spoken in Chiapas. Tzeltal, Tzotzil and Chol are the most widely used, and the later is believed to most closely resemble the one spoken by the Classic Maya.

Many youngsters are now choosing to leave their rural roots, heading to the *maquiladoras* of Mérida, to the megaresorts of Quintana Roo or even to the US. Rather than study Yucatec, many prefer to learn English. But still, there remains a broad, ubiquitous undercurrent of pride in Maya culture: a hopeful sign that the culture will abide.

POPULATION

For more than a millennium the Maya of the Yucatán have intermarried with neighboring and invading peoples. Most of Mexico's population is mestizo (mixture of indigenous and Spanish blood), but the Yucatán has an especially high proportion of pure-blooded Maya, about four times the national average. There are around 1.5 million Maya in southern Mexico, with about 900,000 Yucatec speakers. Yucatán state, with a 59% Maya population, has the highest percentage of indigenous people of any of Mexico's 31 states.

There are 3.7 million people living in the peninsular states. Quintana Roo is the fastest growing of the three, with a 4.7% growth rate. Campeche and Yucatán ring in with 1.6% growth each.

SPORTS

As elsewhere in Mexico, *futbol* (soccer) dominates schoolyards and playing fields around the peninsula. Fans are customarily glued to their TV sets to watch televised matches between Mexico's top teams, such as Guadalajara's Chivas or Mexico City's Águilas. The region finally got a first-division team in 2007 when Atlante moved to Cancún. The other 'big' club in the area was

---

THE BALL GAME

Probably all pre-Hispanic Mexican cultures played some version of the Mesoamerican ritual ball game, the world's first-ever team sport. The game varied from place to place and era to era, but had certain lasting features. Over 500 ball courts have survived at archaeological sites around Mexico and Central America. The game seems to have been played between two teams, and its essence was to keep a rubber ball off the ground by flicking it with hips, thighs, knees or elbows. The vertical or sloping walls alongside the courts were most likely part of the playing area. The game had (at least sometimes) deep religious significance, serving as an oracle, with the result indicating which of two courses of action should be taken. Games could be followed by the sacrifice of one or more of the players – whether winners or losers, no one is sure.

TONGUE TWISTERS: A DIFFICULT DECISION

While Lonely Planet tries its darndest to keep up with linguistic trends, we've decided (purposely) to skip the latest trend in Maya orthography: adding a comma to indicate a glottal stop. The comma was adopted by Maya linguists and historians in 1989 as a vehicle to standardize and legitimize the language. The Maya glottal stop (most often used between two vowels) closely resembles the cockney double 't,' as used in the English pronunciation of bottle. Thus, if we were following the new system, Tikal would be spelled Tik'al, and Chichén Itzá would be spelled Chich'en Itza. It was a tough decision, but in the end we decided to balance out the needs of travelers (signs have yet to be converted to the new orthography) with the need to accurately document language. (See p288 for more on the Maya language.)

---

the Venados de Mérida, but they moved to Guanajuato back in 2005, leaving the rest of the peninsula with a mix of second- and third-division teams, such as the Itzáes of Yucatán, Inter Playa del Carmen, Mérida FC, Corsarios de Campeche, Huracánes de Cozumel and Club Deportivo de Chetumal. The season is divided into two big tournaments: Torneo de Apertura (August to December) and Torneo de Clausura (January to May). Games are played over the weekend; check newspapers for details.

Béisbol (baseball) is popular in Mexico. The level of professional play is quite high, equivalent at least to AAA ball in the USA. The Mexican League season runs from late March to July; among its teams are the Piratas de Campeche (Campeche Pirates), Olmecas de Tabasco (Tabasco Olmecs) and Leones de Yucatán (Mérida Lions), which won the national championship in 2006.

Mexico Online (www .mexonline.com) has good history and culture links, and lots of other information.

Yucatecans are also passionate about bullfights and *charreadas* (similar to rodeos). These events are staples of *ferias* (country fairs) around the peninsula.

RELIGION

Among the region's indigenous populations, ancient Maya beliefs blend and mix nearly seamlessly with contemporary Christian traditions, the values and rituals of the two religions being remarkably similar. Mestizos and criollos are more likely to follow strict Catholic doctrine. And here, like nearly everywhere else in Latin America, Catholicism is fast losing ground to evangelical sects.

Crosses adorned with *huipiles* (woven tunics) are found throughout the peninsula, and are often associated with the cult of the speaking cross.

The Ancient Maya

WORLD-TREE & XIBALBÁ

For the Maya, the world, the heavens and the mysterious 'unseen world' or underworld, called Xibalbá (shi-bahl-*bah*), were all one great, unified structure that operated according to laws of astrology and ancestor worship. The towering ceiba tree was considered sacred. It symbolized the Wakah-Chan (Yaxché, or World-Tree), which united the 13 heavens, the surface of the earth and the nine levels of the underworld of Xibalbá. The World-Tree had a sort of cruciform shape and was associated with the color blue-green. In the 16th century the Franciscan friars required the indigenous population to venerate the cross; this Christian symbolism meshed easily with established Maya beliefs.

In a visit to the church at the Tzotzil village of San Juan Chamula, you may see chanting *curanderos* (healers) carrying out shamanic rites.

POINTS OF THE COMPASS

In Maya cosmology, each point of the compass had special religious significance. East was most important, as it was where the sun was reborn each day; its color was red. West was black because it was where the sun disappeared.

Lavishly illustrated
with sections of friezes,
sculpted figurines, and
painted pottery and other
fine specimens of Maya
art, *The Blood of Kings,*
by Linda Schele and Mary
Ellen Miller, deciphers
glyphs and pictographs
on these objects to elicit
recurring themes of
Classic Maya civilization.

North was white and was the direction from which the all-important rains came, beginning in May. South was yellow because it was the sunniest point of the compass.

Everything in the Maya world was seen in relation to these cardinal points, with the World-Tree at the center, and they were the base for the all-important astronomical and astrological observations that determined fate.

BLOODLETTING

Just as the great cosmic dragon shed its blood, which fell to the earth as rain, so humans had to shed blood to link themselves with Xibalbá.

As illustrated in various Maya stone carvings and painted pottery, the nobility customarily drew their own blood on special occasions, such as royal births or deaths, crop plantings, victories on the battlefield or accession to the throne. Blood represented royal lineage (as it does in other societies), and so the blood of kings granted legitimacy to these events. Often using the spine of a manta ray as a lancet, a noble would pierce his cheek, lower lip, tongue or genitalia and pull a piece of rope or straw through the resulting orifice to extract the sacred substance. Performed for lower-ranking members of the nobility or occasionally before dumbstruck commoners, the excruciating ritual served not only to sanctify the event but to appease the gods, as well as to communicate with them through the hallucinogenic visions that often resulted from such self-mutilation.

When the Christian friars said that the blood of Jesus had been spilled for the common people, the Maya could easily understand the symbolism.

The Maya developed two
separate calendars (see
boxed text, opposite),
one of 260 days, the
second a 365-day cycle
that corresponds to the
solar year. The two cycles
match up every 52 years,
a period referred to as the
Long Count.

SACRED PLACES

Maya ceremonies were performed in natural sacred places as well as in their man-made equivalents. Mountains, caves, lakes, cenotes (limestone sinkholes), rivers and fields were all sacred, and had special importance in the scheme of things. Pyramids and temples were thought of as stylized mountains; sometimes they had secret chambers within them, like the caves in a mountain. A cave was the mouth of the creature that represented Xibalbá, and to enter it was to enter the spirit of the secret world. This is why some Maya temples have doorways surrounded by huge masks: as you enter the door of this 'cave,' you are entering the mouth of Xibalbá.

The plazas around which the pyramids were placed symbolized the open fields or the flat land of the tropical forest. What we call stelae were to the Maya 'tree-stones'; that is, tree-effigies echoing the sacredness of the World-Tree. These tree-stones were often carved with the figures of great Maya kings, for the king was the World-Tree of Maya society.

As these places were sacred, it made sense for succeeding Maya kings to build new and ever grander temples directly over older temples, enhancing

---

SWEATING OUT THOSE EVIL SPIRITS IN A MAYA TEMESCAL

The sweat lodge has always been a cornerstone of indigenous American spiritual life. The Maya, like their brothers to the north, were no different, using the *temescal* for both ceremonial and curative purposes.

The word *temescal* derives from the Aztec word *teme* (to bathe) and *calli* (house). The Maya people used these bathhouses not just to keep clean, but also to heal any number of ailments. Most scholars say they were most likely used during childbirth as well. Large bath complexes have been discovered at several Maya archaeological sites. Ironically, the hygienically suspect conquistadors considered the *temescales* dirty places and strongholds of sin. To this day, they are used by the Maya (and tourists) to bathe and keep those evil spirits away.

THE CELESTIAL PLAN

The ancient Maya were essentially spiritual timekeepers, counting the ticks of the day as they moved toward the end of the universe on December 23, 2012. Every major work of Maya architecture had a celestial plan. Temples were aligned so as to enhance celestial observation of the sun, moon, certain stars or planets, especially Venus. The alignment might not be apparent except at certain conjunctions of the celestial bodies (eg an eclipse), but the Maya knew each building was properly 'placed' and that this enhanced its sacred character.

Temples usually had other features that linked them to the stars. The doors and windows might frame a celestial body at an exact point in its course on a certain day of a certain year. This is the case with the Palacio del Gobernador (Governor's Palace) at Uxmal, which is aligned in such a way that, from the main doorway, Venus would have been visible exactly on top of a small mound some 3.5km away, in the year AD 750. At Chichén Itzá, the observatory building called El Caracol was aligned in order to sight Venus exactly in the year AD 1000.

Furthermore, the main door to a temple might be decorated to resemble a huge mouth, signifying entry to Xibalbá (the secret world or underworld; p41). Other features might relate to the numbers of the calendar round, as at Chichén Itzá's El Castillo. This pyramid has 364 stairs to the top; with the top platform, this makes 365, the number of days in the Maya vague year. (The vague year corresponds to our 365-day solar year, with the difference that it is not adjusted every four years by adding an additional day. Therefore, the seasons do not occur at the same time each year but vary slightly from year to year. For that reason, the Maya solar year is characterized as 'vague.') On the sides of the pyramid are 52 panels, signifying the 52-year cycle of the calendar round. The terraces on each side of each stairway total 18 (nine on either side), signifying the 18 'months' of the solar vague year. The alignment of El Castillo catches the sun and makes a shadow of the sacred sky-serpent ascending or descending the side of El Castillo's staircase on the vernal and autumnal equinoxes (March 20 to 21 and September 21 to 22) each year.

As the Maya civilization flourished, more elaborate temples were built atop smaller, older ones (see opposite).

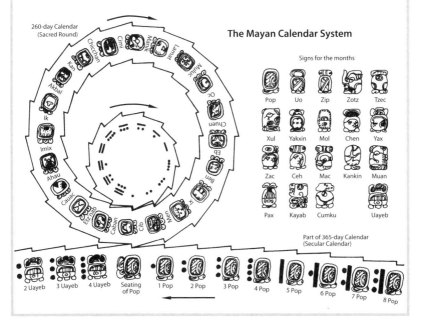

The Mayan Calendar System

260-day Calendar (Sacred Round)

Signs for the months

Pop	Uo	Zip	Zotz	Tzec
Xul	Yakxin	Mol	Chen	Yax
Zac	Ceh	Mac	Kankin	Muan
Pax	Kayab	Cumku		Uayeb

Part of 365-day Calendar (Secular Calendar)

2 Uayeb 3 Uayeb 4 Uayeb Seating of Pop 1 Pop 2 Pop 3 Pop 4 Pop 5 Pop 6 Pop 7 Pop 8 Pop

the sacred character of the spot. The temple being covered over was preserved as it remained a sacred artifact. Certain features of these older temples, such as the large masks on the façades, were carefully padded and protected before the new construction was placed over them.

Ancestor worship and genealogy were very important to the Maya, and when they buried a king beneath a pyramid, or a commoner beneath the floor or courtyard of his or her *na* (thatched Maya hut), the sacredness of the location was increased.

> Ixchel, the moon goddess, was the principal female deity of the Maya pantheon. Today she is linked with the Virgin Mary.

ANIMISM & CATHOLICISM
The ceiba tree's cruciform shape was not the only correspondence the Maya found between their animist beliefs and Christianity. Both traditional Maya animism and Catholicism have rites of baptism and confession, days of fasting and other forms of abstinence, religious partaking of alcoholic beverages, burning of incense and the use of altars.

Contemporary Yucatecans
Today's Maya identify themselves as Catholic but they practice a Catholicism that is a fusion of shamanist-animist and Christian ritual. The traditional religious ways are so important that often a Maya will try to recover from a malady by seeking the advice of a religious shaman rather than a medical doctor. Use of folk remedies linked with animist tradition is widespread in Maya areas.

> Ah Tz'ib are the Maya scribes that wrote the sacred texts of the Maya, including the *Chilam Balam*. H-menob (shamans) and Ah Tz'ib still practice their craft throughout the peninsula.

Roman Catholicism accounts for the religious orientation of around 80% of contemporary Yucatecans, while 11% of the Yucatán's population identifies themselves as Protestants or evangelicals. Congregations affiliated with churches such as the Assemblies of God, the Seventh Day Adventists, the Church of Jesus Christ of Latter Day Saints and Jehovah's Witnesses can also be found in the Yucatán.

ARTS
The Yucatán's arts and crafts scene is enormously rich and varied. The influence of the Maya or Spanish cultures (or both) appears in almost every facet of Yucatecan art, from their dance and music to the clothes and hats they wear.

Pre-Hispanic Art
The Classic Maya, at their cultural height from about AD 300 to 900, were perhaps ancient Mexico's most artistic people. They left countless beautiful stone sculptures, of complicated design and meaning but possessing an easily appreciated delicacy of touch – a talent also expressed in their unique architecture. Subjects are typically rulers, deities and significant events.

Literature

> *Viva Zapata!* (1952) stars Anthony Quinn and Marlon Brando, and traces the story of the Mexican Revolution. Quinn won an Oscar for his supporting role, while Brando, though nominated, was left out in the cold.

Yucatán's earliest known literary work is the *Books of the Chilam Balam of Chumayel*. Written in Maya after the conquest, it is a compendium of Maya history, prophecy and mythology collected by priests from the northern Yucatán town of Chuyamel.

Diego de Landa, the Spanish friar (see boxed text, p35), could be said to have produced the first literary work in Spanish from the Yucatán, *Relación de las Cosas de Yucatán* (An Account of the Things of Yucatán), in which he relates his biased perception of the Maya's ceremonial festivals, daily life and traditions, even as he engineered their eradication.

> ### THE MAYA 'BIBLE': UNRAVELING THE SECRETS OF THE POPOL VUH
>
> The history, prophesies, legends and religious rites of the Maya were preserved on painted codices and through oral traditions. Nearly all of these codices were destroyed during the time of the conquest (only four survive today), effectively cutting the historic record of the Maya. Lucky for Mayanologists, the *Popul Vuh*, known to many as the Maya Bible, recaptured these myths and sacred stories.
>
> The *Popol Vuh* is said to be written by the Quiché Maya of Guatemala, who had learned Spanish and the Latin alphabet from the Dominican friars – the text was written in Latin characters rather than hieroglyphics. The authors showed their book to Francisco Ximénez, a Dominican who lived and worked in Chichicastenango, in Guatemala, from 1701 to 1703. Friar Ximénez copied the Maya book word for word and then translated it into Spanish. Both his copy and the Spanish translation survive, but the original has been lost.
>
> According to the *Popol Vuh*, the great god K'ucumatz created humankind first from mud. But these 'earthlings' were weak and dissolved in water, so K'ucumatz tried again using wood. The wood people had no hearts or minds and could not praise their creator, so they were destroyed, all except the monkeys who lived in the forest, who are the descendants of the wood people. The creator tried once again, this time successfully, using substances recommended by four animals – the gray fox, the coyote, the parrot and the crow. White and yellow corn were ground into meal to form the flesh, and stirred into water to make the blood.
>
> The *Popol Vuh* legends include some elements that made it easier for the Maya to understand certain aspects of Christian belief, including virgin birth and sacrificial death followed by resurrection.

Aside from (unsuccessfully) seeking US intervention against the Maya during the War of the Castes, Justo Sierra O'Reilly is credited with writing what is possibly the first Mexican novel, *La Hija del Judio*. About the ill-fated romance of a Jewish merchant's daughter in colonial Mexico, this superior work of fiction was originally published during the 1840s as a series in Sierra's Campeche newspaper, *El Fénix*, and later published in its entirety.

In more recent times the Yucatecan author Ermilio Abreu Gómez synthesized the peninsula's Maya heritage in fictional works like the novel *Canek: History and Legend of a Maya Hero*, the story of an indigenous laborer's struggle against injustice.

Novelist, playwright and art critic Juan García Ponce, who died in 2003, is perhaps the Yucatán's best-known modern literary figure. *Imagen Primera* (First Image) and *La Noche* (The Night), collections of his short stories, make good starting points for exploring the Mérida-born writer's prolific output.

Music

Two styles of music are traditionally associated with the Yucatán: the *jarana* (p46) and *trova yucateca*.

A type of festive dance music, a *jarana* is generally performed by a large ensemble consisting of two trumpets, two clarinets, one trombone, a tenor sax, timbales and a guiro (percussion instrument made from a grooved gourd). The music pauses for the singers to deliver *bombas* – ad-libbed verses, usually with a humorous double meaning, that are aimed at the object of their affections. A *jarana* orchestra always ends its performances with the traditional *torito*, a vivacious song that evokes the fervor of a bullfight.

A hybrid of Cuban, Spanish, Colombian and homegrown influences, the Yucatecan *trova* is a catchall term for romantic ballads, Cuban claves, tangos, boleros, Yucatecan folk songs and other tunes that can be strummed on a guitar by a *trovador* (troubador). The style is often played by the guitar trios who roam the squares of Mérida, seeking an audience to serenade.

Mel Gibson's Oscar-nominated *Apocalypto* hit theaters in 2006, and was the first major Yucatec-Maya-language film ever. It was filmed mostly in Veracruz.

(The usual serenade consists of five songs.) In any discussion of the *trova,* you're likely to hear the name Guty Cárdenas, nicknamed the 'Yucatecan nightingale.' Cárdenas only recorded for five years during the 1920s, but he's been remarkably influential. In a *trova,* as with *jaranas,* the subject matter is usually a suitor's paean of love to an unattainable sweetheart. March brings the Festival de Trova Yucateca to Mérida.

A more contemporary figure of Yucatecan song is Armando Manzanero, the singer and composer from Mérida. Though Manzanero speaks to an older generation, his songs are still being covered by contemporary pop stars like Luis Miguel and Alejandro Sanz. He is best known for heart-wrenching boleros, such as 'Adoro,' 'Te Extranō,' 'Contigo Aprendí' and 'Somos Novios' (a tune that English speakers are more likely to know as 'It's Impossible'), many of which have taken their place in the canon of Mexican standards.

Guty Cárdenas, un Siglo del Ruiseñor, produced by the prestigious Mexican record label Discos Corasón (www.corason .com), includes a CD and DVD covering the musical career of this seminal Yucatecan composer/ performer.

Dance

The Spanish influence on Maya culture is abundantly evident in the *jarana,* a dance Yucatecans have been performing for centuries. The dance bears more than a passing resemblance to the *jota,* performed in Spain's Alto Aragón region. The movements of the dancers, with their torsos held rigid and a formal distance separating men from women, are nearly identical; however, whereas the Spanish punctuate elegant turns of their wrists with clicks of their castanets, Maya women snap their fingers.

The best place to see dancers perform to the accompaniment of *jarana* is at *vaquerías* – homegrown fiestas held in the atriums of town halls or on haciendas. The women wear their best embroidered *huipiles,* flowers in their hair and white heels; men wear a simple, white cotton outfit with a red bandanna tucked into the waist. In Mérida, *vaquerías* are held weekly in the Plaza de Santa Lucía.

Handicrafts
TEXTILES

The Crafts of Mexico is a gorgeously illustrated coffee-table volume focusing on ceramics and textiles, by Margarita de Orellana and Albertio Ruy Sánchez, editors of the superb magazine *Artes de México.*

Women throughout the Yucatán Peninsula traditionally wear straight, white cotton dresses called *huipiles,* the bodices of which are always embroidered. The tunic generally falls to just below the knee; on formal occasions it is worn with a lacy white underskirt that reaches the ankle. The *huipil* never has a belt, which would defeat its airy, cool design. Light, loose fitting and traditionally made of cotton (synthetics are occasionally used today), these garments are ideally suited for the tropics. Maya women have been wearing *huipiles* for centuries.

Also commonly worn on the peninsula (and similar to the *huipil* in appearance) is the *gala terno,* which is a straight, white, square-necked dress with an embroidered overyoke and hem, worn over an underskirt that sports an embroidered strip near the bottom. It is fancier than a *huipil* and is often accompanied by a delicately hand-knitted shawl.

In addition to *huipiles, galas ternos* and shawls, Maya women throughout the peninsula are known for weaving lovely sashes, tablecloths and napkins.

PANAMA HATS

The classic woven straw hat that most people associate with Panama was made internationally famous in the late 19th century by Ferdinand de Lesseps, builder of the Suez Canal and the brains behind the failed French attempt to build a canal in Panama.

The much-photographed Lesseps was balding when he arrived in Panama, and he found that the light but durable hat provided excellent protection against the sun. Most newspaper photographs taken of him showed the larger-than-life figure looking even worldlier in his exotic headgear. Soon men around the globe began placing orders for the 'panama hat.'

Panama hats originated in Ecuador and were exported to Panama. However, at least as early as the 1880s, residents of Bécal in the Mexican state of Campeche were producing the same style hat. Today more than a thousand people in the small, quiet town of Bécal are still making the hats, which they variously call *panamás* or *jipijapas* (see p214 for details on how the hats are made).

WOODEN CRAFTS

In handicrafts shops across the peninsula, you'll come across beautiful wooden crafts, such as carved wooden panels and galleons.

The ancient Maya made woodcarvings of their many gods, just as they carved the images of their deities in stone. The skill and techniques associated with the artistry survive to this day. The wooden panels are often a meter or more in height and feature a strange-looking character of unmistakably Maya imagination – the image will resemble figures you've seen at Maya ruins. If the carved image is one of a heavily adorned man raising a chalice, most likely you're looking at a representation of Itzamná, lord of the heavens; he's a popular figure on the wooden panels of contemporary Maya.

The Maya – so impressed with the Spanish galleons that arrived on their shores that they made meter-long models of the ships, complete with tiny sails – have been making wooden galleons for generations. Today the galleons that used to haul cargoes of hardwood back to Europe are gone, but the craft of galleon model-making is alive and well in the Yucatán. Campeche is the state most associated with such items, but they are made by accomplished artisans in the states of Yucatán and Quintana Roo as well.

Chloe Sayer's fascinating Arts and Crafts of Mexico *traces the evolution of crafts from pre-Hispanic times to the present, with many fine photos.*

Architecture

Maya architecture is amazing for its achievements but perhaps even more amazing for what it did not achieve. Maya architects never seem to have used the true arch (a rounded arch with a keystone), and never thought to put wheels on boxes for use as wagons to move the thousands of tons of construction materials needed in their tasks. They had no metal tools – they were technically a Stone Age culture – yet could build breathtaking temple complexes and align them so precisely that windows and doors were used as celestial observatories with great accuracy.

The arch used in most Maya buildings is the corbeled arch (or, when used for an entire room rather than a doorway, corbeled vault). In this technique, large flat stones on either side of the opening are set progressively inward as they rise. The two sides nearly meet at the top, and this 'arch' is then topped by capstones. Though they served the purpose, the corbeled arches severely limited the amount of open space beneath them. In effect, Maya architects were limited to long, narrow vaulted rooms.

The Maya also lacked draft animals (horses, donkeys, mules or oxen). All the work had to be done by humans, on their feet, with their arms and backs, without wagons or even wheelbarrows.

Maya pyramids were painted in brilliant red, green, yellow and white colors. And the people of the region often painted their bodies red.

MAYA ARCHITECTURE

Maya architecture's 1500-year history saw a fascinating progression of styles. Styles changed not just with the times, but with the particular geographic area of Mesoamerica in which the architects worked. Not all of the styles can be seen in the Yucatán.

Late Pre-Classic (100 BC to AD 250)

This style is perhaps best exhibited at Uaxactún, north of Tikal in Guatemala's Petén department. Uaxactún's Pyramid E-VII-sub is a fine example of how the architects of what is known as the Chicanel culture designed their pyramid-temples in the time around this period. It's a square stepped-platform pyramid with central stairways on each of the four sides, each stairway flanked by large jaguar masks. The entire platform was covered in a fine white stucco. The top platform is flat and probably bore a temple *na* (hut) made of wooden poles topped with a palm thatch. This temple is well preserved because others had been built on top of it; the later structures fell into ruin and were cleared away to reveal E-VII-sub. Similar Chicanel-style temples were also built at Tikal, El Mirador and Lamanai (in Belize).

Joyce Kelly's An Archaeo-logical Guide to Mexico's Yucatán Peninsula *gives visitors both practical and background information on 91 sites.*

Early Classic (AD 300–600)

The Esperanza culture typifies this phase. In Esperanza-style temples, the king was buried in a wooden chamber beneath the main staircase of the temple; successive kings were buried in similar positions in pyramids built on top of the original.

Of the surviving early Classic pyramids, perhaps the best example is the step-pyramid at Acanceh, just south of Mérida.

Late Classic (AD 600–900)

The most important Classic sites flourished during the latter part of the period. By this time the Maya temple pyramid had a stone building on top, replacing the *na* of wooden poles and thatch. Numbers of pyramids were built close together, sometimes forming contiguous or even continuous structures. Near them, different structures now called palaces were built; they sat on lower platforms and held many more rooms, perhaps a dozen or more.

In addition to pyramids and palaces, Classic sites have carved stelae and round 'altar-stones' set in the plaza in front of the pyramids. Another feature of the Classic and later periods is the ball court, with the sloping playing surfaces of stone covered in stucco.

Of all the Classic sites, Tikal in Guatemala is the grandest restored so far. Here the pyramids reached their most impressive heights and were topped by superstructures (called roofcombs by archaeologists) that made them even taller. As in earlier times these monumental structures were used as the burial places of kings.

Puuc, Chenes & Río Bec (AD 600–800)

Among the most distinctive of the Late Classic Maya architectural styles are those that flourished in the western and southern regions of the Yucatán Peninsula. These styles valued exuberant display and architectural bravado more than they did proportion and harmony – think of it as Maya baroque.

The Puuc style, named for the hills surrounding Uxmal, used facings of thin limestone 'tiles' to cover the rough stone walls of buildings. The tiles were worked into geometric designs and stylized figures of monsters and serpents. Minoan-style columns and rows of engaged columns (half-round cylinders partly embedded in a wall) were also a feature of the style; they were used to good effect on façades of buildings at Uxmal and at the Puuc sites of Kabah, Sayil, Xlapak and Labná. Puuc architects were crazy about Chac, the rain god, and stuck his grotesque face on every temple. At Kabah, the façade of the Palacio de los Mascarones (Palace of the Masks) is covered in Chac masks.

The Chenes style, prevalent in areas of Campeche south of the Puuc region, is similar to the Puuc style, but Chenes architects seem to have enjoyed putting huge masks as well as smaller ones on their façades.

The Río Bec style, epitomized in the richly decorated temples at the ar-chaeological sites between Escárcega and Chetumal, used lavish decoration, as in the Puuc and Chenes styles, but added huge towers to the corners of its low buildings, just for show. Río Bec buildings look like a combination of the Governor's Palace of Uxmal and Temple I at Tikal.

Early Post-Classic (AD 1000–1250)
The collapse of Classic Maya civilization around AD 1000 created a power vacuum that was filled by the invasion of the Toltecs from central Mexico. The Toltecs brought with them their own architectural ideas, and in the process of conquest these ideas were assimilated and merged with those of the Puuc style.

The foremost example of what might be called the Toltec-Maya style is Chichén Itzá. Elements of Puuc style – the large masks and decorative friezes – coexist with Toltec warrior atlantes (male figures used as support-ing columns) and *chac-mools*, odd reclining statues that are purely Toltec and have nothing to do with Maya art. Platform pyramids with broad bases and spacious top platforms, such as the Templo de los Guerreros (Temple of the Warriors), look as though they might have been imported from the ancient Toltec capital of Tula (near Mexico City) or by way of Teotihuacán, with its broad-based pyramids of the sun and moon. Because Quetzalcóatl was so important to the Toltecs, feathered serpents are used extensively as architectural decoration.

Late Post-Classic (AD 1250–1519)
After the Toltecs came the Cocomes, who established their capital at Mayapán, south of Mérida, and ruled a confederation of Yucatecan states during this period. After the golden age of Tikal and Palenque, even after the martial architecture of Chichén Itzá, the architecture of Mayapán is a disappointment. The pyramids and temples are small and crude compared with the glorious Classic structures. Mayapán's only architectural distinc-tion comes from its vast defensive city wall, one of the few such walls ever discovered in a Maya city. The fact that the wall exists testifies to the weak-ness of the Cocom rulers and the unhappiness of their subject peoples.

Tulum, another walled city, is also a product of this time. The columns of the Puuc style are used here, and the painted decoration on the temples must have been colorful. But there is nothing here to rival Classic architecture.

Cobá has the finest architecture of this otherwise decadent period. The stately pyramids here had new little temples built atop them in the style of Tulum.

The Art of Mesoamerica by Mary Ellen Miller is an excellent overview of pre-Hispanic art and architecture.

SPANISH COLONIAL ARCHITECTURE
The conquistadors and Franciscan and Dominican priests brought with them the architecture of their native Spain and adapted it to the conditions they met in the Maya lands. Churches in the largest cities were decorated with baroque elements, but in general the churches are simple and fortress-like. The exploitation of the Maya by the Spaniards led to frequent rebel-lions, and the high stone walls of the churches worked well in protecting the upper classes from the wrath of the indigenous people.

As you travel through the region, you'll see that many churches are plain, both inside and out. These crude and simple borrowings from Spanish architecture are eclipsed by the richness of the religious pageantry that takes place inside the buildings – including many half-Maya, half-Catholic processions, rituals, decorations and costumes.

Food & Drink Mauricio Velázquez de León

I hope you're hungry because in the Yucatán Peninsula you are up for a feast. Yucatecos, and other residents of the Yucatán Peninsula, are enormously proud of their history and cultural background, and they will love to share it with you in the form of a rich-red plate of *cochinita pibil* (pork pibil style), a couple of *panuchos* (small corn tortillas that puff when heated) and a sip of Xtabentún, the so-called liqueur of the gods. The relative geographic isolation from the rest of the country together with a strong Mayan influence have made *la cocina yucateca* the Mexican regional cuisine with the most distinctive personality, and as you travel around the region you will find a cuisine based on ingredients and techniques unheard of anywhere else in Mexico. At first some dishes will resemble specialties that you can find elsewhere in the country, such as tacos or tamales, but soon you will discover that in the Yucatecan kitchen these Mexican-food staples have been transformed with a Mayan and Caribbean flair. Travel further to the south and you'll cross another cultural milestone, where the indigenous population in Chiapas preserves yet a different culinary tradition.

There is a big chance that you landed in this region seduced by the white beaches and crystal-clear waters of Cancún or Playa del Carmen, or to marvel at the architectural and artistic achievements of the Classic Mayan period in ancient cities like Tulum, Uxmal or Chichén Itzá, and there is a reasonable chance that you will find places to eat good, and even great, Yucatecan cuisine in these locations. But if you are determined to embark on a serious culinary escapade, then you have to visit towns like Valladolid, Motul, Campeche, Izamal, Chetumal or Mérida, the peninsula's eating capital.

A regular Monday dish in most Yucatecan homes is *frijol con puerco,* a Yucatecan version of pork and beans. Pork cooked with black beans is served with rice, and garnished with radish, cilantro (coriander) and onions.

STAPLES & SPECIALTIES

The staples of Mexican food – corn, and an array of dry and fresh chilies and beans – are also basic ingredients on the Yucatecan table. Achiote (the seeds from the annatto flower), epazote (a herb called pigweed or Jerusalem oak in the US), *chaya* (a shrub also known as tree spinach), *cat* (a variety of cucumber) and the habanero chili are some regional ingredients. Together with *recados* (local rubs; see boxed text, opposite), these are the building blocks of *la cocina yucateca*.

In the Yucatán Peninsula you will find an array of typical *antojitos* using corn as the base. The word *antojitos* translates as 'little whims, a sudden craving.' But as any Mexican will quickly point out, it is not just a snack. They are more like the Spanish tapas. You can have an entire meal of *antojitos*, or have a couple as appetizers, or yes, eat one as a *tentempíe* (quick bite) before hopping on the bus or while standing outside a bar. A classic Yucatecan *antojito* is *panuchos*. Cooks slit the thin layer of the tortilla and spread beans and a slice of hard-boiled egg inside. Lightly fried, it is then topped with meat or shredded poultry or *cazón* (dogfish) and pickled red onions. In Mayan, *kots'* refer to small stuffed *taquitos,* and that is exactly what *codzitos* are: small fried tacos filled with minced pork and topped with tomato sauce. *Papadzules* are tortillas bathed on a pumpkin-seed sauce, filled with chopped hard-boiled eggs and topped with some drops of pumpkin-seed oil. The peninsula is also distinguished for its variety of tamales. Tamales are made with masa mixed with lard, stuffed with stewed meat, fish or vegetables, wrapped and steamed. The word comes from the Nahuatl word *tamalli* and refers to anything wrapped up. *Tamalitos al vapor* are small tamales filled with pork meat and a sauce made with tomatoes, epazote and achiote, and wrapped

RECADOS

Recado is the generic name used for the local rubs or marinades that combine dry chilies, spices, herbs and vinegar, and are applied to meats and poultry. The Mayan called the *recados* 'kuux,' and they are essential to preparing an array of dishes on the peninsula. Not so long ago you could find *recauderías* (spice-paste stores) in most towns and cities. Today this name is only used to designate some market stalls dedicated to selling spices and dry chilies. Some popular *recados* are *recado blanco* (white), which contains oregano, garlic, cloves, cinnamon, salt, pepper and sour oranges. It's also known as *recado de puchero* because it is used for cooking *puchero*, a hearty stew of beef or chicken, with chayote, zucchini, sweet potatoes and chickpeas. *Recado negro* (black) contains corn tortillas and local chilies that are burned (hence the color) with an array of spices. It's the foundation of one the region's classic dishes *relleno negro*, turkey stuffed with minced pork, dry fruits, tomatoes and epazote, and rubbed with this kind of *recado*. But the most famous *recado* is *recado rojo* (red), containing black and red pepper, oregano, cloves, cinnamon, salt, water and the achiote (annatto) seeds that infuse an intense red color and flavor to *cochinita pibil* (pork pibil style) and other regional favorites. *Recado rojo* is sometimes simply called achiote, but this refers to the prepared paste and not to the achiote flower.

in banana leaves. *El tamal de boda* is made only during weddings, and the *muc bil pollo* is a tamale prepared traditionally during Día de los Muertos (Day of the Dead; see Celebrations, p53). *El brazo de indio* (Indian arm) is a large tamale that can be 28cm long and 10cm wide. It is made by rolling layers of masa and *chaya* leaves.

In the Yucatán some dishes have taken the name of the cities and towns where they were created. Motul is the birthplace of *huevos motuleños*, the famous pair of fried eggs topping a tortilla with beans and covered with a tomato sauce, chopped cheese and ham, and green peas. The *longaniza de valladolid* is a chorizo sausage that has been smoked for up to 12 hours, and the *pollo ticuleño* was born in the city of Ticul. The chicken is rubbed with *recado rojo* and cooked with green peas and *chile dulce* (a local pepper that has no heat). It's served with pickled chilies, potatoes and plantains.

But by far, *cochinita pibil* is the region's most famous dish. In Mayan *pib* means a hole in the ground, and cooking '*al pibil*' is a technique that has been used for centuries in this region to cook all kinds of marinated and nonmarinated meats. Originally it was cooked using venison and it was known as *pibil keh*. Today *lechón* (piglet) is the meat of choice, hence the name *cochinita*, meaning little pig, although many places use meat from adult pigs. It's prepared by rubbing the meat with *recado rojo* that has been thinned using the juice of sour oranges. The meat is then wrapped in banana leaves and cooked underground for as many as eight hours. Most places cook their *cochinita* in traditional ovens, with very good results. It is usually served shredded and topped with red onions that have been pickled with orange juice, vinegar and a dash of sugar. You can make *tacos de cochinita pibil* with corn tortillas or even use it as a filling for *tortas* (sandwiches using *bolillo*, a bread that resembles a French roll). Another popular dish using *recado rojo* is *pavo en escabeche*, where turkey is marinated in the *recado*, then simmered in water and roasted *xcatic chile* (a mild local chili similar to Hungarian wax pepper), and then grilled before serving. *Caldo de pavo* (turkey soup) is also popular in the region, but *sopa de lima* is the favorite Yucatecan soup. This is a local version of chicken soup using tomatoes, *chile dulce*, chopped onion, strips of lightly fried tortillas and lime.

With the Caribbean Sea to the east, the Gulf of Mexico to the west and the Pacific Ocean to the south, you can expect an incredible array of fish and seafood dishes in the Yucatán Peninsula. *Mariscos* (shellfish) and *pescado*

The strongest demand for habanero chili grown in Yucatán comes from Japan. Japanese companies normally buy the chili in its powder form and add it to a wide variety of spicy snacks.

(fish) are prepared *a la ajillo* (in garlic and *guajilllo* chili sauce), *a la plancha* (grilled) or *a la diabla* (with garlic, tomato and *cascabel chile,* a dry moderately hot chili that has a brownish color). Achiote is also used in dishes like *pampano empapelado* (marinated and paper-wrapped pompano), and *tikin-xit,* fish wrapped in banana leaves and grilled, is a local favorite. Crab is famous in the coastal lagoons of the Gulf, such as Celestún and Laguna de Términos, and is served in many forms, especially in *chilpachole* (crab soup with epazote, tomatoes and *chile chipotle* – dried, smoked, jalapenos with a smoky, meaty flavor and moderate heat). In Chiapas *bosto de sardina* (grilled sardines wrapped in banana leaves) is a well-known dish.

DRINKS

Like elsewhere in Mexico, on the peninsula you will find the popular tequila and its cousin mescal. Both spirits are distilled from the agave plant, but the difference is that tequila has to come from blue agave in the central state of Jalisco, and is protected with a Designation of Origin (DO) by the Consejo Regulador del Tequila (the Tequila Regulate Council). Cerveza (beer) is also widely available, and although you can find all national brands, such as Corona and Dos Equis, two local beers stand out: the lager Montejo and the dark León Negra. The practice of a beer served with a wedge of lime in its mouth is not as common in Mexico as it is in foreign bars, and you will find that establishments that serve lime with your beer would most likely offer it on a small plate.

Balché is a Mayan spirit that was offered to the gods during special ceremonies. It is fermented inside the hollow trunk of the *balché* tree with water and honey. In Valladolid, during indigenous weddings, the bride is sprayed with *balché* as a sign of abundance. *Balché* is not commercially available, but another Mayan spirit, *xtabentún,* is easy to find in the region. *Xtabentún* is an anise-flavored liqueur that, when authentic, is made by fermenting honey.

Nonalcoholic

The great variety of fruits, plants and herbs that grow in the Yucatán Peninsula are a perfect fit for the kind of nonalcoholic drinks Mexicans love. *Juguerías*

H IS FOR HOT, HABANERO AND HELP!

That's right, the habanero, the hottest chili grown on our planet, finds its home in Yucatán, and it is a foundation of its cuisine. Does this mean that everything you're going to eat will burn your mouth? Well, no. Despite the fierce reputation of the habanero chili, Yucatecan food is not spicy. The habanero is most commonly found in table salsas, and it is up to you how much to add to the dish. The habanero grown in Yucatán has an international reputation for being a high-quality pepper with a bright-orange color, and the highest number of Scoville Heat Units found in any pepper.

This method, developed by American scientist Wilbur Scoville to measure the piquancy in chilies, quantifies the amount of the chemical compound capsaicin found in chilies. The habanero can have between 100,000 and 500,000 units. As a comparison, a jalapeño chili has between 5000 and 15,000 units and Hungarian hot paprika between 100 and 500 units.

Now, if a little more of what you can tolerate finds its way into your mouth, this is what you need to know: the heat of the habanero is relentless and will spread quickly throughout your mouth. No matter what your instincts tell you, don't drink water, and don't even think about reaching for that beer. Any liquid will spread the flames deeper into your mouth. Instead, eat something that will neutralize the capsaicin: bread, beans or rice are good options, but if you happen to have a chocolate bar with you, eat it. Chocolate is by far the best antidote to cut the burning sensation caused by a hot pepper.

LOVE STORY

According to legend, *balché* was created as an act of love between a beautiful Mayan girl Sak-Nicté (White Flower) and a brave young warrior. As the story goes, the young couple fled their tribe when a powerful cacique (indigenous chief) also declared his love to Sak-Nicté. After days of wandering in the Mayan forest, the lovebirds found a honeycomb. Sak-Nicté and the warrior had a feast with the sweet honey, and decided to save some inside the trunk of a *balché* tree. That night brought rain and thunder, and the water blended with the honey inside the tree creating a luscious beverage.

When the cacique found them, he ordered Sak-Nicté to return to her tribe. The young warrior was devastated and in a desperate attempt to keep her lover at his side, he offered to cook for the cacique a fantastic meal. He accepted and the couple served him a banquet, crowned with the sweet drink they had discovered. The cacique was so impressed with the *balché* that he let the two lovers go, under the condition that they share with him how to prepare it.

(street stalls or small establishments selling all kinds of fresh-squeezed orange, tangerine, strawberry, papaya, beet or carrot juices) are widely available. In some cases they will serve local fruits, like mangoes, *cayumito* (a purple plum-like fruit), *zapote negro* (black fruit with a pear-like consistency) and *marañón* (cashew fruit). *Juguerías* also sell *licuados,* a Mexican version of a milkshake that normally includes banana, milk, honey and fruit. And many serve incredibly creative combinations, such as vanilla, banana and avocado.

Aguas frescas (fresh drinks made with fruit, herbs or flowers) are standard Mexican refreshments. Some of them resemble iced teas. In *agua de tamarindo* the tamarind pods are boiled and then mixed with sugar before chilled, and the *agua de jamaica* is made with dried hibiscus leaves. Others like *horchata* are made with melon seeds and/or rice. Two local favorites are *agua de chia* (a plant from the salvia family) that is typical during Holy Week celebrations in Chiapas, and the leaves from the native shrub *chaya* are mixed with lime, honey and pineapple to create *agua de chaya* on the rest of the peninsula.

In *juguerías* you can expect the water to be purified.

CELEBRATIONS

Food and fiestas go hand-in-hand in Mexico. During the spring *ch´a chaak* ceremony, which takes place in agricultural villages around the peninsula, tortillas and turkey are traditionally offered up to the rain gods and then eaten. The tortillas are made into 'layered cakes,' with ground squash seeds, beans and other vegetables, wrapped in banana leaves and buried to be cooked over charcoals. Turkey and other wild game is cooked in *kol,* a broth thickened with masa. The men drink *balché.*

During Día de los Muertos (Day of the Dead) on 2 November it is traditional in many areas of the peninsula to eat a special tamale called *muc bil pollo.* In Mayan *mukbil* means buried and this is how this tamale is made. Corn masa is mixed with beef broth and placed inside a container covered with banana leaves. The masa is stuffed with chicken and pork meat that has been cooked with achiote, *chile dulce,* epazote, onion and habanero chili, and it is topped with more banana leaves and tied. The tamale is buried and covered with charcoal and sand.

WHERE TO EAT & DRINK

Food on the peninsula is available in many places, whether it be a small *puesto* (street or market stall), a simple cafeteria or a fine restaurant. One thing you should know, though, is that mealtimes in Mexico are different from other countries, and if you're outside one of the major tourist destinations, like Cancún, restaurants close early. *Desayuno* (breakfast) is usually served in restaurants and cafeterias from 8:30am to 11am, and it tends to be on the heavy side. Those who have a light breakfast or skipped it altogether can have an *almuerzo* (a type of brunch) for an *antojito* or another type of quick bite. *Loncherías* (places that serve light meals) are good options for an *almuerzo*. In Mexico the main meal is the *comida*. It's usually served from 2pm to 4:30pm in homes, restaurants and cafés. Places called *fondas* are small, family-run eateries that serve *comida corrida*, an inexpensive prix fixe menu that includes a soup, rice, main dish, beverage and dessert. In some small towns people will have a *merienda*, a light snack between the *comida* and *la cena* (supper). Dinner is served anytime after 7pm and restaurants in small towns won't remain open beyond 8:30pm or 9pm.

Cantinas are the traditional Mexican watering holes. Until recently, women, military personnel and children were not allowed in cantinas, and some cantinas still have a rusted sign stating this rule. Today everybody is allowed, although the more traditional establishments retain a macho edge. Beer, tequila and *cubas* (rum and coke) are served at square tables where patrons play dominoes and watch *futbol* (soccer) games on large TV screens. Cantinas are famous for serving *botanas* (appetizers).

VEGETARIANS & VEGANS

Mexicans think of a vegetarian as a person that doesn't eat meat, and by 'meat' they mean red meat. Many more have never heard the word *veganista*, the Spanish term for vegan. The good news is that almost every city, large or small, has real vegetarian restaurants, and their popularity is increasing. Also, many traditional Mexican and Yucatecan dishes are vegetarian. Be warned, however, that many dishes are prepared using chicken or beef broth, or some kind of animal fat, such as *manteca* (lard). Most waiters would be happy to help you in choosing vegetarian or vegan dishes, but you have to make your requirements clear.

EATING WITH KIDS

In most restaurants in Mexico you will see entire families and their kids eating together, especially on weekends. Waiters are used to accommodating children and will promptly help you with high chairs *(silla para niños* or *silla periquera)*, and in some places they will bring crayons or some other toys to keep kids entertained. Across Mexico it's common to see children having dinner in restaurants after 8pm or 9pm.

EAT YOUR WORDS

For non-Spanish speakers, travel and dining on the Caribbean coast usually pose no problem; English is understood almost everywhere. However, once you leave the tourist bubble, a few words in Spanish will go a long way, and at the same time indicate a respect for the Yucatecans and their culture.

TIPPING & TAXES

A mandatory *impuesto de valor agregado* (IVA, or value-added tax; 15%) is added to restaurant checks in Mexico, but the *propina* (gratuity) is not. The average tip is 15% to 20%, and although some people argue that the tip should be calculated before IVA, it's just easier to tip the same amount, or a bit more, than the amount marked for the IVA. For instance, in a check that marks IVA $82 pesos, a tip between 80 and 100 pesos would be appropriate.

Useful Phrases

Are you open?
    ¿Está abierto?   e·*sta* a·*byer*·to
Are you serving breakfast/lunch/dinner now?
    ¿Ahora, está sirviendo desayuno/la comida/la cena?   a·o·ra e·*sta* ser·*vyen*·do de·sa·*yoo*·no/la
                                                      ko·*mee*·da/la *se*·na

I'd like to see a menu.
    Quisiera ver la carta/el menú.   kee·*sye*·ra ver la *kar*·ta/el me·*noo*
Do you have a menu in English?
    ¿Tienen un menú en inglés?   te·en·nen oon me·*noo* en een·*gles*
I'm a vegetarian.
    Soy vegetariano/a. (m/f)   soy ve·khe·te·*rya*·no/a
I can't eat anything with meat or poultry products, including broth.
    No puedo comer algo de carne o aves, incluyendo caldo.   no *pwe*·do ko·*mer* al·*go* de *kar*·ne o *a*·ves
                                                      een·kloo·*yen*·do *kal*·do

Is it (spicy) hot?
    ¿Es picoso?   es pee·*ko*·so
The check, please.
    La cuenta, por favor.   la *kwen*·ta por fa·*vor*

Food Glossary
MEAT & POULTRY

a la parilla	a la pa·*ree*·ya	grilled
a la plancha	a la *plan*·cha	pan-broiled
albóndigas	al·*bon*·dee·gas	meatballs
aves	*a*·ves	poultry
bistec	*bis*·tek	steak
borrego	bo·*re*·ga	sheep
carne (asada)	*kar*·ne (a·*sa*·da)	meat (grilled beef)
carne de puerco	*kar*·ne de *pwer*·ko	pork
carne de res	*kar*·ne de res	beef
chicharrones	chee·cha·*ro*·nes	deep-fried pork skin
chorizo	cho·*ree*·so	Mexican-style sausage made with chili and vinegar
frijol con puerco	fri·*khol* kon *pwer*·ko	Yucatecan-style pork and beans, topped with a sauce made with grilled tomatoes, and decorated with garnishes; served with rice
jamón	kha·*mon*	ham
lechón	le·*chon*	suckling pig
milanesa	mee·la·*ne*·sa	breaded beef cutlet
pavo	*pa*·vo	turkey
pibil	pee·*beel*	meat wrapped in banana leaves, flavored with achiote, garlic, sour orange, salt and pepper, and baked in a pit oven; the two main varieties are *cochinita pibil* (suckling pig) and *pollo pibil* (chicken)
picadillo	pee·ka·*dee*·yo	a ground beef filling that often includes fruit and nuts
poc-chuc	pok·chook	tender pork strips marinated in sour orange juice, grilled and served topped with a spicy onion relish
pollo	*po*·yo	chicken
puchero	pu·*che*·ro	a stew of pork, chicken, carrots, squash, potatoes, plantains and chayote (vegetable pear), spiced with radish, fresh cilantro and sour orange
tocino	to·*see*·no	bacon
venado	ve·*na*·do	venison, a popular traditional dish

SEAFOOD

calamar	ka·la·*mar*	squid
camarones	ka·ma·*ro*·nes	shrimp
cangrejo	kan·*gre*·kho	large crab
ceviche	se·*vee*·che	raw fish, marinated in lime juice
filete	fee·*le*·te	fillet
langosta	lan·*gos*·ta	lobster
mariscos	ma·*rees*·kos	shellfish
ostiones	os·*tyo*·nes	oysters
pescado	pes·*ka*·do	fish as food
pulpo	*pool*·po	octopus

EGGS

(huevos) estrellados	*(hwe*·vos) es·tre·*ya*·dos	fried (eggs)
huevos motuleños	*hwe*·vos mo·too·*le*·nyos	'Eggs in the style of Motul'; fried eggs atop a tortilla, garnished with beans, peas, chopped ham, sausage, grated cheese and a certain amount of spicy chili
huevos rancheros	*hwe*·vos ran·*che*·ros	fried eggs served on a corn tortilla, topped with a sauce of tomato, chilies and onions
huevos revueltos	*hwe*·vos re·*vwel*·tos	scrambled eggs

SOUP

caldo	*kal*·do	broth or soup
consomé	con·so·*may*	broth made from chicken or mutton base
sopa	*so*·pa	soup, either 'wet' or 'dry' as in rice and pasta
sopa de lima	*so*·pa de *lee*·ma	'lime soup'; chicken broth with bits of shredded chicken, tortilla strips, lime juice and chopped lime

SNACKS

antojitos	an·to·*khee*·tos	'little whims,' corn- and tortilla-based snacks, such as tacos and *gorditas*
empanada	em·pa·*na*·da	pastry turnover filled with meat, cheese or fruits
enchiladas	en·chee·*la*·das	corn tortillas dipped in chili sauce, wrapped around meat or poultry and garnished with cheese
gordita	gor·*dee*·ta	thick, fried tortilla, sliced open and stuffed with eggs, sausage etc, and topped with lettuce and cheese
panuchos	pa·*noo*·chos	Yucatán's favorite snack: a handmade tortilla stuffed with mashed black beans, fried till it puffs up, then topped with shredded turkey or chicken, onion and slices of avocado
papadzules	pa·pad·*zoo*·les	tortillas stuffed with chopped hard-boiled eggs and topped with a sauce of marrow squash (zucchini) or cucumber seeds
papas fritas	*pa*·pas *free*·tas	french fries
quesadilla	ke·sa·*dee*·ya	cheese and other items folded inside a tortilla and fried or grilled
relleno negro	re·*ye*·no *ne*·gro	turkey stuffed with chopped, spiced pork and served in a rich, dark sauce
(queso) relleno	*(ke*·so) re·*le*·no	stuffed (cheese), Dutch edam filled with minced meat and spices
salbutes	sal·*boo*·tes	same as *panuchos* but without the bean stuffing
sope	*so*·pe	thick corn-dough patty lightly grilled, served with salsa, beans, onions and cheese
torta	*tor*·ta	sandwich in a roll, often spread with beans and garnished with avocado slices

DESSERTS

helado	e·*la*·do	ice cream
nieve	*nye*·ve	sorbet
paleta	pa·*le*·ta	popsicle
pastel	pas·*tel*	cake
postre	*pos*·tre	dessert

FRUIT & VEGETABLES

aceituna	a·say·*too*·na	olive
calabacita	ka·la·ba·*see*·ta	squash
cebolla	se·*bo*·lya	onion
champiñones	sham·pee·*nyo*·nes	mushrooms
coco	*ko*·ko	coconut
elote	e·*lo*·te	corn on the cob
ensalada	en·sa·*la*·da	salad
fresa	*fre*·sa	strawberry
frijoles	fri·*kho*·les	beans
guayaba	gwa·*ya*·ba	guava
jícama	*khee*·ka·ma	turnip-like tuber, often sliced and garnished with chili and lime; sweet, crunchy and refreshing
jitomate	khee·to·*ma*·te	tomato
lechuga	le·*choo*·ga	lettuce
limón	lee·*mon*	lemon
maíz	mai·*ees*	corn
papas	*pa*·pas	potatoes
piña	*pee*·nya	pineapple
plátano macho	*pla*·ta·no *ma*·cho	plantain
plátano	*pla*·ta·no	banana
toronja	to·*ron*·kha	grapefruit
verduras	ver·*doo*·ras	vegetables

CONDIMENTS & OTHER FOODS

achiote	a·*cho*·te	reddish paste obtained from annatto seeds
arroz	a·*roz*	rice
azúcar	a·soo·*kar*	sugar
mantequilla	man·te·*kee*·ya	butter
mole	*mo*·le	a handmade chocolate and chili sauce
pan	pan	bread
sal	sal	salt

DRINKS

agua mineral	*a*·gwa mee·ne·*ral*	mineral water or club soda
agua purificada	*a*·gwa poo·ree·fee·*ka*·da	bottled uncarbonated water
atole	a·*to*·le	corn-based hot drink flavored with cinnamon or fruit
café (con leche/lechero)	ka·*fe* (kon *le*·che/le·*che*·ro)	coffee (with hot milk)
café americano	ka·*fe* a·me·ree·*ka*·no	black coffee
caguama	ka·*gwa*·ma	liter bottle of beer
horchata	hor·*cha*·ta	rice drink
jamaica	kha·*may*·ka	hibiscus flower, chief ingredient of *agua de jamaica*, a cold tangy tea
jugo de naranja	*khoo*·go de na·*ran*·kha	orange juice
leche	*le*·che	milk
té de manzanilla	te de man·sa·*nee*·ya	chamomile tea
té negro	te *ne*·gro	black tea

Environment

Arching northward between two seas like the head and shoulders of a *chac-mool* sculpture (as one Yucatecan poet put it), the Yucatán Peninsula has an insular character, in both its physical isolation from the Mexican interior and its distinct topography and wildlife.

THE LAND

Planeta.com (www .planeta.com) brims with information and links for those wanting to delve deeper into Mexico and the Yucatán's flora, fauna and environment.

Separated from the bulk of Mexico by the Gulf of Mexico, and from the Greater Antilles by the Caribbean Sea, the Yucatán Peninsula is a vast, low limestone shelf extending under the sea for more than 100km to the north and west. The eastern (Caribbean) side drops off much more precipitously. This underwater shelf makes Yucatán's coastline wonderful for aquatic sports, keeping the waters warm and the marine life abundant.

Approaching by air, you can easily make out the barrier reef that runs parallel to the Caribbean coastline at a distance of a few hundred meters to about 1.5km. Known variously as the Great Maya, Mesoamerican or Belize Barrier Reef, it's the longest of its kind in the northern hemisphere – and the second largest in the world – extending from southern Belize to Isla Mujeres off the northern coast of Quintana Roo. On the landward side of the reef, the water is usually no more than 5m to 10m deep; on the seaward side it plummets to depths of more than 2000m in the Yucatán Channel running between the peninsula and Cuba.

The peninsula is divided into three states in a 'Y' shape, with the state of Yucatán occupying the upper portion, flanked to the west and east by the states of Campeche and Quintana Roo respectively. Note that while Tabasco and Chiapas are included in this book, they are not part of the Yucatán Peninsula.

Around 3000 cenotes (natural underground pools) dot the Yucatán Peninsula.

Unlike much of Mexico, the Yucatán remains unobstructed by mountains. It rises to no more than a dozen meters above sea level in its northern section, and at its steepest, in the southern interior of Campeche state, only reaches about 300m. About 60km south of Mérida, near Ticul, the flat Yucatán plain gives way to the rolling hills of the Puuc ('hill' in Maya) region.

Capped by a razor-thin crust of soil, the peninsula is less productive agriculturally than elsewhere in Mexico. Formed by cretaceous-era sediments, its porous limestone bedrock does not allow rivers to flow on its surface, except in short stretches near the sea where their roofs have collapsed and in the southernmost reaches of the region where the peninsula joins the rest of Mexico (and Guatemala). Some underground streams don't release their water until well offshore; others empty into lagoons near the sea, such as the lovely Laguna Bacalar in southern Quintana Roo.

A uniquely Yucatecan geological feature, cenotes (pronounced seh-noh-tays) – from the Maya word *d'zonot*, meaning 'water-filled cavern' – are formed by the erosive effects of rainwater drilling down through the porous limestone.

An estimated 3000 of these limestone sinkholes dot the peninsular landscape. Yucatecans have traditionally gotten their fresh water from these natural cisterns, while modern visitors favor their crystalline waters for swimming and snorkeling (see boxed text, p64). South of the Puuc region, the inhabitants draw water from the *chenes* (limestone pools), more than 100m below ground.

HURRICANE ALLEY: THE PATH OF WILMA AND DEAN

Hurricanes have always walloped the Yucatán, but in recent years it feels like they are just getting bigger and badder. Blame global warming, blame Al Gore, blame regularly shifting climate patterns; whatever you decide to blame, the real loser has been the people, plants and animals of the Yucatán.

It started on October 22, 2005, when Hurricane Wilma hit the Yucatán's northeast coast – and stayed there for more than 30 hours. The 13th hurricane of the turbulent 2005 season – and fourth to reach Category 5 status – Wilma vented her worst forces on Isla Holbox, Isla Cozumel, Puerto Morelos and Cancún, causing M$20 billion in damages. Playa del Carmen and the Riviera Maya to the south were left largely unscathed.

Two years later Dean came to town, leveling the town of Mahahual and felling thousands of trees in southern Quintana Roo. For more on the path of Dean, see boxed text, p133.

While residents are slowly recovering from these hurricanes, the environmental wounds inflicted by Wilma and Dean could take much longer to heal. Many trees were uprooted by the storms, leaving dead branches that will serve as fuel for fires, adding to those already left behind in the wake of Hurricane Isidore, which ravaged the state of Yucatán in 2002.

WILDLIFE

The isolation of the Yucatán Peninsula and its range of ecosystems results in an extraordinary variety of plant and animal life, including a number of species that are unique to the region. Whether you like watching exotic birds, following the progress of sea turtles as they nest on the beach, swimming next to manta rays and schools of iridescent fish, or spying wildcats through your binoculars, you'll have plenty to do here.

Animals

BIRDS

For bird-watchers, the Yucatán is indeed a banquet. Over 500 bird species – about half of those found in the whole country – inhabit or regularly visit the peninsula. These include dozens of regional endemics; the island of Cozumel alone boasts three unique species.

Most of the peninsula's birds are represented in the various parks and biosphere reserves, and serious birders should make for at least a few of these. Numerous coastal species can be spotted at the Reserva de la Biósfera Ría Celestún (p180) and Reserva de la Biósfera Ría Lagartos (p198), on the western and eastern ends, respectively, of Yucatán state's coast. The varied panorama is due to a highly productive ecosystem where substantial freshwater sources empty into the Gulf of Mexico. A similarly diverse coastal habitat can be found at the Laguna de Términos (p219) in western Campeche. Parque Nacional Isla Contoy (p96), off the northern coast of Quintana Roo, is a haven for olive cormorants, brown boobies and many other seabirds.

Moving inland, the panorama shifts. The low, dry forests of the Puuc region contain two species of mot-mot, which nest in ruined temples. In the denser forests of the Reserva de la Biósfera Calakmul, train your binoculars on harpy eagles, ocellated turkeys and king vultures.

The Yucatán Peninsula is along the central migratory flyway, and between November and February hundreds of thousands of birds migrate here from harsher northern climes. The region's proximity to the Caribbean Sea also means you'll find island species not seen elsewhere in Mexico.

In late November or early December the environmental group **Ecoturismo Yucatán** (☎ 999-920-2772; www.ecoyuc.com) holds the Toh Festival, an annual birding festival that attracts enthusiasts from far and wide. This bird-a-thon,

The Spanish-language monthly magazine *México Desconocido* points out off-the-beaten track destinations and wildlife-watching spots with copious color photos and maps. Its website (www .mexicodesconocido .mx) includes an English-language section.

Birders should carry *Mexican Birds* by Roger Tory Peterson and Edward L Chalif, or *Birds of Mexico & Adjacent Areas* by Ernest Preston Edwards.

whose name is Maya for the locally seen turquoise-browed mot-mot, is based in Mérida but stages events in various parts of the peninsula.

LAND ANIMALS

To see recently snapped photos of jaguars, pumas and other Yucatán fauna in their habitat, go to the website of the environmental group Pronatura (www.pronatura-ppy .org.mx).

Around a quarter of the mammal species that exist in Mexico roam the Yucatán Peninsula. Some are the last of their breed.

There are jaguars in the forests, although, despite the Maya's traditional fascination with the New World's largest cat, poaching has all but wiped them out in southeastern Mexico. Your best chances of spotting one in the wild are probably in the Reserva de la Biósfera Calakmul (p222) in Campeche state. The peninsula's other native wildcat, the jaguarundi, is also at risk, as are the margay, ocelot and puma, though sightings of the latter aren't all that unusual in southern Yucatán.

The agile spider monkey inhabits some forested areas of the region. It looks something like a smaller, long-tailed version of the gibbon (an ape native to southwest Asia). Another elusive primate, the howler monkey, frequents forest around the ruins of Calakmul and isolated pockets elsewhere. Howlers are more often heard than seen, but you have a fair chance of seeing both them and spider monkeys at Punta Laguna (p132).

Hiking around the forest, you may run into tapirs and piglike peccaries (javelinas), as well as armor-plated armadillos. There are several species of anteater, all with very long, flexible snouts and sharp-clawed, shovel-like front paws – the two tools needed to seek out and enjoy feeding on ants and other insects. The animal's slow gait and poor eyesight make it a common roadkill victim. Besides the *tepezcuintle* (paca) and *sereque* (agouti) – large, tailless rodents – a few species of deer can be found as well, including the smallest variety in North America.

Crocodiles still ply the mangroves near the towns of Río Lagartos and Celestún in Yucatán state. Although their numbers are fast diminishing, plenty of the beady-eyed amphibious reptiles inhabit the Reserva de la Biósfera Sian Ka'an (p133), while smaller numbers lurk up and down the Caribbean coast, including at Laguna Nichupté, which backs onto Cancún's Zona Hotelera.

SEA CREATURES

The Great Maya Barrier Reef, paralleling the length of Quintana Roo's coast, is home to some of the finest snorkeling and diving in the world, a technicolor display of tremendous variety. The coney grouper, for example, is impossible to miss in its bright-yellow suit (it varies in color from reddish brown to sun yellow). The redband parrot fish is easy to recognize by the striking red circle around its eyes and the red band that runs from the eyes to the gills. Butterfly fish are as flamboyant as their name suggests (there are six species in the area), and the yellow stingray has spots that closely resemble the rosettes of a golden jaguar.

Providing an extraordinary backdrop to these brilliant stars of the sea is a vast array of corals. These come in two varieties: hard corals, such as the great star coral, the boulder coral and numerous brain corals; and soft corals, such as sea fans and sea plumes, which are particularly delicate and sway with the current. Successive generations of coral form a skin of living organisms over the limestone reef.

Complementing the experience is a water temperature that seldom dips below 77°F (27°C) and an amazing level of visibility. Because this coast contains not a single exposed river (many underground rivers do present themselves as they near the sea, but they carry very little soil), there's practically no sediment to cloud the water. The crystalline condition is only compromised during or after a storm, and for several weeks around April-May and September-October when reef animals and plants release zillions of eggs and droplets of sperm.

ENDANGERED SPECIES

Pollution, poaching, illegal traffic of rare species and the filling in of coastal areas for yet another resort are taking an enormous toll on the Yucatán's wildlife. Deforestation is also a major threat. While the Maya have practiced slash-and-burn agriculture for more than 2000 years, massive cutting really began to pick up in the 1960s. Since then more than five million hectares of forest have been felled in the Yucatán. Species on the peninsula that are threatened with extinction include five species of cat (the jaguar, puma, ocelot, margay and jaguarundi), four species of sea turtle, the manatee, the tapir and hundreds of bird species, including the harpy eagle, the red flamingo and the jabiru stork.

Various efforts are being made to save these and other endangered creatures from extinction, chiefly by environmental NGOs, such as **The Nature Conservancy** (www.nature.org) and its local partner **Pronatura** (☎ 999-988-4436; www .pronatura-ppy.org.mx; Calle 32 No 269, Col Pinzón, Mérida) This group focuses on preservation of wildlife habitats, particularly in the Ría Celestún, Ría Lagartos and Calakmul biosphere reserves, as well as the promotion of ecotourism. In particular, Pronatura is working to recover jaguar habitat in the area between the Reserva de la Biósfera Ría Lagartos and Isla Holbox, where 120 to 200 of these cats roam.

Tropical Mexico – The Ecotravellers' Wildlife Guide by Les Beletsky is a well-illustrated, informative guide to the land, air and sea life of southeastern Mexico.

Camps at Ría Lagartos, Laguna de Términos and Isla Holbox have been established to promote the survival of the six species of marine turtle that nest on the Yucatán's beaches. Volunteers collect turtle eggs and release hatchlings into the sea, and patrols prevent poachers from snatching eggs that are laid on the beaches. In Punta Laguna (p132) environmental groups are working with local *campesinos* (agricultural workers) to establish protection zones for endangered spider monkeys, which are closely monitored by researchers. The nutrient-rich waters around Isla Holbox attract whale sharks (see boxed text, p97), which are threatened by commercial fishing, and environmentalists have succeeded in getting this area categorized as a protected zone.

Plants

Vegetation varies greatly on the peninsula, with plants falling into four main categories: aquatic and subaquatic vegetation, and humid and subhumid forests. As you move inland from the coast, mangrove swamps are replaced

---

IN FOCUS: THE ENVIRONMENTAL IMPACTS OF MASS TOURISM *Lucy Gallagher*

Pinpointing the main environmental problems in the region is an extremely difficult task as there are so many! In order to accommodate all these workers, towns have mushroomed and, unfortunately, proper infrastructure has not been put in place. As a consequence, some of the main issues are solid-waste management and waste-water management. There is no adequate garbage removal system in most Riviera Maya towns, and the water treatment plants for the 'pueblos' in the region are either nonexistent or redundant. As a result, sewage generally ends up in the underground water systems and cenotes (limestone sinkholes) and then taken out to sea. This black or gray water, rich in nutrients, acts like a fertilizer and increases algal growth in the ocean. The algae, in turn, smothers coral, which has an impact on the entire marine environment.

You can learn more about Mexiconservación at www.mexconservacion.org.

Lucy Gallagher, Marine Projects Director, Mexiconservación

first by a fairly dense forest of low deciduous trees, then by a more jungly zone with tall trees and climbing vegetation and more than a few air plants (but without the soggy underbrush and multiple canopies you'd find further south). The taller trees of the peninsula's southern half harbor more than 100 species of orchid; for the really spectacular blooms, the avid orchid hunter will need to head into the highlands of Chiapas, where the exotic plants thrive at an elevation of about 1000m.

Dispersed among the mango and avocado trees are many annuals and perennials, such as the aptly named *flamboyán* (royal poinciana), bursting into bloom like a red-orange umbrella, and lavender-tinged jacaranda.

NATIONAL PARKS & RESERVES

There are several national parks on the peninsula, some scarcely larger than the ancient Maya cities they contain – Parque Nacional Tulum is a good example of this. Others, such as Parque Nacional Isla Contoy (p96), a bird sanctuary in northeastern Quintana Roo, are larger and have been designated to protect wildlife.

The Selva de Norte, which spans the southern part of the Yucatán Peninsula and northern Guatemala and Belize, is the world's second-largest tropical forest after the Amazon.

The fact that former president Ernesto Zedillo was an avid scuba diver was likely a factor in the creation of several *parques marinos nacionales* (national marine parks) off the coast of Quintana Roo: Arrecifes de Cozumel; Costa Occidental de Isla Mujeres, Punta Cancún y Nizuc; and Arrecifes de Puerto Morelos.

Very large national biosphere reserves surround Río Lagartos, Celestún (both in Yucatán state) and Banco Chinchorro (Quintana Roo), spreading across thousands of hectares. The Reservas de la Biósfera Ría Lagartos (p198) and Ría Celestún (p180) are well known for their diversity of bird and animal species, including large colonies of flamingos, while Banco Chinchorro (p137) contains a massive coral atoll, many shipwrecks and a host of marine species.

Even more impressive are the two colossal Unesco-designated biosphere reserves found in the Yucatán: the Reserva de la Biósfera Calakmul (p222), covering more than 7230 sq km in Campeche, Quintana Roo and Chiapas, as well as parts of Belize and Guatemala, is home to more than 300 species of birds. Jaguars, pumas, tapirs, coatis, peccaries and many other animals also call the preserve home. The Reserva de la Biósfera Sian Ka'an (p133), beginning 150km south of Cancún, covers 6000 sq km, including 100 sq km of the Great Maya Barrier Reef. Its life-forms range from more than 70 species of coral to 350 species of bird (by comparison, there are only 400 species of bird in all of Europe). Crocodiles, pumas, jaguars and jabirus are among the animals calling Sian Ka'an home.

ENVIRONMENTAL ISSUES

Large-scale tourism developments are affecting and sometimes erasing fragile ecosystems, especially along the 'Riviera Maya' south of Cancún. Many hectares of vital mangrove swamp have been bulldozed, and beaches where turtles once laid eggs are now occupied by resorts and condo-mondos. Ironically, tourism development is a major contributor to coastal erosion, as was made evident when 2005's Hurricane Wilma swept away the very beaches (many man-made) that attract hordes of tourists annually. And with the proliferation of new hotels comes the need for freshwater sources, increasing the danger of salinization of the water table. As employment-seekers converge on Quintana Roo's tourist zones, demand for building materials to construct makeshift housing for the burgeoning population is a persistent issue.

Another key issue is the fragmentation of habitat. As patches of jungle shrink with new settlement and construction of new highways, they

---

SMALL FOOTPRINTS, LARGE IMPACT: MORE TIPS TO STAYING GREEN

Travelers can help protect the Yucatán's environment by taking the following steps.

- Hire local guides. Not only does this provide local communities a more ecologically sound way of supporting themselves, it also attaches value to nature and wildlife.

- Avoid places that exploit wildlife for cheap thrills: taking pictures of the kids with a monkey, swimming with dolphins, turtle riding.

- Try to observe wildlife in its natural environment.

- Don't buy souvenirs made from endangered plants and animals that have been acquired illegally. By purchasing these items you aid in their extinction.

- Don't carry off anything that you pick up at the site of an ancient city or out on a coral reef. Don't buy these products if offered by locals.

- When snorkeling or scuba diving, be careful what you touch and where you place your feet; not only can coral cut you, but it's extremely fragile and takes years to grow even a finger's length.

- Keep water use down, especially in areas that have signs requesting you to do so. Most of the Yucatán Peninsula has limited water reserves, and in times of drought the situation can become grave.

---

become isolated and species become trapped in smaller habitats. Animals' movements are restricted and the gene pool cannot flow beyond the borders of their fragmented habitat.

Mexico's largest oil field, the Cantarell complex, is in the Bay of Campeche 85km off the shore of Ciudad del Carmen. In 2007 there was an 11,700-barrel oil spill in the bay. The oil will affect the marine life and birdlife of the region, but at the time of publication there were no reliable reports as to the extent of the damage. The Cantarell field is also yielding less oil than it did in the past, leading the company to seek new sources in the Alacranes reef off the coast of Progreso, and at Laguna de Términos, where further habitat destruction is feared.

And, of course, you can't underplay the effects global warming may be having on the peninsula. Over the past few years hurricanes seem to have grown in strength in the region, with both Dean and Wilma creating massive damage (see boxed text, p59).

Through the efforts of nongovernmental environmental groups, such as Pronatura, the level of protection on reserves has increased in recent years, and new reserves have been established and corridors extended. In 2004, for example, 370,000 acres of threatened forest in the Reserva de la Biósfera Calakmul was permanently protected. However, Yucatán's protected zones and reserves actually encompass private *ejido* (communally owned land) occupied by *campesinos*, whose activities, particularly cattle raising and logging, may infringe upon the environment. Seeking a solution, some environmental organizations have begun training *ejido* inhabitants as guides for ecotourism activities, thus providing alternative livelihoods. Such programs are under way in the Reserva de la Biósfera Calakmul and on Isla Holbox.

Think before you drink! Around 2.7 million tons of plastic are used to bottle water each year. Stay green by asking your hotelier to provide water coolers or by carrying your own water filter.

Yucatán Outdoors

Most visitors come to the Yucatán for the beaches, leaving the rest of the peninsula wide open for exploration and adventure. Come here to rip across warm surf beneath the wind-filled parabola of a kiteboard; dive into the aquatic wonderworlds inhabited by resplendent corals and technicolor schools of fish; leap from limestone ridges into the crystalline waters of Yucatán's mysterious, otherworldly cenotes (limestone sinkholes containing fresh water); or get sweaty (we mean really sweaty) as you cut your way through jungle trails to lost pyramids.

Yucatán is home to the second-largest barrier reef in the world, making this a world-class diving and snorkeling destination.

The Yucatán's amazing biological preserves offer hikers, kayakers and other outdoor wanderers the chance to spot birds and animals few people still see in the wild. Even the quickest of detours brings you face to face with everything you thought you'd only see on television, or invest yourself a bit more for a once-in-a-lifetime multiday trek or kayak.

Whatever your pleasure, be it the heart-stopping rush hanging on to a jungle-canopy zipline or a quiet stroll along a romantic, secluded beach at sunset, the Yucatán has what you're looking for. Don't hesitate to step outside the lines or do something on the spur of the moment. Those moments are likely to be the best ones of your whole trip.

DIVING & SNORKELING

The cenotes of Cuzamá are the most frequently photographed sinkholes of the peninsula.

Without a doubt, diving and snorkeling are the area's top activity draw. The Caribbean is world famous for its wonderful coral reefs and translucent waters full of tropical fish. The Yucatán's reefs stretch from the northeastern tip near Isla Contoy and as far south as Belize. Isla Cozumel (p108), once a pilgrimage site of the Maya and all but abandoned except for a small fishing community, was brought to the world's attention by Jacques Cousteau in 1961, shortly after the perfection of the Aqua-Lung. Guided by local fishermen, Cousteau was able to show – for the first time – the astounding richness of Cozumel's reefs, sparking in many who see it a lifelong passion for diving.

Although Cozumel was hammered by two hurricanes (Emily and Wilma) in 2005, most of the island's diveable reefs, and all of the deeper ones, remained unharmed. Unsurprisingly, it was the snorkeling sites that were hardest hit; yet, thanks to the tireless efforts of the local diving community (whose livelihood depends on the health of the reefs) and to the resilience

---

DIVING CENOTES

When you find yourself yawning at the green morays, eagle rays, dolphins, sea turtles, nurse sharks and multitudinous tropical fish, you're ready to dive a cenote (a deep limestone sinkhole containing water). Hook up with a reputable dive shop and prepare for (in the immortal words of Monty Python) 'something completely different.'

You'll be lucky if you see four fish on a typical cenote dive. Trade brilliance for darkness, blue for black, check that your regulator is working flawlessly and enter a world unlike anything you've ever dived before. Soar around stalactites and stalagmites, hover above cake-frosting formations and glide around in tunnels that will make you think you're in outer space.

Keep in mind these are fragile environments. Avoid applying sunscreen or insect repellent right before entering. Use care when approaching, entering or exiting, as the rocks are often slippery. Loud noises such as yelling disturb bats and other creatures – though most people find themselves subdued by the presence in these caverns. In rare cases, tourists have been seriously injured or killed by climbing on the roots or stalactites.

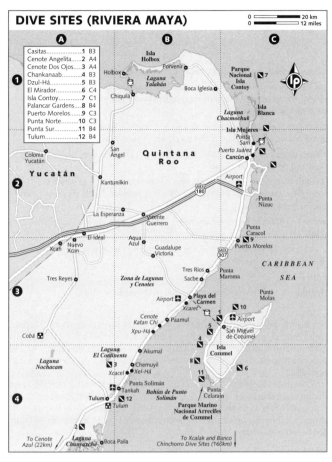

DIVE SITES (RIVIERA MAYA)

Casitas....................1	B3
Cenote Angelita........2	A4
Cenote Dos Ojos......3	A4
Chankanaab.............4	B3
Dzul-Há...................5	B3
El Mirador................6	C4
Isla Contoy...............7	C1
Palancar Gardens.......8	B4
Puerto Morelos.........9	C3
Punta Norte............10	C3
Punta Sur..............11	B4
Tulum...................12	B4

of this amazing ecosystem, things are returning to normal. If you're a diver heading to this area, Cozumel's Punta Sur and Palancar Gardens (see boxed text, p113) are must-sees. Snorkelers will want to check out Dzul-Há and Casitas, both of which are near the town of San Miguel de Cozumel. Hurricanes are not the only weather-related issue for divers, though. In Cozumel, *nortes* (storms bringing wind and rain from the north) can blow so strongly that the harbormaster closes ports – sometimes for days. While this won't affect the ferry between Cozumel and Playa del Carmen, it can wreck diving plans.

Though Cozumel is a must-see, serious divers will be happy to know that there are great dives to be enjoyed all along the eastern coast of the Yucatán Peninsula. Cancún, Isla Mujeres, Puerto Morelos, Playa del Carmen and Xcalak are all prime places to plan a diving vacation. The Banco Chinchorro (see 'Digging Out After Dean, the Big Picture', p133), the largest coral atoll in the northern hemisphere, was hard-hit by Hurricane Dean in 2007. At the time of publication, there was no news regarding the damage to the reef, so call a local operator (p137) before visiting.

Cenotes and lagoons are fragile ecosystems. Most environmentalists urge visitors to not wear sunscreen when entering these miraculous bodies.

RESPONSIBLE DIVING & SNORKELING

Please consider the following tips when diving and help preserve the ecology and beauty of reefs:

- Never use anchors on the reef, and take care not to ground boats on coral.

- Avoid touching or standing on living marine organisms or dragging equipment across the reef. Polyps can be damaged by even the gentlest contact. If you must hold on to the reef, only touch exposed rock or dead coral.

- Be conscious of your fins. Even without contact, the surge from fin strokes near the reef can damage delicate organisms. Take care not to kick up clouds of sand, which can smother them.

- Practice and maintain proper buoyancy control. Major damage can be done by divers descending too fast and colliding with the reef.

- Take great care in underwater caves. Spend as little time in them as possible as your air bubbles may be caught within the roof and thereby leave organisms high and dry. Take turns to inspect the interior of a small cave.

- Resist the temptation to collect or buy corals or shells or to loot marine archaeological sites (mainly shipwrecks).

- Ensure that you take home all your rubbish and any litter you may find as well. Plastics in particular are a serious threat to marine life.

- Do not feed the fish.

- Minimize your disturbance of marine animals. Never ride on the backs of turtles.

The Cozumel Dive Guide (www.cozumeldiveguide.com) offers great maps and descriptions of the area's dives. And a little shameless plug: Lonely Planet has a dive guide to the region, too.

Most of the places listed earlier are also great snorkeling spots. The best snorkeling is generally reached by boats, but the areas near Akumal, Isla Mujeres and Cozumel all offer pretty decent beach-accessed spots. Inland you can dive or swim in some of the Yucatán's famed cenotes (see boxed text, p124).

Most dive shops expect that you have your own equipment. If you do rent diving equipment, try to make sure that it's up to standard. And remember that coral reefs and other marine ecosystems are particularly fragile environments. For tips on caring for them and other tips for responsible diving, see boxed text, above.

KAYAKING

For those who like to keep their head above water, consider renting a kayak and exploring the shoreline or a mangrove swamp. Yucatán's coastal lagoons and sheltered bays make for magnificent kayaking, and there's often interesting wildlife to be seen among the mangrove thickets. It's uncommon to see manatees (unheard of now in the Cancún area) but possible in the protected reserves near Punta Allen (p134) and Xcalak (p137), if you're lucky. Even if you don't see a manatee, you'll spot amazing bird life: herons, egrets, storks, bitterns, and (in the right places) even flamingos or roseate spoonbills, ducks and migratory shorebirds as you glide the unpaddled pathways.

You'll find that many hotels and inns have kayaks for rent or for guests' use. Hostal del Pirata (p209) in Campeche arranges kayaking trips to Reserva de la Biósfera Los Petenes, a network of mangroves north of the city, and around the Isla de Jaina, which is an archaeological site on a small island up the coast. The Laguna de Términos in southern Campeche was a good kayaking spot, but a 2007 oil spill in the Bay of Campeche may have put an end to that. You'll want to call ahead to see how the region is faring. Kayaking tours in northern Quintana Roo can be booked through Playa del Carmen's

Alltournative (p105). In the south, book tours through Community Tours Sian Ka'an (p134).

You can rent equipment for DIY adventures all along the Caribbean coast at Cancún, Isla Holbox, Tres Ríos or at Playa Palancar near Cozumel. You can also get out onto the water at Rancho Punta Venado, Bahías de Punta Solimán, Tankah and Xcalak. The Laguna de Bacalar offers some freshwater adventure opportunities.

KITEBOARDING & WINDSURFING

The same winds that can make a dive challenging or even cause it to be canceled are a kitesurfer's dream. Strong northeast winds made Isla Holbox (p96) a prime spot for kiteboarding – though the region's protected status has put a temporary moratorium on the sport – but the whole Riviera Maya and the beaches near Progreso (p183) also see good winds. The beaches east of Progreso are much less crowded than those of Tulum (p122) or Cancún. But use care, especially when sunbathers might be within the range of a crashing kite. There's nothing like a lawsuit to spoil an otherwise fantastic vacation. It's Mexico, so don't assume that your instructor is licensed or on the lookout for dangers. Before setting off, check carefully for above-water obstacles, both moving and stationary. Check in and around the water for swimmers, boats and so on. Ask where the reef is and whether there are any other underwater obstacles that could pose a problem. In all but the biggest tourist centers of Quintana Roo – Cancún, Playa del Carmen, Cozumel and Isla Mujeres – you'll need your own equipment.

What about windsurfing? Well, with all that great wind you'd think there'd be lots of windsurfer rentals around (you remember, those things with a real sail?) but they're becoming scarce. Some cabanas or beachside hotels still rent them (or have ones you're welcome to use). But if you're an old-school, die-hard windsurfer and you're planning on finding a rig, you might need to call around or check online (unless you're going to bring your own).

If surfing is your thing, then you're in the wrong spot, barney. But the windward side of Cozumel does offer a few waves bigger than what you'd see in a toilet bowl.

February and March are the worst months for norte *winds, which can close ports and frustrate divers, but are great news for kiteboarders.*

HIKING

Hiking is a wonderful way to enjoy Yucatán's many outdoor delights. Any of the region's inland reserves make great hiking spots. Ruin-hoppers will find that even relatively flat areas, such as Chichén Itzá (p186), offer one or two hours of strenuous – even difficult – walking, especially around the midday heat. Bring a hat and lots of water. Less visited areas, such as Dzibanché (p145) and Kohunlich (p146), offer beautiful vistas from the tops of the structures, and lots of small trails through truly awesome jungle. The walking tours on Isla Contoy (p96) afford great opportunities to see birdlife.

FINDING A DIVE SHOP & STAYING SAFE

There's no such thing as a free dive. Beware of dive shops that promise certification after just a few hours' instruction. Make sure the dive shop is certified by **PADI** (www.padi.com), **NAUI** (www .naui.com) or **FMAS** (www.fmas.org.mx), the internationally recognized Mexican diving organization, and that its accreditation is up to date. If you don't have your own equipment, ask to see theirs before you commit. And ask to talk with your dive master before you leave. Make sure you feel comfortable with them: after all, it's your life. Lastly, remember that it's wise to know the locations of the nearest decompression chambers and the emergency telephone numbers, and to avoid diving less than 18 hours before a high-altitude flight.

Hiking tours are also available through companies located in the larger towns, such as Mérida (p157), Xpujil (p225) and San Cristóbal de Las Casas (p235). Many companies combine walks in national parks with visits to Maya sites. The tour operator in Xpujil offers weeklong jungle treks through the Reserva de la Biósfera Calakmul (p225) for those who just can't get enough of being bitten by mosquitoes.

The highlands of Chiapas are a great place for hiking, though you'll want to exercise extreme caution here given the current political situation. The Selva Lacandona (Lacandon Jungle; see boxed text, p242) is one of the most biodiverse spots in Mexico.

Yucatán also offers DIY-style hikes at just about anywhere you feel like parking the car. Ruined haciendas, overgrown jungle trails, a mile of flotsam-studded coastline – the wonders of Yucatán's outdoors are limited mainly by your own imagination and what you have time for.

That said, remember that this is the boonies: prepare carefully if you're going to be heading off the beaten track. Tell someone where you're headed and when you're due back, and bring relevant maps, a cell phone and GPS. Valuables left in a car are unlikely to be stolen, especially once you're outside the bigger cities, but it's a possibility. Actual muggings are even rarer, but it's always safer to travel as part of a group. More likely are problems with scorpions (painful, but not deadly), vipers (yep, deadly) or (wouldn't this make a great story?) crocodiles – in Celestún's estuaries they can reach a length of 6m (though this is rare). Even in the well-traveled spots such as the Ruta Puuc ruins there are poorly marked sinkholes: a wrong step could snap a leg or even plop you into an inescapable chamber below. Have fun, but keep the thinking cap on.

> Alternative and agro-tourism are on the rise throughout the peninsula. You can learn more about Quintana Roo's rural tourism alternatives at www.puertaverde.com.mx.

CYCLING

The relatively flat terrain of most of the Yucatán Peninsula can make pedaling an attractive option, though it's best to steer clear of busy roads where possible. Valladolid has a nice 5km bike trail to its nearby cenotes (p194). Campeche has a bike trail along its *malecón* (seafront promenade; p208) that would make for a pleasant spin. The secondary roads throughout the peninsula are all good biking spots, and most Maya living in the countryside get around on utilitarian tricycles. Mérida (p149) closes its downtown streets on Sundays to make room for cyclists and street vendors.

Bicycles are available for rent at the hostels in Campeche (p208), Isla Mujeres (p95), Cozumel (p118), Tulum (p128), Cobá (p129), Río Lagartos (p199) and Valladolid (p196).

For tips on cycling in the Yucatán, see above.

WATCHING WILDLIFE & BIRDS

In the Yucatán you can head inland into jungle so remote that it still has populations of jaguars, known only because of the occasional discoveries of half-eaten spider monkeys. Reserva de la Biósfera Calakmul (p222) and Punta Laguna (p132) offer your best chances of seeing a jaguar in the wild, but (seriously) don't get your hopes up. At Punta Laguna, native guides take you on a walking tour that will most probably include sightings of spider and howler monkeys. Extended trips may be possible, too, but should only be undertaken by expert trekkers who have ample experience.

> Nonprofit Amigos de Isla Contoy (www.islacontoy.org) has good information on visiting the island bird sanctuary.

Both Calakmul (p222) and Laguna de Términos (p219) are prime birding spots. Reserva de la Biósfera Calakmul has 235 different kinds of birds, of which 76% are resident species, including the ocellated turkey, a large bird with rainbow plumage like a peacock. Similar birding experiences can be found at Río Lagartos (p198) and Celestún (p180).

Spotting manatees is difficult but may be possible on a kayaking trip (see p66), which is also a great way to see birdlife. You can swim with whale sharks (see boxed text, p97) off the coast of Isla Holbox.

For more information on what you can see and where, check p59.

FISHING

The Caribbean coast has some good sport fishing, and the areas around Punta Allen (p134) and Xcalak (p137) are famous for their catch-and-release fly-fishing. Further north, fishing can be done on Isla Mujeres and around Cozumel. In Yucatán state, the popular areas are Río Lagartos (p198) and San Felipe (p200).

ZIPLINING & OTHER ADRENALINE RUSHES

Ziplining has become popular in recent years, and many of the cenote adventures also offer (or include) the adrenaline-filled, bird's-eye dangle over the jungle canopy. It's not as heart-stopping as bungee jumping or parachuting, but it's a whole lot safer and still pretty good fun. Hidden Worlds, which offers cave tours in its cenote park (p120), also has ziplining, as do many of the tour operators out of Cancún and Playa del Carmen.

All-terrain vehicle (ATV) and off-road tours are other possible outdoor thrills that are offered and often touted; however, weigh the potential fun with the clear and obvious environmental destruction that ATVs cause: tearing up trails, destroying plant and animal life. They are especially harmful to the fragile dune ecologies, as many of the plants that prevent the sand from shifting or blowing away can be killed with a single footstep, let alone a wheel of a vehicle. We feel most readers will want to find less destructive ways to enjoy their time in Yucatán, so ATV-specific tour operators have not been listed. Those who want to rent one, however, will have no problem finding a place that offers ATVs.

THE QUIET OUTDOORS

OK, so you're reading all this thinking, 'Every time I feel adrenaline it's right before I throw up… isn't there something relaxing I can do outside?' Of course there is. Even for folks who aren't adrenaline junkies, Yucatán offers great opportunities for quiet outdoor fun. The shallow waters between Isla Mujeres' Playa Norte and Punta Norte (p90) are perfect for low-key, no-current splashing and wading, and would be perfect for anyone with kids in tow. And Yucatán is blessed with hundreds of miles of beaches perfect for combing. Few things are nicer than softly padding your way along the beach as the sun sets (or rises).

By putting the guidebook down and exploring the little-known sights beyond the 'Lonely Planet Trail,' you create a more sustainable model for tourism.

DELVE DEEPER INTO NATURE – VOLUNTEER

One of the best ways to get up close and personal with wildlife is by volunteering your time – or money – to protect it. For more volunteer opportunities in the region, see boxed text, p264.

■ **AmeriSpan** (www.amerispan.com) Offers volunteer opportunities in environmental education and other areas.

■ **Mexiconservación** (www.mexiconservacion.org) This NGO dedicated to coastal preservation often looks for volunteers to study the reefs and coasts of Quintana Roo.

■ **Pronatura** (www.pronatura-ppy.org.mx) An environmental NGO that seeks volunteers to work with sea-turtle nesting areas in the Yucatán and in other projects.

■ **Vive Mexico** (www.vivemexico.org) NGO that coordinates international social, ecological and cultural work camps in Mexico.

Progreso (p183), Río Lagartos (p198) and Celestún (p179) all offer beautiful beaches. Between Mahahual (p136) and Xcalak (p137) there are lovely stretches of sand, fringed by palm trees and strewn with coral and conch shells, though there's also an amazing (sometimes fascinating!) amount of trash. Some of the hotels in this area employ full-time beach-cleaners to wander through every few hours and keep their sections clean.

There's plenty of golf to be found here, especially in Quintana Roo – some would say too much. A whole lot of mangrove forest is sacrificed to create the courses here. Wouldn't it be better to take up a less detrimental sport like co-ed naked blue whale spearing?

Parks and plazas are an integral part of Mexican and Yucatecan life, one that's often overlooked as we travelers dash about from one must-see sight to another. Yet few activities offer a better insight into the lifestyle and character of a town than a few hours spent people-watching in an outdoor park. It's a great opportunity to chat with locals: put the guidebook down for a while and get their suggestions on where to eat or what to see.

Quintana Roo

You'd think that as one of Mexico's most visited states, it'd be impossible to find a bit of solitude in Quintana Roo. But beyond the 'hit-me-baby-one-more-time' clubs of Cancún and 'McMaya' theme parks of the Riviera Maya, you just might find your own quiet piece of paradise.

There are talcum-powder beaches stretching all the way from Cancún to the Belizean border, unassuming Caribbean islands protected by the world's second-largest barrier reef, and impressive Maya sites throughout this long-arching sliver of limestone, salt and sea.

It's the peninsula's super state, highly developed, heavily touristed, easy to get around and chock-full of adventure opportunities – from exploring the depths of the region's numerous cenotes (limestone sinkholes filled with fresh water) and world-class dive sites to beating your own path to seldom-visited ruins such as Dzibanché and Kohunlich in the Maya heartland.

Most trips to Quintana Roo (kin-tah-nah *roh*) will begin and end in Cancún. Chicer-than-thou Playa del Carmen, Cozumel (truly a diver's delight) and Isla Mujeres round out the not-at-all-off-the-beaten-track-but-still-a-pretty-damned-good-place-to-spend-your-vacation fairylands of Quintana Roo.

Several hurricanes (Wilma, Emily and Dean, just to name the biggies) have slammed into the region in recent years. And widespread tourism development along the coast has also taken its environmental toll on the fragile reefs and coastal lagoons of the area, but Quintana Roo is too big now to be knocked out by mere hurricane winds. It'll take at least a dozen greedy real-estate developers and a couple million more complacent visitors to signal the death knell.

HIGHLIGHTS

- Set out for a morning bird-watching mission from the remote Costa Maya beach town of **Xcalak** (p137), heading out a bit later for a dive at **Banco Chinchorro** (p137)

- Stay out till dawn in one of the happening beachfront clubs in **Playa del Carmen** (p107), taking the ferry across to **Isla Cozumel** (p108) the next day for a snorkel and a swim

- Take a whale shark excursion from **Isla Holbox** (see boxed text, p97)

- Go iguana-spotting among the mysterious, spectacularly situated ruins of **Tulum** (p124)

- Marvel at Jurassic-like jungles amid the mysterious ruins of **Kohunlich** (p146) and **Dzibanché** (p145)

- POPULATION: 1.14 MILLION
- AREA: 50,351 SQ KM

QUINTANA ROO

CANCÚN

☎ 998 / pop 526,700

Unlike many cities in the world, Cancún just isn't afraid. It's unabashed and unapologetic, and in that lies its high-gloss charm. So send in the Maya dancers, swashbuckling pirates and beer-chugging US spring breakers. Cancún can take it. But can you?

Like Las Vegas, Ibiza or Dubai, Cancún is a party city that just won't give up. Top that off with a pretty damned good beach and you have one of the western hemisphere's biggest tourist draws, bringing in as many as four million visitors (mostly from the US) annually. And with four million visitors each year you have crime and corruption, over-the-top, outrageously overhyped tourist traps, clamor and clutter. You also have a boomtown economic juggernaut, and an accidental metropolis with a growing culinary sophistication. There are a few hip nightspots in the old downtown area and even some relatively authentic market areas.

Cancún isn't for everyone, and this type of mass tourism certainly won't interest many Lonely Planet–style travelers. But as long as you're here, might as well dig into the kitsch and crap that make this city unique.

HISTORY

When you look around at the giant hotels and supermalls it's hard to imagine that pre-1970s there was nothing here but sand and fishermen. In the 1970s Mexico's ambitious planners decided to outdo Acapulco with a brand-new, world-class resort located on the Yucatán Peninsula. The place they chose was a deserted sand spit located offshore from the little fishing village of Puerto Juárez, on the peninsula's eastern shore: Cancún. Vast sums were sunk into landscaping and infrastructure, yielding straight, well-paved roads, potable tap water and great swaths of sandy beach.

Hurricanes Wilma and Emily whipped into town in 2005, destroying area hotels, flooding much of the city and carrying off much of Cancún's precious beach sand. Nearly M$200 million later, the beaches are back, the hotels are up and running, and Cancún is ready to get you drunk and get you tanned.

ORIENTATION

Cancún consists of two very distinct areas: Ciudad Cancún (downtown) and Isla Cancún (the Zona Hotelera).

The airport is about 8km south of the downtown. Puerto Juárez, the main port for passenger ferries to Isla Mujeres, is about 3km north of downtown. Punta Sam, the dock for the slower car ferries to Isla Mujeres, is about 7km north of downtown. Irregular services leave from the Zona Hotelera.

Ciudad Cancún

Ciudad Cancún is where you should stay if you're looking to save a bundle. Prices are reasonable (for Cancún, that is) and food is great: seafood and traditional Yucatecan fare. Beaches are about 20 minutes away via Route 1 city buses, but there's also plenty to do and see in the centro itself. The main north–south thoroughfare is Avenida Tulum, a wide boulevard lined with banks, shopping centers and restaurants. Park Las Palapas is quiet and safe, a great place for an afternoon picnic or an evening stroll. Shopaholics will enjoy the colorful markets, which offer jewelry, handicrafts and souvenirs, as well as a variety of inexpensive Mexican food.

Plaza Las Américas, on Avenida Tulum at the south edge of the centro, is a vast modern shopping mall that includes the Liverpool and Chedraui department stores, a multiplex cinema, a food court and a salsa dance club. Don't confuse it with Plaza América, a small, aging arcade on Avenida Cobá with a few airline offices.

Zona Hotelera

The Zona Hotelera is what most people think of when they say 'Cancún': the sandy spit that encloses a scenic lagoon on one side and has the Caribbean's azure-greens on the other. Its main road, Blvd Kukulcán, is a four-lane divided avenue that leaves Ciudad Cancún and heads eastward for a few kilometers passing condominium developments, several hotels and shopping complexes, to Punta Cancún (Cancún Point) and the Centro de Convenciones (Convention Center).

From Punta Cancún, the boulevard heads south for about 13km, flanked on both sides for much of the way by huge hotels, shopping centers, dance clubs and many restaurants and bars, to Punta Nizuc (Nizuc Point). Here it turns westward and then rejoins the mainland,

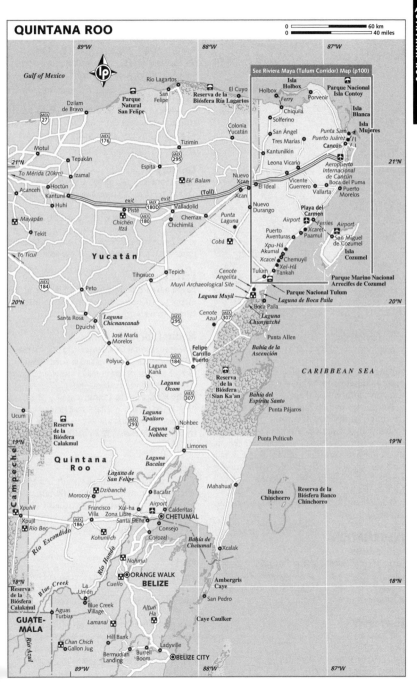

QUINTANA ROO

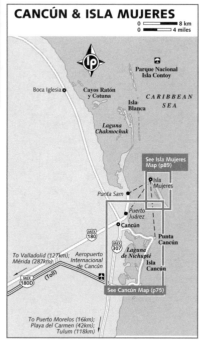

cutting through light tropical forest for a few more kilometers to its southern terminus at Cancún's international airport.

Addresses in the Zona Hotelera are refreshingly simple: instead of a street name (usually Blvd Kukulcán anyway) a kilometer distance from the 'Km 0' roadside marker at the boulevard's northern terminus in Ciudad Cancún is given. Each kilometer is similarly marked. Most bus drivers will know the location you're heading but, if in doubt, you can just ask to be dropped off at the appropriate kilometer marker.

INFORMATION
Bookstores
Fama (Map p77; ☎ 884-6541; Av Tulum 105 SM 22 M4 Lotes 27 & 27A) Magazines, atlases and books in several languages. The store is downtown near the southern end of Tulipanes.

Emergency
Cruz Roja (Red Cross; ☎ 884-1616)
Fire (☎ 060)
Police (Map p75; ☎ 060; Blvd Kukulcán)
Tourist Police (☎ 885-2277)

Immigration
Instituto Nacional de Migración (Immigration Office; Map p77; ☎ 881-3560; cnr Av Náder 1 & Av Uxmal; 9am-1pm Mon-Fri) For visa and tourist-card extensions. Enter the left-hand, southernmost of the two offices.

Internet Access
Hotels can charge as much as M$50 per 15 minutes. Internet cafés in Cancún centro are plentiful, speedy and cheap, costing M$15 per hour or less.

Laundry
Lava y Seca (Map p77; ☎ 892-4789; Crisantemos 20; 9am-6pm Mon-Sat) Downtown; charges M$15 per kilogram.
Lavanderia Lagoon (Map p75; ☎ 044 999-883-1129; Paseo Pok-Ta-Pok; 9am-8pm Mon-Sat) All the resorts in the Zona offer laundry service, but Lavanderia Lagoon charges M$15 per kilogram and takes two hours.

Left Luggage
Pay-in-advance lockers (per 24hr M$70) are at the airport, just outside customs at the international arrivals area.

Medical Services
American Medical Care Center (Map p75; ☎ 884-6133; Plaza Quetzal, Blvd Kukulcán Km 8) Has bilingual (Spanish and English) doctors and 24-hour emergency care. Major US insurance plans are accepted.
Centro Medico Caribe Cancún (Map p77; ☎ 883-9257; Av Yaxilan 74A; 24hr) A small facility on the roundabout on Av Yaxilan with 24-hour assistance.
Hyperbaric Chamber (☎ 892-7680; Alcatraces 44; 24hr)

Money
There are several banks with ATMs on Avenida Tulum (including a Banamex and two Bancomers), between Avenidas Cobá and Uxmal. Cancún's international airport also has ATMs and money exchange; for more details see p86.

Post
There is no post office in the Zona Hotelera, but most hotels' reception desks sell stamps and will mail letters. There's a FedEx office in the bus terminal (Map p77).
Main post office (Map p77; ☎ 884-1418; cnr Avs Xel-Há & Sunyaxchén; 8am-6pm Mon-Fri, 9am-1pm Sat) Downtown at the edge of Mercado 28. You can also post mail in the red postal boxes sprinkled around town; collection frequency varies.

CANCÚN

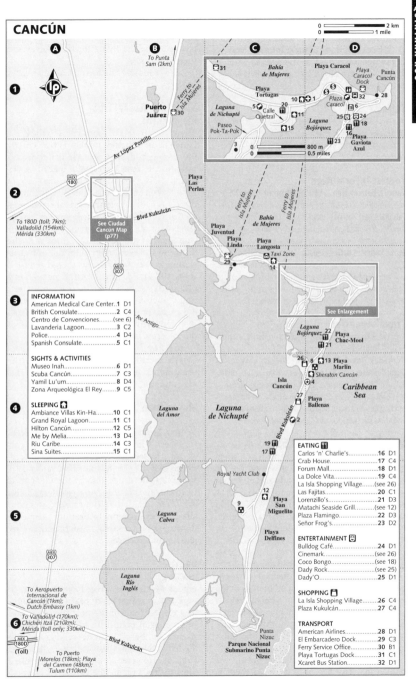

0 —————— 2 km
0 —————— 1 mile

INFORMATION
American Medical Care Center.**1** D1
British Consulate.....................**2** C4
Centro de Convenciones.......(see 6)
Lavandería Lagoon................**3** C2
Police..................................**4** D4
Spanish Consulate.................**5** C1

SIGHTS & ACTIVITIES
Museo Inah...........................**6** D1
Scuba Cancún........................**7** C3
Yamil Lu'um.........................**8** D4
Zona Arqueológica El Rey.......**9** C5

SLEEPING
Ambiance Villas Kin-Ha.........**10** C1
Grand Royal Lagoon.............**11** C1
Hilton Cancún......................**12** C5
Me by Melia.........................**13** D4
Riu Caribe...........................**14** C3
Sina Suites..........................**15** C1

EATING
Carlos 'n' Charlie's...............**16** D1
Crab House...........................**17** C4
Forum Mall..........................**18** D1
La Dolce Vita........................**19** C4
La Isla Shopping Village.......(see 26)
Las Fajitas...........................**20** C1
Lorenzillo's..........................**21** D3
Matachi Seaside Grill...........(see 12)
Plaza Flamingo.....................**22** D3
Señor Frog's.........................**23** D2

ENTERTAINMENT
Bulldog Café.........................**24** D1
Cinemark............................(see 26)
Coco Bongo.........................(see 18)
Dady Rock...........................(see 25)
Dady'O................................**25** D1

SHOPPING
La Isla Shopping Village........**26** C4
Plaza Kukulcán.....................**27** C4

TRANSPORT
American Airlines..................**28** D1
El Embarcadero Dock............**29** C3
Ferry Service Office..............**30** B1
Playa Tortugas Dock.............**31** C1
Xcaret Bus Station................**32** D1

Telephone

Phoning by Voice Over Internet Protocol (VOIP) can be done at most internet cafés.
Call Center (Map p77; Av Cobá 5) At Soberanis Hostal. Offers good rates on international calls and calls to other parts of Mexico.

Toilets

Many internet cafés have a small bathroom in back, free for internet users. Cleanliness varies. Or strut your way into a hotel lobby restroom.

Tourist Information

Cancún Convention & Visitors Bureau (Map p77; ☎ 884-6531; Av Cobá; ☉ 9am-2pm & 4-7pm Mon-Fri) This place near Avenida Tulum, Ciudad Cancún, has ample supplies of printed material and usually a fairly knowledgeable English-speaker in attendance.
State tourism office (Sedetur; Map p77; ☎ 884-8073; Pecari 23; ☉ 9am-9pm Mon-Fri) The Convention & Visitors Bureau's parent is mysteriously tucked away near Avenida Cobá, a fair walk south of the center, but its information is good and includes all of Quintana Roo.

Travel Agencies

In the Zona Hotelera, most big hotels have travel agencies.
Nómadas Travel (Map p77; ☎ 892-2320; www .nomadastravel.com; Av Cobá 5) Downtown, next to the Soberanis Hostal, Nómadas is a student-oriented agency that books and makes changes to air tickets, makes some reservations for accommodations on the Yucatán Peninsula and offers packages to Cuba, among other services.

DANGERS & ANNOYANCES

The biggest safety danger in Cancún isn't street crime – it's the streets themselves. Traffic speeds by along narrow roads and pedestrians (often drunk) are frequently injured. A night spent clubbing is more likely to lead to a poked eye or twisted ankle than a mugging; however, if anyone *does* demands money, don't argue with them. Most violent incidents have involved fights where tourists or locals have actively put themselves in danger.

Theft of valuables left unattended is a possibility, but no more so than in other parts of the world. Use prudence, keeping vital items with you or leaving them in a hotel safe, and you'll avoid problems. Napping sunbathers may wake up to find cameras or wallets gone; don't leave anything unattended on the beach.

Hawkers can be quite irritating but are not dangerous. The best way to avoid them is to just keep walking. As frustrating as this may be, remember that these vendors are just trying to make a living for themselves and their families.

See p78 for information on Cancún's water hazards.

SIGHTS & ACTIVITIES

Maya Ruins

There are two sets of Maya ruins in the Zona Hotelera and, though neither is particularly impressive, both are worth a look if time permits. In the **Zona Arqueológica El Rey** (Map p75; admission M$34; ☉ 8am-5pm), on the west side of Blvd Kukulcán between Km 17 and Km 18, there's a small temple and several ceremonial platforms. The other, much smaller, site is **Yamil Lu'um** (Map p75; admission free), atop a beachside knoll in the parklike grounds near the Sheraton Cancún hotel. Only the outward-sloping remains of the weathered temple's walls still stand, but the ruin makes for a pleasant venture, as much for its lovely setting as anything else. To reach the site visitors must pass through either of the hotels flanking it or approach it from the beach – there is no direct access from the boulevard.

The tiny Maya structure and *chac-mool* (Maya sacrificial stone sculpture) in the beautifully kept grounds of the Sheraton hotel are authentic.

Museo Inah

Closed for the past two years from Hurricane Wilma damage (even the museum's director doesn't know when it'll be opening its doors), **Museo Inah** (Map p75; ☎ 883-0305; admission M$35; ☉ 9am-8pm Tue-Fri, 10am-7pm Sat & Sun) is on the south side of the Centro de Convenciones in the Zona Hotelera. Skulls exhibiting the deformities caused intentionally by Maya parents to beautify their children are a bit creepy but also on display are jewelry and artifacts.

Beaches

ACCESS

Under Mexican law you have the right to walk and swim on every beach in the country except those within military compounds. In practice, it is difficult to approach many stretches of beach without walking through the lobby of a hotel, particularly in the Zona Hotelera. However, as long as you look like a tourist (this shouldn't be hard, right?), you'll

CIUDAD CANCÚN

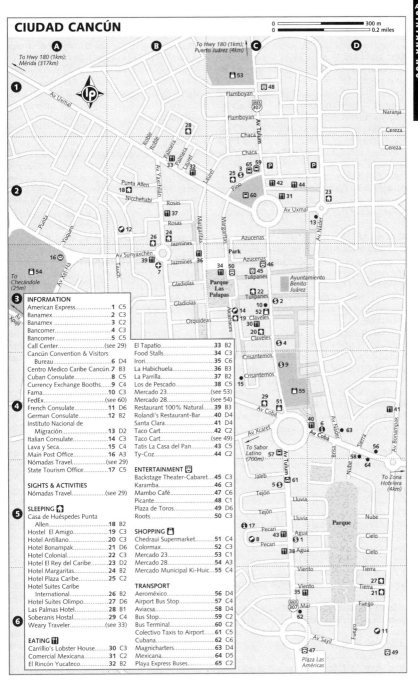

QUINTANA ROO

usually be permitted to cross the lobby and proceed to the beach.

Starting from Ciudad Cancún in the north-west, all of Isla Cancún's beaches are on the left-hand side of the road (the lagoon is on your right). The first beaches are Playa Las Perlas, Playa Juventud, Playa Linda, Playa Langosta, Playa Tortugas and Playa Caracol; after you round Punta Cancún, the beaches to the south are Playa Gaviota Azul, Playa Chac-Mool, Playa Marlin, the long stretch of Playa Ballenas, Playa San Miguelito and finally, at Km 17, Playa Delfines. Delfines is about the only beach with a public parking lot big enough to be useful; unfortunately, its sand is coarser and darker than the exquisite fine, white sand of the more northerly beaches.

BEACH SAFETY

Cancún's ambulance services respond to as many as a dozen near-drownings per week. The most dangerous beaches seem to be Playa Delfines and Playa Chac-Mool. Though rare, accidents with kiteboards, paragliders or jet skis can happen; be aware of other beachgoers at all times.

Though the surf is usually gentle, undertow is a possibility, and sudden storms (called *nortes*) can blacken the sky and sweep in at any time without warning. A system of colored pennants warns beachgoers of potential dangers:

Blue Normal, safe conditions.
Red Unsafe conditions; use a swimming pool instead.
Yellow Use caution, changeable conditions.

Water Sports

For decent snorkeling, you need to travel to one of the nearby reefs. Resort hotels, travel agencies and various tour operators in the area can book you on day-cruise boats that take snorkelers on the barrier reef, as well as to other good sites in the region. To see the relatively sparse aquatic life off Cancún's beaches, you can rent equipment for about M$100 a day from most luxury hotels. Most of the major resorts rent kayaks and the usual water toys; a few make them available to guests free of charge.

Scuba Cancún (Map p75; ☎ 849-5226; www.scuba cancun.com.mx; Blvd Kukulcán Km 5.2), a family-owned and PADI-certified (Professional Association of Diving Instructors) dive operation with many years of experience, was the first dive shop in Cancún. It offers a Cancún snorkeling tour for M$290 and a variety of dive options (including cenote, night and nitrox dives), as well as fishing trips, at reasonable prices (one/two tank M$594/740, equipment rental extra). The bilingual (English and Spanish) staff are safety oriented and environmentally aware; there are Japanese- and Korean-speaking instructors on call as well.

CENOTES

There are a handful of nice cenotes just outside of Puerto Morelos (see p100), along what tourist-brochure writers are calling the Ruta de Los Cenotes (that's right, that's the Route of the Cenotes). One of the newer cenote discoveries, **Taj Mahal**, is south of Playa del Carmen. It's a doable dive, snorkel, or even a chance to just go 'wow.'

CANCÚN FOR CHILDREN

With such easy access to sand, sea and swimming pools, most kids will have a blast in Cancún. Some hotels offer babysitting or day-care services – be sure to check in advance if these are needed. Remember that the sun, strong enough to scald even the thickest of tourist hides, can be even more damaging for kids or babies: make sure your children are properly protected.

If the beach gets boring or you want a change of scene, the theme parks of Xel-Há (p120) or Xcaret (p118) make a good day trip. Xcaret in particular has a highly suspect environmental record, hardly the 'eco-paradise' its brochure touts. For a bit more culture, head over to Chichén Itzá (p186) or Cobá (p130) for the day.

TOURS

Most hotels and travel agencies work with companies that offer tours to surrounding attractions. Popular day trips are Chichén Itzá, Cobá, Tulum, and the theme parks at Xel-Há and Xcaret. Often local touts at the hotels and agencies are paid only in commissions, so if you chat with someone and decide to take the tour later, be sure to take the time to find the same person who assisted you or they may not get paid.

Nómadas Travel (Map p77; ☎ 892-2320; www .nomadastravel.com; Av Cobá 5) is a popular agency that operates out of the lobby of Soberanis Hostal downtown. It offers a choice of reasonably priced packages to popular destinations.

DAY-TRIPPER: THREE GREAT EXCURSIONS FROM CANCÚN

Go ahead, leave the all-inclusive for a day to check out the world beyond the little yellow wristband. And a quick sustainable travel tip: skip the group tour, using that extra dough to hire a local guide and buy some crafts. Staying the night in your destination will bring even more money into the local community.

- Chichén Iztá (p186) – rent a car so you can take the old highway through Valladolid. Stop in the small Maya communities along the way for out-of-sight *panuchos* (tortillas stuffed with mashed beans, topped with shredded turkey or chicken and avocado).

- Isla Mujeres (p88) – take the ferry from Puerto Juárez to save money. Check out the turtle farm in the morning, then swing up north to a sweet little swimming spot near the Avalon Reef Club.

- Nuevo Durango and beyond – make your own way through the Maya hinterland as you explore small villages such as Nuevo Durango, and forgotten cenotes that don't even make it into the guidebooks. If you ask nicely, locals will often put you up in a *palapa* (thatched palm-leaf-roofed shelter). Bring your own hammock and a sense of adventure.

SLEEPING

Almost all hotels offer discounts in the 'low' season, but at many places there are up to five different rates: Christmas and New Year are at a premium you can count on, but there are high rates in March and April for US spring break, Easter, and even July and August (when locals have their holidays). Ask if there is a 'promotion,' too, as many places may be willing to deal. Many Zona Hotelera spots offer internet specials, so it's best to book ahead of time if you want to stay near the beach.

Wherever possible in the following listings, simple low- and high-season prices are detailed; more complex schemes are represented by a price range unless otherwise specified; and peak-season rates may be higher.

Ciudad Cancún

BUDGET

'Budget' is a relative term; prices in Cancún are higher for what you get than most anywhere else in Mexico. There are many cheap lodging options within a few blocks of the bus terminal northwest on Avenida Uxmal. The area around Parque Las Palapas has numerous hostels and budget digs as well. Hotel hawkers tend to waylay anyone exiting the bus station, sometimes going so far as to insult people heading to other hotels. Just say 'No' and keep heading to the place you planned on.

Weary Traveler (Map p77; ☎ 887-0191; www.weary travelerhostel.com; Palmera 30; dm fan/air-con M$100/110; ⊠ ☒ ▣) The cramped shared rooms could use a bit of work, but the Weary Traveler has all the basic ingredients to make a good hostel:

a cool rooftop terrace kitchen area for swilling beers and swapping tales, a big breakfast buffet, lots of guests from around the globe and a friendly owner. Ask about private rooms for rent down the street.

Las Palmas Hotel (Map p77; ☎ 884-2513; Palmera 43; dm/d M$100/300; ☒) A family-run affair, the Palmas has a clean downstairs dorm room with much-appreciated air-con. There's a handful of bright, cheery and affordable rooms upstairs. Continental breakfast includes freshly squeezed orange juice. If you are looking to get away from the backpacker scene for a bit, then stay here. If not, head over to Weary Traveler–landia or the hostels near Parque Las Palapas.

Hostel El Amigo (Map p77; ☎ 892-7056; 29 Alcatrazes; dm fan/air-con; M$120/140; ☒ ▣) Right on the corner of Parque Las Palapas, this small hostel has shiny new shared rooms, a quiet sitting area for postbeach cervezas and, of course, the requisite computers. The dorms have fewer beds than at other hostels, meaning you won't meet tons of travelers, but will probably get a better night's sleep.

Soberanis Hostal (Map p77; ☎ 884-4564, 800-101-0101; www.soberanis.com.mx; Av Cobá 5; dm/d M$120/590; ▣) It's good value with a nice location, and is a fun place to meet friends. All rooms have very comfortable beds, tiled floors, cable TV and nicely appointed bathrooms. Though primarily a midrange hotel, the Soberanis also has four-bed 'hostel' rooms with the same amenities as the regular rooms, including a free continental breakfast. The cafeteria serves affordable lunches and dinners and the hotel also has a bar, internet facilities (per hour M$10), a phone center, a tour agency and also a student-oriented travel agency.

ourpick Hotel Colonial (Map p77; ☎ 884-1535; Calle Tulipanes 22; d fan/air-con M$350/450; ⚡) Perhaps the best buy in its price range, the Colonial has a central courtyard, superclean rooms with traditional textile bedspreads, and a pleasant central courtyard. Get a room toward the back as the street noise in this party district can be a bit much.

Casa de Huéspedes Punta Allen (Map p77; ☎ 884-0225; www.puntaallen.da.ru; Punta Allen 8; s/d M$400/450) On a side street that's a bit dicey after dark, this friendly, family-run guesthouse has ample rooms, spotless tiles and nice bathrooms. From Avenida Uxmal, walk south along Avenida Yaxchilán and take the first right.

MIDRANGE

Midrange in Cancún is a two-tiered category; the Ciudad Cancún area is much cheaper than the Zona Hotelera and only a short R-1 bus ride away from the Zona's beaches.

Hotel Suites Olimpo (Map p77; ☎ 884-0875; www.hotelolimpo.com.mx; Av Bonampak 221 SM4; s/d M$450/600; ⚡ 🖳) Beds are a bit sproingy, but the rooms are clean and include phone and cable TV. Some have kitchenettes, and some are noisier than others. It's right across from Hotel Bonampak, and there's a rambling, rather scraggly green area around the corner.

Hotel Antillano (Map p77; ☎ 884-1132, 800-288-7000; www.hotelantillano.com; Claveles 1; d M$500-700; ⚡ 🖳) A large beige shoebox with a groovy-groupie-bebop feel just off Avenida Tulum, this is a very pleasant and quiet place with a relaxing lobby, nice pool, good central air-con and cable TV. Rooms on Avenida Tulum are noisier than those in the back. Rates include a welcome drink, continental breakfast and a Zona Hotelera beach pass.

ourpick Hotel El Rey del Caribe (Map p77; ☎ 884-2028; www.reycaribe.com; cnr Avs Uxmal & Náder; d M$630-820; ⚡ ⚡ 🖳 ♨) El Rey is a true eco-tel that composts, employs solar collectors and cisterns, uses gray water on the gardens and even has a few composting toilets. This is a beautiful spot with jungly courtyard, azure swimming pool and small Jacuzzi. Many of the 31 rooms have a fully equipped kitchenette; all have comfortable beds, hairdryers and safes (you can use your own lock). Two children under 11 can stay for free, and it offers good prices in low season.

Hotel Bonampak (Map p77; ☎ 884-0280; www.hotelbonampak.com; Av Bonampak 225 SM4; r M$690; ⚡ 🖳 🖳) Not a speck of character, but this motel is good value: the pool is sunny, the wide stairways are airy and fresh, the rooms are spotless and many have small balconies. Ask for a room overlooking the pool to avoid the road noise. There's wi-fi in the lobby.

Hotel Suites Caribe Internacional (Map p77; ☎ 884-3999; www.caribeinternacional.com; cnr Avs Sunyaxchén & Yaxchilán; d/tr M$790/840; ⚡ 🖳 🖳) This six-story hotel boasts 80 rooms with cable TV. The junior suites have two comfortable beds, a sofa and kitchenette. Amenities include secure parking, a small pool in an agreeable courtyard, and a restaurant and bar. Rates are often negotiable here; try asking for a discount.

Hotel Plaza Caribe (Map p77; ☎ 884-1377, in the USA 866-294-8514; www.hotelplazacaribe.com; Calle Pino; d M$840-990; ⚡ 🖳) Directly across from the bus terminal between Avenidas Tulum and Uxmal, this all-business hotel offers 166 comfortable rooms with full amenities, including a pool and restaurant. Rooms have white-tile floors and comfy beds; baths are clean but overchlorinated. The *palapa* (thatched, palm-leaf-covered shelter) bar is a nice place to sip a drink on a hot day.

TOP END

Hotel Margaritas (Map p77; ☎ 884-9333, 800-537-8483; www.margaritascancun.com; cnr Avs Yaxchilán & Jazmines; s & d M$1300, tr M$1500; ⚡ 🖳 🖳) The curvaceous swimming pool is eye-catching. The 100 guestrooms are clean but musty, so check and see if one with a balcony is available. If so, they air out nicely. This place is across the street from the Suites Caribe and also sports six floors. There's a (pricey) restaurant, a decent bar, Jacuzzi and helpful staff.

Zona Hotelera
MIDRANGE

Hotels near Blvd Kukulcán in the Zona Hotelera are close to cheap, convenient transportation. Both the following hotels are on Laguna Nichupté rather than the sea.

Sina Suites (Map p75; ☎ 883-1017; www.cancunsinasuites.com.mx; Quetzal 33; ste M$800-2000; ⚡ 🖳) Right on the lagoon, this is a great deal in low season, when prices drop by as much as 20%. The hotel was completely renovated after Hurricane Wilma, and its 36 spacious suites are still lookin' good: each with two double beds, a separate living room (with a sofa bed) and satellite TV, a kitchen and 1½ bathrooms. Bring some friends to save money. This gleaming white hotel also has a pool and restaurant surrounded by Brady Bunch–inspired astroturf.

Grand Royal Lagoon (Map p75; ☎ 883-2749; www .grlagoon.com; Quetzal 8A; r & studio M$900; 🆇 🅡) A breezy place with cable TV and safes; most rooms have two double beds, while some have kings. Some studios come with a kitchenette and balcony, and an outdoor ping-pong table makes for fun. The hotel has a small pool, and guests have use of the Fat Tuesday beach club. The hotel is 100m off Blvd Kukulcán Km 7.7.

TOP END

All of the resorts described below are in the Zona Hotelera and border the Caribbean. Guestrooms come equipped with air-con and satellite TV, and many have balconies with sea views. Many hotels offer all-inclusive packages, often at reasonable rates if you're willing to forgo eating or entertainment elsewhere. Often the best room rates are available through booking hotel-and-airfare packages: shop around.

Ambiance Villas Kin-Ha (Map p75; ☎ 891-5400; www .ambiancevillas.com; Blvd Kukulcán Km 8; r M$1460/1570; 🆇 🅧 🅡 🅹) A great family spot, Kin-Ha offers day care and babysitting, plus a 'kids' club' designed to let parents relax while the kids are occupied. You'll never need to leave the hotel's grounds (though we think you should), as there are 136 big rooms and suites in five buildings in this rolling complex. All rooms feature a balcony and two double beds or one king-sized bed…or you can just use the beachside mattresses. There are bars, markets, travel and car-rental agencies and more on the premises. Prices listed are for European plans, but you can arrange an all-inclusive stay.

Hilton Cancún (Map p75; ☎ 881-8000; www.hilton .com; Blvd Kukulcán Km 17; d M$1700; 🆇 🅡 🅢) This used to be one of the granddaddies of the strip, but lately it's being upstaged by young upstarts such as the Melia. Still, you get seven cascading pools, a beautiful Zen-inspired garden spa, and yoga on the beach. The blue-and-turquoise bed throws are attractive, matching the ocean view outside. And the price is right – even in high season.

Me by Melia (Map p75; ☎ 881-2500; www.mebymelia .com; Blvd Kukulcán Km 12; d low/high season M$1780/3200; 🆇 🅧 🅡 🅢) 'Enough about you, let's talk about me!' That's the philosophy at this uber-

modern, expressionist-inspired hotel. It won't suit everyone, but if you prefer clean lines over your standard Cancún baroque, then Me is the place for you. Only half the rooms have ocean views, and it just ain't worth it to pay this much and not have a view of the Caribbean blue.

Riu Caribe (Map p75; ☎ 848-7850; www.riu.com; Blvd Kukulcán Km 5.5; s low/high season M$1900/2140, d M$2690/3860; 🆇 🅧 🅡 🅢) Riu rules the Riviera Maya – they're everywhere. This particular Riu has 541 rooms (all with ocean views), including 60 junior suites, and a family-friendly atmosphere. All come with private terraces that overlook a dazzling swimming pool and 200m of beach. The lobby is gorgeous, with a nice view of the water, pretty tiled floors and stained-glass ceiling. Prices listed are all-inclusive; room-only rates are not available.

EATING
Ciudad Cancún

Restaurants in Ciudad Cancún range from ultra-Mexican taco joints to fairly expensive eateries.

BUDGET

Cancún's downtown area has lots of good budget eats. Mercados 23 and 28 have a number of tiny eateries, and Parque Las Palapas has some food stands. Few nonalcoholic options beat cantaloupe or watermelon juices; ask for *agua de melón* or *agua de sandia* and you'll feel like you're sipping chilled rainbow juice.

Los de Pescado (Map p77; Av Tulum 32; meals M$16-75; 🕙 10am-5:30pm) It's easy to order at this restaurant as there are only two choices: ceviche or tacos. Knock either back with a beer or two, and you'll see why this is one of the best budget spots in Ciudad Cancún. With its thatched roof, you can tell the owners take a certain pride in their work – that's why this is always the most crowded restaurant on the block.

Santa Clara (Map p77; ☎ 884-9548; Av Bonampak 157; cones M$30-40; 🕙 9am-10pm) There's a pleasant patio at this little café specializing in ice cream. It also serves coffee and various sweet dishes. There's milk and cheese as well, all locally produced.

Ty-Coz (Map p77; ☎ 884-6060; Av Tulum; sandwiches M$30-40; 🕙 9am-11pm Mon-Sat) A bakery-café just north of the Comercial Mexicana supermarket. It has granite tabletops and a pleasing

STRETCH YOUR BUDGET

For self-catering, try **Comercial Mexicana** (Map p77; cnr Avs Tulum & Uxmal), a centrally located supermarket close to the bus station. It has a good selection of produce, meats, cheeses and cookies.

The main market is set back from the street, west of the post office. Its official name is long; locals simply call it Mercado Veintiocho (Mercado 28; Map p77). Another market, Mercado 23 (Map p77), is a bit north of the bus station and offers inexpensive, nontouristy shopping. Most eateries are in the inner courtyard and open from about 7:30am to 6pm daily.

Inexpensive Mexican food can also be found at the food stalls in the northeast corner of Parque Las Palapas, and at two good taco carts operating in the evening – one at the north edge of the Comercial Mexicana parking lot (across Avenida Tulum from the bus terminal) and the other at the southeast edge of the Plaza de Toros (Bullring) parking lot, at Avenidas Sayil and Bonampak.

ambience, and serves good coffee, baguettes and croissants, as well as sandwiches made with a variety of meats and cheeses. There's also a spot near Km 7.5 on Blvd Kulkulkán.

Tatis La Casa del Pan (Map p77; ☎ 892-3877; cnr Pecari & Av Tulum; breakfast M$35-50, sandwiches & light dishes M$30-60; ☯ 7am-8pm Mon-Fri, 7am-3pm Sat) Friendly and fun, with art on the walls and a great selection of wholesome fare. Come here for coffee and espresso that might be your last good cup of coffee before heading off into the rest of Yucatán. The crêpes are *delicioso.*

El Tapatío (Map p77; ☎ 887-8317; cnr Avs Uxmal & Palmera; dishes M$40-90, set meals M$35; ☯ 9am-11:30pm) Touristy but good – a popular choice for hostel-goers, who suck down the mammoth fruit and veggie juices, shakes and smoothies at any time of day.

El Rincón Yucateco (Map p77; Av Uxmal 24; dishes M$40-100; ☯ noon-10pm Mon-Sat) A reasonably priced Yucatecan place that's across from Hotel Cotty, serving a nice variety of favorites along with very weak 'American'-style coffee. *Sopa de lima* ('lime soup'; chicken soup with lime) is light: a good option for anyone nursing a stomach problem (or a hangover).

MIDRANGE

As with budget restaurants, the Ciudad Cancún area has a wider variety of midpriced places than the Zona Hotelera.

Restaurant 100% Natural (Cien por Ciento Natural; Map p77; ☎ 884-0102; Av Sunyaxchén; mains M$40-150; ☯ 7am-11pm; V) Vegetarians and health-food nuts delight at this health-food chain near Avenida Yaxchilán, which serves juice blends (try the 'Crazy Yog' or the 'Vampiro'), a wide selection of yogurt-fruit-vegetable combinations, and brown rice, pasta, fish

and chicken dishes. The on-site bakery turns out whole-wheat products, and the entire place is very nicely decorated and landscaped. Service is excellent – at times even too attentive.

our pick Checándole (Map p77; ☎ 884-7147; Av Xpujil 6 SM 27; mains M$50-130; ☯ noon-8pm) If you can only eat at one restaurant in Cancún, then you should eat here. It's a bit away from the city center, but well worth the extra effort. Dressed up with a *palapa* roof, Checándole specializes in *chilango* (Mexico City) cuisine. The *menu del día* (fixed three-course meal) is just M$45 – great value. If it's offering *pollo en mole poblano* (chicken smothered in a handmade chocolate and chili sauce), you should definitely go for it.

Rolandi's Restaurant-Bar (Map p77; ☎ 884-4040; Av Cobá 12; mains M$70-140; ☯ 1pm-12:30am) A Swiss-Italian eatery with a wood-fired pizza oven, between Avenidas Tulum and Náder just off the southern roundabout. It serves elaborate pizzas, spaghetti plates and a range of northern Italian dishes.

La Parrilla (Map p77; ☎ 884-8193; Av Yaxchilán 51; mains M$70-370; ☯ noon-2am) Any Cancún eatery founded before the saccharine 1980s gets to call itself venerable. And La Parrilla (founded in 1975) should get a capital 'V.' A traditional Mexican restaurant popular with locals and tourists alike, it serves a varied menu from all over Mexico, with Yucatecan specialties thrown in. Try the tasty *calamares al mojo de ajo* (squid in garlic sauce), steaks or sautéed grouper. *Mole* (a Spanish sauce) enchiladas and delicious piña coladas both run about M$60. If you're lucky, a waiter will serve you beer, balancing it on his head from the bar to your table.

Irori (Map p77; ☎ 892-3072; Av Tulum 226; rolls M$50-100, nigiri pair M$30-70, teppanyaki meals M$100-340; ☺ 1-11pm Mon-Sat, 1-7pm Sun; ☂) Enjoy the show as the chef slices and dices the night away at this Japanese-run restaurant serving sushi and many other Japanese favorites in an intimate and nicely decorated setting. There's even a kids' menu if you've got sushi-scoffing rugrats in tow.

TOP END

Restaurants in this category offer better value than those in the Zona Hotelera.

Carrillo's Lobster House (Map p77; ☎ 884-1227; Claveles 35; shrimp & fish dishes M$120-200, lobster dishes M$380) Try Carrillo's Plato Cozumel if you're looking for something a bit special. This somewhat formal restaurant has air-con indoors and is fan-cooled outdoors, and entertainment is provided by mariachis. Follow the good smells leading to the blue building and you'll be in the right place.

our pick **La Habichuela** (Map p77; ☎ 884-3158; Margaritas 25; mains M$150-420) An elegant restaurant with a lovely courtyard dining area, just off Parque Las Palapas. The specialty is shrimp and lobster in curry sauce served inside a coconut with tropical fruit, but almost anything on the menu is delicious. The seafood ceviche and *tapa al ajillo* (potatoes in garlic) are mouthwatering. The gorgeous aquarium in the lobby makes for a very attractive wait (reservations are advised). Finish with lime sorbet splashed with Xtabentún, a Yucatecan anise-flavored liqueur.

Zona Hotelera

BUDGET

For budget eats in the Zona Hotelera, try the food courts at any large mall. La Isla Shopping Village, Plaza Flamingo and the Forum Mall (all Map p75) hold other options to get a bite, including pizzas and burgers. There's a Checándole in Plaza Flamingo.

Las Fajitas (Map p75; Blvd Kulkulcán Km 7.5; mains M$12-75; ☺ 7am-8pm Mon-Sat, 7am-5pm Sun) It offers a complete breakfast for just M$30, and you can get fresh *mahimahi* (a type of fish) fillets for M$75 (they worked out a deal with a local diver to get fresh fish) – not a bad deal for the Zona Hotelera. But there's a catch: it's roadfront on Blvd Kulkulcán, meaning you'll be sucking down more exhaust than cerveza. Still, it's the best budget spot on the strip!

MIDRANGE

The Zona Hotelera is a vast swath of mainly Tex Mex–style places catering to the just-flew-in crowd. Prices are higher and quality is generally lower than what you'll find in Ciudad Cancún. A number of places cater to a young crowd, with conga lines where waiters cheer and pour watery tequila down dancers' throats as they weave by. So you'll either want to head *for* or *away from* **Señor Frog's** (Map p75; Blvd Kulkulcán Km 9.8; dishes M$100-200) and **Carlos 'n Charlie's** (Map p75; Blvd Kulkulcán Km 5.5; dishes M$100-180) for that kind of dining experience.

TOP END

'Pay-per-view' takes on a whole different meaning in the Zona Hotelera. Though there are many establishments in this category, their prices sometimes reflect their location and what's outside the window more than the quality of food.

La Dolce Vita (Map p75; ☎ 885-0161; www.cancunitalianrestaurant.com; Blvd Kulkulcán Km 14.6; pizzas M$125-150, mains M$145-450; ☺ noon-11pm) One of Cancún's fanciest Italian restaurants, it

---

VANESSA'S PICKS

Despite all our 'authority and attitude,' Lonely Planet authors will never know the local dining scene as well as the locals themselves. That's why we got together with Cancún local Vanessa Trava and 10 of her closest friends to see where Cancún's young professionals choose to dine. Call ahead for reservations.

La Barbacoa de la Tulum If you love tacos, head to this cheap cantina in the Plaza de Toros.
La Favola (☎ 889-9180) Exquisite Italian dining.
La Troje (☎ 887-9556) It's *muy caro* (expensive), but the excellent international cuisine is worth it.
Manyee (☎ 881-5900) Go for the delicious wraps.
Marakame Café (☎ 887-1010) For international flavor with live music.
Mocambo (☎ 883-0398) For fresh seafood.
Salute (☎ 881-5556) An eclectic mix of Mediterranean and Mexican fare.

offers white wicker chairs and soft, romantic lighting, plus great lagoon views and attentive staff. Try the chicken with sun-dried tomatoes and finish with crêpes Suzette (for two). With a bottle of red, white or rosé this could be the start or the finish of a wonderful day.

Crab House (Map p75; ☎ 885-3936; Blvd Kukulcán Km 14.8; dishes M$140-200; 🕑 1-11:30pm) Offers a lovely view of the lagoon that complements the seafood. The long menu includes many shrimp and fillet-of-fish dishes. Crab and lobster are priced by the pound.

Matachi Seaside Grill (Map p75; ☎ 881-8047; Blvd Kukulcán Km 17; mains M$220-450) The Matachi is a stylish, intimate place inside the Hilton, right on the beach. It offers a variety of Mexican and Asian-inspired cuisine, seafood, sushi and other creative dishes. It also has one of the best views in town.

Lorenzillo's (Map p75; ☎ 883-1254; Blvd Kukulcán Km 10.5; mains M$190-440; 🕑 1pm-12:30am) Reputed by locals to be Cancún's best seafood restaurant, Lorenzillo's gives you 19 separate choices for your lobster presentation, including a taste-bud-popping chipotle plum and tamarind sauce. Facing the lagoon, it's a good sunset joint.

ENTERTAINMENT

Many of the clubs and restaurants are open for drinks for much of the day.

Clubs

CIUDAD CANCÚN

Ciudad Cancún clubs are generally mellower than those in the rowdy Zona Hotelera. Stroll along Avenida Yaxchilán down to Parque Las Palapas and you are sure to run into something (or somebody) you like.

GAY & LESBIAN CANCÚN

Cancún is well known for its lively gay and lesbian scene (though there's more for gay men than women), meaning there's plenty to do most nights. Here's but a pinch of what's out there.

Backstage Theater-Cabaret (Map p77; ☎ 887-9106; Tulipanes 30) Backstage features drag shows, strippers (male and female), fashion shows and musicals. Terrific ambience, joyful crowd.

Karamba (right) Popular with cross-dressers.

Picante (right) More for talkers than dancers.

Roots (Map p77; ☎ 884-2437; Tulipanes 26; admission Fri & Sat M$50; 🕑 6pm-1am Mon-Sat) Pretty much the hippest bar in Ciudad Cancún, Roots features jazz, reggae or rock bands and the occasional flamenco guitarist. It's also a pretty decent restaurant, serving pasta, salads, seafood and meat dishes, with main dishes running M$80 to M$160. Thursday seems to be the best night for catching nice tunes with a crowd.

Mambo Café (Map p77; ☎ 887-7891; Plaza Las Américas; admission women/men M$30/50; 🕑 10pm-6am Thu-Sun) Upstairs from the food court in the middle of the huge mall on the southern stretch of Avenida Tulum. It features live salsa, Cuban and other Caribbean music and is very popular with Cancún's young people. Thursday is ladies' night.

Sabor Latino (off Map p77; ☎ 892-1916; cnr Avs Xcaret & Tankah; admission women/men M$40/60, Wed free; 🕑 10:30pm-6am, closed Sun-Tue low season) On the 2nd floor of Chinatown Plaza, this is another happening club. Its live acts feature Dominican salsa and other tropical styles.

Karamba (Map p77; ☎ 884-0032; cnr Azucenas & Av Tulum; 🕑 10pm-6am Thu-Sun) A venerable standby above the Club Sandwich Café, it has frequent drink specials. Admission ranges from free to M$70. Come here for a varied crowd of gays, lesbians and cross-dressers.

Picante (Map p77; Av Tulum 20; 🕑 9pm-6am) Set back from Avenida Tulum a few blocks north of Avenida Uxmal, this place isn't as 'spicy' as its name suggests, but it is a longtime neighborhood gay bar. It often features movies shown at high volume until about 1am, when the dance music comes on.

Built into the **Plaza de Toros** (Bullring; Map p77; cnr Avs Bonampak & Sayil) are several bars, some with music, that draw a largely local crowd.

ZONA HOTELERA

The club scene in the Zona Hotelera is young, loud and booze-oriented – the kind that often has an MC urging women to display body parts to hooting and hollering crowds. Carlos 'n Charlie's and Señor Frog's (both p83) have dancing in the evenings. Most of the dance clubs charge around M$200 admission, which may include two or three drinks; admission with open-bar privileges (ie drink all you want) is M$200 to M$250, rising to M$400 to M$500 during spring break. Though some clubs open as early as 5:30pm, most don't get hopping much before midnight.

INSIDE THE SEEDY SEX-TOURISM TRADE

In recent years an alarming number of tourists are visiting Mexico not for the beaches and booze, but for the brothels.

As if this weren't bad enough, now Mexico is being used as a bridge to bring sex slaves, often underage, into the US, Japan and other developed countries, according to reports by Reuters.

Depending on what news source you look at, there are as many as 5000 child sex slaves in Mexico – calling them prostitutes just makes it sound too much on the up-and-up. The age of consent varies from region to region based on local laws, but is as low as 12 in some areas and under certain circumstances (people in the countryside get married young). On the whole, however, the general trend is toward creating a higher age of consent of 18 years. Prostitution is legal in most parts of the country (prostitutes must be 18 or older); however, this hasn't stopped pedophilia rings from profiteering in the trade of children.

Things may be changing. New laws in the US have made it possible to prosecute Americans who have had sex with children even if it occurred outside of its borders. And public awareness of and indignation about this issue has grown, even in Mexico.

If you're serious about your partying, consider a 'Party Hopper Package,' available at most of the lobby tour offices or at other travel agents downtown. Usually M$400 to M$500 will buy all you can drink at four or five of the popular clubs; some packages include van transportation.

The following four clubs are clustered along the northwest-bound side of Blvd Kukulcán, all within easy stumbling distance of each other. Be careful crossing the street.

Coco Bongo (Map p75; ☎ 883-5061; Forum Mall; ✆ 10:30pm-5am) This is often the venue for MTV's coverage of spring break, and tends to be a happening venue just about any day of the week. The club opens with celebrity impersonators, dancers and circus acts (clowns, acrobats and the like) for an hour or so, then the rock, pop and hip-hop start playing.

Dady'O (Map p75; ☎ 800-234-9797; Blvd Kukulcán Km 9; ✆ 10pm-4:30am) Opposite the Forum Mall, this is one of Cancún's more elaborate dance clubs. The setting is a five-level black-walled faux cave with a two-level dance floor and what seem like zillions of laser beams and strobes. The predominant beats are Latin, house, techno, trance and hip-hop, and the crowd is mainly 20-something.

Dady Rock (Map p75; ☎ 883-3333; Blvd Kukulcán Km 9; ✆ 5:30pm-3:30am) A steamy rock-and-roll club – it plays techno on occasion – next door to Dady'O and attracting a slightly older crowd than its neighbor. Admission is free until 10pm.

Bulldog Café (Map p75; ☎ 883-1133, ext 544; Blvd Kukulcán Km 9; ✆ 10pm-late) Bills itself as 'the home of rock and roll,' and features live bands and a jumbo Jacuzzi that's made to look a bit like a cenote but is really just a showcase for bikini-clad staff to splash around. Look for the giant bulldog sign outside and you'll know you've found the right place.

Cinemas
Cinemark (Map p75; ☎ 883-5603; La Isla Shopping Village) In general, Hollywood movies are shown in English with Spanish subtitles; however, English-language children's movies are usually dubbed in Spanish. Ticket prices run about M$40 for children and adults.

SHOPPING
Neither Ciudad Cancún nor the Zona Hotelera fits the bill as a bargain-hunter's paradise – still, Cancún can be a great place to shop for souvenirs and jewelry.

Plaza Kukulcán (Map p75; Blvd Kukulcán Km 13) The largest (and definitely among the stuffiest, attitude-wise) of the indoor malls is chichi Plaza Kukulcán. Of note here is the huge art gallery (taking up nearly half of the 2nd floor); the many stores selling silverwork; and La Ruta de las Indias, a shop featuring wooden models of Spanish galleons and replicas of conquistadors' weaponry and body armor. But all is not lost; the plaza has a bowling alley and a large food court.

La Isla Shopping Village (Map p75; Blvd Kukulcán Km 12) Unique among the island's malls, this is an indoor-outdoor place with canals, an aquarium, ultramodern parasol structures and enough other visual distractions to keep even the most inveterate hater of shopping amused. For tipplers on your list, consider picking up a bottle of Xtabentún, a Yucatecan anise-flavored liqueur.

Mercado Municipal Ki-Huic (Map p77; Av Tulum) This warren of stalls and shops carries a wide variety of souvenirs and handicrafts.

Colormax (Map p77; ☎ 887-4625; Av Tulum 22; ✆ 9am-9pm Mon-Sat, 10am-6pm Sun) Colormax, just north of Calle Claveles, offers a wide assortment of film. It does developing as well.

Locals head to either Mercado 28 (Map p77) or Mercado 23 (Map p77) for clothes, shoes, inexpensive food stalls, hardware items and so on. Of the two, Mercado 23 is the least frequented by tourists. If you're looking for a place *without* corny T-shirts, this is the place to go.

Across Avenida Tulum from Colormax is the Chedraui supermarket (Map p77); the upstairs clothing department here sometimes has souvenir-grade items at very affordable prices.

GETTING THERE & AWAY
Air

Cancún's **Aeropuerto Internacional de Cancún** (off Map p77; ☎ 886-0047) is the busiest in southeastern Mexico. The airport has a few ATMs: the best place to change money is the Banamex bank along the back wall outside the domestic baggage-claim area (behind the coffee shop); it has an ATM and offers good exchange rates. Opposite the bank are (inconvenient) pay-in-advance baggage lockers costing M$70 for 24 hours (a tip is appreciated, but optional). There's wi-fi access and a free, Spanish-only public internet terminal that has sticky, punch-button keys.

Cancún is served by many direct international flights; for more information see p266. Between Mexicana de Aviación and its subsidiary, Click Mexicana, there is at least one and up to eight daily flights to each of the following destinations: Mexico City (one way M$1350, 2¼ hours), Oaxaca ($1700, direct, four hours), Tuxtla Gutiérrez (M$2168, one stop, six hours), Villahermosa (M$1699, one stop, 2½ hours) and Mérida (M$2698, direct, one hour). Click Mexicana offers flights daily to Mérida, and six to Cozumel. It also flies twice daily to Havana, Cuba (round-trip only, M$3198), but you can get better package deals through local travel agents. US visitors heading to Cuba should pay particular attention to the recent US crackdown on agencies and visitors organizing trips to Cuba. Cubana,

the Cuban national airline, has daily flights as well.

Aviacsa, a regional carrier based in Tuxtla Gutiérrez, has direct flights from Cancún to Mexico City (one way M$887, two hours), with connections for Oaxaca, Tapachula (M$1780, five hours), Tuxtla Gutiérrez (M$1900, five hours) and Villahermosa (M$1750, four hours), as well as points in central and northern Mexico.

Magnicharters flies direct to Monterrey, Mexico City, Guadalajara and León.

Taca Airlines flies from Cancún direct to Flores, Guatemala (round-trip M$2540, two hours), connecting to points in Central America several times a week.

If you intend to fly from Cancún to other parts of Mexico, reserve your airline seat ahead of time to avoid any unpleasant surprises. The following airlines are represented in Cancún:

Aeroméxico (Map p77; ☎ 287-1868; Av Cobá 80) Just west of Avenida Bonampak.

American Airlines (Map p75; ☎ 800-904-6000; Hotel Fiesta Americana Coral Beach, Blvd Kukulcán Km 8.7) Has an airport counter as well.

Aviacsa (Map p77; ☎ 887-4214; Av Cobá 39) Also has an airport counter.

Azteca (☎ 886-0831) Airport counter.

Click Mexicana (☎ 884-2000) Airport counter.

Continental Airlines (☎ 886-0006, 800-900-5000; www.continental.com) Airport counter.

Copa (☎ 886-0653) Airport counter.

Cubana (Map p77; ☎ 887-7210; Av Tulum)

Delta Airlines (☎ 800-123-4710, 886-0668) Airport counter.

Magnicharters (Map p77; ☎ 884-0600; Av Náder 93)

Mexicana de Aviación (Map p77; ☎ 881-9090, 800-801-2010; Av Cobá 39) 800-801-2010

Northwest (☎ 800-907-4700) Airport counter.

Taca Airlines (☎ 886-0008; www.taca.com) Airport counter.

United Airlines (☎ 800-003-0777; www.united.com) Airport counter.

US Airways (☎ 800-007-8800; www.usairways.com) Airport counter.

Boat

There are several points of embarkation to reach Isla Mujeres from Cancún by boat. From Punta Sam (off Map p77) costs M$15, Puerto Juárez (Map p75) costs M$35, and leaving from the Zona Hotelera (Map p75) costs about M$70. You'll need to head to Chiquilá to get to Isla Holbox. While there

BUS SERVICES FROM CANCÚN

Destination	Cost (M$)	Duration (hr)	Departures
Chetumal	210	5½–6½	many buses
Chichén Itzá	140	3–4	hourly 2nd-class Oriente buses 5am–5pm
Chiquilá (for Isla Holbox)	70	3½	Mayab buses at 7:50am & 12:40pm, Noreste buses at 1:45pm
Felipe Carrillo Puerto	130	3½–4	8 1st-class Ado buses & hourly 2nd-class Mayab buses
Mérida	200–270	4–6	15 UNO & ADO GL buses, hourly 2nd-class Oriente buses (5am–5pm)
Mexico City 1060 (Terminal Norte)	24	2	ADO buses
Mexico City (TAPO)	1100	22–24	1 ADO & 4 ADO GL buses
Palenque	490	12–13	4 buses
Playa del Carmen	34	1–1¼	Riviera every 15min 5am–midnight, many Playa Express & Mayab buses; see also buses to the airport, p88
Puerto Morelos	12–17		Use Playa del Carmen buses
Ticul	190–220	6	6 Mayab buses
Tizimín	85	3–4	9 2nd-class Noreste & Mayab buses
Tulum	62	2¼–3	many Riviera, Playa Express & other buses
Valladolid	110	2–3	many buses
Villahermosa	540	12	11 buses
Xcaret	30	1½	many buses; uses Playa Express or Mayab buses (bus will leave you 1km from Xcaret's main gate)

are ferries to Cozumel from Cancún, you are better off getting there from Playa del Carmen's dock.

See p95 for details of boats to Isla Mujeres and p98 for boats to Isla Holbox.

Bus

Cancún's modern bus terminal occupies the wedge formed where Avenidas Uxmal and Tulum meet. Upon leaving you'll be asked by every taxi driver if you want a ride; you'll also be approached by hotel hawkers pushing 'deals.' Despite this, it's a safe area and you'll be fine walking around. Across Pino from the bus terminal, a few doors from Avenida Tulum, is the ticket office and miniterminal of Playa Express, which runs air-conditioned buses down the coast to Tulum approximately every half-hour until early evening, stopping at major towns and points of interest along the way. Riviera covers the same ground with its 1st-class (though not necessarily better) service.

ADO (☎ 884-5542) sets the 1st-class standard, while UNO, ADO GL and Super Expresso provide luxury services. Mayab provides good 'intermediate class' (modern, air-con buses, tending to make more stops than 1st class) to many points. Oriente's 2nd-class air-con buses often depart and arrive late.

Noreste buses vary in quality; some are pretty shabby indeed.

The staff at the ADO/Riviera information counter in the bus terminal provide good information on many of the bus services and are available 24 hours. The table (above) shows some of the major routes serviced daily.

Car

Rental-car agencies with facilities at the airport include: **Alamo** (☎ 886-0179), **Avis** (☎ 886-0222), **Budget** (☎ 884-6955), **Dollar** (☎ 886-0179) and **Hertz** (☎ 884-1326). You can receive better rates if you reserve ahead of time, but it doesn't hurt to do comparison shopping after arriving and before signing your original agreement.

You're better off leaving the rental car parked inside Cancún and walking or catching a bus to most places in town till you're ready to get out of town. Be warned also that Hwy 180D, the 238km *cuota* (toll road) running much of the way between Cancún and Mérida, costs M$329 for the distance and has only two exits before the end. The first, at Valladolid, costs M$194 to reach from Cancún and the second, at Pisté (for Chichén Itzá), is an additional M$48.

GETTING AROUND
To/From the Airport

White TTC buses to Ciudad Cancún (M$80) leave the airport about every 20 minutes between 5:30am and 11:30pm, stopping in both the domestic and international terminals. A straight line drawn from the exit of the international arrivals terminal (past all the vans) reaches the small lot and its ticket booth decorated with a Coca-Cola sign. Once in town, the buses travel up Avenida Tulum and will stop most anywhere you ask. One central stop is across from the Chedraui supermarket on Avenida Cobá (not to be confused with the Chedraui further south in Plaza Las Américas).

Going to the airport from Ciudad Cancún, the same TTC airport buses (Aeropuerto Centro) head south on Avenida Tulum. You can flag them down anywhere it's feasible, from well north of the bus terminal to well south of Avenida Cobá.

Comfortable *colectivos* (shared vans) depart from the curb in front of the international terminal about every 15 minutes for the Zona Hotelera and Ciudad Cancún; they charge M$110 per person. If volume allows, they will separate passengers into Ciudad Cancún and Zona groups. Otherwise, depending who's going exactly where, they may head downtown first and then to the Zona. Going the opposite way, via Punta Nizuc, can take up to 45 minutes from the airport to Ciudad Cancún.

Cheaper ADO shuttles leave from the domestic terminal side, charging M$35 to go downtown or M$65 direct to Playa del Carmen. Riviera also runs nine express 1st-class buses from the airport to Playa del Carmen between 7am and 7:30pm (M$80, 45 minutes to one hour). The service is direct and tickets are sold at a counter that is located in the international section of the airport.

Regular taxis into town or to the Zona Hotelera cost up to M$450 (up to four people) if you catch them right outside the airport. If you follow the access road out of the airport, however, and past the traffic-monitoring booth (a total of about 300m), you can often flag down an empty taxi leaving the airport that will take you for much less (you can try for M$50) because the driver is no longer subject to the expensive regulated airport fares.

Colectivo taxis head to the airport from a stand in front of the Hotel Cancún Handall on Avenida Tulum about a block south of Avenida Cobá. These operate from 6am to 9pm (but check beforehand), charge M$20 per person and leave when full. The official rate for private taxis from town is M$200.

Bus

To reach the Zona Hotelera from Ciudad Cancún, catch any bus with 'R1', 'Hoteles' or 'Zona Hotelera' displayed on the windshield as it travels along Avenida Tulum toward Avenida Cobá, then eastward on Avenida Cobá. The one-way fare is M$6.50, but since change is often unavailable this varies between M$6 and M$7. Having correct change in advance makes things easier.

To reach Puerto Juárez and the Isla Mujeres ferries, catch a Ruta 13 ('Pto Juárez' or 'Punta Sam'; M$4) bus heading north on Avenida Tulum. Some R1 buses make this trip as well; tickets cost M$6.50.

Taxi

Cancún's taxis do not have meters. Fares are set, but you should always agree on a price before getting in; otherwise you could end up paying for a 'misunderstanding.' From Ciudad Cancún to Punta Cancún is M$80, to Puerto Juárez M$30. Hourly and daily rates should run about M$150 to M$120 and M$700 to M$800 respectively.

NORTH OF CANCÚN

Except for the roads feeding Cancún's megalopolis, the rest of north and northwestern Yucatán is a tangle of roadless jungle, uninhabited except in small pockets. Islands – Isla Mujeres, Isla Contoy and Isla Holbox – are the main tourist draws. Isla Mujeres has good beaches and is more laid-back than Cancún; Contoy is a bird sanctuary; and Holbox has diverse wildlife (it's a great place to swim with whale sharks) and a friendly community of fisherfolk and hammock-weavers. All three are worth a peek if you have the time, and both Isla Mujeres and the slightly more distant Isla Contoy are doable as day trips even if you're based in Cancún.

ISLA MUJERES
☎ 998 / pop 14,000

If you are going to visit just one of Quintana Roo's islands, then Isla Mujeres (Island of Women) is probably the place for you. It's not as crowded as Cozumel, yet offers more to do and see than in chiller-than-thou Holbox. Sure, there's quite a few ticky-tack tourist shops, but folks still get around by golf cart and the crushed-coral beaches are better than those of Cozumel or Holbox.

The little island lies just north of Cancún and is an ideal day trip or a destination in its own right. There's not much here and that's the whole point: come to bask in quiet shallows or stretch out on the sand, to snorkel or scuba dive, or just to put the sunglasses on and open that book you've been dying to finish. Come sunset, there's plenty of tasty options for your dinner, and the nightlife scene moves at a good clip.

The Pintando Isla Mujeres program has invited 400 artists from all around the world to paint many of the town's buildings, brightening up the streets and making for fun walks.

History

A glimpse at the sunbathers on the beach will have you thinking the moniker 'Island of Women' comes from the bikini-clad tourists; however, the name Isla Mujeres goes at least as far back as Spanish buccaneers, who (legend has it) kept their lovers in safe seclusion here while they plundered galleons and pillaged ports on the mainland. An alternate theory suggests that in 1517, when Francisco Hernández de Córdoba sailed from Cuba and arrived here to procure slaves, the expedition discovered a stone temple containing clay figurines of Maya goddesses; it is thought Córdoba named the island after the icons.

Today some archaeologists believe that the island was a stopover for the Maya en route to worship their goddess of fertility, Ixchel, on Isla Cozumel. The clay idols are thought to have represented the goddess. The island may also have figured in the extensive Maya salt trade, which extended for hundreds of kilometers along the coastline.

Orientation

The island is 8km long, 150m to 800m wide and 13km from Cancún's Zona Hotelera. You'll find most of the restaurants and hotels in the town of Isla Mujeres, with the pedestrian mall on Hidalgo serving as the focal point. The ferry arrives in the town proper on the island's northern tip. On the southern tip are the lighthouse and vestiges of the Maya temple. The two are linked by Avenida Rueda Medina, a loop road that more or less

follows the coast. Between them are a handful of small fishing villages, several saltwater lakes, a string of westward-facing beaches, a large lagoon and a small airstrip.

The eastern shore is washed by the open sea, and the surf there is dangerous. The most popular sand beach (Playa Norte) is at the northern tip of the island.

Information

The following places are all in Isla Mujeres Town.

BOOKSTORES

Mañana (☎ 044 998-866-4347; cnr Matamoros & Guerrero; ☒ 10am-7pm) This café has some nice offerings, and swaps or sells, depending on your needs.

EMERGENCY
Police (☎ 877-0082)

INTERNET ACCESS
Internet café (cnr Matamoros & Guerrero; per hr M$15; ☺ 9am-10pm Mon-Sat) As yet unnamed.

LAUNDRY
Tim Pho (☎ 877-0529; cnr Juárez & Abasolo; ☺ 7am-9pm Mon-Sat, 8am-2pm Sun) Friendly and cheap: up to 4kg takes two hours and costs M$50.

MEDICAL SERVICES
Medical center (Guerrero) Between Madero and Morelos.

MONEY
Several banks are directly across from the Zona Hotelera ferry dock. Most exchange currency, have ATMs and are open 8:30am to 5pm Monday to Friday and 9am to 2pm Saturday.
HSBC (Av Rueda Medina)

POST & TELEPHONE
The island has an abundance of Telmex card phones.
Post office (☎ 877-0085; cnr Guerrero & López Mateos; ☺ 9am-4pm Mon-Fri)

TOURIST INFORMATION
Immigration office (☎ 877-0189; Av Rueda Medina; ☺ 9am-5pm Mon-Fri, 9am-noon Sat & Sun) Next door to the tourist information office, but frequently has a sign up that reads 'Sorry, gone to Cancún.'
Tourist information office (☎ 877-0767; Av Rueda Medina; ☺ 8am-8pm Mon-Fri, 9am-2pm Sat & Sun) There's no sign, but the office is located between Madero and Morelos next to the Migracíones office. It offers a number of brochures, and one member of its friendly staff speaks English; the rest speak Spanish only.

Sights & Activities
BEACHES & SWIMMING
Once you reach **Playa Norte**, the island's main beach, you won't want to leave. Its warm shallow waters are the color of blue-raspberry syrup and the beach is crushed coral. Unlike the outer beach, Playa Norte is safe and the water is only chest-deep even far from shore. If you tire of sunbathing, cool off with something frosty at one of the many bars.

Five kilometers south of town is **Playa Lancheros**, the southernmost point served by local buses. The beach is less attractive than Playa Norte, but it sometimes has free musical festivities on Sunday. A taxi ride to Lancheros is M$20.

Another 1.5km south of Lancheros is **Playa Garrafón**, with translucent waters, colorful fish and no sand. Unfortunately the reef here has been heavily damaged by hurricanes and careless visitors. The water can be very choppy, sweeping you into jagged areas, so it's best to stay near shore. Avoid the over-hyped and overpriced Parque Natural (which has constructed a horrendous eyesore of an observation tower that has you praying for a hurricane) and visit instead **Hotel Garrafón de Castilla** (☎ 877-0107; Carretera Punta Sur Km 6; admission M$20; ☺ 9am-5pm), which provides chairs, umbrellas, showers and baths for the entrance fee. Snorkeling gear is M$60 extra. It has a roped-off swimming area as well as a restaurant and snack bar. The hotel rents lockers and towels, and offers snorkeling tours to the offshore reef for M$200. Taxis from town cost M$50.

HACIENDA MUNDACA
This **hacienda** (Av Rueda Medina; admission M$10; ☺ 9am-5pm) is at the large bend in Avenida Rueda Medina, about 4km south of the town. Its story is perhaps more intriguing than the ruins that remain. A 19th-century slave trader and reputed pirate, Fermín Antonio Mundaca de Marechaja, fell in love with a local woman known as La Trigueña (Brunette). To win her, Mundaca built a two-story mansion complete with gardens and graceful archways, as well as a small fortification.

But while Mundaca was building the house, La Trigueña married another islander. Brokenhearted, Mundaca died and his house, fortress and garden fell into disrepair. Some documents indicate that Mundaca died during a visit to Mérida and was buried there. Others say he died on the island, and indeed there's a grave in the town cemetery that supposedly contains his remains. Despite the skull and crossbones on his headstone (a common memento mori) there's no evidence in history books that Mundaca was ever a pirate. Instead, it is said he accumulated his wealth by transporting slaves from Africa to Cuba, where they were forced to work in mines and sugarcane fields.

Today the mostly ruined complex has some walls and foundations, a large central pond, some rusting cannons and a partially rebuilt

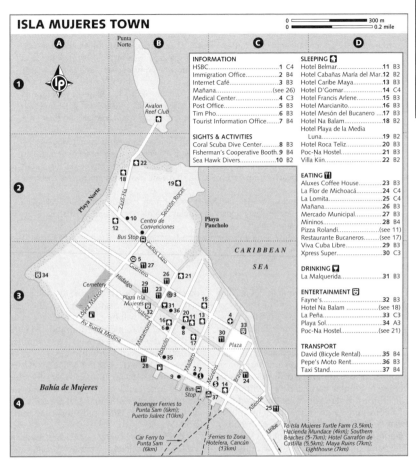

ISLA MUJERES TOWN

0 ——————— 300 m
0 ——————— 0.2 mile

INFORMATION
HSBC..1 C4
Immigration Office...................2 B4
Internet Café............................3 B3
Mañana..............................(see 26)
Medical Center.........................4 C3
Post Office................................5 B3
Tim Pho....................................6 B3
Tourist Information Office.......7 B4

SIGHTS & ACTIVITIES
Coral Scuba Dive Center.........8 B3
Fisherman's Cooperative Booth.9 B4
Sea Hawk Divers....................10 B2

SLEEPING
Hotel Belmar..........................11 B3
Hotel Cabañas María del Mar.12 B2
Hotel Caribe Maya.................13 B3
Hotel D'Gomar......................14 C4
Hotel Francis Arlene...............15 B3
Hotel Marcianito....................16 B3
Hotel Mesón del Bucanero....17 B3
Hotel Na Balam......................18 B2
Hotel Playa de la Media
   Luna..................................19 B2
Hotel Roca Teliz.....................20 B3
Poc-Na Hostel........................21 B3
Villa Kiin...............................22 B2

EATING
Aluxes Coffee House...............23 B3
La Flor de Michoacá...............24 C4
La Lomita...............................25 C4
Mañana..................................26 B3
Mercado Municipal................27 B3
Mininos.................................28 B4
Pizza Rolandi...................(see 11)
Restaurante Bucaneros.......(see 17)
Viva Cuba Libre......................29 B3
Xpress Super...........................30 C3

DRINKING
La Malquerida........................31 B3

ENTERTAINMENT
Fayne's..................................32 B3
Hotel Na Balam ....(see 18)
La Peña..................................33 C3
Playa Sol...............................34 A3
Poc-Na Hostel...................(see 21)

TRANSPORT
David (Bicycle Rental)............35 B4
Pepe's Moto Rent..................36 B3
Taxi Stand..............................37 B4

house. At the southern end stand a gateway and a small garden. You can still make out the words *Entrada de La Trigueña* (La Trigueña's Entrance) etched into the impressive stone arch of the gate.

The shady grounds make for pleasant strolling (bring insect repellent), and a small zoo is scattered across them, holding local fauna. Kids may find it fun; adults may want to unlock the cages.

Hacienda Mundaca is easily reached by bus or bike; a taxi from town will cost M$30.

PUNTA SUR
At the south end of the island you'll find a romantic lighthouse, modern sculpture garden and the severely worn remains of a

temple dedicated to Ixchel, Maya goddess of the moon and fertility. The lightkeeper will sometimes let you climb to the top for amazing views – remember to tip. In 1988 Hurricane Gilbert nearly finished the ruins off; what was left was pummeled by Emily and Wilma in 2005, and there's now little to see other than the sculpture garden, the sea and, in the distance, Cancún. Unless you're desperate to pay the steep entry fee (M$50), head left before the lighthouse and enjoy the view from the small dirt parking lot. From Isla Mujeres Town, a taxi costs M$50.

DIVING & SNORKELING
Many of the diving and snorkeling sites in the Cancún/Isla Mujeres area were affected by

QUINTANA ROO

DREAM GREEN BY VISITING ISLA MUJERES TURTLE FARM

Although they are endangered, sea turtles are still killed throughout Latin America for their eggs and meat, which is considered a delicacy. Three species of sea turtle lay eggs in the sand along Isla Mujeres' calm western shore, and they are now being protected – one *tortuga* (little turtle) at a time.

In the 1980s, efforts by a local fisherman led to the founding of the **Isla Mujeres Tortugranja** (Isla Mujeres Turtle Farm; ☎ 877-0595; Carretera Sac Bajo Km 5; admission M$30; ☺ 9am-5pm; ♿), 5km south of town, which protects the turtles' breeding grounds and places wire cages around their eggs to protect against predators.

Hatchlings live in three large pools for up to a year, then are tagged for monitoring and released. Because most turtles in the wild die within their first few months, the practice of guarding them through their first year greatly increases their chances of survival. Moreover, the turtles that leave this protected beach return each year, which means their offspring receive the same protection.

There are several hundred sea turtles, ranging in weight from 150g to more than 300kg. The farm also has a small but good-quality aquarium, displays on marine life and a gift shop. Tours are conducted in Spanish and English.

If you're driving, cycling or walking from the bus stop, bear right at the 'Y' just beyond Hacienda Mundaca's parking lot (the turn is marked by a tiny sign). The facility is easily reached from town by taxi (M$30).

Hurricanes Emily and Wilma in 2005. That said, hurricane damage is part of natural reef ecology, and the reefs are now growing anew. Within a short boat ride of the island there's a handful of lovely dives, such as **Barracuda**, **La Bandera**, **El Jigueo** and **Manchones**. You can expect to see sea turtles, rays and barracuda, along with a wide array of hard and soft corals. A popular nonreef dive is **Ultrafreeze** (or El Frío), where you'll see the intact hull of a 60m-long cargo ship – thought to have been deliberately sunk in 30m of water. It's 90 minutes by boat northeast of Isla Mujeres. The name of the site is due to the unusually cool water found there. A rental 3mm shorty wetsuit will barely keep you warm; consider asking for a hood if you tend to get chilled while diving.

Snorkeling with whale sharks (M$1250) is the latest craze on the island. The season runs from July through September. It can get a bit crazy with several boats circling one whale shark, but they try to limit the number of swimmers in the water to three people (including one guide). Sea Hawk Divers, Coral Scuba Dive Center and the Fisherman's Cooperative Booth (see right) all offer whale shark trips. (For more information on whale sharks, see boxed text, p97.)

To protect and preserve the reefs, a M$20 fee is charged for all diving and swimming. Please pay it, as this money is used to preserve natural patrimony. At all of the reputable dive centers you need to show your certification card, and you will be expected to have your own gear. Equipment rental adds M$100 to the prices listed here; you'll pay another M$100 if you need a wetsuit.

Sea Hawk Divers (☎ /fax 877-0296; www.isla-mujeres.net/seahawkdivers; Carlos Lazo) offers dives for M$450 (one tank) to M$600 (two tanks), a resort course for M$850, PADI Open Water certification (M$3200) and snorkeling tours from M$250.

Coral Scuba Dive Center (☎ 877-0763; www.coralscubadivecenter.com; Hidalgo), between Abasolo and Madero, offers dives for M$290 to M$590, snorkel trips for M$220 and a variety of courses.

The fisherfolk of Isla Mujeres have formed a cooperative to offer snorkeling tours of various sites from M$200, including the reef off Playa Garrafón, and day trips to Isla Contoy for M$500. You can book through the **Fisherman's Cooperative Booth** (☎ 877-1363; Av Rueda Medina) in a *palapa* steps away from the dock. Booking here ensures your money goes to locals.

DEEP-SEA FISHING

The fishing cooperative (see above) offers trips to fish for marlin, swordfish and dorado from M$500/1500 per hour/half-day, including bait and tackle, soft drinks, snacks and beer.

Sleeping

The 'high season' rates cover roughly mid-December through March. During this period you can expect many places to be booked solid by noon (even earlier during Easter week). US spring break (March to early April) is another peak time.

All the sleeping options given here are in Isla Mujeres Town.

BUDGET

our pick **Poc-Na Hostel** (☎ /fax 877-0090; www.pocna .com; cnr Matamoros & Carlos Lazo; sites per person M$65, dm with/without card M$90/110, d M$240-350; ✱ 💻) Only moments away from one of the island's nicest beaches and decorated with shells and hibiscus flowers, Mexico's oldest youth hostel ranks among the country's best. It has fan-cooled six-, eight- and 10-bed co-ed dorms as well as women's dorms and a few air-con doubles. The large main common area has hammocks to chill in and an excellent sound system putting out tunes till the wee hours. The property extends through 100m of sand and coconut palms to the edge of the Caribbean and the hostel's own beach bar. Though there are no cooking facilities for guests, the kitchen serves good, inexpensive food (and beer and wine).

Hotel Roca Teliz (☎ 877-0407; jccanopus@hotmail .com; cnr Hidalgo & Abasolo; s low/high season M$100/160, d low/high season M$160/250; ✱) Good budget digs, especially for solo travelers, the 'Rock' has a cool central courtyard, dark but clean rooms, and is located right on the Hidalgo pedestrian mall. Add M$100 for air-con.

Hotel Caribe Maya (☎ 877-0684; Madero 9; d with fan/air-con M$250/300; ✱) The old blue tiles need replacing, but this place offers rooms that, though a bit musty, are solid value even in the high season.

Hotel Marcianito (☎ 877-0111; Abasolo 10; r M$300-350) The 'Little Martian' is a neat, tidy and non-pod-people-owned hotel with 13 slightly dark, fan-cooled rooms that have a bit too much air freshener. Upper-floor rooms are the more expensive ones. Plaid quilts seem cutely out of place.

MIDRANGE

Hotel D'Gomar (☎ 877-0541; Av Rueda Medina 150; d with fan M$350, with air-con low/high season M$500/650; ✱) A friendly place facing the ferry dock between Morelos and Bravo, this has four floors of attractive, ample and well-maintained rooms

with double beds (air-con rooms have two) and large bathrooms. Most have hammocks, and both coffee and water are free. The mirror in the stairway gives warped, funhouse-style reflections as you head to your room.

Hotel Belmar (☎ 877-0430; www.rolandi.com; Hidalgo 110; d with air-con low/high season M$350/950, ste with Jacuzzi M$950/1340; ✱) Above the Pizza Rolandi restaurant and run by the same friendly family. All rooms are comfy and well kept, with tiled floors and (some) balconies. Prices span four distinct seasons.

Hotel Mesón del Bucanero (☎ 877-1222, 800-712-3510; www.bucaneros.com; Hidalgo 11; d M$400-700; ✱) Above Restaurant Bucaneros, between Abasolo and Madero. Its nicely decorated rooms (most with air-con) all have TVs and are priced according to their various combinations of beds, balcony, tub and fridge – one even has a blender and toaster. Rooms air out nicely if the windows are opened.

Villa Kiin (☎ 877-1024; www.villakiin.com; Calle Zazil-Ha s/n; d low season M$400-1290, high season M$990-1690) This is the best buy in this price range. Beautiful cabanas right by the beach offer something similar to what's in Tulum, while palm-shaded hammocks and a common kitchen make it easy to do nothing all afternoon.

Hotel Francis Arlene (☎ /fax 877-0310; Guerrero 7; r with fan/air-con low season M$450/550, high season M$550/650; ✱) This place offers comfortable, good-sized, pastel-and-white rooms with fan and fridge. Most have a king-sized bed or two doubles, and many have balconies and sea views. The lounging frog sculptures will either seem hokey or cute. Either way they kinda fit right in.

TOP END

All rooms in this category have air-con.

Hotel Playa de la Media Luna (☎ 887-0759; www .playamedialuna.com; Sección Rocas, lotes 9 & 10, Punta Norte; r M$950-1500; ✱ 💻) The older, cheaper rooms (M$400 to M$600) are a pretty good deal as you get to use the hotel's pool, though the beds are a bit sproingy. The rooms in the new house are a bit fancier, some with ocean views, all featuring bedspreads that should have left this world when *Three's Company* went off the air. Big spenders should head next door to the Hotel Secreto.

Hotel Cabanas María del Mar (☎ 877-0179; www .cabanasdelmar.com; Carlos Lazo 1; d low season M$750-990, high season M$1100-1300; ✱ 💻) Near Playa Norte, it has 73 rooms with firm beds and 'pretty in

QUINTANA ROO

pink' bedspreads. All have balconies or terraces, many with sea or pool views and lovely tiled bathrooms. A lush courtyard, restaurant and swimming pool top things off. Rates include continental breakfast.

Hotel Na Balam (☎ 877-0279; www.nabalam.com; Calle Zazil-Ha 118; r low/high season M$1500/2400, ste M$3000/3600; ❄ ⚊) Butterflies flit around the beautiful hibiscus and palm garden, and many rooms face Playa Norte. All rooms are decorated with simple elegance and have safes, hammocks, private balconies or patios…and no TVs. The hotel offers yoga and meditation classes as well as massage services, and has a pool and restaurant. There's also entertainment here (opposite).

Eating

Mercado Municipal (Town Market; Guerrero) Inside the remodeled market are a couple of stalls selling hot food cheap – a plate of chicken *mole* and rice, or tuna with olives in a tortilla, can go for as little as M$15. Other stalls sell a variety of produce, and a juice stand serves up liquid refreshments. Four open-air restaurants out the front serve simple, filling meals at fair prices.

La Flor de Michoacán (cnr Hidalgo & Bravo; juices M$8-M$15; ❄ 9am-9pm) Near the plaza, this is the place to go for excellent and inexpensive milkshakes, fruit drinks and shaved ices.

Aluxes Coffee House (Matamoros; bagels M$20, sandwiches M$40-50; ❄ 8am-10pm Wed-Mon) Aluxes serves bagels with cream cheese, sandwiches, muffins, and hot and iced coffee. Between Guerrero and Hidalgo.

ourpick Mañana (☎ 877-0555; cnr Matamoros & Guerrero; dishes M$20-70; ❄ 8am-4pm; Ⓥ) A good-vibe place with colorful hand-painted tables, superfriendly service and some excellent veggie options – the hummus and veggie baguette is the restaurant's signature dish – Mañana is perhaps the best lunch spot on the island. It also has coffee, *licuados* (blends of fruit or juice with water or milk, and sugar) and some Middle Eastern dishes. There's a book exchange, too.

Restaurante Bucaneros (☎ 877-0126; Hidalgo; mains M$26-120, set meals M$120; ❄ 7am-11pm) Below the Hotel Mesón del Bucanero between Abasolo and Madero, this is a fan-cooled, mostly outdoor restaurant with a pleasing ambience and a variety of alcoholic and nonalcoholic tropical shakes and drinks. The best deal is the *menú especial* (set menu), which gives

you a choice of several mains accompanied by soup or salad and a dessert.

La Lomita (Juárez; mains M$40-120; ❄ 9am-10:30pm Mon-Sat) The 'Little Hill' serves good, cheap Mexican food in a small, colorful setting between Allende and Uribe. Seafood and chicken dishes predominate. Try the fantastic bean and avocado soup, or ceviche.

Viva Cuba Libre (Calle Hidalgo Plaza Almendros; mains M$60-90; ❄ 5pm-midnight Tue-Sun) It competes for decibel levels with neighboring restaurants, but really, we all like Cuban *son* (a type of dance) more than bad disco remixes, don't we? Apart from that, you get a well-deserved break from Mexican fare with *ropa vieja* (slow-cooked shredded beef), Cuban lobster and other Caribbean favorites. *Mojitos* (Cuban mint, lime and rum cocktails) are two for M$50. Viva Cuba indeed!

Mininos (Av Rueda Medina; mains M$60-130; ❄ 11am-9pm) A tiny, colorfully painted shack with a sand floor right on the water, Mininos dishes up cocktails of shrimp, conch and octopus, as well as heaping plates of delicious ceviche and seafood soups.

Pizza Rolandi (☎ 877-0430; Hidalgo; mains M$70-120, pizzas M$60-130; ❄ 8am-11pm) Below the Hotel Belmar, between Abasolo and Madero, it bakes very good thin-crust pizzas and calzones in a wood-fired oven. The menu also includes pasta, fresh salads, fish, good coffee and some Italian specialties – definitely *don't* come here looking for Mexican.

Xpress Super, a chain supermarket on the plaza, has a solid selection of groceries, baked goods and snacks.

Drinking & Entertainment

Isla Mujeres' highest concentration of nightlife is along Hidalgo, and hot spots on or near the beach form an arc around the northern edge of town. Loud disco-bar-restaurants open and close seasonally on Hidalgo, usually to be replaced by something almost the same. If no hours are listed you can assume the venue opens in the afternoon and doesn't close until at least midnight.

Poc-Na Hostel (cnr Matamoros & Carlos Lazo; ❄ sunset-sunrise) Has a beachfront joint with bonfires and more hippies than all the magic buses in the world. It's a scene, but it's a chill, cooled-out scene.

Fayne's (Hidalgo; ❄ 5pm-midnight) One of the latest disco-bar-restaurants, often featuring live reggae, salsa and other Caribbean sounds. Near Matamoros.

La Malquerida (☎ 877-1639; cnr Hidalgo & Matamoros; ☒ 10am-midnight) Seems pricier than it could be and doesn't have the view the beach bars do, but it's open daily and sometimes has live music.

Playa Sol (Playa Norte; ☒ 9am-10pm or whenever) A happening spot day and night, with volleyball, a soccer area and good food and drinks at decent prices. It's a great spot to watch the sunset, and in high season bands play reggae, salsa, merengue or other danceable music. Just follow the beach to the party.

Hotel Na Balam (Calle Zazil-Ha) Caters to an older set, and has a beach bar that's a popular spot on weekend afternoons (every other week in the off-season), with live music, dancing and a three-hour-long happy hour.

La Peña (Guerrero; ☒ 7:30pm-3am or later) This English-run club features the sound of waves, lots of wood and a nice pool table. Off the north side of the plaza, it has a great atmosphere and a fabulous music mix. Some say it's the best in town.

Getting There & Away

There are several points of embarkation to reach Isla Mujeres. The following description starts from the northernmost port and progresses southeast (see Map p75). To reach Puerto Juárez or Punta Sam from Ciudad Cancún, catch any bus (M$4) displaying those destinations and/or 'Ruta 13' as it heads north on Avenida Tulum. Some R1 (Zona Hotelera; M$6.50) buses make the trip as well; ask before boarding.

PUNTA SAM

Car ferries, which also take passengers, depart from Punta Sam (off Map p77), about 8km north of Cancún center, and take about an hour to reach the island. Departure times are 8am, 11am, 2:45pm, 5:30pm and 8:15pm from Punta Sam; and 6:30am, 9:30am, 12:45pm, 4:15pm and 7:15pm from Isla Mujeres. Walk-ons and vehicle passengers pay M$15; drivers are included in the fare for cars (M$190), vans (M$240), motorcycles (M$75) and bicycles (M$60). If you're taking a car in high season (believe us, you don't need one), it's good to get in line an hour or so before departure time. Tickets go on sale just before the ferry begins loading.

PUERTO JUÁREZ

Just over 4km north of Ciudad Cancún (15 minutes by bus) is Puerto Juárez (Map p75). Enclosed, air-con express boats depart from here for Isla Mujeres (one way M$35, 25 minutes) every 30 minutes from 6am to 8:30am, then hourly until 9:30pm with a final departure at 11pm; they rarely leave on time.

ZONA HOTELERA

Services from the following two spots in the Zona Hotelera change names and schedules frequently; ask your concierge to check for you before heading out to catch boats from any of the following places. All take about 25 minutes to reach Isla Mujeres.

El Embarcadero

Shuttles depart from this dock at Playa Linda (Map p75) four times daily in low season, between 9:30am and 1:30pm, returning from Isla Mujeres at 10:30am, 1:30pm, 3:30pm and 5:15pm. The one-way fare (M$75) includes soft drinks. High season sees up to seven departures each way. El Embarcadero is a beige building between the Gran Costa Real Hotel and the channel, on the mainland side of the bridge (Blvd Kukulcán Km 4).

Playa Tortugas

The **Isla Shuttle** (☎ 883-3448) leaves from the dock on Playa Tortugas (Map p75) on Blvd Kukulcán Km 6.35 at 9:15am, 11:30am, 1:45pm and 3:45pm, returning from Isla Mujeres at 10:15am, 12:30pm, 3:30pm and 6:30pm. The one-way fare is M$90.

Getting Around

With all rented transportation it's best to deal directly with the shop supplying it. They're happier if they don't have to pay commissions to touts, and the chances for misunderstandings are fewer. Rates are usually open to negotiation.

BICYCLE

Cycling is a great way to get around the island. Many bicycles are single-speed, with coaster (ie push-back-on-the-pedal) brakes; these give you a good workout on the gradual hills. A number of shops rent bikes for about M$20/80 per hour/day. Arrive early in the day to get your pick of the better ones and take the time to have the seat adjusted properly. Some places ask for a deposit of about M$100.

David (☎ 044 998-860-0075; Av Rueda Medina), near Abasolo, has a decent selection.

BUS & TAXI

Local buses depart about every 25 minutes (but don't bank on it) from next to the Centro de Convenciones (near the back of the market) or from the ferry dock and head along Avenida Rueda Medina, stopping along the way. Get taxis from the stand at the dock or flag one down. You can get to the entrance of Hacienda Mundaca, within 300m of the Turtle Farm (Tortugranja), and as far south as Playa Lancheros (1.5km north of Playa Garrafón). Taxi rates are set by the municipal government and posted at the taxi stand just south of the passenger ferry dock. As always, agree on a price before getting in.

MOTORCYCLE & GOLF CART

Take a look around before you rent. The island is tiny and you can walk from the dock to any part of the town in 15 minutes. Two-wheeled motorized transportation can be dangerous; even on sedate Isla Mujeres people get seriously injured or die in bike mishaps. Inspect the vehicle carefully before renting. Costs vary, and are sometimes jacked up in high season, but generally start at about M$100 per hour, with a two-hour minimum, M$300 all day (9am to 5pm) and M$350 for 24 hours.

Many people find golf carts a good way to get around the island, and caravans of them can be seen tooling down the roads. They average M$150/450 per hour/day and M$550 for 24 hours. A good, no-nonsense place for both bikes and golf carts is **Pepe's Moto Rent** (☎ 877-0019) on Hidalgo between Matamoros and Abasolo.

PARQUE NACIONAL ISLA CONTOY

Spectacular Isla Contoy is a bird-lover's delight: a national park and sanctuary that is an easy day trip from Isla Mujeres. About 800m at its widest point and more than 7km long, it has dense foliage that provides ideal shelter for more than 100 species of bird, including brown pelicans, olive cormorants, turkey birds, brown boobies and frigates, as well as being a good place to see red flamingos, snowy egrets and white herons.

Most of the trips stop for snorkeling both en route to and just off Contoy, which sees about 1500 visitors a month. Bring binoculars, mosquito repellent and sun block.

The trip gives you about two hours of free time to explore the island's two interpretive trails, skim through materials in the visitors center and to climb the 27m-high observation tower. For M$100 per person, a park biologist will take you on a tour of Laguna Puerto Viejo, a prime nesting site; funds go toward park upkeep and research projects. Contact the **park headquarters** (☎ 998-877-0118) on Isla Mujeres. **Amigos de Isla Contoy** (www.islacontoy.org) has a website with good information on the island's ecology.

Getting There & Away

Daily visits to Contoy are offered by the **Fisherman's Cooperative Booth** (Map p91; ☎ 998-877-1363; Av Rueda Medina) on Isla Mujeres. The trip (M$500 per person) lasts from 9am to 5pm and includes a light breakfast, lunch (with fish caught en route), snorkeling (gear provided), park admission, scientific information on the island, and your choice of purified water, soft drinks or beer.

ISLA HOLBOX

☎ 984 / pop 2000

Isn't life great when it's low-fi and low-rise? That's the attitude on friendly Isla Holbox (hol-bosh) with its sandy streets, colorful Caribbean buildings, and lazing, sun-drunk dogs. There's so little to do here, in fact, that even the bars close at 8pm or 9pm (at least during low season). Holbox is thus a welcome refuge for anyone looking to just get away from it all ('all' likely meaning the hubbub of Cancún!).

The island is about 30km long and from 500m to 2km wide, with seemingly endless beaches, tranquil waters and a galaxy of shells in various shapes and colors. Lying within the 1.54 sq km Yum Balam reserve, Holbox is home to more than 150 species of bird, including roseate spoonbills, pelicans, herons, ibis and flamingos. The waters are abundant with fish, and dolphins can be seen year-round. In summer, whale sharks congregate relatively nearby in unheard-of quantities. And strong northerly winds could make for great kite-boarding and windsurfing (at press time both these activities were prohibited; ask before you set sail).

The water is not the translucent turquoise common to Quintana Roo beach sites, because here the Caribbean mingles with the darker Gulf of Mexico. The island's dark-

---

A GAME OF DOMINOES – SWIM WITH THE WHALE SHARKS

Between mid-May and mid-September, massive whale sharks congregate around Isla Holbox to feed on plankton. They are the largest fish in the world, weighing up to 15 tons and extending from gaping mouth to arching tail as long as 15m. Locals call them dominoes because of their speckled skin.

The best time to swim with these gentle giants is in July. A trip will cost you M$800, plus M$20 to visit the marine reserve. During the shoulder seasons, you can get up to a dozen boats rotating around a single whale shark. It's unpleasant for both shark and swimmer, so think twice about taking a tour during this season.

The World Wildlife Fund has been working with the local community since 2003 to develop responsible practices for visiting the whale sharks, trying to balance the economic boon of these tours with the environmental imperatives of protecting a threatened species.

When swimming with the whale shark only three swimmers (including your guide) are allowed in the water at a time. You are not allowed to touch the fish, and are required to wear either a life jacket or wetsuit to ensure you do not dive below the shark.

Willy's Tours (☎ 875-2008; holbox@hotmail.com, Av Tiburón Ballena), near Mini Súper Besa, offers tours swimming with whale sharks (M$800 per person), birding (M$800 to M$1200 per boat), crocodile spotting (M$2270 per boat) and fishing (M$3500 per boat). Boats can accommodate six to 12 people. Ask to stop for a quick snorkel on the way back from your trip – the guides will normally agree to this.

---

water lagoon on the south side inspired the Maya to name it Holbox or 'black hole.' During the rainy season there are clouds of mosquitoes: bring repellent and be prepared to stay inside for a couple of hours after dusk.

Orientation & Information

Golf carts are big here, but walking to the town square from the dock only takes about 15 minutes. Keep going and you'll hit the beach. Budget hotels and most of the town's restaurants are clustered around the plaza. A few cabanas are further out along the island's northern shore in what locals call the Zona Hotelera. Nobody uses street names, but Calle Juárez connects the town with the ferry dock.

Note that the island has no bank or ATM, and many places to stay and eat do not accept credit cards. Bring more cash than you think you'll use, then double that amount.

Cyber@Shark (☎ 875-2044; per hr M$15; ☼ noon-midnight Mon-Fri, 10am-midnight Sat & Sun) offers internet and VOIP/phone connections.

Dial ☎ 066 for police, fire or medical assistance.

Many hotels will book tours of the area's attractions. Posada Mawimbi (p98) offers canoe and kayak trips to the other side of the island, as well as motorboat trips toward the central areas of the island.

Sleeping

Isla Holbox is the perfect place to bring a book and lounge in a hammock under some palm trees. Not surprisingly, cabanas are everywhere, but the town plaza has some reasonable hotels. Remember that many budget options and some midrange ones have either no hot water or have it only at certain times of the day. The first three listings are utilitarian concrete constructions inland from the beach. The Mawimbi and Tortugas are newer, Italian-run places at the edge of the beach, using lots of varnished hardwood, timbers and thatch. If you're taking a taxi, make sure the driver brings you to the place you've requested.

Posada La Raza (☎ 875-2072; Juárez; s with fan/air-con M$250/400, d with fan/air-con M$350/500; ☒) A modest, clean, one-story place on the west side of the parque. Rooms have one double and one single bed. Fan-cooled rooms have ceiling and pedestal fans, making for good circulation. Guests have use of a small kitchen and hand-laundry facilities, and can hang clothes or sunbathe on the roof.

Posada d'Ingrid (☎ 875-2070; www.posadadingrid .com; r with air-con M$350-500; ☒) A friendly bright-blue place one block west and one block north of the northwest edge of the parque. All six rooms have hot water and TV; there's a simple *palapa* in the courtyard.

Posada Los Arcos (☎ 875-2072; saul954@hotmail.com; Juárez; d with fan M$350, with air-con M$400-550; ☒) Next

QUINTANA ROO

door to Posada La Raza, this is a touch more upscale. Unfortunately, cracks in the doorframes mean tons of mosquitoes can easily get in (a problem easily remedied by buying a mosquito coil and burning it near the door before you go to bed). Its rooms are located around a central courtyard and all have hot and cold water. Rates rise by 50% in summer.

Posada Mawimbi (☎ /fax 875-2003; www.mawimbi .net; d low/high season M$400/600, ste M$800-1000; 🙂) Mosquito nets are a welcome luxury in this pleasant two-story place just off the beach and about three blocks east of Juárez. The standard rooms have a fan and comfortable beds, while the suites offer air-con (not really necessary). Many rooms also have a balcony and hammock, and some have kitchenettes. Blue-and-yellow tiled sinks make even shaving a pleasure. Conch lamps light the walkways after dark – a beautiful finishing touch.

our pick Hotel La Palapa (☎ 875-2121; www.hotella palapa.com; d low/high season M$500/700; 🙂) Arguably the best midrange option on the island, Palapa is brand-spanking new, and offers cozy beachfront rooms, private patios (complete with hammocks) and a cloistered beach area complete with an outdoor *fogata* (fireplace). The staff are efficient and friendly, and it's located right near the restaurants of the town's center, 100m east of Juárez along the beach.

Hotelito Casa Las Tortugas (☎ /fax 875-2129; www.holboxcasalastortugas.com; r low season M$500-800, high season M$700-1100) Has the same rustic but refined style as its neighbor, the Mawimbi, with an even greater abundance of charming touches, particularly in the bathrooms. Many rooms have kitchenettes and balconies, with hammocks to laze in outside. There's a beach-front café that serves the complimentary continental breakfast.

Villas Delfines (☎ /fax 875-2197; www.holbox.com; bungalows low season M$900-1500, high season M$1200-1500) This eco-tel on the beach about 1km east of town composts waste, catches rainwater and uses solar power. Its large beach bungalows are built on stilts, fully screened and fan-cooled. The hotel rents kayaks and has a restaurant that offers very reasonable meal plans. It's great for those going green, but the accommodations are not quite as *accommodating* as other lodgings in this price category.

Eating

The influx of Italians has been good for gourmets. Italian, seafood and lobster meals are all good, but eat early, especially in the off-season. Many places close by 9pm.

La Isla del Colibrí (breakfast M$35-60, mains M$50-160; 🕑 8am-1pm & 5-10:30pm) A small restaurant in a gaily painted, Caribbean-style wooden house on the southwest corner of the parque. It serves huge fruit plates, breakfasts (and coffee), *licuados*, juices and a variety of meat and seafood dishes.

Edelín Pizzería & Restaurant (pizzas M$50-150, mains M$40-100; 🕑 11am-midnight) On the southeast corner of the plaza, it serves good, Sardinian-style pizza, as well as *tortas* (sandwich in a roll), ceviches, fish fillets, shrimp and lobster; beer costs M$15.

our pick Los Pelicanos (☎ 998-192-4575; meals M$60-200; 🕑 5pm-midnight, closed Mon) Half a block south from the plaza's southeast corner, this friendly eatery is lauded by locals as the best restaurant in town. The house specialty is homemade pasta with your choice of sauce. It serves up other Italian favorites and a smattering of seafood dishes, including a pepper-seared tuna and a delicious fish soup. The friendly international owners give you free bruschetta to kick off the meal, and there's a good selection of Italian wines.

Buena Vista Grill (☎ 875-2102; meals M$100-200; 🕑 11am-9pm) This casual eatery next to Faro Viejo has plastic chairs, but serves up grilled fish specialties including whole grilled fish or fillets wrapped in banana leaves. The day varies.

Getting There & Around

A *barco* (boat) ferries passengers (M$40, 25 minutes) to Holbox from the port village of Chiquilá nine times daily from 5am to 6pm in winter, 6am to 7pm in summer. Buses departing Chiquilá usually wait for the boat to arrive. Smaller, faster and wetter *lanchas* (motorboats) make the crossing whenever anyone's willing to pay M$250 for the entire boat (up to about six people with gear; the fare is higher after dark).

Two Mayab buses – with no bathroom, so use the grungy one in the nearby restaurant (M$3) beforehand if you think you'll need to go – leave Cancún daily for Chiquilá (M$70, 3½ hours) at 7:50am and 12:40pm. There's also an Oriente bus from Valladolid (M$70, 2½ hours) at 2:45am. From Mérida, take an overnight Noreste bus to Chiquilá (M$124, seven hours) at 11:30pm.

QUINTANA ROO

OFF THE MAP – ALTERNATIVE TOURISM ON THE RISE IN QUINTANA ROO

Many Maya communities are beginning to welcome tourism – it may be the only way to maintain their language and culture as mass migration to boom towns such as Cancún draws away the best and brightest, and children ask to study English rather than Yucatec.

Organizations such as **Puerta Verde** (www .puertaverde.com.mx) are helping these communities build tourist infrastructure. Two of the program's projects can be found on the road to Chiquilá in the towns of Solferino and San Ángel. You can go kayaking, cycling or learn about medicinal plants in San Ángel. Further north, Solferino has an orchid garden, jungle camping spots and canopy tours.

Taking a taxi from Cancún is another possibility; you may be able to get a taxi for M$600.

Buses (all 2nd class) leave Chiquilá for Cancún (M$70) at 7:30am and 1:30pm; Tizimín (M$50) at 7:30am, 1:30pm and 4:30pm; Valladolid (M$70) at 5:30am; and Mérida (M$124) at 5:30am.

If you're driving you can either park your vehicle in the Chiquilá parking lot for M$30 per day (8am to 6pm or any fraction thereof), take your chances parking it on the pier (which is crowded in high season) or try to catch the infrequent car ferry to Holbox. Since you won't need the car on the island, leaving it on the mainland is a better option.

Holbox' sand streets see few autos, but golf carts have become ubiquitous and, for many residents, rather annoying. If you need one, try **Rentadora El Brother** (☎ 875-2018; cart per hr/day/24hr M$100/600/800), on Juárez near the beach – but consider using your walking shoes instead.

RIVIERA MAYA

The Riviera Maya (Tulum Corridor) is a strip of coastline that stretches from Cancún in the north to the town of Tulum, about 135km southward. Once a beautiful stretch of undeveloped jungle, stunning coastline and barrier coral reef, it is now fast becoming a strip of giant all-inclusive resort hotels.

Undaunted by hurricanes or efforts by locals to prevent such incursions, megatels are scooping up the mangrove swamps and turning them into golf courses. 'Ecoparks' are also booming. The developers buy giant swaths of acreage under the guise of being 'environmental,' then turn them into theme-based tourist traps, many of which charge exorbitant entry fees.

That said, the parts along the way that aren't developed to death are quite beautiful. Tulum is worth a visit. Its ruins – perched above a perfect beach – are simply breathtaking. Playa del Carmen has exciting nightlife and some great food. And Cozumel remains one of the world's top diving destinations. Qualified divers will find exhilarating cavern-diving opportunities in the Riviera Maya area, and the cenotes, Yucatán's natural limestone caves, are spectacular.

Stop in the small towns along the Riviera Maya or head inland to catch glimpses of the Mexico that tourism forgot.

PUERTO MORELOS
☎ 998 / pop 3000

Halfway between Cancún and Playa del Carmen, Puerto Morelos retains its quiet, small-town feel despite the building boom north and south of town. While the village offers enough restaurants and bars to keep you entertained by night, it's really the shallow Caribbean waters that draw visitors here. Brilliantly contrasted stripes of bright green and dark blue separate the shore from the barrier reef – a tantalizing sight for divers and snorkelers – while inland a series of excellent cenotes beckon the adventurous. Unfortunately, Hurricanes Wilma and Emily knocked down most of the beach's lovely palms – those naughty girls. In their munificence, they did leave behind the sparkling sand beaches.

Like many resort towns along the coast, Puerto Morelos used to be a fishing village. Today it retains that laid-back appeal, but development is on the rise, including plans for a new cruise-ship port. There's a nice market just a few minutes' walk from the plaza, with a great selection of crafts, hammocks and reasonably priced souvenirs.

Orientation & Information
Puerto Morelos' central plaza is 2km east of Hwy 307 nearly at the end of the main road

QUINTANA ROO

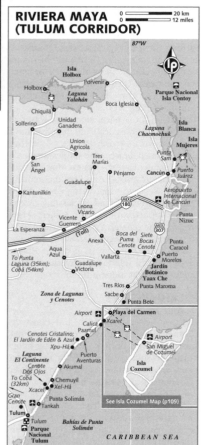

RIVIERA MAYA (TULUM CORRIDOR)

Lavanderia 'Vicar' (☎ 206-9055; Av Gomez M5L6; ☿ 7am-9pm) charges M$15 per kilogram.

Goyo Morgan, of **Goyo's** (☎ 221-2679), on the plaza, offers jungle tours (adult/child under 12 years M$400/200). He can be difficult to locate at times, but is a wealth of information about the area, especially edible and medicinal jungle plants. He also offers *temescal* (bathhouse) sessions. See p42 for more on *temescal*.

Sights & Activities
DIVING & SNORKELING

The barrier reef that runs along most of the coast of Quintana Roo is only 600m offshore here, providing both divers and snorkelers with views of sea turtles, sharks, stingrays, eagle rays, moray eels, lobsters, staghorn and brain corals and, of course, loads of colorful tropical fish. Several sunken ships make great wreck diving, and the dive centers have cenote trips as well.

Keep in mind (if you're a do-it-yourselfer) that any divers or snorkelers are required to pay M$20 for an entry bracelet to the marine park; if you're snorkeling, you need a personal flotation device. While the proximity of the reef makes it a tempting destination for beach-based swimmers, strong currents and lots of boat traffic can be hazardous. You're best off hiring a boat from the dock (M$250) or arranging to tag along with a dive center group as they head out.

You'll find dive shops in Hotel Ojo de Agua and Hotel del Cid.

Dive Puerto Morelos (☎ 206-9084; www.divepuerto morelos.com; ☿ 8am-7pm) offers snorkeling, diving and cenote trips, or it costs M$3250 for PADI certification. It often closes during the low season.

CENOTES

For chilling cenote action, check out the 'eco-park' **Boca del Puma** (☎ 577-6420; www.bocadelpuma .com; ♿), 16km west of Puerto Morelos, near the village of Vallarta, or **Siete Bocas** (admission M$50; ♿), 13km west of Puerto Morelos, which has seven mouths and some serious tourism development going on.

Sleeping

Hotels can be surprisingly full even at non-peak times, so call or book ahead if at all possible.

Posada Amor (☎ 871-0033; www.posadaamor.com; s & d from M$380, tr & q M$500) About 100m south-

into town (the main dock is the true end of the road). The town, all of three streets wide from east to west, stretches several blocks to the north of the plaza and about three long blocks south.

Alma Libre (☎ 871-0713; www.almalibrebooks.com; ☿ 10am-3pm & 6-9pm Tue-Sat, 4-9pm Sun, closed Jul-Sep) has more than 20,000 new and used books. The friendly owners are also a great resource for information about the area.

The HSBC ATM stands off the northeast corner of the plaza.

Computips (per hr M$15; ☿ 9am-8:30pm Mon-Fri, 3-8:30pm Sat & Sun), an air-con internet place on the plaza, is one of several Puerto Morelos internet cafés.

west of the plaza, it has been in operation for many years. The simple white-walled rooms have some creative touches, and ocean-blue bedspreads seem just right. There's a shady back area with tables and plenty of plants, the restaurant offers good meals, and there's a friendly expat bar. Prices drop by 15% from May to October.

Posada El Moro (☎ 871-0159; www.posadaelmoro .com; Av Gomez; s/d M$500/750; ⛶) It has cheery geraniums in the halls and courtyard, and white walls with red trim. Rooms are slightly stuffy, and some have kitchenettes. All have couches that fold out into futons, and there's a small plunge pool. Rates include continental breakfast. Prices drop substantially in low season. All in all, you're probably better off at the Amor.

Hotel Ojo de Agua (☎ 871-0027; www.ojo-de-agua .com; 1-/2-bed r with air-con M$600/700, with fan & kitchenette M$800) Offers 33 rooms in a fairly modern building on a nice stretch of beach. It's about three blocks north of the plaza and has its own restaurant, which offers a nice buffet breakfast.

Hotel Hacienda Morelos (☎ /fax 871-0448; www .haciendamorelos.com; d M$890; ⛶ ⛶) On the waterfront about 150m south of the plaza, it has 15 very appealing, breezy rooms with sea views, kitchenettes and air-con, as well as a small pool and a good restaurant. This is a great value.

Ceiba del Mar (☎ 872-8060; www.ceibadelmar.com; d M$3700; ⛶ ⛶) OK, it's probably out of most folks' price ranges, but it's worth knowing about, as it's one of the classiest hotels on the Riviera Maya. There's a day-spa that's open to 'outsiders.' It's 2km north of town on the beach.

Eating

Tío's (dishes M$15-30; ⏰ 6am-11pm) A modest, friendly place directly across from the lighthouse, just off the northeast corner of the plaza. It serves great fish tacos in the morning (three for M$18!), and good Yucatecan and Mexican dishes the rest of the time, such as *panuchos* (tortilla stuffed with mashed beans, fried, then topped with shredded turkey or chicken, onion and slices of avocado), *salbutes* (same as *panuchos* but without the bean stuffing), *sopa de pollo* (chicken soup) and *tortas*.

Le Café d'Amancia (sandwiches M$20-40; ⏰ 8am-3pm & 6-10pm; ⓥ) This is a spotlessly clean place with pleasing ambience on the southwest corner of the plaza. It serves bagels, sandwiches, pies, coffee, and fruit and veggie *licuados.* There's internet machines (formerly known as computers) upstairs.

Mama's Bakery (☎ 845-6810; mains M$30-60; ⏰ 7:30am-2pm) At Mama's try the kiwi-raisin muffins, great carrot cake or the signature sticky buns. Yum! It also offers egg dishes and wonderful smoothies. This intimate, friendly place is a bit hard to find, but don't give up – it's well worth the short walk from the square. Heading north along Gómez, go about four blocks and look on your left for the bamboo wind chimes under the *palapa.* The small sign is easy to overlook.

Hola Asia (☎ 871-0679; mains M$70-120; ⏰ 1-10pm Wed-Mon) On the south side of the plaza, this has become a local institution. Once a tiny café, it has expanded yearly and now serves Japanese sushi, Thai, Chinese and Indian dishes. General Tso's chicken and whole Thai fish are favorites. There's a bar and large dining area upstairs.

John Gray's Kitchen (☎ 871-0665; Av Niños Héroes L6; mains M$100-200; ⏰ 6-10pm Mon-Sat) One block west and two blocks north of the plaza, this 'kitchen' turns out some truly fabulous food. John, the personable owner-chef, has won international acclaim. The eclectic menu changes frequently and may include duck breast with chipotle-tequila-honey sauce, fresh fish with baked tomatoes and kalamata olive sauce, and an array of scrumptious desserts.

Entertainment

Puerto Morelos' nightlife scene is pretty chill. You can hop in a taxi or bus for a night of raunchy fun in neighboring Playa del Carmen if you just can't stand the quiet. Some of the restaurants have bars and live music, and some stay open late.

Don Pepe's (☎ 871-0613; ⏰ noon-3am) This is an old standby, popular with the mellow set and karaoke masters. Come here to hang out, talk, watch the plaza or catch live music if it happens to be on.

Café Finca la Chiquilla (Av Rojo Gomez s/n; ⏰ 8am-10pm or later) This place, directly across from Don Pepe's, is one of a kind, a great little spot with occasional live music, a full bar, and coffee that is not only freshly ground and roasted, but even *grown and picked* by the owners from their coffee plantation in Puebla.

It's very popular with locals and tourists alike. Meals are also served for M$40 to M$70.

Next to Posada Amor, the following bookend bars are popular with expats:

Bara, Bara (☺ noon-1am) Appeals to a younger crowd.

Que Hora Es (☺ noon-1am)

Shopping

One of the best reasons to come to Puerto Morelos is to hit the artisans market, one block south of the plaza's west corner. You can find authentic Tixkokob hammocks, fine jewelry, pottery and clothing at much better prices than you'll see in Playa del Carmen or Cancún. It's refreshingly low-key, and you can often see the craftspeople at work. Mauricio Soriano is the person to find for hammocks. He will explain the different types and offers a wide variety of styles to choose from. See p163 for more information on hammocks.

Getting There & Away

Most Playa Express and Riviera buses that travel between Cancún and Playa del Carmen drop you on the highway. Some Mayab buses enter town; the Riviera bus running between Cancún airport and Playa del Carmen will sometimes enter the town on request. The 2nd-class bus fare from Cancún is M$17. *Colectivos* cost M$4.

Taxis are usually waiting at the turnoff to shuttle people into town, and there's often a taxi or two near the plaza to shuttle people back to the highway. Many drivers will tell you the fare is per person or overcharge in some other manner; strive for M$20 for the 2km ride, for as many people as you can stuff in.

JARDÍN BOTÁNICO

Two kilometers south of the turnoff for Puerto Morelos is the **Jardín Botánico Yaax Che** (admission M$70; ☺ 9am-5pm Mon-Sat; ♿), a 60-hectare nature reserve with nearly 3km of trails through several native habitats. The garden has sections dedicated to epiphytes (orchids and bromeliads), palms, ferns, succulents (cacti and their relatives), ornamental plants and plants used in traditional Maya medicine. The flora is identified in English, Spanish and Latin. The preserve also holds a large animal population, including the only coastal troops of spider monkeys left in the region. Birders come to observe the many migratory and resident bird species. A lookout tower affords views over the mangrove to Puerto Morelos and the sea.

For the anthropologically minded, the preserve has re-creations of a Maya house and a *chiclero* camp (temporary shelters where locals lived while extracting sap from the 'zapote' or chicle tree; the sap was boiled down and used as the base for chewing gum), as well as some genuine Maya ruins (c AD 1400). Bring insect repellent. Buses may be hailed directly in front of the garden.

TRES RÍOS

Tres Ríos (☎ 998-887-8077; www.tres-rios.com; Hwy 307 Km 54) is not open to the public, nor will it ever be, according to resort spokespeople. Rather, it will be a superexclusive ecoresort, and open only to guests of the Hacienda Tres Ríos, slated to open in the summer of 2008.

PUNTA BETE

Punta Bete, a rocky, reef-hugged point 65km south of Cancún, is reached by a dirt road that runs past a large new housing development and weaves 2.5km from Hwy 307 (turn at the sign for Xcalacoco) before reaching the sea. North and south of the stubby point there are beautiful and occasionally wide stretches of beach upon which sit a few small, low-profile hotels, a few restaurants and a superpricey resort.

Coco's Cabanas (☎ /fax 998-887-5470; www.tulum resorts.com; r low/high season M$700/850; ☀) consists of five nicely decorated cabanas with electricity, fan, good beds and hammocks. It's a short walk from the beach and has a bar, a small pool, a pleasant garden area and a restaurant.

The hotels and restaurants in Punta Bete are within walking distance of each other, but you're best off getting here by rental car or taxi.

PLAYA DEL CARMEN

☎ 984 / pop 100,380

Playa del Carmen, now the third-largest city in Quintana Roo – its population more than doubled over the past five years – is the hippest city on all of the Yucatán Peninsula. Sitting coolly on the lee side of Cozumel, the town's beaches are jammed with superfit Europeans – they let Americans in, too, if they meet the weight requirements! The waters aren't as clear as those of Cancún or Cozumel, and the beach sands aren't quite as champagne-powder-perfect as they are further north, but still Playa (as it's locally known) grows and grows.

Strolling down Playa del Carmen's pedestrian mall, Quinta Avenida (Fifth Ave), is a fabulous game of see-and-be-seen. It's where the beautiful people go – a city of fashion and fitness, understated chic and European cool.

The town is ideally located: close to Cancún's international airport, but far enough south to allow easy access to Cozumel, Tulum, Cobá and other worthy destinations. The reefs here are excellent, and offer diving and snorkeling close by. Look for rays, moray eels, sea turtles and a huge variety of corals. The lavender sea fans make for very picturesque vistas.

With daily cruise-ship visitors, Playa is starting to feel like a mass-tourism destination, but it retains its European chic, and one need just head two blocks west of the hoity-toity pedestrian mall to catch real glimpses of Mexico.

Orientation

Playa is mostly laid out on an easy, one-way grid. Quinta Avenida (*keen*-ta) is the most happening street in town, especially along its pedestrian stretch (the tourist zone). La Nueva Quinta (New Fifth Ave) is also called La Zona Italiana for the number of Italians operating businesses here. It begins on Calle 22 and stretches north for 10 blocks. It's not as happening as the old Quinta, but probably will be in a year or two. The main bus terminal is at the intersection of Quinta

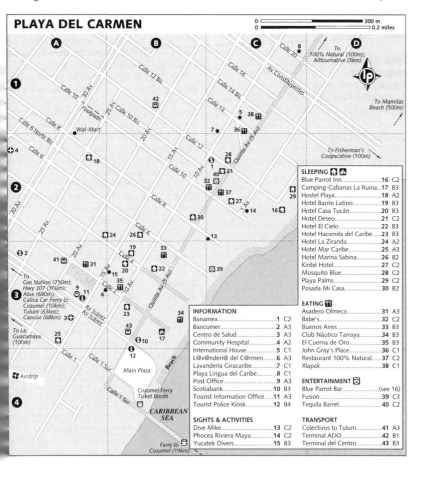

PLAYA DEL CARMEN

0   300 m
0   0.2 miles

To 100% Natural (100m); Alltournative (3km)

To Mamitas Beach (500m)

To Fisherman's Cooperative (100m)

To Gas Station (250m); Hwy 307 (300m); Alux (680m); Calica Car Ferry to Cozumel (10km); Tulum (63km); Cancún (68km)

To La Guacamaya (100m)

Main Plaza

Airstrip

Cozumel Ferry Ticket Booth

Beach

CARIBBEAN SEA

Ferry to Cozumel (19km)

INFORMATION	
Banamex	1 C2
Bancomer	2 A3
Centro de Salud	3 A3
Community Hospital	4 A2
International House	5 C1
L@v@nderi@ del C@rmen	6 A3
Lavandería Giracaribe	7 C1
Playa Lingua del Caribe	8 C1
Post Office	9 A3
Scotiabank	10 B3
Tourist Information Office	11 A3
Tourist Police Kiosk	12 B4

SIGHTS & ACTIVITIES	
Dive Mike	13 C2
Phocea Riviera Maya	14 C2
Yucatek Divers	15 B3

SLEEPING	
Blue Parrot Inn	16 C2
Camping-Cabanas La Ruina	17 B3
Hostel Playa	18 A2
Hotel Barrio Latino	19 B3
Hotel Casa Tucán	20 B3
Hotel Deseo	21 C2
Hotel El Cielo	22 B3
Hotel Hacienda del Caribe	23 B3
Hotel La Ziranda	24 A2
Hotel Mar Caribe	25 A3
Hotel Marina Sabina	26 B2
Kinbé Hotel	27 C2
Mosquito Blue	28 C2
Playa Palms	29 C2
Posada Mi Casa	30 B2

EATING	
Asadero Olmeca	31 A3
Babe's	32 C2
Buenos Aires	33 B3
Club Náutico Tarraya	34 B3
El Cuerna de Oro	35 B3
John Gray's Place	36 C1
Restaurant 100% Natural	37 C2
Xlapak	38 C1

ENTERTAINMENT	
Blue Parrot Bar	(see 16)
Fusion	39 C3
Tequila Barrel	40 C2

TRANSPORT	
Colectivos to Tulum	41 A3
Terminal ADO	42 B1
Terminal del Centro	43 B3

QUINTANA ROO

THOSE MYSTERIOUS ALUXES

Aluxes (a-loosh-es) are Yucatecan forest sprites, and many of the Maya still believe they can bring good or bad luck, even death, to those around them. Therefore, when forests are cleared, whether to make a field or build a house, offerings of food, alcohol and even cigarettes are made to placate them.

Avenida and Juárez, but there is another one further away on Calle 12.

Some people are afraid that leaving the tourist zone will result in instant death, or at least a quick mugging. Unless you're being stupid, you've got little to fear, and the quiet side streets have a wealth of restaurants and cheap hotels.

Information

EMERGENCY

Ambulance, fire & police (☎ 066)
Tourist police kiosk (☎ 873-2656; 24hr) Guards the north corner of the main plaza.

INTERNET ACCESS

There are enough internet cafés in Playa to keep Bill Gates in fancy khakis for the rest of his life.

LAUNDRY

L@v@nderi@ del C@rmen (Calle 2 No 402; 8am-10pm Mon-Sat) Conveniently has an internet café in front of the lavandería. Between Calle 10 and Calle 15.
Lavandería Giracaribe (10 Av; 8am-9pm Mon-Sat) Costs M$14 a kilogram. Between Calle 12 and Calle 14.

MEDICAL SERVICES

In a medical emergency dial ☎ 066.
Centro de Salud (☎ 873-0493; cnr 15 Av & Av Juárez)
Community Hospital (35 Av)

MONEY

These are some of the many banks around town.
Banamex (cnr Calle 12 & 10 Av)
Bancomer (Av Juárez)
Scotiabank (Quinta Av)

POST

Post office (cnr 15 Av & Av Juárez; 9am-4pm Mon-Fri)

TOURIST INFORMATION

Tourist information office (☎ 873-2804; cnr Av Juárez & 15 Av; 9am-8:30pm Mon-Fri, 9am-5pm Sat & Sun) Well stocked with brochures and usually staffed by a speaker of English, Italian and German.

Dangers & Annoyances

Playa is generally safe: you are very unlikely to experience street crime or muggings. However, pickpockets do circulate, especially in crowded dance clubs. Never leave valuables unattended on the beach, especially on the isolated stretches to the north. Run-and-grab thefts while victims are swimming or sleeping on isolated beaches are a common occurrence (the jungle has eyes).

Sights & Activities

DIVING & SNORKELING

In addition to great ocean diving, all of the following outfits offer cenote dives (for more on nearby cenotes, see boxed text, p119).

Dive Mike (☎ 803-1228; www.divemike.com; Calle 8), between Quinta Avenida and the beach, offers snorkeling tours by boat to reefs and a secluded beach for M$350 including refreshments and all gear. To tag along on a dive boat is M$100. Ask the staff about cenote snorkel tours (M$500). English, German, French, Italian, Danish, Norwegian, Swedish and Spanish are spoken.

At **Phocea Riviera Maya** (☎ 873-1210; www.phocearivieramaya.com; 1 Av) French, English and Spanish are spoken. **Yucatek Divers** (☎ 803-1363; www.yucatek-divers.com; 15 Av), between Calle 2 and Calle 4, has German, French, English, Spanish and Dutch speakers, and offers handicapped/limited-mobility dives.

BEACHES

Beachgoers will agree that it's pretty darn nice here. You can swim on Playa's lovely white-sand beaches nearly anywhere: just head down to the ocean, stretch out and enjoy. Numerous restaurants front the beach in the tourist zone; flag down a waiter if you need something frosty to beat the heat. Nights are breezy, sometimes chilly, so bring more than just a bathing suit if you're planning on going for a midnight stroll.

If crowds aren't your thing, go north of Calle 38, where a few scrawny palms serve for shade. Here the beach extends for uncrowded kilometers, making for good camping, but you need to be extra careful with your belongings, as thefts are a possibility.

Many women go topless in Playa (though it's not a common practice in most of Mexico, and generally frowned upon by locals – except the young bucks, of course). **Mamita's Beach**, north of Calle 28, is considered the best place to free the girls.

FISHING

Playa used to be a fishing village, and you can still go out on small skiffs in search of kingfish, tarpon, barracuda, and maybe even a sailfish. April to July is the best time.

Fisherman's Cooperative (☎ 984-130-9892; kabul yuc@hotmail.co), at the beachfront kiosk near Avenida Constituyentes, runs four-hour trips from M$1800 to M$2100.

Courses

Playa has a couple of good language schools. While it makes more sense to study Spanish in a place such as Mérida, where English is not so widely spoken, you can't beat practicing your Spanish by ordering margaritas beachfront. (Hint: '*dos margaritas por favor*' will do the trick, and you didn't even have to pay for a single class. Don't worry Lonely Planet's got your back!)

International House (☎ 803-3388; www.ihriviera maya.com; Calle 14) Offers homestays (the best way to learn a language), a small residence hall and Spanish lessons. Twenty hours of instruction per week costs M$2000. Residence hall rooms are M$300 per night (you can stay there even if you aren't taking classes). Homestays are M$280 per night, including two meals, but you have to be studying with the school.

Playa Lingua del Caribe (☎ 873-3876; www.playa lingua.com; Calle 20) Offers 20-hour-per-week classes for around M$1850. It also offers occasional classes in Maya language, stone carving, cooking, and even salsa dancing.

Tours

Alltournative (☎ 873-2036; www.alltournative.com; Av 38 Norte, L3 M200; ◷ 9am-7pm Mon-Sat) offers packages include ziplining, rappelling and kayaking, as well as custom-designed trips. It also takes you to nearby Maya villages for an 'authentic' experience, that could easily be had on your own.

Sleeping

Surprisingly affordable hotels can be found even in the tourist zone, and a number of hostels offer dorm-style lodging in the M$100 range. Thus, a week, even a month in Playa can be affordable – and once you're here you'll find excuses to stay. You can find great deals by heading away from the beach on Calle 4, Calle 6 and Calle 8 and looking beyond the tourist zone.

BUDGET

Camping-Cabanas La Ruina (☎ /fax 873-0405; laruina @prodigy.net.mx; Calle 2; sites or hammock spaces per person M$100, d with bathroom M$300-550, d without bathroom M$200; ▣) Pitch your tent or hang your hammock in a large lot near the beach. It's very casual, and beach gear can be stored (insecurely) in the courtyard. Some rooms have ceiling fans, some have air-con – the cheapest are bare and bleak, the most expensive front the beach.

Hostel Playa (☎ 803-3277; www.hostelplaya.com; Calle 8; dm/d/tr M$120/300/450) While it's a bit away from the center, this is Playa's best youth hostel. The best thing about this spirited place is the ambience: it has a huge, central common area, great kitchen, and both beer and spirits are allowed until 12:30am, when people either head to bed or go out to the clubs. No meals are served, but there's free coffee and bottled water (M$10 to fill a water bottle), and the staff are extremely helpful and have great suggestions on what to see and do.

Hotel Marina Sabina (☎ 873-0113; www.mariasabina hotel.com; Calle 6 btwn Av 5 & 10; dm M$120, s/d M$450/550) It's not great, but it's better than the other hostels in the area. The cramped rooms aren't worth it, but the hostel space isn't so bad. Plus, you're right next to Quinta Avenida, so you'll definitely get the chance to party on.

Hotel Mar Caribe (☎ 873-0207; cnr 15 Av & Calle 1; r low season M$200-350, high season M$350-550; ▣) A simple, secure and very clean nine-room place with mostly fan-cooled rooms (there are three rooms with air-con). The owners speak French, Spanish and some English. One can almost imagine Steinbeck working on a novel at one of the dark wooden tables.

MIDRANGE

Posada Mi Casa (☎ 873-1972; posada1@prodigy.net .mx; cnr Quinta Av & Calle 8; d low season M$400-500, high season M$500-600; ▣) A very reasonable option right in the center of the Zona, the Mi Casa has spotless tiled-floor rooms and large bathrooms, though some rooms could use an extra chair…or even a chair at all. The friendly owners will let you leave luggage in a back room even after you've checked out.

Hotel La Ziranda (☎ 873-3933; www.hotellaziranda .com; Calle 4; r with air-con low/high season M$400/700; ✖) This place was constructed in late 2000. Its two peach-colored buildings have 15 nice rooms, all with balconies or terraces and two double beds or one king. Trees have been left in place and several walkways have holes to allow them to grow. Fan-cooled rooms are M$100 cheaper.

Hotel Barrio Latino (☎/fax 873-2384; www.hotel barriolatino.com; Calle 4; d low season M$400-500, high season M$700-900; ✖ 💻) Offers 16 clean, colorful rooms with good ventilation, ceiling fans, tiled floors, bathrooms and hammocks (in addition to beds). The friendly Italian owners speak English and Spanish, the place is often full and the front gate is always kept locked. Discounted rates for extended stays. Rates include breakfast, and guests get to make free international calls at certain times of day.

Hotel Casa Tucán (☎/fax 873-0283; www.casatucan .de; Calle 4; r low season M$450-650, high season M$500-650; ✖ ☝) This German-run hotel is a warren of 29 rooms of several types. Rooms have fans or air-con, a couple have kitchenettes, and the cheapest don't have bathrooms. The Tucán has a swimming pool, a pleasant tropical garden and a café serving good, affordable food. Between Avenidas 10 and 15.

Hotel El Cielo (☎ 873-1227; www.hotelcielo.com; Calle 4; d low/high season M$550/1150; 💻) On the low-end of Playa's new chic boutiques is the Cielo. Funky, modern rooms come with creamsicle-and-red bed covers and hand-painted azulejos (a welcomed rustic touch in an otherwise modern environment). There are plans to make a lounge upstairs. It's between Avenidas 10 and Quinta.

our pick **Kinbé Hotel** (☎ 873-0441; www.kinbe.com; Calle 10; d low/high season M$640/830, ste M$1220/1690; ✖) An Italian-owned and operated hotel, it has 29 clean, simple but elegant rooms with lovely aesthetic touches, azure bedspreads, a gorgeous lush courtyard garden and a breezy rooftop terrace with fab views from the 3rd floor. It's near 1 Avenida.

Playa Palms (☎ 803-3908; www.playapalms.com; Av 1 Bis; d low/high season M$720/1330; 💻 ☝) A rip-roaring deal in low season (get the best price online), Playa Palms is right on the beach. The shell-shaped rooms have balconies that look out to the ocean past the curly-whirly dip pool. Go with the cheaper studios to get the best views at the best price. All rooms have kitchenettes.

TOP END

Hotel Hacienda del Caribe (☎ 873-3132; www.hacienda delcaribe.com; Calle 2 No 130; d low/high season M$670/900; ✖ ☝) This Mexican-run place was built in 2000. Its bright-yellow, quiet, comfortable rooms have lovely décor, air-con and cable TV. Many have balconies. The courtyard has a small pool with hydromassage, and parking in a nearby lot is free while you stay.

Blue Parrot Inn (☎ 206-3350, in USA 800-435-0668; Calle 12; r low season M$1240-2840, high season M$2330-5370; ✖ ☝) Many of the charming units have terraces, sea views and full kitchens. But it's a bit pricey to not be right on the ocean. It also has an immensely popular bar (opposite).

Hotel Deseo (☎ 879-3620; www.hoteldeseo.com; cnr Quinta Av & Calle 12; d M$1680-2380; ✖ 💻 ☝) If you can still afford your rock-and-roll lifestyle, then you're going to love the hi-fi lounge atmosphere of Deseo. There's a very chill lounge and plunge pool right in front of your blindingly white room (white is evidently the color of desire). Pay a bit more for an upstairs balcony room, and be prepared to stay up late.

Mosquito Blue (☎ 873-1245; www.mosquitoblue .com; Quinta Av; r low season M$2090-4050, high season M$2720-4750; ✖ 💻 ☝) Between Calle 12 and Calle 14. Strives for – and at times achieves – ultrachicness. Its cloistered interior boasts two pools and courtyards, a bar and restaurant, and very nicely decorated rooms furnished in Indonesian mahogany. Art and artistic touches abound throughout the hotel, which has junior and master suites as well as the standard and deluxe rooms.

Eating

As happens in other tourist-oriented places on the Yucatán Peninsula, some Playa restaurants add a service charge to the bill. You are not required to pay it; however, a 10% to 15% tip for good service is appreciated.

El Cuerna de Oro (cnr Calle 2 & 10 Av; set meals M$30-50; ☺ 7am-10pm) Hearty, homestyle set meals are served in this casual eatery near the bus station. You get a giant portion of your selected dish (the three or four options change nightly) plus rice, beans and unlimited refills of the nightly drink, such as hibiscus water or iced tea. The breakfasts are skippable.

our pick **Restaurant 100% Natural** (☎ 873-2242; cnr Quinta Av & Calle 10; mains M$35-100; ☺ 7am-11pm; ✓) The trademarks of this quickly establishing chain – vegetable- and fruit-juice blends, salads, various vegetable and chicken dishes and other healthy foods – are delicious and filling. There's another branch on the corner of Quinta Avenida and Calle 22.

Babe's (Calle 10; mains M$50-100; ☿ noon-11:30pm Mon-Sat, 5-11:30pm Sun) Babe's serves some excellent Thai food, including a yummy homestyle *tom kha gai* (chicken and coconut-milk soup) brimming with veggies. Excellent Vietnamese salad (with shrimp and mango) is another specialty. Most dishes can be done vegetarian, and to mix things up a bit the Swedish cook has some tasty Greek items on the menu as well. There's another Babe's along the Nueva Quinta.

Club Náutico Tarraya (☎ 873-2040; Calle 2; mains M$50-120; ☿ noon-9pm) One of the few restaurants in Playa del Carmen that dates from the 1960s. It continues to offer good seafood at decent prices in a casual place on the beach with a nice view.

La Guacamaya (cnr Calle 1 Sur & Av 30; meals M$60 ☿ noon-10pm Mon-Sat, noon-5pm Sun) Locals love this large open-air restaurant. Veggies beware, if it doesn't have hoofs, it's unlikely to make it on the menu. Try the *tablazo*, a monstro mixed grill with every cut of meat imaginable for less than M$100.

Xlapak (☎ 879-3595; Quinta Av; meals M$70-180; ☿ 8am-11pm) Serves delicious food at unbelievably low prices. Lunch and dinner consists of a starter, a main dish (accompanied by rice, steamed veggies and garlic bread) and a dessert. Try the chicken with *chaya* (a spinachlike green) salsa and wash it down with one of a wide selection of juices and drinks. The restaurant is very nicely done up like a Maya temple, with faithfully rendered reproductions of Maya murals on the walls and plants everywhere. It's between Calle 14 and Calle 14 Bis.

Buenos Aires (☎ 873-2751; Calle 6; mains M$90-240; ☿ noon-11:30pm) In a new location, this Argentinean-owned steak house is well known for its *parrilla*, an all-you-can-eat smorgasbord (M$350 for two people). Waiters bring your meat to you on a skewer. You can also sample ribs, empanadas, burgers and other 'lighter' fare.

John Gray's Place (☎ 803-3689; www.johngrayrestaurants.com; Calle Corazón 5TA; mains M$110-250; ☿ 6-11pm Mon-Sat) The sister restaurant to John Gray's Kitchen in Puerto Morelos, it has a dark-wood bar downstairs, and the same spectacular food. Crab cakes melt on the tongue, set off by a dash of Asian vinaigrette and a few cilantro leaves. Chicken with cilantro pesto is a favorite.

Norah Jones croons in the background as you polish off your glass of wine. Calle Corazón is between Calle 12 and Calle 14.

Alux (☎ 803-2936; Av Juárez; mains M$120-140; ☿ 7pm-2am) About three blocks west of Hwy 307, the Alux is an amazing must-visit. It's a restaurant-lounge situated in a cavern: stalactites, stalagmites, pools and all. Candles and dim electric lights illuminate numerous nooks and crannies converted into sofalike seating. Wander through, have a bite to eat or a drink and revel in the atmosphere. It offers live music nightly at 10pm, and a party on Saturday night. Snacks are M$40 to M$90.

Head out of the tourist zone to find cheap, quality eats such as great grilled chicken from **Asadero Olmeca** (Calle 2; mains M$30; ☿ 7am-6pm), next to the Tulum-bound *colectivos*. There's a ton of cheap food stands on Avenida 10 between Calle 8 and Calle 10 near the center. Choose between tacos, kebabs and pizza.

Entertainment

Venues here come and go, so ask around if you're wondering where the party is (or where it isn't). You'll find everything from mellow, tranced-out lounge bars to classic rock-and-roll places. Here are a few options we found fun.

Tequila Barrel (☎ 873-1061; Quinta Av; ☿ 8am-2am) With a large dancing area in back, this sparkling clean bar and grill between Calles 10 and 12 pours a huge selection of tequila and other spirits, and spins old rock and Motown CDs.

Blue Parrot Bar (☎ 873-0083; Calle 12; ☿ 11am-4am) This is the Blue Parrot Inn's immensely popular open-sided *palapa* beachfront bar with swing chairs, a giant outdoor dance stage, indoor section if the weather's bad…and lots of sand.

our pick **Fusion** (Calle 6; ☿ until late) Groove out beachside under that Playa moon at Fusion. There's live music most nights.

Getting There & Away
BOAT

Ferries to Cozumel (M$110 one way) leave at 6am, 8am, 9am, 10am, 11am, 1pm, 3pm, 5pm, 6pm, 7pm, 9pm and 11pm. The air-conditioned catamaran takes about a half-hour, depending on weather. Buy tickets at the booth on Calle 1 Sur. An open-air boat (same ticket price but running less regularly) takes 45 minutes to an hour; it operates mostly in the summer season.

BUS SERVICES FROM PLAYA DEL CARMEN

Destination	Cost (M$)	Duration (hr)	Departures
Cancún	34	1	numerous 4am-midnight
Cancún international airport	80	1	frequent ADO buses 8am-6:15pm
Chetumal	18-18.80	5-5½	9 ADO buses 6:15am-11:56pm, numerous Mayab buses 1:30am-11:15pm
Chichén Itzá	18	3-4	1 ADO bus at 8am
Cobá	68	1-1¾	ADO buses at 8am & 9am
Mérida	310	5	Frequent ADO buses; ADO GL at 4pm, 9:30pm & 11:45pm
Palenque	540	12-13	ADO GL at 7pm
San Cristóbal de Las Casas	780	16-18	ADO GL at 7pm
Tulum	22	1	frequent Riviera & Mayab buses
Valladolid	77-140	2½-3½	Mayab at 7:30am & 2:30pm

BUS

Playa has two bus terminals; each sells tickets and provides information for at least some of the other's departures. The newer one, **Terminal ADO** (20 Av), just east of Calle 12, is where most 1st-class buslines arrive and depart. Riviera's buses (which don't entirely deserve the designation '1st-class' anyhow) use the old terminal. A taxi from Terminal ADO to the main plaza will run about M$15.

The old bus station, **Terminal del Centro** (cnr Av Juárez & Quinta Av), gets all the 2nd-class (called *'intermedio'* by such lines as Mayab) services. Riviera buses to Cancún and its airport have a separate ticket counter on the Avenida Juárez side of the terminal. The table (above) shows some distances, travel times and prices for buses.

COLECTIVOS

Colectivos are a great option for cheap travel southward to Tulum (M$25, 45 minutes). They depart from Calle 2 near 20 Avenida as soon as they fill (about every 10 or 15 minutes) from 5am to 10pm. They will stop anywhere along the highway between Playa and Tulum, charging a minimum of M$10. Luggage space is somewhat limited, but they're great for day trips.

ISLA COZUMEL

☎ 987 / pop 73,200

Cozumel is too resilient, too proud to give into the Señor Frog's of this world. And leaving the tourist area – and the Señor Frog's merchandise megamart behind – you still see an island of quiet cool and genuine authenticity. Garages still have shrines to the Virgin, there's a spirited Caribbean pathos, and of course there's some tourist things to do, such as diving down to some of the best damned reefs in the world.

A hugely popular diving spot since 1961, when Jacques Cousteau, led by local guides, showed its spectacular reefs to the world, Cozumel lies 71km south of Cancún. Measuring 53km by 14km, it is Mexico's largest island. Called Ah-Cuzamil-Peten (Island of Swallows) by its earliest inhabitants, Cozumel has become a world-famous diving and cruise-ship destination. Hurricane Wilma did some serious damage to the snorkeling sites around the island – while they are still beautiful, it will take years for them to recover completely. Fortunately, most of the deep-water reefs missed the brunt of the storm. The squadrons of eagle rays have dwindled due to overfishing of the shellfish stocks – no shellfish, no eagle rays.

While diving and snorkeling are the main draws, the tourist zone offers lots of shopping 'deals' (often not very cheap), and a pleasant town square in which to spend the afternoon. In February there is a festive Carnaval, which brings dancers festooned with feathers out into the streets. It's not Rio, but it's still fun. There are some small Maya ruins and a few eco-themed parks.

The less-visited, windswept far side of the island has beautiful beaches and a few large waves. Rent a scooter or convertible bug and head over for a picnic lunch, but watch the currents if you head out for a swim or surf.

History

Maya settlement here dates from AD 300. During the post-Classic period Cozumel flourished as a trade center and, more importantly, a ceremonial site. Every Maya woman living on the Yucatán Peninsula and beyond was expected to make at least one pilgrimage here to pay tribute to Ixchel, the goddess of fertility and the moon, at a temple erected in her honor. Archaeologists believe this temple was at San Gervasio, a bit north of the island's geographical center.

At the time of the first Spanish contact with Cozumel (in 1518, by Juan de Grijalva and his men), there were at least 32 Maya building groups on the island. According to Spanish chronicler Diego de Landa, a year later Hernán Cortés sacked one of the Maya centers but left the others intact, apparently satisfied with converting the island's

population to Christianity. Smallpox introduced by the Spanish wiped out half the 8000 Maya and, of the survivors, only about 200 escaped genocidal attacks by conquistadors in the late 1540s.

The island remained virtually deserted into the late 17th century, its coves providing sanctuary for several notorious pirates, including Jean Lafitte and Henry Morgan. In 1848 indigenous people fleeing the War of the Castes began to resettle Cozumel. At the beginning of the 20th century the island's (by then mostly mestizo) population grew, thanks to the craze for chewing gum. Cozumel was a port of call on the chicle export route, and locals harvested the gum base on the island. After the demise of chicle

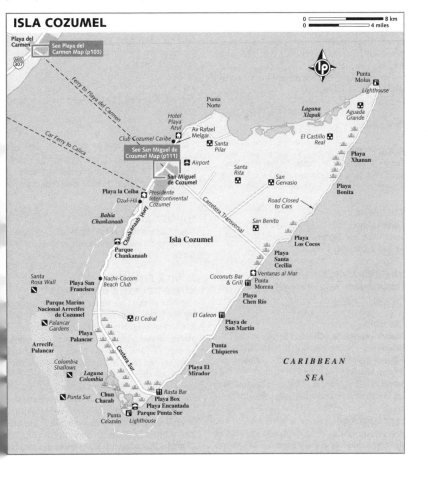

Cozumel's economy remained strong owing to the construction of a US air base here during WWII.

When the US military departed, the island fell into an economic slump, and many of its people moved away. Those who stayed fished for a living until 1961, when Cousteau's documentary broadcast Cozumel's glorious sea life to the world. The tourists began arriving almost overnight.

Orientation & Information

It's easy to make your way on foot around the island's only town, San Miguel de Cozumel. The waterfront boulevard is Avenida Rafael Melgar; along Melgar south of the main ferry dock (Muelle Fiscal) is a narrow sand beach. The main plaza is opposite the ferry dock. The airport is 2km northeast. Much of the roads in the town's center were under construction as of press time, but local authorities say they should be back to normal soon.

An excellent documentary on Cozumel diving is available at www.cozumelnatural treasure.com.

The following places are all in San Miguel de Cozumel.

BOOKSTORES

Fama (☎ 872-5020; Av 5 Norte; ☺ 9am-10pm Mon-Sun) Carries books and periodicals in English and Spanish. Between Avenida Benito Juárez and Calle 2 Norte.

EMERGENCY

Tourist police Patrols the island and staffs a kiosk (open 8am to 11pm) one-quarter of a block inland on Calle 11 Sur from Avenida Rafael Melgar.

INTERNET ACCESS

Phonet (Av Benito Juárez 5; per hr M$15; ☺ 8am-11pm Mon-Sun)

LAUNDRY

Express Lavandería (☎ 872-2932; Calle Dr Adolfo Rosado Salas; ☺ 8am-9pm Mon-Sat, 8:30am-4pm Sun) Self-serve washing and drying costs M$50 per load. Between Avenidas 5 and 10 Sur.

Servi-Lav (☎ 872-3951; Av 10 Norte; ☺ 8am-8pm Mon-Sat) Charges M$10 per kilogram. Between Calles 6 and 8.

LEFT LUGGAGE

A convenience store at the landward end of the ferry dock stores luggage for M$20 per day, but the shelves used are not big enough for a full-sized backpack.

MEDICAL SERVICES

There are at least two hyperbaric chambers in San Miguel.

Buceo Médico Mexicano (☎ 872-1430; fax 872-1848; Calle 5 Sur) Between Avenida Rafael Melgar and Avenida 5 Sur.

Cozumel Hyperbaric Research (☎ 872-0103; Calle 6 Norte) Between Avenida 5 and Avenida 10 Norte, in the Médica San Miguel clinic.

MONEY

ATMs are the best way to get quick cash. For currency exchange, try any of the banks near the main plaza, such as Banorte or HSBC. All are open 8am or 9am to 4:30pm Monday to Friday and on Saturday morning. The many *casas de cambio* (currency-exchange houses) around town may charge as much as 3.5% commission (the bank rate is 1%) to cash a traveler's check.

POST

Post office (cnr Calle 7 Sur & Av Rafael Melgar; ☺ 9am-5pm Mon-Fri)

TELEPHONE

The Telecomm office, near the post office, handles faxes, money orders and such. Telmex card phones are abundant around town and are often cheaper than making calls at internet cafés.

TOURIST INFORMATION

Tourist information office (☎ 869-0211; ☺ 8am-8pm) Operates kiosks at the passenger ferry, cruise-ship and car-ferry docks.

Sights & Activities
MUSEO DE LA ISLA DE COZUMEL

Exhibits at the fine **Museo de la Isla de Cozumel** (☎ 872-1434; Av Rafael Melgar; admission M$30; ☺ 8am-5pm) in San Miguel present a clear and detailed picture of the island's flora, fauna, geography, geology and ancient Maya history. Thoughtful and detailed signs in English and Spanish accompany the exhibits. It's a good place to learn about coral before hitting the water, and it's one not to miss before you leave the island. A courtyard in the back contains a *na* (thatched Maya hut) with someone in attendance who will explain (in Spanish) the various elements that made up Maya domestic life: the

SAN MIGUEL DE COZUMEL

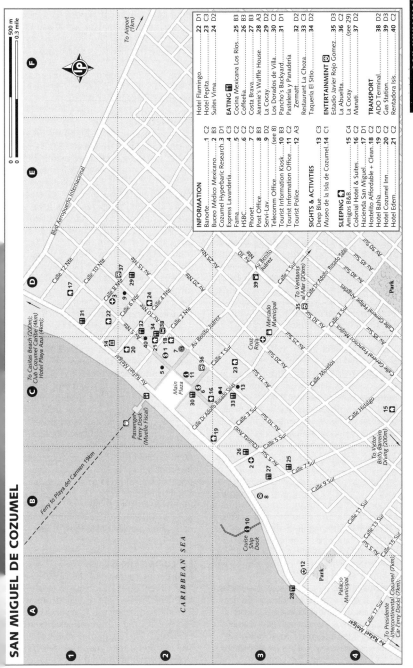

INFORMATION	
Banorte	1 C2
Buceo Médico Mexicano	2 B3
Cozumel Hyperbaric Research	3 D1
Express Lavandería	4 C3
Fama	5 C2
HSBC	6 C2
Phonet	7 C2
Post Office	8 B3
Servi-Lav	9 D2
Telecomm Office	(see 8)
Tourist Information Kiosk	10 B3
Tourist Information Office	11 C2
Tourist Police	12 A3

SIGHTS & ACTIVITIES	
Deep Blue	13 C3
Museo de la Isla de Cozumel	14 C1

SLEEPING	
Amigos B&B	15 C4
Colonial Hotel & Suites	16 C2
Hacienda San Miguel	17 D1
Hostelito Affordable + Clean	18 C2
Hotel Bahía	19 C2
Hotel Cozumel Inn	20 C3
Hotel Edem	21 C2

EATING	
Cocina Mexicana Los Rios	25 B3
Coffeelia	26 B3
Costa Brava	27 B3
Jeannie's Waffle House	28 A3
La Cocay	29 D2
Los Dorados de Villa	30 C2
Pancho's Backyard	31 D1
Pastelería y Panadería	
Zermatt	32 D2
Restaurant La Choza	33 C3
Taquería El Sitio	34 D2

Hotel Flamingo	22 D1
Hotel Pepita	23 C3
Suites Vima	24 D2

ENTERTAINMENT	
Estadio Javier Rojo Gomez	35 D3
La Abuelita	36 C2
La Cocay	(see 29)
Manatí	37 D2

TRANSPORT	
ADO Terminal	38 D2
Gas Station	39 D3
Rentadora Isis	40 C2

toys, utensils, foodstuffs, a raised garden bed for kitchen herbs and more.

DIVING

Despite the massive hit of Hurricane Wilma, Cozumel – and its 65 surrounding reefs – remains one of the most popular diving destinations in the world. 'It will take 10 years without a hurricane for the reef to get back in shape,' says Deep Blue's Pedro Venegas. '[But] even a year after Wilma, the reef's recuperation was incredible.'

It has fantastic year-round visibility (commonly 30m or more) and a jaw-droppingly impressive variety of marine life that includes spotted eagle rays, moray eels, groupers, barracudas, turtles, sharks, brain coral and some huge sponges. The island has strong currents (normally around 3 knots), making drift dives the standard, especially along the many walls. Even when diving or snorkeling from the beach you should evaluate conditions and plan your route, selecting an exit point down-current beforehand, then staying alert for shifts in currents. Always keep an eye out (and your ears open) for boat traffic as well. It's best not to snorkel alone away from the beach area.

Prices vary, but in general expect to pay about M$880 for a two-tank dive (less if you bring your own buoyancy control device and regulator), M$650 for an introductory 'resort' course and M$4000 for PADI open-water certification. Multiple-dive packages and discounts for groups or those paying in cash can bring these rates down significantly. For more information, pick up a copy of Lonely Planet's *Diving & Snorkeling Cozumel*, with detailed descriptions of local dive sites.

There are scores of dive operators on Cozumel. The following are some reputable ones that come recommended. All limit the size of their groups to six or eight divers, and take pains to match up divers of similar skill levels. Some offer snorkeling and deep-sea fishing trips as well as dives and diving instruction. Those out of the center will provide transport.

Deep Blue (☎ /fax 872-5653; www.deepbluecozumel .com; cnr Av 10 Sur & Calle Dr Adolfo Rosado Salas) This PADI, National Association of Underwater Instructors (NAUI), Technical Diving International (TDI) and International Association of Nitrox and Technical Divers, Inc (IANTD) operation has very good gear and fast boats that give you a chance to get more dives out of a day.

Victor Brito Barreiro (☎ /fax 872-3223; www.angel fire.com/ga/cozumeldiving) Based south of town. Victor is head of Cozumel's diving instructors association and has many years of experience. Highly recommended.

If you encounter a decompression emergency, head immediately to one of Cozumel's two hyperbaric chambers (p110).

SNORKELING

Good snorkeling can be found at Casitas just north of San Miguel de Cozumel and Dzul-Há to the south. Snorkelers are required to pay M$20 for park admission. The best snorkeling sites are reached by boat. A half-day boat tour will cost from M$350 to M$500. Most strictly snorkeling outfits operating in town go to one of three stretches of reef near town, all accessible from the beach. If you go with a dive outfit instead, you can often get to better spots, such as Palancar Reef or the adjacent Colombia Shallows, near the island's southern end. **Ramón Zapata** (☎ 044 987-100-2256) runs snorkeling trips leaving from Playa Palancar for about M$250 per person, but you'll need to make your own way to the beach.

You can save on boat fares (and see fewer fish) by walking into the gentle surf north of town. One good spot is Hotel Playa Azul, 4km north of the turnoff to the airport; its *palapas* offer shade, and it has a swimming area with a sheltering wharf and a small artificial reef. If you'd like to sit at one of the *palapas* the waiters ask only that you buy a drink or a bite to eat. Next door to the south, the **Club Cozumel Caribe** (☎ 800-833-5971, www.clubcozumelcaribe.info) has underwater cement statuary that makes for some interesting snorkeling. It has a decent beach and pool, and, as of press time, you didn't need to pay anything to get in. You will need to fork over some cash, however, to don snorkel gear (M$50) or test your mettle on the rock-climbing wall (M$350). It also has a snack bar.

EXPLORING THE ISLAND

In order to see most of the island you will have to rent a vehicle or take a taxi; cyclists will need to brave the regular strong winds. The following route will take you south from San Miguel, then counterclockwise around the island. There are some places along the way to stop for food and drink, but it's good to bring water all the same.

COZUMEL'S TOP DIVE SITES

Ask any dive operator in Cozumel to name the best dive sites in the area and the following names will come up time and again.

Santa Rosa Wall

This is the biggest of the famous sites. The wall is so large most people are able to see only a third of it on one tank. Regardless of where you're dropped, expect to find enormous overhangs and tunnels covered with corals and sponges. Stoplight parrot fish, black grouper and barracuda hang out here. The average visibility is 30m and minimum depth 10m, with an average closer to 25m. Carry a flashlight with you, even if you're diving at noon, as it will help to bring out the color of coral at depth and illuminate the critters hiding in crevices. Hurricane Wilma left shallower spots with uncovered coral, but for the most part it is unharmed.

Punta Sur Reef

Unforgettable for its coral caverns, each of which is named, this reef is for experienced, properly certified divers only. Before you dive be sure to ask your dive master to point out the Devil's Throat. This cave opens into a cathedral room with four tunnels, all of which make for some pretty hairy exploration. Only advanced divers should consider entering the Devil's Throat, but anyone who visits Punta Sur Reef will be impressed by the cave system and the butterfly fish, angelfish and whip corals that abound here.

Colombia Shallows

Also known as Colombia Gardens, Colombia Shallows lends itself equally well to snorkeling and scuba diving. Because it's a shallow dive (maximum depth 10m, average 2m to 4m), its massive coral buttresses covered with sponges and other resplendent life-forms are well illuminated. The current at Colombia Gardens is generally light to moderate. This and the shallow water allows you to spend hours at the site if you want, and you'll never get bored spying all the elkhorn coral, pillar coral and anemones that live here.

Palancar Gardens

Also known as Palancar Shallows, and thus one of the spots that sustained serious Wilma damage, this dive can be appreciated by snorkelers due to the slight current usually found here and its modest maximum depth (20m). The Gardens consists of a strip reef about 25m wide and very long, riddled with fissures and tunnels. The major features here are enormous stovepipe sponges and vivid yellow tube sponges, and you can always find damselfish, parrot fish and angelfish around you. In the deeper parts of the reef, divers will want to keep an eye out for the lovely black corals.

Sad to say, access to many of Cozumel's best stretches of beach has become limited. Resorts and residential developments with gated roads create the most difficulties. Pay-for-use beach clubs occupy some other prime spots, but you can park and walk through or around them and enjoy adjacent parts of the beach without obligation. Sitting under their umbrellas or otherwise using the facilities requires you to fork out some money, either a straight fee or a *consumo mínimo* (minimum consumption of food and drink), which can add up to a pretty ridiculous M$150 per person in some places. It's not always strictly applied, especially when business is slow.

Several sites along the island's west coast offer horse riding (most of the horses look ready to keel over). The asking price is M$160 an hour; bargain hard.

Parque Chankanaab

A popular snorkeling spot, especially when cruise ships are in port, is **Parque Chankanaab** (admission M$160; ⏰ 7am-6pm; ♿). However, there's not a lot to see in the water beyond some brightly colored fish and deliberately sunken artificial objects. The beach is a nice one, though, and 50m inland is a limestone lagoon surrounded by iguanas and inhabited by turtles. You're not allowed to swim or snorkel here, but it's picturesque all the same. The beach is lined with *palapas* and fiberglass lounge chairs, and you can rent snorkel and dive equipment.

Dolphin shows are included in the admission price, as is the use of dressing rooms, lockers and showers. There's a small archaeological park containing replica Olmec heads and Maya artifacts, a small museum featuring objects from Chichén Itzá, and a botanical garden with 400 species of tropical plants. Other facilities include a restaurant, a bar and snack shops. A taxi from town costs M$100 one way.

El Cedral

This Maya ruin is the oldest on the island. It's the size of a small house and has no ornamentation, but costs nothing to visit and is easy to reach, unlike San Gervasio and other ruins on Cozumel. It's 3.5km down a signed paved road that heads off to the left (east) a kilometer or two south of Nachi-Cocom's access road, hiding amid a forest of pole structures painted yellow and white and erected as souvenir stalls. El Cedral is thought to have been an important ceremonial site; the small church standing next to the tiny ruin today is evidence that the site still has religious significance for locals.

Playa Palancar

About 17km south of town, Palancar is another great beach. It has a beach club renting hydro bikes, kayaks, snorkel gear and sailboats, plus a restaurant and a dive operation. Near the beach, Arrecife Palancar (Palancar Reef) has some very good diving (it's known as Palancar Gardens), as well as fine snorkeling (Palancar Shallows), though the shallow spots were marked by Wilma. See boxed text, p113, for more information.

Parque Punta Sur

The southern tip of the island has been turned into a rather overpriced **'ecotouristic park'** (☎ 872-0914; admission M$100; 🕙 9am-5pm). Visitors board an open vehicle for the 3km ride to visit picturesque Celarain lighthouse and the small nautical museum at its base. Another vehicle carries visitors to **Laguna Colombia**, part of a three-lagoon system that is the habitat of crocodiles and many resident and migratory waterfowl. Crocs can be seen (when they feel like it) from shore, via a trail through mangrove or a bridge over the lagoon.

East Coast

The eastern shoreline is the wildest part of the island and presents some beautiful seascapes and many small blowholes (there's a bunch around Km 30.5). Swimming is dangerous on most of the east coast because of riptides and undertows. With a bit of care you can sometimes swim at Punta Chiqueros, Playa Chen Río and Punta Morena.

As you travel along the coast, consider stopping for lunch or a drink at the Rasta Bar (Km 29.5), El Galeon (Km 43.1) or Coconuts Bar & Grill (Km 43.5). El Galeon rents surf and boogie boards for M$200 and M$70 per hour, respectively. Or just bring a picnic lunch and plan on having the beach to yourself.

Punta Molas

Beyond where the east-coast highway meets the Carretera Transversal, intrepid travelers may take a poorly maintained, infrequently traveled and almost impossible to find track toward Punta Molas, the island's northeast point, accessible only by all-terrain vehicles (ATV) or on foot. If you head up this road be aware that you can't count on flagging down another motorist for help in the event of a breakdown or accident, and most rental agencies' insurance policies don't cover any mishaps on unpaved roads. Word on the street is that Donald Trump has plans to build in the area, but the road was officially closed to cars and 4WDs as of press time. About 17km up the road are the Maya ruins known as **El Castillo Real**, and a few kilometers further is **Aguada Grande**. Both sites are quite far gone, their significance lost to time. In the vicinity of Punta Molas are some fairly good beaches and a few more minor ruins.

San Gervasio

This **Maya complex** (admission M$60; 🕙 7am-4pm) is Cozumel's only preserved ruins, and a prime example of the local government's efforts to milk dollars out of cruise-ship passengers. San Gervasio is thought to have been the site of the sanctuary of Ixchel, goddess of fertility, and thus an important pilgrimage site at which Maya women – in particular prospective mothers – worshipped. But its structures are small and crude, and the clay idols of Ixchel were long ago destroyed by the Spaniards.

Sleeping

All hotel rooms come with private bathroom and fan, unless otherwise noted. Almost all places raise their rates at Christmas and Easter. 'High season' is mid-December to mid-April, but whatever the season, if business is slow, most places are open to negotiation.

BUDGET

The following listings are in San Miguel de Cozumel.

ourpick Hostelito Affordable + Clean (☎ 869-8157; www.hostelito.com; Av 10; dm M$120, d M$350) The name says it all: brand-spanking new Hostelito is affordable *and* clean. There's one shared dorm room downstairs for boys and girls with bamboo privacy screens, giant lockers and amazingly clean showers. (How's that for truth in advertising?) Upstairs you'll find a great terrace, kitchen and common area, as well as a six-person group room and two doubles. It has wi-fi and luggage storage and is located between Avenida Benito Juárez and Calle 2 Norte on Avenida 10.

Hotel Edem (☎ 872-1166; Calle 2 Norte No 124; d with fan/air-con M$180/320; 🕸) Great location and saintly rates make the Edem a prime deal. It has a turtle-filled fountain and a friendly Siamese cat, and the no-nonsense senora keeps the doors locked after 9pm. Rooms are clean and simple, with hammock hooks and scaldingly hot showers. There's a deposit for the threadbare towels (like anyone would run off with them).

Hotel Cozumel Inn (☎ 872-0314; fax 872-3156; Calle 4 Norte; d with fan/air-con M$320/370; 🕸 🖳) A green building with 26 well-maintained rooms with good beds, and a small (sometimes suspect!) swimming pool, the Cozumel is a good deal, especially in high season. Mustiness airs out quickly. Find it between Avenida Rafael Melgar and Avenida 5 Norte.

Hotel Pepita (☎ /fax 872-0098; Av 15 Sur; d low/high season M$350/400; 🕸) The HP's owner, Maria Teresa, takes pride in her work, and it shows. This is the best economic hotel in the city. It's friendly, with well-maintained rooms grouped around a garden. All have two double beds, refrigerators and air-con (many catch a good breeze), and there's free morning coffee.

MIDRANGE

The following listings are in San Miguel de Cozumel.

Suites Vima (☎ /fax 872-5118; Av 10 Norte; s/d M$400/500; 🕸 🖳) Has spotless and spacious modern rooms with tiled floors, Barney Rubble–hard beds, good air-con and bathrooms, fridges, tables and chairs. The décor is mint green, highlighted by other pastels. A small swimming pool with a current to swim against lies in a green area in back. No kids aged under 13, please.

Amigo's B&B (☎ 872-3868; www.cozumelbedandbreakfast.net; Calle 7 Sur No 57; d/tr/q Jan 4-Apr 30 M$650/750/850, Sep & Oct M$400/500/600, May 1-Aug 31 & Nov 1-Dec 20 M$500/600/700; 🕸 🖳 🖳) Has a large garden, wifi access, an inviting pool and a good lounging area stocked with reading material. It's worth the hike from the center to enjoy one of the three well-appointed, cottage-style rooms here. All have air-con and full kitchenettes and rates include a good breakfast. Book ahead.

Hotel Bahía (☎ 872-9090, 800-227-2639; www.suitesbahia.com; cnr Av Rafael Melgar & Calle 3 Sur; d with balcony/ocean view M$660/800; 🕸 🖳) Offers some rooms with sea views and balconies. All rooms have the same amenities and general setup as the Colonial (they're under the same management). Rates include continental breakfast.

Colonial Hotel & Suites (☎ 872-9090, 800-227-2639; www.suitescolonial.com; Av 5 Sur; ste low/high season M$720/850; 🕸) This place is down a passageway off Avenida 5 Sur between Calles 1 Sur and Dr Adolfo Rosado Salas. It features lovely studios and nice, spacious, one-bedroom 'suites' (beds are separated from the rest of the room by low partitions) with kitchenettes. All rooms have cable TV, fridge and air-con, and lots of varnished-wood touches. Rates include coffee and pastries.

Hotel Flamingo (☎ 872-1264; www.hotelflamingo.com; Calle 6 Norte 81; r low season M$750-1500, high season M$850-1600; 🕸) The colorful Hotel Flamingo is a nicely decorated place with spacious air-conditioned rooms (some with fridges) sporting direct-dial phones. Common areas include a leafy courtyard where you can eat breakfast, a 2nd-floor pool table, a bar and a rooftop sun deck with good sea views. Wifi access makes it a good choice for laptoptoters. Make reservations via the internet to save a few pesos.

Hacienda San Miguel (☎ 872-1986; www.haciendasanmiguel.com; Calle 10; r Sep-Dec 18 M$850-1300, Jan-Aug from M$1050; 🕸) It's a quiet place built and furnished to resemble an old hacienda, and niceties such as bathrobes and continental breakfast served in your room make this very good value. It offers divers' packages, and long stays can bring rates down by amazing amounts – check the web for deals.

TOP END

Several kilometers north and south of town are a few big luxury resort hotels. All rooms in this category have air-con.

Ventanas al Mar (☎ 105-2684; www.ventanasalmar .biz; Costera Oriente Km 43.5; r low/high season M$940/1050; 🅿) Notable as it's the only windward hotel on the island, Ventanas al Mar might be right for you if you are looking to get away from it all (way away from it all). After dark you'll need to go into town as the windward-side restaurants are closed. But the rooms offer great ocean views, and nice touches such as hand-painted tiles. Beware: the constant wind is enough to drive you batty.

Presidente Intercontinental Cozumel (☎ 872-9500; www.intercontinental.com; Carretera a Chankanaab Km 6.5; r from M$2000; 🅿 🏊) This is one of the island's oldest luxury hotels. It has a lovely beach and 253 posh guestrooms, many with sea views, set amid tropical gardens and swimming pools. Wild (large!) iguanas roam the grounds. Unlike the all-inclusives further south, the Presidente is sufficiently close to town to allow you several dining options; truth be told, the city has grown south around the hotel.

Hotel Playa Azul (☎ 869-5160; www.playa-azul.com; Carretera a San Juan Km 4; d from M$2350, ste from M$2800; 🅿 🏊) This is in the sedate area north of town on its own pretty little stretch of beach (it's not deep but it's a gem), and there's good snorkeling (the current is sometimes strong). All rooms have a sea view, a balcony or terrace, and one king or two queen beds. The hotel has a bar, restaurant and gorgeous pool, and guests can play golf free at a nearby course. There's still a mandatory M$250 cart fee though.

Eating
BUDGET

Head out of the 'zone' for the best food in Cozumel, and maybe even discover your own greasy spoon. Cheapest of all eating places are the little market *loncherías* (lunch stalls) next to the Mercado Municipal on Calle Dr Adolfo Rosado Salas between Avenida 20 and Avenida 25 Sur. Most offer soup and a main

course for around M$30, with a large selection of dishes available; ask about the cheap *comida corrida* (fixed-price menu) not listed on the menu.

Taquería El Sitio (Calle 2 Norte; M$15-30; 🕑 7am-1pm) For scrump-diddily-umptious tacos and *tortas*, head over to El Sitio. It has fancy-upped the canopy-covered eating area with a mural of a cruise ship and jumping dolphins. It's two doors east of Hotel Edem.

Pastelería y Panadería Zermatt (cnr Av 5 Norte & Calle 4 Norte; bread M$20; 🕑 7am-8:30pm Mon-Sat) Bakes pastries, cakes, pizzas and whole-wheat breads and serves decent coffee. Unlike many Mexican bakeries, it does its cooking in the early morning.

our pick Coffeelia (☎ 872-7402; Calle 5 Sur; breakfast M$40-70, set meals M$57; 🕑 7:30am-11pm Mon-Sat, 8am-1pm Sun; Ⓥ) A great way to start or finish the day: head over to Coffeelia for warm smiles and delicious food – and great coffees, including espressos. Coffeelia (rhymes with Ophelia) is a focal point for Cozumel's art community. The menu includes quiche, good salads and vegetarian dishes, and organic Chiapas coffee roasted fresh locally. Thursday is story night in the pleasant garden area.

Cocina Mexicana Los Ríos (☎ 044 987-800-9043; cnr Quinta Av & Calle 7; mains M$30-40; 🕑 7am-5pm Mon-Sat) Ceviches, chicken and seafood: all simple and good. Red plastic furniture and Bellafonte tunes are part of this cheap, clean café not far from the post office. *Comida corridas* are M$30 (a smokin' deal), and get you a main, a soup, tortillas, soda or other nonalcoholic drinks and dessert.

Costa Brava (☎ 869-0093; Calle 7 Sur No 57; mains M$50-120; 🕑 6:30am-11pm) Painted in bright, preschool primary colors, this casual place with its lovely Virgencita shrine has good prices on lobster dishes, chicken and shrimp.

Jeannie's Waffle House (☎ 878-4647; cnr Av Rafael Melgar & Calle 11 Sur; breakfast dishes M$55-80, sandwiches M$50-60; 🕑 7am-7pm) The views of the water are great from the outdoor patio. Jeannie's serves waffles, of course, plus hash-brown potatoes, eggs, sandwiches and other tidbits. Great frozen coffees beat the midday heat.

Los Dorados de Villa (☎ 872-0196; Calle 1 Sur; mains M$50-120; 🕑 8am-midnight) Near the edge of the plaza, it specializes in food from the Distrito Federal (Mexico City and surroundings), but has a wide variety of Mexican dishes including seafood and cuts of meat. The spinach crêpes are great as are the complimentary chips.

MIDRANGE

Restaurant La Choza (☎ 872-0958; cnr Dr Adolfo Rosado Salas & Av 10 Sur; mains M$80-170; ⏰ 7am-10:30pm) An excellent and popular restaurant specializing in authentic regional cuisine. All mains come with soup. La Choza sometimes offers a *comida corrida* (M$100) in the afternoon.

TOP END

Pancho's Backyard (☎ 872-2141; cnr Av Rafael Melgar & Calle 8 Norte; mains M$110-160; ⏰ 10am-11pm Mon-Sat, 4-10:30pm Sun) Very atmospheric, set in a beautifully decorated inner courtyard. The food's not bad either, focusing on international favorites and (drumroll please) seafood.

La Cocay (☎ 872-5533; Calle 8 Norte No 208; mains M$110-230; ⏰ 1-11pm Mon-Sat) Romantic, coconut-scented candlelight and an intimate atmosphere make this snazzy restaurant a lot of fun. Sit at the bar sipping a good single malt or find a quiet table in the corner (or the back garden) to chat with someone special. The menu changes seasonally, but focuses on light, Mediterranean-influenced fare. The welcoming owners, Gary and Kathy Klein, seem to know every guest by name.

Entertainment

San Miguel de Cozumel's nightlife is quiet and subdued. Most restaurants are open for drinks, but by 11pm things wind down. Try the plaza first if you're looking to mingle with the wilder cruise-ship crowd. You are best off asking around, as the clubs change frequently.

Estadio Javier Rojo Gomez (cnr Dr Adolfo Rosada Salas & Av 30 Sur) Hosts rock concerts, *lucha libre* (professional wrestling) matches and just about any other event you can think of. Most events happen on the weekends, but ask around.

La Cocay (☎ 872-5533; Calle 8 Norte No 208; ⏰ 1-11pm Mon-Sat) A great place for an after-dinner drink and has nice ambience, with candles and a high ceiling.

La Abuelita (cnr Calle 1 Sur & Av 10 Sur) Grab a drink with locals at the 'little grandma.' Turns out granny is quite an enterprising lady: there's an Abuelita Dos *and* Tres in other parts of town.

Manati (cnr Calle 8 Norte & Av 10 Norte) Get there early for the *comida corrida* or stay late to listen to live music (Thursday to Saturday) in this cute bistro-bar combo.

Getting There & Away

AIR

Some airlines fly direct from the USA; European flights are usually routed via the USA or Mexico City. **Continental Airlines** (☎ 800-900-5000, in USA & Canada 800-231-0856; www.continental.com) has direct flights from Newark and Houston. **Delta Airlines** (☎ 800-123-4710, in USA & Canada 800-241-4141; www.delta.com) has a direct flight from Atlanta. **Mexicana de Aviación** (☎ 800-801-2010; www.mexicana.com) flies direct to Mexico City, Miami and Dallas. There are currently no direct flights from Cancún to Cozumel; you'll need to fly through Mexico City. In the end, you're better off taking a bus-ferry combo.

BOAT

Passenger ferries run to Cozumel from Playa del Carmen, and vehicle ferries leave the Calica facility (officially known as the Terminal Marítima Punta Venado) south of Playa del Carmen. However, the vehicle ferry does not take rentals. Unless you're driving your own car, use the Playa passenger ferry (M$110 one way) instead. There's normally a passenger ferry every hour to and from Cozumel, depending on the season. The ferry runs from 6am to midnight. Schedules are not set in stone, but currently there are six departures from Cozumel for Calica between 4:30am and midnight. Six ferries return from Calica between 2am and 9pm. Sundays have four departures in each direction. Fares are M$500 for cars and M$800 for a van-sized vehicle (both fares include the driver's passage). You need to line up at least one hour before departure (earlier is better, they say).

BUS

OK, it may sound silly, but you can actually get long-distance bus tickets in advance at the **ADO terminal** (☎ 872-1706; cnr Av 10 & Calle 2 Norte; ⏰ 6:30am-9pm). Tickets are for services from the **Playa del Carmen Terminal del Centro** (Map p103; cnr Juárez & Quinta Av) for all over Yucatán and Mexico.

Getting Around

TO/FROM THE AIRPORT

The airport is about 2km northeast of town. You can take a *colectivo* from the airport into town for about M$70 (slightly more to the hotels south of town), but you'll have to take a taxi (M$120 from town to M$200 from southern hotels) to return to the airport.

BICYCLE

A full day's bicycle rental typically costs M$80 to M$150 (depending on season), and can be a great way to get to the northern and southern beaches on the west side of flat Cozumel. The completely separate bicycle/scooter lane on the Chankanaab Hwy sees a good deal of car traffic from confused tourists and impatient cab drivers, so be careful.

CAR

A car is the best way to get to the island's further reaches, and you'll get plenty of offers to rent one. All rental contracts should automatically include third-party insurance (*daños a terceros*), which runs about M$100 per day. Check that taxes are included in the price you're quoted – they often are not. Collision insurance is usually about M$150 extra with a M$5000 deductible for the cheapest vehicles. Rates start at around M$450 all-inclusive, though you'll pay more during late December and January. There are plenty of agencies around the main plaza, but prices drop about 50% from the dock to the fringes of the tourist zone.

When renting, check with your hotel to see if it has an agreement with any agencies, as you can often get discounts. Note that some agencies will deduct tire damage (repair or replacement) from your deposit, even if tires are old and worn. Be particularly careful about this if you're renting a 4WD for use on unpaved roads; straighten out the details before you sign. And always check your car's brakes before driving off.

One fairly no-nonsense place, with cars in good shape, is **Rentadora Isis** (☎ 872-3367; Av 5 Norte), between Calles 2 and 4 Norte. VW Beetles rent for around M$300 for 24 hours, with little seasonal variation in prices.

If you rent, observe the law on vehicle occupancy. Usually only five people are allowed in a vehicle. If you carry more, the police will fine you. You'll need to return your vehicle with the amount of gas it had when you signed it out or pay a premium. This can be tricky as agencies usually don't rent out cars with full tanks. There's a gas station on Avenida Benito Juárez five blocks east of the main square.

MOTORCYCLE

Solo touring of the island by motorcycle or scooter is OK provided you have experience with them and with driving in Mexico. Two people on a bike is asking for trouble, though, as the machines' suspension will be barely adequate for one. Many auto drivers speed and pass aggressively on Cozumel, and it has its share of *topes* (speed bumps). Riders are injured in solo crashes nearly every day, and deaths, usually involving other vehicles, are not uncommon. That said, rental opportunities abound, with prices ranging from M$180 to M$400 a day (depending on the agency, the season, volume of business and whether the stars are aligned properly), but you may be able to haggle down to less, with third-party insurance and tax included. Collision insurance is not usually available for motorcycles: you break, you pay.

To rent, you must have a valid driver's license and leave a credit-card slip or put down a deposit (usually M$1000). There is a helmet law and it is enforced.

Rentadora Isis (left) rents scooters for M$180 per day – you need to return them before dark.

TAXI

Some locals refer to the 'taxi mafia'; as in some other towns on the Yucatán Peninsula, the taxi syndicate on Cozumel wields a good bit of power. Fares in and around town are M$30 per ride; luggage may cost extra. Carry exact change as drivers often 'can't' provide it.

XCARET

Once a precious spot open to all, **Xcaret** (☎ 984-871-5200; www.xcaret.com; adult/child 5-12yr M$676/338, with buffet & snorkel gear M$971/481; ☉ 8:30am-9pm; ♿), pronounced shkar-*et*, is 10km south of Playa del Carmen and has been turned into a heavily Disneyfied 'ecopark.' Cruise-ship passengers often swear by the place, but the contrived, premium-priced 'beauty' here doesn't compare with the wealth of authentic and often free options available to those who don't mind veering off the beaten path. The park also has a mixed environmental record. Despite encouraging good ecological practices for visitors (like not wearing sunscreen while swimming in delicate lagoons) and financing a number of environmental research projects with visitor revenues, the resort reportedly imported its sand beach, which can wreak environmental mayhem on neighboring reefs. It also used explosives to clear natural debris when building the park, according to a report by Ron Mader on www.planeta.com. So should you go? Kids

---

DETOUR: CRISTALINO CENOTE

On the west side of the highway south of Playa del Carmen is a series of cenotes (limestone sinkholes/caverns filled with water) that you can visit and usually swim in for a price. Among these is **Cristalino Cenote** (adult/child M$40/20; ⊙6am-5:30pm), just south of the Barceló Maya Resort. It's easily accessible, only about 70m from the entrance gate, which is just off the highway. The well-tended cenote has mangrove on one side and a large open section you can dive into by climbing a ladder up to a ledge above it. The water extends about 20m into an overhung, cavelike portion.

Two more sinkholes, Cenote Azul and El Jardín de Edén, are just south of Cristalino along the highway. But Cristalino is the best of the three.

---

will surely enjoy the aquarium, turtles and dolphins, but you may be better off taking them to a truly natural environment to enjoy the wonders of, well, nature.

Buses for Xcaret leave from the Zona Hotelera in Cancún (Map p75).

RANCHO PUNTA VENADO

This delightful spot for **horse riding** (☎ 998-887-1191; www.puntavenado.com; ⊙8am-5pm) is about 5km south of Xcaret and 2km further east of the highway. The ranch sits on some 8 sq km of land, much of it virgin jungle, and has a cenote and a 3km-long stretch of isolated beach. In addition to guided horse tours (M$500 per person, maximum group size 20 people) you can also make arrangements to snorkel, kayak or (if you must) ATV. In the course of a ride you're likely to see monkeys, deer, coatis and various other mammals, as well as crocodiles, snakes and lots of birds, including the occasional toucan. The horses are well cared for and the owners are very hospitable.

PAAMUL

Paamul, 87km south of Cancún, is a de facto private beach on a sheltered bay. Like many other spots along the Caribbean coast, it has signs prohibiting entry to nonguests, and parking is limited.

The attractions here are great diving and a sandy, palm-fringed beach, which, though lovely, has many small rocks, shells and spiked sea urchins in the shallows offshore; take appropriate measures. A large recreational vehicle (RV) park here is greatly favored by snowbirds; the 'BC' license plates you see are from British Columbia, not Baja California. An attractive alabaster sand beach lies about 2km north.

Scuba-Mex (☎/fax 984-875-1066; www.scubamex .com) offers diving trips to any of 30 superb

sites at very reasonable prices (with your gear/ gear rental M$290/390).

Paamul Hotel (☎ 999-925-9422; www.paamul .mx; d & cabanas low/high season M$600/1000; ⊠) has eight beachfront rooms with good beds and air-con, and 10 lovely, spacious cabanas built on stilts. Each cabana has two beds, a ceiling fan, hot-water bathroom and a veranda. Gaps in the wooden floors provide additional ventilation, and a serene atmosphere prevails.

Giant sea turtles come ashore here at night in July and August to lay their eggs. If you run across one during an evening stroll along the beach, keep your distance and don't turn your flashlight on or you might scare it away. Do your part to contribute to the survival of these endangered turtles; let them lay their eggs in peace.

If you come by bus, it's a 500m walk from the highway to the hotel and beach.

XPU-HÁ

Xpu-há (shpoo-*ha*) is a beach area about 95km south of Cancún that extends for several kilometers. It's reached by numbered access roads (most of them private).

Hotel Villas del Caribe (☎ 984-128-4260; www.xpu hahotel.com; cabanas M$650-750, r M$800-900), at the end of X-4 (Xpu-há access road 4), is a laid-back place sitting on a handsome stretch of beach whose northern reaches are nearly empty. All rooms have a terrace or balcony and are very clean and quiet, with fans and good beds; most have hammocks as well. Guests can participate in yoga and meditation classes, and the hotel offers meal plans at its good on-site restaurant.

AKUMAL

Famous for its beautiful beach and large, swimmable lagoon, Akumal (Place of the Turtles) does indeed see some sea turtles come ashore to lay their eggs in the summer, although fewer and fewer arrive each year thanks to resort development. Akumal is one of the Yucatán Peninsula's oldest resort areas and consists primarily of pricey hotels, condominiums and residential developments (occupied mostly by Americans and Canadians) on nearly 5km of wide beach bordering four consecutive bays. With the exception of Villa Las Brisas, all sights and facilities are reached by taking the first turnoff, Playa Akumal, as you come south on the highway. It's about 500m from the highway to the entrance.

Activities

Although increasing population is taking its toll on the reefs that parallel Akumal, diving remains the area's primary attraction. Hurricane Dean also reportedly did some minor damage to the area's reef, though we were unable to independently verify this when we passed through town. Ask about conditions before you commit to a trip.

Dive trips and deep-sea fishing excursions are offered by **Akumal Dive Shop** (☎ 984-875-9032; www.akumal.com). It also offers snorkeling trips to the reef and beaches unreachable by car for M$250; fishing is M$1500 and diving M$700.

At the northern end of Akumal, **Laguna Yal-Kú** (adult/child M$75/40; ☒ 8am-5:30pm; ☒) is a beautiful lagoon 2km from the Playa Akumal entrance. The rocky lagoon, without a doubt one of the region's highlights, runs about 500m from its beginning to the sea. It is home to large schools of brightly colored fish, and the occasional visiting turtle and manta ray. There is a tasteful sculpture garden along the shore. Showers, parking and bathrooms are included in the admission price, lockers are an extra M$20, and snorkel gear and life jackets each cost M$50 to rent. Cabs from the Playa Akumal entrance charge about M$60 to the lagoon. In an effort to protect the lagoon's fragile environment, sun block is prohibited.

You can also simply find a place to park and snorkel or swim on your own, as the shallow waters are pretty and fun. Close to the shore you will not have problems with currents, though at times the surf can be rough.

Sleeping & Eating

Villa Las Brisas (☎ /fax 984-876-2110; www.aventuras-akumal.com; r M$450-2300) On the beach in Aventuras Akumal, this is an attractive, modern place with two hotel-type rooms, some one- and two-bedroom condos and a studio apartment – all under two roofs. Room prices vary greatly by category and season. The friendly owners Horacio and Kersten speak five Western languages! The turnoff is 2.5km south of the turnoff for Playa Akumal.

Que Onda (☎ 984-875-9101; www.queondaakumal.com; r low/high season M$700/900; ☒ ☒) It's set amid an expanse of greenery in a fairly residential area only 50m from Laguna Yal-Kú. The six fan-cooled rooms have white-tiled floors and great beds; some have sofas, and the upstairs ones have terraces. The hotel also offers a gorgeous pool, free internet access, bicycles and snorkeling gear, and half-price admission to the lagoon. The restaurant serves delicious pasta.

Just outside the entrance to Playa Akumal are two minimarkets that stock a good selection of inexpensive food. La Cueva del Pescador restaurant, inside and just north of the entrance, serves three meals daily. Que Onda has a nice restaurant and serves coffees from 11am to 4pm. Dinner is served from 5pm to 10pm; the bar closes around midnight.

XEL-HÁ

Once a pristine natural lagoon brimming with iridescent tropical fish and ringed on three sides by untouched mangroves, **Xel-Há** (☎ 998-883-3293; ww.xel-ha.com; adult/child 5-11yr M$382/264; ☒ 9am-6pm; ☒), pronounced shell-hah, is now a private park with landscaped grounds, developed cenotes, caves, nature paths, underwater walks with oxygen helmet (at additional cost), several restaurant-bars and more. Like Xcaret, its main competitor, it's overpriced and you are better off with the less expensive or free alternatives that abound.

Underwater Cave Tours

About 1km south of Xel-Há is the turnoff for **Cenote Dos Ojos**, which provides access to the enormous Dos Ojos cave system. You can take guided snorkel and dive tours of some amazing underwater caverns, floating past illuminated stalactites and stalagmites in an eerie wonderland. With an aggregate length of nearly 57km, it's the third-largest underwater cave system in the world. **Ox Bel Ha** and **Nohoch Nah Chich** (about 97km and 61km total length, respectively) are relatively nearby. Divers have tried for years to find a passage linking Dos Ojos and Nohoch Nah Chich to prove them to be one humongous system. They succeeded in linking Nohoch with one of its outlets to the sea (at Cenote Manatí in Tankah). While that was going on, new kid on the block Ox Bel Ha was found to be really big.

Hidden Worlds (☎ 984-877-8535; www.hidden worlds.com.mx) is an American-run outfit offering guided snorkeling tours for M$400, and one-/two-tank dives for M$500/900. The snorkeling price includes a flashlight, wetsuit, equipment and transportation to the cenotes on a unique 'jungle mobile.'

Another way to see part of the system is through the **Dos Ojos** (⊗ 8am-4:30pm) operation, a short distance north of Hidden Worlds. It's run by the Maya community that owns the land. The entrance fee is M$100 and snorkeling gear is M$70 more. You can dive here as well, if accompanied by a certified cave diver.

See p124 for details of more great cenotes in this area.

BAHÍAS DE PUNTA SOLIMÁN

These two beautiful, protected bays are separated by a narrow point, 123km south of Cancún and 11km north of Tulum. The area offers good wildlife-watching, kayaking, snorkeling and dining opportunities.

A few hundred meters in after the signed turnoff from Hwy 307, you can bear left (north) to reach **Oscar y Lalo's** (☎ 984-804-6973; mains M$60-100; ⊗ 10am-8pm), a picturesque restaurant that has the entire Bahía Solimán to itself. The kitchen puts out heaping plates of food, including fish fillets and barracuda steaks. Chicken fajitas are also on offer, and couples can order elaborate specials such as king crab stuffed with lobster and shrimp.

Oscar rents **kayaks** for around M$100 per hour; you can paddle out to the reef that shelters the entire mouth of the bay and snorkel or bird-watch. The dense mangrove around the 150m stretch of (somewhat spiky) white beach breeds quite a few mosquitoes and sand flies; you'll want a tent with very good screens if you're **camping** (sites per person M$30).

Back on the main access road, heading straight a short distance beyond the turnoff for Oscar's brings you to an intersection. Continuing straight here leads to the end of the point via a road that splits and rejoins itself a few times. The little-traveled track makes a great **nature walk**: you can see both bays, and birding in the perennially dry mangrove area is terrific. Birds of interest here

include Yucatán vireos, Yucatán woodpeckers, rose-throated tanagers, black catbirds and orange orioles. If you're very lucky you may spot one of the pumas seen in the area from time to time.

Turning right (south) at the intersection rather than going straight takes you along the edge of the bay on the other side of the point, also named **Bahía Solimán** (though some call it Bahía de San Francisco). It has terrific coral heads, tons of colorful fish, plenty of grouper and reef sharks, and the occasional sea turtle and even tuna.

A number of beach houses, some quite luxurious, line the road. Most of them rent by the week, at well over M$10,000. A good website for house rentals in the area is www.locogringo.com.

Maya Jardin (☎ 984-125-8806; www.mayajardin.com; d M$1250-1900; ⊠ ♨) is on the southern end of the bay, and offers large rooms, free kayaks and snorkel gear to explore the bay.

The road continues south beyond another point past residential lots then continues into the Tankah area and loops back northwest to rejoin the highway.

Most people get to Punta Solimán by car, or by taking a bus to Tulum and a taxi from there.

TANKAH

A few kilometers south of the Hwy 307 turnoff for Punta Solimán is the turnoff for Tankah, which also has a picturesque stretch of beach and accommodations that have the sea for a front yard and mangrove out the back.

Besides the attractions of beach and reef, Tankah offers **Cenote Manatí**, named for the gentle 'sea cows' that used to frequent it. Used to. It's actually a series of seven cenotes connected by a channel that winds through the mangrove a short distance before heading back underground briefly to reach the sea. The snorkeling's great, as is the birding, and both are free.

To reach the places described here, turn east at the 'Casa Cenote' sign, go 700m, then turn left and head north up the coast. You'll come to Tankah Inn first, then Casa Cenote, which is less than 2km from the highway.

Room rates vary seasonally and the ranges given here don't include the Christmas (and for some, Easter and Thanksgiving) peaks. High season is roughly mid-December to late April.

Tankah Inn (☎ 984-100-0703, in USA 918-582-3743; www.tankah.com; d low/high season M$1100/1510) has five comfortable rooms with tiled floors; the beds, bathrooms and cross-ventilation are all good. A large upstairs kitchen, dining room and common area have splendid views. It offers diving, snorkeling, yoga classes, Spanish lessons and more.

Casa Cenote (☎ 998-874-5170; www.casacenote.com; ste with breakfast & dinner low/high season M$990/2250; 🐾) is just across the road from Cenote Manatí, leading many people to apply the hotel's name to the water feature. Its seven beachside *casitas* (small houses) are lovingly done up with Maya touches, and each has a screened sliding glass door leading to its own little terrace with hammock. The restaurant serves fresh seafood, with a Texas-style barbecue on Sunday.

TULUM
☎ 984 / pop 14,790

Tulum's spectacular coastline – with all its confectioner-sugar sands, jade-green water, balmy breezes and bright sun – makes it one of the top beaches in Mexico. Where else can you get all that *and* a dramatically situated Maya ruin? There's also excellent diving, fun cenotes, great snorkeling, and a variety of lodgings and restaurants to fit every budget.

There is one big drawback. The town center, where the really cheap eats and sleeps are found, sits right on the highway, making if feel more like a truck stop than a tropical paradise. This said, both Cobá to the west and the massive Reserva de la Biósfera Sian Ka'an to the south make doable day trips.

Hurricane Dean brought some minor damage to Tulum's beachfront cabanas, but most places should be up and running by the time you read this.

Orientation

Tulum lies some 135km south of Cancún and is spread out over quite a large area. Approaching from the north on Hwy 307 the first thing you reach is Crucero Ruinas, where the old access road (closed to vehicle traffic about 100m in from the highway) heads in a straight line about 800m to the ruins' ticket booth. About 400m further south on Hwy 307 (past the gas station) is the new entrance for vehicles going to the ruins; it leads to a parking lot. Another 1.5km south on the highway brings you to

the Cobá junction; turning right (west) takes you to Cobá, and turning east leads about 3km to the north–south road servicing the Zona Hotelera, the string of waterfront lodgings extending for more than 10km south from the ruins. This road eventually enters the Reserva de la Biósfera Sian Ka'an, continuing some 50km past Boca Paila to Punta Allen.

The town center, sometimes referred to as Tulum Pueblo, strides the highway (called Avenida Tulum through town) south of the Cobá junction.

Information

Tulum has Telmex pay phones, numerous currency-exchange booths (one with an ATM), and an **HSBC bank** (Av Tulum; 🕒 8am-5pm Mon-Sat) offering good exchange rates and an ATM open 24 hours.

The **post office** (Av Tulum; 🕒 9am-3:30pm Mon-Fri), between Satelite and Centauro, is about five blocks north of the bus terminal.

There are numerous internet cafés (M$15 per hour) on Avenida Tulum.

Community Tours Sian Ka'an (☎ 114-0750; www .siankaantours.org; Av Tulum), between Orión and Centauro, runs tours to the magnificent Reserva de la Biósfera Sian Ka'an stopping at various ancient Maya sites.

Dangers & Annoyances

Tulum is generally safe and locals welcome tourists. However, if you nod off on the beach, your valuables (and even nonvaluables) may disappear. Do not listen to touts who wait near the T-junction of the beach and offer inexpensive cabanas – there truly is no such thing as a free lunch. And bring your own lock if you plan on staying in the cheap, no-frills beachfront cabanas.

Sights & Activities
DIVING & SNORKELING

Cenote Dive Center (☎ 871-2232; www.cenotedive.com; Av Tulum) is a recommended outfit specializing in guided cavern dives and also offering cave dives, and cenote and cavern snorkeling trips. The staff speak English, Spanish, German and Scandinavian languages.

The dive shop at Zazil-kin (p127) is a PADI, National Association of Cave Diving (NACD) and TDI operation offering low-cost reef dives and renting snorkel gear for M$100 per day.

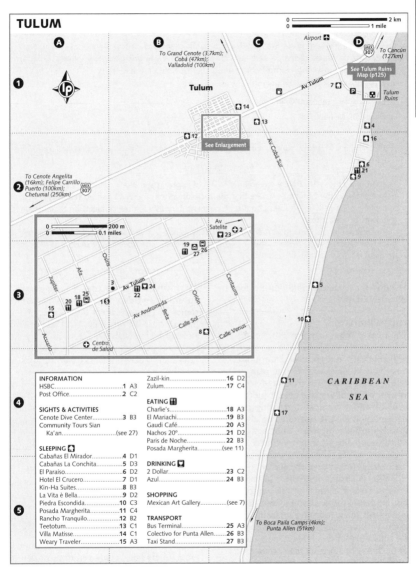

TULUM

To Grand Cenote (3.7km);
Cobá (47km);
Valladolid (100km)

Airport
To Cancún (127km)

Tulum

To Tulum Ruins
Map (p125)

Av Tulum

Av Coba Sur

See Enlargement

To Cenote Angelita
(16km); Felipe Carrillo
Puerto (100km);
Chetumal (250km)

Tulum Ruins

Av Satelite

Av Tulum

Av Andromeda

Calle Sol

Calle Venus

Centro de Salud

CARIBBEAN SEA

To Boca Paila Camps (4km);
Punta Allen (51km)

INFORMATION		
HSBC	1	A3
Post Office	2	C2

SIGHTS & ACTIVITIES		
Cenote Dive Center	3	B3
Community Tours Sian		
Ka'an	(see 27)	

SLEEPING		
Cabañas El Mirador	4	D1
Cabañas La Conchita	5	D3
El Paraíso	6	D2
Hotel El Crucero	7	D1
Kin-Ha Suites	8	B3
La Vita è Bella	9	D2
Piedra Escondida	10	C3
Posada Margherita	11	C4
Rancho Tranquilo	12	B2
Teetotum	13	C1
Villa Matisse	14	C1
Weary Traveler	15	A3

Zazil-kin	16	D2
Zulum	17	C4

EATING		
Charlie's	18	A3
El Mariachi	19	B3
Gaudi Café	20	A3
Nachos 20º	21	D2
Paris de Noche	22	B3
Posada Margherita	(see 11)	

DRINKING		
2 Dollar	23	C2
Azul	24	B3

SHOPPING		
Mexican Art Gallery	(see 7)	

TRANSPORT		
Bus Terminal	25	A3
Colectivo for Punta Allen	26	B3
Taxi Stand	27	B3

Snorkeling or swimming from the beach is possible and fun, but be extra careful of boat traffic (a dive flag is a good idea), as the strip between the beach and reef offshore is traveled by dive boats and fishermen. If there's a heavy wind onshore, strong currents can develop on the lee side of the reef. Inexperienced swimmers should stay close to shore.

Cenote Angelita

This spectacular cenote is most notable to divers for the unique, curious, even eerie layer of hydrogen sulfide that 'fogs' the water about halfway through the descent. Look up and see the sunlight filtering down through ancient submerged tree branches that are wonderfully creepy – like outstretched witches' arms.

THE YUCATÁN PENINSULA'S TOP FIVE CENOTES

One look and it's easy to see why the Maya thought cenotes were sacred: fathomless cerulean pools, dancing shafts of light, a darkened chamber. Even if you don't buy the spiritual aspects, they're still awe-inspiring examples of nature's beauty. Here's our five faves:

■ A two-tank dive at Dos Ojos (p120)

■ Diving or swimming at Gran Cenote (p129)

■ Diving Taj Mahal (p78)

■ Sinking through eerie layers of 'foggy' water in Angelita (p123)

■ Plunging into the cool triple cenotes of Cuzamá after a jouncy ride by a horse-pulled train cart (p175)

Keep in mind these are fragile environments. Avoid applying sun block or insect repellent right before entering the cenote. Be aware that the rocks are often slippery. Loud noises disturb bats and other creatures. In rare cases, tourists have been seriously injured or killed by climbing on the roots or stalactites.

For more information about Yucatán's fascinating cenotes, pick up a copy of Steve Gerrard's book *The Cenotes of the Riviera Maya*, a beautiful paperback with spectacular photos as well as detailed information about each listing.

The dive is deep and should only be done by experienced divers.

TULUM RUINS

The **ruins of Tulum** (admission M$45; ⏰ 8am-5pm) preside over a rugged coastline, a strip of brilliant beach and green-and-turquoise waters that will make you want to tear up that return ticket home. It's true the extents and structures are of a modest scale and the late post-Classic design, workmanship and ornamentation are inferior to those of earlier, more grandiose projects – but wow, those Maya occupants must have felt pretty smug each sunrise. Iguanas are everywhere, and many act as if they own the place.

Tulum is a prime destination for large tour groups. To best enjoy the ruins without feeling like part of the herd, you should visit them either early in the morning or late in the afternoon. Parking costs M$40 for cars and M$80 for vans and pickups. A M$20 train takes you to the ticket booth from the entrance, or just hoof the 300m. Taxi cabs from town charge M$35 and can drop you off at the old entrance road, about an 800m walk from the ticket booth. There's a less-used foot entrance just north of Cabañas El Mirador.

History

Most archaeologists believe that Tulum was occupied during the late post-Classic period (AD 1200–1521) and that it was an important port town during its heyday. The Maya sailed up and down this coast, maintaining trading routes all the way down into Belize. When Juan de Grijalva sailed past in 1518, he was amazed by the sight of the walled city, its buildings painted a gleaming red, blue and yellow and a ceremonial fire flaming atop its seaside watchtower.

The ramparts that surround three sides of Tulum (the fourth side being the sea) leave little question as to its strategic function as a fortress. Several meters thick and 3m to 5m high, the walls protected the city during a period of considerable strife between Maya city-states. Not all of Tulum was situated within the walls. The vast majority of the city's residents lived outside them; the civic-ceremonial buildings and palaces likely housed Tulum's ruling class.

The city was abandoned about 75 years after the Spanish conquest. It was one of the last of the ancient cities to be abandoned; most others had been given back to nature long before the arrival of the Spanish. But Maya pilgrims continued to visit over the years, and indigenous refugees from the War of the Castes took shelter here from time to time.

'Tulum' is Maya for 'wall,' though its residents called it Zama (Dawn). The name Tulum was apparently applied by explorers during the early 20th century.

Exploring the Ruins

Visitors are required to follow a prescribed route around the ruins. From the ticket booth, head along nearly half the length of Tulum's enormous **wall**, which measures approximately 380m south to north and 170m along its sides. Just before reaching the northwest corner, you enter the site through a breach in the wall. The **tower** at the corner, once thought to be a guard post, is now believed by some to have been a type of shrine.

Heading east you'll reach the **Casa del Cenote**, named for the small pool at its southern base, where you can sometimes see the glitter of little silvery fish as they turn sideways in the murky water. A small tomb was found in the casa. Walk south toward the bluff holding the **Templo del Dios del Viento** (Temple of the Wind God) – roped off at the time of research – which provides the best views of El Castillo juxtaposed with the sea below.

Below the Wind God's hangout is a lovely little stretch of **beach**. It's quite swimmable when conditions are good, but take note of the lifeguards and the warning flags. After your dip, head west to **Estructura 25**, which

has some interesting columns on its raised platform and, above the main doorway (on the south side), a beautiful stucco frieze of the Descending God. Also known as the Diving God, this upside-down, part-human figure appears elsewhere at Tulum, as well as at several other east-coast sites and Cobá. It may be related to the Maya's reverence for bees (and honey), perhaps a stylized representation of a bee sipping nectar from a flower.

South of Estructura 25 is **El Palacio**, notable for its X-figure ornamentation. From here, head east back toward the water and skirt the outside edge of the central temple complex (keeping it to your right). Along the back are some good views of the sea. Heading inland again on the south side, you can enter the complex through a corbeled archway past the restored **Templo de la Estela** (Temple of the Stela), also known as the Temple of the Initial Series. Stela 1, now in the British Museum, was found here. It was inscribed with the Maya date corresponding to AD 564 (the 'initial series' of Maya hieroglyphs in an inscription gives its date). At first this confused archaeologists, who believed Tulum had been

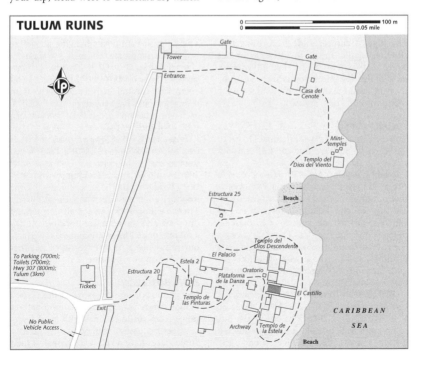

settled several hundred years later than this date. It's now thought that Stela 1 was brought to Tulum from Tankah, a settlement 4km to the north dating from the Classic period.

At the heart of the complex you can admire Tulum's tallest building, a watchtower appropriately named **El Castillo** (The Castle) by the Spaniards. Note the Descending God in the middle of its façade, and the Toltec-style 'Kukulcanes' (plumed serpents) at the corners, echoing those at Chichén Itzá. To the Castillo's north is the small, lopsided **Templo del Dios Descendente**, named for the relief figure above the door.

Walking west toward the exit will take you to the two-story **Templo de las Pinturas**, constructed in several stages around AD 1400–1450. Its decoration was among the most elaborate at Tulum and included relief masks and colored murals on an inner wall. The murals have been partially restored but are nearly impossible to make out. This monument might have been the last built by the Maya before the Spanish conquest and, with its columns, carvings and two-story construction, it's probably the most interesting structure at the site.

Sleeping

The biggest choice, aside from budget, is whether to stay in the town center or out along the beach. Both have their advantages: most of the daytime action is at the beach or the ruins, while at night people tend to hit the restaurants and bars in town.

TULUM PUEBLO

You have to use a taxi (or hitchhike) to get to the beach. If you crave sand and surf, consider staying along the Zona Hotelera.

Rancho Tranquilo (☎ 871-2784; www.ranchotranquilo .com.mx; Av Tulum s/n; dm M$120, r from M$250-480) A nice option for those looking for hostel-type lodging, Rancho Tranquilo offers a mix of cabanas, dorms and rooms in a low-key, desert-landscaped garden. There's a covered common area and free breakfast. It can get a bit noisy, and for those without wheels it's quite far south on Avenida Tulum, and pretty dark late at night.

ourpick **Weary Traveler** (☎ 871-2390; www.weary traveler.info; Av Tulum; dm M$120, r with/without bathroom M$350/300; 🐾 🖳) Turn right out of the bus station and walk one block south to this fun hostel. A great place to meet friends, the

Weary Traveler is known for a full breakfast that includes fruit, eggs, bread, coffee and condiments. There's internet, a shuttle to the beach, and a great central courtyard with hammocks and picnic benches. It even has its own bar. Chilly, pull-style showers and a lack of any shelving for toiletries are the only downsides.

Hotel El Crucero (☎ 871-2610; www.el-crucero.com; Crucero Ruinas; dm M$85-100; d with fan/air-con M$350/450; 🐾 🖳) You'll feel welcome and well-taken-care-of at this friendly hotel. Dorm rooms have bathrooms and lockers, while air-con rooms are done up in themes, such as the Mexican Mural, Jungle Room and the Lizard Lounge. The hotel has a garden area plus a bar and restaurant, and internet access. You can rent bicycles and store bags as well. It's a 10-minute walk to the ruins, and 15 minutes to the beach. The hotel can arrange low-impact bicycle tours to cenotes. Local artist Enrique Diaz has a gallery here (see Shopping, p128).

Villa Matisse (☎ 871-2636; shuvinito@yahoo.com; Av Satelite No 19; d low/high season M$400/500) Funky patchwork quilts add a splash of color to the glaringly white, clean rooms at the Matisse. Little details such as seashell bouquets and fresh plants add an intimacy and closeness. There's even hammocks hanging above the beds in the fan-cooled rooms – a nice touch.

Kin-Ha Suites (☎ /fax 871-2321; www.hotelkinha.com; Orión; d with fan/air-con M$600/750; 🐾) While it's a bit overpriced, this Italian-run joint has pleasant rooms surrounding a small courtyard garden, each with a hammock out front. It's between Calles Sol and Venus.

Teetotum (☎ 745-8827; www.teetotumhotel.com; Av Cobá Sur; r low/high season M$750/1250) There's just four rooms in this retro-hip boutique hotel 200m south of Avenida Tulum, with everything bordering on the supermaude, like the bright orange and green vinyl headboards. There are iPod docks, an upstairs lounge and dip pool, and the restaurant is excellent. It's a bit overpriced for not being on the beach, but a fun place to stay if you've got that groovy-groupie syndrome.

ZONA HOTELERA

Quality and price are so varied here that it's best to look before you decide. Accommodations range from rustic cabanas with sand floors to pricey bungalows with pricier restaurants. Some places have no electricity, or shut their generators off at 9pm or 10pm; many have no phone.

The cheapest way to sleep in cabanas is to have your own hammock and mosquito net; if you don't, several of the inexpensive places rent them for about M$30 a night. In the cheapest places you'll have to supply your own towel and soap, and water, hot water, and even electricity may be erratic. Bedbugs, sand fleas and mosquitoes are all a possibility. Bring repellent or consider burning a noxious mosquito coil near your door. Nights can be darned cold if there's a breeze blowing.

The following picks are ordered north to south. The last four listings are all south of where the road from town (and Cobá) meets the Tulum–Punta Allen road, forming a T-intersection (referred to hereafter as 'the T').

Cabañas El Mirador (☎ 879-6019; elfishi@hotmail.com; cabana with hammock/bed M$130/250) The closest place to the ruins, the Mirador rents tiny 4m-by-3m cabanas that feel a bit like jail cells – they even stink a little bit. Go for a hammock bungalow as the rooms with beds aren't worth the extra money. There's a decent restaurant with great views sitting up and back from the beach.

Zazil-kin (☎ 124-0082; cabanas with/without bathroom M$670/400) About a 10-minute walk from the ruins, this is a popular place. It has a dive center, a basketball court, a restaurant-bar-disco and a nice stretch of beach. All structures in this little Smurf village are very tidy and nicely painted – Papa Smurf would be proud. The cabanas' poles have been filled in with concrete, which makes them more secure (bring your own lock) but hinders ventilation. Be warned that the disco plays music at very high volumes sometimes until 1am or 2am.

El Paraíso (☎ 137-9066; r with fan low/high season M$900/1300) Has 10 rooms in a one-story hotel-style block, each with two good beds, private hot-water bathroom, fine cross-ventilation and 24-hour electricity. The restaurant is very presentable, with decent prices, and the level beach, with its palm trees, *palapa* parasols, swing-chaired bar and soft white sand, is among the nicest you'll find on the Riviera Maya.

La Vita è Bella (☎ 871-3501; www.lavitaebella-tulum.com; bungalows low/high season M$1000/2500, s & d without bathroom M$350) A few hundred meters south of El Paraíso, it offers lovely bungalows with tiled floors, big comfy beds, well-screened sliding doors, good bathrooms with colorful basins and wide verandas with hammocks.

All overlook a narrow but nice beach with beach umbrellas and chairs. It's Italian-run (surprise!), so the restaurant serves delicious handmade pastas and thin-crust pizza from its wood-fired oven. Kiteboarding lessons are also offered.

Cabañas La Conchita (fax 871 2092; www.differentworld.com; d low/high season M$1200/1600) About 2km south of the T across from some souvenir shops, the 'Little Shell' has eight units: three freestanding and five in two-story structures. Ask for the beachfront cabana with the vaulted *palapa* roof and '*muy romantico*' mosquito netting. Rates include a big breakfast. When sending a fax to Cabañas La Conchita make sure to mark it 'Attn: La Conchita.'

Piedra Escondida (☎ 100-3826; www.piedraescondida.com; r low/high season M$1250/2350) Offers very good service in its large rooms. All have bathrooms and balconies or porches and are nicely decorated; some have excellent views. La Piedra also has a pleasing *palapa*-style restaurant-bar, and shares a small beach with neighboring hotels.

Posada Margherita (☎ 100-3780; www.posadamargherita.com; Km 4.5; d low/high season M$1300/2000) Unlike many so-called 'eco-tels' everything here is totally solar- or wind-powered – even the kitchen, which makes amazing food using mainly organic ingredients. All rooms have tiled floors, good bug screening, 24-hour lights and a terrace or balcony with hammock. The beach here is wide and lovely. The excellent restaurant was being renovated at press time, but should now be up and running. The hotel also has something virtually unheard of on the Yucatán Peninsula: wheelchair access.

Zulum (☎ 801-0314; www.xulumhotels.com; Boca Paila Km 6.5; r low/high season M$1000/2500) This is an upscale joint with well-appointed rooms. The rooms facing the beach are worth the price, while those without ocean views are just a bit *caro* (expensive) for what they offer.

Eating
TULUM PUEBLO
All of the following places are on Avenida Tulum (Hwy 307). To escape the tourist traffic, consider putting the guidebook down for a second, leaving the main drag and finding a nice, quiet, friendly *taquería* (taco place) on a side street.

Gaudi Café (cnr Av Tulum & Jupiter; mains M$20-60; ☷ 7am-10pm) Just south of the bus station on the same side of the street, Gaudi Café offers great fresh-squeezed juices and good coffee. Spotlessness and relaxing music make it a great way to start the morning.

ourpick El Mariachi (Av Tulum; mains M$65-90; 7am-3am) Staff ask you your name when you walk into this tidy little eatery and bar. It seems like a small thing, but it's a barometer for the excellent service and tasty traditional food you are about to enjoy. Popular with locals and tourists alike, this open-air spot delivers yummy slow-cooked pork enchiladas, fresh grilled fish and about every cut of meat you could imagine. Find it between Orion and Centauro.

París de Noche (☎ 871-2532; Av Tulum; mains M$70-140; 11am-11pm Mon-Fri, 7am-11pm Sat & Sun) Serves some big portions, so bring an appetite or a friend. The French owner won a *Time Out* award at the restaurant he ran in London. He serves a mix of French and Mexican dishes (as well as steaks and seafood) that include escargots, ceviche, and a delicious green salad with chèvre that's a full meal in itself. There's often two-for-one drink specials and a tasty *comida corrida*.

Charlie's (☎ 871-2573; Av Tulum; mains M$85-140; 7:30am-11pm Tue-Sun) An old standby with attractive conch-shell décor and a wall made of old glass bottles, it's near the bus station and offers your choice of indoor or courtyard dining. The food is largely Mexican, with a selection of salads thrown in.

ZONA HOTELERA

Most of the hotel restaurants also welcome nonguests.

Posada Margherita (☎ 100-3780; mains M$80-250) This hotel's restaurant is candlelit at night, making it a beautiful, romantic place to dine. The fantastic food, including pasta, is made fresh daily and the wines are excellent. It's on the Tulum–Punta Allen road.

Nachos 20° (☎ 100-5067; Km 2.5; lunch mains M$80, dinner mains M$80-160; 8am-9pm) Another appealing option. North of the T-junction on the Tulum–Punta Allen road, it has tables on a rocky bluff above the water, offering some fabulous views.

SELF-CATERING

Two small supermarkets provide an alternative to eating out: the Stop 'n Go, 100m east of Hwy 307 on the road to Cobá, and the Super Mar Caribe, about four blocks north of the bus terminal.

Drinking & Entertainment

Azul (Av Tulum; 6pm-late) Bathed in white with strips of blue neon, this lounge/disco heats up late. It's next to París de Noche.

2 Dollar (Av Tulum) Despite the name, this is a locals' watering hole. It's generally a boys-only club, and there are a few seats outside away from the blaring music.

Shopping

Avenida Tulum is lined with shops offering many items (hammocks, blankets, handicrafts) that you'll see everywhere. Prices drop drastically the further you go from the bus station – up to 50%.

Mexican Art Gallery (☎ 745-8979; inf_art@hot mail.com; 9am-6pm Mon-Sat) Located at the Hotel El Crucero, this gallery features the brightly colored work of local artist Enrique Diaz, whose motto is to 'paint the colors of Tulum.' His art is vivid and fun, a variety of portraits and landscapes that seem vaguely Picasso-esque.

Getting There & Away

The bus terminal (just a waiting room, really) is toward the southern end of town. When leaving Tulum, you can also wait at Crucero Ruinas for intercity buses and the *colectivos* to Playa del Carmen. The table (opposite) shows some travel times and prices for buses leaving Tulum.

If you're headed for Valladolid, be sure your bus is traveling the short route through Chemax, not via Cancún. *Colectivos* leave from Avenida Tulum for Playa del Carmen (M$25, 45 minutes), Punta Allen (at 2pm), and *colectivos* for Felipe Carrillo Puerto (M$45, one hour) leave from just south of the hostel.

Getting Around

Except for the shuttles operated from the youth hostels, there are no *colectivos* out to the beach. You either hitch, ride a taxi, rent a bike or walk. And it's a long walk.

Bicycles can be a good way to get around and usually cost M$150 a day.

Taxi fares are fixed and pretty cheap; from either of the two taxi stands in Tulum Pueblo (one south of the bus terminal, which has fares posted; the other four blocks north on the opposite side of the street) to the ruins is M$35. Fares to most cabanas mentioned here are M$35 to M$50.

BUS SERVICES FROM TULUM

Destination	Cost (M$)	Duration	Departures
Cancún	54-67	2hr	numerous buses
Chetumal	107-140	3½-4hr	every 2hr
Chichén Itzá	101	3½hr	2 ADO buses at 9am & 2:30pm
Cobá	30	45min	about 5 ADO or Mayab buses 7am-6pm
Felipe Carrillo Puerto	60	1½hr	numerous buses, consider taking a *colectivo*
Mahahual	122	4hr	ADO bus at 11:30am
Mérida	172	4hr (avoid 2nd-class buses which take much longer)	numerous services daily
Playa del Carmen	34	1hr	numerous buses
Valladolid	60	2hr	5 ADO & 5 Mayab buses 1:25am-6pm

GRAN CENOTE

A little over 3km from Tulum on the road to Cobá is Gran (Grand) Cenote, a worthwhile stop on your way between Tulum and the Cobá ruins, especially if it's a hot day. You can snorkel (M$80) among small fish and see underwater formations in the caverns here if you bring your own gear. A cab from downtown Tulum costs around M$50 one way, or it's an easy bike ride.

COBÁ

Though not as large as some of the more famous ruins, Cobá is 'cool' because you feel like you're in a *Raiders of the Lost Ark* flick. It's set deep in the jungle and many of the ruins have yet to be excavated. Walk along ancient *sacbé* pathways (stone-paved avenues; *sacbeob* is the plural in Maya), climb up vine-covered mounds, and ascend to the top of Nohoch Mul for a spectacular view of the surrounding jungle.

From an over-the-top sustainable tourism perspective, it's great to stay the night in small communities such as Cobá. The money you spend goes straight to the local economy, encouraging continued rural stewardship and minimizing the mass migration to tourist cities such as Cancún. Hiring local guides, buying local crafts and simply stopping here for lunch also help.

History

Cobá was settled earlier than Chichén Itzá or Tulum, and construction reached its peak between AD 800 and 1100. Archaeologists believe that this city once covered 50 sq km and held 40,000 Maya.

Cobá's architecture is a mystery; its towering pyramids and stelae resemble the architecture of Tikal, which is several hundred kilometers away, rather than the much nearer sites of Chichén Itzá and the northern Yucatán Peninsula.

Some archaeologists theorize that an alliance with Tikal was made through marriage to facilitate trade between the Guatemalan and Yucatecan Maya. Stelae appear to depict female rulers from Tikal holding ceremonial bars and flaunting their power by standing on captives. These Tikal royal females, when married to Cobá's royalty, may have brought architects and artisans with them.

Archaeologists are also baffled by the extensive network of *sacbeob* in this region, with Cobá as the hub. The longest runs nearly 100km from the base of Cobá's great Nohoch Mul pyramid to the Maya settlement of Yaxuna. In all, some 40 *sacbeob* passed through Cobá, parts of the huge astronomical 'time machine' that was evident in every Maya city.

The first excavation was lead by the Austrian archaeologist Teobert Maler in 1891. There was little subsequent investigation until 1926, when the Carnegie Institute financed the first of two expeditions led by Sir J Eric S Thompson and Harry Pollock. After their 1930 expedition, not much happened until 1973, when the Mexican government began to finance excavation. Archaeologists now estimate that Cobá contains some 6500 structures, of which just a few have been excavated and restored, though work is ongoing.

Orientation & Information

The tiny, tranquil village of Cobá, 2.5km west of the Tulum–Chemax road, has a small, cheap hotel; several small, simple and

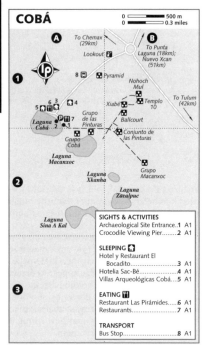

COBÁ

SIGHTS & ACTIVITIES
Archaeological Site Entrance...**1** A1
Crocodile Viewing Pier........**2** A1

SLEEPING
Hotel y Restaurant El
Bocadito.............................**3** A1
Hotelia Sac-Bé....................**4** A1
Villas Arqueológicas Cobá...**5** A1

EATING
Restaurant Las Pirámides.....**6** A1
Restaurants.........................**7** A1

TRANSPORT
Bus Stop..............................**8** A1

low-cost restaurants; and the upscale Villas Arqueológicas Cobá (Club Med) hotel.

Be careful not to picnic beside the lake, as it has large crocodiles. If you want to snap a picture of a croc, try looking for one near Villas Arqueológicas Cobá in early afternoon from the pier.

The **archaeological site entrance** (admission M$45; 8am-5pm;), at the end of the road on the southeast corner of Laguna Cobá, has a parking lot that charges M$15 per car. Be prepared to walk several kilometers on paths, depending on how much you want to see. If you arrive after 11am you'll feel a bit like a sheep in a flock. Bring insect repellent and water; the shop next to the ticket booth sells both at reasonable prices. There is a drink stand within the site near the Nohoch Mul pyramid.

A short distance inside, at the Grupo Cobá, is a concession renting bicycles at M$30 per day. These can only be ridden within the site, and are useful if you really want to get around the further reaches; also they're a great way to catch a breeze and cool off. If the site is crowded, however, it's probably best to walk. Pedi-trikes (two people and driver cost M$95

per day) are another popular option for those who are tired or have limited mobility.

You may want to buy a book on Cobá before coming. On-site signage and maps are minimal and cryptic. Guides near the entrance size you up and ask whatever they think you're worth; tours generally run about M$200 to M$400. Guides drop their prices inside the gate, so pay admission first and avoid bargaining out in the parking lot. The Nohoch Mul pyramid is the only structure the public is allowed to climb.

Sights

GRUPO COBÁ

Walk just under 100m along the main path from the entrance and turn right to get to **La Iglesia** (The Church), the most prominent structure in the Cobá Group. It's an enormous pyramid; if you were allowed to climb it, you could see the surrounding lakes (which look lovely from above on a clear day) and the Nohoch Mul pyramid.

Take the time to explore Grupo Cobá; it has a couple of corbeled-vault passages you can walk through. Near its northern edge, on the way back to the main path and the bicycle concession, is a very well-restored **juego de pelota** (ball court).

GRUPO MACANXOC

About 500m beyond the *juego de pelota*, the path forks. Going straight gets you to the Grupo Macanxoc, a group of stelae that bore reliefs of royal women who are thought to have come from Tikal. They are badly eroded, and it's a 1km walk, but the flora along the way is interesting.

GRUPO DE LAS PINTURAS

You can reach the Grupo de las Pinturas (Paintings Group) by heading 200m toward the Grupo Macanxoc and turning left. If you're on a bike, you'll have to park it here and return to it (this is the case at a few other spots as well). The temple here bears traces of glyphs and frescoes above its door and remnants of richly colored plaster inside.

You approach the temple from the southeast. Leave by the trail at the northwest (opposite the temple steps) to see two stelae. The first of these is 20m along, beneath a *palapa*. Here, a regal figure stands over two others, one of them kneeling with his hands bound behind him. Sacrificial captives lie beneath the feet of a ruler at the base. You'll need to use your imagination, as this and most of the other stelae here are quite worn. Continue along the path past another badly weathered stela and a small temple to rejoin the Nohoch Mul path and turn right (or, if you rented a bike, turn around or go left to retrieve it).

GRUPO NOHOCH MUL

Continuing northeast you will reach another ball court on the right side of the path. Look at the ground in the center of the court to spot a carved stone skull (the winner or the loser of the ball game?) and the carved relief of a jaguar. More weathered stelae lie at the north end. After the ball court, the track bends between piles of stones – a ruined temple – and you reach a junction of sorts. Turn right (east) and head to the structure called **Xaibé**. This is a tidy, semicircular stepped building, almost fully restored. Its name means 'the Crossroads,' as it marks the juncture of four separate *sacbeob*.

Going north from here takes you past Templo 10 and Stela 20. The exquisitely carved stela – worn, but not nearly so badly as the others – bears the date AD 730 and a familiar theme: a ruler standing imperiously over two captives. In front of it is a modern line drawing depicting the original details.

By this time you will have noticed **Nohoch Mul** (Big Mound) just to the north. Also known as the Great Pyramid, which sounds a lot better than Big Mound, Nohoch Mul reaches a height of 42m, making it the second-tallest Maya structure on the Yucatán Peninsula. Calakmul's Estructura II, at 45m, is the tallest.

Climbing the old steps can be scary for some; see boxed text, p172, for tips.

Two diving gods are carved over the doorway of the temple at the top (built in the post-Classic period, AD 1100–1450), similar to the sculptures at Tulum. The view from up top is over many square kilometers of flat scrubby forest, with peeks of lake, and Xaibé as the sole visible Maya structure. Still, it's inspiring.

After descending, walk past Templo 10 and turn right to make a loop back to the ruined-temple junction. In all it's a 1.4km, half-hour walk back to the site entrance.

Sleeping & Eating

There's no organized campsite, but you can try finding a place along the shore of the lake, which is inhabited by crocodiles (local children can show you a safe swimming spot).

Hotel y Restaurant El Bocadito (☎ 984-264-7070; s/d M$100-150) Just north of the Laguna Cobá, at the entrance to town, this place has very basic, fan-cooled rooms all with private bathrooms. Chickens cluck and dogs wander around. The restaurant (mains around M$60) is well run and serves basic food, including an affordable set menu. It will store luggage while you visit the ruins. El Bocadito also serves as Cobá's bus terminal.

Hotelita Sac-bé (☎ 984-206-7140; s/d with fan M$250, with air-con M$400; 🖳) Clean and friendly, the Sac-bé is on the opposite side of the street from El Bocadito and about 100m closer to the main road heading out of town. The chickens are a bit noisy in the morning, but it has nice hot showers and comfortable, springy beds.

Villas Arqueológicas Cobá (☎ 984-206-7000; cob ccrecol@clubmed.com; s/d/tr M$860/1000/1450; 🖳 🖳)

BODY ARTISTS: CRANIAL DEFORMATION, PIERCING & TATTOOS

Take a second to imagine what a Maya at the height of the Classic period must have looked like. Their heads were sloped back, their ears, noses, cheeks and sometimes even genitals were pierced. Their eyes were crossed and their bodies were tattooed. These were, indeed, some of the first body artists.

Cranial deformation was one of the Maya's most odd forms of body art, and was most often performed to indicate social status. Mothers would bind the head of their infant (male or female) tightly to a board while the skull was still soft. By positioning the board either on top of or behind the head, the mother could shape the skull in many ways – either long and pointy (known as 'elongated' – think *Cone Heads*) or long and narrow, extending back rather than up (known as 'oblique' – think *Alien*). As the infant grew older and the bones calcified, the headboard was no longer needed: the skull would retain its modified shape for life. Apparently, compressing the skull did not affect the intelligence or capabilities of the child. Both practices became less and less common after the Spanish arrived.

A Club Med hotel next to the lake, it was built to resemble an old hacienda, with red-tiled floors and rooms grouped around a large inner courtyard with an expansive swimming pool. The restaurant is surprisingly afford-able and serves good Yucatecan cuisine, but the rooms are too small for the price. It has a small Maya ruin – yes it's for real – out back by the tennis courts.

Restaurant Las Pirámides (mains M$60) A few doors down from Villas Arqueológicas Cobá, it has good lake views and friendly service.

Several small restaurants by the site's park-ing lot serve inexpensive meals.

Getting There & Away

Most buses serving Cobá swing down almost to the lake to drop off passengers before turning around. Buses run six to eight times daily between Tulum and Cobá (M$30); six of these also serve Playa del Carmen (M$68, one to 1¾ hours). Buses also run to Valladolid (M$26, 45 minutes) and Chichén Itzá (M$52, 1½ hours).

Day-trippers from Tulum can reach Cobá by forming a group to split the cost of a taxi, which costs about M$500 round-trip, includ-ing two hours at the site.

The road from Cobá to Chemax is arrow-straight and in good shape. If you're driving to Valladolid or Chichén Itzá this is the way to go.

PUNTA LAGUNA

Punta Laguna is a fair-sized lake with a small Maya community nearby, 20km northeast of Cobá on the road to Nuevo Xcan. The forest around the lake supports populations of spi-der and howler monkeys, as well as a variety of birds, and contains small, unexcavated ruins and a cenote. A surprising jaguar population was recently discovered, though chances of seeing one are very slim. Toucans sometimes flit across the road.

A **tourist cooperative** (☎ 986-861-4094) charges M$40 for entrance to the lake area, and about M$200 per hour for guided visit, which is your best chance of spotting simians. Arrive at dusk or dawn to further increase your chances. The local community is increasing its tourist offerings in an effort to keep the town's youth from fleeing to work in Señor Froglandia. The new activities include a zipline tour (M$125), a repel into a nearly pitch-black cenote (M$200) and a shamanic

ceremony (M$125) at a 'traditional' altar that's been erected fortuitously right on the trail to the lake. While these are fun, the best activity is renting a canoe (M$60 per hour) to explore the lake, an eerily beautiful sight when shrouded in morning mist.

Intrepid travelers can call ahead and reserve a *palapa* for the night. Or bring your own tent and camp out near the lake. Camping or a *palapa* costs around M$60 per night. It's best to bring your own hammock and a mosquito net. Like any rural commu-nity, Punta Laguna offers a unique oppor-tunity to learn about the local indigenous culture, and community leaders say travelers should consider studying Maya with local women (the price varies). There's a restau-rant near the cenote, but it rarely opens, so consider bringing your own food.

Public transportation is so sparse as to be nonexistent. In a car, you can reach Punta Laguna by turning southwest off Hwy 180 at Nuevo Xcan and driving 26km, or by heading 18km northeast from the Cobá junction.

SOUTHERN QUINTANA ROO

Whether you're going by rental car or star-ing out a bus window, you'll notice the landscape is different the further south you go. The trees get taller and the birds more colorful, until you reach the southern border with Belize where you'll be in real, honest-to-goodness jungle (well, if you're not in a sugarcane field). Hurricane Dean did some serious damage to the area (see opposite), but things are recovering quickly.

Quintana Roo's capital Chetumal is the only 'Mexican' city in Quintana Roo, and it feels different: somehow more visceral, more real. It has a fairly good Maya history museum, a number of nice restaurants and a cool local music scene.

Merely sideswiped by Dean, the '*muy tranquilo*' (very tranquil) coastal towns of Punta Allen and Xcalak offer access to great birding, diving and snorkeling along this relatively pristine stretch of coast. Beautiful Laguna Bacalar provides fine escapes for people looking to get away from it all. And in the interior, the seldom-visited ruins of

---

DIGGING OUT AFTER DEAN – THE BIG PICTURE

Hurricane Dean, the ninth-largest Atlantic hurricane on record, slashed his way into the region on August 21, 2007. The Category 5 plowed straight through the small coastal town of Mahahual, destroying nearly 80% of the town's buildings as well as the cruise-ship dock, the town's main economic driver.

Chetumal, Punta Allen, and the areas around Laguna Bacalar all sustained damage at the hands of Dean, as did the remote Maya ruins of Dzibanché and Kohunlich. Thankfully, most of the tourist infrastructure in these areas was undamaged, though many of the trees around the remote ruins were felled by the strong winds.

In all the Mexican government reported M$8 billion in damage and 14 hurricane-related deaths. But the region is recovering and the government has pledged M$30 million toward reconstruction. Unlike Wilma, Dean did not destroy the major asset of these coastal areas: the sugary sand beaches. And as of press time, all the towns were back welcoming tourists.

Many of the road signs in the area were twisted and torn by Dean's winds, so you'll need to exercise caution on the roads. And there are fears that the reefs, especially the once magnificent Banco Chinchorro, may have been damaged during the storm. As of press time reports were splotchy, but some Mexican papers cited minor damage to the reefs near Akumal and Chinchorro. Refer to specific regional headings to learn more about life after Dean.

Word on the street is that the Mexican tourism authorities are going to use this as a chance to begin some major development projects in the region. Best to get there now before the cruise ships return!

Dzibanché and Kohunlich seem all the more mysterious without the tour vans. Go in the early morning and you'll likely share the spot with vultures, leaf-cutter ants, mist, and possibly an agouti or two.

This part of Quintana Roo will mostly appeal to people who want to see a section of Caribbean Mexico before it gets developed. But you'd best hurry, as big plans are in the works to rebuild this region after Dean, creating a second Riviera Maya of sorts, only they're calling it the Costa Maya. Those developer types sure are creative, aren't they?

TULUM TO PUNTA ALLEN

Punta Allen sits at the end of a narrow spit of land that stretches south nearly 40km from its start below Tulum. There are some charming beaches along the way, with plenty of privacy, and most of the spit is within the protected, wildlife-rich Reserva de la Biósfera Sian Ka'an. Hurricane Dean whipped the region pretty good, and the beaches were littered with debris when we passed through.

The road can be a real muffler-buster between gradings, especially when holes are filled with water from recent rains, making it impossible to gauge their depth. The southern half, south of the bridge at Boca Paila, is the worst stretch – some spots require experienced off-road handling or you'll sink into a meter of sand. It is doable even in a non-4WD vehicle, but bring along a shovel and boards just in case, and plan on returning that rental with a lot more play in the steering wheel.

There's an entrance gate to the reserve about 10km south of Tulum. Entrance is M$21. At the gate, there's a short nature trail taking you to a rather nondescript cenote (Ben Ha). The trail's short, so go ahead and take a second to have a gander.

This is where DIY adventure really takes off. Bring a couple hammocks, lots of water, a sixer of cerveza, and mosquito nets for remote coastal camping. Around 30km from the entrance gate is an excellent camping spot with the lagoon on one side and glorious blue ocean on the other.

At the time of research, one *colectivo* made the three-hour trip daily, leaving Tulum center at 2pm and arriving in Punta Allen about 5pm. Another leaves Punta Allen for Tulum at 3pm. You may also be able to come on a launch via the mainland, though that is more expensive and less frequent.

Reserva de la Biósfera Sian Ka'an

More than 5000 sq km of tropical jungle, marsh, mangroves and islands on Quintana Roo's coast have been set aside by the Mexican government as a large biosphere reserve. In

1987 the UN classified it as a World Heritage site – an irreplaceable natural treasure.

Sian Ka'an (Where the Sky Begins) is home to howler monkeys, anteaters, foxes, ocelots, pumas, crocodiles, eagles, raccoons, tapirs, peccaries, giant land crabs, jaguars and hundreds of bird species, including *chocolateras* (roseate spoonbills) and some flamingos. There are no hiking trails through the reserve; it's best explored with a professional guide.

Community Tours Sian Ka'an (Map p123; ☎ 984-114-0750; www.siankaantours.org; Av Tulum, Tulum) runs tours out of Tulum that include pickup in the Zona Hotelera. Tours include a guided walk of the interpretive trail at the Muyil archaeological site south of Tulum, and a boat trip or float trip through Lagunas Muyil, Chunyaxché and Boca Paila via an ancient Maya trade route along a natural channel. On the way you can see abundant birdlife and visit little-known Maya temples. It also offers snorkeling, birding and fishing trips further into the reserve. Trips cost between M$950 and M$1100. There are discounts for children under 12.

If you can get to Punta Allen, three locals with training in English, natural history, interpretation and birding conduct bird-watching, snorkeling and nature tours, mostly by boat, for about M$1000 for five to six people: **Baltazar Madera** (☎ 984-871-2001, in Tulum 984-879-8234); **Marcos Nery** (☎ 984-871-2424), reachable through the local phone exchange; and Chary Salazar (inquire in town at her eponymous restaurant). The latter two are experts on endemic and migratory bird species, and Chary also does walking tours when she's available.

Punta Allen

The town of Javier Rojo Gómez is more commonly called by the name of the point 2km south. Hurricane Gilbert nearly destroyed the town in 1988, and there was some damage, and a lot of wind-scrubbed palms, after Hurricane Dean. But Punta Allen is still walking tall. This is truly the end of the road, the 400-some-odd residents mostly work as fishermen – some working in restaurants popular with day-trippers. The village sports a laid-back ambience reminiscent of the Belizean cays. There's also a healthy reef 400m from shore that offers snorkelers and divers wonderful sights.

The area is known primarily for its catch-and-release bonefishing; tarpon and snook are very popular sportfish as well. The guides

listed for Sian Ka'an (left), as well as cooperatives in town (inquire at Galletanes or Vigía Grande eateries), do fishing trips for about M$2000, including lunch. There's also a fishing outfit just north of town called **Pesca Maya** (☎ 998-883-4204; www.pescamaya.com; ☯ 5am-10pm), which does daily saltwater fly-fishing runs and has a restaurant for guests only.

An hour's tour of the lagoon, including turtles, bird-watching and a quick snorkel, costs M$400 to M$500. You'll be offered trips by one of the three co-ops. Encourage your captain not to get so close to birdlife that he scares it away. Though very rare, manatee spottings are possible.

There are no ATMs or internet cafés in town. Electricity generally works between 11am and 2pm, and 4pm and midnight.

SLEEPING & EATING

Posada Sirena (☎ 984-877-8521; www.casasirena.com; d M$400-600) Offers fully furnished cabanas with kitchens and hot-water showers. The rooms are simple and very big; some sport sitting areas and hammocks. There's no maid service, and the Posada can arrange tours.

Cuzán (☎ 983-834-0353; www.flyfishmx.com; r M$500-900) Just south of the town's center along the main road, Cuzán has ocean-front cabanas – one set on the fusil lodge of an old boat. There are cheaper cabins away from the beach. It also offers fishing and snorkeling trips.

Vigía Grande and Galletanes are among several of the town's dining choices, both close to the water and both owned by co-ops. They serve Mexican dishes and seafood, naturally including lobster. Neither has a phone and opening hours vary based on whether any customers are there.

GETTING THERE & AWAY

The best way to reach Punta Allen by public transportation is by *colectivo* out of Tulum: one leaves daily from Tulum center at 2pm and arrives about three hours later. Driving in a rental car is another option, but prepare for 5km/h to 10km/h speeds and more than a few transmission-grinding bumps.

FELIPE CARRILLO PUERTO
☎ 983 / pop 21,530

Now named for a progressive governor of Yucatán, this crossroads town 95km south of Tulum was once known as Chan Santa Cruz the rebel headquarters during the War of the

Castes. Besides its historical and cultural significance, Carrillo Puerto has few attractions other than the only gas station, bank and hotels for some distance around. There's a main square with a clocktower, church and cultural center. Come nighttime, the square fills up as locals take spins around the park in an age-old tradition known as *paseando* (taking a walk). Watching this simple anachronism may be enough to keep you occupied for hours – you can even take a couple of trips around the plaza yourself.

History

In 1849, when the War of the Castes turned against them, the Maya of the northern Yucatán Peninsula made their way to this town seeking refuge. Regrouping, they were ready to sally forth again in 1850 when a 'miracle' occurred. A wooden cross erected at a cenote on the western edge of the town began to 'talk,' telling the Maya they were the chosen people, exhorting them to continue the struggle against the Spanish and promising victory. The talking was actually done by a ventriloquist who used sound chambers, but the people looked upon it as the authentic voice of their aspirations.

The oracular guided the Maya in battle for more than eight years, until their great victory conquering the fortress at Bacalar. For the latter part of the 19th century, the Maya in and around Chan Santa Cruz were virtually independent of governments in Mexico City and Mérida.

A military campaign by the Mexican government retook the city and the surrounding area at the beginning of the 20th century (see boxed text, p37), and the talking cross's shrine was desecrated. Many of the Maya fled to small villages in the jungle and kept up the fight into the 1930s; some resisted even into the 1950s.

Carrillo Puerto today remains a center of Maya pride. The talking cross, hidden away in the jungle for many years following the Mexican takeover, has been returned to its shrine, and Maya from around the region still come to visit it, especially on May 3, the day of the Holy Cross.

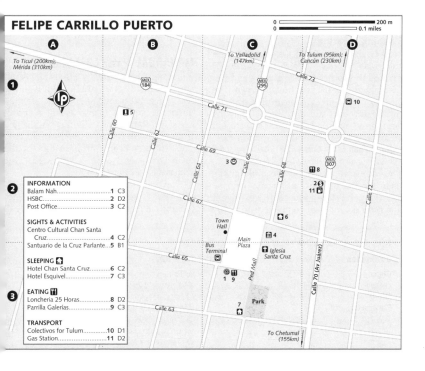

FELIPE CARRILLO PUERTO

0 — 200 m
0 — 0.1 miles

To Ticul (200km);
Mérida (310km)

To Valladolid
(147km)

To Tulum (95km);
Cancún (230km)

To Tulum (95km);
Cancún (230km)

To Chetumal
(155km)

MEX 184
MEX 295
MEX 307

Calle 73
Calle 71
Calle 69
Calle 67
Calle 65
Calle 63
Calle 60
Calle 62
Calle 64
Calle 66
Calle 68
Calle 70 (Av Juárez)
Calle 72
Ped Mall

Town Hall
Main Plaza
Bus Terminal
Iglesia Santa Cruz
Park

INFORMATION
Balam Nah.....................................1 C3
HSBC...2 D2
Post Office....................................3 C2

SIGHTS & ACTIVITIES
Centro Cultural Chan Santa
   Cruz...4 C2
Santuario de la Cruz Parlante....5 B1

SLEEPING
Hotel Chan Santa Cruz...............6 C2
Hotel Esquivel.............................7 C3

EATING
Loncheria 25 Horas.....................8 D2
Parrilla Galerías...........................9 C3

TRANSPORT
Colectivos for Tulum.................10 D1
Gas Station.................................11 D2

QUINTANA ROO

Information

Balam Nah (Calle 65; ✆ 8am-1am) On the plaza, it offers slow, cheap internet.

HSBC (cnr Calles 70 & 69) Has an ATM.

Post office (Calle 69; ✆ 9am-4pm Mon-Fri)

Sights

The **Santuario de la Cruz Parlante** (Sanctuary of the Talking Cross) is five blocks west of the gas station on Hwy 307. There's no sign at the site, but you can't miss the stone wall with a gate. Some of the town's residents do not like strangers in the sanctuary, and may try to take your camera if they see you using it here. The building, a thatch roof set over walls, is next to a small cenote and set on a rock slope. A sign on the door says no one may enter wearing a hat or shoes.

More accessible is the **Centro Cultural Chan Santa Cruz** (admission free; ✆ 8am-9:30pm Mon-Fri, 8am-1pm & 6-8pm Sat & Sun), on the plaza, which has art exhibitions, workshops and the occasional exhibit on the War of the Castes. Be sure to check the mural outside, expressing the conviction that the war is not lost, and displaying accomplishments of Maya culture.

Sleeping & Eating

Hotel Esquivel (✆ 834-0344; hotelesquivelfcp@todito .com; cnr Calles 63 & 68; d with fan/air-con M$300/380; ✖) Around the corner from the plaza and bus terminal, this is the best hotel in town. The air-con rooms are a good deal, with very clean bathrooms and tiled floors, while the fan rooms have good beds and showers, but are dark, windowless and over-perfumed.

Hotel Chan Santa Cruz (✆ 834-0021; www.hotel chansantacruz.com; cnr Calles 67 & 68; d M$360-400; ✖) The rooms are just a bit too pink, giving them the feel of Martha Stewart's jail cell. But they are clean, and there's a mighty fine central courtyard complete with gaudy statuary. In the lobby there's an air-hockey table (and we said there was nothing to do in Carrillo Puerto at night!).

Loncheria 25 Horas (Calle 69; items M$20; ✆ 24hr) Dirt cheap without being dirty, this casual eatery sports plastic chairs and the fumes of passing trucks (it's across from the gas station), but had a giant selection of eggs, sandwiches, tacos and smoothies.

Parrilla Galerías (✆ 834-0313; Calle 65; mains M$40-80) On the plaza, it has the look of a more upscale spot, but serves beer for M$15 and tacos for M$40 for three. The house specialty is a *parrilla* with lots of accompaniments (M$185 for three people).

Getting There & Away

Most buses serving Carrillo Puerto are *de paso* (they don't originate there). The table (below) shows some of the routes.

Colectivos leave for Playa del Carmen (M$110, two hours) and Tulum (M$45, one hour) from Hwy 307 just south of Calle 73.

Check your fuel before heading to or leaving Carrillo Puerto. There are few, if any, gas stations between here and Valladolid (Hwy 295), Chetumal (Hwy 307), Tulum (Hwy 307) or José María Morelos (Hwy 184). The one in Mahahual is a 50km detour.

MAHAHUAL & THE COSTA MAYA

Hurricane Dean virtually razed the coastal city of Mahahual (see p133), but it is slowly recovering. We passed by just weeks after the hurricane, and the town was still in recovery stage. Rather than eliminate Mahahual from the book entirely, which would only cause further economic hardship for the town's residents, we decided to reupdate the material closer to press time.

Now that Mahahual no longer has a cruiseship port – though plans are in place to rebuild it – it may be a bit more welcoming to

BUS SERVICES FROM FELIPE CARRILLO PUERTO			
Destination	Cost (M$)	Duration (hr)	Departures
Cancún	100-130	3½-4	10 1st-class buses, hourly 2nd-class buses to 9pm
Chetumal	54-94	2-3	8 1st-class & 13 2nd-class buses
Mérida	134-146	5½	11 2nd-class buses, 1st class at 3pm
Playa del Carmen	68-76	2½	9 1st-class buses, hourly 2nd-class buses to 9pm
Ticul	100	4½	11 2nd-class buses; change there for Uxmal
Tulum	44-5	1½	9 1st-class buses, hourly 2nd-class buses to 9pm, consider taking a *colectivo*

independent-minded travelers, with great beaches, excellent diving nearby, and a fairly laid-back Caribbean appeal. More significantly, Mahahual offers access to **Banco Chinchorro**, the largest coral atoll in the northern hemisphere. Some 45km long and up to 14km wide, Chinchorro's western edge lies about 30km off the coast, and dozens of ships have fallen victim to its barely submerged ring of coral. According to early reports, the Banco Chinchorro may have sustained some serious damage at the hands of Dean. While the reports are splotchy at best – and we were unable to independently verify the information – the mangroves of the above-water portion of the atoll were destroyed, only the ranger hut left standing.

The atoll and its surrounding waters were made a biosphere reserve (the Reserva de la Biósfera Banco Chinchorro) to protect them from depredation. But the reserve lacks the personnel and equipment needed to patrol such a large area, and many abuses go undetected.

There is a ban on wreck dives as many are too shallow (or too looted) for good diving. But there are plenty of other things to see around the bank: coral walls and canyons, rays, turtles, giant sponges, grouper, tangs, eels and, in some spots, reef, tiger and hammerhead sharks. There's good snorkeling as well, including **40 Cannons**, a wooden ship in 5m to 6m of water. Looters have taken all but about 25 of the cannons, and it can only be visited in ideal conditions. The prohibition on wreck dives doesn't apply to snorkelers.

Dreamtime Dive Center (☎ 983-834-5823; www.dreamtimediving.com; malecón), 2.7km south of Mahahual, runs trips to stretches of the barrier reef and offers PADI courses.

Sleeping & Eating

Addresses are given as distances from the military checkpoint at the north entrance to town.

Las Cabanas del Doctor (☎ 983-832-2102; Km 2; cabanas with/without bathroom M$350/250) Across the street from the beach, it offers several fairly simple dwellings. Prices rise by about M$100 in December and Easter week.

Posada Pachamama (☎ 983-834-5842; www.posadapachamama.net; Km 1; r M$550-750) Located across from the football field, which will become the town plaza on the first street behind the

malecón (waterfront boulevard), this small comfortable hotel also has a pizzeria.

Posada de los 40 Cañones (www.los40canones.com; Km 1.5; r M$600-M$1800) This Italian-owned hotel on the new malecón on the south side of downtown is clean and comfortable with a beach club and restaurant. Suites are available.

Doña Marí (mains M$30-50) Septuagenarian Doña Marí is tough as nails. She began digging out the day after the hurricane hit, and eventually moved her operation to the corner of Huchanango and Calle Sierra. Her restaurant still serves tasty fish fillets prepared in various styles, accompanied by beans and tortillas.

Restaurante Mahahual (☎ 983-834-5849; mains M$50; ⏱ 7am-8pm) Reasonably priced food at the north end of the pedestrian malecón. Refresh with a colossal limonada (lime with soda water) or have a meal. Service is on Mexican time.

Getting There & Around

Mahahual is 127km south of Felipe Carrillo Puerto, and approximately 100km northeast of Bacalar. A new ADO bus terminal (a stop, really, operating between 5:30am and 6pm daily) has made getting here easier than ever, though the buses are infrequent. They depart here for Chetumal (M$50, 2½ hours, 6am, 12:30pm and 6pm) and Cancún (M$170, five hours, 8:30am and 6pm), with an additional departure at 3pm on Sunday and Monday. There's a Pemex gas station if you need to fill your tank.

XCALAK

The rickety wooden houses, beached fishing launches and lazy gliding pelicans make this tiny town plopped in the middle of nowhere a perfect escape. Despite its proximity to Hurricane Dean's Ground Zero in Mahahual, Xcalak (ish-kah-lak) escaped the brunt of the storm. And blessed by virtue of its remoteness and the Chinchorro barrier reef (preventing the creation of a cruise-ship port), Xcalak may yet escape the development boom.

After Dean, the inner portions of the coastal reefs near Xcalak are reportedly in better shape than the outer sections, which were hammered by heavy seas (waves reached up to 5m). Ask around before you commit to a tour. Xcalak also offers easy access to the Banco Chinchorro.

If diving isn't your thing, there's still plenty to do. Come here to walk in dusty streets and sip frozen drinks while frigates soar above translucent-green lagoons. Explore a mangrove swamp by kayak, or just doze in a hammock and soak up some sun. Perhaps best of all, you won't hear a single offer for hammocks or Cuban cigars. And, though tiny, Xcalak boasts a few nice restaurants and an easygoing mix of foreigners and local fishermen.

The mangrove swamps stretching inland from the coastal road hide some large lagoons and form tunnels that invite kayakers to explore. They and the drier forest teem with wildlife and, as well as the usual herons, egrets and other waterfowl, you can see agouti, jabiru (storks), iguanas, javelinas (peccaries), parakeets, kingfishers, alligators and more. Unfortunately, the mangrove also breeds mosquitoes and some vicious *jejenes* (sand flies). There's a remote Maya ruin on the western side of the lagoon. Your hotelier can tell you how to get there.

Xcalak is seeing negative population growth. Specializing in coconuts, it was an important port during the War of the Castes, and the town even had a cinema until a series of hurricanes wiped everything away. Today, there's no signs of getting a bank, grocery store or gas station anytime soon, so stock up before you come.

Aventuras Xcalak to Chinchorro Dive Center (☎ 983-839-8865; www.xtcdivecenter.com), about 300m north of town on the coast road, offers dive and snorkel trips (from M$650) to the wondrous barrier reef just offshore, and to Banco Chinchorro (three-tank dive M$1750, not including rental gear). It also rents diving equipment and offers PADI open-water certificates for M$3850, NAUI and SDI instruction, as well as fishing and birding tours.

Sleeping

The following places are among a handful on the old coastal road leading north from town (mostly run by Americans or Canadians). All have purified drinking water, ceiling fans, 24-hour electricity (from solar or wind with generator backup), bikes and/or sea kayaks for guest use, and private hot-water bathrooms. The first three have docks to swim off, and most arrange fishing excursions.

High season here is mid-December to mid-April (with very slight variations). Most places don't accept credit cards without prior

arrangements, and are best contacted through their websites or via email. Addresses here are expressed in kilometers north along the coast from town.

Villas La Guacamaya (☎ 983-839-8608; www.villa laguacamaya.com; Km 10; d low/high season M$500/1000; 🖳) You'll be greeted by an exuberant parrot at this quiet place 10km north of Xcalak. It has two bright green rooms that face the sea and share use of a fully equipped gourmet kitchen. Each room has a double and a single bed. There's also a separate apartment with kitchen set back from the beach, and a fourth, smallish room with a double bed and a lovely bathroom. It also offers bikes, kayaks and snorkel gear for guest use.

Hotel Tierra Maya (www.tierramaya.net; Km 2; r low/high season M$600/800, r with ocean view low/high season M$800/900) A modern beachfront hotel featuring six lovely rooms (three quite large), each tastefully appointed and with many architectural details. Each of the rooms has mahogany furniture and a balcony facing the sea – the bigger rooms even have small refrigerators. Mains at the pleasant restaurant are around M$160. Rates include a continental breakfast.

Casa Carolina (www.casacarolina.net; Km 2.5; d low/high season M$750/950) A bright, cheery yellow, the Casa has four guestrooms with large, hammock-equipped balconies facing the sea. Each room has a kitchen with fridge, and the bathrooms try to outdo one another with their beautiful Talavera tile. All levels of scuba instruction (NAUI) are offered here, as well as recreational dives at the barrier reef. Rates include continental breakfast, and there's massage on offer.

Sonrisa (www.playasonrisa.com; Km 7; cabanas from M$950) Sonrisa offers 'clothing optional' European-style sunbathing for couples – and couples only. Come here to lose the tan lines in a low-key, casual setting that includes simple cabanas, a bar-restaurant and friendly owners. Note that the cancellation penalties are steep, so read the website carefully and make sure of your plans. Rates include a continental breakfast.

Eating

Food in Xcalak tends to be tourist-grade seafood or Mexican, though the Leaky Palapa is a delectable exception.

Leaky Palapa (meals M$50-120; 🕐 5-10pm Fri-Mon) Chef and owner, Marla and Linda, have turned an old standby into a new sensation serving wonderful meals such as lobster in caramel ginger sauce. Opinion was unanimous that this was the best place to go to treat your taste buds. It's about three blocks west of the plaza.

Lonchería Silvia's (mains M$35-90; 9am-10pm) About three blocks south of the plaza and a block in from the coast, Silvia's serves mostly fish fillets and ceviche, and keeps pretty regular hours. The long menu doesn't mean that everything is available. You'll likely end up having the fish.

Getting There & Around

Cabs from Limones cost about M$500 (including to the northern hotels). Buses cost M$30, the same as to Mahahual even though they travel an hour longer.

Driving from Limones, turn right (south) after 55km and follow the signs to Xcalak (another 60km). Keep an eye out for the diverse wildlife that frequents the forest and mangrove; a lot of it runs out into the road.

A taxi sporadically works the town, serving the northern hotels for M$100 and available for hire for excursions to further destinations. The coastal road between Mahahual and Xcalak was closed at press time.

LAGUNA BACALAR

Laguna Bacalar comes as a surprise in this region of tortured limestone and scrubby jungle. More than 60km long with a bottom of sparkling white sand, this crystal-clear lake offers opportunities for camping, swimming, kayaking, bird-watching and simply lazing around. Hurricane Dean scrubbed the town clean, felling a number of trees, but things were recovering nicely on our last pass.

The small, sleepy town of Bacalar lies east of the highway, 125km south of Felipe Carrillo Puerto and 39km north and east of Chetumal. It's the only settlement of any size on the lake, and is noted mostly for its old Spanish fortress and popular *balneario* (swimming facility). There's not a lot else going on, but that's why people like it here. A growing number of foreigners (chiefly Americans and Canadians) have been buying up lakeside lots.

The fortress above the lagoon was built to protect citizens from raids by pirates and the local indigenous population. It also served as an important outpost for the Spanish in the War of the Castes. In 1859 it was seized by Maya rebels, who held the fort until Quintana

Roo was finally conquered by Mexican troops in 1901. Today, with formidable cannons still on its ramparts, the fortress remains an imposing sight. It houses a **museum** exhibiting colonial armaments and uniforms from the 17th and 18th centuries.

The **balneario** (admission M$5; 10am-7pm) lies a few hundred meters north along the *costera* (waterfront avenue) below the fort. There are some small restaurants along the avenue and near the *balneario*, which is very busy on weekends.

La Costera South

The *costera* (also known as Calle 1) winds south several kilometers along the lakeshore from Bacalar town to Hwy 307 at Cenote Azul.

Just shy of the south end of the *costera* is **Cenote Azul**, a 90m-deep natural pool on the southwest shore of the lake. It's 200m east of Hwy 307, so many buses will drop you nearby.

Sleeping

All the following places are along the *costera* and are listed from north to south.

Los Coquitos (sites per person M$40) A nice camping area on the lakeshore, run by a family who lives in a shack on the premises. You can camp in the dense shade of the palm trees, enjoy the view of the lake from the *palapas* and swim from the grassy banks.

Casita Carolina (/fax 983-834-2334; www.casita carolina.com; d M$250-450, palapas M$450) This is a delightful place about 1½ blocks south of the fort. It has a large lawn leading down to the lake, five fan-cooled rooms and a deluxe *palapa* that sleeps up to four. Guests can explore the lake in the Casita's kayaks. It's best reached by taking a bus into Bacalar and walking or catching a taxi.

Hotel Laguna (983-834-2206; www.hotellaguna bacalar.com; d M$420;) This clean, cool, turquoise place is hospitable. It boasts a small swimming pool, a restaurant, a bar and excellent views of the lake. Some rooms are showing their age. It's 2km south of Bacalar town along the *costera* and only 150m east of Hwy 307, so if you're traveling by bus on the highway you can ask the driver to stop at the turnoff.

Amigos B&B Laguna Bacalar (987-872-3868; www.bacalar.net; d M$500;) Brought to you by the same hospitable family that runs Amigos B&B in Cozumel, this ideally located lakefront property (about 500m south of the fort) has five spacious guestrooms and a comfy shared common area. You can save M$100 by skipping the breakfast.

Hostel Ximba Li (☎ 983-834-2516; cnr Av 3 & Calle 30; dm M$70) This simple new hostel is located a couple of blocks from the lake and a short walk to town. Breakfast included.

Eating

Of the few places to eat right in town, Orizaba's at the northwest corner of the plaza is a good choice. Serving consistently good Yucatecan meals, the lake-view restaurant at quaintly kitsch Hotel Laguna is popular. The restaurant at Balneario Ejidal serves fresh ceviche and good grilled fish.

Getting There & Away

Southbound 2nd-class buses go through Bacalar town on Calle 7, passing a block uphill from the central square (el parque), which is just above the fort and has a taxi stand. Northbound 2nd-class buses run along Calle 5, a block downhill from Calle 7. Most 1st-class buses don't enter town, but many will drop you along Hwy 307 at the turnoffs to Hotel Laguna and Cenote Azul; check before you buy your ticket.

Minibuses from Chetumal to the town of Bacalar (M$20, 45 minutes, 39km) depart from the terminal on Primo de Verdad at Hidalgo about once an hour from 5am to 9pm.

If you're driving from the north and want to reach the town and fort, take the first Bacalar exit and continue several blocks before turning left (east) down the hill. From Chetumal, head west to catch Hwy 307 north; after 25km on the highway you'll reach the signed right turn for Cenote Azul and the costera.

AROUND BACALAR

A few kilometers north of Bacalar town, right next to the highway, is **Puerto del Cielo Hotel y Restaurante** (r M$400; ✗ ⚱), which offers 12 air-con rooms with hot-water bathrooms and TV. A swimming pool overlooks Laguna Bacalar, but the water is two shades greener than that of the lake. The restaurant specializes in chicken and fish dishes.

Further north, and 3.2km off the highway, is **Federico's Laguna Azul** (fax 983-834-2035; www .laguna-azul.de; sites per person M$35, screened palapas M$25, cabanas M$250), a serene, secluded spot located on the north end of Laguna Bacalar. It has a

variety of accommodations, including three well-built and screened cabanas with good private bathrooms, perfect mattresses, tiled floors and a hammock; places to pitch tents or hammocks; eight RV sites with hookups; and immaculate shared bathrooms with hot and cold water. You can rent kayaks here, and eat at the family-style restaurant (you generally eat what's cooking, though it often will prepare other, simple dishes).

The German owner speaks Spanish and very good English, and checks for incoming faxes and email at least once a week. The unpaved road in comes off the east side of Hwy 307, 200m south of the southernmost *tope* (speed bump) in Pedro A Santos, which is about 6km south of the Mahahual junction. You can ask to be let off 2nd-class buses either at the speed bump (and walk the 3.2km in) or in Pedro Santos itself, to take the town's one taxi.

CHETUMAL
☎ 983 / pop 136,800

The capital city of Quintana Roo, Chetumal has stylish, friendly people, some decent restaurants, and a lively music scene. Best of all, this town is for real. It's not dolled up; it's just a quiet provincial capital going about its daily paces. Hurricane Dean displaced many of Chetumal's inhabitants, but with a bit of lumber, some tarpaulins, sweat, rummaged nails and a few quick-drying tears, the town is quietly rebuilding. None of the major tourist areas were affected.

The bayside esplanade hosts carnivals and events, and the modern Maya museum is impressive (though a bit short on artifacts). Impressive Maya ruins, amazing jungle and the border to neighboring Belize are all close by. Though sightings are infrequent (there are no tours), manatees can sometimes be seen in the rather muddy bay or nearby mangrove shores.

Carnaval (late February/early March) is particularly lively in Chetumal. Colorful nightly parades bring locals into the streets to watch floats and plumed dancers pass by.

Before the Spanish conquest, Chetumal was a Maya port for shipping gold, feathers, cacao and copper to the northern Yucatán Peninsula. After the conquest, the town was not actually settled until 1898, when it was founded to put a stop to the illegal trade in arms and lumber carried on by the descendants of the War of the Castes rebels. Dubbed Payo Obispo, the town changed its name to Chetumal in 1936. In 1955, Hurricane Janet virtually obliterated it.

The rebuilt city is laid out on a grand plan with a grid of wide boulevards along which traffic speeds (be careful at stop signs).

Orientation & Information

Chetumal is a large city but remains (thanks largely to its network of wide, one-way streets) very drivable, almost unheard of in a state capital. The southern edge is bordered by the water. The main street, Avenida Héroes, divides the city into east and west sides, ending at the waterfront. Obregón parallels the bay and leads, heading westward, first to a *glorieta* (traffic circle), then to the airport, then to the turn for Belize.

Most of the hotels and restaurants listed are clustered around the Avenida Héroes/ Obregón intersection.

EMERGENCY
Ambulance, fire & police (☎ 066)

INTERNET ACCESS
Arba (☎ 832-2581; Efraín Aguilar; per hr M$10; ☺ 8am-1am Mon-Sat, 8am-midnight Sun) Several other similar cafés are nearby.

MEDICAL SERVICES
Both of these places can handle medical emergencies.
Cruz Roja (☎ 832-0571; cnr Avs Independencia & Héroes de Chapultepec)
Hospital Morelos (☎ 832-4595) Just northeast in the same block.

MONEY
There are several banks and ATMs around town, including an ATM inside the bus terminal.
Cambalache (Av Héroes) Between Calles Plutarco Elías and Ignacio Zaragoza. A currency exchange.
HSBC (San Francisco de Asís supermarket; ☺ 8am-6pm Mon-Sat) Currency exchange. With adjacent ATM, it's just east of the bus terminal, a few kilometers north of downtown.

POST
Post office (☎ 832-2281; cnr Plutarco Elías Calles & Av 5 de Mayo; ☺ 9am-4pm Mon-Fri)

TELEPHONE
There is no shortage of public phones around town, from which you can place international calls. The bus terminal also has an international phone and fax service.
Telmex (Calle Lazaro Cárdenas; ☺ 8am-6pm Mon-Fri) Between Avenidas Independencia and Benito Juárez. It's possible to place long-distance calls and send faxes here.

TOURIST INFORMATION
City tourist office (☎ 835-0860; cnr Blvd Bahía & Av Miguel Hidalgo; ☺ 9am-3pm Mon-Sat) Near the waterfront; dispenses advice.
Immigration office (☎ 832-6353; Av Héroes; ☺ 9am-1pm Mon-Fri) Far north of downtown, on the left about four blocks north of Avenida Insurgentes (and the bus terminal). It's open for tourist-card extensions and such.
Tourist information kiosk (☺ 9am-8pm) In the bus terminal, this is usually staffed by an English-speaker and offers a map of the city and information on hotels.

Dangers & Annoyances

Chetumal is generally safe, but be cautious just the same, especially if walking alone late at night. Crime does happen, but it is rarely aimed at tourists.

If you are heading south to Belize be sure to read the boxed text, p146.

Well-dressed swindlers sometimes pretend to be travelers in trouble. If you listen long enough they will ask for money for a bus ticket to somewhere expensive, such as Acapulco.

Sights
MUSEO DE LA CULTURA MAYA
The **Museo de la Cultura Maya** (☎ 832-6838; Av Héroes; admission M$50; ☺ 9am-7pm Sun-Thu, 9am-8pm Fri & Sat) is the city's claim to cultural fame – a bold showpiece beautifully conceived and executed.

It's organized into three levels, mirroring Maya cosmology. The main floor represents this world; the upper floor the heavens; and the lower floor Xibalbá, the underworld. The various exhibits (labeled in Spanish and English) cover all of the Mayab (lands of the Maya), not just Quintana Roo or Mexico, and seek to explain the Maya way of life, thought and belief. Scale models show the great Maya buildings as they may have appeared, including a temple complex set below Plexiglas you can walk over. Though artifacts are in short supply there are replicas of stelae and a burial chamber from Honduras' Copán, reproductions of the murals found in Room 1 at Bonampak, and much more. Ingenious mechanical and computer

QUINTANA ROO

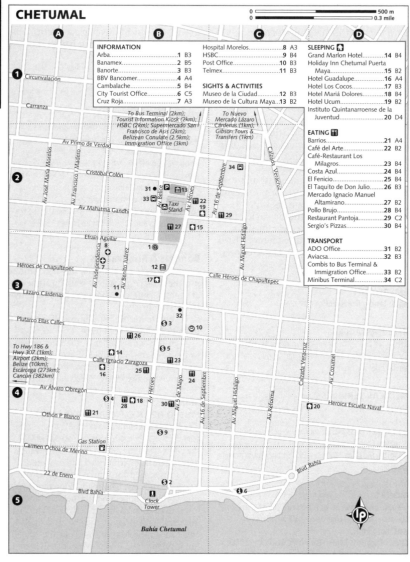

CHETUMAL

0 / 500 m
0 / 0.3 mile

INFORMATION
Arba...............................1 B3
Banamex.........................2 B5
Banorte..........................3 B3
BBV Bancomer.................4 A4
Cambalache.....................5 B4
City Tourist Office............6 C5
Cruz Roja........................7 A3
Hospital Morelos.............8 A3
HSBC..............................9 B4
Post Office.....................10 B3
Telmex..........................11 B3

SIGHTS & ACTIVITIES
Museo de la Ciudad.........12 B3
Museo de la Cultura Maya..13 B2

SLEEPING
Grand Marlon Hotel..........14 B4
Holiday Inn Chetumal Puerta
   Maya.........................15 B2
Hotel Guadalupe..............16 A4
Hotel Los Cocos...............17 B3
Hotel Mariá Dolores...........18 B4
Hotel Ucum.....................19 B2
Instituto Quintanroense de la
   Juventud.....................20 D4

EATING
Barrios...........................21 A4
Café del Arte...................22 B2
Café-Restaurant Los
   Milagros......................23 B4
Costa Azul......................24 B4
El Fenicio........................25 B4
El Taquito de Don Julio......26 B3
Mercado Ignacio Manuel
   Altamirano...................27 B2
Pollo Brujo......................28 B4
Restaurant Pantoja...........29 C2
Sergio's Pizzas.................30 B4

TRANSPORT
ADO Office......................31 B2
Aviacsa..........................32 B3
Combis to Bus Terminal &
   Immigration Office.........33 B2
Minibus Terminal..............34 C2

To Bus Terminal (2km);
Tourist Information Kiosk (2km);
HSBC (2km); Supermercado San
Francisco de Asís (2km);
Belizean Conulate (2.5km);
Immigration Office (3km)

To Nuevo
Mercado Lázaro
Cárdenas (1km);
Gibson Tours &
Transfers (1km)

Bahía Chetumal

---

displays illustrate the Maya's complex calendrical, numerical and writing systems.

The museum's **courtyard**, which you can enter for free, has salons for temporary exhibits of modern artists (such as Rufino Tamayo), paintings reproducing Maya frescoes and a *cinemuseo* (cinema showing historic films) giving free film showings. In the middle of the courtyard is a *na* with implements of daily Maya life on display: gourds, grinders and a metate. Just walk past the ticket window.

Look for a bronze bust in the middle of Avenida Héroes, just east of the museum's entrance. It depicts Jacinto Pat, one of the Maya leaders who planned the insurrection that became the War of the Castes.

MUSEO DE LA CIUDAD

The **Museo de la Ciudad** (Local History Museum; Héroes de Chapultepec; admission M$10; 9am-7pm Tue-Sun) is small but neatly done, displaying historic photos, military artifacts and old-time household items (even some vintage telephones and a TV). All labels are in Spanish but, even if you don't read the language, it's worth visiting for 15 minutes of entertainment.

Sleeping

Instituto Quintanarroense de la Juventud (832-0525; Heroica Escuela Naval; sites M$30, dm M$50) Between Calzada Veracruz and Avenida Cozumel. The price is hard to beat, and kind Spanish-speaking staff will assist with information. Downsides include showers that tease with a minute of warmth before turning icy, many toilets flood or don't flush, and most stalls don't have doors. The beds are OK, the rooms are a bit stuffy, and there are single-sex and couples rooms.

Hotel Ucum (832-0711, 832-6186; Av Mahatma Gandhi 167; d with fan/air-con M$200/$350;) This fine motel-like place looks like it may have once been used as a Jackie Chan movie set. And despite the unfortunate name (a town in Campeche), it offers pretty decent rooms, a (slightly milky) swimming pool and a restaurant serving good, inexpensive food.

Hotel María Dolores (832-0508; Av Álvaro Obregón 206; s M$220; d without/with air-con M$240/270) Follow the 'Duke of Ducks' to this little pink-and-aquamarine hotel west of Avenida Héroes. The beds are a bit saggy, but some of the fan-cooled rooms are a good size and there's off-street parking and a free water jug in the lobby (an enviro-traveler's delight).

Hotel Guadalupe (832-8649; Calle Ignacio Zaragoza 226; s/d with fan M$250/280, r with air-con M$400;) You could eat dinner off the spotless floors of this hotel's spick-and-span rooms. Despite the cleanliness, the rooms are slightly stale but air out quickly. Peach-pink walls make the place cheery, and the staff are very friendly.

our pick Grand Marlon Hotel (285-3279; hotel_grandmarlon@hotmail.com; Av Juárez 88; d M$500;) With modern clean lines, a rather funky pool area (complete with Astroturf and a luke-warm Jacuzzi), the 'Grand' almost achieves 'hip boutique' status. And the simple, stylish rooms are an excellent deal for the price. Or, you can save a few pesos by heading across the street to the plain ol' Marlon.

Hotel Los Cocos (832-0544; www.hotelloscocos.com .mx; cnr Av Héroes & Calle Héroes de Chapultepec; d with air-con & TV M$750, ste M$1600;) Has a great location and a seriously disco-mirrored lobby that gets your inner Dirk Diggler's mojo rising. There's also a nice swimming pool, wireless access, a guarded parking lot and a popular sidewalk restaurant. Rooms have fridges, but are a bit small and musty for the price.

Holiday Inn Chetumal Puerta Maya (835-0400; www.holimaya.com.mx; Av Héroes 171; d M$1300, ste M$1690-3630;) The best in town, with comfortable rooms that overlook a small courtyard, a swimming pool set amid tropical gardens, and a restaurant and bar. The Maya sun mirror in the lobby adds interesting flair.

Eating & Drinking

El Taquito de Don Julio (Plutarco Elías Calles 220; tacos M$8-12, mains M$50-70; noon-5pm & 7pm-1am Mon-Sat) This is an airy, simple dining room and a good spot for night owls. The small tacos cost slightly more with cheese; other menu offerings include cheap snacks, *tortas* and vegetarian brochettes (M$35).

Barrios (cnr Othón P Blanco & Independencia; mains M$10-50; 8am-2pm Mon-Sat) Great little eatery with Mexican favorites such as *salbutes* or quesadillas and *cebada* (a refreshing barley drink).

Café del Arte (Av Héroes 171; snacks M$20-50; 8am-1pm & 7-10pm) This is a pretty hip joint right across the street from the museum. The friendly owner, Raquel, offers up good snacks and coffee drinks, and is also a painter. Many of her pieces adorn the walls.

Café-Restaurant Los Milagros (832-4433; Calle Ignacio Zaragoza; breakfast M$25-70, mains M$40-60; 7:30am-9pm Mon-Sat, 7:30am-1pm Sun) Serves great espresso and food indoors and outdoors. A favorite with Chetumal's student and intellectual set, it's also a place to play chess or dominoes, chat, or observe a local radio program being broadcast from one of the tables.

Restaurant Pantoja (832-3957; cnr Avs Mahatma Gandhi & 16 de Septiembre; mains M$30-70; 7am-7pm) A popular, family-run restaurant serving breakfasts, enchiladas and a variety of meat dishes. It offers a M$40 *menu del día*. Although fan-cooled, it gets a bit warm in the afternoon.

Pollo Brujo (837 4747; Av Álvaro Obregón 208; half-/whole chicken M$42-77; 10am-10pm) West of Hotel María Dolores. Only chicken is served in this joint; take it with you or dine in the air-con salon. Service is with a snarl.

El Fenicio (cnr Av Héroes & Calle Ignacio Zaragoza; mains $35-90; 24hr) Come here at 11pm and you'll feel like you've stepped into a Hopper painting: the yellow light, the few solitary diners hunched over a meal. The food, a selection of mainly Mexican fare, is tasty and served promptly. Flan and decent American-style coffee are a tasty way to finish the day.

Sergio's Pizzas (☎ 832-2991; cnr Avs Álvaro Obregón & 5 de Mayo; pizza M$45-170, mains M$60-160; 🔀) A well air-conditioned place serving pizzas and cold beer in frosted mugs, plus Mexican and continental dishes, steaks and seafood, complemented by an extensive wine list.

Costa Azul (☎ 129-2002; Calle Ignacio Zaragoza 166; mains M$60-120; 🕑 11:30am-8pm) Popular *palapa*-topped bar-restaurant with a fun Caribbean-Chetumalan vibe. Just plastic chairs and (sometimes) a mariachi or two.

Across from the Holiday Inn is the Mercado Ignacio Manuel Altamirano and its row of small, simple eateries serving inexpensive meals. Similar is the upstairs area in the **Nuevo Mercado Lázaro Cárdenas** (Calzada Veracruz).

Supermercado San Francisco de Asís, just east of the bus terminal, has a wide selection of groceries, and is a department store besides.

Getting There & Away

AIR

Chetumal's small airport is roughly 2km northwest of the city center along Avenida Obregón.

Aviacsa (☎ 01-800-771-6733; www.aviacsa.com; cnr Lázaro Cárdenas & Av 5 de Mayo) flies to Mexico City once a day Sunday to Friday.

For flights to Belize City (and on to Flores, to reach Tikal) or to Belize's cays, cross the border into Belize and fly from Corozal.

BUS

The main bus terminal is about 2km north of the center, near the intersection of Avenidas Insurgentes and Belice. Services are provided by Deluxe Omnitur del Caribe, Maya de Oro and Super Expresso; ADO and Cristóbal Colón (1st class); and (2nd class) TRT, Sur and Mayab (a cut above), among others. The terminal has lockers (in the store against the east wall, near the pay toilets), a bus information kiosk (open until 3pm), an ATM, a cafeteria and shops.

BUS SERVICES FROM CHETUMAL

Destination	Cost (M$)	Duration	Departures
Bacalar	20	45min	hourly minibuses from minibus terminal; many Mayab buses from main terminal
Belize City, Belize	100	3-4hr	18 1st- & 2nd-class Novelos & Northern buses depart from Nuevo Mercado 4:30am-6:30pm, some depart main terminal 15min later
Campeche	170-250	6½-9hr	1 ADO bus at noon, TRT buses at 4:15am & 2:15pm
Cancún	180-210	5½-6½hr	many buses
Corozal, Belize	35	1hr with border formalities	18 1st- & 2nd-class Venus & other buses depart Nuevo Mercado 4:30am-6:30pm, some depart main terminal 15min later
Escárcega	120-160	4-6hr	5 buses 4:15am-10:30pm
Felipe Carrillo Puerto	54-90	2-3hr	many buses
Flores, Guatemala (for Tikal)	290	8hr	5 Servicio San Juan, Linea Dorado & Mundo Maya buses 6:20am-2:30pm
Mahahual	50	4hr	2nd-class buses at 4am, 6am & 3:15pm
Mérida	180-250	6-8hr	8 Omnitur del Caribe & Super Expresso buses, 3 Mayab buses
Orange Walk, Belize	30-45	2¼hr	18 1st- & 2nd-class Novelos & Northern buses depart Nuevo Mercado 4:30am-6:30pm, some depart main terminal 15min later
Palenque	280	7-8hr	4 Altos & Colón buses
Playa del Carmen	140-180	4½-6hr	many buses
Ticul	155	6hr	6 Mayab buses
Tulum	110-144	3½-4hr	many buses
Valladolid	140	6hr	6 Mayab buses
Veracruz	620	16hr	2 ADO buses
Villahermosa	330	7-9hr	5 ADO buses
Xcalak	66	5hr	2nd-class buses at 4am, 6am & 3:15pm
Xpujil	55-78	2-3hr	9 buses 4:15am-10:30pm

You can also buy tickets for some lines and get information about most bus services at the **ADO office** (Av Belice; ☼ 6am-10pm), just west of the Museo de la Cultura Maya.

Many local buses, and those bound for Belize, begin their runs from the Nuevo Mercado Lázaro Cárdenas, on Calzada Veracruz at Confederación Nacional Campesina (also called Segundo Circuito), about 10 blocks north of Avenida Primo de Verdad. From this market, most 1st-class Belize-bound buses continue to the long-distance terminal and depart from there 15 minutes later; the 2nd-class buses don't. Tickets can be purchased on board the buses or (1st-class only) at the main terminal.

The **minibus terminal** (cnr Avs Primo de Verdad & Miguel Hidalgo) has services to Bacalar and other nearby destinations. Departures listed in the table (opposite) are from the main terminal unless otherwise noted.

TAXI

Gibson Tours & Transfers (www.gibsontoursandtransfers.com) charges M$250/500 to the border/Corozal. Though pricier than a bus, its taxi can wait for you and it can assist with border problems (see boxed text, p146).

Getting Around

From anywhere in town taxis charge a flat fare of M$20. From the traffic circle at Avenida Héroes, you can also get a *combi* (van) for M$3 to the town center via the Santa Maria or Calderitas eastbound buses. To reach the terminal from the center, catch a *combi* from Avenida Belice behind the Museo de la Cultura Maya. Ask to be left at the *glorieta* at Avenida Insurgentes. Head left (west) to reach the terminal. The immigration office is about 800m north of the *glorieta*. (Ask for the *oficina de inmigración.*)

CORREDOR ARQUEOLÓGICO

The Corredor Arqueológico comprises the archaeological sites of Dzibanché and Kohunlich. After Hurricane Dean, Dzibanché was closed due to heavy treefall. It's open now, but the site is missing many of the trees that made it so great. Kohunlich also suffered serious treefall, but has remained open to the public.

Sights

DZIBANCHÉ

Though it's a chore to get to, this **archaeological site** (admission M$37; ☼ 8am-5pm) is definitely

---

TINY TRAILBLAZERS

The small trails you'll see crisscrossing the cleared areas in many of the ruins baffle observant visitors. What made them? A rodent? To get the answer right you have to think tiny: ants.

Leaf-cutter ants, to be specific. Sometimes marching up to several kilometers from their colony, leaf-cutter ants walk in single file along predetermined routes, often wearing down a pathway over a period of months or years. Patient observers can often see the tiny landscapers at work, carrying fingernail-sized clippings back home. Though they can bite if molested, these ants are generally harmless and should be left in peace to do their work.

---

worth a visit for its secluded, semiwild nature. While many of the trees were toppled by Dean, the site is recovering, and the temples withstood the blasting (those Maya were some bee's-knees architects!).

Dzibanché (dzee-ban-*chay*; literally, 'writing on wood') was a major city extending more than 40 sq km, and on the road in you pass huge mounds. The site itself is not completely excavated.

The first restored structure you come to is Edificio 6, the **Palacio de los Dinteles** (Palace of the Lintels), which gave the site its name. This is a perfect spot to orient yourself for the rest of the site: facing Edificio 6's steps, you are looking east. It's a pyramid topped by a temple with two vaulted galleries; the base dates from the early Classic period (AD 300–600), while the temple is from the Late Classic period (AD 600–900). Climb the steps and stand directly under the original lintel on the right (south) side of the temple. Looking up you can see a Maya calendrical inscription with the date working out to AD 733. This is some old wood.

On descending, head to your left (south) and thread between a mound on the right and a low, mostly restored, stepped structure on the left. This structure is Edificio 16, **Palacio de los Tucanes**; in the center from the side you first approach on are the visible remains of posts that bore a mask. The path then brings you into **Plaza Gann**. Circling it counterclockwise takes you past Edificio 14 (stuck onto the north side of a larger building), decorated at the base with *tamborcillos* (little drums), in Late Classic

Río Bec style – look up the dirt hill to see them. The larger building to the south is Edificio 13, **Templo de los Cautivos**, so named for the carvings in its steps of captives submitting to whatever captives submitted to in those days. This seems to be the dominant (if you'll pardon the pun) theme in most Maya stelae.

On the east side of the plaza is Dzibanché's highest structure, the **Templo de los Cormoranes** (Temple of the Cormorants; Edificio 2), whose upper structure has been restored. The lower part is covered in greenery. A vaulted passage beckons halfway up, but at last pass it was forbidden to climb the temple.

Exit the plaza by climbing the stone steps to the north of Edificio 2. At the top of the stairs is **Plaza del Xibalbá** (Plaza of the Underworld), though it's higher than Plaza Gann.

Opposite Palacio Norte is, of course, Palacio Sur, and from here you can see more of Edificio 2, but the most notable building is across the plaza: Edificio 1, the **Templo del Buho** (Temple of the Owl). It had an inner chamber with a stairway leading down to another chamber, in which were found the remains of a Very Important Personage (VIP) and burial offerings. The nearly 360-degree views from the very top of the temple (it's a bit dicey, so be careful) are quite impressive. You can see Grupo Lamay to the west and you may spot Kinich-Ná, more than 2km to the northwest.

Kinich-Ná

Part of Dzibanché but well removed from the main site, Kinich-Ná consists of one building. But what a building: the megalithic Acrópolis held at least five temples on three levels, and a couple more dead VIPs with offerings. The site's name derives from the frieze of the Maya sun god once found at the top of the structure. It's an easy drive of 2km along a narrow but good road leading north from near Dzibanché's visitors center.

KOHUNLICH

The most accessible of the corridor's ruins has nearly 200 mounds still covered in vegetation. The surrounding jungle was a thick tangle of half-felled trees at last pass. The speed of vegetation regeneration in this tropical area means that it should be well on its way to recovery by the time this book hits the shelves. The **archaeological site** (admission M$40, guide M$250; ☺ 8am-5pm) sits on a carpeted green. Drinks are sometimes sold at the site, and it has toilets.

NO-MAN'S-LAND

'No-Man's-Land' is the strip of territory after the Mexican exit but before you've crossed into Belize. Many tourists head to Chetumal expecting to make a quick zip across the border and back to renew their tourist card. While most tourists cross without problem, the occasional unscrupulous official will invent an excuse to not let you through even though it is perfectly legitimate.

Often they'll say there's a 'minimum 72-hour stay in Belize.' (There isn't.) Or they'll claim that you need a Mexican re-entry stamp for them to let you through. (You don't.) Sometimes they'll say that Belize doesn't welcome day trips, as 'tourists don't spend enough money in their country.' (The Belizean consulate says trips, even day trips, across the border are perfectly fine, as do the Mexican officials.)

If a guard decides to single you out, there's not a lot you can do other than pay up or beg your way back into Mexico and try again. The following should help:

- Group up with other foreign travelers.
- Get visas and other papers stamped at the Belize office in Chetumal prior to crossing.
- Don't disclose that you're intending a day trip.
- Even if you are not planning to return to Mexico, if you have more than a few days left on your tourist card you can have it prestamped for a re-entry by Mexican exit officials. This costs only M$100 and is a good way to ensure a smooth crossing onward.
- Often the yellow-shirted guards are more understanding and helpful than the white-shirted officials behind the desk.
- Crossing back into Mexico, be sure to check that your Belize exit stamp is clear and easy to read, with the official's signature and the date written inside.

The ruins, dating from both the late pre-Classic (AD 100–200) and the early Classic (AD 300–600) periods, are famous for the great **Templo de los Mascarones** (Temple of the Masks), a pyramid-like structure with a central stairway flanked by huge, 3m-high stucco masks of the sun god. The thick lips and prominent features are reminiscent of Olmec sculpture. Of the eight original masks, only two are relatively intact following the ravages of archaeological looters.

The masks themselves are impressive, but you can only see them from close up because the large thatch coverings that have been erected to protect them from further weathering obscure the view. Try to imagine what the pyramid and its red masks must have looked like in the old days as the Maya approached them across the sunken courtyard at the front.

A few hundred meters southwest of Plaza Merwin are the **27 Escalones** (27 Steps), the remains of an extensive residential area.

The hydraulic engineering used at Kohunlich was a great achievement; 90,000 of the site's 210,000 sq meters were cut to channel rainwater into Kohunlich's once enormous reservoir.

Getting There & Away

The turnoff for Dzibanché from Hwy 186 is about 44km west of Chetumal, on the right just after the Zona Archeológica sign. From there it's another 24km north and east along a pot-holed road. It's quite passable in a passenger car, but watch for livestock, sun-drunk iguanas and birdlife. Just after the tiny town of Morocoy you'll need to turn right again. It's easy to miss the sign unless you're looking for it.

Kohunlich's turnoff is 3km west along Hwy 186 from the Dzibanché turnoff, and the site lies at the end of a paved 8.5km road. It's a well-paved straight shot from the highway.

At the time of writing, there was no public transportation running directly to either of the sites. They're best visited by car, though Kohunlich could conceivably be reached by taking an early bus to the village of Francisco Villa near the turnoff, then either hitchhiking or walking the 8.5km to the site. To return by bus to Chetumal or head west to Xpujil or Escárcega you must hope to flag down a bus on the highway; not all buses will stop.

Taxis can be rented per hour in Chetumal for as little as M$200; a group could pile in and split the cost.

Tour operators in Xpujil (p225) offer trips to Kohunlich and Dzibanché for M$750.

ZONA LIBRE

A bustling free-trade zone sprawling over 24 muddy hectares in a no-man's-land between the borders of Belize and Mexico, the Zona Libre draws thousands of Mexicans seeking cheap liquor and cigarettes, knockoff clothing and CDs and other shiny things.

Minibuses depart from their terminal in Chetumal at the corner of Avenidas Primo de Verdad and Hidalgo about every half-hour between 6am and 9pm, charging M$8 for the 20-minute trip. If traffic is bad at the border you can get off and walk over the bridge, then turn left; you can't miss it. Walking back you may need to show your passport, but usually officials will just ask where you've been and wave you through.

SOUTH TO BELIZE & GUATEMALA

Corozal

☎ 501 / pop 8800

This fairly laid-back town, 18km south of the Mexico–Belize border, is an appropriate introduction to English-speaking Belize. There's a simple plaza in the center, a waterfront and a lot of chickens running around. Visitors might want to check out the butterfly farm, take a boat trip to neighboring islands from Thunderbolt Dock or visit the smallish Santa Rita archaeological site just minutes away from town. A Belize Bank with an ATM is at the plaza.

The following places are within a five-minute walk from the bus stop.

Corozal Guest House (☎ 422-0634; Av 6 No 22; US$22.50; ✗) makes big claims to be 'Your Friendly Guest House,' and indeed it is. It's clean and simple, with spacious rooms, towels and soap.

Both **Al's Cafe** (☼ 8am-3pm) and **Patty's Bistro** (☼ 8am-3pm) offer inexpensive Belizean meals for around US$3.

Gilharry Bus service, across the street, has US$4 rides to the Belize–Mexico border. From Corozal you can take buses to Melchor de Mencos, Guatemala, which will take you to Flores and the Maya supersite of Tikal. You can also head to Belize City.

Yucatán State

A wild undercurrent, writhing like a liquid goddess, resides beneath the scrub jungle, pyramids and rolling hills of Yucatán state.

You feel her tides as you walk beneath the towering Maya pyramids of Chichén Itzá and Uxmal, imagining the rich waves of history, slaughter, deceit, fame and famine that rolled through these mighty power centers. She ebbs and flows in the intact colonial cities of Mérida, Valladolid and Izamal as *huipil* (woven tunic)-clad mestizas mingle with trendy students, factory workers, tourists and the wealthy elite as they ply the streets of the peninsula's modern-day cultural crossroads. She gurgles and spits and purges and pulls in the bird-clogged estuaries along the coasts, and underground in the vast system of caves and cenotes (limestone sinkholes) that pock the region.

Sitting regally on the northern tip of the peninsula, Yucatán state sees less mass tourism than her flashy neighbor, Quintana Roo. She is sophisticated and savvy, and the perfect spot for travelers more interested in cultural exploration than beach bumming. Sure, there are a few nice beaches in Celestún and Progreso, but most people come to this area to explore the ancient Maya sites peppered throughout the region, like the Ruta Puuc, which will take you to four or five ruins in just a day.

Visitors also come to experience the past and present in the cloistered corners of colonial cities, to visit henequen haciendas lost to time (or restored by caring hands to old glory), and to discover the energy, spirit and subtle contrasts of this authentic corner of southern Mexico.

HIGHLIGHTS

- Marvel at colonial architecture, take a few Spanish-language courses or attend a free concert in **Mérida** (opposite), the cultural capital of the peninsula
- Find out why they named **Chichén Itzá** (p186) the 'seventh modern wonder of the world,' or why **Ek'Balam** (p196) should have at least made the list
- Scan the salty horizon for flamingos, harpy eagles and crocodiles among the mangroves of **Reserva de la Biósfera Ría Celestún** (p180) or **Río Lagartos** (p198)
- Bump your way through the countryside on a horse-drawn train cart, stopping to dive into the sparkling azure riffs of the cenotes of **Cuzamá** (p175)
- Spin off the tourist track to the less-visited areas around **Valladolid** (p193) and the remote archaeological sites of the **Ruta Puuc** (p172)

- POPULATION: 1,818,948
- AREA: 39,340 SQ KM

MÉRIDA

☎ 999 / pop 781,146

Since the Spanish conquest, Mérida has been the cultural capital of the entire peninsula. At times provincial, at others *'muy cosmopolitano,'* it is a town steeped in colonial history, with narrow streets, broad central plazas and the region's best museums. It's also a perfect hub to kick off your adventure into the rest of Yucatán state. There are cheap eats, good hostels and hotels, thriving markets and goings-on just about every night somewhere in the downtown area.

Long popular with European travelers looking to go beyond the hubbub of Quintana Roo's resort towns, Mérida is not an 'undiscovered Mexican gem' like some of the tourist brochures claim. Simply put, it's a tourist town, but a tourist town too big to feel like a tourist trap. And as the capital of Yucatán state, Mérida is also the cultural crossroads of the region, and there's something just a smidge elitist about the people who live here. They've got a damned nice town, and they know it.

HISTORY

Francisco de Montejo (the Younger) founded a Spanish colony at Campeche, about 160km to the southwest, in 1540. From this base he took advantage of political dissension among the Maya (see boxed text, p174), conquering T'ho (now Mérida) in 1542. By decade's end Yucatán was mostly under Spanish colonial rule.

When Montejo's conquistadors entered T'ho, they found a major Maya settlement of lime-mortared stone that reminded them of the Roman architecture in Mérida, Spain. They promptly renamed the city and proceeded to build it into the regional capital, dismantling the Maya structures and using the materials to construct a cathedral and other stately buildings. Mérida took its colonial orders directly from Spain, not from Mexico City, and Yucatán has had a distinct cultural and political identity ever since.

During the War of the Castes (p36), only Mérida and Campeche were able to hold out against the rebel forces. On the brink of surrender, the ruling class in Mérida was saved by reinforcements sent from central Mexico in exchange for Mérida's agreement to take orders from Mexico City.

Mérida today is the peninsula's center of commerce, a bustling city that has benefited greatly from the *maquiladoras* (low-paying, for-export factories) that opened in the 1980s and 1990s, and the tourism industry that picked up during those decades. This success means the town grows more each year, with immigrants flooding in from all around Mexico. There's even a large Lebanese community in town. This still being the provinces, locals refer to the Lebanese as Turks.

ORIENTATION

The Plaza Grande, as Méridanos call the main square, has been the city's heart since the time of the Maya. Though Mérida now sprawls several kilometers in all directions, most of the services and attractions for visitors are within five blocks of the Plaza Grande. Following the classic colonial plan, the square, holding the cathedral and seats of government, is ringed by several barrios (neighborhoods). Each barrio has its park and church (side by side), usually bearing the same name: for example Iglesia de Santiago is next to Parque de Santiago in Barrio de Santiago. Locals orient themselves and often give directions referring to the barrios.

Odd-numbered streets run east–west; even-numbered streets run north–south. House numbers may increase very slowly, and addresses are usually given in this form: 'Calle 57 No 481 x 56 y 58' (between streets 56 and 58).

From 8pm Saturday to 11pm Sunday, Calles 60 and 62 are closed to motor vehicles between Plaza Grande and Calle 55.

INFORMATION

Bookstores

Librería Dante (☎ 928-3674; Calle 59 btwn Calles 60 & 62; ⏰ 8am-9:30pm Mon-Sat, 10am-6pm Sun) Has a small selection of paperbacks in English, as well as some guidebooks, and a large selection of archaeology books in English, French, German and Spanish. The company has other branches throughout the city, including one on Plaza Grande (☎ 928-2611) on the corner of Calle 61 and Calle 62.

Emergency

Emergency (☎ 066)
Fire (☎ 924-9242)
Police (☎ 925-2034)
Red Cross (☎ 924-9813)
Tourist police (☎ 925-2555 ext 260)

YUCATÁN STATE

YUCATÁN STATE

YUCATÁN STATE

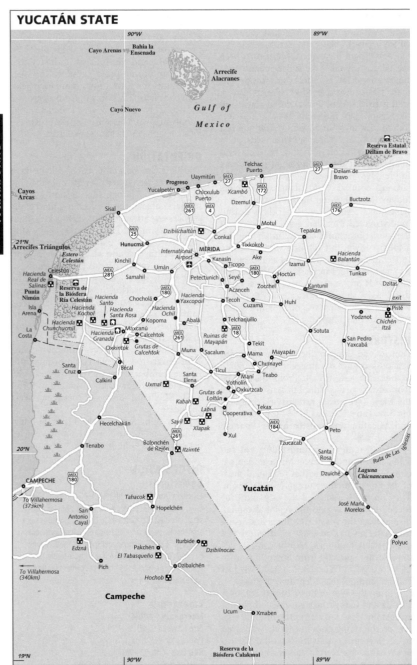

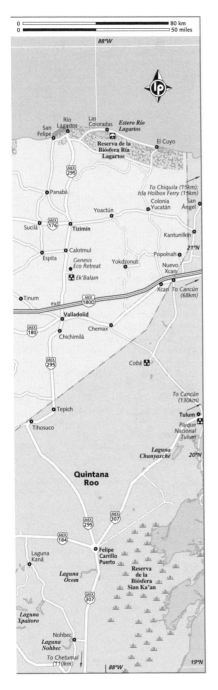

Internet Access

Most internet places around town charge M$10 per hour. Plans are in the works to make the entire downtown Plaza Grande a wi-fi hotspot.

Laundry

Most upmarket hotels offer overnight laundry service.

Lavandería La Fe (☎ 924-4531; Calle 64 btwn Calles 55 & 57; ☺ 8am-6pm Mon-Fri, 8am-2pm Sat) Charges M$40 per 3kg load (less for smaller loads).

Media

Yucatán Today (☎ 927-8531; www.yucatantoday.com; Calle 39 No 483 int 10 btwn Calles 54 & 56) A Spanish-English magazine devoted to tourism in Yucatán. Pick up a copy of the magazine or visit the website for great tips and useful information.

Medical Services

Hospital O'Horán (☎ 924-4800, 924-1111; Av de los Itzáes) For most treatments (including prescriptions and consultations) you're best off going to a private clinic. Ask at your consulate or hotel for a recommendation.

Money

Banks and ATMs are scattered throughout the city. There is a cluster of both along Calle 65 between Calles 60 and 62, one block south of the Plaza Grande. *Casas de cambio* (money-exchange offices) offer faster service and longer hours than banks, but often with poorer rates.

Post

Main post office (☎ 928-5404; Calle 53 No 469 btwn Calles 52 & 54; ☺ 9am-4pm Mon-Fri, for stamps only 9am-1pm Sat)

Postal service booth Airport (☺ Mon-Fri); CAME bus terminal (Calle 70 btwn Calles 69 & 71; ☺ Mon-Fri)

Telephone

Card phones can be found throughout the city. Internet cafés also offer Voice Over Internet Protocol (VOIP)–based phone services.

Toilets

There are pay toilets in the **CAME bus terminal** (Calle 70 btwn Calles 69 & 71). The free museums are also good spots to unburden yourself. Bring your own toilet paper, and be sure all used paper is put in the trashcan, not flushed (the drains can't cope).

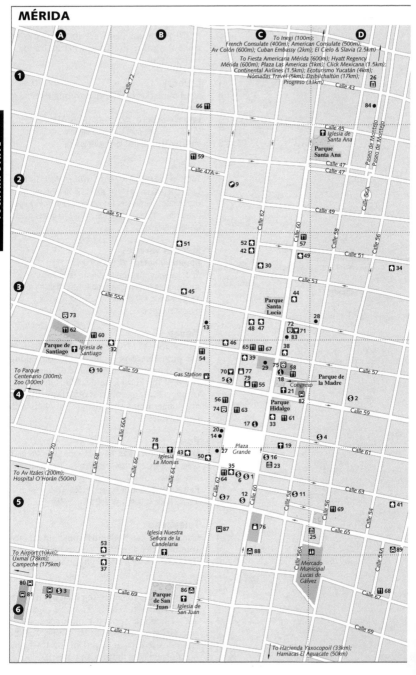

MÉRIDA

YUCATÁN STATE

Tourist Information

The tourist information booths at the airport and the CAME bus terminal have coupons for lodging discounts and hotel suggestions. Three tourist offices downtown have more current information, brochures, bus schedules and maps.

City tourist office (☎ 942-0000 ext 80119; Calle 62 on Plaza Grande; ☯ 8am-8pm Mon-Sat, 8am-2pm Sun) Just south of the main entrance to the Palacio Municipal, it is staffed with helpful English speakers. It offers free walking tours of the city at 9.30am (see p157).

State tourist office (☎ 930-3101; Calle 61 on Plaza Grande; ☯ 8am-9pm) In the entrance to the Palacio de Gobierno. It usually has an English speaker on hand.

Tourist Information Center (☎ 924-9290; cnr Calles 60 & 57A; ☯ 8am-9pm) Less than two blocks north of the state tourist office, on the southwest edge of the Teatro Peón Contreras, this office is used for training tourism students. There's always an English speaker on hand, and sometimes a speaker of Italian or French.

Travel Agencies

Nómadas Travel (☎ 948-1187; www.nomadastravel .com.mx; Prolongación Paseo de Montejo No 370, Colonia Benito Juárez Norte) It's out of the way in the north of town, but it books flights and offers services for student travelers.

DANGERS & ANNOYANCES

Guard against pickpockets, bag snatchers and bag slashers in the town's markets and when you're in any crowded area. Outright muggings are very rare. Much more scary are the buses that travel at breakneck speed along the narrow streets; sidewalks are often narrow and crowded.

Hawkers are annoying but generally harmless. Mérida's **Policía Turística** (Tourist Police; ☎ 925-2555 ext 260) wear brown-and-white uniforms and are your best bet if you've been robbed; during the day you can almost always find an officer at the Palacio de Gobierno or elsewhere on the Plaza Grande.

SIGHTS
Plaza Grande

'El Centro' is one of the nicest plazas in Mexico. Huge laurel trees shade the park's benches and wide sidewalks, and it is surrounded by a bustle of pedestrians who shop or sip coffee at the many open-air cafés. It was the religious and social center of ancient T'ho; under the Spanish it was the Plaza de Armas, the parade ground, laid out by

Francisco de Montejo (the Younger). A ceremony is held daily marking the raising and lowering of the Mexican flag. On Sunday hundreds of Méridanos take their paseo (stroll) here, and there's a cultural exhibit – normally dance or live music – nearly every night.

CATEDRAL DE SAN ILDEFONSO

On the plaza's east side, on the site of a former Maya temple, is Mérida's hulking, severe **cathedral** ([icon] 6am-noon & 4-7pm), begun in 1561 and completed in 1598. Some of the stone from the Maya temple was used in its construction. The massive crucifix behind the altar is **Cristo de la Unidad** (Christ of Unity), a symbol of reconciliation between those of Spanish and Maya heritage. To the right over the south door is a painting of Tutul Xiú, cacique (indigenous chief) of the town of Maní, paying his respects to his ally

Francisco de Montejo at T'ho (de Montejo and Xiú jointly defeated the Cocomes; Xiú converted to Christianity, and his descendants still live in Mérida).

In the small chapel to the left of the altar is Mérida's most famous religious artifact, a statue called **Cristo de las Ampollas** (Christ of the Blisters). Local legend says the statue was carved from a tree that was hit by lightning and burned for an entire night without charring. It is also said to be the only object to have survived the fiery destruction of the church in the town of Ichmul (though it was blackened and blistered from the heat). The statue was moved to the Mérida cathedral in 1645.

Other than these items, the cathedral's interior is largely plain, its rich decoration having been stripped away by angry peasants at the height of anticlerical fervor during the Mexican Revolution.

AROUND THE CATHEDRAL

South of the cathedral, housed in the former archbishop's palace, is the **Museo de Arte Contemporáneo** (Macay; ☎ 928-3236; Calle 60 btwn Calles 61 & 63; admission free; ◷ 10am-6pm Sun-Thu, 10am-8pm Fri & Sat). This attractive museum holds permanent exhibits of Yucatán's most famous painters and sculptors, as well as revolving exhibits by local craftspeople.

Casa de Montejo (Palacio de Montejo; ◷ 9am-4pm Mon-Fri, 10am-2pm Sat) is on the south side of the Plaza Grande and dates from 1549. It originally housed soldiers but was soon converted into a mansion that served members of the Montejo family until 1970. Today it houses a Banamex bank, and you can enter and look around during bank hours. At other times content yourself with a close look at the façade, where triumphant conquistadors with halberds hold their feet on the necks of generic barbarians (though they're not Maya, the association is inescapable). Typical of the symbolism in colonial statuary, the vanquished are rendered much smaller than the victors; works on various churches throughout the region feature big priests towering over or in front of little Indians. Also gazing across the plaza from the façade are busts of Montejo the Elder, his wife and his daughter.

Across the square from the cathedral is Mérida's **Palacio Municipal** (City Hall). Originally built in 1542, it was twice refurbished, in the 1730s and the 1850s. Adjoining it is the **Centro Cultural Olimpo**, Mérida's municipal cultural center. Attempts to create a modern exterior for the building were halted by government order, to preserve the colonial character of the plaza. The ultramodern interior serves as a venue for music and dance performances (see p163), as well as other exhibitions. Schedules for performances and frequent film showings are posted outside.

On the north side of the plaza, the **Palacio de Gobierno** (admission free; ◷ 8am-10pm) houses the state of Yucatán's executive government offices (and one of its tourist information centers). It was built in 1892 on the site of the palace of the colonial governors. Be sure to have a look inside at the murals painted by local artist Fernando Castro Pacheco. Completed in 1978, they were 25 years in the making and portray a symbolic history of the Maya and their interaction with the Spaniards.

Mercado Municipal Lucas de Gálvez & Museo de la Ciudad

Mérida's main market, **Mercado Municipal Lucas de Gálvez** (Municipal Market; cnr Calles 56A & 67), is an ever-evolving mass of commerce, with stalls selling everything from *panuchos* (a fried tortilla stuffed with beans and topped with meat and veggies) to ponchos. The surrounding streets are all part of the large market district. This is a great place to stop for lunch as you tour the city, but watch for pickpockets, purse snatchers and bag slashers.

The **Museo de la Ciudad** (City Museum; ☎ 923-6869; Calle 56 btwn Calles 65 & 67; admission free; ◷ 9am-8pm Tue-Fri, 9am-2pm Sat & Sun) is housed in the old post office and offers a great reprieve from the hustle, honks and exhaust of this market neighborhood. There are exhibits tracing back the city's history to pre-conquest days up through the henequen *belle époque* and into the 20th century (for more on henequen, see boxed text, p181).

Calle 60

A block north of the Plaza Grande, beyond shady Parque Hidalgo, rises the 17th-century **Iglesia de Jesús**, also called Iglesia de la Tercera Orden. Built by the Jesuits in 1618, it is the sole surviving edifice from a complex of buildings that once filled the entire city block.

North of the church is the enormous bulk of the **Teatro Peón Contreras** (cnr Calles 60 & 57; ◷ visitors 9-6pm Tue-Sat), built between 1900 and 1908, during Mérida's henequen heyday. It boasts a main staircase of Carrara marble, a dome with faded frescoes by Italian artists, and various paintings and murals throughout the building.

Across Calle 60 from the theater is the main building of the **Universidad de Yucatán**. The modern university was established in the 19th century by Governor Felipe Carrillo Puerto and General Manuel Cepeda Peraza.

A block north of the university is pretty little **Parque Santa Lucía** (cnr Calles 60 & 55), with arcades on the north and west sides. When Mérida was a lot smaller, this was where travelers would get on or off the stagecoaches that linked towns and villages with the provincial capital. The **Bazar de Artesanías**, the local handicrafts market, is held here at 11am on Sunday.

DAY-TRIPPER

Mérida is a great base for day trips into the countryside. By staying in local communities you'll help create a more sustainable model for tourism, encouraging local businesses and providing an incentive for folks to reinvest in their communities, traditions and culture. That said, it's sometimes nice to return to the sophistication and comfort of the capital. Here are some worthwhile trips:

■ **Cuzamá** Three amazing cenotes (limestone sinkholes) accessed by horse-drawn cart (p175). The cost for a group of four is around M$150.

■ **Ruta Puuc** Ruin yourself by visiting all five sites (including megadraw Uxmal) in one day (p172). Trip lasts about eight hours and costs around M$330 per person. Extend your trip by visiting **Mayapán** (p174) and the **Loltún caves** (p174).

■ **Celestún** Head out early to catch a mangrove birding tour (p180). It's about M$228 per person, including the boat trip. Bring a bunch of friends to save money! For a bit more dough, you can visit the ruined haciendas along the way.

■ **Dzibilchaltún & Progreso** Visit the ruins and cenote for about M$80 (p182) or extend your trip for an afternoon of beach time in Progreso (p183).

■ **Put the guidebook down** Close this book for a day and find adventure in the spirited offbeat towns and wilderness areas of Yucatán's backroads (for our tips, see boxed text, p175).

Paseo de Montejo

Paseo de Montejo, which runs parallel to Calles 56 and 58, was an attempt by Mérida's 19th-century city planners to create a wide boulevard similar to the Paseo de la Reforma in Mexico City or the Champs Élysées in Paris. Though more modest than its predecessors, the Paseo de Montejo is still a beautiful swath of green, relatively open space in an urban conglomeration of stone and concrete. There are rotating sculpture exhibits along the paseo.

Europe's architectural and social influence can be seen along the paseo in the fine mansions built by wealthy families around the end of the 19th century. The greatest concentrations of surviving mansions are north of Calle 37, and on the first block of Avenida Colón west of Paseo de Montejo.

Museo Regional de Antropología

The massive Palacio Cantón houses the **Museo Regional de Antropología** (Regional Anthropology Museum of the Yucatán; ☎ 923-0557; cnr Paseo de Montejo & Calle 43; admission M$37; ☯ 8am-8pm Tue-Sat, 8am-2pm Sun). Construction of the mansion lasted from 1909 to 1911, and its owner, General Francisco Cantón Rosado (1833–1917), lived here for only six years before his death. The palacio's splendor and pretension make it a fitting symbol of the grand aspirations of Mérida's elite during the last years of the *porfiriato*, the period from 1876 to 1911 when Porfirio Díaz held despotic sway over Mexico.

The museum covers the peninsula's history since the age of mastodons. Exhibits on Maya culture include explanations (many in Spanish only) of such cosmetic practices as forehead-flattening (done to beautify babies) causing eyes to cross, and sharpening teeth and implanting them with tiny jewels. If you plan to visit archaeological sites near Mérida, you can study the exhibits here – some with plans and photographs – covering the great Maya cities of Mayapán, Uxmal and Chichén Itzá, as well as lesser-known sites such as the marvelous Ek' Balam. There's also a good bookstore with many archaeological titles.

Parque Centenario

About 12 blocks west of the Plaza Grande lies the large, verdant **Parque Centenario** (admission free; ☯ 6am-6pm Tue-Sun), bordered by Avenida Itzáes, which leads to the airport and becomes the highway to Campeche. The park's **zoo** (admission free; ☯ 6am-6pm Tue-Sun) features the fauna of Yucatán, as well as some exotic species. To get there, take a bus west along Calle 61 or 65.

Museo de Arte Popular de Yucatán

The **Museo de Arte Popular de Yucatán** (Yucatecan Museum of Popular Art; cnr Calle 50A & Calle 57 in the Casa Molina; admission M$30; ☯ 9:30am-4:30pm Tue-Sat, 9am-2pm Sun) is six blocks east of the Plaza Grande in a building built in 1906. There's a small rotating exhibit downstairs that features pop art from around Mexico, but honestly, you're better off heading to any artisan market in the countryside – you'll see the same style of work, and it won't cost you a single peso, unless you want to buy something. The upstairs exhibits don't have any explanatory signs yet, but they give you an idea of how locals embroider *huipiles*, carve ceremonial masks and weave hammocks.

Across the plaza from the museum is **Iglesia La Mejorada**, a large 17th-century church. The building just north of it was a monastery (El Convento de La Mejorada) until the late 19th century. It now houses an architectural school, but visitors are sometimes allowed to view the grounds.

COURSES

The **Centro de Idiomas del Sureste** (CIS; ☎ 923-0954; www.cisyucatan.com.mx; Calle 52 No 455 btwn Calles 49 & 51) offers Spanish-language courses. You can also often find a private tutor through your hostel.

TOURS

City Tours

The **city tourist office** (☎ 942-0000 ext 80119; Calle 62 on Plaza Grande) offers free daily guided walking tours of the historic center (sometimes in English), focusing on Plaza Grande.

Tours depart at 9.30am from in front of the Palacio Municipal.

Transportadora Turística Carnaval (☎ 927-6119) conducts two-hour guided tours of Mérida in English and Spanish on its Paseo Turístico bus (M$75) departing from Parque Santa Lucía (on the corner of Calles 55 and 60) at 10am, 1pm, 4pm and 7pm Monday to Saturday, and 10am and 1pm Sunday. You can buy your tickets ahead of time at nearby Hotel Santa Lucía, among other places.

Regional Tours

Turitransmérida (☎ 928-1871; www.turitransmerida .com.mx; cnr Calles 55 & 58) is one of the largest of the many agencies offering group tours to sites around Mérida, including Celestún, Chichén Itzá, the Ruta Puuc and Izamal. Prices cost M$300 to M$450.

The owners of reputable **Ecoturismo Yucatán** (☎ 920-2772; www.ecoyuc.com.mx; Calle 3 No 235) are passionate about both sharing and protecting the state's natural treasures. Trips focus on archaeology, birding, natural history, biking and kayaking. One-day excursions cost around M$1200; eight-day jungle tours M$20,150.

Many hotels will book these tours, as will **Nómadas Youth Hostel** (☎ /fax 924-5223; www.nomadas travel.com; Calle 62 No 433), which also arranges

---

SIGNS O' THE TIMES

Visitors to Mérida will notice small, artistic plaques on the corners of some buildings beside major intersections. The ceramic plaques are located about 3m above the sidewalk – about where you'd expect to see a street sign if signposts weren't used.

Indeed the plaques, which feature paintings of people, animals and other subjects with their Spanish names underneath, are old-fashioned Mérida street signs. For example, on the building housing a Burger King (cnr Calles 59 & 60), you'll see a painted figure of a dog and, just below it, the words *el perro* (the dog).

Signs like this one were placed on corner buildings during colonial days by conquistadors trying to teach the native populace some Spanish. The signs reflected the streets' local names. Unfortunately, all of the original plaques disappeared over time; the several dozen you see today were affixed to buildings relatively recently by city officials hoping to increase tourism and maintain a piece of history. Although new, the plaques are said to closely resemble the originals, and their locations are supposedly historically accurate.

A sign on the corner of Calles 65 and 60, for example, shows an old lady. The sign was posted at that particular location because local people knew the street as 'the old lady's street' on account of an elderly woman who had once worked in a bakery near the corner.

Likewise, the 'two faces' sign found at the junction of Calles 65 and 58 has its origin in a liar who lived nearby. The 'headless man' street (look for the sign on the corner of Calles 67 and 60) took its name from a man who had the misfortune of being under a window when it broke and was beheaded by a falling piece of glass.

a variety of other tours, from DIY trips in your rented car or on public transportation (with written instructions) to nearly all-inclusive (some meals) trips in private buses. Many tours include lodging at other hostels as well as insurance. Nómadas will help to match up travelers into groups for sharing cars and costs.

ATS buses conducts a day tour to Uxmal, Kabah and the Ruta Puuc sites, beginning from the Terminal de Segunda Clase in Mérida at 8am. See p170 for details.

FESTIVALS & EVENTS

Anniversary of the Universidad de Yucatán For most of February the Universidad de Yucatán celebrates its anniversary with free performances by the Ballet Folklórico, concerts of Afro-Cuban music and *son* (Mexican folk music that blends elements of indigenous, Spanish and African musical styles), and other manifestations of Yucatán's cultural roots.

Carnaval Prior to Lent, in February or March, and features colorful costumes and nonstop festivities. It's celebrated with greater vigor in Mérida than anywhere else in Yucatán state.

Festival de Trova Yucateca This festival celebrates *trovas,* romantic ballads. For more on *trovas,* see p45. Held in March.

Semana Santa (Holy Week) A major celebration in Mérida over Easter week. The main feature of the celebrations is the city's Passion Plays.

Between September 22 and October 14, *gremios* (guilds or unions) venerate the Cristo de las Ampollas (Christ of the Blisters) statue in the cathedral with processions.

Exposición de Altares de los Muertos A big religious tradition. Throughout Mexico families prepare shrines to welcome the spirits of loved ones back to earth. Many Maya prepare elaborate dinners outside their homes, and Mérida observes the occasion with festivities and displays in the town center from 11am on November 1 until 11am the next day.

SLEEPING

From about December 15 to January 6, and during Semana Santa (Easter week), many midrange and top-end hotels raise their prices by 10% to 20%. These times and during July and August (which also see price increases at some places) tend to be the busiest; it's wise to book ahead. Rates quoted in the following listings are for the low season.

When business is slow many places will offer discounts, some without being asked (it never hurts to ask for a *descuento* if it's not offered, but don't be cruel). If you're arriving at the CAME bus terminal, check at the tourist information booth for flyers offering hotel discounts.

Budget

Rooms in this category have fans unless otherwise noted; spending the extra money for air-con is well worth it in the hotter months. Many dirt-cheap places don't have toilet seats.

our pick Nómadas Youth Hostel (☎ /fax 924-5223; www.nomadastravel.com; Calle 62 No 433 at Calle 51; dm M$85, s or d with/without bathroom M$240/200; P 🖳) This is Mérida's Backpacker's Central, and the best hostel in the city. There are mixed and women's dorms, as well as private rooms. All rates include breakfast, and guests have use of a fully equipped kitchen with fridge and purified water, 24-hour hot showers, internet and hand-laundry facilities. It even has free salsa classes and it's planning on building a pool out back. Luggage lockers are free while you stay, and M$15 a day while you travel. Bring mosquito repellent and earplugs, as the front rooms can get traffic noise.

Hostel Zocalo (☎ 924-5223; Calle 63 No 508; dm M$100, s/d M$140/230; 🖳) Great location and a beautiful old colonial building make this hostel unique. Its owners are lovingly restoring it by hand. It has firm beds and a simple breakfast is included. The hosts offer a wealth of information about the area.

Hostal del Peregrino (☎ 924-5491; www.hostaldel peregrino.com; Calle 51 No 488; dm M$130, d M$400) On a quiet street, it's earthy, homey and tasteful. For the price, you're probably better off at Nómadas, but if you're looking to get away from the groovy-groupie backpacker scene, this may be the place for you. Breakfast is included in the price, and it offers low-season discounts and wi-fi.

Hotel Los Arcos (☎ 924-9728; Calle 63 btwn Calles 62 & 64; s/d M$170/230; P 🔀) Peach pink with frosting-cake colors, this clean hotel offers pretty good value for budget hunters. The slightly dark rooms have OK bathrooms and beds, good screens and nice décor. Some rooms have air-con.

Hotel y Restaurant San José (☎ 928-6657; san -jose92@latinmail.com; Calle 63 btwn Calles 62 & 64; s/d/tr M$140/160/180, with air-con M$260/280/300; 🔀) The walls are crumbling in this fading hotel 30m west of the Plaza Grande, but with a lot of elbow grease and a bit of heavy detergent staff manage to keep the place spick-and-span. The 30 good-sized rooms are all set well off the street. It offers value and is a favorite with visiting Mennonites.

Hotel Casa Becil (☎ 924-6764; hotelcasabecil @yahoo.com.mx; Calle 67 No 550C btwn Calles 66 & 68; s/d/tr M$180/220/260, d with air-con M$300-330; ✖) Almost a hostel but not quite, the Casa Becil's friendly owner calls it a 'BBC,' for breakfast, bed and coffee. It offers very inexpensive, clean rooms with a fully equipped kitchen downstairs, an intimate courtyard, a sun deck, beautiful tiled floors, left-luggage service, book exchange, tours and more. The rooms are breezy, without a hint of stuffiness, and the owner speaks excellent English.

Hotel del Mayab (☎ 928-5174; Calle 50 No 536A btwn Calles 65 & 67; s/d with fan M$250/270, with air-con M$350/400; ✖ P ✖) This place is clean and low-key, and offers off-street parking. Streetside rooms can be noisy, but interior rooms are quiet, and the hotel has a large swimming pool.

Posada del Ángel (☎ 923-2754; Calle 67 No 535 btwn Calles 66 & 68; s/d/tr/q with fan M$200/270/340/410, with air-con M$260/340/420/550; ✖ P) A neocolonial hotel three blocks northeast of the CAME bus terminal, it offers rooms with good beds and crisp, clean sheets; it's quieter here than at most other hotels in the area.

Hotel Dolores Alba (☎ 928-5650; fax 928-3163; www .doloresalba.com; Calle 63 btwn Calles 52 & 54; r without air-con M$260, d with air-con M$420-490; ✖ ✖ P) Rooms are on three floors (with an elevator) around two large courtyards. Those in the new, modern wing are quite large, with good beds and TV, and face the lovely pool. The hotel has secure parking and is quiet, well managed and friendly.

ourpick Casa Ana B&B (☎ 924-0005; www.casaana .com; Calle 52 No 469 btwn Calles 53 & 51; r M$300-450; ✖ ✖) Though out of the way, Casa Ana is an intimate escape and the best budget B&B in town. It features a small natural-bottom pool and a cozy overgrown garden complete with Cuban tobacco plants (memories of home for the Cuban owners, no doubt). The rooms are spotless, with clean sheets, Mexican hammocks and (whew) nice mosquito screens.

Alvarez Family Guest House (☎ 924-3060; casa .alvarez@hotmail.com; Calle 62 No 448 btwn Calles 51 & 53; s/d M$350/400, d with air-con M$500; ✖) Impeccably clean and in a family's home, this 'hostel plus' offers a friendly, one-of-the-family ambience,

nice showers, spotless baths and laundry. The guesthouse is full of beautiful antiques, including an old cylinder-style gramophone player, which Enrique, the accommodating owner, may demonstrate on request.

Midrange

Compared with many parts of the peninsula, many of Mérida's midrange places provide surprising levels of comfort for the price.

Hotel Trinidad (☎ 923-2033; www.hotelestrinidad .com; Calle 62 No 464 btwn Calles 55 & 57; d M$400; ✖) Occupies a colonial house and a newer wing, and has a variety of rooms, each with its own unique décor and charm. Some rooms have good kitchenettes, most have air-con, and there's even a rooftop Jacuzzi. It has great common areas (including two courtyards, one with a lovely garden), a billiard table, a book exchange, a small café, 24-hour tea, luggage storage, and guests have use of the pool at the nearby Hotel Trinidad Galería. All rates include continental breakfast.

Hotel Santa Lucía (☎ /fax 928-2672, in USA 1-800-560-2445; hstalucia@prodigy.net.mx; Calle 55 No 508 btwn Calles 60 & 62; s/d/tr M$400/450/500; ✖ P ✖) Across from the park of the same name, this hotel is clean, secure and popular, and has an attractive lobby. The pool is small but clean, and the rooms have TV and phone. Rates include breakfast. Someone here really likes potted plants.

Hotel Trinidad Galería (☎ 923-2463; www.hoteles trinidad.com; Calle 60 No 456 near Calle 51; r with/without air-con M$400/300, ste M$450-550; ✖ ✖ P) It's like walking into the 'General's Labyrinth' or a Salvador Dali Dream. Odd – at times freakish – artwork and statuary gather dust in every corner of this rambling hotel. You will either love this wacky place or find it disquieting. The rooms vary considerably: some are dark and musty, while others offer well-vented bathrooms with good mosquito screens; all have original artwork and interesting posted rules, which include: 'All deaths will be reported to the authorities.' The art is the main reason to come here, a refreshing change from the usual framed poster. Even if you don't stay, it's worth popping your head in.

Hotel Aragón (☎ /fax 924-0242; www.hotelaragon .com; Calle 57 No 474 btwn Calles 52 & 54; s/d M$450/480; ✖ ✖ P) The common areas of this hotel are great, with a large courtyard and a narrow pool along one side. If only it followed the same theme in the modern, rather stagnant rooms. Still the room rates include a continental breakfast and purified water, making this a solid value option.

Hotel Montejo (☎ 928-0390; fax 924-2692; www .hotelmontejo.com; Calle 57 btwn Calles 62 & 64; s/d/tr with air-con $440/510/560; 🔀) This is an eclectic, one-of-a-kind hotel with a central courtyard loaded with 400-year-old stone columns. Its big, clean rooms with classic colonial doors and tiled bathrooms are distributed around the courtyard on two floors. It's a bit overpriced for what you get.

Hotel Medio Mundo (☎ /fax 924-5472; www.hotel mediomundo.com; Calle 55 No 533 btwn Calles 64 & 66; d with fan M$600, r/ste with air-con M$750; 🔀 🖳) This former private residence has been completely remodeled and painted in lovely colors. Its 12 ample, simply furnished rooms have super-comfortable beds, tiled floors, beautiful tiled sinks, great bathrooms and plenty of natural light. One of the two courtyards has a small swimming pool, the other a fountain. The well-traveled, charming hosts prepare large, delicious 'Continental Plus' breakfasts (M$80) and make their guests feel like part of the family.

Casa Mexilio (☎ /fax 928-2505, in USA 800-538-6802; www.casamexilio.com; Calle 68 No 495 btwn Calles 57 & 59; r M$550-850, ste M$1200; 🔀 🖳 P) It occupies a well-preserved, historic house with a maze of quiet, beautifully appointed rooms (some with fan, some air-con), a small bar and a postage-stamp-sized pool with Jacuzzi. All room rates include a full breakfast in the period dining room, and the hotel serves dinner as well.

Hotel Maison Lafitte (☎ 928-1243; www.maison lafitte.com.mx; Calle 60 No 472; d/tr M$750/800; 🖳) The Maison Lafitte offers a full buffet breakfast in its rates, has friendly staff and a nice location – central but still away from it all. The building was once an old colonial house and has a lush garden and a clean, heart-shaped pool. The rooms are a bit bland, but the sit-down showers are a fun luxury.

Gran Hotel (☎ 924-7730; fax 924-7622; www.granhotel demerida.com.mx; Calle 60 No 496 btwn Calles 59 & 61; s/d M$710/850, tr & q M$1350; 🔀) This was indeed a grand hotel when built in 1901; it's a bit faded now but retains many elegant and delightful decorative flourishes. The 28 rooms have period furnishings; some overlook Parque Hidalgo. There's no pool, making it a bit overpriced, but who needs a pool when you're staying at the Gran?

Hotel Colonial (☎ 923-6444; fax 928-3961; www .hotelcolonial.com.mx; Calle 62 No 476 btwn Calles 57 & 59; d/tr M$760/850; 🔀 🖳) The Colonial features 73 comfortable rooms in a fairly modern building with a small clover-shaped pool and perhaps Mexico's smallest bar. 'Promocion' (promotion) rates can drop the prices by up to M$150. It's recently renovated a few rooms; ask for a newer room.

ourpick Los Arcos Bed & Breakfast (☎ 928-0214; www.losarcosmerida.com; Calle 66 btwn Calles 49 & 53; s/d M$850/950; 🖳 🖳) Certainly not for minimalists – there's art on every wall and in every corner – Los Arcos is a lovely, gay-friendly B&B with two guestrooms at the end of a drop-dead gorgeous garden and pool area. Parrots, chihuahuas, a Jacuzzi and palm trees add to the décor. Rooms have an eclectic assortment of art and antiques, excellent beds and bathrooms, and come stocked with CD players, bathrobes and sarongs. All guests have access to the internet and a huge CD library. Rates include a full, hot breakfast.

Top End

During nonpeak times, walk-in rates may be cheaper than booking in advance.

Hotel Casa del Balam (☎ 924-2150, in USA or Mexico 800-624-8451; fax 924-5011; www.casabalam.com; Calle 60 No 488; d M$1200; 🔀 🖳) This place is centrally located and has a great pool and large, quiet colonial-style rooms. It often offers hefty discounts during quiet times.

Hotel Hacienda Mérida (☎ 924-4363; www.hotel haciendamerida.com; Calle 62 btwn Calles 51 & 53; r M$1500-1750; 🔀 🖳) A new entrant in the upscale boutique category, the Hacienda is lovely by night with illuminated columns leading you past the pool to your classically styled chambers. By day you can see that the hotel still needs a bit of work to qualify for the hefty price tag. Still, it beats staying in a heartless business hotel for most.

Hyatt Regency Mérida (☎ 942-0202; fax 925-7002; www.hyatt.com; Av Colón 344; d from M$1700; 🔀 🖳 P) Not far from the Fiesta Americana Mérida (another good top-end bet), the 17-story Hyatt offers some of Mérida's chichiest hotel digs, with some 300 rooms, tennis courts, a gym and steam bath, and a great pool with swim-up bar.

EATING

As in other touristed areas of the Yucatán Peninsula, many restaurants in Mérida have begun adding a service charge (usually 10%) to the bill.

Budget

Our pick **Mercado Municipal Lucas de Gálvez** (cnr Calles 56A & 67) Mérida's least-expensive eateries are in the Mercado Municipal Lucas de Gálvez; most are open from early morning until early evening. Upstairs joints have tables and chairs and more varied menus; main-course platters of beef, fish or chicken go for as little as M$12. Look for *recados* (spice pastes). Downstairs at the north end are some cheap *taquerías* (taco joints), where you sit on a stool at a narrow counter, while near the south end are *coctelerías* (seafood shacks, specializing in shellfish cocktails) serving shrimp, octopus and conch cocktails, as well as ceviche starting at around M$20.

Mercado Municipal No 2 (Calle 57) Numero Dos is a less crowded, but still cheap and good market on the north side of Parque de Santiago, packed with juice stalls, *loncherías* (simple restaurants often only open for lunch) and even a cheap ice-cream place.

Fe y Esperanza (☎ 241-0995; Calle 60 No 452 cnr Calle 51; tacos & tortas M$8-28; 7:30am-5:30pm Mon-Sat) This popular hole-in-the-wall offers simple snacks like tacos and *tortas* (sandwich in a roll). High spenders can go upscale with a set lunch (M$28) with your choice of meat, rice, beans, salad and *agua fresca* fruit juice. The service is super-friendly.

La Flor de Santiago (☎ 928-5591; Calle 70 btwn Calles 57 & 59; mains $30-60; 7am-11pm) Chiapas coffee is served in incongruous, chipped Willow-ware cups in this cafeteria-style eatery. The guacamole is near perfect, and there is a wide selection of Mexican comfort foods, such as chicken tamales or turkey soup. A Saturday or Sunday breakfast buffet costs M$60. It's all good, and the friendly, no-nonsense waiters are obliging.

La Casa del Cheesecake (cnr Calle 47 & 66; cake slice M$15-20; 9am-7pm Mon-Fri, 9am-3pm Sat) This veritable institution offers cheesecakes, whole or by the slice, in an array of funky flavors that may include peach or even Kahlua.

El Trapiche (☎ 928-1231; Calle 62 No 491 btwn 59 & 61; mains M$26-50; 8am-midnight) A great place close to El Centro, El Trapiche has cheap Mexican eats in a casual environment that includes passing visits by just about every peddler around. As you eat, you can stock up on Cuban cigars or Chiapas belts or jewelry. If you don't want to buy anything and just want to eat, choose a table in the back near the fountain. Pitchers of *agua de melon* (cantaloupe blended with water and a touch of sugar) cost only M$45.

A few blocks east of the Plaza Grande are side-by-side **supermarkets** (Calle 56 btwn Calles 63 & 65) as well as a branch of **Super Bodega** (cnr Calles 67 & 54A), a market–department store chain.

Both markets are great spots to pick up ingredients for a sumptuous DIY dinner or picnic lunch.

For good, cheap breakfasts, try a selection of *panes dulce* (sweet rolls and breads) from one of Mérida's several bakeries, such as **Panificadora Montejo** (Calle 62) on the corner of the main plaza. A full bag of goodies usually costs no more than M$25.

Midrange

Il Caffé Italiano (☎ 928-0093; Calle 57A btwn Calles 58 & 60; mains M$75-150; 8am-midnight Mon-Sat) It's an Italian-style café with nice espressos, good

---

ASK A LOCAL: LAURA'S PICKS

Laura Alonzo Fuentes is a vegetarian who grew up in an affluent corner of Mérida. She now lives in the US, but we caught up with her before she left to see where Mérida's young professionals dine – all of these spots are outside the downtown area and offer good eats for carnos and vegos alike. Call for directions and reservations, or make your own top five.

- **100% Natural** (☎ 948-4254) A great spot for vegos, with fresh smoothies and homemade bread.
- **La Bologna** (☎ 926-2505) Italian class. As the great H Simpson might say 'mmmm, bologna.'
- **La Habichuela** (☎ 926-3626) Fancy modern takes on classic dishes.
- **La Tratto** (☎ 927-0434) Miami-style open-air dining.
- **Trotters** (☎ 942-0202) For stylish international cuisine.

mains and very interesting desserts: the straw-berries with balsamic vinegar and ice cream is something completely different.

Pop Cafetería (☎ 928-6163; Calle 57 btwn Calles 60 & 62; breakfast M$28-48, mains M$35-90; ◷ 7am-midnight Mon-Sat, 8am-midnight Sun) There's an Art Deco bebop feel to this little cafeteria-style restau-rant, which serves cheap breakfast combina-tions and a good variety of Mexican dishes; try the chicken in dark, rich *mole* (a handmade chocolate and chili sauce; M$45).

Main Street (☎ 923-6850; Calle 60 btwn Calles 59 & 61; breakfast M$50-80, mains M$60-140; ◷ 7am-11pm) On the edge of Parque Hidalgo, this eatery serves generous, reasonably priced breakfasts, as well as ample portions of pasta and other dishes, including mediocre pizza. The outdoor tables offer prime people-watching opportunities.

Amaro (☎ 928-2451; www.restauranteamaro.com; Calle 59 btwn Calles 60 & 62; mains M$55-100; ◷ 11am-1am or 11pm if it's slow; **V**) A romantic dining spot, especially at night, when there's usually a duo performing ballads. It's set in the courtyard of the house in which Andrés Quintana Roo – poet, statesman and drafter of Mexico's Declaration of Independence – was born in 1787. The service and food are good (but check your bill carefully), and the menu includes Yucatecan dishes and a variety of vegetarian plates, as well as some continental dishes, crêpes and pizzas.

Pane e Vino (☎ 928-6228; Calle 62 btwn Calles 59 & 61; mains M$70-100; ◷ 6pm-midnight Tue-Sun; **V**) This Italian-run joint serves tasty antipasti and salads (with olive oil and balsamic vinegar if you wish), lasagna, fish, meat and a selection of respectable wines by the glass or bottle. The star attractions are the fresh handmade pasta dishes, which vary daily and usually include gnocchi, ravioli and fettuccine.

Restaurante Kantún (☎ 923-4493; Calle 45 btwn Calles 64 & 66; mains M$60-120; ◷ noon-7pm Tue-Sun) The Kantún serves some of the best sea-food in town. Main dishes are all prepared to order and delicately seasoned or sauced; try the *filete Normanda*, a fillet stuffed with smoked oysters and topped with anchovies. There are a few meat offerings for nonfishy types. The service is friendly and attentive, if almost formal at times.

Top End
Restaurante Pórtico del Peregrino (☎ 928-6163; Calle 57 btwn Calles 60 & 62; mains M$70-140; ◷ noon-midnight) There are several pleasant, traditional-style

dining rooms (some with air-con) sur-rounding a small courtyard in this upscale eatery. Yucatecan dishes such as *pollo pibil* (chicken flavored with achiote sauce and wrapped in banana leaves) are its forte, but you'll find many international dishes and a broad range of seafood and steaks as well. *Mole poblano,* a chocolate and chili sauce, is a house specialty, as is artery-clogging *queso relleno* (Dutch cheese stuffed with spiced ground beef).

Alberto's Continental Patio (☎ 928-5367; cnr Calles 64 & 57; mains M$70-170, set dinners M$240-280; ◷ 1-11pm Mon-Sat, 6-11pm Sun; **V**) Alberto's offers yet more colonial-courtyard (as well as in-door) dining. The setting is extremely atmos-pheric, chockablock with religious artifacts, Maya ceramic figures and greenery. Middle Eastern dishes such as hummus, babaga-noush and tabbouleh are served with pita bread, and can be a welcome change from Mexican food. The steaks, poultry and sea-food are also good, as is the service. Tipplers will appreciate the fine brandy selection.

DRINKING
It's impossible not to find a beer or bar in Mérida; if you're really desperate, ask anyone on the street to point the way to a nearby watering hole. Most of the restaurants listed earlier serve drinks or have their own bars.

KY60 (Calle 60 btwn Calles 55 & 57; free admission; ◷ 9pm-3am) Surprisingly, despite the men-wearing-construction-outfits Village People vibe, this is not a gay bar. It's got good pool tables and is popular with guys and gals, gays and straights, locals and tourists, prob-ably because of its reasonably priced beers, which seem to be a universal attraction.

People not needing something alcoholic can try:

Jugos California (☎ 923-4142; Calle 63 No 502; juices US$1.10-2.50; ◷ 7am-10pm) On the corner next to the bread shop Panificadora Montejo, this cheery yellow-and-blue tiled place of-fers great fresh juices and smoothies, served with friendly smiles.

El Hoyo (☎ 928-1531; Calle 62 No 487; coffees US$1.60-2.50; ◷ 8am-11:30pm Mon-Sat) This is the best place for cheap espressos and lattes, plus chessboards and books if you want to hang out. A small courtyard at the back has beautiful tilework. The Nutella crêpe is a unique specialty.

ENTERTAINMENT

Mérida offers many folkloric and musical events in parks and historic buildings, put on by local performers of considerable skill. Admission is free except as noted in the following reviews. Check with one of the tourist information offices to confirm schedules and find out about special events; the website www.yucatantoday.com offers monthly news and often highlights seasonal events.

Centro Cultural Olimpo (☎ 924-0000 ext 80152; cnr Calles 62 & 61) Offers something nearly every night, from films to concerts to art installations.

Caribbean Blue (☎ 923-2279; Calle 60 btwn Calles 57 & 55; admission M$30; 10pm-3:30am) One of a cluster of bars on this block that has music and dancing, with a live nine-piece salsa band most nights. The crowd is fairly young, with a mix of locals and visitors.

Take a taxi to the Prolongación de Montejo, where you'll have your choice of bumping discos and uberchic lounges. Most charge admission. **El Cielo** (☎ 944-5127; Prolongación de Montejo btwn Calle 25 & Av Campestre) is a locals' favorite, as is the nearby **Slavia** (☎ 926-6587; Prolongación de Montejo s/n).

Mérida has several cinemas, most of which show first-run Hollywood fare in English, with Spanish subtitles (ask '¿inglés?' at the ticket office if you need to be sure), as well as other foreign films and Mexican offerings. Cinema tickets cost about M$45 for evening shows, M$25 for matinees. Try the following:

Cines Rex (Calle 57 btwn Calles 70 & 72)
Teatro Mérida (Calle 62 btwn Calles 59 & 61)

YUCATÁN STATE

YUCATECAN HAMMOCKS: THE ONLY WAY TO SLEEP

The fine strings of Yucatecan hammocks make them supremely comfortable. In the sticky heat of a Yucatecan summer, most locals prefer sleeping in a hammock, where the air can circulate around them, rather than in a bed. Many inexpensive hotels used to have hammock hooks in the walls of all guestrooms; many still do.

Yucatecan hammocks are normally woven from strong nylon or cotton string and dyed in various colors. There are also natural, undyed cotton versions. Some sellers will try to fob these off as henequen (also called sisal) or jute, telling you it's much more durable (and valuable) than cotton, and even that it repels mosquitoes. Don't be taken in; real henequen hammocks are very rough and not something you'd want near your skin. Silk hammocks are no longer made, but a silk-rayon blend has a similar feel.

Hammocks come in several widths (each shop seems to have slightly different names and numbers for them), and though much is made of the quantity of pairs of end strings they possess, a better gauge of a hammock's size and quality is its weight. The heavier the better. A *sencilla* (for one person) should be about 500g and cost around M$120. The *doble* (double size, big enough for a large man) is about 700g to 800g and costs roughly M$150 to M$200. Next comes the *matrimonial* (queen size, big enough for two people to snuggle) at 1100g (M$220) and *familiar* (king size, big enough for two people, a dog, a cat and a goldfish – but we doubt you'll really be able to fit the whole family in it; up to about 1500g, M$270). De croché (very tightly woven) hammocks can take several weeks to produce and cost double or triple the prices given here.

Many stores can also sell mosquito netting for an additional M$150 or so. And before you leave, ask staff to show you how to fold it – only fishing line takes longer to untangle.

You can save yourself a lot of trouble by shopping at a hammock store with a good reputation. Getting away from the heavily touristed areas helps. In Mérida, **Hamacas El Aguacate** (☎ 928-6469; cnr Calles 58 & 73) has quality hammocks and decent prices, and there's absolutely no hard sell. In Quintana Roo, check out Puerto Morelos' artisans market (p102), where high-quality Tixkokob hammocks are sold.

Some of the best (and best-priced) hammocks are produced in prisons, but a less-depressing excursion is to venture out to the village of Tixkokob, near Mérida, to watch hammocks being woven. The senora at **Hamacas El Gallito** (☎ 999-996-5612; cnr Calles 21 & 14; 10am-8pm) is very helpful, though she doesn't speak English. A bus runs regularly from the **Progreso bus terminal** (Calle 62 No 524 btwn Calles 65 & 67) in Mérida.

SHOPPING

Mérida is a fine place for buying Yucatecan handicrafts. Purchases to consider include guayaberas (short-sleeved sports shirts) and traditional Maya clothing, such as the colorful, embroidered *huipiles,* panama hats and, of course, the wonderfully comfortable Yucatecan hammocks (see boxed text, p163).

During the last days of February or the beginning of March (the dates vary) is Kihuic, a market that fills the Plaza Grande with handicraft artisans and their wares from all over Mexico.

Mercado Municipal Lucas de Gálvez (cnr Calles 56A & 67) Mérida's main market is a great spot to pick up that perfect piece of kitsch.

Handicrafts

Casa de las Artesanías (☎ 928-6676; Calle 63 btwn Calles 64 & 66; ☽ 9am-8pm Mon-Sat, 9am-2pm Sun) One place to start looking for handicrafts is this government-supported market for local artisans selling just about everything. Prices are fixed and a bit high.

Artesanías Bazar García Rejón (cnr Calles 65 & 60) Concentrates a wide variety of products into one area of shops.

Miniaturas (☎ 928-6503; Calle 59 btwn Calles 60 & 62; ☽ 10am-8pm) Here you'll find lots of small Día de los Muertos (Day of the Dead) tableaux, tinwork and figurines of every sort, from ceramics to toy soldiers. They all have two thing in common: they're easy to pack and have nothing to do with Yucatecan artisan traditions! The store is definitely fun to browse and prices are fixed at a fair rate, so you needn't worry about bargaining.

Clothing & Panama Hats

Camisería Canul (☎ 923-5661; Calle 62 btwn Calles 57 & 59; ☽ 8:30am-9pm Mon-Sat, 10am-1pm Sun) A good place for guayaberas and *huipiles.* It has been in business for years, offers fixed prices and does custom tailoring.

The Campeche town of Bécal is the center of the hat-weaving trade (see p214), but you can buy good examples of the hatmaker's art in Mérida. Prices range from a few dollars for a hat of basic quality to M$80 or more for top quality. The Casa de las Artesanías has only very low-quality examples; the Artesanías Bazar García Rejón is a much better bet.

GETTING THERE & AWAY

Air

Mérida's tiny but modern airport is a 10km, 20-minute ride southwest of the Plaza Grande off Hwy 180 (Avenida de los Itzáes). It has car-rental desks, an ATM and currency-exchange booth, and a **tourist information booth** (☽ 9am-5pm) that helps mainly with hotel reservations.

Most international flights to Mérida are connections through Mexico City or Cancún. Nonstop international services are provided by Aeroméxico (daily from Los Angeles, thrice weekly from Miami), Continental Airlines and Northwest Airlines (both from Houston, total eight times weekly). Most domestic flights are operated by small regional airlines, with a few flights by Aeroméxico and Mexicana de Aviación. The following airlines are represented in Mérida:

Aeroméxico (☎ 800-021-4010; www.aeromexico.com); Mérida (☎ 920-1293) Flies to Mexico City, Los Angeles and Miami.

Aviacsa (☎ 800-006-2200; www.aviasca.com.mx); Mérida (☎ 925-6890) Flies to Mexico City.

Click Mexicana (☎ 800-112-5425; www.clickmx.com); Mérida (☎ 946-1366; Paseo de Montejo 500B) Flies between Mérida and Cancún, Veracruz and Villahermosa, with connections to Tuxtla Gutiérrez, Havana and other destinations.

Continental Airlines (☎ 800-900-5000; www.continental.com); Mérida (☎ 946-1888; Paseo Montejo No 437 at Calle 29) Flies nonstop between Houston and Mérida.

Delta Airlines (☎ 800-123-4710, reservations toll-free in USA; www.delta.com) Nonstop service from Miami.

Mexicana de Aviación (☎ 924-6633, 800-801-2010; www.mexicana.com; Paseo de Montejo 493) Nonstop flights to Mexico City.

Northwest Airlines (☎ 800-907-4700 in Mexico; www.nwa.com) Flies to Houston.

Bus

Mérida is the bus transportation hub of the Yucatán Peninsula. See the table (opposite) for prices and more information. Take care with your gear on night buses and those serving popular tourist destinations (especially 2nd-class buses); we have received many reports of theft on the night runs to Chiapas and of a few daylight thefts on the Chichén Itzá and other routes.

There are a number of bus terminals, and some lines operate from (and stop at) more than one terminal. Tickets for departure from one terminal can often be bought at another, and destinations overlap greatly among bus lines. Some lines offer round-trip tickets to nearby towns that reduce the fare quite a bit. Following are some of the terminals, the bus lines operating from them and areas served.

CAME bus terminal (☎ reservations 924-8391; Calle 70 btwn Calles 69 & 71) Sometimes referred to as the 'Terminal de Primera Clase,' Mérida's main bus terminal has (mostly 1st-class) buses to points around the Yucatán Peninsula and places such as Campeche, Mexico City, Palenque, San Cristóbal de Las Casas and Villahermosa. CAME has card phones and an ATM and runs counters for tourist, bus and hotel information. The baggage check is open 6am to midnight daily and charges M$5 for storage from 6am to noon, M$10 for all day.

Fiesta Americana Mérida (☎ 924-0855; Av Colón near Calle 56A) A small 1st-class terminal on the west side

of the hotel complex servicing guests of the luxury hotels on Avenida Colón, north of the city center. ADO GL and Super Expresso services run between here and Cancún, Campeche, Chetumal and Playa del Carmen.

Noreste bus terminal (Calle 67 btwn Calles 50 & 52) LUS, Occidente and Oriente bus lines use this terminal. Destinations served from here include many small towns in the northeast part of the peninsula, including Tizimín and Río Lagartos; frequent services to Cancún and points along the way; as well as small towns south and west of Mérida, including Celestún (served by Occidente), Ticul, Ruinas de Mayapán and Oxkutzcab. Some Oriente buses depart from Terminal 69 and stop here; others leave directly from here (eg those to Izamal and Tizimín).

Parque de San Juan (Calle 69 btwn Calles 62 & 64) From all around the square and church, vans and *combis*

YUCATÁN STATE

BUS SERVICES FROM MÉRIDA

Destination	Fare ($M)	Duration (hr)	Departures
Campeche (short route)	122	2½-3½	hourly ADO buses, 3 ADO GL buses, ATS 2nd-class bus every 30min to 7:15pm
Cancún	150-260	4-6	16 2nd-class Oriente buses, 20 deluxe Super Expresso buses & many other buses
Celestún	44	2	15 2nd-class Occidente buses from Noreste bus terminal
Chetumal	170-250	6-8	2 ADO buses from CAME bus terminal, 5 2nd-class Mayab buses, 3 super-deluxe Caribe Express buses from Terminal de Segunda Clase
Chichén Itzá	54-80	1¾-2½	3 Super Expresso & hourly 2nd-class Oriente Cancún-bound buses stop at Chichén Itzá or nearby Pisté
Cobá	94-106	3½-4	Oriente bus at 5:20am
Escárcega	150-176	5-5½	4 ATS, many 2nd-class Sur buses
Felipe Carrillo Puerto	134-146	5½-6	8 Mayab, 2 ATS buses
Izamal	27	1½	frequent 2nd-class Oriente buses from Noreste bus terminal
Mayapán Ruinas	31	1½	15 LUS buses btwn 5:30am & 8pm from Noreste bus terminal, continuing to Oxkutzcab
Mexico City (Norte)	858-1136	19	ADO bus at midnight
Palenque	316-332	8-9	1 deluxe Maya de Oro bus at 8:30am, 3 ADO buses, 1 Occidente bus at 7:15pm
Playa del Carmen	258-310	4½-8	10 deluxe Super Expresso buses, 1 ADO GL bus at 1:30pm, numerous Mayab buses
Progreso	12.50	1	frequent buses 5:30am-10pm from the Progreso bus terminal, shared taxis (some with air-con) from a parking lot on Calle 60 btwn Calles 65 & 67
Río Lagartos	70-110	3-4	3 1st- & 2nd-class Noreste buses from 9am
Ruta Puuc (round-trip)	126	8	1 2nd-class ATS bus at 8am (stops 30min at each site)
Ticul	40	1¾	frequent Mayab buses, some TRP buses; frequent cheaper & quicker *combis* from Parque de San Juan from 5am-10pm
Tizimín	83	2½-4	6 1st- & 2nd-class Noreste buses (for Isla Holbox connect in Tizimín)
Tulum	172	4	Super Expresso bus at 6:30am, 11am & 1pm; there is 2nd-class service to Tulum, but it takes much longer
Uxmal	39	1-1½	15 2nd-class ATS buses, round-trip available
Valladolid	66-112	2½-3½	hourly buses, including Super Expresso, 2nd-class Oriente & ATS

(vans or minibuses) depart for Dzibilchaltún, Muna, Oxkutzcab, Tekax, Ticul and other points.

Progreso bus terminal (Calle 62 No 524 btwn Calles 65 & 67) Progreso has a separate bus terminal here, serving Progreso.

Terminal de Segunda Clase (Calle 69) Also known as Terminal 69 (Sesenta y Nueve) or simply Terminal de Auto-buses, this terminal is located just around the corner from the CAME bus terminal. ADO, Mayab, Oriente, Sur and TRT run mostly 2nd-class buses to points in the state and around the peninsula. The terminal has a baggage check room.

Car

The most flexible way to tour the many archaeological sites around Mérida is by rental car, especially if you have two or more people to share costs. Assume you will pay a total of M$550 to M$650 per day (tax, insurance and gas included) for short-term rental of a cheap car. Getting around Mérida's sprawling tangle of one-way streets and careening buses is better done on foot or on a careening bus.

Several agencies have branches at the airport as well as on Calle 60 between Calles 55 and 57, including **Budget** (☎ 925-1900; www .budgetcancun.com), **Avis** (☎ 946-1524; www.avis.com.mx) and **Hertz** (☎ 946-2554; www.hertz.com.mx). All rent for about M$350 to M$500 a day. You'll get the best deal by booking ahead of time over the internet.

See p87 for details of the expensive toll highway between Mérida and Cancún.

GETTING AROUND
To/From the Airport

Bus 79 (Aviación) travels between the airport and the city center every 15 to 30 minutes until 9pm, with occasional service until 11pm. The half-hour trip (M$4) is via a roundabout route; the best place to catch the bus to the airport is on Calle 70, south of Calle 69, near the CAME bus terminal.

Transporte Terrestre (☎ 946-1529) provides speedy service between the airport and the city center, charging M$100 per carload (same price for hotel pick-up). A taxi from the city center to the airport should cost about M$80 (but it's hard to get this price *from* the airport, so walk out to the main street and flag one down or else prepare to pay M$200).

Bus

Most parts of Mérida that you'll want to visit are within five or six blocks of the Plaza Grande and are thus accessible on foot. Given the slow speed of city traffic, particularly in the market areas, travel on foot is also the fastest way to get around.

City buses are cheap at M$4, but routes can be confusing. Most start in suburban neighborhoods, skirt the city center and terminate in another distant suburban neighborhood. To travel between the Plaza Grande and the upscale neighborhoods to the north along Paseo de Montejo, catch the Ruta 10 on Calle 57 between Calles 58 and 60, a block north of the Parque Hidalgo, or catch a 'Tecnológico,' 'Hyatt' or 'Montejo' bus on Calle 60 and get off at Avenida Colón. To return to the city center, catch any bus heading south on Paseo de Montejo displaying the same signs and/or 'Centro.' Many will let you off on Calle 58 north of Calle 61.

Taxi

Taxis in Mérida are not metered. Rates are fixed, with a M$30 minimum fare, which will get you from the bus terminals to all downtown hotels. Most rides within city limits do not exceed M$60. Taxi stands can be found at most of the barrio parks, or dial ☎ 982-1504 or ☎ 982-1171; service is available 24 hours (dispatch fees cost an extra M$10 to M$20).

SOUTH OF MÉRIDA

There's a lot to do and see south of Mérida. The major draws are the old henequen plantations, some still used for cultivating leaves, and the well-preserved Maya ruins like Uxmal and the lesser-known sites along the Ruta Puuc. Beyond these tourist draws you'll find seldom-visited cenotes and caves, and traditional villages where life still moves at an agrarian pace: women still wear *huipiles* and speak Yucatec, and their men still bike out to cut firewood or shoot a pheasant for dinner. The smell of tortillas mixes with the citrus-like smell of the semi-arid plants that call the region home. It's a rough-and-tumble landscape, and one of the few spots on the peninsula where you'll actually find a few hills.

HACIENDA YAXCOPOIL

This **hacienda** (☎ 999-910-4334; Hwy 261; admission M$50; ☼ 8am-6pm Mon-Sat, 9am-1pm Sun) is 33km southwest of central Mérida. A vast estate that grew and processed henequen, many of its numerous French Renaissance–style buildings have undergone picturesque restorations. There's a small 17th-century museum offering glimpses at the (now defunct) giant rasping machines that turned the leaves into fiber. Frequent buses pass Yaxcopoil running between Mérida and Ticul, but it's easiest to drive here.

HACIENDA OCHIL

Lying about 44km south of Mérida, **Hacienda Ochil** (☎ 999-910-6035; Hwy 261 Km 176; admission M$20; ☒ 9am-6pm; ☻) provides a fascinating, though basic, look at how henequen was grown and processed. From the parking lot follow the 'truck' tracks – used by the small wheeled carts to haul material to and from the processing plant – to the right around the parklike, restored portion of the hacienda. You'll pass workshops where you might see locals fashioning handicrafts for sale and a small henequen museum with exhibits illustrating the cultivating, harvesting and processing of the plant. These include pieces of machinery and photos of hacienda life. Iguanas abound.

The *casa de máquinas* (machine house) and smokestack still stand, and Ochil also has a **restaurant** (mains M$80-100), bar, a small cenote and a henequen patch. Mayab runs 2nd-class buses between Mérida and Muna (M$25, one hour) that will drop you at Ochil's parking lot.

GRUTAS DE CALCEHTOK

The **Calcehtok caves** (☒ 9:30am-3:30pm Mon-Fri, 8am-5pm Sat & Sun; ☻) are said by some to comprise the longest dry-cave system on the Yucatán Peninsula. More than 4km have been explored so far, and two of the caves' 25 vaults exceed 100m in diameter (one has a 30m-high 'cupola'). The caves hold abundant and impressive natural formations, human and animal remains and plenty of artifacts, including many *haltunes* (stone basins carved by the Maya to catch water). Archaeologists have found and removed ceramic arrowheads, quartz hammers and other tools, and you can still see low fortifications built by the Maya who sheltered here during the War of the Castes.

The opening of the main entrance is an impressive 30m in diameter and 40m deep, ringed by vegetation often buzzing with bees. It's about 1m deep in bat guano at the bottom (some visitors wear dust masks to avoid infection from a fungus on the guano). There's nothing to stop you from exploring on your own (and possibly getting lost), but you'd be wise to employ one of the six guides, all members of the Cuy family, whose great-grandfather rediscovered the caves in 1840. They carry lanterns and flashlights.

You can opt for a basic tour or an adventure package – one that involves belly-crawling, rope descents to see human skeletons and possibly the 7m long by 20cm wide 'Pass of Death,' or 'El Parto' (The Birth: you figure it out). Tours last one to six hours and cost from M$200 for four people. Wear sturdy shoes.

The caves are 75km southwest of Mérida off Hwy 184, a few kilometers south of the town of Calcehtok. They are best reached by car.

OXKINTOK

Archaeologists have been excited about the ruins of **Oxkintok** (admission M$30; ☒ 8am-5pm) for several years. Inscriptions found at the site contain some of the oldest known dates in the Yucatán, and indicate the city was inhabited from the pre-Classic to the post-Classic period (300 BC to AD 1500), reaching its greatest importance between AD 475 and 860.

Three main groups of the approximately 8-sq-km site have been restored thus far, all near the site entrance. Though much of the rebuilding work looks like it was done with rubble, you can see examples of Oxkintok, Proto-Puuc and Puuc architecture. The highest structure (15m) is Ma-1, **La Pirámide**, in the Ah-May group, which provides good views of the area. Probably the most interesting structure is **Palacio Chich** (Estructura Ca-7), in the Ah-Canul group, for its original stonework and the two columns in front carved with human figures in elaborate dress. Recently researchers discovered a labyrinth beneath La Pirámide, which unfortunately is closed to the public. You can see the blocked-off entrance quite clearly from the (facing the front) right side, about halfway up.

The ruins are reached by road by taking a west-leading fork off the road to the Grutas de Calcehtok (see left for info on getting to the Grutas de Calcehtok).

UXMAL

Pronounced oosh-mahl, **Uxmal** (admission M$95, parking M$10, guides M$400; ☒ 8am-5pm; ☻) is one impressive set of ruins, easily ranking among the top Maya archaeological sites (and unfortunately most-visited). It is a large site with

YUCATÁN STATE

some fascinating structures in good condition and bearing a riot of ornamentation. Adding to its appeal is Uxmal's setting in the hilly Puuc region, which lent its name to the architectural patterns in this area. *Puuc* means 'hills,' and these, rising up to about 100m, are the first relief from the flatness of the northern and western portions of the peninsula.

History

Uxmal was an important city in a region that encompassed the satellite towns of Sayil, Kabah, Xlapak and Labná. Although Uxmal means 'Thrice Built' in Maya, it was actually constructed five times.

That a sizable population flourished in this dry area is yet more testimony to the engineering skills of the Maya, who built a series of reservoirs and *chultunes* (Maya cisterns) lined with lime mortar to catch and hold water during the dry season. First settled about AD 600, Uxmal was influenced by highland Mexico in its architecture, most likely through contact fostered by trade. This influence is reflected in the town's serpent imagery, phallic symbols and columns. The well-proportioned Puuc architecture, with its intricate, geometric mosaics sweeping across the upper parts of elongated façades, was strongly influenced by the slightly earlier Río Bec and Chenes styles.

The scarcity of water in the region meant that Chac, the rain god or sky serpent, carried a lot of weight here. His image is ubiquitous at

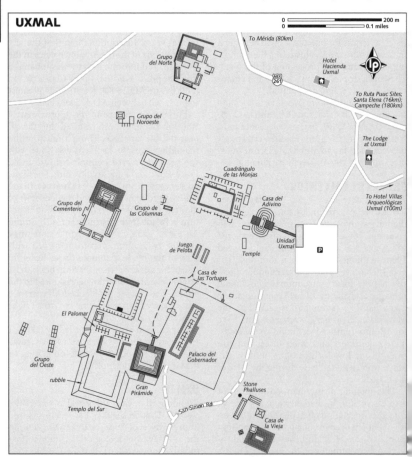

UXMAL

0 _____ 200 m
0 _____ 0.1 miles

To Mérida (80km)

Grupo
del Norte

Hotel
Hacienda
Uxmal

MEX
261

To Ruta Puuc Sites;
Santa Elena (16km);
Campeche (180km)

Grupo del
Noroeste

The Lodge
at Uxmal

Cuadrángulo
de las Monjas

Casa del
Adivino

To Hotel Villas
Arqueológicas
Uxmal (100m)

Grupo del
Cementerio

Grupo de
las Columnas

Unidad
Uxmal

P

Juego
de Pelota

Temple

Casa de
las Tortugas

El Palomar

Palacio del
Gobernador

Grupo
del Oeste

Stone
Phalluses

rubble

Gran
Pirámide

San Simón Rd

Casa de
la Vieja

Templo del Sur

the site in the form of stucco masks protruding from façades and cornices. There is much speculation as to why Uxmal was abandoned in about AD 900; a severe drought may have forced the inhabitants to relocate.

Rediscovered by archaeologists in the 19th century, Uxmal was first excavated in 1929 by Frans Blom. Although much has been restored, there is still a good deal to discover.

Information

The site is entered through the modern Unidad Uxmal building, which holds an air-conditioned restaurant, a small museum, shops selling souvenirs and crafts, an auditorium, bathrooms, an ATM and a left-luggage facility. Also here is Librería Dante, a bookstore that stocks an excellent selection of travel and archaeological guides, and general-interest books on Mexico in English, Spanish, German and French; the imported books are very expensive.

The 45-minute sound-and-light show begins nightly at 8pm in summer and 7pm in winter, and costs M$30. It's in Spanish, but you can rent devices with English, French, German or Italian translations (beamed via infrared) for M$25. Specify the language you need or it may not be broadcast. You'll need to repay the M$10 parking fee if you return for the show.

Sights

CASA DEL ADIVINO

As you climb the slope to the ruins, the Casa del Adivino comes into view. This tall temple (the name translates as 'Magician's House'), 39m high, was built in an unusual oval shape. It gives rather a bad first impression of Uxmal to the visitor, consisting of round stones held rudely together with lots of cement. What you see is a restored version of the temple's fifth incarnation. Four earlier temples were completely covered in the final rebuilding by the Maya, except for the high doorway on the west side, which remains from the fourth temple. Decorated in elaborate Chenes style (a style that originated further south), the doorway proper forms the mouth of a gigantic Chac mask.

Climbing the temple is not allowed.

CUADRÁNGULO DE LAS MONJAS

The 74-room, sprawling Nuns' Quadrangle is directly west of the Casa del Adivino.

Archaeologists guess variously that it was a military academy, royal school or palace complex. The long-nosed face of Chac appears everywhere on the façades of the four separate temples that form the quadrangle. The northern temple, grandest of the four, was built first, followed by the southern, then the eastern and then the western.

Several decorative elements on the exuberant façades show signs of Mexican, perhaps Totonac, influence. The feathered-serpent (Quetzalcóatl, or in Maya, Kukulcán) motif along the top of the west temple's façade is one of these. Note also the stylized depictions of the *na* (traditional Maya thatched hut) over some of the doorways in the northern and southern buildings. Take plenty of time to look around here; the amount of detail is almost overwhelming.

Passing through the corbeled arch in the middle of the south building of the quadrangle and continuing down the slope takes you through the **Juego de Pelota** (Ball Court). From here you can turn left and head up the steep slope and stairs to the large terrace. If you've got time, you could instead turn right to explore the western **Grupo del Cementerio** (which, though largely unrestored, holds some interesting square blocks carved with skulls in the center of its plaza), then head for the stairs and terrace.

CASA DE LAS TORTUGAS

To the right at the top of the stairs is the House of the Turtles, which takes its name from the turtles carved on the cornice. The Maya associated turtles with the rain god, Chac. According to Maya myth, when the people suffered from drought so did the turtles, and both prayed to Chac to send rain.

The frieze of short columns, or 'rolled mats,' that runs around the temple below the turtles is characteristic of the Puuc style. On the west side of the building a vault has collapsed, affording a good view of the corbeled arch – remember that the Maya never mastered keystone arch design – that supported it.

PALACIO DEL GOBERNADOR

The Governor's Palace, with its magnificent façade nearly 100m long, has been called 'the finest structure at Uxmal and the culmination of the Puuc style' by Mayanist Michael D Coe. The buildings have walls filled with rubble, faced with cement and then covered in a thin veneer of limestone squares; the lower part of the façade is plain, the upper part festooned with stylized Chac faces and geometric designs, often latticelike or fretted. Other elements of Puuc style are decorated cornices, rows of half-columns (as in the House of the Turtles) and round columns in doorways (as in the palace at Sayil). Stones forming the corbeled vaults in Puuc style are shaped somewhat like boots.

GRAN PIRÁMIDE

Though it's adjacent to the Governor's Palace, a sign by the steps of the Gran Pirámide (Great Pyramid) warns 'it is dangerous to go up' from the rear of the palace. Most visitors ignore the sign and take the shortcut from the palace's southwest corner. If you don't feel comfortable doing this, retrace your route to go back down the hillside stairs and then keep turning left following the base of the platform until you reach the pyramid's steps.

The 32m-high pyramid has been restored only on its northern side. Archaeologists theorize that the quadrangle at its summit was largely destroyed in order to construct another pyramid above it. That work, for reasons unknown, was never completed. At the top are some stucco carvings of Chac, birds and flowers.

EL PALOMAR

West of the Gran Pirámide sits a structure whose roofcomb is latticed with a pattern reminiscent of the Moorish pigeon houses built into walls in Spain and northern Africa – hence the building's name, which means the Dovecote or Pigeon House. The nine honeycombed triangular 'belfries' sit on top of a building that was once part of a quadrangle. The base is so eroded that it is hard for archaeologists to guess its function.

CASA DE LA VIEJA

Off the southeast corner of the Palacio del Gobernador's platform is a small complex, largely rubble, known as the Casa de la Vieja (Old Woman's House). In front of it is a small *palapa* (thatched-roof shelter) sheltering several large phalluses carved from stone. Don't get any ideas; the sign here reads 'Do not sit.'

Tours

ATS buses depart Mérida's Terminal de Segunda Clase at 8am on a whirlwind excursion to the Ruta Puuc sites (p172) plus Kabah and Uxmal, heading back from Uxmal's parking lot at 2:30pm. This 'tour' is transportation only; you pay all other costs. The time spent at each site is enough to get only a brief acquaintance, though some say the two hours at Uxmal is sufficient, if barely. The cost is M$126 for the whole deal, or M$78 if you want to be dropped off only at Uxmal in the morning and picked up in the afternoon.

More organized tours of Uxmal and other sites can be arranged in Mérida. See p157 for more details.

Sleeping & Eating

There is no town at Uxmal, only several top-end hotels. Cheaper lodgings can be found in Santa Elena (opposite), 16km away, or in Ticul (p177), 30km to the east.

Hotel Villas Arqueológicas Uxmal (☎ /fax 997-974-6020, in the USA 800-514-8244; www.clubmed.com; d/tr M$860/1060; 😕 🔊) This Club Med is a good family spot, with a pool, tennis courts and billiards, but the rooms are rather small and the beds are curiously sproingy (must be the humidity). It's also the cheapest joint around, and it has a good library to check out Catherwood's amazing Uxmal illustrations in the book *Incidents of Travel in Yucatan*.

Hotel Hacienda Uxmal (☎ 997-976-2012, in the USA 800-235-4079; www.mayaland.com; d with air-con low season M$880-1480, high season M$1480; 😕 🔊) This Mayaland Resort is 500m from the ruins. It housed the archaeologists who explored and restored Uxmal. Wide, tiled verandas, high ceilings, great bathrooms and a beautiful swimming pool make this a very comfortable place to stay. There are even rocking chairs to help you kick back after a hard day of exploring.

The Lodge at Uxmal (☎ 997-976-2010, in the USA 800-235-4079; www.mayaland.com; d May-Oct M$2200-2850, Nov-Apr M$3940-4900; 🔊 😕) This Mayaland Resort is Uxmal's newest luxury hotel. The Hacienda's rooms are a bit nicer, but you can't beat the easy access to the ruins. The pool is equally delicious, as are the monstro tubs – some rooms even have Jacuzzis. Don't suppose Stephens and Catherwood enjoyed such luxury when they passed through the area in the late 1830s.

Getting There & Away

Uxmal is 80km from Mérida. Most buses plying the inland route between Mérida and

Campeche will drop you off at Uxmal, Santa Elena, Kabah or the Ruta Puuc turnoff. But when you want to leave, passing buses may be full (especially on Saturday and Monday).

If you're going from Uxmal to Ticul, first take a northbound bus to Muna (M$5, 20 minutes), from where you can catch one of the frequent buses to Ticul (M$8, 30 minutes).

SANTA ELENA

The nearest town to Uxmal is Santa Elena. It was originally called Nohcacab, and was virtually razed in 1847 in the War of the Castes. *'Ele-na'* means burnt houses in Maya. The Mexican government changed the name to Santa Elena in a bold PR stunt. There's a small **museum** (admission M$10; 8am-7pm) dedicated to a gruesome find: 18th-century child mummies found buried beneath the adjoining cathedral, and some henequen-related exhibits. Go for a little DIY adventure by heading 4km outside of town to the Mulchic pyramid; locals can tell you how to get there. If time permits, try asking if you can take in the view from the roof of the cathedral.

At **Bungalows Sacbé** (985-858-1281, 997-978-5158; www.sacbebungalows.com.mx; d M$230-290) there's a nice garden, and all the rooms have fans, good screens and decent beds. Each room has an excellent book with information about local activities, flora and fauna. The friendly Mexican and French owners serve a good, cheap breakfast (M$50). To get here, ask the bus driver to drop you off at the *campo de béisbol* (baseball field) *de Santa Elena*. It's about 200m south of the town's southern entrance.

Flycatcher Inn (997-107-4126, 997-102-0865; www.flycatcherinn.com; d M$400-500, ste or cottage M$600) features six squeaky-clean rooms, an enormous master suite and a separate cottage. All have great porches, supercomfy imported beds, plus hammocks, excellent screenage and great bathrooms. A large breakfast is included in the rates. The owners, a local Maya and his American wife, have kept most of the five hectares of land around the inn undeveloped, and a number of bird and animal species can be seen here, including the flycatchers that gave their name to the place. The inn's driveway is less than 100m north of Santa Elena's southern entrance; there's a bus stop just across the highway from it, near Restaurant El Chac-Mool.

On Hwy 261 at the southern entrance to Santa Elena, **Restaurant El Chac-Mool** (999-996-2025; mains M$40-60; 8am-9pm) is a friendly place serving Yucatecan food that includes a hearty vegetarian plate of rice, beans and fried bananas. It has a little store, too.

Locals say **The Pickled Onion** (mains M$60-100; odd hr) is the best restaurant in town. It's located just before the turnoff to Sacbé Bungalows, but is often closed.

Santa Elena is 16km southeast of Uxmal and 8km north of Kabah – for details of bus services from Uxmal, see opposite; from Ticul, see p177.

KABAH

These **ruins** (admission M$34; 9am-5pm), 23km southeast of Uxmal, are right astride Hwy 261. The guard shack–souvenir shop–office sells snacks and cold drinks. The bulk of the restored ruins are on the east side of the highway.

On entering, head to your right to climb the stairs of the structure closest to the highway, **El Palacio de los Mascarones** (Palace of the Masks). Standing in front of it is the Altar de los Glifos, whose immediate area is littered with many stones carved with glyphs. The palace's façade is an amazing sight, covered in nearly 300 masks of Chac, the rain god or sky serpent. Most of their huge curling noses are broken off; the best intact beaks are at the building's southern end. These noses may have given the palace its modern Maya name, Codz Poop (Rolled Mat; it's pronounced more like 'Codes Pope' than some Elizabethan curse).

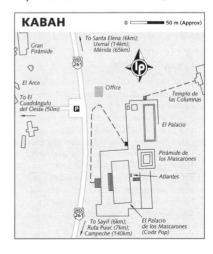

KABAH   0 ⊢━━━━ 50 m (Approx)

To Santa Elena (6km);
Uxmal (14km);
Mérida (65km)

Gran Pirámide

MEX 261

El Arco

Office

To El Cuadrángulo del Oeste (50m)

P

Templo de las Columnas

El Palacio

Pirámide de los Mascarones

Atlantes

MEX 261

To Sayil (6km);
Ruta Puuc (7km);
Campeche (140km)

El Palacio de los Mascarones (Codz Pop)

When you've had your fill of noses, head north and around to the back of the Poop to check out the two restored **atlantes** (an atlas – plural 'atlantes' – is a male figure used as a supporting column). These are especially interesting, as they're some of the very few three-dimensional human figures you'll see at the Maya sites covered in this book. One is headless and the other wears a jaguar mask atop his head.

Descend the steps near the *atlantes* and turn left, passing the small **Pirámide de los Mascarones**, to reach the plaza containing **El Palacio**. The palace's broad façade has several doorways, two of which have a column in the center. These columned doorways and the groups of decorative *columnillas* (little columns) on the upper part of the façade are characteristic of the Puuc architectural style.

Steps on the north side of El Palacio's plaza put you on a path leading about 200m through the jungle to the **Templo de las Columnas** (watch out for the 'tourist trap' on the way – a person-sized hole in the middle of the pathway). This building has more rows of decorative columns on the upper part of its façade.

West of El Palacio, across the highway, a path leads up the slope and passes to the south of a high mound of stones that was once the **Gran Pirámide** (Great Pyramid). The path curves to the right and comes to a large restored **monumental arch**. It's said that the *sacbé*, or cobbled and elevated ceremonial road, leading from here goes through the jungle all the way to Uxmal, terminating at a smaller arch; in the other direction it goes to Labná. Once, all of the Yucatán Peninsula

was connected by these marvelous 'white roads' of rough limestone.

At present nothing of the *sacbé* is visible, and the rest of the area west of the highway is a maze of unmarked, overgrown paths leading off into the jungle.

There's good, affordable lodging about 8km north of Kabah at Bungalows Sacbé and the Flycatcher Inn; for details, see p171.

Getting There & Away

Kabah is 104km from Mérida. For details of bus services from Uxmal, see p170, and p157 for details on tours. You only get about a 25-minute visit on the ATS excursion bus.

Buses will usually make flag stops at the entrance to the ruins. Many visitors come to Kabah by car and may be willing to give you a lift out.

RUTA PUUC

Just 5km south of Kabah on Hwy 261, a road branches off to the east and winds past the ruins of Sayil, Xlapak and Labná, eventually leading to the Grutas de Loltún. This is the Ruta Puuc (Puuc Route), and its sites offer some marvelous architectural detail and a deeper acquaintance with the Puuc Maya civilization.

For details of bus services from Uxmal, see p170, and p177 for details on catching the ATS excursion bus, the only regularly scheduled public transport on the route. During the busy winter season it's often possible to hitch rides from one site to the next. The best way to appreciate the sites is by rented car or taxi, especially if you plan on taking time at each site.

Sayil

The ruins of **Sayil** (admission M$34; ☾ 8am-5pm) are 4.5km from the junction of the Ruta Puuc with Hwy 261.

Sayil is best known for **El Palacio**, the huge three-tiered building with a façade some 85m long and reminiscent of the Minoan palace on Crete. The distinctive columns of Puuc architecture are used here over and over, either as supports for the lintels, as decoration between doorways and as a frieze above them, alternating with huge stylized Chac masks and 'descending gods.' The building was under renovation when we passed through, but the project is slated to

---

PYRAMID SCHEME

It's tempting to skirt the (often unpoliced) signs that prohibit climbing, but please climb only where it's allowed. Be careful, and if you're worried about heights, give this sure-fire technique a try: zigzag up or down the steps, making diagonal passes to either side of the stairway. Once you master this style, you'll never descend again using the embarrassing sit-and-bump-down-on-your-butt method, or the painful trip-and-fall-to-your-near-death method, which is why most of the pyramids are closed to climbing in the first place.

be finished before this book hits the shelves. Ascending the *palacio* beyond its first level was not allowed at press time.

Taking the path south from the palace for about 400m and bearing left, you come to the temple named **El Mirador**, whose rooster-like roofcomb was once painted a bright red. About 100m beyond El Mirador, beneath a protective *palapa,* is a stela bearing the relief of a fertility god with an enormous phallus, now sadly weathered.

Grupo Sur is a bit further, and offers beautifully jungle-covered ruins with tree roots twisting through the walls.

Xlapak

From the entrance gate at Sayil, it's 6km east to the entrance gate at **Xlapak** (admission free; 8am-5pm). The name means 'Old Walls' in Maya and was a general term among local people for ancient ruins.

The ornate **palacio** at Xlapak (shla-pak) is quite a bit smaller than those at Kabah and Sayil, measuring only about 20m in length. It's decorated with the inevitable Chac masks, columns and colonnettes and fretted geometric latticework of the Puuc style. The building is interesting and on a bit of a lean. Plenty of mot-mots brighten up the surrounding forests.

Labná

If you're short on time, **Labná** (admission M$34; 8am-5pm) is the Ruta Puuc site not to miss. Its setting on a flat, open area is striking, and if no one has been through before you for a while, at each doorway you approach you're likely to startle groups of long-tailed mot-mots into flight. Between the birds and the vegetation growing atop the palace, you can almost imagine yourself one of the first people to see the site in centuries. OK, you may need to squint a bit to ignore the trimmed grass.

Archaeologists believe that at one point in the 9th century, some 3000 Maya lived at Labná. To support such numbers in these arid hills, water was collected in *chultunes* (Maya cisterns). At Labná's peak there were some 60 *chultunes* in and around the city; several are still visible. From the entrance gate at Xlapak, it's 3.5km east to the gate at Labná.

EL PALACIO

The first building you come to at Labná is one of the longest in the Puuc region, and

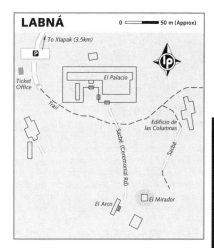

LABNÁ 0 ⸻ 50 m (Approx)

To Xlapak (3.5km)
El Palacio
Ticket Office
Trail
Edificio de las Columnas
Sacbé (Ceremonial Rd)
Sacbé
El Arco
El Mirador

much of its interesting decorative carving is in good shape, thanks in part to a massive renovation project completed in 2006. On the west corner of the main structure's façade, straight in from the big tree near the center of the complex, is a serpent's head with a human face peering out from between its jaws, the symbol of the planet Venus. Toward the hill from this is an impressive Chac mask, and nearby is the lower half of a human figure (possibly a ballplayer) in loincloth and leggings.

The lower level has several more well-preserved Chac masks, and the upper level contains a large *chultún* that still holds water. The view of the site and the hills beyond from there is impressive.

From the palace a limestone-paved *sacbé* leads to El Arco.

EL ARCO

Labná is best known for its magnificent arch, once part of a building that separated two quadrangular courtyards. It now appears to be a gate joining two small plazas. The corbeled structure, 3m wide and 6m high, is well preserved, and the reliefs decorating its upper façade are exuberantly Puuc in style.

Flanking the west side of the arch are carved *na* with multitiered roofs. Also on these walls, the remains of the building that adjoined the arch, are lattice patterns atop a serpentine design. Archaeologists believe a high roofcomb once sat over the fine arch and its flanking rooms.

EL MIRADOR

Standing on the opposite side of the arch and separated from it by the *sacbé* is a pyramid known as El Mirador, topped by a temple. The pyramid itself is largely stone rubble. The temple, with its 5m-high roofcomb, is well positioned to be a lookout, thus its name.

GRUTAS DE LOLTÚN

About 15km north and east of Labná, a sign points left to the Grutas de Loltún, 5km further northeast. The road passes through lush orchards and some banana and palm groves, an agreeable sight in this dry region.

The **Grutas de Loltún** (Loltún Caverns; admission M$54, parking M$10; �9am-5pm; 🚻), one of the largest dry-cave systems on the Yucatán Peninsula, provided a treasure trove of data for archaeologists studying the Maya. Carbon dating of artifacts found here reveals that the caves were used by humans 2200 years ago. Chest-high murals of hands, faces, animals and geometric motifs were apparent as recently as 20 years ago, but so many people have touched them that scarcely a trace remains, though some handprints have been restored. A few pots are displayed in a niche, and an impressive bas-relief, El Guerrero, guards the entrance. Other than that, you'll mostly see floodlit limestone formations, or the poorly aimed floodlights shining into your eyes.

To explore the labyrinth, you must take a scheduled guided tour at 9:30am, 11am, 12:30pm, 2pm, 3pm or 4pm, but they may depart earlier if enough people are waiting, or switch to English if the group warrants it (tours are usually in Spanish). The services of the guides are included in the admission price, though they expect a small tip afterwards. Tours last about one hour and 20 minutes, with lots of lengthy stops. Some guides' presentations are long on legends (and jokes about disappearing mothers-in-law) and short on geological and historical information.

Food is available at the *parador turístico* (roadside restaurant) across the highway from the caves' parking lot. A tiny shop near the entrance sells snacks, water and beer.

Getting There & Away

Renting a car is the best option for reaching the Grutas, and once you're out of Mérida it's easy going on pretty good roads.

There is a bus service to Oxkutzcab (osh-kootz-kahb; M$44, 1½ hours), with departures at 8:30am and 12:30pm, from the Noreste bus terminal in Mérida. Loltún is 7km southwest of Oxkutzcab, and there is usually some transportation along the road. *Camionetas* (pickups) and *camiones* (trucks) charge about M$10 for a ride

A taxi from Oxkutzcab may cost M$100 or so one way.

RUINAS DE MAYAPÁN

These **ruins** (admission M$27; �8am-5pm) are some 50km southeast of Mérida. Though far less impressive than many Maya sites, Mayapán is historically significant, its main attractions

---

THE RISE OF MAYAPÁN & THE DEATH WARRANT OF MAYA INDEPENDENCE

The rise of Mayapán played an integral role in the ultimate demise of Maya rule in the region. The city was supposedly founded by Kukulcán (Quetzalcóatl) in 1007, shortly after the former ruler of Tula arrived in Yucatán. His dynasty, the Cocom, organized a confederation of city-states that included Uxmal, Chichén Itzá and many other notable cities. Despite their alliance, animosity arose between the Cocomes of Mayapán and the Itzáes of Chichén Itzá during the late 12th century, and the Cocomes stormed Chichén Itzá, forcing the Itzáe rulers into exile. The Cocom dynasty emerged supreme in all of northern Yucatán.

Cocom supremacy lasted for almost 250 years, until the ruler of Uxmal, Ah Xupán Xiú, led a rebellion of the oppressed city-states and overthrew Cocom hegemony. The capital of Mayapán was utterly destroyed and remained uninhabited ever after.

But struggles for power continued in the region until 1542, when Francisco de Montejo (the Younger) conquered T'ho and established Mérida. At that point the current lord of Maní and ruler of the Xiú people, Ah Kukum Xiú, proposed to Montejo a military alliance against the Cocomes, his ancient rivals. Montejo accepted, and Xiú was baptized as a Christian, taking the name Francisco de Montejo Xiú (original, no?). The Cocomes were defeated and – too late – the Xiú rulers realized that they had signed the death warrant of Maya independence.

LEAVING THE TOURIST TRAIL BEHIND: DIY ADVENTURE IN YUCATÁN

This book only touches the surface of the great adventures to be had in this region. Here's some ideas to get you started as you leave the guidebook behind for a few days of DIY adventure.

- **Tekit** is just off the road to Mayapán and has a cenote worth visiting.

- Friar Diego de Landa burnt 5000 idols, 13 altars, 27 religious and historic codices, and 197 ceremonial vases in an auto-da-fé in 1562 in the town of **Maní**. The town has a nice cathedral and the Príncipe de Tutul-Xiu restaurant's *poc chuc* is so popular that families will drive all the way here from Mérida to dive into the tender-as-a-baby's-butt slow-cooked pork.

- **La Ruta de Los Conventos** is a new tourist route taking you to colonial-era convents in the towns of Maní, Oxkutzcab, Teabo, Mama, Chumayel, Tekax and Yotholín.

- The seldom-visited town of **Yodznot,** west of Chichén Itzá on the old highway, is developing grassroots tourism.

---

are clustered in a compact core and visitors usually have the place to themselves. It is one of few sites where you can ascend to the top of the pyramid for a nice view.

Don't confuse the ruins of Mayapán with the Maya village of the same name, some 40km southeast of the ruins, past the town of Teabo.

Exploring the Site

The city of Mayapán was large, with a population estimated to be around 12,000; it covered 4 sq km, all surrounded by a great defensive wall, a testament to the bellicose époque, which was its heyday. More than 3500 buildings, 20 cenotes and traces of the city wall were mapped by archaeologists working in the 1950s and in 1962. The late post-Classic workmanship is inferior to that of the great age of Maya art.

Among the structures that have been restored is the **Castillo de Kukulcán**, a climbable pyramid with fresco fragments around its base and, at its rear side, friezes depicting decapitated warriors. The reddish color is still faintly visible. The **Templo Redondo** (Round Temple) is vaguely reminiscent of El Caracol at Chichén Itzá. Close by is Itzmal Chen, a cenote that was a major Maya religious sanctuary.

Getting There & Away

The Ruinas de Mayapán are just off Hwy 18, a few kilometers southwest of the town of Telchaquillo. LUS runs hourly 2nd-class buses between 5:30am and 8pm from the Noreste bus terminal in Mérida (M$14 each way, 1½ hours) that will let you off near the entrance to the ruins and pick you up on your way back.

Again, you may want to consider renting a car to get here.

CENOTES DE CUZAMÁ

Three kilometers east of the town of Cuzamá, accessed from the small village of Chunkanan, are the **Cenotes de Cuzamá** (for horse, driver, & up to 4 people M$150; 9am-5pm), a series of three amazing limestone sinkholes accessed by horse-drawn railcart in an old henequen hacienda.

The fun, horse-drawn ride will jar your fillings loose while showing you attractive scenes of the surrounding, overgrown agave fields. Iguana sightings are a sure bet here, but keen eyes can also see vultures or caracaras, as well as other birds, lizards and the occasional rabbit or two. One of the cenotes is featured in much of Yucatán's tourist literature, and all three are spectacular, with rope-like roots descending along with ethereal shafts of light to the crystal-clear, deep-blue water. Though you may find yourself sharing a dip with other bathers, it's more likely that the drivers will time the trip so that you have most of the swimming to yourself. Several have steep stairways or ladders that are often slippery, so use caution at all times.

It's possible to rent a *palapa* in Chunkanan for around M$130, but bring your own hammock and mosquito net.

To get here by car, take Hwy 180 toward Cancún until you get to a turnoff for Ticopo on the right; after Akankeh (there's a small pyramid here), bear left to reach Cuzamá. From there, head east at the cathedral for 3km to the cenotes. Signs will lead the way, and keep your eyes peeled for kids, dogs, livestock and sun-drunk iguanas…all will be on the road at some point. Shared vans leave for Cuzamá (M$30 round-trip, two hours) from Mérida's Parque de San Juan. If you use the vans, you'll need to take a peditrike from the van stop to Chunkanan, an additional M$10.

TICUL

☎ 997 / pop 31,147

Ticul, 30km east of Uxmal, is the largest town in this ruin-rich region. It's dusty and quiet, with certainly no nightlife other than perhaps a watering hole, but it has hotels and restaurants and transportation, and makes an attractive base for day trips to nearby ruins, though people going by public transportation to the Ruta Puuc sites will need to go to Muna or Santa Elena first. Ticul is also a center for fine *huipil* weaving, and ceramics made here from the local red clay are renowned throughout the Yucatán.

Orientation & Information

Ticul's main street is Calle 23, sometimes called 'Calle Principal', starting from the highway and going past the *mercado* (market) to the main plaza, Plaza Mayor. A **post office** (8am-2:30pm Mon-Fri) faces the plaza, as do two banks, Banamex and HSBC, with ATMs. Telmex has an office here.

Several internet cafés are dotted around near the town center. **Café Trovadores** (internet per hr M$10, coffee M$20; 9am-9pm) has a few computers, and sells coffee and pastries.

Sights & Activities

Because of the number of Maya ruins in the vicinity, from which to steal building blocks, and the number of Maya in the area 'needing' conversion to Christianity, Franciscan friars built many churches in the region. Among them is Ticul's **Iglesia de San Antonio de Padua**, construction of which dates from the late 16th century. Although looted on several occasions, the church has some original touches, among them the stone statues of friars in primitive style flanking the side entrances and a Black Christ altarpiece ringed by crude medallions.

Diagonally opposite the Plaza Mayor is the recently built Plaza de la Cultura, which is all cement and stone but nevertheless an agreeable place to take the evening breeze,

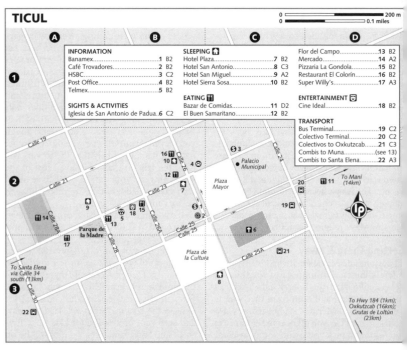

TICUL

INFORMATION		SLEEPING		Flor del Campo	13	B2
Banamex	1 B2	Hotel Plaza	7 B2	Mercado	14	A2
Café Trovadores	2 B2	Hotel San Antonio	8 C3	Pizzaria La Gondola	15	B2
HSBC	3 C2	Hotel San Miguel	9 A2	Restaurant El Colorín	16	B2
Post Office	4 B2	Hotel Sierra Sosa	10 B2	Super Willy's	17	A3
Telmex	5 B2					
		EATING		ENTERTAINMENT		
SIGHTS & ACTIVITIES		Bazar de Comidas	11 D2	Cine Ideal	18	B2
Iglesia de San Antonio de Padua	6 C2	El Buen Samaritano	12 B2			
				TRANSPORT		
				Bus Terminal	19	C2
				Colectivo Terminal	20	C2
				Colectivos to Oxkutzcab	21	C3
				Combis to Muna	(see 13)	
				Combis to Santa Elena	22	A3

enjoy the view of the church and greet passing townspeople.

Saturday mornings in Ticul are picturesque: Calle 23 near the market is closed to motorized traffic, and the street fills with three-wheeled cycles transporting shoppers between the market and their homes.

Sleeping

Hotel San Miguel (Calle 28 No 295D; s/d M$100/130; P) Near the market, the friendly management offers worn, simple rooms (some musty) with fan and bathroom. The beds put a spring in your sleep, but maybe not in your step the next day.

Hotel Sierra Sosa (☎/fax 972-0008; Calle 26 No 199A; s M$150, d/tr M$170/190, air-con extra M$60;) The Sierra Sosa is just northwest of the Plaza Mayor. It's friendly and a bit run-down, but has good beds and OK bathrooms.

Hotel San Antonio (☎ 972-1983; cnr Calles 25A & 26; s M$260, d/tr M$300/350; P) A clean lobby with TV and shiny tiled floors sets a good impression that is confirmed by rooms with decent beds; some rooms have great views of the Plaza de la Cultura. The hotel lacks character, but here in Ticul, that's kind of reassuring. All rooms have TV, phone and clean bathroom – there's also off-street parking and a pleasant restaurant.

Hotel Plaza (☎ 972-0484; www.hotelplazayucatan.com; cnr Calles 23 & 26; d/ste M$360/460;) Spacious rooms with white-tiled floors, firm beds and small but fun balconies make this a nice choice. The old building adds character, though the street-facing rooms are sometimes noisy. You could eat off the bathroom floors. Laundry service, wi-fi, phone and pickup/drop-off in Mérida are additional reasons to consider staying here.

Eating

Flor del Campo (☎ 972-1875; cnr Calles 23 & 28; juice M$8-15; 6:30am-9pm Mon-Sat, 6:30am-3pm Sun) Juice up for the day at this tiny place, which just has chilled juices (no smoothies). It's like sipping a part of the rainbow.

El Buen Samaritano (Calle 23) Bakes bread and sweet rolls.

Restaurant El Colorín (☎ 972-0094; Calle 26 No 199B; set meal M$35; 7am-9pm) A cheap restaurant, half a block northwest of Plaza Mayor, offering homemade meals.

Pizzaria La Gondola (☎ 972-0112; Calle 23 No 208; mains M$40-90; 8am-1pm & 5-11pm) A clean place on the corner that's open late, it has sandwiches and slightly pricey pizzas with the usual plethora of toppings. 'Order by number' options make it easy for non-Spanish speakers to get exactly what they want.

Super Willy's (Calle 23) Across from the market, this is a small supermarket with a big variety of groceries and household items.

Ticul's lively **mercado** (Calle 28A btwn Calles 21 & 23) provides all the ingredients for picnics and snacks, and offers nice photo ops, too. It also has lots of those wonderful eateries where the food is good, the portions generous and the prices low. Stalls at the new **Bazar de Comidas** (cnr Calles 25 & 24) serve inexpensive prepared food.

Entertainment

Cine Ideal (Calle 23 btwn Calles 26A & 28) shows mostly Spanish-dubbed films.

Getting There & Away

BUS, COLECTIVO & TAXI

Ticul's 24-hour **bus terminal** (Calle 24) is behind the massive church. Mayab runs frequent 2nd-class buses between Mérida and Ticul (M$40, 1½ hours) from 4:30am to 9pm. Mayab and ADO run 11 buses to Felipe Carrillo Puerto (M$100, four hours), frequent ones to Oxkutzcab (M$8 to M$12) and five daily to Chetumal (M$150, six hours). There are also eight Mayab buses to Cancún daily (M$210, six hours), three of which also serve Tulum (M$150) and Playa del Carmen (M$170). ADO and Super Expresso have less frequent 2nd- and 1st-class services, respectively, to some of these destinations.

Colectivos (shared vans) go direct to Mérida's Parque de San Juan (M$33, 1½ hours) from their shiny new **colectivo terminal** (cnr Calles 24 & 25) as soon as they're full between 5am and 7:30pm. _Combis_ for Oxkutzcab (M$10, 30 minutes) leave from Calle 25A on the south side of the church between 7am and 8:30pm.

Colectivos to Santa Elena (M$10), between Uxmal and Kabah, depart from Calle 30 between 6:15am and 7:30pm. They take Hwy 02 and drop you in Santa Elena to catch another bus northwest to Uxmal (15km) or south to Kabah (3.5km).

You can take a _combi_ or bus to Muna (M$10) from in front of Flor del Campo on Calle 23 near Calle 28, and then south to Uxmal. Ruta Puuc–bound travelers can

---

UNDERSTANDING THE MODERN MAYA

The area between Ticul and Tihosuco is truly the Maya heartland. Indeed, the Maya in these parts entered the 21st century continuing to honor the gods of rain, wind and agriculture, just as their ancestors had done before them.

Yucatán state has the second-highest percentage of indigenous-language speakers in all of Mexico, after Oaxaca. But the number of Maya speakers is rapidly declining. In 2000, 37% of Yucatecans spoke Maya, just five years later only 33.9% claimed they spoke the language. So where have all the Maya gone? Many have moved to big tourist cities like Cancún, while others have moved all the way up to the US. Many small Maya communities are beginning to welcome tourists in an effort to keep young folks from fleeing to the cities. It's ironic, but inviting foreigners in may prove the best way to maintain traditions.

The homes of today's rural Maya are still rectangular wood-framed huts with lean-to roofs of palm. The walls are made of bamboo poles or branches, and the spaces between the poles are often filled with mud to keep pests out. Contemporary Maya prefer hammocks to beds, just like their ancestors.

Anywhere from a stone's throw to an hour's walk from a Maya hut is a *milpa* (corn field). Corn tortillas remain a staple of the Maya diet, but the Maya also raise pigs and turkeys and produce honey, squash and other crops, which they sell from town markets. Many of the younger generation, particularly men, hitchhike out to work for a week in the larger towns such as Playa del Carmen or Cancún and return for a day or two on long weekends or holidays. A *small* family will have about five children.

---

catch a 6:30am bus from Ticul to Muna and pick up the ATS tour bus (M$50) for Labná, Sayil, Xlapak, Kabah and Uxmal at 9am on its way from Mérida. It returns to Muna at 3pm. Any of the buses leaving Ticul before 8am for Muna (or Mérida) will get you to Muna in time to catch the ATS Ruta Puuc bus. Another way would be to catch a *colectivo* from Ticul to Santa Elena, then walk a few blocks to Hwy 261, cross it and wait for the Ruta Puuc bus to come by at about 9:30am.

Alternatively, for M$550 you can get a taxi in Ticul that will stop at the Grutas de Loltún, Labná, Sayil, Xlapak, Kabah and Uxmal, and wait for you while you see each place. If you wish to stay at Uxmal for the 7pm sound-and-light show, the cost is M$100.

CAR

The quickest way to Uxmal, Kabah and the Ruta Puuc sites is via Santa Elena. From central Ticul, go west to Calle 34 and turn south; it heads straight to Santa Elena.

Those headed east to Quintana Roo and the Caribbean coast can take Hwy 184 from Ticul through Oxkutzcab to Tzucacab and José María Morelos (which has a gas station). At Polyuc, 130km from Ticul, a road turns left (east), ending after 80km in Felipe Carrillo Puerto. The right fork of the road goes south to Laguna Bacalar.

Between Oxkutzcab and Felipe Carrillo Puerto or Bacalar there are few restaurants or gas stations, and no hotels. Mostly you see small, typical Yucatecan villages, with their traditional Maya thatched houses, *topes* (speed bumps), agricultural activity and iguanas.

TICUL TO TIHOSUCO

The route from Ticul to Tihosuco, in Quintana Roo, is seldom traveled by tourists. Some might say, 'There's nothing to see.' But others will welcome the opportunity to travel through farmland and jungle and see glimpses of Maya life that have remained the same for centuries. Part of the route is called La Ruta de los Conventos (The Route of the Convents), as each of these tiny villages has a cathedral or church, many in beautiful disrepair. Prepare to hear mainly Maya, though many people speak Spanish as well.

The towns of Oxkutzcab, Tekax and Tihosuco offer budget accommodations. Beyond Oxkutzcab, the towns along this route are linked by *combis* and, less frequently, local buses; they may be hailed from the roadside.

Oxkutzcab

Located 16km southeast of Ticul, Oxkutzcab is renowned for its daily produce market and colonial church. Markets were the principal means of trade for the ancient Maya, and the peninsula's indigenous people still travel from the countryside to central communities to exchange produce at stalls beside a main square. Oxkutzcab is such a community.

Here, alongside Hwy 184, which becomes a slow-moving, two-lane road as it passes through the town center, the visitor can't miss seeing the magnificent **Franciscan mission**, out front of which is the sprawling produce market.

The church is remarkable mostly for its ornamental façade, at the center of which is a stone statue of St Francis, the mission patron. The church, which was constructed at a snail's pace from 1640 to 1693, is also remarkable for its magnificent altarpiece. Indeed, it's one of only a few baroque altarpieces in the Yucatán to survive the revolts that have occurred since its construction.

A mural in the plaza across from the market depicts inquisitor Friar Diego de Landa's auto-da-fé in Maní, when he burnt thousands of idols (see boxed text, p35).

Hotel Puuc (☎ 997-975-0103; cnr Calles 55 & 44; s/d M$230/280; P ⊠) offers a great deal for the price, with air-con in every business-hotel-style room. The beds are Flintstone firm, and there's a pretty good restaurant downstairs.

Tekax

Unlike the church at Oxkutzcab, the one in Tekax has been looted a couple of times, initially during the War of the Castes and later during the Mexican Revolution.

Situated in an increasingly prosperous area, due to a successful crop switch from corn to sugarcane and citrus, Tekax residents recently replaced the church's damaged floor with a beautiful tiled floor and added a lovely new stone altar. According to *Maya Missions: Exploring the Spanish Colonial Churches of Yucatán*, a fabulous book by Richard and Rosalind Perry, during construction of the church one of the church's belfries collapsed, burying (and presumably crushing) the many indigenous laborers under tons of rubble. Miraculously, as local legend has it, no one lost their life in the collapse.

Also noteworthy is the shape of the church, which undoubtedly was constructed of materials taken from nearby Maya temples. The general form of the church is that of a three-tiered pyramid. Possibly the architecture was based on the Maya structure from which the blocks were taken.

Tihosuco

Tihosuco, located inside the state of Quintana Roo, was a major military outpost for the Spanish during the late 16th century and for 300 years thereafter. During this time the town came under numerous Maya assaults, and in 1686 it was attacked, though not sacked, by pirates led by legendary Dutch buccaneer Lorencillo.

During many of those attacks, the Spaniards retreated to the heavily fortified 17th-century church at the town center, which for much of its life served as both a house of God and an arsenal and stronghold. But the town and church fell to rebel hands in 1866 following a long siege, and much of the magnificent building was gutted. What remains of the once-great church is still worth investigating. Services are still held inside, as in many other roofless churches in the region.

Also in Tihosuco, housed in an 18th-century building one block straight ahead of the church, is the **Museo de la Guerra de Castas** (Museum of the War of the Castes; admission M$5; ☺ 10am-6pm Tue-Sun). It does a good job of detailing the more than three centuries of oppression suffered by the Maya on the peninsula, but only a couple of explanations are translated into English. There's a small botanical garden here as well.

From Tihosuco, it's a fast ride up Hwy 295 to Valladolid (p193). Going the other way, Hwy 295 goes south to Felipe Carrillo Puerto (p134).

WEST & NORTH OF MÉRIDA

CELESTÚN
☎ 988 / pop 6423

West of Mérida, Celestún is a sleepy sun-scorched fishing village that moves at a turtle's pace – and that's the way locals like it. There's a pretty little square in the center of the town and some nice beaches (though the water is a bit turbid), but the real draw here is Reserva de la Biósfera Ría Celestún, a wildlife sanctuary abounding in waterfowl, with flamingos as the star attraction.

It makes a good beach-and-bird day trip from Mérida, and it's also a great place to kick back and do nothing for a few days, especially if you've become road weary. Fishing boats dot the appealing white-sand beach that stretches to the north for kilometers, and afternoon breezes cool the town on most days. Celestún is sheltered by the peninsula's southward curve, resulting in an abundance of marine life and less violent seas during the season of *nortes* (winds and rains arriving from the north).

Orientation & Information

All you need to know is that Calle 11 is the road into town (it comes due west from Mérida), ending at Calle 12, the road paralleling the beach, along which lie most of the restaurants and hotels. Don't plan on using high-speed internet here, and bring lots of cash as there are no banks or ATMs.

Sights & Activities

RESERVA DE LA BIÓSFERA RÍA CELESTÚN

The 591-sq-km Reserva de la Biósfera Ría Celestún is home to a huge variety of animals and birdlife, including a large flamingo colony.

The best months to see the flamingos are from March or April to about September, outside the season of the *nortes*. Morning is the best time of day, though from 4pm onward the birds tend to concentrate in one area after the day's feeding, which can make for good viewing.

Tours

In Celestún, you can hire a boat for bird-watching either from the bridge on the highway into town (about 1.5km inland) or from the beach itself. Boats depart from outside Restaurant Celestún, at the foot of Calle 11. The restaurant's beachfront *palapa* is a pleasant place to wait for a group to accumulate, rather than the tiny *palapa* at the boats themselves. Otherwise, Turitransmérida in Mérida organizes flamingo tours (for details, see p157).

Unfortunately, hiring a boat can be a frustrating experience, and a lesson in false expectations. Knowing what to expect will save you some frustration. First, operators tend to try to collect as many people as possible, often telling one couple 'Sure, the tour will leave at 8:30am,' and another couple 'We'll wait for you until 9am.' Prices are often quoted assuming eight passengers, but if only four or six people show up that means the quoted price

rises, often to the irritation of people who've waited 30 minutes to an hour. You can solve this problem by coming up with a group of eight on your own.

Trips from the beach last 2½ to three hours and begin with a ride along the coast for several kilometers, during which you can expect to see egrets, herons, cormorants, sandpipers and many other bird species. The boat then turns into the mouth of the *ría* (estuary) and passes through a 'petrified forest,' where tall coastal trees once belonging to a freshwater ecosystem were killed by saltwater intrusion long ago and remain standing, hard as rock.

Continuing up the *ría* takes you under the highway bridge where the other tours begin and beyond which lie the flamingos. Depending on the tide, the hour and the season, you may see hundreds or thousands of the colorful birds. Don't encourage your captain to approach them too closely; a startled flock taking wing can result in injuries and deaths (for the birds). In addition to taking you to the flamingos, the captain will wend through a 200m mangrove tunnel and visit one or both (as time and inclination allow) of the freshwater cenote-springs welling into the salt water of the estuary, where you can take a refreshing dip.

Currently, a boat from the beach costs M$1200 to operate; the average price with eight people ends up around M$150 per passenger. If it's just you and a friend, try asking for M$1000 for the boat. If you remember that trips happen on Mexican time, you'll enjoy it a lot more.

Tours from the bridge, where there is a parking lot, ticket booth and a place to wait for fellow passengers, are slightly cheaper and last about 1½ hours. For M$140 per passenger (maximum six passengers), you get to see the flamingos, mangrove tunnel and spring. It's also possible to add a trip from the bridge south to the 'petrified forest,' for an additional M$100 per passenger and a total time of about 2½ hours.

With either the bridge or beach option, your captain may or may not speak English. An English-speaking guide can be hired at the bridge for about M$200 per hour; this reduces the maximum possible number of passengers, of course. Bring snacks, water and sunscreen for the longer tours. There is no bank in town, and neither credit cards nor traveler's checks are accepted by the tour operators.

BEACH & BIRDING

North of town, beyond the small navy post, you'll find more secluded stretches of beach. In the same area, but inland of the road, lies a large section of scrub stretching east to the estuary that also provides good birding opportunities. South and east of town, toward the abandoned Hacienda Real de Salinas, is another good area for nature observation. Flamingos, white pelicans, cormorants, anhingas and many other species frequent the shores and waters of the *ría* (river).

HACIENDA REAL DE SALINAS

This abandoned hacienda a few kilometers south and east of town once produced dyewood and salt, and served as a summer home for a Campeche family. It's 5km in from the mouth of the estuary. Out in the *ría* you can see a cairn marking an *ojo de agua dulce* (freshwater spring) that once supplied the hacienda.

The buildings are decaying in a most scenic way; you can still see shells in the wall mixed into the building material, as well as pieces of French roof tiles that served as ballast in ships on the way from Europe. Many intact tiles with the brickworks' name and location, Marseille, are still visible in what's left of the roofs. The hacienda makes a good bicycle excursion from town. Coming south, go left

at the Y junction, or turn right to reach El Lastre (The Ballast), a peninsula between the estuary and its western arm. Flamingos, white pelicans and other birds are sometimes seen here. If the water is high enough, it's possible to ask your flamingo tour captain to try stopping here on the way back from the birds.

Sleeping

Celestún's hotels are all on Calle 12, within a short walk of one another. The following list runs from south to north. Try to book ahead if you want a sea view, especially on weekends.

Hostel Ría Celestún (☎ 916-2597; hostelriacelestun @hotmail.com; cnr Calles 12 & 13; dm M$60-70, s/d low season M$80/100, high season M$100/180; 🖳) This hostel offers a good cheap sleep, with single-sex or mixed fan-cooled dorms (slightly dusty), kitchen and laundry facilities, a courtyard and TV room for common areas, bicycle rentals and internet access. The staff are great sources of info about the area, and can provide directions for doing just about anything.

Hotel Sofía (☎ in Mérida 999-189-8959; Calle 12; s/d M$150/300; 🅿) The rooms smell a bit, but they are pretty well maintained and a decent value. It also has secure parking and the owners let guests use the (hand) laundry facilities.

Hotel María del Carmen (☎ /fax 916-2170; cnr Calles 12 & 15; d with fan/air-con M$250/300; 🖳 🅿) This place

YUCATÁN STATE

HENEQUEN: A SMELLY, BITTER HARVEST

Yucatán state would have been little more than a provincial backwater if it weren't for a spiky son-of-a-bitch-of-a-plant named Agave Fourcroydes. Some call it henequen, others call it sisal; call it what you will, the up-to-2m-high lanced-leaved plant used to create strong maritime rope was chlorophyll gold from the late 19th century to the end of WWI for the 'sisal barons' of Yucatán.

Today henequen is still cultivated in the region; however, cheap synthetics and imported Brazilian fibers are now dominating the market. But the state still has its hand in the production of sisal ropes: the fibers from Brazil are now woven into rope in the *maquiladoras* (for-export factories) around the state. You will normally smell a henequen plant before you see it, as they emit a putrid, excremental odor. And just like in the old days when indigenous labor was employed under slave conditions, the *maquiladoras* of today still create huge profit margins, while paying employees only M$44 per day.

Once planted, henequen can grow virtually untended for seven years. Thereafter, the plants are stripped for fiber, yielding about 25 leaves annually. A plant may be productive for upwards of two decades. To get at the fibrous interior, the leaves are cut off by machete, taken to a factory and crushed between heavy rollers. The pulpy vegetable matter is scraped away to reveal fiber strands up to 1.5m in length, which are slightly stretchable and resistant to marine organisms.

Growing henequen on the peninsula is still economically viable, if barely. The decline has been hard on the few Maya farm workers who still struggle to keep the defibering machines operating on a few former haciendas. The town of Ake, east of Mérida, has one of only three remaining working rasping machines in the region.

has 14 clean and pleasant beachfront rooms tucked behind a picturesque maroon-colored false front; rooms on the upper floors have balconies facing the sea. Prices drop when things are slow.

Hotel Los Manglares (☎ 998-916-2156; www.hotel manglares.com; Calle 12, 1km north of Calle 11; d M$850, cabana M$1600; 🔀 🖭 🅿 🐾) While the architecture doesn't blend perfectly with the laid-back feel of town, this is a nice upscale choice. The rooms all have sea views and private balconies. The well-appointed cabanas have minikitchens, Jacuzzis and a small common area, making them perfect for families.

Eating

Celestún's specialties are crab, octopus, small shrimp from the lagoon and, of course, fresh fish. Restaurants close early (7:30pm or so) on weeknights.

Restaurante Chivirico (cnr Calles 11 & 12; mains M$60-120; 🕙 10am-7:30pm) A large place with wicker chairs and a TV with Spanish soaps as its ambience, the Chivirico has excellent seafood and is well worth a visit. The *ensalada de jaiba* (crab salad; M$60) is delicious.

Restaurant Los Pamponos (Calle 12, just north of Calle 11; mains M$60-120; 🕙 11am-7pm) A tranquiloer-than-thou joint on the beach, this is a great spot for afternoon drinks on the sand. Try the octopus ceviche or a fish fillet stuffed to the brim with shellfish.

La Playita (mains M$70-120; 🕙 10am-7pm) It's right on the (sometimes windy) beach with great views. Cheap seafood and ceviche are its main draw.

Getting There & Away

Buses from Mérida head for Celestún (M$44, two hours) 17 times daily between 5am and 8pm from Noreste bus terminal. The route terminates at Celestún's plaza, a block inland from Calle 12. Returning buses also run from 5am to 8pm.

By car from Mérida, the best route to Celestún is via the new road out of Umán.

RUINED HACIENDAS ROUTE

A fascinating alternative return route if you're driving out of Celestún is to turn south off Hwy 281 where a sign points to Chunchucmil. The road has frequent potholes along the 25km stretch to Chunchucmil, which is the name of both a ruined henequen hacienda and a nearby Maya archaeological site.

You should ask locally before visiting any of these haciendas. A land dispute kicked off protests in Chunchucmil in 2007. Paying local boys a small tip to show you around goes a long way to ease the mounting tensions regarding who, in fact, owns (and therefore has the right to develop) these haciendas.

After Chunchucmil the road is in good shape (look for the covered Maya mounds as you drive away), and about every 5km passes another ruined hacienda – easy to spot as there's a *futbol* (soccer) pitch in front of each one – all the way to Hacienda Granada, shortly before the road hits old Hwy 180. Several buildings are pretty hard to see from the road, so you'll need to stop frequently to really give them their due. There are two **talleres de arte popular** (pop art workshops) near the church in Granada. Stop by from 10am to 6pm (Monday to Saturday) to watch local women create *jipijapa* (palm frond) hats and baskets.

Hacienda Santa Rosa (☎ 999-910-4852; www.star wood.com/luxury; r M$3290, ste M$4090-4660) is the only hacienda in the area that has been converted into a hotel. The 11 rooms show amazing variety; some have private walled gardens with bathtubs or plunge pools.

DZIBILCHALTÚN

About 17km north of downtown Mérida (a 25-minute drive), **Dzibilchaltún** (Place of Inscribed Flat Stones; admission M$63, children under 13yr free; 🕙 8am-5pm, 5:30am-5pm at equinox) was the longest continuously utilized Maya administrative and ceremonial city, serving the Maya from 1500 BC or earlier until the European conquest in the 1540s. At the height of its greatness, Dzibilchaltún covered 15 sq km. Some 8500 structures were mapped by archaeologists in the 1960s; only a few of these have been excavated and restored. In some ways it's unimpressive if you've already seen larger places, such as Chichén Itzá or Uxmal, but twice a year humble Dzibilchaltún shines. At sunrise on the equinoxes (approximately March 21 and September 22), the sun aligns directly with the main door of the **Templo de las Siete Muñecas** (Temple of the Seven Dolls), which got its name from seven grotesque dolls discovered here during excavations. As the sun rises, the temple doors glow, then 'light up' as the sun passes behind. It also casts a cool square beam on the crumbled wall behind.

Whether you come to strike a Y-shaped 'feel the pyramid power' pose, to snap a picture or just to see what the fuss is about, it's pretty impressive – many who've seen both feel the sunrise here is more spectacular than Chichén Itzá's famous snake (p188), and is well worth getting up at the crack of dawn to witness.

Enter the site along a nature trail that terminates at the modern, air-conditioned **Museo del Pueblo Maya** (8am-4pm Tue-Sun), featuring artifacts from throughout the Maya regions of Mexico, including some superb colonial-era religious carvings and other pieces. Exhibits explaining Maya daily life and beliefs from ancient times until the present are labeled in Spanish and English. Beyond the museum, a path leads to the central plaza, where you'll find an open chapel that dates from early Spanish times (1590–1600).

The **Cenote Xlacah** is more than 40m deep. In 1958 a National Geographic Society diving expedition recovered more than 30,000 Maya artifacts, many of ritual significance, from the cenote. The most interesting of these are now on display in the site's museum. South of the cenote is **Estructura 44** – at 130m it's one of the longest Maya structures in existence.

Parking costs M$10. Minibuses and *colectivos* depart frequently from Mérida's Parque de San Juan for the village of Dzibilchaltún Ruinas (M$8, 30 minutes), a little over 1km from the museum. Taxis will cost around M$120 round-trip.

PROGRESO

969 / pop 35,519

If Mérida's heat has you dying for a quick beach fix, or you want to see the longest wharf (7km) in Mexico, head to Progreso (also known as Puerto Progreso). The beach is fine, well groomed and long; however, except for the small *palapas* erected by restaurants, it's nearly shadeless and is dominated by the view of the wharf, giving it a rather industrial feel. Winds can hit here full force off the Gulf in the afternoon and can blow well into the night, which should mean good kiteboarding and windsurfing, but currently there's neither unless you've brought your own rig. As with other Gulf beaches, the water is murky; visibility even on calm days rarely exceeds 5m. None of this stops Méridanos from coming in droves on weekends, especially in summer. Even on spring weekdays it can be difficult to find a room with a view. Once or twice a week

the streets flood with cruise-ship tourists, but the place can feel empty on off nights, which makes a refreshing change.

There's also a strong evangelical presence here, so on Sunday prepare to see families in their finest clothes heading to church. You're as likely to be approached by people offering pamphlets (sometimes even in English) about redemption as by hammock sellers.

Orientation & Information

Downtown Progreso's streets have new signs in anticipation of the tourist boom, and its confusing dual numbering system has largely been eliminated. Even-numbered streets run east–west; odd ones north–south. The bus terminal, on Calle 29, is west of Calle 82, a block north (toward the water) from the main plaza. From the plaza on Calle 80, it's six short blocks to the waterfront *malecón* (boulevard; Calle 19) and *muelle* (wharf); along the way are two Banamex banks, one with an ATM.

Internet cafés offering so-so access are sprinkled everywhere, especially around the bus terminal and Calles 29 and 78. Some stay open until 9pm, others as late as 1am, charging about M$15 per hour.

Sleeping & Eating

All hotels and restaurants listed are no more than 11 blocks north and east of the bus terminal. Head inland to get cheaper, more authentic eats.

Hotel Miralmar (935-0552; Calle 27 No 124 at Calle 76; s/d with fan M$230/260, d with air-con M$330;) You're probably better off down by the beach, but if you want to keep it real in town, this is a good budget bet. Four blocks inland, it has mostly comfortable beds, decent bathrooms and good natural light. Rooms on the upper floor have better ventilation and private bathrooms, in curious prefab clover-shaped units.

Hotel Tropical Suites (935-1263; fax 935-3093; cnr malecón & Calle 70; d/tw with fan M$250/300, with air-con M$250/350;) Across the street from Hotel Real del Mar, this seaside hotel has 21 tidy, nonmusty, smallish rooms, some with sea views. The 1st-floor rooms facing the street don't afford much privacy.

Hotel Real del Mar (935-0798; cnr malecón & Calle 70; s/d M$200/300, seaside d M$550;) There's large balconies offering panoramic ocean views on both floors of this sprawling hotel. The décor is nice, with tiled floors, a small fountain and a tropical green-and-yellow paint job, and the satiny sheets are '*muy romantico.*'

Restaurant Mary Doly (Calle 25 btwn Calles 74 & 76; breakfast M$18-30, mains M$30-80; 🕑 7am-9pm) Near Hotel Miralmar, this is a homey place with good, cheap seafood and meat dishes and breakfasts. The freshly squeezed orange juice is very refreshing.

Restaurant El Cordobes (☎ 935-2621; cnr Calles 80 & 31; mains M$45-90; 🕑 6am-midnight) Also near Hotel Miralmar, this locals' joint is on the north side of the plaza in a 100-year-old building. Weak 'American' coffee is served quickly, with a warm smile, and it's a perfect place to relax for a bit, sluice down a cerveza and look out on the main plaza.

Restaurant Los Pelícanos (☎ 935-5378; cnr malecón & Calle 70; mains M$55-100, special dishes M$200; 🕑 8am-midnight Mon-Sat, 8am-8pm Sun) By Hotel Real del Mar, Los Pelícanos has a shady terrace, sea views, a good menu and moderate prices, considering its location. It's usually very windy. Peaches and cream is a satisfying way to finish a meal.

Getting There & Away

Progreso is 33km north of Mérida along a fast four-lane highway that's basically a continuation of the Paseo de Montejo. The **bus station** (Calle 29, btwn Calles 80 & 82) has numerous Mérida-bound buses from 5:20am to 10pm. For bus information to Progreso from Mérida, see p164.

EAST OF PROGRESO

Heading east from Progreso, Hwy 27 parallels the coast for 70km, to Dzilam de Bravo, before turning inland. It's a beautiful drive, and you'll pass miles of mixed mangrove clumps and notice that on the right (south) the mud takes on a pink color. Unsurprisingly, this area is named the Laguna Rosada (Pink Lagoon). Heading east from Dzilam, the road continues a further 100km to hit the coast at the charming fishing village of San Felipe (p200).

On the seaward side (the north) of the Rose Lagoon things are less pristine with a lot of new timeshares, condo-mondos and hotels. Local fishing communities are taking a big hit as prices rise with the tourism and second-home boom. But things are still pretty laid-back here. It might even be a good spot to do a little guerrilla camping on the beach. Remember, the beach is public property in Mexico.

The most interesting bits of this area are relatively close to Progreso and are best explored by car. **Telchak Puerto** (below) is the best place to base operations in the region.

At **Uaymitún** a tall wooden observation tower at the edge of the lagoon allows you to watch flamingos, as well as ibis, herons, spoonbills and other waterfowl.

The buildings thin out beyond Uaymitún, and about 16km east of it a road heads south from the coast some 3km across the bird-riddled lagoon to the turnoff for the ruins of **Xcambó**, a Maya salt-distribution center with a few reconstructed structures. While it's technically free to visit the ruins, the caretaker will ask for a small donation.

Following the road south beyond the ruins turnoff takes you into grassy marshland with cattails and scatterings of palm trees, a beautiful landscape providing ample opportunities for bird-spotting without even getting out of the car.

Continuing south on this road takes you back to civilization at Motul, from where you can head in any number of directions: east and south to Izamal, west and north to the Dzibilchaltún ruins, southwest to Tixkokob and its beautiful hammocks (see boxed text, p163), or west and south to Mérida via Conkal, whose Convento de San Francisco de Asís now houses the new **Museo de Arte Sacro** (admission free; 🕑 9am-6pm Tue-Sat, 9am-2pm Sun). This is a small but well-done museum of religious art and artifacts, including 18th- and 19th-century altarpieces and carvings of saints, good historical and archaeological exhibits detailing the foundation (and later restoration) of Yucatán's monasteries, and contemporary profane and religious artwork. Some of the latter is surprisingly racy. All labeling is in Spanish. Be sure to check out the architecture of the convent itself, including the *noria* (irrigation system) out back.

Telchac Puerto

There really isn't much to do in Telchac Puerto but sit on the brown-sand beach, suck the briny air and wait for the earth to turn another rotation. The town, just a few kilometers east of the turnoff to Xcambó on the road to Dzilam, is a good place to base yourself for adventures along this forgotten-but-not-totally-lost coast. There are no ATMs or banks here, and it's best to arrive by car. Locals recommend Tiburón Restaurant in the town center.

The simple **Hotel Libros y Sueños** (☎ 991-917-4125; www.l-y-s.net; Calle 23 No 200; s/d with fan M$200/250) has a big English-language library, clean rooms and wi-fi, and it's just a block away from the beach.

The monstro all-inclusive **Hotel Reef Yucatán** (☎ 999-941-9494; www.reefyucatan.com; Zona Hotelera Telchac Puerto; r per person M$990; ☒ ☒ P) has 150 rooms, a big swimming pool and a pretty damned good beach. Expect boilerplate all-inclusive rooms, service and food.

EASTERN YUCATÁN STATE

Scrub jungle, intact colonial cities, cenotes aplenty and Yucatán's largest coastal estuary are but a few of the attractions in the eastern portion of this state. Oh, and then there's the seventh modern wonder of the world, Chichén Iztá, as well as a smattering of less-visited (but nonetheless impressive) Maya ruins.

IZAMAL
☎ 988 / pop 15,100

In ancient times Izamal was a center for the worship of the supreme Maya god, Itzamná, and the sun god, Kinich-Kakmó. A dozen temple pyramids were devoted to these or other gods. No doubt these bold expressions of Maya religiosity are why the Spanish colonists chose Izamal as the site for an enormous and impressive Franciscan monastery, which still stands at the heart of this town, located about 70km east of Mérida.

The Izamal of today is a quiet provincial town, nicknamed La Ciudad Amarilla (The Yellow City) for the traditional yellow buildings that spiral out from the center like a budding daisy. It's easily explored on foot, and horse-drawn carriages add to the city's charm. Making a trip here even easier is the excellent tourist map, available in several languages (English and Spanish are always available, but there's also French, German and even Japanese), describing various walking tours and locations where handicraft demonstrations take place.

Sights & Activities
When the Spaniards conquered Izamal, they destroyed the major Maya temple, the Ppapp-Hol-Chac pyramid, and in 1533

began to build from its stones one of the first monasteries in the western hemisphere. Work on **Convento de San Antonio de Padua** (admission free; �), 6am-8pm) was finished in 1561. Under the monastery's arcades, look for building stones with an unmistakable maze-like design; these were clearly taken from the earlier Maya temple.

The monastery's principal church is the **Santuario de la Virgen de Izamal**, approached by a ramp from the main square. The ramp leads into the **Atrium**, a huge arcaded courtyard in which the **fiesta of the Virgin of Izamal** takes place each August 15. There's a **sound-and-light show** (admission M$40; ☽ 8:30pm Tue, Thu & Sat) here three nights a week.

At some point the 16th-century **frescoes** beside the entrance of the sanctuary were completely painted over. For years they lay concealed under a thin layer of whitewash until a maintenance worker who was cleaning the walls discovered them recently. The church's original altarpiece was destroyed by a fire believed to have been started by a fallen candle. Its replacement, impressively gilded, was built in the 1940s. In the niches at the stations of the cross are some superb small figures.

In the small courtyard to the left of the church, look up and toward the Atrium to see the original sundial projecting from the roof's edge. A small **museum** (☽ 10am-1pm & 3-6pm Mon-Sat, 9am-4pm Sun) at the back commemorates Pope John Paul II's 1993 visit to the monastery. He brought with him a silver crown for the statue of the patron saint of Yucatán, the Virgin of Izamal.

The monastery's front entrance faces west; it's flanked by Calles 31 and 33 on the north and south, respectively, and Calles 28 and 30 on the east and west. The best time to visit is in the morning, as the church is occasionally closed during the afternoon siesta.

Southeast of the convent on the plaza is the small **Museo de los Grandes Maestros del Arte Mexicano** (Calle 31 No 201; admission free; ☽ 10am-6pm Tue-Sat, 10am-5pm Sun), an art museum and gallery showcasing pop art from around Mexico. It's also worth taking the time to visit the **talleres de arte** (artisan workshops) found throughout the city. Your little yellow map will lead the way to adventures and cultural attractions beyond the scope of this book.

Three of the town's original 12 Maya **pyramids** have been partially restored. The largest

---

PUEBLOS AND PLACES OFF THE MAP

There's a ton of good off-the-map adventures to be had in and around town. Here are a few of our favorites:

- **Cuauhtémoc** A small community 6km south of Izamal on an extension of Calle 24, with a 17th-century chapel.

- **Kimbilá** Located 8km west of Izamal on an extension of Calle 31, this town is famous for its embroidery.

- **Iztamatul, Habuk, Chaltún Há & beyond** They've discovered some 80 pre-Hispanic structures within the city limits. Habuk, Itzamatul and Chaltún Há are just a few. They are all free to the public, and you can hire a guide at the tourist center.

(and the third largest in Yucatán) is the enormous **Kinich-Kakmó**, three blocks north of the monastery. You can climb it for free.

If you want a real jungle experience, ask at the **tourist center** (☎ 988-954-0009, Calle 30 No 323) for Esteban Abán, the jewelry maker, who offers guided trips to Ox-Huadz, an unexcavated ruin. You'll need to make arrangements at least a day in advance, depending on Abán's availability, but the trip offers great birding and Indiana Jones–style ruin-hunting. You can also rent bikes at the tourist center.

Sleeping & Eating

Posada Flory (☎ 954-0562; Calle 30 No 267, cnr Calle 22; s/d M$180/250; ❄) There's a nice little center patio in this small, uberclean budget hotel, probably the best low-end deal in town. You can air-con yourself for a few extra pesos.

Macan Ché (☎ /fax 954-0287; www.macanche.com; Calle 22 No 305; d M$380-600; ❄ ▢ ☑) It's about three long (yes, long!) blocks east of the monastery (take Calle 31 toward Cancún and turn right on Calle 22) to this very Zen boutique hotel, which has a cluster of cottages and a small 'cenote' pool in a woodsy setting. The most expensive of the 12 rooms has air-con and a kitchenette. Rates include a big breakfast. Free wi-fi and Local Area Network (LAN) for guests.

El Toro (Calle 31 No 303; mains M$60-90; ❄ 8am-midnight) At the southeast corner of the roundabout in front of the monastery, this

small family-run establishment specializes in Yucatecan fare (with a few international favorites thrown in to keep the tourists happy). Try a twist on the traditional with the *pozole con coco* (Maya corn stew with coconut overtones).

Several *loncherías* occupy spaces in the market on the monastery's southwest side.

Getting There & Away

Oriente operates frequent buses between Mérida and Izamal (M$27, 1½ hours) from the Noreste bus terminal. There are buses from Valladolid (M$41, two hours) as well. Coming from Chichén Itzá you must change buses at Hoctún. Izamal's bus terminal is two short blocks west of the monastery.

CHICHÉN ITZÁ
☎ 985

The most famous and best restored of the Yucatán Maya sites, **Chichén Itzá** (Mouth of the Well of the Itzáes; admission M$95, parking M$10, sound-&-light show M$30, guide M$500-600; ❄ 8am-6pm summer, 8am-5:30pm winter), while tremendously overcrowded – every gaper and his grandmother is trying to check off the new seven wonders of the world – will still impress even the most jaded visitor. Many mysteries of the Maya astronomical calendar are made clear when one understands the design of the 'time temples' here. Other than a few minor passageways, climbing on the structures is not allowed.

At the **vernal and autumnal equinoxes** (March 20 to 21 and September 21 to 22), the morning and afternoon sun produces a light-and-shadow illusion of the serpent ascending or descending the side of El Castillo's staircase. The site is mobbed on these dates, however, making it difficult to see, and after the spectacle, parts of the site are sometimes closed to the public. The illusion is almost as good in the week preceding and following each equinox (and draws much smaller crowds), and is re-created nightly in the sound-and-light show year-round. Some find the spectacle fascinating, others think it's overrated. Either way, if you're in the area around the equinox and you've got your own car, it's easy to wake up early for Dzibilchaltún's fiery sunrise (see p182) and then make it to Chichén Itzá by midafternoon, catching both spectacles on the same day.

The heat, humidity and crowds can be fierce; try to do your exploration of the site (especially around El Castillo) either early in the morning or late in the afternoon.

History

Most archaeologists agree that the first major settlement at Chichén Itzá, during the Late Classic period, was pure Maya. In about the 9th century, the city was largely abandoned for reasons unknown. It was resettled around the late 10th century, and shortly thereafter it is believed to have been invaded by the Toltecs, who had migrated from their central highlands capital of Tula, north of Mexico City. The bellicose Toltec culture was fused with that of the Maya,

incorporating the cult of Quetzalcóatl (Kukulcán, in Maya). You will see images of both Chac-Mool, the Maya rain god, and Quetzalcóatl, the plumed serpent, throughout the city.

The substantial fusion of highland central Mexican and Puuc architectural styles makes Chichén unique among the Yucatán Peninsula's ruins. The fabulous El Castillo and the Plataforma de Venus are outstanding architectural works built during the height of Toltec cultural input.

The sanguinary Toltecs contributed more than their architectural skills to the Maya. They elevated human sacrifice to a near obsession, and there are numerous carvings of the bloody ritual in Chichén demonstrating this.

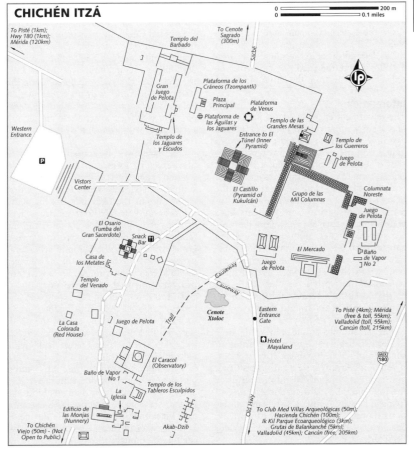

After a Maya leader moved his political capital to Mayapán while keeping Chichén as his religious capital, Chichén Itzá fell into decline. Why it was subsequently abandoned in the 14th century is a mystery, but the once-great city remained the site of Maya pilgrimages for many years.

Orientation

Most of Chichén's lodgings, restaurants and services are arranged along 1km of highway in the village of Pisté, to the western (Mérida) side of the ruins. It's 1.5km from the ruins' main (west) entrance to the nearest hotel (Pirámide Inn) in Pisté, and 2.5km from the ruins to Pisté's village plaza, which is shaded by a huge tree. Buses to Pisté generally stop at the plaza; you can make the hot walk to and from the ruins in 20 to 30 minutes.

On the eastern (Cancún) side, it's 1.5km from the highway along the access road to the eastern entrance to the ruins; three top-end hotels line the road, the closest being only about 100m from the entrance.

Information

The western entrance has a large parking lot and a big visitors center. Facilities include two bookstores with a good assortment of guides and maps, a restaurant serving decent if somewhat pricey food, a Banamex ATM, Telmex card phones, excellent free bathrooms and, around the corner from the ticket counter, a free *guardaequipaje* (room for storing luggage) where you can leave your belongings while you explore the site.

As at most sites, filming with a video camera costs M$35 extra, and tripods require a special permit from Mexico City. Hold on to your wristband ticket; it gives you in-and-out privileges and admission to that evening's sound-and-light show. Explanatory plaques around the site are in Spanish, English and Maya.

The 45-minute sound-and-light show in Spanish begins at 8pm each evening in summer and 7pm in winter. It costs M$30 if you don't already have a ruins wristband, and it counts toward the admission price the following day. Devices for listening in English, French, German or Italian translations (beamed via infrared) rent for M$25. Specify the language you need or it may not be broadcast.

Sights
EXPLORING THE RUINS
Visitors Center

The visitors center has a small but worthwhile **museum** (🕙 8am-5pm), with sculptures, reliefs, artifacts and explanations in Spanish, English and French.

The **Chilam Balam Auditorio**, next to the museum, sometimes has video shows about Chichén and other Mexican sites. The picture quality can be truly abominable, but the aircon is great. In the central space of the visitors center stands a scale model of the archaeological site, and off toward the toilets is an exhibit on Edward Thompson's excavations of the Cenote Sagrado.

El Castillo

As you approach from the visitors center into the site, El Castillo (also called the Pyramid of Kukulcán) rises before you in all its grandeur. The first temple here was pre-Toltec, built around AD 800, but the present 25m-high structure, built over the old one, has the plumed serpent sculpted along the stairways and Toltec warriors represented in the doorway carvings at the top of the temple. You won't get to see these temple-top carvings as you are not allowed to ascend the pyramid.

The structure is actually a massive Maya calendar formed in stone. Each of El Castillo's nine levels is divided in two by a staircase, making 18 separate terraces that commemorate the 18 20-day months of the Maya vague year. The four stairways have 91 steps each; add the top platform and the total is 365, the number of days in the year. On each façade of the pyramid are 52 flat panels, which are reminders of the 52 years in the Maya calendar round. See boxed text, p43, for more on the Maya calendar.

To top it off, during the spring and autumn equinoxes, light and shadow form a series of triangles on the side of the north staircase that mimic the creep of a serpent (note the carved serpent's heads flanking the bottom of the staircase).

The older pyramid *inside* El Castillo boasts a red jaguar throne with inlaid eyes and spots of jade; also lying behind the screen is a *chac-mool* figure. The entrance to **El Túnel**, the passage up to the throne, is at the base of El Castillo's north side. You can't go in, though.

DREDGING CHICHÉN'S SACRED CENOTE

Around 1900 Edward Thompson, a Harvard professor and US consul to Yucatán, bought the hacienda that included Chichén Itzá for M$750. No doubt intrigued by local stories of female virgins being sacrificed to the Maya deities by being thrown into the site's cenote, Thompson resolved to have the cenote dredged.

He imported dredging equipment and set to work. Gold and jade jewelry from all parts of Mexico and as far away as Colombia was recovered, along with other artifacts and a variety of human bones. Many of the artifacts were shipped to Harvard's Peabody Museum, but some have since been returned to Mexico.

Subsequent diving expeditions in the 1920s and 1960s turned up hundreds of other valuable artifacts. It appears that all sorts of people, including children and old people, the diseased and the injured, and the young and the vigorous, were forcibly obliged to take an eternal swim in Chichén's Cenote Sagrado.

The cenote is reached by walking about 200m north from the Platforma de Venus.

Gran Juego de Pelota

The great ball court, the largest and most impressive in Mexico, is only one of the city's eight courts, indicative of the importance of the games held here. The court, to the left of the visitors center, is flanked by temples at either end and is bounded by towering parallel walls with stone rings cemented up high.

There is evidence that the ball game may have changed over the years. Some carvings show players with padding on their elbows and knees, and it is thought that they played a soccerlike game with a hard rubber ball, with the use of hands forbidden. Other carvings show players wielding bats; it appears that if a player hit the ball through one of the stone hoops, his team was declared the winner. It may be that during the Toltec period the losing captain, and perhaps his teammates as well, were sacrificed (and you thought your dad was hard on you in Little League).

Along the walls of the ball court are stone reliefs, including scenes of decapitations of players. The court exhibits some interesting acoustics – a conversation at one end can be heard 135m away at the other, and a clap produces multiple loud echoes.

Templo del Barbado & Templo de los Jaguares y Escudos

The structure at the northern end of the ball court, called the Temple of the Bearded Man after a carving inside of it, has some finely sculpted pillars and reliefs of flowers, birds and trees. The Temple of the Jaguars and Shields, built atop the southeast corner of the ball court's wall, has some columns with carved rattlesnakes and tablets with etched

jaguars. Inside are faded mural fragments depicting a battle.

Plataforma de los Cráneos

The Platform of Skulls (*tzompantli* in Náhuatl, a Maya dialect) is located between the Templo de los Jaguares and El Castillo. You can't mistake it, because the T-shaped platform is festooned with carved skulls and eagles tearing open the chests of men to eat their hearts. In ancient days this platform was used to display the heads of sacrificial victims.

Plataforma de las Águilas y los Jaguares

Adjacent to the *tzompantli*, the carvings on the Platform of the Eagles and Jaguars depict those animals gruesomely grabbing human hearts in their claws. It is thought that this platform was part of a temple dedicated to the military legions responsible for capturing sacrificial victims.

Cenote Sagrado

From the *tzompantli*, a 300m rough stone road runs north (a five-minute walk) to the huge sunken well that gave this city its name. The Sacred Cenote is an awesome natural well, some 60m in diameter and 35m deep. The walls between the summit and the water's surface are ensnared in tangled vines and other vegetation. There are ruins of a small steam bath next to the cenote, as well as a modern drinks stand with toilets. See boxed text, above, for the historical details.

Grupo de las Mil Columnas

This group to the east of El Castillo takes its name, which means 'Group of the Thousand

YUCATÁN STATE

Columns', from the forest of pillars stretching south and east. The star attraction here is the **Templo de los Guerreros** (Temple of the Warriors), adorned with stucco and stone-carved animal deities. At the top of its steps is a classic reclining *chac-mool* figure – you're no longer allowed to ascend to it.

Many of the columns in front of the temple are carved with figures of warriors. Archaeologists working in 1926 discovered a Temple of Chac-Mool lying beneath the Temple of the Warriors.

You can walk through the columns on its south side to reach the **Columnata Noreste**, notable for the 'big-nosed god' masks on its façade. Some have been reassembled on the ground around the statue. Just to the south are the remains of the **Baño de Vapor** (Steam Bath or Sweat House) with an underground oven and drains for the water. The sweat houses were regularly used for ritual purification.

El Osario

The Ossuary, otherwise known as the Bonehouse or the Tumba del Gran Sacerdote (High Priest's Grave), is a ruined pyramid to the southwest of El Castillo. As with most of the buildings in this southern section, the architecture is more Puuc than Toltec. It's notable for the beautiful serpent heads at the base of its staircases. A square shaft at the top of the structure leads into a cave beneath it that was used as a burial chamber; seven tombs with human remains were discovered inside. These days a snack bar with telephone and toilets stands nearby.

El Caracol

Called El Caracol (The Snail) by the Spaniards for its interior spiral staircase, this observatory, to the south of the Ossuary, is one of the most fascinating and important of all Chichén Itzá's buildings (but, alas, you can't enter it). Its circular design resembles some central highlands structures, although, surprisingly, not those of Toltec Tula. In a fusion of architectural styles and religious imagery, there are Maya Chac rain-god masks over four external doors facing the cardinal points. The windows in the observatory's dome are aligned with the appearance of certain stars at specific dates. From the dome the priests decreed the times for rituals, celebrations, corn-planting and harvests.

Edificio de las Monjas & La Iglesia

Thought by archaeologists to have been a palace for Maya royalty, the so-called Edificio de las Monjas (Nunnery), with its myriad rooms, resembled a European convent to the conquistadors, hence their name for the building. The building's dimensions are imposing: its base is 60m long, 30m wide and 20m high. The construction is Maya rather than Toltec, although a Toltec sacrificial stone stands in front. A smaller adjoining building to the east, known as La Iglesia (The Church), is covered almost entirely with carvings. Currently, on the far side at the back there are some passageways that are still open, leading a short way into the labyrinth inside. They are dank, slippery, smell of bat urine and it's easy to twist an ankle, but Indiana Jones wannabes will think it's totally cool.

Akab-Dzib

East of the Nunnery, the Puuc-style Akab-Dzib is thought by some archaeologists to be the most ancient structure excavated here. The central chambers date from the 2nd century. The name means 'Obscure Writing' in Maya and refers to the south-side annex door, whose lintel depicts a priest with a vase etched with hieroglyphics that have never been translated.

Chichén Viejo

Old Chichén comprises largely unrestored ruins, scattered about and hidden in the bush south of the Nunnery. The predominant architecture is Maya, with Toltec additions and modifications. At the time of research, the public was not allowed to enter the area.

CENOTE IK KIL

About 3km east of the eastern entrance to Chichén Itzá is the turnoff for **Ik Kil Parque Ecoarqueológico** (☎ 858-1525; adult/child M$60/30; ☼ 8am-6pm), whose cenote has been developed into an OK swimming spot. For anyone who's visited some of the other cenotes this will seem touristy, dirty and expensive; those who're heading back to Cancún or anyone with mobility difficulties will probably enjoy peeking, as it offers some idea of what makes cenotes so unusual and there are good stairs with some handrails. As with other cenotes in the region, do not pull on the roots that hang down into the water. It took them a long time to get there.

Small cascades of water plunge from the high limestone roof, which is ringed by greenery. A good buffet lunch costs an extra M$120 (beverages extra). Get your swim in by no later than 1pm to beat the tour groups. The grounds also hold five lovely **cabanas** (up to 8 people M$1000-2000; ⊠) with Jacuzzi.

GRUTAS DE BALANKANCHÉ

In 1959 a guide to the Chichén ruins was exploring a cave on his day off when he came upon a narrow passageway. He followed the passageway for 300m, meandering through a series of caverns. In each, perched on mounds amid scores of glistening stalactites, were hundreds of ceremonial treasures the Maya had placed there 800 years earlier: ritual *metates* and *manos* (grinding stones), incense burners and pots. In the years following the discovery, the ancient ceremonial objects were removed and studied. Eventually most of them were returned to the caves, and placed exactly where they were found.

The turnoff for the **caverns** (admission Mon-Sat M$54, Sun M$20; ☼ ticket booth 9am-5pm) is 5km east of Chichén Itzá (about 5km southeast of Cenote Ik Kil) on the highway to Cancún. Second-class buses heading east from Pisté toward Valladolid and Cancún will drop you at the Balankanché road. The entrance to the caves is 350m north of the highway.

Outside the caves you'll find a good **botanical garden** (displaying native Yucatecan flora with information on the medicinal and other uses of the trees and plants), a small museum, a shop selling cold drinks and souvenirs, and a ticket booth with free luggage storage. The museum features large photographs taken during the exploration of the caves, and descriptions (in English, Spanish and French) of the Maya religion and the offerings found in the caves. Also on display are photographs of modern-day Maya ceremonies called Ch'a Chaac, which continue to be held in all the villages on the Yucatán Peninsula during times of drought and consist mostly of praying and making numerous offerings of food to Chac.

Compulsory 40-minute tours (minimum six people, maximum 20) have melodramatic recorded narration that is nearly impossible to make out and is not very informative, but if you'd like it in a particular language, English is at 11am, 1pm and 3pm; Spanish is at 9am, noon, 2pm and 4pm; and French is at 10am.

Be warned that the cave is unusually hot, and ventilation is poor in its further reaches. The lack of oxygen (especially after a few groups have already passed through) makes it difficult to draw a full breath until you're outside again.

Sleeping

Don't hesitate to haggle for a bed in the low season (May, June, September and October), when prices drop. Hwy 180 is known as Calle 15A on its way through Pisté.

BUDGET

Pirámide Inn (☎ 851-0115; www.chichen.com; Calle 15A No 30; per person hammock or tent sites M$40, d M$410; ⊠ ⊡) Next to the eastern bus stop in Pisté. They're into world peace here, and so are we! Campers can pitch a tent or hang a hammock under a *palapa*, enjoy the inn's pool and watch satellite TV in the lobby. Campers also have use of tepid showers, clean shared toilet facilities and a safe place to stow gear. The 42 spacious rooms have good bathrooms and two spring-me-to-the-moon double beds. The hotel also has a book exchange, swimming pool, Maya-style sweat lodge, and a restaurant serving international and vegetarian cuisine. You're as close as you can get to the ruins for cheap, though it's still a hike of about 3km. Animals are welcome.

Posada Olalde (☎ 851-0086; cnr Calles 6 & 17; s/d M$200/250, bungalows M$200) Two blocks south of the highway by Artesanías Guayacán, this is the best of Pisté's several *posadas* (inns). It has clean, quiet and attractive rooms, a few twiddling parakeets and four decent-sized bungalows. Some toilets are missing seats. All accommodations are fan-cooled (though there were plans to install air-con), and the friendly manager speaks Spanish and English, as well as some German and Maya.

Posada Poxil (☎ 851-0116; Calle 15A; s/d/tr M$150/200/250) At the western end of Pisté, this posada has seven bright and cheery rooms with good light, towels that have seen better days, and fans. There's also an inexpensive restaurant serving big breakfasts (M$35) and Yucatecan dishes. The hot water is 'solar heated,' not a bit warmer than tepid. Alas no toilet seats!

Posada Chac-Mool (☎ 851-0270; Calle 15A; s/d with fan M$200/270, with air-con M$350/410; ⊠) Just east of Hotel Chichén Itzá and on the opposite (south) side of the highway in Pisté, Chac-Mool has

YUCATÁN STATE

fairly basic doubles with good screens. Some rooms have air-con to augment the fans.

MIDRANGE

Pirámide Inn (☎ 851-0115; www.chichen.com; Calle 15A No 30; d M$410; ✷ ☒) See the review on p191.

Hotel Chichén Itzá (☎ 985-851-0022; fax 985-851-0023; www.mayaland.com; Calle 15A No 45; r fan only M$300, r M$600-1000; ✷ ☒ ⚏) On the west side of Pisté, this hotel has 42 pleasant rooms with tiled floors and old-style brick-tiled ceilings. Rooms in the upper range face the pool and the nicely landscaped grounds, and all have firm beds and minibars. Parents may bring two kids under 13 years for free.

TOP END

All of these hotels are close to the archaeological zone's eastern entrance.

Club Med Villas Arqueológicas (☎ 856-6000, in the USA 800-514-8244; www.clubmed.com; d/tr/ste M$810/1010/1370; ✷ ☒) A Club Med hotel, this is 300m from the east entrance. It is an exact clone of the villas at Cobá and Uxmal, a walled hacienda-style complex sporting a profusion of red floor tiles, a library with billiard table, and 40 smallish but comfortable rooms recently upgraded with nice touches of marble and tile.

Hacienda Chichén (☎ in Mérida 999-924-2150, in the USA 800-624-8451; www.haciendachichen.com; d M$1700-2200; ✷ ☒) About 300m from the ruins' entrance, this is on the grounds of a 16th-century estate. The hacienda's elegant main house and ruined walls make a great setting, and huge ceiba trees offer welcome shade. The archaeologists who excavated Chichén during the 1920s lived here in bungalows, which have been refurbished and augmented with new ones.

Hotel Mayaland (☎ 851-0100, in the USA 800-235-4079; www.mayaland.com; d/ste/royal ste M$1700/2500/3450; ✷ ☒) Less than 100m from the ruins' entrance – from the lobby and front rooms you can look out at El Caracol. The rooms, pools and garden bungalows are nicely built and well appointed, but when you're at El Caracol you'll wish the management hadn't cut an ugly swath through the jungle just so hotel patrons could have a nicer view.

Eating

The highway through Pisté is lined with more than 20 eateries, large and small. The cheapest are the market stalls on the main plaza opposite the large tree.

Restaurant Sayil (☎ 851-0033; mains M$35-70; ☽ 7am-9pm) A recently renovated old standby, with a pleasant garden and simple but tasty regional fare. It's attached to the new Felix Inn.

Xunan (☎ 851-0131; Calle Principal s/n; mains M$40-90; ☽ 7am-9pm) Service is a bit slow, but this colorful eatery (at the front of a souvenir stand) offers good food at reasonable prices and is a nice change from the tourist buffets. Portions are generous.

Restaurant Hacienda Xaybe'h (☎ 851-0039; buffet lunch & dinner M$110; ☽ 7:30am-6:30pm; Ⓥ ⚏) Set a block back from the highway opposite Hotel Chichén Itzá, this is a large, rather fancy place with nice grounds. It's popular with tours and the food is a bit overpriced; the selection of salads makes it a good option for vegetarians. Diners can use the swimming pool free of charge!

Getting There & Away

Oriente has ticket offices near the east and west sides of Pisté, and 2nd-class buses passing through town stop almost anywhere along the way. Many 1st-class buses only hit the ruins and the west side of town, close to the toll highway.

When they're running on schedule, Oriente's 2nd-class buses pass through Pisté bound for Mérida (M$52, 2½ hours) hourly between 8:15am and 4:15pm. Hourly Oriente buses to Valladolid (M$36, 50 minutes) and Cancún (M$80, 4½ hours) pass between 7am and 5:30pm. There is a service to Cobá (M$52, 1½ hours) as well.

First-class buses serve Mérida (M$80, 1¾ hours, 2:25pm and 5pm), Cancún (M$140, 2½ hours, 4:30pm), Tulum (M$101, 2½ hours, 8am and 4:30pm) and Playa del Carmen (M$180, four hours).

Shared vans to Valladolid (M$20, 40 minutes) pass through town regularly.

Getting Around

During Chichén Itzá's opening hours, 1st- and 2nd-class buses serve the ruins (check with the driver), and they will take passengers from town for about M$6 when there's room. For a bit more, 2nd-class buses will also take you to the Cenote Ik Kil and the Grutas de Balankanché (be sure to specify your destination when buying your ticket).

If you plan to see the ruins and then head directly to another city by 1st-class bus, buy your bus ticket at the visitors center before hitting the ruins, for a better chance of getting a seat.

There is a taxi stand near the west end of town; the price to the ruins is M$25. There are usually taxis at Chichén's parking lot.

VALLADOLID
☎ 985 / pop 45,868

Also known as the Sultaness of the East, Yucatán's third-largest city is known for its quiet streets and sun-splashed, pastel walls. She certainly is one sultry babe, and it's worth staying here for a few days or even a week as the provincial town makes a great hub for visits to Río Lagartos, Chichén Itzá, Ek' Balam and a number of nearby cenotes. The city resides at that magic point where there's plenty to do, yet it still feels small, manageable and affordable. Slow down for a day by renting a bicycle and tootle out to the nearby cenotes. Sit on a bench in one of the many squares and watch men play board games or kids chase pigeons. Buy a dollar's worth of fresh tortillas and let an afternoon pass lazily by.

History

Valladolid has seen its fair share of turmoil and revolt. The city was first founded in 1543 near the Chouac-Ha lagoon some 50km from the coast, but it was too hot and there were way too many mosquitoes for Francisco de Montejo, nephew of Montejo the Elder, and his merry band of conquerors. So they upped and moved the city to the Maya ceremonial center of Zací (sah-*kee*), where they faced heavy resistance from the local Maya. Eventually the Elder's son – Montejo the Younger – ultimately took the town. The Spanish conquerors, in typical fashion, ripped down the town and laid out a new city following the classic colonial plan.

During much of the colonial era, Valladolid's physical isolation from Mérida kept it relatively autonomous from royal rule, and the Maya of the area suffered brutal exploitation, which continued after Mexican independence. Barred from entering many areas of the city, the Maya made Valladolid one of their first points of attack following the 1847 outbreak of the War of the Castes (p36) in Tepich. After a two-month siege, the city's defenders were finally overcome. Many fled to the safety of Mérida; the rest were slaughtered.

Today Valladolid is a prosperous seat of agricultural commerce, augmented by some light industry and a growing tourist trade. Many Vallisetanos speak Spanish with the soft and clear Maya accent.

Orientation & Information

The old highway passes through the town center, though most signs urge motorists toward the toll road north of town. To follow the old highway eastbound, take Calle 41; westbound, take Calle 39. To preserve the colonial flavor of the town center, Valladolid has limited the posting of signs by businesses to those approved by the city. This can sometimes make it difficult to find an establishment; you need to keep a keen eye out for small cardboard signs on open doors.

Various banks (most with ATMs) near the town center are generally open 9am to 5pm Monday to Friday and 9am to 1pm Saturday. The main plaza, Parque Francisco Cantón Rosado, has banks of Telmex card phones in each corner.

High-speed internet is available at numerous small cafés in and around the town center; all charge around M$10 per hour and are open 9am-ish to as late as midnight.

Hospital Valladolid (☎ 856-2883; cnr Calles 49 & 52; ☼ 24hr) Near the Convento de Sisal, it handles emergencies.

Main post office (cnr Calles 39 & 40; ☼ 8:30am-3pm Mon-Fri)

Tourist office (☼ 9am-9pm Mon-Sat, 9am-noon Sun) On the east side of the plaza, it is frequently unattended and provides mediocre information.

Sights

TEMPLO DE SAN BERNARDINO & CONVENTO DE SISAL

The **Templo de San Bernardino** (Church of San Bernardino; ☼ 8am-noon & 5-9pm) and the Convento de Sisal are about 700m southwest of the plaza. They were constructed between 1552 and 1560 to serve the dual functions of fortress and church.

You may have to knock on the church's left-hand door to gain admittance, or someone may approach and offer you a short tour in exchange for a gratuity. Either way, it's worth peeking inside. Its charming decoration includes beautiful rose-colored walls,

YUCATÁN STATE

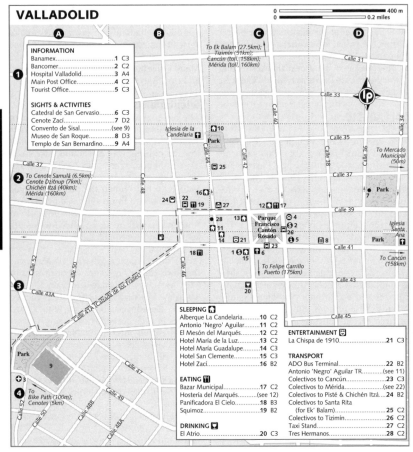

VALLADOLID

0 — 400 m
0 — 0.2 miles

INFORMATION
Banamex.....................1 C3
Bancomer...................2 C2
Hospital Valladolid........3 A4
Main Post Office...........4 C3
Tourist Office...............5 C3

SIGHTS & ACTIVITIES
Catedral de San Gervasio....6 C3
Cenote Zací..................7 D2
Convento de Sisal...........(see 9)
Museo de San Roque.........8 D3
Templo de San Bernardino....9 A4

To Ek Balam (27.5km);
Tizimín (51km);
Cancún (toll, 158km);
Mérida (toll, 160km)

Iglesia de la
Candelaria

Parque
Francisco
Cantón
Rosado

To Cenote Samulá (6.5km);
Cenote Dzitnup (7km);
Chichén Itzá (40km);
Mérida (160km)

To Mercado
Municipal
(50m)

Iglesia
Santa
Ana

To Felipe Carrillo
Puerto (175km)

To Cancún
(158km)

To
Bike Path (100m);
Cenotes (5km)

SLEEPING
Alberque La Candelaria........10 C2
Antonio 'Negro' Aguilar........11 C2
El Mesón del Marqués.........12 C2
Hotel María de la Luz..........13 C2
Hotel María Guadalupe.........14 C3
Hotel San Clemente............15 C3
Hotel Zaci....................16 B2

EATING
Bazar Municipal...............17 C2
Hostería del Marqués..........(see 12)
Panificadora El Cielo..........18 B3
Squimoz......................19 B2

DRINKING
El Atrio......................20 C3

ENTERTAINMENT
La Chispa de 1910............21 C3

TRANSPORT
ADO Bus Terminal............22 B2
Antonio 'Negro' Aguilar TR....(see 11)
Colectivos a Cancún...........23 C3
Colectivos a Mérida..........(see 22)
Colectivos a Pisté & Chichén Itzá....24 B2
Colectivos a Santa Rita
(for Ek' Balam)..............25 C2
Colectivos a Tizimín..........26 C2
Taxi Stand...................27 C2
Tres Hermanos................28 C2

arches, some recently uncovered 16th-century frescoes and a small image of the Virgin on the altar. These are about the only original items remaining; the grand wooden *retablo* (altarpiece) dates from the 19th century. The adjacent convent is often closed to the public; your best bets for gaining entrance to it are during the vacation periods of Easter week, August and Christmas (December 14 to January 6). It's well worth a visit. The walled grounds hold a cenote with a vaulted dome built over it and a system of channels that once irrigated the large garden.

If you're arriving by bicycle, note that it's prohibited to ride on the wide concrete paths leading from the street to the church.

MUSEO DE SAN ROQUE

Previously a church, the **Museo de San Roque** (Calle 41 btwn Calles 38 & 40; admission free; 9am-9pm) has models and exhibits relating the history of the city and the region. Other displays focus on various aspects of traditional Maya life.

CENOTES

Among the region's several underground cenotes is **Cenote Zací** (Calle 36, enter from Calle 39; admission M$25; 8am-6pm), set in a park that also holds traditional stone-walled thatched houses and a small zoo. People swim in Zací, though being mostly open it contains some dust and algae. Look in the water for catfish or overhead for a bat or two.

A bit more enticing but less accessible is **Cenote Dzitnup** (Xkekén; admission M$25; ⏀ 8am-5pm), 7km west of the plaza. It's artificially lit and very swimmable, and a massive limestone formation dripping with stalactites hangs from its ceiling. Across the road about 100m closer to town is **Cenote Samulá** (admission M$25; ⏀ 8am-6pm), a lovely cavern pool with *álamo* roots stretching down many meters from the middle of the ceiling to drink from it. The *ejido* (indigenous communal landholding) that maintains both cenotes charges M$35 for use of a video camera in either one.

Pedaling a rented bicycle (see p196) to the cenotes takes about 20 minutes. By bike from the town center take Calle 41A (Calzada de los Frailes), a street lined entirely with colonial architecture, which leads past the Templo de San Bernardino and the convent. Keep to the right of the park, then turn right on Calle 49. This opens onto tree-lined Avenida de los Frailes and hits the old highway. Turn left onto the *ciclopista* (bike path) paralleling the road to Mérida. Turn left again at the sign for Dzitnup and continue for just under 2km; Samulá will be off this road to the right and Dzitnup a little further on the left.

Shared vans from in front of Hotel María Guadalupe (on Calle 44) go to Dzitnup for M$10. Taxis from Valladolid's main plaza charge M$100 for the round-trip excursion to Dzitnup and Samulá, with an hour's wait. You also can hop aboard a westbound bus; ask the driver to let you off at the Dzitnup turnoff, then walk the final 2km (20 to 30 minutes) to the site. Dzitnup has a restaurant and drinks stand. Otherwise, bring a picnic.

MERCADO MUNICIPAL

On Calle 32, this is a good, authentic Mexican market where locals come to shop for cheap clothing, homewares, meat, produce and what-have-you, and to eat at inexpensive *taquerías*. The east side is the most colorful, with flowers and stacks of fruit and vegetables on offer. Most of the activity takes place between 6am and 2pm.

Sleeping

Most hotels are on or near the main plaza, Parque Francisco Cantón Rosado.

BUDGET

Albergue La Candelaria (☎ /fax 856-2267; fidery @chichen.com.mx; Calle 35 No 201F; dm with/without hostel card or ISIC M$80/88, d M$160/200; ▣) The HI-affiliated hostel was closed when we passed through, but locals said it would be reopening. Prices were last updated in 2006.

Antonio 'Negro' Aguilar (☎ 856-2125; Calle 44 btwn Calles 39 & 41; r M$150) This cantankerous old character rents the cheapest separate rooms in town, and they are actually pretty clean. For details, stop by his bike-rental shop (p196), which is not so clean.

Hotel María Guadalupe (☎ 856-2068; hotelmaria guadalupe@prodigy.net.mx; Calle 44 No 198A; d/tr M$220/270) This airy hotel has eight simple and clean fan-cooled rooms, which though a bit dark are not musty. The management is friendly and provides purified water. There's a nice common area upstairs to meet fellow travelers or sip something cold after a hot day.

Hotel Zací (☎ /fax 856-2167; www.hotelzaci.com; Calle 44 No 191; s/d/tr with fan M$240/350/410, with air-con M$340/400/450; ▨) Someone here really loves calla lilies. The 60 rooms with mock-colonial décor are spread around a green courtyard. Some rooms are a bit musty, but they air out.

MIDRANGE

The hotels listed here have restaurants, free secure parking facilities and swimming pools.

Hotel San Clemente (☎ /fax 856-2208; www.hotel sanclemente.com.mx; Calle 42 No 206; s/d/tr with fan M$300/360/410, with air-con M350/390/470; ▨ ▣) Offers good value and boasts 64 rooms with optional air-con and décor nearly identical to the Zací's, minus the calla lilies. The bathrooms are a bit dirty, but it's still a solid deal. There's a central courtyard.

Hotel María de la Luz (☎ /fax 856-2071; www.maria delaluzhotel.com; Calle 42 No 193; d/tr/q M$400/480/520; ▨ ▣) The beds are a bit concave and damp, but if the Zací or San Clemente are full, you might want to check out this spot. The restaurant is actually pretty good, and serves margaritas that (at least initially) pack a punch.

El Mesón del Marqués (☎ 856-2073; fax 856-2280; www.mesondelmarques.com; Calle 39 No 203; d standard/ superior M$580/710; ▨ ▣) It's only worth staying in this hotel if you're willing to up the ante for the superior rooms with their crispy-clean bedspreads, quaint blue-and-yellow tilework and firm mattresses. There's also a charming old courtyard and the fine Hostería del Marqués restaurant (p196), and wi-fi is available.

Eating & Drinking

Valladolid has a few good bakeries, including **Panificadora El Cielo** (Calle 41 btwn Calles 44 & 46; breads M$2-10; ⏰ 7am-noon & 3-9pm).

Bazar Municipal (cnr Calles 39 & 40) This place is a collection of market-style cookshops at the plaza's northeast corner, popular for their big, cheap breakfasts. At lunch and dinner some offer *comidas corridas* (set meals) – check the price before you order. El Amigo Casiano, on the left side nearly at the back, is good, super-cheap and always crowded; it's closed for the day by 2pm. Lonchería Canul, at the very back, stays open much later and serves good food accompanied by tasty salsas.

Squimoz (☎ 856-4156; Calle 39 No 219 btwn Calles 44 & 46; mains M$20-50; ⏰ 7am-10pm Mon-Sat, 7am-3pm Sun) A delightful little shop just a few doors east of the ADO bus terminal, Squimoz offers cakes, pastries and good espresso drinks, and has a nice rear courtyard. Its rich, creamy flan is one of Yucatán's best.

Hostería del Marqués (☎ 856-2073; El Mesón del Marqués, Calle 39 No 203; mains M$50-130; ⏰ 7am-11pm) Probably the best restaurant in town for lunch and dinner, where you can dine in the tranquil colonial courtyard with its bubbling fountain, or the air-con salon looking onto it. It also offers some vegetarian choices, and steaks priced by weight.

El Atrio (Calle 42 No 205; drinks M$10-40; ⏰ 6pm-midnight) This new café and grill has a very chill atmosphere with comfy sofas in a colonial-era *casona* (large old house). There's a patio out back.

Entertainment

Following a centuries-old tradition, dances are held in the main plaza from 8pm to 9pm Sunday, with music by the municipal band or other local groups. This is not aimed at tourists, though they're more than welcome.

La Chispa de 1910 (☎ 856-2668; Calle 41 No 201; ⏰ 5pm-1am Mon-Thu, 5pm-2am Fri-Sun) Sparks fly at this bar-restaurant that often features live music. Test your pipes by singing 'Besame Mucho' on karaoke nights (Thursday to Saturday).

Getting There & Away

BUS

Valladolid's main bus terminal is the convenient **ADO bus terminal** (cnr Calles 39 & 46). The principal services are Oriente, Mayab and Expresso (2nd class), and ADO and Super Expresso (1st class).

Cancún (M$70 to M$110, two to three hours, many buses)
Chetumal (M$140, six hours, five Mayab buses)
Chichén Itzá/Pisté (M$36, 45 minutes, 14 Oriente Mérida-bound buses between 7:15am and 5:30pm) Buses stop near ruins during opening hours.
Chiquilá (for Isla Holbox) (M$70, 2½ hours, Oriente bus at 2:45am)
Cobá (M$26, 45 minutes, four buses)
Izamal (M$41, two hours, two buses at 12:45pm and 3:50pm)
Mérida (M$74 to M$110, two to three hours, many buses)
Playa del Carmen (M$78 to M$140, 2½ to 3½ hours, eight buses)
Tizimín (M$20, one hour, 12 buses)
Tulum (M$47 to M$60, two hours, six buses)

COLECTIVOS

Often faster, more reliable and more comfortable than 2nd-class buses are the *colectivos* that leave for various points as soon as their seats are filled. Most operate from 7am or 8am to about 7pm. Direct services to Mérida (from the ADO bus terminal; M$60) and Cancún (from in front of the cathedral; M$70) take a little over two hours – confirm they're nonstop, though. *Colectivos* for Pisté and Chichén Itzá (M$20, 40 minutes) leave across the road from the ADO bus terminal, and for Tizimín from the east side of the main plaza. *Colectivos* for Ek' Balam (M$30) leave from Calle 44, between Calles 35 and 37.

Getting Around

Bicycles are a great way to see the town and get out to the cenotes. **Tres Hermanos** (Calle 44 btwn Calles 39 & 41; ⏰ 7:30am-8pm Mon-Sat, 7:30am-2pm Sun) and **Antonio 'Negro' Aguilar** (☎ 856-2125; ⏰ 7am-7pm) rent bikes for about M$8 per hour. If you want a motor behind your wheels, taxis charge M$100 per hour.

EK' BALAM

The turnoff for fascinating **Ek' Balam** (admission M$27, guide M$250; ⏰ 8am-5pm) is 17km north of Valladolid, from where the archaeological site is a further 6km east. Vegetation still covers much of the area, but excavations and restoration continue to add to the sights, including an interesting ziggurat-like structure near the entrance, as well as a fine arch and a ball court.

Most impressive is the gargantuan **Acrópolis**, whose well-restored base is 160m long and holds a 'gallery,' actually a series of separate chambers. Built atop the base is Ek' Balam's massive main pyramid, reaching a height of 32m and sporting a huge jaguar mouth with 360-degree dentition. Below the mouth are stucco skulls, while above and to the right sits an amazingly expressive figure. On the right side stand unusual winged human figures (some call them Maya angels), whose hands are poised in gestures looking for all the world like Hindu/Buddhist *mudras* (ritual hand movements used in Hindu religious dancing; also gesture of Buddha figure). It's enough to make you wonder, either about connections between ancient civilizations or the artistic license taken by the restoration crew, though much of the plaster is supposed to be original.

The view from the top of the pyramid is fantastic as well. Across the flat terrain you can make out the pyramids of Chichén Itzá and Cobá.

From the Ek' Balam parking lot you can visit the **X-Canche Cenote** (☎ 985-107-4774; admission M$30, bike rental M$70, bike, rappel & kayak tour M$110; ☷ 8am-5pm). It's worth the extra dough to take the fun rappel and kayak tour.

The town of Ek' Balam itself is worth a visit, if only to see what a fairly traditional Maya village looks like. There are two nice hotels, as well as a handful of artisan stands along the main plaza, which also serves as the town's soccer field.

Sleeping & Eating

ourpick **Genesis Eco-Retreat** (☎ 985-852-7980; www .genesisretreat.com; d M$400-600; ☐ ☒ ☷ ☑) The Genesis Eco-Retreat offers B&B intimacy in a quiet, ecofriendly setting. This is a true ecotel: gray water is used for landscaping, some rooms are naturally cooled, insects are controlled by a crack squadron of mosquito-hating ducks and there's even an entire wall made out of plastic bottles. The place is postcard-beautiful – there's a chilling dip pool and *temescal* steam bath on-site – and offers delicious veggie meals. The hotel is sometimes closed between September and early October.

Dolcemente Ek' Balam (☎ /fax 045-985-103-6073; dolcementeekbalam@gmail.com; d M$500) It lacks a bit of soul, but Dolcemente does have a fine collection of super-clean fan-cooled rooms. The yummy restaurant specializes in (you guessed it) Italian fare.

Getting There & Away

It's possible to catch a *colectivo* from Calle 44 between Calles 35 and 37 in Valladolid for Ek' Balam (M$30). A round-trip taxi ride from Valladolid with an hour's wait at the ruins will cost around M$250.

TIZIMÍN

☎ 986 / pop 44,151

Tizimín is dusty and 'authentic,' meaning that you won't find much here that's designed with the tourist in mind. That doesn't make it less of a place to investigate, however, and some travelers may find Tizimín a refreshing change if they've just come from Playa del Carmen or Cancún. Most travelers will be bound for Río Lagartos, San Felipe and Isla Holbox, as there isn't much that warrants an overnight stay. Still, the tree-filled Parque Principal is pleasant, particularly at sundown.

The city fills with people from outlying ranches during its annual fair to celebrate **Día de los Reyes Magos** (Three Kings' Day), which lasts from January 1 to 15.

Two great colonial structures – **Parroquia Los Santos Reyes de Tizimín** (Church of the Three Wise Kings) and its former **Franciscan monastery** (the ex-convento) – are worth having a look while you're waiting for your bus connection. They're on opposite sides of Calle 51, reached by walking two blocks south on Calle 48, which itself is a block west of the bus terminals.

The church fronts Tizimín's main plaza, the Parque Principal, which has an HBSC with ATM and currency exchange on its southwest side.

Sleeping & Eating

Posada María Antonia (☎ 863-2857; Calle 50 No 408; r with air-con M$220; ☷) Just south of the church, it has 12 bare-bones rooms, each holding up to four people.

Hotel San Carlos (☎ 863-2094; hsancarlos@hotmail .com; Calle 54 No 407, btwn Calles 51 & 53; r with air-con M$290; ☷) Two blocks west of the plaza, this is the nicest hotel in town. All the air-con rooms have private patios looking onto the shared garden area.

Market (cnr Calles 47 & 48) The market, half a block west of the Noreste bus terminal, has the usual cheap eateries.

Pizzería César's (Calle 50; pizza M$30-60, mains M$60-110; ☷ 8am-1am) A popular joint near the Posada María Antonia, it serves inexpensive pasta

YUCATÁN STATE

dishes, sandwiches and burgers in addition to pizza and steak.

Getting There & Away

Oriente and Mayab, both offering 2nd-class services, share a **bus terminal** (Calle 47 btwn Calles 48 & 46) just east of the market. **Noreste bus terminal** (Calle 46), offering 1st- and 2nd-class services, is just around the corner.

Cancún (M$85, three to 3½ hours, 15 Mayab and Noreste buses)

Izamal (M$55, 2½ hours, Oriente bus at 5:30am, 11am and 4pm)

Mérida (M$83, 2½ to 3½ hours, 2nd-class Noreste buses at 5:30am, 9am, 2:30pm, 4pm and 5pm)

Río Lagartos/San Felipe (M$20 to M$25, one hour, six Noreste buses between 6am and 4:15pm, some *colectivos*) Some buses continue 12km west to San Felipe (same price).

Valladolid (M$20, one hour, 16 Oriente buses between 5:30am and 7:30pm)

Taxis to Río Lagartos or San Felipe charge about M$250, and leave from outside both bus terminals. The drivers can be asked to wait for you for M$100 per additional hour.

RÍO LAGARTOS

☎ 986 / pop 2127

On the windy northern shore of the peninsula, sleepy Río Lagartos (Alligator River) is a fishing village that also boasts the densest concentration of flamingos in Mexico, supposedly two or three flamingos per Mexican, if one believes the math. Lying within the **Reserva de la Biósfera Ría Lagartos**, this mangrove-lined estuary also shelters 334 other species of resident and migratory birds, including snowy egrets, red egrets, tiger herons and snowy white ibis, as well as a small number of the once-numerous crocodiles that gave the town its name. It's a beautiful area. At the right time of year you can see numerous species of birds without even getting out of your vehicle.

The Maya knew the place as Holkobén and used it as a rest stop on their way to Las Coloradas, a shallow part of the vast estuary that stretches east almost to the border of Quintana Roo. There they extracted precious salt from the waters, a process that continues on a much vaster scale today. Spanish explorers mistook the narrowing of the *ría* (estuary) for a *río* (river) and the crocs for alligators, and the rest is history. Hurricane Isadore destroyed much of the mangrove forest in 2002, but it's slowly recovering.

Less than 1km east of town, on the edge of the estuary, a natural *ojo de agua dulce* (natural spring) has been developed into a swimming hole. A sometimes-empty tourist kiosk sits at the end of Calle 10 by the waterfront.

Orientation & Information

Most residents aren't sure of the town's street names, and signs are few. The road into town is the north–south Calle 10, which ends at the waterfront Calle 13. There's no bank or ATM in town, so bring lots of cash.

Flamingo, Shorebird & Wildlife Tours

The brilliant orange-red flamingos can turn the horizon fiery when they take wing. Depending on your luck, you'll see either hundreds or thousands of them. The best months for viewing them are June to August. The four primary haunts, in increasing distance from town, are Punta Garza, Yoluk, Necopal and Nahochín (all flamingo feeding spots named for nearby mangrove patches).

To see the flamingos, you'll need to rent a boat and driver. You'll see more birdlife if you head out at sunrise or around 4pm. Prices vary by boat, group size (maximum six) and destination. A one-hour trip costs around M$500, and two to three hours is M$700. In addition, the reserve charges visitors a M$20 admission fee. Plan on packing something to eat the night before, as most restaurants open long after you'll be on the water.

You can negotiate with one of the eager men in the waterfront kiosks near the entrance to town; it's nearly impossible to get through town without being approached by someone. They speak English and will connect you with a captain (who usually doesn't). The best guides are to be found at **Restaurante-Bar Isla Contoy** (☎ 862-0000); driving into town, turn left on Calle 19 at the sign for the restaurant-bar. From the bus terminal, head to the water and turn left (west).

FLAMINGO ETIQUETTE

Although the sight of flamingos taking to the wing is impressive, for the well-being of the birds, please ask your boat captain not to frighten the birds into flight. You can generally get to within 100m of the birds before they walk or fly away.

CELEBRATING LA FERIA DE SANTIAGO AND DÍA DE LA MARINA

Río Lagartos knows how to party, and two festivals, La Feria de Santiago and Día de la Marina, are well worth checking out. **La Feria de Santiago**, the patron-saint festival of Río Lagartos, is held mid-July. A bullfight (really bullplay) ring is erected in the middle of town during the weeklong event, and every afternoon anyone who wishes is able to enter it and play matador with a young bull. The animal is not killed or even injured, just made a little angry at times. Don't turn your back to it or it will knock you down. Call a hotel in town to find out when the festival is being held.

Another big annual event in Río Lagartos is the **Día de la Marina** (Day of the Marine Force), which is always on June 1. On this day, following 9am Mass, a crown of flowers is dedicated to the Virgin and is carried from the church to a boat, where it is then taken 4km out to sea and placed in the water as an offering to all the fishermen who have perished at sea.

The boats, not incidentally, are heavily decorated on this day, and tourists are welcome to ride to the site for free. Just ask if you can go, and be friendly and respectful. A tip for their kindness, following the service, is always appreciated (M$50 to M$100 per visitor).

If time permits, seek out **Ismael Navarro** (☎ 862-0000; www.riolagartosexpeditions.com) or **Diego Núñez Martínez** (diego2909@yahoo.com), two licensed guides with formal training as naturalists. They speak English, Spanish and Italian and are up to date on the fauna and flora in the area, including the staggering number of bird species, for which they have books and the official Yucatán Peninsula checklist.

Besides their flamingo expeditions, Ismael takes four-hour shorebird tours along the mudflats in winter. Diego offers catch-and-release fly-fishing trips for tarpon and snook, and can help with lodgings reservations. Both also offer land tours for birding as well as night rides looking for crocodiles and, from May to September, sea turtles.

For M$200 you can get a boat to take you across the lagoon for a couple of hours on the beach.

Sleeping & Eating

Posada Las Gaviotas (☎ 862-0507; Calle 12 with the riverfront; d M$250) This simple budget option right on the riverfront offers clean fan-cooled rooms bathed in avocado green. There are no toilet seats.

Posada Isla Contoy (☎ 862-0000; www.riolagartoexpeditions.com; Calle 19 No 134, cnr Calle 14; s/d M$200/350; 🍴) Next to the restaurant Isla Contoy (ask there to see the rooms), this hotel has five very simple rooms. You can pay a bit extra for the air-con, which doesn't really work anyway. That's OK as there are fans overhead and a boob box with local programming to keep you company.

Hotel Villas de Pescadores (☎ 862-0020; villa_pescadores@prodigy.net.mx; Calle 14 & Calle 9; d with fan/air-con M$400/500; 🍴) Near the water's edge, this nice hotel offers nine very clean rooms, each with good cross-ventilation (all face the estuary), two beds and a fan. Upstairs rooms have balconies, and there's a rickety spiral staircase leading up to a rooftop lookout tower where adventurous guests can (careful on those stairs!) watch the sun set or sip a relaxing beverage. Guests planning on an early morning flamingo trip can ask for breakfast to be prepared before they head off (an additional M$35 to M$60). The owner rents bicycles and canoes as well, and there's a new restaurant on-site.

Restaurante-Bar Isla Contoy (Calle 19; mains M$50-100; 🕐 8am-9pm) A popular eatery at the waterfront, this is a good place to meet other travelers and form groups for the boat tours. Lobster, at market price, is a delicious specialty.

Getting There & Away

Several Noreste buses run daily between Tizimín (M$20 to M$25, one hour), Mérida (M$110, three to four hours) and San Felipe (M$10, 20 minutes). Noreste and Mayab also serve Cancún (M$120, three to four hours) three times daily.

EAST OF RÍO LAGARTOS

The road between Río Lagartos and El Cuyo often washes out in rainy season, but it's normally passable in dry season (even with a non-4WD vehicle). Ask locally before you take the trip (you'll need your own wheels), which is truly a birder's delight. It's best to take the trip early in the morning, when you are likely to see egrets, blue heron, osprey and gaggles of pink flamingos. If you do stop to observe wildlife, be as quiet as possible and remember that there are crocodiles in the shallows, as well as venomous snakes: don't let that great roseate spoonbill photo opportunity send you to the hospital.

Start your trip by turning east at the junction about 2km south of Río Lagartos. About 8km from the junction, on the south side of the road, is the beginning of a 1km **interpretive trail** to Petén Tucha (a *petén* is a hummock or rise often forming around a spring). You should register at the biosphere reserve's office near the junction before walking the trail.

Continuing east on the road 4km beyond the trailhead you'll reach a bridge over a very narrow part of the estuary. Fishermen cast nets here, and you can sometimes see crocs lurking in the water (look for dead horseshoe crabs on the bridge). Another 6km beyond this is **Las Coloradas**, a small town housing workers who extract salt from the vast shallow lagoons of the same name that stretch eastward for kilometers on the south side of the road. The salt is piled in gleaming mounds that look like icebergs, up to 15m high, and from a distance it appears oddly incongruous, as if you've arrived in the Arctic despite the blistering heat.

The road turns to sand after Las Coloradas, but you can still make it to El Cuyo most times of year. You may consider spending a few Robinson Crusoe days on the beach here, but the brown sands are pretty littered with trash. The unique vegetation includes century plants, an agave species that lives quietly for decades before sending up a tall stalk that blossoms, in turn triggering the final demise of the plant. These are different from the henequen agaves that you see further south.

El Cuyo

At the end of the road, El Cuyo has a clear white-sand beach, muddy waters, and curiously smells a bit like old socks. The town sees a few local tourists looking for a short beach vacation, but not many foreigners pass through. Maybe this is the off-the-beaten-track spot you were looking for all this time.

Cabañas Mar y Sol (☎ 986-853-4062; cabana M$350), one block west of the town square,

has very simple and clean cabins occupying a large swath of green grass that heads straight down to the beach. Some even have hot water and cable TV. La Cochinita restaurant is attached to the hotel and is quite popular with locals.

You can get here by the coastal road east from Río Lagartos. If the road is out, reach El Cuyo by heading back towards Tizimín and then turning left (east) at the first paved road, heading toward Yoactún. Follow this through savanna-like grassy ranchland until you come to a T-junction at Colonia Yucatán. Head left (north) and you'll arrive in El Cuyo.

At El Cuyo the road passes through broad expanses of grassy savanna with palms and some huge-trunked trees, passing the site of the original founding of Valladolid, in 1543. At Colonia Yucatán, a little over 30km south of El Cuyo, you can head east to pick up the road to Chiquilá and Isla Holbox (or in the opposite direction to Hwy 180) or west to Tizimín. Public transportation through all of this is scarce. Hitchhiking may be possible, but a rental car is by far the better way to go.

SAN FELIPE
☎ 986 / pop 1769

San Felipe is a fishing village seldom visited by travelers, about 12km west of Río Lagartos, notable for its orderly streets, cheery Caribbean feel and painted wooden houses. With its laid-back air, this is a good alternative to staying in Río Lagartos. Getting there you'll pass primarily swampy mangrove-dotted lagoons, and perhaps surprise a turtle or two crossing the road. Its beach lies across the mouth of the estuary, at Punta Holohit, and the mangroves there and on the western edge of town are a bird-watcher's paradise. Just looking out the windows of the town's one hotel you can see white and brown pelicans, terns, cormorants, great blue herons, magnificent frigate birds and jabirus (storks).

The beach, though not great, usually has *palapas* providing shade. *Lancheros* (boat owners) charge M$100 per boatload (round-trip) to take passengers across, or M$800 for a half-day fishing or birding trip.

At the corner of Calles 12 and 13 is a simple **shed** (internet per hr M$8) with five or six computers with dial-up connections. It's run by a very kind young man with a health problem and this café helps him support himself.

Hotel San Felipe de Jesús (☎ 862-2027; hotelsf@hot mail.com; d M$400-450, with balcony M$490) is a friendly, clean and cleverly constructed hotel at the edge of San Felipe's harbor. To get there, turn left at the water and proceed about 200m. Six of the 18 rooms are large and have private balconies and water views (it's definitely worth the extra pesos for these rooms). The restaurant offers good seafood at low prices.

Six buses from Tizimín pass through Río Lagartos and continue to San Felipe (M$20 to M$22, 1½ hours) each way. The bus ride from Río Lagartos (M$10) takes 20 minutes. You can take a taxi from Tizimín to San Felipe for M$250, but you will possibly need to arrange return pickup in advance or pay the driver an hourly rate to wait until you're ready to return.

Campeche State

Tucked into the southwestern corner of the Yucatán Peninsula like a forgotten stepdaughter, Campeche is home to vast stretches of tangled jungle, some of the region's least visited and most imposing Maya ruins, forgotten pastoral villages, bird-choked coastal lagoons and an inspiring colonial-era capital city. It's the least touristed of the Yucatán's states, and in that lies its provincial, lost-land charm.

In the northeastern Chenes region and other remote corners, women still don *huipiles* (colorfully embroidered tunics), and Yucatec is widely spoken. The backroads of this northern region bring you to forgotten underground wonderworlds, the massive restored Edzná archaeological site and a handful of smaller, less-traveled Maya ruins.

This is also the wildest corner of the Peninsula, and the Reserva de la Biósfera Calakmul is Mexico's largest reserve. Here you can spot toucans, monkeys and even the occasional big jungle cat. And beyond the cacophonous roar of the howlers and hiccuping frogs rise massive Maya ruined cities such as Calakmul and Becán. Along the coast, the Laguna de Términos is great for birding, and beach bums revel in the solitude on forgotten beaches.

The southern coast of Campeche was affected by an oil spill in October 2007, and boomtowns such as Ciudad del Carmen are changing the spirit (and environment) of the region. Nevertheless, the age-old grace of the *campechanos* (residents of Campeche) abides. And the walled city of Campeche, without a doubt the best-preserved colonial capital on the peninsula, remains the cultural epicenter of the region, offering a great jumping-off point for your adventure into the offbeat hinterland.

HIGHLIGHTS

- Feel the burn as you haul yourself up the massive pyramid at **Calakmul** (p222), heavy-nosed toucans soaring past toward their treetop jungle hideaways

- Stroll through history as you cruise the colonial-era streets of **Campeche** (p204), with their pastel-hued edifices and arching ramparts

- Stop to test out your Yucatec in Maya strongholds along the old route to Mérida, visiting **Hochob** (p217) and the **Chenes sites** (p217) along the way

- Find your little patch of foggy-bottomed paradise on one of the region's lost beaches around **Playa Varadero** (p219)

- Head out for an afternoon birding mission on the **Laguna de Términos** (p219)

- POPULATION: 754,730
- AREA: 56,798 SQ KM

CAMPECHE

☎ 981 / pop 211,671

Campeche is a colonial fairyland, its walled city center a tight enclave of perfectly restored pastel buildings, narrow cobblestone streets, fortified ramparts and well-preserved mansions. Added to Unesco's list of World Heritage sites in 1999, the state capital has been so painstakingly restored you wonder if it's a real city. Nearly 2000 structures have been renovated. But leave the city's walls and you'll find a real Mexican provincial capital complete with a frenetic market, a quiet *malecón* (waterfront boulevard) and old fishing docks.

Relatively few tourists visit the city, meaning the town retains its authenticity – it's not a tourist trap, at least not yet. And the big-hearted and proud *campechanos* are likely to show you an unobtrusive and reserved hospitality not seen in other regional capitals such as Chetumal or Mérida.

Besides the numerous mansions built by wealthy Spanish families during Campeche's heyday in the 18th and 19th centuries, two segments of the city's wall have also survived, as have no fewer than seven of the *baluartes* (bastions or bulwarks) that were built into it. Two perfectly preserved colonial forts guard the city's outskirts, one of them housing the Museo de la Arquitectura Maya, an archaeological museum with world-class pieces.

The city's central location on the Gulf of Mexico makes it the perfect jumping-off point for adventures to the Chenes sites, Edzná and neighboring beaches. Come back at night to enjoy the gauzy light of the illuminated church and other central landmarks.

HISTORY

Once a Maya trading village called Ah Kim Pech (Lord Sun Sheep-Tick), Campeche was first briefly approached by the Spaniards in 1517. Resistance by the Maya prevented the Spaniards from fully conquering the region for nearly a quarter-century. Colonial Campeche was founded in 1531, but later abandoned due to Maya hostility. By 1540, however, the conquistadors had gained sufficient control, under the leadership of Francisco de Montejo (the Younger), to found a permanent settlement. They named the settlement Villa de San Francisco de Campeche.

The settlement soon flourished as the major port of the Yucatán Peninsula, but this made it subject to pirate attacks (see boxed text, p207). After a particularly appalling attack in 1663 left the city in ruins, the king of Spain ordered construction of Campeche's famous bastions, putting an end to the periodic carnage.

Today the economy of the city is largely driven by fishing and, increasingly, tourism, which to some extent have funded the downtown area's renovation.

ORIENTATION

Though the bastions still stand, the walls have been mostly razed and replaced by Avenida Circuito Baluartes, which rings the city center (Centro Histórico) as the walls once did. In the classic colonial plan, the center is surrounded by barrios (neighborhoods), each with its own church and square. Particularly charming are San Román, Guadalupe and Santa Ana.

The streets in the central grid follow a numbered sequence: inland-oriented streets have odd numbers and perpendicular ones even.

A multilane boulevard with bicycle and pedestrian paths extends along Campeche's shoreline, from the Fuerte de San Miguel (San Miguel Fort) in the southwest to Fuerte de San José (San José Fort) in the northeast. Graced by a series of monuments, the boulevard is commonly referred to as La Costera or the *malecón*, though the stretch closest to the city center is officially named Avenida Adolfo Ruiz Cortínez.

INFORMATION

Internet Access

All of the hostels and quite a few hotels provide online services, and 'cibers' abound in the Centro Histórico.

Laundry

Same-day laundry service is available at the following locations.

Kler Lavandería (Calle 16 No 305; per kilogram M$10; ☽ 8am-6pm Mon-Fri, 8am-4pm Sat)

Lavandería Antigua (Calle 57; per kilogram M$15; ☽ 8am-4pm Mon-Sat) Between Calles 12 and 14.

Medical Services

In an emergency, call one of the following.

Cruz Roja (Red Cross; ☎ 815-2411; cnr Av Las Palmas & Ah Kim Pech) Some 3km northeast of downtown.

Emergency (☎ 066)

Hospital Dr Manuel Campos (☎ 811-1709; Av Circuito Baluartes Norte) Between Calles 14 and 16.

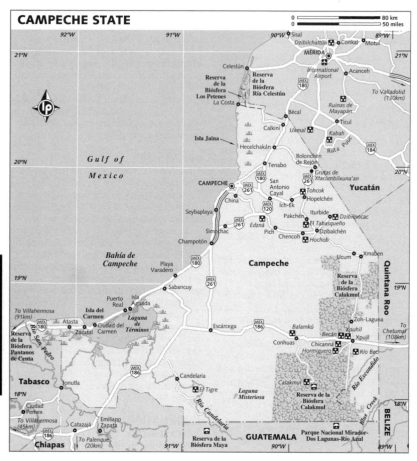

Money

Campeche has numerous banks with ATMs, open 8am to 4pm Monday to Friday, 9am to 2pm Saturday.

Post

Central post office (cnr Av 16 de Septiembre & Calle 53; 8:30am-3:30pm Mon-Fri)

Tourist Information

Coordinación Municipal de Turismo (☎ 811-3989; www.ayuntamientodecampeche.gob.mx; Calle 55 No 3; 9am-9pm) Next to the cathedral, the municipal tourist office is the more useful of the two information centers.

Secretaría de Turismo (☎ 816-6767; Plaza Moch Couoh; 9am-9pm) Service is inconsistent here though staff will gladly hand you some brochures.

SIGHTS & ACTIVITIES
Plaza Principal

Shaded by spreading carob trees, and ringed by tiled benches with broad footpaths radiating from a *belle époque* kiosk, Campeche's appealingly modest central square started life in 1531 as a military camp. Over the years it became the focus of the town's civic, political and religious activities and remains the core of public life. *Campechanos* come here to chat, smooch, have their shoes shined or cool off with a dish of ice cream after the heat of the day. The plaza is seen at its best on weekend evenings, when it's closed to traffic and concerts are staged (see p211).

The plaza is surrounded by suitably fine buildings. On the northern (seaward) side stands a replica of the old government center, now housing the modern **Biblioteca de Campeche** (State Library; ☺ 9am-2:30pm & 3-8:30pm Mon-Fri, 9am-noon Sat). The impressive porticoed building on the opposite side housed an earlier version of the city hall; it is now occupied by shops and restaurants.

CATEDRAL DE NUESTRA SEÑORA DE LA PURÍSIMA CONCEPCIÓN

Dominating the Plaza Principal's east side is the two-towered **cathedral** (admission free; ☺ 7am-noon & 4-6pm). The limestone structure has stood on this spot for more than three centuries, and it still fills beyond capacity most Sundays. Statues of St Peter and St Paul occupy niches in the baroque façade; the sober, single-nave interior is lined with colonial-era paintings.

CENTRO CULTURAL CASA NÚMERO 6

During the pre-revolutionary era, when the mansion was occupied by an upper-class *campechano* family, **Número 6** (Calle 57 No 6; admission M$5; ☺ 9am-9pm) was a prestigious plaza address. Wandering the premises, you'll get an idea of how the city's high society lived back then. The front sitting room is furnished with Cuban pieces of the period. Inside are exhibition spaces and a good bookstore.

Baluartes

After a particularly blistering pirate assault in 1663 (see p207), the remaining inhabitants of Campeche set about erecting protective walls around their city. Built largely by indigenous labor with limestone extracted from nearby caves, the barrier took more than 50 years to complete. Stretching more than 2.5km around the urban core and rising to a height of 8m, the hexagonal wall was linked by eight bulwarks. The seven that remain display a treasure trove of historical paraphernalia, artifacts and indigenous handicrafts. You can climb atop the bulwarks and stroll sections of the wall for sweeping views of the port.

Two main entrances connected the walled compound with the outside world. The **Puerta del Mar** (Sea Gate; cnr Calles 8 & 59) provided access from the sea, opening onto a wharf where small craft delivered goods from ships anchored further out. (The shallow waters were later reclaimed so the gate is now several blocks from the waterfront.) The **Puerta de Tierra** (Land Gate; Calle 18; admission free; ☺ 9am-9pm), on the opposite side, was opened in 1732

as the principal ingress from the suburbs. It is now the venue for a sound-and-light show (p211).

Designed to protect the Puerta del Mar, the **Baluarte de Nuestra Señora de la Soledad** was the largest of the bastions completed in the late 1600s. Appropriately, it was named for the patron saint of sailors. This bulwark contains the fascinating **Museo de la Arquitectura Maya** (Calle 8; admission M$27, free Sun; ☺ 8am-7:30pm Tue-Sun), the one must-see museum in Campeche. It provides an excellent overview of the sites around Campeche state and the key architectural styles associated with them. Five halls display stelae taken from various sites, accompanied by graphic representations of their carved inscriptions with brief commentaries in flawless English.

Completed in 1704 – the last of the bulwarks to be built – the **Baluarte de Santiago** (cnr Calles 8 & 49; admission M$10; ☺ 9am-9pm) houses the **Jardín Botánico Xmuch Haltún**, a botanical garden with numerous endemic plants. Unless you're really into plants, it's not worth the entrance fee.

Named after Spain's King Carlos II, the **Baluarte de San Carlos** houses the **Museo de la Ciudad** (Calle 8; admission M$27; ☺ 8am-7:30pm Tue-Sun). This small but worthwhile museum chronologically illustrates the city's tempestuous history via well-displayed objects: specimens of dyewood, muskets, a figurehead from a ship's prow and the like. The dungeon downstairs alludes to the building's use as a military prison during the 1700s.

Directly behind Iglesia de San Juan de Dios, the **Baluarte de San Pedro** (cnr Avs Circuito Este & Circuito Baluartes Norte; admission free; ☺ 9am-9pm) served a postpiracy defensive function when it repelled a punitive raid from Mérida in 1824. Carved in stone above the entry is the symbol of San Pedro: two keys to heaven and the papal tiara. Climb the steep ramp to the roof and look between the battlements to see San Juan's cupola. Downstairs, the **Museo y Galería de Arte Popular** (Museum & Gallery of Folk Art; admission free; ☺ 9am-9pm Mon-Sat, 9am-2pm Sun) displays beautiful indigenous handicrafts.

Once the primary defensive bastion for the adjacent Puerta de la Tierra, the **Baluarte de San Francisco** (Calle 18; admission to both San Francisco & San Juan M$20; ☺ 9am-2pm & 4-7pm Mon-Sat, 9am-2pm Sun) houses a small arms museum. Down the street is the **Baluarte de San Juan** (Calle 18; admission with San Francisco ticket free; ☺ 8am-7:30pm Tue-Sun), the smallest of the

CAMPECHE

0 ──────── 300 m
0 ──────── 0.2 miles

INFORMATION
Banamex 1 C3
Banco Santander Mexicano.....2 B2
Central Post Office...................3 C2
Coordinación Municipal de
    Turismo...............................4 B2
Hospital Dr Manuel Campos....5 D3
Inegi.......................................6 A3
Kler Lavandería.......................7 B4
Lavandería Antigua.................8 C3
Secretaría de Turismo.............9 A3

Gulf of Mexico

CAMPECHE STATE

Parque de
las Banderas

Mansión
Carvajal

**Parque del
IV Centenario**

Plaza
Moch-Couoh

Plaza de la
República

Plaza
Principal

Palacio de
Gobierno

Palacio
Legislativo

Palacio
Municipal

**Iglesia
Dulce
Nombre
de Jesús**

*To Clubs & Discos (1km);
Las Mañanitas (2km);
Museo Arqueológico de
Campeche (3.5km);
Fuerte de San
Miguel (3.5km);*

*Paseo de
los Héroes*

**Iglesia de
San Juan
de Dios**

*To Iglesia de
San Román (350m);
Universidad Autónoma
de Campeche (2km);
Centro de Español
y Maya (2km)*

*Centro de
Convenciones
Campeche XXI*

*To Plaza Cuatro de Octubre (1.2km);
Parador Gastronómico
de Cocteleros (2km);
Los Piratas/Estadio Nelson Barrera (3km);
Isla de Jaina (32km);
Mérida (toll road, 177km)*

*To Fuerte Museo
San José del
Alto (2.5km);
Cruz Roja (3km)*

*To Plazuela de
San Francisco (650m);
Cenaduría Portales (650m)*

*To 2nd-class Bus
Terminal (400m)*

Alameda

*To Main Bus Terminal (2km); Airport (5.5km); Edzná (60km);
Mérida (long route, 235km); Ciudad del Carmen (toll road, 237km)*

SIGHTS & ACTIVITIES
Baluarte de Nuestra Señora de la
    Soledad......................(see 20)
Baluarte de San Carlos........(see 21)
Baluarte de San Francisco........10 C4
Baluarte de San Juan...............11 B5
Baluarte de San Pedro.........(see 22)
Baluarte de Santa Rosa...........12 A4
Baluarte de Santiago...............13 C2
Biblioteca de Campeche...........14 B2
Catedral de Nuestra Señora de la
    Purísma Concepción............15 C3
Centro Cultural Casa Número 6....16 B3
Ex-Templo de San José............17 A3
Instituto Campechano..............18 A3
Jardín Botánico Xmuch Haltún...(see 13)
Monument to the City Gates.......19 A3
Museo de la Arquitectura Maya....20 B2
Museo de la Ciudad.................21 A3
Museo y Galería de Arte Popular....22 D4
Novia del Mar........................23 C1
Old Baseball Stadium..............24 B2
Pedro Sáinz de Baranda Monument....25 B2
Puerta de Tierra......................26 C4
Puerta del Mar.......................27 B3
Tranvía de la Ciudad...............28 B3
Xtampak Tours.......................29 B3

SLEEPING
Hostal del Pirata.....................30 C4
Hostal La Parroquia................(see 41)
Hotel América........................31 B3
Hotel Castelmar......................32 B3
Hotel Colonial........................33 C3
Hotel del Mar.........................34 B2
Hotel del Paseo......................35 A3
Hotel López...........................36 B3
Hotel Maya Campeche.............37 C4
Hotel Plaza Campeche.............38 C2
Hotel Reforma........................39 B3
Monkey Hostel........................40 B3

EATING
Café La Parroquia...................41 C3
Chef Color.............................42 C3
Lonchería Las Mañanitas..........43 D2
Marganzo..............................44 B3
Mercado Principal.................(see 52)
Mundo Natural.......................45 B3

Taquería Los Patitos................46 B3

DRINKING
La Casa Vieja.........................47 B3
Lafitte's..............................(see 34)
Salón Rincon Colonial..............48 C4

ENTERTAINMENT
Claustro del Instituto de Campeche....49 B3
Iguana Azul...........................50 C3
Puerta de Tierra....................(see 26)

SHOPPING
Bazar Artesanal......................51 C1
Mercado Principal...................52 D4

TRANSPORT
Local Bus Stop........................53 C4
Maya Rent a Car...................(see 34)
Payless Car Rental................(see 35)
Sur Champotón Terminal..........54 C4

RIBALD TALES: THE MARAUDING PIRATES OF CAMPECHE

Where there's wealth, there are pirates. This was no less true in the 1500s as it is today. And Campeche, which was a thriving chicle, timber and dyewood port in the mid-16th century, was the wealthiest place around.

Such riches did not escape the notice of pirates, who first attacked Campeche only six years after the town's founding. For two centuries, they terrorized the growing city. Ships were attacked, the port was invaded, citizens robbed, women raped and buildings burned – typical pirate stuff. The buccaneers' hall of shame counted the infamous John Hawkins, Diego the Mulatto, Barbillas and the notorious 'Pegleg' (Pata de Palo) himself. In their most gruesome assault, in early 1663, the various pirate hordes set aside rivalries to converge as a single flotilla upon the city, massacring Campeche's citizens.

This tragedy finally spurred the Spanish monarchy to take preventive action, but it was another five years before work on the 3.5m-thick ramparts began. By 1686 a 2.5km hexagon incorporating eight strategically placed bastions surrounded the city. A segment of the ramparts extended out to sea so that ships literally had to sail into a fortress to gain access to the city.

With Campeche nearly impregnable, pirates turned to other ports and ships at sea. In 1717 the brilliant naval strategist Felipe de Aranda began a campaign against the buccaneers, and eventually made this area of the Gulf safe from piracy. Of course, all that wealth from chicle and timber was being created using indigenous slaves, leading one to question: who were the real pirates, anyway?

seven, containing a permanent exhibition on the history of the bulwarks. And the **Baluarte de Santa Rosa** (cnr Calles 14 & Circuito Baluartes Sur; admission free; 10am-3pm & 6-9pm), a couple of blocks to the northwest, has Campeche's art gallery.

Ex-Templo de San José

Faced with flamboyant blue-and-yellow tiles, the **Ex-Templo de San José** (former San José church; cnr Calles 10 & 63; admission M$15; 9am-3pm & 3:45-8:30pm Tue-Sun) is a wonder to behold; note the lighthouse, complete with weather vane, atop the right spire. Built in the early 18th century by Jesuits who ran it as an institute of higher learning until they were booted out of Spanish domains in 1767, it now serves as an exhibition space. It belongs to the Instituto Campechano, the university to which it's attached.

Museo Arqueológico de Campeche & Fuerte de San Miguel

Campeche's largest colonial fort, facing the Gulf of Mexico some 4km southwest of the city center, is now home to the excellent **Museo Arqueológico de Campeche** (Campeche Archaeological Museum; admission M$34; 9am-7:30pm Tue-Sun). Here you can admire findings from the sites of Calakmul and Edzná, and from Isla de Jaina, an island north of town once used as a burial site for Maya aristocracy.

Stunning jade jewelry and exquisite vases, masks and plates are thematically arranged

in 10 exhibit halls. The star attractions are the jade burial masks from Calakmul. Also displayed are stelae, seashell necklaces and clay figurines.

Equipped with a dry moat and working drawbridge, the fort itself is a thing of beauty. The roof deck, ringed by 20 cannons, affords wonderful harbor views.

Buses marked 'Lerma' or 'Playa' depart from the market and travel counterclockwise around the Circuito before heading down the *malecón*. The access road to the fort is 4km southwest of the Plaza Moch-Couoh. Hike 700m up the hill (bear left at the fork). Otherwise, take a taxi (M$35) or the *tranvía* (trolley; see p208).

Fuerte Museo San José del Alto

San Miguel's northern counterpart, built in the late 18th century, sits atop the Cerro de Bellavista. From the parapets you can see where the town ends and the mangroves begin. Cross a drawbridge over a moat to enter the neatly restored fortress. Inside, a **museum** (Av Francisco Morazán; admission M$27, Sun free; 8am-7pm Tue-Sun) illustrates the port's maritime history through ship models, weaponry and other paraphernalia, including a beautiful ebony rudder carved in the shape of a hound.

To get there, catch a local, green 'Josefa,' 'Bellavista' or 'Morelos' bus from the side of the market.

CAMPECHE STATE

Malecón

A popular path for joggers, cyclists, strolling friends and cooing sweethearts, the **malecón**, Campeche's waterfront promenade, makes a breezy sunrise ramble or sunset bike ride.

A series of monuments along the 2.5km stretch allude to various personages and events in the city's history. Southwest of the Plaza Moch-Couoh stands a statue of Campeche native **Justo Sierra Méndez**, a key player in the modernization of Mexico's educational system. Northeast up the *malecón* is a **sculpture** representing the city's two forts, San Miguel and San José. In front of the Plaza Moch-Couoh is a **monument** of the walled city's four gates. A block past the Hotel del Mar is a monumental sculpture of native son **Pedro Sáinz de Baranda**, who played a key role in defeating the Spanish at their last stronghold in Veracruz, thus ending the War of Independence. Just beyond the Centro de Convenciones Campeche, the girl gazing out to sea is the **Novia del Mar**. According to a poignant local legend, the *campechana* fell in love with a foreign pirate and awaits his return. About 1km further north, the **Plaza Cuatro de Octubre** (October 4 Plaza) commemorates the date of the city's 'founding,' depicting the fateful meeting of a Maya cacique (chief, who was evidently lost, since it took Montejo to found the city), the conquistador Francisco de Montejo and a priest. At the *malecón*'s northern end is the seafood restaurant complex known as the Parador Gastrónomico de Cockteleros (p210).

While there are no real beaches to speak of in town, by the time you get down to Las Mañanitas (p210), just over 2km to the southwest, the water is clear enough for **swimming**.

COURSES

Universidad Autónoma de Campeche Centro de Español y Maya (CEM; etzna.uacam.mx/cem/principal.htm; Av Agustín Melgar), one block east of the *malecón*, offers four- to eight-week summer language courses. Homestays can be arranged. Drop by to sit in on classes or check the notice board for Spanish teachers.

TOURS

Monkey Hostel, Hostal La Parroquia and Hostal del Pirata will all arrange tours and/ or shuttle services to the Maya sites. Hostal del Pirata also offers kayaking tours of Isla de Jaina and the Reserva de la Biósfera

Los Petenes (M$300 per person), as well as tarpon-fishing expeditions.

Tranvía de la Ciudad (adult M$80, child under 10yr free; ☿ hourly 9am-1pm & 5-9pm) Three different tours by motorized *tranvía* depart from Calle 10 beside the Plaza Principal daily; all last about 45 minutes. On the same schedule, the trolley called 'El Guapo' goes to the Fuerte de San Miguel or its twin on the north side of town, the Fuerte de San José. (Note that the fort tours do not leave time to visit the museums within them.) Buy tram tickets and check schedules at the booth just inside the plaza from the trolley stop.

Xtampak Tours (☎ 811-6473; xtampak_7@yahoo .com.mx; Calle 57 No 14; ☿ 8am-4pm & 5:30-8:30pm) Offers comprehensive city tours at 9am and 4pm daily (M$250 per person, four hours), as well as archaeological tours to Edzná (M$180), the Chenes sites (M$750) and eastern Campeche. You pay extra (M$700) for a bilingual guide, who can lead groups of up to seven people. Overnight packages are available to Calakmul and Río Bec.

FESTIVALS & EVENTS

Carnaval Campeche pulls out all the stops for Carnaval in February, with at least a week of festivities leading up to 'Sábado de Bando' (Carnaval Saturday, date varies), when everyone dresses up in outrageous costumes and parades down the *malecón*. The official conclusion is a week later, when a pirate effigy is torched and hurled into the sea, followed by much revelry in front of the Concha Acústica (bandshell) in the Barrio de San Román.

Feria de San Román September 14. This festival honors the beloved Cristo Negro (Black Christ) of the Iglesia de San Román. Fireworks and Ferris wheels take over the zone, just southwest of the center, along with beauty contests, boxing matches and a music-and-dance competition that brings in traditional ensembles from around the peninsula.

Día de Nuestra Señora de Guadalupe December 12. Pilgrimages from throughout the peninsula travel to the Iglesia de Guadalupe, 1.5km east of the Plaza Principal and Mexico's second-most-visited shrine, next to the Virgin of Guadalupe.

Festival del Centro Histórico Held throughout December with a jazz festival toward the end of the month. Coincides with Día de Nuestra Señora de Guadalupe on December 12.

SLEEPING

Budget

Campeche's three hostels all offer laundry services, free internet and complimentary breakfast, plus bicycle rentals and tours of archaeological sites.

our pick **Monkey Hostel** (☎ 811-6605; www.hostal campeche.com; cnr Calles 10 & 57; dm M$80, r without bathroom M$200; ▢) You can't beat the view of the plaza and cathedral from Campeche's longest-established and most popular hostel. The international social scene is enhanced by cozy common areas with bar, hammocks and well-worn sofas, and friendly bilingual staff. The beds are firm, but they don't have individual fans, which can make for a hot night.

Hostal del Pirata (☎ 811-1757; piratehostel@hotmail.com; Calle 59 No 47; dm M$90, r with/without bathroom M$230/210; 🖳) A block from the Puerta de Tierra, this Hostelling International (HI) affiliate is ensconced in Campeche's historic center, and the building itself is a 17th-century relic. Though it hasn't attained the Monkey's popularity, the Pirata's neatly kept premises may appeal to more fastidious travelers. Occupying a modern annex, dorms and 'semiprivate' rooms share modest facilities with cramped showers. The beds border on mashed-potato firmness, but you get your own fan.

Hostal La Parroquia (☎ 816-2530; www.hostalparroquia.com; Calle 55; dm M$90, d/q without bathroom M$200/300; 🖳) Half a block from the Plaza Principal, Campeche's newest hostel resides in a magnificent late-1500s mansion. Rooms with original stone walls and exposed wooden beams flank a grand hallway that opens onto a pleasant patio with small kitchen and adjacent lawn for sunbathing. Of the three hostels, it offers the best complimentary breakfast scheme: fresh fruit, toast and coffee at the café next door.

Hotel Reforma (☎ 816-4464; Calle 8 No 257; s M$120-250, d M$300; 🔀) Just off the Plaza Principal, this ancient hotel in a 400-year-old building has all the potential in the world. As is, it's a rather bizarre place. Enormous upstairs rooms have modern tiled bathrooms, high ceilings and great balconies, if you can handle the traffic noise. The threadbare sheets leave something to be desired. Rates vary with inclusion of TV, hot water and/or air-con; the complex scheme is posted over the reception desk.

Hotel Colonial (☎ 816-2222; Calle 14 No 122; s M$170, d M$180-200; 🔀) Time stands still within this stubbornly low-tech establishment, a budget traveler's haven for six decades. Indeed, little seems to have changed since it was occupied by king's lieutenant Miguel de Castro in the colonial era. Zealously maintained rooms surround a tranquil tiled courtyard with wicker-backed rockers and a central *aljibe* (rainwater cistern).

Hotel Maya Campeche (☎ 816-8053, 800-561-3730; www.mayacampechehotel.com.mx; Calle 57 No 40;

s/d M$380/440; 🔀 🖳) This small, boutique-style hotel in the heart of the walled city has a romantic, pseudo-colonial atmosphere and at-times taciturn staff. Fifteen rooms and painted wall motifs face a narrow courtyard.

Midrange

Hotel América (☎ 816-4576; www.hotelamericacampeche.com; Calle 10 No 252; s/d/tr M$420/480/540; 🔀) A large central hotel, the América has an impressive interior, with arcaded corridors surrounding a handsome courtyard where a complimentary breakfast is served. The 48 drab, all-business rooms clash with the charm and warmth of the common areas, but are clean and simply utilitarian.

ourpick Hotel López (☎ /fax 816-3344; www.hotellopezcampeche.com; Calle 12 No 189; d/tr/q M$490/540/590; 🔀 🖳) This elegant hotel is the best buy in the midrange category, though it lacks the charm of other colonial-styled digs. Comfortably appointed rooms open onto art-deco balconies around oval courtyards and exuberant gardens. There's a lovely new dip pool out back, where you can chill out while checking your emails with the wi-fi hookup.

Hotel del Paseo (☎ 811-0100; www.hoteldelpaseo.com; Calle 8 No 215; s/d/tr/q M$500/570/680/770; 🔀) Named for its proximity to the pleasant *paseo* (promenade) that connects the historic center with the Barrio San Román, this modern option has an interior promenade too, with street lamps, shops and a bar, all beneath your balcony.

Hotel Castelmar (☎ 811-1204; www.castelmarhotel.com; Calle 61 No 2; s/d/ste M$750/850/1050; 🔀) Once an army barracks, the Castelmar has been operating as a hotel for 100 years now. A recent remodeling job upped the casual refinement of this small hotel. Oversized crucifixes and other colonial-era-inspired ornaments add to the charm, as do the amazingly thick walls. Just try to scream – nobody will hear you.

Top End

Hotel Plaza Campeche (☎ 811-9900; www.hotelplazacampeche.com; cnr Calle 10 & Circuito Baluartes; r M$890, junior ste M$2120; 🔀 🖳 🛒) Just outside the historic center on the lovely Parque del IV Centenario, the Plaza caters to business travelers. It aims for Euro elegance with faux French furniture, a sumptuous dining room and attentive bellhops. The spacious rooms have soothing color schemes.

Hotel del Mar (☎ 811-9191; www.delmarhotel.com.mx; Av Adolfo Ruiz Cortínez 51; r with city/sea view M$950/1320; 🐾 🖳 🖭) The Miami-style Hotel del Mar, on the *malecón*, exudes luxury and a beachy glow. Rooms with sea views have balconies. There's a popular downstairs bar.

EATING

Taquería Los Patitos (Calle 8 No 289; tortas & trancas M$6-14; 🕙 7:30am-3pm) Chow down with the longshoremen at this friendly hole-in-the-wall, where overseer Doña Hilaria fills *tortas* (sandwiches in rolls) and *trancas* (baguettes stuffed with roast pork) with a variety of scrumptious fillings, such as shark-and-egg salad and *salpicón de res* (shredded beef salad). Don't miss the exotic fruit juices.

Lonchería Las Mañanitas (Calle 49B No 3; snacks & soups M$9-25, mains M$70-120; 🕙 6pm-midnight Thu-Tue) At the Portales de San Martín, a block north of Avenida Circuito Baluartes Norte, this place serving regional snacks under the arcades of the plaza is a popular gathering place for families and friends. The festive mood is buoyed by a steady stream of *panuchos* (tortillas filled with black beans), tamales and bowls of turkey soup.

Las Mañanitas (cnr Avenidas Resurgimiento & Lopez Mateos; panuchos M$9, mains M$70-120; 🕙 noon-1am) With great ocean views some 2km southwest of downtown, this place is perfect for sunset cocktails or a casual lunch or dinner. It serves basically the same menu as the city-center location (Lonchería Las Mañanitas), but the atmosphere burns two degrees hotter.

Mundo Natural (cnr Calles 8 & 61; juices M$18, salads M$20; 🕙 7am-4pm Mon-Fri, 8am-1pm Sat; 🅥) This open-air 'natural foods' bar opposite the Palacio de Gobierno prepares fresh juice combos, hefty salads and *sandwichónes* (very large double- or triple-decker sandwiches that are sliced into snack-sized sections).

Cenaduría Portales (☎ 811-1491; Calle 10, Portales de San Francisco 86; trancas M$20, soups M$25; 🕙 6pm-midnight) A relaxed place outside the walls, alongside the delightful Plazuela de San Francisco in the barrio of the same name. It specializes in regional dishes. On warm evenings, an ice-cold goblet of coconut *horchata* (a rice-based drink) really hits the spot.

Chef Color (☎ 811-4455; cnr Calles 55 & 12; full/half lunch platter M$25-40; 🕙 10am-6pm) This Central American–style eatery serves up large platters of toothsome fare from a steam table. The list of *guisados* (main courses) might include potato croquettes and Cuban-inspired *ropa vieja*

SKIP THE TOURIST TRAPS & DIG INTO TRADITIONAL CAMPECHANO CUISINE

Travelers who take their eating seriously will find plenty of good options in Campeche, but steer clear of the numerous tourist-oriented restaurants, which generally serve dull, overpriced fare. Such places are recognizable as they're empty when not occupied by tour groups.

On Saturday and Sunday the best place to sample Campeche cuisine is the Plaza Principal. Before sundown, stalls set up around the plaza to offer an impressive variety of home-cooked fare at reasonable prices. You can sample regional specialties such as *pibipollo* (chicken tamales traditionally cooked underground), *brazo de reina* (tamales with chopped *chaya* greens mixed into the dough) and *pan de cazón* (layers of shark and tortillas laced with a tomato-based sauce), plus various desserts and cold teas.

Though startlingly rustic compared with Campeche's spruced-up center, the main market, **Mercado Principal** (Circuito de Baluartes Este; 🕙 7am-5pm), across the street from the Baluarte de San Pedro, offers some terrific snacks. At the Calle 53 entrance, regional-style tamales are dispensed from big pots in the morning. Inside, take a battered stool at Taquería El Amigo Carlos Ruelas and order a *tranca* – a baguette stuffed with *lechón* (roast pork) – and an ice-cold glass of *agua de lima* (sweet lemon drink). In the adjacent circular market building a number of *cocina economica* (basic eatery) stalls ring the interior rotunda.

ourpick **Parador Gastrónomico de Cockteleros** (Av Pedro Sainz de Baranda; shrimp cocktails M$40-100, fish M$50-90; 🕙 9am-6:30pm), on the north end of the *malecón*, 2.5km from the Plaza Principal, is the place to partake of the bountiful seafood netted daily from the Gulf. About 20 thatched-roof restaurants all serve pretty much the same thing: shellfish cocktails and fried fish. Ask to see the day's catch and make your selection; a medium-sized fish goes for about M$50. Most places give you free starters such as fried shrimp or crab legs.

LA LOTERÍA

'Twenty-three, melons'...'47, volcano'... '41, rocking chair'...'78, rose'...'two, dove.'

It's Saturday night in Campeche, and the tables in front of the cathedral are already full for the ritual game of *la lotería,* held every Saturday and Sunday evening from 6pm to 10pm. The litany of icons is chanted through a cheap microphone by a woman in a *huipil* (colorfully embroidered tunic), as she picks up numbered balls from the spinner cage and places them upon a panel of 90 pictures.

A bingo-like game of European origin that uses numbered images, *la lotería* has been played on the peninsula since the 19th century. John L Stephens' *Incidents of Travel in Yucatan* has a good description of the game as he observed it played at a fiesta in Mérida in 1841. The action now may not be as heated as he describes, but the old folks can get pretty excited when one of them finishes a row.

At a peso per card, most anyone can afford to play a card or four. Players usually mark the images on their cards with bottle caps from a plastic container on the table. A variation on bingo is that markers can be placed in a variety of patterns: in addition to the usual rows, players can arrange their five markers in the form of a 'V,' a pair of scissors, or several kinds of crosses. The first person to form one of these patterns takes the pot, which can get pretty hefty as the evening progresses.

('old clothes,' shredded beef in salsa) accompanied by fried plantains, beans and rice.

Café La Parroquia (☎ 816-2550; Calle 55 No 8; breakfast combos M$30-40, lunch specials M$35; ⏰ 24hr) Any time of day – or night – your table awaits at this classic coffee house with a dozen ceiling fans, attentive waiters in white coats, and continuous Televisa broadcasts. Not just tourists but local geezers in guayaberas (short-sleeved sports shirts) hang out here for hours on end. In addition to the breakfast packages and daily lunch specials (served 10:30am to 6pm), there's a full list of regional faves such as *pollo en escabeche* (chicken marinated in vinaigrette-style sauce).

Marganzo (☎ 813-8981; Calle 8 No 267; mains M$40-150; ⏰ 7am-11pm) OK, so we told you to avoid the tourist joints, but this touristy spot is worth its mustard. Very sweet waitresses start you off with complimentary shredded manta ray, octopus salad, salsa, garlic cream and chips. From there, dig through the extensive menu, which offers everything from international fare to a regional tasting menu (M$140). There's live music and dances at night, and a pretty decent wine list (this being the provinces and all).

DRINKING

La Casa Vieja (☎ 811-8016; Calle 10 No 319A; ⏰ 8:30am-12:30am) There's no better setting for an evening cocktail than La Casa Vieja's colonnaded balcony overlooking the Plaza Principal. Seek dinner elsewhere, however; the restaurant is aimed primarily at the tour-bus trade.

Salón Rincon Colonial (☎ 816-8376; Calle 59 No 60; ⏰ noon-8pm) With ceiling fans high over an airy hall and a solid wood bar amply stocked with rum, this Cuban-style drinking establishment appropriately served as a location for *Original Sin,* a 2001 movie with Antonio Banderas that was set in Havana. Just across the way from the Puerta de Tierra, the classic bar was until recently a male-only enclave. The *botanas* (drinking snacks) are exceptionally fine; you get a different selection with each round.

Lafitte's (☎ 811-9191; www.delmarhotel.com.mx; Hotel del Mar, Av Ruiz Cortínes 51; ⏰ till 2am) Hotel del Mar's downstairs bar is one of Campeche's more popular nightspots. Waitstaff here dress like pirates.

ENTERTAINMENT

There's invariably someone performing on the Plaza Principal every Saturday and Sunday evening from around 6:30pm, be it a rock-and-roll band, pop-star impersonator, traditional dance troupe or a folk trio. On Sunday, the Banda del Estado (State Band) kicks off the program, performing Campeche classics, show music, marches and other rousing fare. Try to arrive early for a good seat.

Also on weekends, tables are set up from 6pm to 10pm in front of the cathedral and library for *la lotería* (a bingolike game; see above).

Puerta de Tierra (tickets M$50; ⏰ 8pm Tue, Fri & Sat) Incidents from Campeche's pirate past are re-enacted several nights a week in the Land Gate. It's a Disneyesque extravaganza with lots of cannon blasts and flashing lights. The tale is told in four languages.

Universidad Autónoma de Campeche (Av Agustin Melgar) Has revolving art exhibits, plays and art-house movies (M$25) at the Cine Teatro Universitario Joaquín Lanz.

Catch a free weekday concert, dance or folklore exhibit at the **Claustro del Instituto de Campeche** (Calle 12).

Nightclubs

For Campeche's hottest nightlife, head 1km south from the city center along the malecón past the Torres del Cristal. Here you'll find a bunch of great bars, cafés and discos. Locals recommend Margarita's House, popular with the older karaoke set; the hip lounge Rooms; Café Solé for an easy-going 'Friends' night; and Millennium disco if you want to get a little raucous.

Iguana Azul (☎ 816-3978; Calle 55 No 11; ☯ 6pm-2am Mon-Sat) Toward the weekend this casual restaurant across from Café La Parroquia hosts local cover bands and jazz combos in its colonial courtyard.

Sports

Los Piratas (☎ 816-6071; www.piratasdecampeche.com.mx; tickets M$50-80) Campeche's Mexican Baseball League team plays every other week during the March-to-July season at the Estadio Nelson Barrera on the north end of town. Tickets can be purchased at the old baseball stadium on Calle 57, across from the Baluarte de Nuestra Señora de la Soledad.

SHOPPING

Bazar Artesanal (Plaza Ah Kim Pech; ☯ 10am-10pm) The state-run Folk Art Bazaar, down by the *malecón* near the Centro de Convenciones Campeche, offers one-stop shopping for regional crafts. One section of the market is reserved for demonstrations of traditional craft techniques. Prices are set – no bargaining.

Mercado Principal (Av Circuito Baluartes Este; ☯ 7am-5pm) Prowl around the main market and survey the spices and herbs, exotic fruit, honey and chilies. Bonetería Bazar Puebla has a good selection of *huipiles* and guayaberas.

GETTING THERE & AWAY

Air

The airport is 6km southeast of the center. **Aeroméxico** (☎ 823-4044, 800-021-4010) flies to Mexico City at least twice daily.

Bus

Campeche's **main bus terminal** (☎ 816-2802; Av Patricio Trueba 237), usually called the ADO or 1st-class terminal, is about 2.5km south of Plaza Principal via Avenida Central. Buses provide 1st-class and deluxe service to Mérida, Cancún, Chetumal (via Xpujil), Palenque, Veracruz and Mexico City, as well as 2nd-class service to Sabancuy (M$75), Hecelchakán (M$23), Candelaria (M$114) and points in Tabasco.

The **2nd-class terminal** (☎ 816-2802; Av Gobernadores 289), often referred to as the 'old ADO' station, is 1.5km east of the Mercado Principal. Second-class buses to Hopelchén, Bolonchén, Xpujil and Bécal (M$35) depart from here.

CAMPECHE STATE

BUS SERVICES FROM CAMPECHE

Destination	Fare (M$)	Duration (hr)	Departures
Bolonchén de Rejón	50	3	5 daily from 2nd-class terminal
Cancún	340	7	7 ADO direct daily
Chetumal via Xpujil	260	6	1 ADO at noon daily, buses from 2nd-class terminal at 8:15am & 10pm
Ciudad del Carmen	120-160	3	ADO roughly hourly, 1 deluxe ADO-GL at noon
Hopelchén	37	1½	hourly until 5pm from 2nd-class terminal
Mérida via Bécal	105-125	2½	ADO approx every 30min, 1 deluxe ADO-GL at 6:30pm
Mérida via Uxmal	90-140	4½	5 Sur from 2nd-class terminal
Mexico City	900-1060	17	6 ADO daily, 1 deluxe ADO GL
Palenque	220-270	6	3 ADO daily, 1 OCC, 1 deluxe ADO-GL at 11:30pm
San Cristóbal de Las Casas	360-410	9	1 OCC daily, 1 deluxe ADO-GL at 11:30pm
Villahermosa	230-330	6	multiple ADO daily, 1 deluxe ADO-GL at 4:30pm
Xpujil	130-170	5	1 ADO at noon daily, 5 Sur from 2nd-class terminal

To get to the new terminal, catch any 'Las Flores,' 'Solidaridad' or 'Casa de Justicia' bus by the post office. To the 2nd-class terminal, catch a 'Terminal Sur' or 'Ex-ADO' bus from the same point.

The Sur Champotón terminal across from the Alameda has rural buses to Champotón and Edzná.

The destinations in the table (opposite) are from the 1st-class terminal unless otherwise noted.

Car & Motorcycle

If you're heading for either Edzná, the long route to Mérida or the fast toll road going south, take Calle 61 to Avenida Central and follow signs for the airport and either Edzná or the *cuota* (toll road). For the non-toll route south, just head down the *malecón*. For the short route to Mérida go north on the *malecón*.

Coming to Campeche from the south via the *cuota,* turn left at the roundabout signed for the *universidad,* and follow that road straight to the coast. Turn right up the *malecón* and you will arrive instantly oriented.

In addition to some outlets at the airport, several car-rental agencies can be found downtown. Rates are generally higher than in Mérida or Cancún.

Maya Rent A Car (☎ 811-9191; Hotel del Mar, Av Ruiz Cortínez 51)

Payless Car Rental (☎ 816-4214; Hotel del Paseo, Calle 10 No 288, interior 3)

GETTING AROUND

Local buses originate at the market or across Avenida Circuito Baluartes from it and go at least partway around the Circuito before heading to their final destinations. The fare is M$4.50.

Taxis charge a set rate of M$25 (M$35 after dark) for rides within the city; by the hour they're around M$100. Tickets for authorized taxis from the airport to the center (M$80) are sold from a booth in the terminal. To request a taxi, call ☎ 815-5555 or ☎ 816-6666.

Consider renting a bicycle for a ride along the *malecón* or through the streets of the Centro Histórico. All of Campeche's hostels rent bicycles at reasonable rates.

Drivers should note that even-numbered streets in the Centro Histórico take priority, as indicated by the red (stop) or black (go) arrows at every intersection.

CAMPECHE TO MÉRIDA VIA HIGHWAY 180

The *ruta corta* (short route) is the fastest way between the two cities, and it's the route more traveled by buses. Hwy 261, the longer alternative via Kabah and Uxmal, is covered by buses out of Campeche's 2nd-class terminal.

HECELCHAKÁN
☎ 996 / pop 9974

Bicycle taxis with canvas canopies noise-lessly navigate the tranquil central plazas of Hecelchakán, a delightful village 60km northeast of Campeche that is known for its culinary pleasures and excellent small museum. Hecelchakán's inhabitants, which include a Mennonite community, are primarily devoted to agriculture, while a few are employed in the clothing *maquiladora* (low-paying, for-export factory).

A **tourist information office** (☎ 827-0071), inside the Casa de Cultura on the left side of the church, opens up occasionally.

Dating from the 16th century, the **Iglesia de San Francisco de Asis** on the main plaza seems massive for a town this size. The former Franciscan monastery is worth entering to admire the wood-beam ceiling and striking iconography of the altar, with flaming hearts flanking a crucifix.

The **Museo Arqueológico del Camino Real** (admission M$27; ☺ 9:30am-5:30pm Wed-Mon, 9:30am-4pm Tue), on the north corner of the plaza, contains a small but compelling collection of ceramic art excavated from Isla de Jaina, a tiny island due west of Hecelchakán that flourished as a commercial center during the 7th century. Portraying ballplayers, weavers, warriors and priests, the extraordinary figurines on display here paint a vivid portrait of ancient Maya life. There's also a collection of stelae in the courtyard.

Residents of the capital customarily make the trip up just for Hecelchakán's famous snacks. In the mornings, outside the church, little **pavilions** serve up *cochinita pibil* (barbecued suckling pig wrapped in banana leaves) and *relleno negro* (turkey stuffed with chopped pork and laced with a rich, dark chili sauce) in tacos or baguettes, along with *horchata* (a rice-based drink) and *agua de cebada* (a barley beverage served with a spoon).

> ### BÉCAL'S UNDERGROUND – DISCOVER THE ROOTS OF THE JIPIJAPA HAT
>
> While on the surface Bécal may look like a somnolent Campeche town, underground are people laboring away at the traditional craft of hat making. Called *jipijapas* by the inhabitants of Bécal, the soft, pliable hats that constitute its principal industry have been woven by townsfolk from the fibers of the *huano* palm tree since the mid-19th century, when the plants were imported from Guatemala by a Catholic priest.
>
> The stalk of the plant is cut into strands to make the fibers; the quality of the hat depends on the fineness of the cut. The work is done in humid limestone caves that provide just the right atmosphere for shaping the fibers, keeping them moist and pliable. There's at least one cave on every block, generally reached by a hole in the ground in someone's backyard. Though often no bigger than a bedroom, the caves may be occupied by a half-dozen Maya-speaking weavers at a time. Once exposed to the relatively dry air outside, the panama hat is surprisingly resilient and resistant to crushing. Prices for the hats range from around M$200 for coarsely woven hats to more than M$900 for very fine work.

Hotel Margarita (☎ 827-0472; Calle 20 No 80; s/d/tr with fan M$120/140/160, with air-con M$210/250/270; 🔁), on the main drag about 200m from the plaza, is a 'family' establishment – no booze or friends of guests allowed. There's an internet café next door.

ATS buses from Campeche's 2nd-class terminal stop here en route to Mérida every half-hour till around 10pm (M$20, one hour). In addition, blue *colectivos* (shared vans) shuttle passengers between Campeche's Mercado Principal and Hecelchakán's plaza every 15 minutes for M$22.

BÉCAL

Bécal, about 90km north of Campeche just before you enter the state of Yucatán, is a center of the Yucatán's panama-hat trade. About one-third of the adult population makes their living weaving *jipijapas,* as the soft, pliable hats are known locally. The finest hats are destined for export to connoisseurs in foreign cities. The tranquil town clearly identifies with its stock-in-trade, as is made obvious by the centerpiece of its plaza.

For more on *jipijapas,* see boxed text (above). To find out where *jipijapas* are crafted and sold in town, hail a bicycle taxi (M$10) on Bécal's plaza and ask the rider for his recommendation. The workshop of Senor Valdemero, opposite the *secundaria* (high school) about 1km south from the plaza, is one of numerous recommendable options.

In early May the **Fiesta de Flor del Jipi** is celebrated with dancing and bullfights.

From Campeche's 2nd-class terminal, ATS buses bound for Mérida stop in Bécal's main plaza (M$45, two hours).

The rest of the route between here and Mérida is covered in the Yucatán State chapter (see p166).

CAMPECHE TO MÉRIDA VIA HIGHWAY 261

A perfect day trip from Campeche, or a nice backroad drive on your way to Mérida, this route takes you past traditional Maya villages to many of the state's best archaeological sites. It's often referred to as the Ruta Chenes (Chenes Route), for the *chenes* (wells) that give the region its name. All of Campeche's archaeological sites are open daily from 8am to 5pm.

EDZNÁ

If you only have the time or inclination to visit just one archaeological site in northern Campeche, **Edzná** (☎ 555-150-2591; admission M$37) should be your top pick. Get there early to avoid the crowds, and remember that Sunday is free for Mexican nationals, so the site gets overcrowded.

Edzná's massive complexes were built by a highly stratified society that flourished from approximately 600 BC to the dawn of the colonial era. During that period the people of Edzná built more than 20 complexes in a mélange of architectural styles, installing an ingenious network of water collection and irrigation systems. After its demise in the 15th century, the site remained unknown until its rediscovery by *campesinos* (agricultural workers) in 1906.

Edzná means 'House of the Itzáes,' in reference to a predominant governing clan of Chontal Maya origin. Edzná's rulers recorded significant events on stone stelae. Around 30 stelae have been discovered adorning the site's principal temples, a handful are on display underneath a *palapa* (thatched palm-leaf-roofed structure) just beyond the ticket office.

A path from the *palapa* leads about 400m through vegetation and then through the Anexo de los Cuchillos beside the **Plataforma de los Cuchillos** (Platform of the Knives), a residential complex highlighted by Puuc architectural features. The name is derived from an offering of silica knives found within.

Crossing a *sacbé* (stone-paved avenue), you arrive at the main attraction, the **Plaza Principal**. Measuring 160m long and 100m wide, the Plaza Principal is surrounded by temples. On your right as you enter from the north is the **Nohochná** (Big House), a massive, elongated structure topped by four long halls likely used for administrative tasks, such as the collection of tributes and the dispensation of justice.

Across the plaza is the Gran Acrópolis, a raised platform holding several structures, including Edzná's major temple, the 31m-high **Edificio de los Cinco Pisos** (Five-Story Building). The current structure is the last of four remodels and was done primarily in the Puuc style. It rises five levels from its base to the roofcomb and contains many vaulted rooms. A great central staircase of 65 steps, some with well-preserved glyphs along their bases, goes right to the top. Climbers are rewarded with sweeping views of the whole complex and surrounding jungle canopy.

Southeast of Plaza Principal is the **Templo de Los Mascarones** (Temple of the Masks), with a pair of reddish stucco masks underneath a protective *palapa*. Personifying the gods of the rising and setting sun, these extraordinarily well-preserved faces display dental mutilation, crossed eyes and huge earrings, features associated with the Maya aristocracy.

There's a fairly tasteful **sound-and-light show** (M$110) Friday and Saturday nights beginning at 8pm.

Cabañas Ecoturísticas Usahasil (☎ 981-829-4842; cabanas M$150), 1km north of the Edzná turnoff on Hwy 120 in Poblado No-Yaxche, is the only place to stay near the ruins. A public-relations

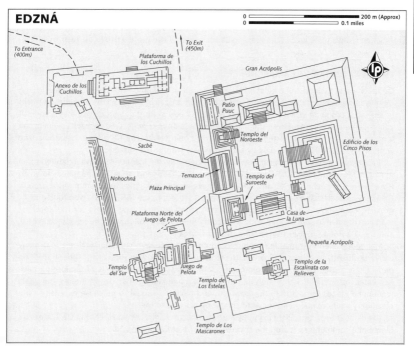

EDZNÁ

0   200 m (Approx)
0   0.1 miles

To Entrance (400m)

To Exit (450m)

Plataforma de los Cuchillos

Gran Acrópolis

Anexo de los Cuchillos

Patio Puuc

Sacbé

Templo del Noroeste

Edificio de los Cinco Pisos

Nohochná

Temazcal

Templo del Suroeste

Plaza Principal

Plataforma Norte del Juego de Pelota

Casa de la Luna

Pequeña Acrópolis

Templo del Sur

Juego de Pelota

Templo de Los Estelas

Templo de la Escalinata con Relieves

Templo de Los Mascarones

schlock would call it rustic… We call it the only place to stay in the area. There are a few roadside stands serving food directly opposite the Cabañas' entrance.

Getting There & Away

From Campeche, dilapidated buses leave from outside the Sur Champotón terminal at 7am and 11:15am, returning from the site at 1pm and 4pm (M$20, one hour). Most drop you 200m from the site entrance; ask before boarding. Schedules vary, so check the day before you travel.

Xtampak Tours (☎ 981-811-6473; xtampak_7 @yahoo.com.mx; Calle 57 No 14, Campeche; ☯ 8am-4pm & 5:30-8:30pm) provides an hourly shuttle service from Campeche to Edzná (M$180, minimum two passengers) as well as guided tours of the site.

Leaving the site by car, you can either go north on Hwy 120 to pick up Hwy 261 east to Hopelchén, or alternatively head toward Dzibalchén and the Chenes site of Hochob by going south to Pich, then east to Chencoh, 54km from Edzná over a decent but little-used road.

HOPELCHÉN

☎ 996 / pop 6500

The municipal center for the Chenes region, Hopelchén (Maya for 'Place of the Five Wells')

makes a pleasant base for visiting the various archaeological sites in the vicinity while also providing a glimpse of everyday life in a small Campeche town.

A **tourist information office** (☎ 822-0089; Calle 20; ☯ 8am-3pm) in the Casa de Cultura, two blocks north of the main plaza, is staffed by English speakers. To get online, visit **Cyber 23** (Calle 23), a block west of the bus station.

On a typical morning here, Maya *campesinos* and Mennonites congregate under box-shaped laurels as bicycle taxis glide past. Opposite the central plaza, the **Parroquia de San Antonio de Padua**, dating from the 16th century, features an intricate *retablo* (altarpiece), with a gallery of saints and angels amid lavishly carved pillars. Herbalists, midwives and shamans practice traditional Maya medicine at the **Consejo Local de Médicos Indigenas** (Colmich, Calle 8), five blocks east of the plaza.

Hotel Arcos (☎ 100-8782; Calle 23 s/n; s/d/tr M$130/190/260; ✿), next door to the bus terminal, is a convenient no-frills option. The rooms are immaculately clean, and you can add air-con and TV for M$100. You can also sling your hammock from the hooks on the wall.

For a good *caldo de pollo* (chicken soup), try the stalls on Plaza Chica, open mornings from 7am and evenings till 1am.

THE MENNONITES OF CAMPECHE

Campeche is in the midst of a quiet invasion by an unlikely community – the Mennonites. Seeing them waiting in bus stations, hanging about the main plazas of villages, crowding pickup trucks or sharing a *caguama* of Sol (liter bottle of Mexican beer) in front of a store, you may wonder if you've somehow stumbled onto the set of *Little House on the Prairie*. Clad in black coveralls and long-sleeved flannel shirts in the midday heat, the men tower over their Maya neighbors. The women wear dark floral-print dresses and straw hats with broad ribbons.

Tracing their origins to 16th-century Reformist Germany, the Mennonites have inhabited some northern Mexican states since the 1920s. Drawn by cheap land, they first migrated down to Hopelchén, Campeche, in 1983 and since then have established agricultural communities around Dzibalchén, Hecelchakán and Edzná. Once they've settled in, the Mennonites work relentlessly, growing corn, melons and other crops, raising cattle and producing cheese for the domestic market. They live in *campos* (self-contained communities with their own schools and churches), and speak among themselves in a form of Low German.

Mennonite men customarily fraternize and conduct business with the Mexicans and many converse fluently in colloquial Spanish (the women only speak with their own). Though they are generally accepted by the local community, some *campechanos* (residents of Campeche) have expressed resentment at the Mennonite invasion, complaining that the 'Menonas' buy *ejido* (communal) lands for less than they're worth and have the capital to purchase expensive farm machinery while *campechanos* have to scrape by with lesser means.

The film *Luz Silenciosa* (Silent Light) by Mexican director Carlos Reygadas looks at life in Mexico's Mennonite communities. It won the coveted Jury Prize at Cannes in 2007.

Getting There & Away

The terminal is served by 2nd-class Sur buses, with daily departures to/arrivals from Campeche (M$37, 1½ hours, hourly), Mérida via Bolonchén (M$70, 1½ hours, five services), and Xpujil (M$90, three hours, one at 8pm). In addition, blue *colectivos* run continuously between Campeche's 2nd-class terminal (M$35) and Hopelchén, stopping at villages along the way.

Drivers can strike southward to Dzibalchén and Xpujil, stopping along the way to check out the Maya ruins at El Tabasqueño, Dzibilnocac and Hochob. Travelers heading for bankless Xpujil: there's a Bancomer with ATM next to the Palacio Municipal on the smaller plaza. Xpujil-bound drivers should fill up in town.

AROUND HOPELCHÉN

Tohcok is a walkable 3km northwest of Hopelchén. Of the 40-odd structures found at this **site** (admission free), the only one that has been significantly excavated displays features of the Puuc and Chenes styles. The custodian can point out a *chultún* (Maya underground cistern), one of around 45 in the zone.

Some of the most significant caves in the peninsula are found 31km north of Hopelchén, shortly before you reach the town of Bolonchén de Rejón. The local Maya have long known of the existence of the **Grutas de Xtacumbilxuna'an** (admission M$50; ✆ 10am-5pm Tue-Sun; ♿), a series of underground cenotes in this water-scarce region. In 1844 the caves were 'discovered' by the intrepid John L Stephens and Frederick Catherwood, who depicted the Maya descending an incredibly high rope-and-log staircase to replenish their water supply. Today the cenote is dry but Xtacumbilxuna'an (*shtaa-koom-bcel-shoo-nahn*) is open for exploration and admiration of the vast caverns and incredible limestone formations within. A light-and-sound extravaganza accompanies the tour; skip the headphones and verbal commentary in six languages (something about the legend of the hidden lady for whom the caves are named). While the lighting helpfully picks out some of the more spectacular stalactites and stalagmites, the soundtrack only detracts from the experience. Instead, listen to the sounds of mot-mots echoing off the walls as you descend.

Sur buses traveling between Hopelchén and Mérida will drop you at the cave entrance before Bolonchén (M$15, 25 minutes). In addition,

colectivos depart for Bolonchén from the north side of Hopelchén's plaza, passing nearby the caves. Check with the driver for return times.

Hwy 261 continues north into Yucatán state to Uxmal, with a side road leading to the ruins along the Ruta Puuc.

CHENES SITES

Northeastern Campeche state is dotted with more than 30 sites in the distinct Chenes style, recognizable by the monster motifs around doorways in the center of long, low buildings of three sections, and temples atop pyramidal bases. Most of the year you'll have these sites to yourself. The three small sites described below make for an interesting single-day trip if you have your own vehicle or you can take a tour from Campeche with **Xtampak Tours** (✆ 981-811-6473; xtampak_7@yahoo.com.mx; Calle 57 No 14, Campeche; ✆ 8am-4pm & 5:30-8:30pm).

Supposedly named after a local landowner from Tabasco, **El Tabasqueño** (admission free; ✆ 8am-5pm) boasts a temple-palace (Estructura 1) with a striking monster-mouth doorway, flanked by stacks of eight Chac masks with hooked snouts. Estructura 2 is a solid freestanding tower, an oddity in Maya architecture. To reach El Tabasqueño, go 30km south from Hopelchén. Just beyond the village of Pakchén, there's an easy-to-miss sign at a turnoff on the right; follow this rock-and-gravel road 2km to the site.

Approximately 60km south of Hopelchén near the village of Chencoh, **Hochob** (admission M$27; ✆ 8am-5pm), 'the place where corn is harvested,' is among the most beautiful and terrifying of Chenes-style sites. Considered a classic example of the Chenes style, the Palacio Principal (Estructura 2, though signposted as 'Estructura 1') is on the north side of the main plaza. It's faced with an elaborate doorway representing Itzamná, lord creator of the ancient Maya, as an open-jawed rattlesnake. Facing Estructura 2 across the plaza, Estructura 5 has a pair of raised temples on either end of a long series of rooms; the better-preserved temple on the east side retains part of its perforated roofcomb.

To reach Hochob, turn right (south) about 500m west of Dzibalchén and drive the 10km to Chencoh, then the remaining 4km over a paved, though much deteriorated, road to the site. The small complex stands on a platform at the top of a snaking trail of circular steps.

Though it only has one significant structure, **Dzibilnocac** (admission free; ✆ 8am-5pm) possesses an

---

TRADITIONAL HARVEST: THE SWEET HISTORY OF MAYA HONEY

The Yucatán's flowers yield a sweet, mellifluous harvest, and bees have held an exalted place throughout its honeyed history. At the time of the conquest, records show that the Maya produced vast amounts of honey and Yucatecan villages paid tribute to the Spanish in honey, which was valued more for its curative properties than as a sweetener. Bees were important in the Maya pantheon: bee motifs appear in the surviving Maya codices, and the image of Ah Mucenkab, god of bees, is carved into the friezes of Chichén Itzá, Tulum and Sayil.

Mexico remains the world's No 4 producer of honey, and the nectar of the Yucatán is especially coveted for its blend of flavors and aromas, a result of the diversity of the region's flowers. Many *campesinos* (agricultural workers) keep bees to supplement their agricultural output. However, the stingless variety known to the ancient Maya has long since been supplanted by European bees, which in turn are being pushed aside by the more aggressive African bees, notorious among handlers for their nasty sting.

One Maya women's cooperative in the village of Ich-Ek, near Hopelchén, wants to preserve the ancient heritage. **Koolel Kab** (Women Who Work with Bees; ☎ 996-822-0073) produces honey with indigenous *melipona* bees, which take up residence in hollow trees. Using techniques much like those of their ancestors, the women place sections of tree trunk under a shelter, capping each end of the trunk with mud. An average trunk yields 12L of honey, which is marketed chiefly for its medicinal properties as throat lozenges, eye drops, soaps and skin creams.

---

eerie grandeur that merits a visit. Unlike the many hilltop sites chosen for Chenes structures, Dzibilnocac ('big painted turtle' is one translation) is on a flat plain, like a large open park. As Stephens and Catherwood observed back in 1842, the many scattered hillocks in the zone, still unexcavated today, attest to the presence of a large city. The single clearly discernible structure is A1, a palatial complex upon a 76m platform with a trio of raised temples atop rounded pyramidal bases. The best preserved of the three, on the east end, has fantastically elaborate monster-mask reliefs on each of its four sides and the typically piled-up Chac masks on three of the four corners.

Dzibilnocac is located beside the village of Iturbide (also called Vicente Guerrero), 20km northeast of Dzibalchén. From Campeche's 2nd-class terminal, there are nine buses daily to Iturbide via Hopelchén (M$60, three hours), but there's no place to stay here so you'll need to make it back to Hopelchén by nightfall.

The rest of the route between here and Mérida is covered in the Yucatán State chapter (see p167).

SOUTHWESTERN COAST

This lonely coast gets very little tourism. Heading down from Campeche city you pass small fishing villages and deserted white-sand beaches, finally hitting the Laguna de Términos, a vast mangrove-fringed lagoon home to riots of migratory birds and a prime sea-turtle nesting spot.

First-class ADO buses cover the three-hour journey between Campeche city and Ciudad del Carmen, while both ADO and 2nd-class ATS buses service points in-between.

CHAMPOTÓN

pop 27,325

Champotón, at the mouth of the river of the same name, has great historical significance as the landing place of the first Spanish exploratory expedition from Cuba, led by Francisco Hernández de Córdoba, in 1517. Probably seeking a source of water along the river, the Spaniards were assailed by warriors under the command of the cacique Moch Couoh, forcing them to retreat. Hernández de Córdoba died shortly after his return to Cuba from wounds he received at Champotón, which from then on was known as the 'Bahía de la Mala Pelea' (Bay of the Bad Fight).

Now considered a truck stop between Ciudad del Carmen and Campeche, Champotón sustains itself mainly on fishing, and perhaps the best reason to stop is to sample its abundant seafood. Try **Cocktelería Las Brisas del Boxito** (Av Colosio; ❤ 8am-6pm & 8pm-1am), an open-air tent south of the town center serving an outstanding *sopa de mariscos* (seafood soup) packed with octopus, shrimp and

CAMPECHE STATE

conch. Another good bet is the string of *coctelerías* (seafood shacks, specializing in shellfish cocktails) under thatched roofs about 2km north of town.

Two roads head south from Campeche to Champotón: a meandering coastal route (free) and a direct toll road (M$53).

From Champotón, Hwy 261 leads 84km south to Escárcega.

CHAMPOTÓN TO SABANCUY

From Champotón, Hwy 180 continues southwest along the coast. This sparsely developed stretch of seafront is fringed with usually deserted **beaches** that are ideal for shell-searching expeditions, pelican watching and an occasional dip in the shallow aquamarine waters. There are a few rest stops along the way, including at **Playa Varadero**, about 60km south of Champotón, with cold beer and a few thatched shelters suitable for hanging hammocks, a privilege that will cost around M$5.

LAGUNA DE TÉRMINOS

The largest lagoon in the Gulf of Mexico area, the Laguna de Términos comprises a network of estuaries, dunes, swamps and ponds that together form a uniquely important coastal habitat.

Red, white and black mangroves fringe the lagoon, and the area is an important nesting ground for six species of marine turtle and numerous migratory birds. Encompassing not only wildlife habitat but also the state's second-largest city and Mexico's principal oil-production center, the lagoon's ecosystem remains threatened by various environmental dangers, and in 1994 it was designated a Flora and Fauna Protection Area. The area's fragile ecosystem was dealt a heavy blow when oil from a damaged rig in the Gulf of Mexico came ashore in October 2007, arriving at several beaches in Campeche and Tabasco. The extent of environmental damage from the 11,700-barrel spill was not known at press time.

Hemmed in by a narrow strip of land that is traversed by Hwy 180, the lagoon can be explored from various points along the way.

Sabancuy
pop 6290

One base for exploring the lagoon is Sabancuy, a truly picturesque fishing village on the lower side of an estuary that branches off the lagoon's northeastern end. Sabancuy is 2km from the coast, across the estuary via two bridges. You enter onto the village's cute little waterfront plaza, the focus of activity.

Facing the estuary, 15km from town by motorboat, are the extensive ruins of the old **Hacienda de Tixchel**, a cattle ranch and sugar plantation from the late colonial period. The ruins are maintained by Sabancuy's fishermen, who provide transport there. To hire a boat to the hacienda (M$400), it's best to reserve in advance: phone **Dr José de Jesús Ambrosio Reyes** (☎ 982-825-0128), or go to the Farmacia de Jesús, one block up from the plaza on the right side of the church.

About six blocks from the waterfront, the minimally managed **Hotel Aguilar Salas** (☎ 982-731-5258; cnr Aldama & Manuel López; r with/without air-con M$230/190; 🅿 🔲) has a faded façade but modern rooms inside with pretty tiled floors and wood shutters. Rooms in back, overlooking the pool, are the best.

A pair of good seafood eateries can be found at Sabancuy's beach, right across the highway from the bridge. **El Crucero** (meals M$30-70; 🕙 8am-5pm), the humbler of the two, whips up an exceptional *caldo de pescado* (fresh fish in a cilantro broth), as well as fried snapper in garlic or chili sauce.

Sabancuy is easily reached by bus from Campeche (M$75, two hours, five daily 1st-class ADO) or Ciudad del Carmen (M$50, 1¼ hours, five daily ADO).

Sabancuy to Ciudad del Carmen

Another 39km down Hwy 180, at the threshold of the Canal Grande where the Laguna de Términos drains into the sea, you reach **Isla Aguada**, a primitive fishing community with a gas station and an old lighthouse. Tiny mangrove islands dot the lagoon here, and birders can arrange an excursion to the **Isla de Pájaros**, where thousands of herons, gulls and magnificent frigate birds converge at sunset. Inquire at the **Comisaría** (☎ 938-109-3983), near Parque Benito Juárez, to hire a motorboat out to the island; a two-hour excursion for up to eight people costs M$800. **Hotel Playa Punta Perla** (☎ 938-382-1063; r M$320; 🔲 🔲 🖦) faces a stretch of deserted white-sand beach on Isla Aguada's Gulf side. With cheerfully painted two-level blocks amid palm-lined grounds, and fresh shrimp and oysters from the lagoon served under the shade of *palapas,* it's the sort of place that fills up at Easter and stays empty the rest of the year.

From Isla Aguada, the 3.2km Puente La Unidad (M$47) spans the strait for access to Isla del Carmen and Ciudad del Carmen, a 46km drive further west.

CIUDAD DEL CARMEN

☎ 938 / pop 154,200

Campeche state's second-biggest city occupies the western end of a narrow island between the Gulf of Mexico and the Laguna de Términos. Though its self-proclaimed title, 'Pearl of the Gulf,' is open to dispute, Ciudad del Carmen is very much a bustling, prosperous seaside town, with freighters anchored in the harbor and salty breezes caressing the *malecón*.

With the discovery of oil in the 1980s, investment poured in, the population swelled, and the 3.8km-long Puente Zacatal (Zacatal Causeway) was completed in 1994, linking the city with the rest of Mexico.

Though Ciudad del Carmen rarely sees foreign tourists, it does have a renowned and colorful **Carnaval** celebration, which makes for a fabulous experience. Another exciting event is the **Festival de Nuestra Señora de Carmen**, which kicks off July 16 when the port's patron saint is taken on a cruise around the harbor, and continues till the end of the month.

Orientation & Information

Ciudad del Carmen takes up the western part of Isla del Carmen, with the center of town at its western extremity and the main plaza and *malecón* facing the channel that connects the lagoon to the Gulf. Near the southwestern corner of the island, the Puente Zacatal extends westward 3.8km across the strait toward Tabasco.

Cyber Café Inbox (Calle 33 No 10; internet per hr M$10; ۞ 8am-9:30pm) Check email and make inexpensive long-distance phone calls here.

Municipal Tourism Office (☎ 384-2413; Calle 20 s/n, cnr Calle 31; ۞ 8am-4pm) Small module inside the city hall with a few brochures.

Sights & Activities

Parque Zaragoza, the central plaza, has a handsome 19th-century kiosk. On its north side is the c 1856 **Santuario de la Virgen del Carmen**, which pays homage to the patron saint of sailors. Vestiges of Carmen's earlier prosperity remain in the **19th-century mansions** of chicle barons along Calles 22 and 24, going south from the plaza.

Playa Norte on the Gulf of Mexico has shallow green waters rolling in lazily to a flat, expansive beach with coarse sand. After the heat of the day, join the crowds promenading through the plaza, buy a bag of *enamoradas* (cream-filled pastries) and enjoy the sunset serenade as grackles settle into the huge laurels on the plaza.

Sleeping

Rates tend to be higher here than elsewhere on the pPeninsula.

Hotel Zacarias (☎ 382-0121; Calle 24 No 58; s/d M$210/270) It's right across from the cathedral on the main square, which means it's a cinch to find this joint. The rooms are bare-bones but clean, and many have balconies overlooking the plaza, a nice way to pass a few hours of people-watching.

Hotel Playa Dorado (☎ 382-4450; Av Paseo del Mar 8; r M$310; ۞ ۞) At Playa del Norte, this older lodging has a homey, well-kept feel and a large swimming pool out back. Unfortunately, since Pemex erected offices between the property and the beachfront, the balconies have lost their appeal.

Hotel Las Villas (☎ 384-1154; Calle 28 No 116; s/d M$410/470; ۞) There are 10 rooms in this cute little hotel right off the west side of the plaza. The spacious rooms have large beds with brand-new comforters and spick-and-span bathrooms, perfect for your inner Don Limpio (Mr Clean). Go for an upstairs room to avoid the noise. There's a cozy café upstairs.

Eating

At the foot of the Puente Zacatal, the zone called La Puntilla has a string of fine seafood restaurants.

La Fuente (☎ 382-0666; Calle 20 No 203; tamales M$13, snacks M$25; ۞) Almost meriting a visit to Carmen in itself, this classic waterfront café is a busy gathering place for families and domino players. It's an excellent spot to sample regional snacks such as *tamales torteados* (tamales dyed orange by achiote seeds, served with red sauce and a bowl of red onions) or huge *pibipollo* (chicken tamales traditionally cooked underground).

El Último Recurso (☎ 384-1275; Calle 28 No 118; set lunch M$40; ۞ 6am-9pm) Near the central plaza, this workingman's lunch hall has daily stick-to-your-ribs specials, such as lentil potage (Monday) and *pollo en pipian* (chicken in squash-seed sauce, Saturday). Fire things up with the house *salsa habanera* (habanero chili salsa), served in covered jars.

Restaurante El Marino (☎ 384-1583; Calle 20 No 2; fish M$100-150; ☷ 10am-7pm) This large open-air hall affords terrific views of the bridge as a backdrop for fresh snapper fillets or crab, served in empanadas or whole with garlic sauce.

Getting There & Away

Interjet (☎ 01 800-011-2345; www.interjet.com.mx) has flights to/from Toluca daily (except Saturday) for under M$500 one way.

Both 1st-class ADO and 2nd-class Sur buses use Ciudad del Carmen's modern **terminal** (☎ 382-0680; Av Periférica s/n), a 15-minute taxi ride (M$25, after dark M$30) east of the main plaza. Some key destinations:

Campeche (M$130 to M$160, three hours, hourly 1st-class ADO buses, one deluxe ADO-GL bus)
Mérida (M$250 to M$290, five hours, 11 ADO buses, two ADO-GL buses)
Mexico City (M$680 to M$820, 13½ hours, six ADO buses, two ADO-GL buses)
Villahermosa (M$110 to M$170, three hours, an ADO bus every 45 minutes until 11pm, four ADO-GL buses)

ATASTA PENINSULA

West of Ciudad del Carmen across the Puente Zacatal is this lushly tropical peninsula. A scarcely visited ecological wonderland, it stretches along a thin strip between the Gulf and a network of small mangrove-fringed lagoons that feed into the Laguna de Términos. Various waterfront seafood shacks prepare crab and shrimp pulled out of the lagoon. **Atasta Mangle Tours** (☎ 938-286-7026), about 1km east of the village of Atasta, offers two-hour boat excursions for up to eight people for around M$700. Howler monkeys, manatees and river turtles may be spotted along the journey through the estuarine waterway. If you have your own kayak, Atasta Mangle Tours may take you to areas that make great exploring. You'll need one of its guides to prevent you from getting lost.

ESCÁRCEGA TO XPUJIL

Hwy 186 heads nearly due east across south-central Campeche state, climbing gradually from east of the ugly truck-stop town of Escárcega to a broad, jungly plateau and descending again to finally reach Chetumal,

---

DETOUR: EL TIGRE

Off Hwy 186 heading southwest from Escárcega is one of Campeche's most recently uncovered Maya sites, **El Tigre** (☎ 555-150-1722; admission M$30; ☷ 8am-5pm). Archaeologists are almost certain it is none other than Itzamkanac, legendary capital of the Itzáes (see p32 for more on the Itzáes), though much remains to be explored. Unlike other Campeche sites, El Tigre occupies a wetlands environment crisscrossed by rivers, with two well-excavated pyramids amid swaying palms and diverse birdlife. From Candelaria take the road east to Monclova; a short distance beyond the village of Estado de México is the turnoff to the site. Buses will only take you to Candelaria.

---

in Quintana Roo. The highway passes near several fascinating Maya sites including historically significant Calakmul and through the ecologically diverse and archaeologically rich Reserva de la Biósfera Calakmul. The largest settlement on the road between Escárcega and Chetumal is Xpujil. The only gas station in the same stretch is about 5km east of Xpujil.

Calakmul and most of the other sites in this section can be visited by taxis hired in Xpujil or tours booked either in Xpujil (p225) or with companies in Campeche city (see p208).

Among the region's archaeological sites, the Río Bec architectural style predominates. It is actually a hybrid of styles fusing elements from the Chenes region to the north and Petén to the south. Río Bec structures are characterized by long, low buildings divided into three sections, with a huge 'monster' mouth glaring from a central doorway. The façades are decorated with smaller masks and geometric designs. At each end are tall, smoothly rounded towers with banded tiers supporting small false temples flanked by extremely steep, nonfunctional steps.

BALAMKÚ

'Discovered' only in 1990, **Balamkú** (☎ 555-150-2081; admission M$30; ☷ 8am-5pm) boasts a remarkably ornate, stuccoed frieze that bears little resemblance to any of the known decorative elements in the Chenes or Río Bec styles.

CAMPECHE STATE

Well-preserved with traces of its original red paint, the frieze is a richly symbolic tableau that has been interpreted as showing the complementary relationship between our world and the underworld. Along the base of the scene, stylized seated jaguars (referred to in the temple's Maya name) represent the earth's abundance. These figures alternate with several grotesque fanged masks, upon which stand amphibian-like creatures (toads or crocodiles?) that in turn support some royal personages with fantastically elaborate headdresses. Readers of Spanish can find more details in the explanatory diagrams that front the frieze.

The solid stone that hid the frieze for centuries has been replaced with a protective canopy with slit windows that let in a little light. The door is kept locked, but the site custodian will usually appear to open it and give you a tour (no flash photography allowed).

Balamkú is 60km west of Xpujil (2km past the Calakmul turnoff), then 3km north of the highway along a fissured road.

CALAKMUL

A major city during Maya times, **Calakmul** (☎ 555-150-2073; admission M$37, road maintenance fee per car M$40, local tax per person M$20; ☉ 8am-5pm) was 'discovered' in 1931 by American botanist Cyrus Lundell. The site bears comparison in size and historical significance to Tikal in Guatemala, its chief rival for hegemony over the southern lowlands during the Classic era.

A central chunk of its 72-sq-km expanse has been consolidated and partially restored but, owing to ecological considerations, clearing has been kept to a minimum. Most of the city's approximately 7200 remnants lie covered in jungle; exploration and restoration are ongoing. You can get a Calakmul map online at mayaruins.com/calakmul/calakmul_map.html.

Visiting Calakmul is as much an ecological as an historical experience. Lying at the heart of the vast, untrammeled **Reserva de la Biósfera Calakmul** (which covers close to 15% of the state's total territory), the ruins are surrounded by rainforest, with cedar, mahogany, sapodilla and rubber trees dotting a seemingly endless canopy of vegetation. While wandering amid the ruins, you may glimpse wild turkeys, parrots and toucans among the 230 bird species that reside or fly through here. You may also come across peccaries, agoutis

or howler monkeys, as well as numerous lizards and snakes. Five of the six wildcats found in Mexico inhabit the reserve, including the sacred jaguar. The earlier in the day you come, the more wildlife you're likely to spot.

History

From about AD 250 to 695, Calakmul was the leading city in a vast region known as the Kingdom of the Serpent's Head. Its decline began with the power struggles and internal conflicts that followed the defeat by Tikal of Calakmul's King Garra de Jaguar (Jaguar Claw). Calakmul flourished again in the Late Classic period by forming alliances with the Río Bec powers to the north.

As at Tikal, there are indications that construction occurred over a period of more than a millennium. Beneath Edificio VII, archaeologists discovered a burial crypt with some 2000 pieces of jade, and tombs continue to yield spectacular jade burial masks; many of these objects are on display in Campeche city's Fuerte de San Miguel. The cleared area of Calakmul holds at least 120 carved stelae, the oldest dating from 435 BC, registering key events such as the ascent to power of kings and the outcome of conflicts with rival states.

Sights

From the ticket booth at the end of the road to the ruins is about a 1km walk through the woods. Arrows point out three suggested walks, a long, medium and short route. The short route leads straight to the Gran Plaza; the long route directs you through the Gran Acrópolis before sending you to the main attractions.

The **Gran Plaza**, with loads of stelae in front of its buildings (Estructura V has the best ones), makes a good first stop, and climbing the enormous **Estructura II**, at the south side of the plaza, is a must. Each of this pyramid's sides is 140m long, giving it a footprint of just under 2 hectares – one of the largest known Maya structures. After a good climb you'll reach a temple occupying what appears to be the top of the building, but you have to go around it to the left to reach the real apex. From here, more than 50m above the forest floor, you'll enjoy magnificent views over the jungle canopy to the photographable Estructura I to the southeast and north across the plaza to Estructura VII. Facing southwest, you'll be looking toward the Maya city El

Mirador, in neighboring Guatemala, and with the aid of binoculars you may be able to spot that site's towering El Tigre pyramid. Work was under way to create a tunnel to a frieze in an inner chamber of the pyramid. The tunnel was slated for completion in 2008.

A path on the left (east) side of Estructura II leads past the palatial **Estructura III**, with a dozen rooms atop a raised platform. Archaeologists found a tomb inside the 5th-century structure that contained the body of a male ruler of Calakmul surrounded by offerings of jade, ceramics and shell beads, and wearing not one but three jade mosaic masks (one each on his face, chest and belt). Walking south you come to **Estructura I**, Calakmul's second great pyramid, which is about as tall as Estructura II. (Lundell named the site Calakmul, Maya for 'two adjacent mounds,' in reference to the pair of then-unexcavated pyramids that dominated the site.) The steep climb pays off handsomely with more top-of-the-world views.

A trail leading west from Estructura I around the back of Estructura II takes you to the **Gran Acrópolis**, a labyrinthine residential zone with a ceremonial sector containing a ball court. From the northern perimeter of this zone, you head east and follow the path back to the entrance.

Sleeping & Eating

Rangers allow camping at the Semarnat post, open from 6am, 20km down the road from the Conhuas; they appreciate a donation if you use the shower and toilets. Bear in mind that it can get chilly on this plateau in winter months – up to three blankets' worth.

Campamento Yaax'che (☎ 983-871-6064; ciitcalak mul@prodigy.net.mx; site per person M$50, with tent from M$100) More than just a campground, Yaax'che, 7km along the access road, is the base for tours by Servidores Turísticos Calakmul (p225), a training center for local guides and an experiment in sustainable ecotourism. You can rent a prepitched tent or set up your own under a thatched shelter. There's no electricity and facilities are primitive – douse-yourself showers and lime decomposition latrines. Regional fare is prepared over wood fires with variable results.

Villas Puerta Calakmul (☎ 988-884-3278, 001-786-206-9492; www.puertacalakmul.com.mx; cabanas low/high season M$950/1200; ☒) This jungle lodge 700m from the highway turnoff is designed for those who want to get into nature without roughing it too much. Fifteen spacious bungalows with jungly décor and overhead fans spread out from the main cabin, where you can dine on a forest-view terrace until 8pm. A small, kidney-shaped pool at the far end keeps filling up with leaves, a sore point with the beleaguered staff.

Getting There & Away

Xtampak Tours (p208) in Campeche and Río Bec Dreams (p224) near Chicanná run tours to Calakmul.

By car, the turnoff to Calakmul is 56km west of Xpujil, and the site is 60km south of the highway at the end of a decent paved road. A toll of M$40 per car (more for heavier vehicles) and M$20 per person is levied by the *municipio* (township) of Calakmul at the turnoff from Hwy 186. You'll need to register at the Semarnat post.

CHICANNÁ

Aptly named 'House of the Snake's Jaws,' this Maya **site** (☎ 555-150-2071; admission M$30; ☒ 8am-5pm) is best known for one remarkably well-preserved doorway with a hideous fanged visage. Located 11km west of Xpujil and 400m south of the highway, Chicanná is a mixture of Chenes and Río Bec architectural styles buried in the jungle. The city attained its peak during the Late Classic period, from AD 550 to 700, as a sort of elite suburb of Becán.

Beyond the admission pavilion, follow the rock paths through the jungle to **Estructura XX** (AD 830), which boasts not one but two monster-mouth doorways, one above the other. The top structure is impressively flanked by rounded stacks of crook-nosed Chac masks.

A five-minute walk along the jungle path brings you to Grupo C, with what remains of some of the earliest buildings. Continue along the main path about 120m northeast to reach the main plaza. Standing on the east side is Chicanná's famous **Estructura II**, with its gigantic Chenes-style monster-mouth doorway, believed to depict the jaws of the god Itzamná, lord of the heavens, creator of all things. Also worth examining here are the painted glyphs to the right of the mask. When you're done snapping photos, take the path leading from the right corner of Estructura II to reach nearby **Estructura VI** with some beautiful profile masks upon the façade and a well-preserved roofcomb. Circle around back, noting the red-painted blocks of the west wing, then turn right to hike back to the main entrance.

CAMPECHE STATE

our pick **Río Bec Dreams** (☎ 983-124-0501; www
.riobecdreams.com; Hwy 186 Km 142; cabanas with/without
bathroom M$800/420) provides unquestionably
the best accommodations in the area. This
Canadian-run jungle lodge has thatched-
roofed 'jungalows' sharing a bathhouse and
cabanas with private bathrooms in the woods.
Environmentally sound facilities include com-
posting toilets, rainwater collection devices
and solar electricity. There's a delightful
open-air restaurant serving Euro-Canadian
cuisine and a low-key bar with an excellent
library, all set amid lovingly designed gardens.
Enthusiastic and knowledgeable promoters of
the zone, owners Rick and Diane also conduct
highly recommended tours of Calakmul, Río
Bec and other sites in the area. Look for the
flags on the north side of the highway 2km
west of Chicanná.

BECÁN

Located 8km west of Xpujil and 500m north
of the highway, this must-visit site (☎ 555-150-
2069; admission M$30; ⏰ 8am-5pm) contains three
separate architectural complexes. You should
set aside at least two hours to explore it properly. The Maya word for 'canyon' or 'moat' is
becán, and indeed a 2km moat snakes its way
around this major site, with seven causeways
providing access to the 12-hectare complex.
The elaborate defense suggests the militaristic
nature of the city which, from around AD 600
to 1000, was a regional capital encompassing
Xpujil and Chicanná. A strategic crossroads
between the Petenes civilization to the south
and Chenes to the north, Becán displays architectural elements of both, with the resulting
composite known as the Río Bec style.

You enter the complex via the western
causeway, skirting Plaza del Este on your left –
more about that later. Proceed through a
66m-long arched passageway and you will
emerge onto the Plaza Central, ringed by
three monumental structures. The formidable **Estructura IX**, on the plaza's north side,
is Becán's tallest building at 32m. Though
its steeply ascending southern staircase may
be tempting, you are not supposed to climb
it. You may, however, scale **Estructura VIII**,
the huge temple on your right with a pair
of towers flanking a colonnaded façade at
the top. It's a great vantage point for photos of Estructura IX and views of the Xpujil
ruins to the east. Across the plaza from VIII
is **Estructura X**, with fragments of an Earth

Monster mask still visible around the central
doorway. The other side of X opens onto the
west plaza, with a ritual ball court. As you
loop around Estructura X to the south, check
out the encased stucco mask on display.

From this point you are routed through
woods to still another massive edifice, **Estructura
I**, which takes up one side of the eastern plaza.
Its splendid south wall is flanked by a pair of
amazing Río Bec towers rising 15m. Ascend
the structure on the right side and follow the
terrace alongside a series of vaulted rooms
back to the other end, where a passage leads
you into the Plaza del Este. The most significant structure here is **Estructura IV**, on the opposite side of the plaza; experts surmise it was
a residence for Becán's aristocrats. A stairway
leads to an upstairs courtyard ringed by seven
rooms with cross motifs on either side of the
doorways. Finally, you descend the north
façade of Estructura IV, with more intricately
decorated panels, completing the circle.

XPUJIL

☎ 983 / pop 3222

The truck-stop hamlet of Xpujil (shpu-heel)
lies at the intersection of east–west Hwy 186
and the road north to Hopelchén (and eventually Mérida). From this junction westward
are the ruins of Xpuhil (less than 1km), Becán
(8km), Chicanná (11.5km) and Balamkú
(60km); to the south are the remote sites of
Río Bec and Hormiguero. While hardly an
attractive base for visiting these sites, Xpujil
does offer an internet café, a guide service, a
handful of hotels, some unexceptional eateries and a taxi stand, all within 1km of the bus
depot. The only gas station between Escárcega
and Chetumal is 5km east of town. What
Xpujil does not have is a bank or ATM.

A far more appealing base is the village of
Zoh-Laguna, 10km north along the Hopelchén
road. Though easily accessible from Xpujil by
taxi (M$30), it is sufficiently removed from the
highway for a peaceful night's sleep. During
the 1940s the now-somnolent village boomed
as a logging center. Zoh-Laguna's interesting
history is illustrated photographically in its
small **museum** (admission free; ⏰ 8am-3pm Mon-Fri),
opposite Hotel Bosque Modelo.

Xpuhil (Xpujil) Ruins

Within walking distance of the town of a
similar name, **Xpuhil** (admission M$30; ⏰ 8am-5pm)
boasts a surreal skyscraper that is a striking

CAMPECHE STATE

example of the Río Bec style. The three towers (rather than the usual two) of Estructura I rise above a dozen vaulted rooms. The central tower, soaring 53m, is the best preserved. With its banded tiers and impractically steep stairways leading up to a temple that displays traces of a zoomorphic mask, it gives a good idea of what the other two must have looked like back in Xpuhil's 8th-century heyday. Go around back to see a fierce jaguar mask embedded in the wall below the temple.

The site's entrance is on the west edge of town on the north side of Hwy 186, at the turnoff for the airport.

Tours

Rick and Diane at Río Bec Dreams (opposite), near Chicanná, provide 4WD tours with well-informed commentary to Calakmul, Río Bec and some lesser-known sites such as Oxpemul and Manos Rojas. They charge M$800 to M$1000 for an eight- to 10-hour day, depending on driving time and accessibility of the site. You don't need to be staying at Río Bec Dreams to join the tour.

Servidores Turísticos Calakmul (☎ 871-6064; ciitcalakmul@prodigy.net.mx; Carretera Escárcega-Chetumal Km 153; ☺ 9am-2pm & 3-7pm Mon-Sat), around 200m east of the Xpujil junction, provides ecotours led by trained guides from nearby communities. In addition to tours of Maya sites in the area, it also offers nature walks, plant identification, bird-watching and horse tours, photo safaris and rural tourism experiences such as visits to beekeepers and organic farms. On one popular excursion you can observe millions of bats emerging from a cenote. One-day tours to Calakmul for up to 10 people cost M$550. It also runs extended camping tours for around M$310 per day. Reservations for the latter should be made a month in advance. Look for head honchos Fernando and Leticia at the office or the Yaax'che campground (p223) along the road to Calakmul.

Sleeping & Eating

The nicest and most reasonably priced accommodations are in Zoh-Laguna, 10km north of Xpujil. They are all contactable by dialing ☎ 200-125-6587, the village's central phone booth; say what hotel you want and wait a few minutes. All of the Xpujil options are along the main highway; have earplugs handy at bedtime.

ZOH-LAGUNA

Hotel Bosque Modelo (bosquemodelocalakmul@hotmail .com; r M$120) This small wooden structure is a typical leftover from the mid-20th-century logging boom. There are six simple rooms with single beds and hammock hooks. This is where the French archaeologists have stayed when working on the Río Bec site.

Cabañas El Viajero (cabanas M$140, r M$250; ❄) Travelers can choose from neat little cabins or more luxurious air-conditioned rooms across the street. All meals are prepared in the sparkling kitchen.

Cabañas Mercedes (s/d M$150/250) The best value place in the area has 13 thoughtfully designed bungalows with ceiling fans and large, tiled bathrooms. Good home-cooked meals are served in the thatched-roof dining hall. Don Antonio is both a gracious and well-informed host, who can take you to the major Maya sites in the area.

XPUJIL

Cabañas de Don Jorge (☎ 871-6128; cabanas M$100) Don Jorge's rustic but perfectly acceptable clapboard cabins sit up on a hill behind his store-eatery, Cocina Económica Xpujil, which can be found opposite the entrance to the Xpuhil ruins.

Hotel Calakmul (☎ 871-6029; 2-person cabanas without bathroom M$200, d with air-con M$450; ❄) About 350m west of the junction, this sterile roadside motel has standard tiled units plus a handful of cramped bungalows out the back. The restaurant, though, comes highly recommended.

THE ROAD TO RUINS

Maya sites around Xpujil are most conveniently reached by organized tour (see left) or taxi. The following taxi fares are for the round trip from Xpujil; add M$60 per hour for waiting while you're visiting the site. You can usually negotiate a fare to several sites on the same route for little more than the fare to one.

- Balamkú: M$600
- Becán: M$75
- Calakmul: M$600
- Chicanná: M$75
- Hormiguero: M$180

CAMPECHE STATE

EXPLORE THE RÍO BEC ARCHAEOLOGICAL SITES

Río Bec (8am-5pm) is the designation for an agglomeration of small sites, 70 at last count, in a 100-sq-km area southeast of Xpujil. The very remoteness of the site and ongoing excavations give it a certain buzz and mystique that's lacking in the established sites. Couple this with the fact that it's nearly impossible to get here during the rainy season and you have the makings for a real adventure.

Grupo B has some of the best-restored buildings, particularly the magnificent **Estructura I**, dating from around AD 700. Discovered in 1907 by French archaeologist Maurice de Périgny, who named the site after a nearby water source, this palatial structure features a pair of typical tiered towers crowned by matching temples with crosss motifs on their sides. Much of the current restoration work is being done at Grupo A, to the north of Grupo B. Its main structure is a 15m-long **palace** with intact towers and unusual bas-relief glyphs on the lower panels.

Access to the sites is from the collective farm of Ejido 20 de Noviembre. To get there, turn south off Hwy 186, about 10km east of the Xpujil junction, and follow a potholed road 5km to the community and its U'lu'um Chac Yuk Nature Reserve. From there, a very rough road leads 13km further south to the site. It's only passable when dry and even then you need a high-clearance vehicle. Furthermore, the way is unsigned with many twists and turns. You're best off hiring a guide with a 4WD truck. It's possible to arrange this in Xpujil or at the *ejido;* the going rate is M$600 to M$700. A taxi from Xpujil's main junction to the *ejido* will charge M$60 for drop-off service; negotiate waiting time. Alternatively, check with Río Bec Dreams (p224) near Chicanná.

Aside from the hotel restaurants, there are various greasy spoons clustered around the bus station and roadside *taquerías* (taco places) toward the Xpuhil ruins. Try Antojitos Mimi, opposite Hotel Calakmul, for some pretty fine *salbutes* (tortilla topped with shredded turkey or chicken, onion and slices of avocado) and an ice-cold *agua de jamaica* (a cold tangy tea made from hibiscus flowers).

Getting There & Around

No buses originate in Xpujil, so you must hope to luck into a vacant seat on one passing through. The **bus terminal** (871-6027) is just east of the Xpujil junction, on the north side of the highway.

Campeche (M$78 to M$160, 5½ hours, via Escárcega one 1st-class Ado bus at 1:45pm and two 2nd-class Sur buses, via Hopelchén one Sur bus)

Cancún (M$280, 6½ hours, two ADO buses)

Chetumal (M$70, 1½ hours, three ADO buses and one Sur bus)

Escárcega (M$90, two hours, seven ADO buses)

Hopelchén (M$90, three hours, one Sur bus at 4am)

Palenque (M$220, six hours, one 1st-class OCC bus at 9:40pm or change at Escárcega for a 1pm ADO bus to Palenque)

For Becán, Hormiguero, Calakmul or other sites you will need to book a tour or hire a cab.

See boxed text, p225, for taxi rates. The taxi stand is on the north side of the junction.

AROUND XPUJIL

Hormiguero

Though not easy to reach, **Hormiguero** (555-150-2075; admission M$30; 8am-5pm) has many mind-blowing buildings that will impress even the most jaded explorer. An old site, with buildings dating as far back as AD 50, the city (whose name is Spanish for 'anthill') flourished during the late Classic period.

As you enter you'll see the 50m-long **Estructura II**. The facade's chief feature is a very menacing Chenes-style monster-mouth doorway, jaws open wide, set back between a pair of classic Río Bec tiered towers. Walking around the back of the building you can see solid intact Maya stonework and the remains of several columns. Follow the arrows 60m to the north to reach **Estructura V**, with a much smaller but equally ornate open-jawed temple atop a pyramidal base. Climb the right side for a closer look at the incredibly detailed stonework, especially along the corner columns that flank the doorway.

This site is reached by heading 14km south from Xpujil junction, then turning right and going 8km west on what was once a paved road, still passable except following heavy rains.

Tabasco & Chiapas

Mismatched siblings, the neighboring states of Tabasco and Chiapas are almost a study in opposites. Smaller Tabasco – between central Mexico and the Yucatán Peninsula – is less diverse than Chiapas, and prone to flooding, as demonstrated by the catastrophic flood of October 2007 (see boxed text, p228). A largely flat, steamy, well-watered lowland, it has fewer visitors, but those who do drop in discover a place with fascinating pre-Hispanic heritage from the Olmec and Maya civilizations, a relaxed tropical lifestyle, an entertaining capital city in Villahermosa, and a unique environment of enormous rivers, endless wetlands and good Gulf of Mexico beaches.

In Chiapas, pine-forest highlands, wildlife-rich rainforest jungles and well-preserved co-lonial cities highlight a region of incredible variety. Palenque and Yaxchilán are evocative vestiges of powerful Maya kingdoms, and the presence of modern Maya a constant reminder of the region's rich and uninterrupted history. The colonial architecture of San Cristóbal de Las Casas and Chiapa de Corzo gives way to fertile plots of coffee and cacao in the south-western region known as the Soconusco, and for outdoor adventurers, excursions to Laguna Miramar and the Cañón del Sumidero are unmissable.

HIGHLIGHTS

- Scaling the jungly hills and soaring Maya temples of **Palenque** (p240)
- Strolling the high-altitude cobblestone streets of **San Cristóbal de Las Casas** (p231)
- Cruising through the waterway and sheer high rock cliffs of the spectacular **Cañón del Sumidero** (see boxed text, p245)
- Hiking in and lazing away a few splendid days at the mountain-ringed **Laguna Miramar** (see boxed text, p245)
- Admiring the mysterious art of the ancient Olmecs at **Villahermosa** (p228) and **La Venta** (p228)

- POPULATION: TABASCO 2 MILLION; CHIAPAS 4.3 MILLION
- AREA: TABASCO 25,267 SQ KM; CHIAPAS 74,211 SQ KM

TABASCO

Few travelers linger in Tabasco longer than it takes to see the outstanding Olmec stone sculpture in Villahermosa's Parque-Museo La Venta. But staying a little longer will reveal a very rewarding slice of the real Mexico, with few other tourists, some intriguing pre-Hispanic sites (both the Olmecs and the Maya flourished here), and a large and lively capital city.

In late October and early November 2007, prolonged heavy rainfall led to major floods here, submerging a whopping 80% of the state. The federal government quickly mobilized food distribution and emergency shelters, and relief donation centers sprouted up nationwide as people pitched in to head off the humanitarian crisis. Though the floodwaters have receded, full economic recovery is expected to take years. By early 2008 most infrastructure, attractions and travelers' services were already up and running.

VILLAHERMOSA

☎ 993 / pop 673,000

This sprawling, flat, hot and humid city, with over a quarter of Tabasco's population, was never the 'beautiful town' its name implies, but it takes advantage of its position on the winding Río Grijalva, with a welcome riverside leisure development a couple of blocks from the pedestrianized city center. Still, when the river burst its banks and engulfed the city in 2007, the result looked like New Orleans after Hurricane Katrina.

TABASCO FLOODS OF 2007

Due to the severe flooding that hit the state of Tabasco during the time of this book's research, making all routes nearly impassable, our author could not access the state. Our research for this section consisted of personal contacts by phone and internet, and input from local citizens and fellow travelers. At the time of publication, the state was still in recovery. While we've tried our best to ensure the text is current and useful to travelers, some of these listings may be out of date.

Orientation

The central area, known as the Zona Luz, extends north–south from Parque Juárez to the Plaza de Armas, and east–west from the Río Grijalva to roughly Calle 5 de Mayo. The main bus terminals are between 750m and 1km to its north.

Parque-Museo La Venta lies 2km northwest of the Zona Luz, beside Avenida Ruíz Cortines, the main east–west highway crossing the city. West of Parque-Museo La Venta is the Tabasco 2000 district of modern commercial and government buildings.

Information

Hospital Cruz Roja (☎ 315-5555; Av Sandino s/n)
Main post office (Sáenz 131; ☼ 9am-3pm Mon-Fri, 9am-1pm Sat)
Tourist office (Av Ruíz Cortines; ☼ 8am-4pm Tue-Sun) In the Parque-Museo La Venta.

Sights

The fascinating outdoor **Parque-Museo La Venta** (☎ 314-1652; Av Ruíz Cortines; admission M$40; ☼ 8am-5pm, last admission 4pm, zoo closed Mon; ♿) was created in 1958, when petroleum exploration threatened the highly important ancient Olmec settlement of La Venta in western Tabasco. Archaeologists moved the site's most significant finds, including three colossal stone heads, to Villahermosa. The park features a **zoo**, **sculpture trail** and **sound-and-light show** (admission M$100; ☼ hourly 7-10pm, closed Mon).

Next to the park entrance, the **Museo de Historia Natural** (☎ 31421-75; admission M$15; ☼ 8am-4pm Tue-Sun) has quite well-set-out displays on dinosaurs, space, early humanity and Tabascan ecosystems (all in Spanish). The park is 3km from the Zona Luz.

The **Regional Anthropology Museum** (☎ 312-6344; Periférico Carlos Pellicer; admission M$25; ☼ 9am-5pm Tue-Sun) is a little dilapidated and poorly labeled (in Spanish only), but still holds some interesting exhibits. The museum is 1km south of the Zona Luz.

Tours

Turismo Nieves (☎ 314-1888; reservaya@turismonieves .com.mx; Sarlat 202; ☼ 8am-7pm Mon-Sat) offers a range of comprehensive tours around Tabasco.

Sleeping & Eating

Hotel Oriente (☎ 312-0121; fax 312-1101; Madero 425; s/d/tr with fan M$220/250/360, with air-con M$300/330/420; ❄) The Oriente is a well-run downtown hotel, with comfortable, spick-and-span rooms.

Hotel Olmeca Plaza (☎ 358-0102, 800-201-09-09; www.hotelolmecaplaza.com; Madero 418; r Mon-Thu M$750, Fri-Sun M$590; Ⓟ Ⓧ Ⓧ 🖳 🖳) The classiest downtown hotel also has an open-air pool and well-equipped gym. Rooms are modern and comfortable.

Market (Hermanos Bastar Zozaya s/n; 🕙 5am-7pm) Fresh vegetables, chilies, fish, meat and big dollops of local atmosphere.

Riviera Villahermosa (☎ 312-4468; Constitución 104; mains M$75-160; 🕙 1pm-2am Mon-Sat, noon-6pm Sun) The Euro-Mex menu is pretty good, and the air-conditioned 4th-floor setting with floor-to-ceiling windows overlooking the river is spectacular.

Getting There & Away

AIR

Villahermosa's **Aeropuerto Rovirosa** (☎ 356-0157) is 13km east of the city center, off Hwy 186. Nonstop or one-stop direct flights to/from Villahermosa include the following destinations: Cancún (Click Mexicana, flies daily), Houston, Texas (Continental Airlines, flies daily), Mérida (Aviacsa and Click Mexicana, flights daily), Mexico City (Aeroméxico, Aviacsa and Mexicana de Aviación, eight or more flights daily), Monterrey (Aeroméxico and Aviacsa, both with one nonstop flight daily), Oaxaca (Click Mexicana, flies daily), Tuxtla Gutiérrez (Click Mexicana, flies daily) and Veracruz (Aeroméxico, flies daily).

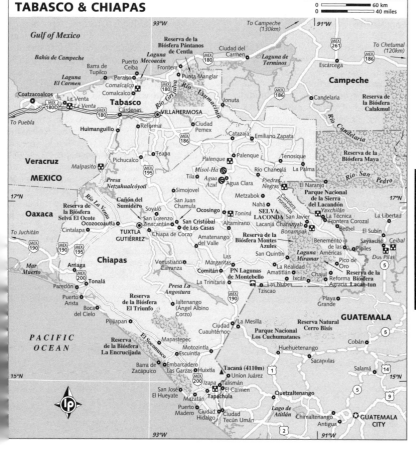

BUS & COLECTIVO TAXI

The 1st-class **ADO bus terminal** (☎ 312-8422; Mina 297) is 750m north of the Zona Luz and has a luggage room. Deluxe and 1st-class UNO, ADO and OCC buses run from here, as well as a few 2nd-class services. For a sample of departures from the ADO bus terminal (most in the evening), see the table (below).

Getting Around

A taxi from the airport to the city center costs around M$180 (M$150 from the city to the airport) and takes about 25 minutes. Any taxi ride within the area between Avenida Ruíz Cortines, the Río Grijalva and Paseo Usumacinta costs M$15. *Combi* (a catch-all term used for taxi, van and minibus services regardless of vehicle type) rides within the same area are M$5.

AROUND VILLAHERMOSA

Comalcalco

☎ 933 / pop 40,000

The impressive ruins of ancient **Comalcalco** (admission M$35; ☺ 10am-4pm) make a visit to this hot, bustling town, 51km northwest of Villahermosa, worthwhile. This Maya site is unique because many of its buildings are constructed of bricks and/or mortar made from oyster shells. Comalcalco was at its peak between AD 600 and 1000, when ruled by the Chontals. It remained an important center of commerce for several more centuries.

The museum at the entrance has a fine array of sculptures and engravings of human heads, deities, glyphs and animals, such as crocodiles and pelicans.

The site is 1km (signposted) off the Comalcalco–Paraíso road. Vans to the turnoff (M$5) stop outside Comalcalco's ADO bus terminal (for details, see right). A taxi to the site costs around M$20.

The **Hotel Copacabana** (☎ 334-1933, 800-224-77-77; www.hotelcopacabana.com.mx; cnr Juárez & Serdán; s/d M$595/712; P 🔀) is the best hotel in town.

GETTING THERE & AWAY

Comalcalco's **ADO bus terminal** (☎ 334-0007; cnr López Mateos & Monserrat) by the clock tower (El Reloj) is on the main road, 300m east of the town center. It has 1st- and 2nd-class buses to Villahermosa (M$54, 1½ hours, seven daily), Paraíso (M$15, 20 minutes, 25 daily), Frontera (M$66, 2½ hours, three daily) and more distant destinations.

Reserva de la Biósfera Pántanos de Centla

This 3030-sq-km biosphere reserve protects a good part of the wetlands around the lower reaches of two of Mexico's biggest rivers, Río Usumacinta and Río Grijalva. These lakes, marshes, rivers, mangroves, savannas and forests are an irreplaceable sanctuary for countless creatures, including the West Indian manatee and Morelet's crocodile (both endangered), six kinds of tortoise, tapir, ocelots, jaguars, howler monkeys, 60 fish species, including the *pejelagarto,* and 230 bird species – not to mention 15,000 people scattered in 90 small waterside villages.

A paved, and in parts rough, road follows the broad winding Río Usumacinta, right across the reserve from the Río Grijalva bridge near Frontera, eventually reaching the town of Jonuta (from which other roads lead to the major east–west Hwy 186). Ten kilometers along this road, **Punta Manglar** (☎ 913-403-9763; Hwy Frontera–Jonuta Km 10; ☺ 9am-4pm Tue-Sun) is an embarkation point for boat-and-foot **excursions** (☎ 913-403-9842; up to 7 people M$500; ☺ trips 6am-7pm) into the mangroves, where you should see crocodiles, iguanas, birds and, with luck, howler monkeys.

The reserve's visitors center, the **Centro de Interpretación Uyotot-Ja** (☎ 993-313-9362; Carretera Frontera–Jonuta Km 12.5; admission M$25; ☺ 9am-4pm Tue-Sun), is a further 2.5km along the road.

Gray *combis* and *colectivos* (shared vans) from Calle Madero in Frontera (*combis* half

BUS SERVICES FROM VILLAHERMOSA

Destination	Fare ($M)	Duration (hr)	Departures
Campeche	278-318	6-7	17 daily
Cancún	550-960	12-14	21 daily
Mérida	390-608	8-9	19 daily
Palenque	95	2½	13 daily
San Cristóbal de Las Casas	204	7	2 daily
Tuxtla Gutiérrez	200-240	4-8	13 daily

TABASCO & CHIAPAS

EXPLORE MORE OF TABASCO

This section only scratches the surface of the adventures to be had here. For more info, visit www.lonelyplanet.com or try out some of these DIY adventures:

▪ **Cacao Haciendas** Discover the past at Hacienda La Luz, just west of Comalcalco's central plaza.

▪ **Gulf Beaches** Explore around Puerto Ceiba, where you can take boat rides into Laguna Mecoacán. Or cruise the lost roads along the **Barra de Tupilco**.

▪ **La Venta** While most of the cool artifacts have been moved to the museum in Villahermosa, this site, 128km west of Villahermosa, is still worth a visit.

▪ **Malpasito** Up in Tabasco's beautiful and mountainous far southwestern corner, tiny Malpasito is the site of mysterious ancient Zoque ruins.

▪ **Southern Tabasco** Explore riverside swimming holes and caves, using Teapa, 50km south of Villahermosa, as your base.

---

a block south of the plaza, and *colectivos* 1½ blocks south of the plaza) charge M$10 for the 15-minute trip to Punta Manglar or Uyotot-Ja. Some continue to Jonuta (M$50, three hours), where buses leave for Villahermosa, Palenque and other destinations.

CHIAPAS

Chilly pine forest highlands, sultry rainforest jungles and attractive colonial cities exist side by side within Mexico's southernmost state, a region awash in the legacy of Spanish rule and the remnants of ancient Maya kingdoms. The state has the second-largest indigenous population in the country, and the modern Maya of Chiapas form a direct link to the past, with a traditional culture that persists to this day. Many indigenous communities rely on subsistence farming and have no running water or electricity, and it was frustration over lack of political power and their historical mistreatment that fueled the Zapatista rebellion, putting a spotlight on the region's distinct inequities.

Chiapas contains swaths of wild green landscape that have nourished its inhabitants for centuries. From the Selva Lacandona (Lacandon Jungle) to the biosphere reserves of El Triunfo and Selva El Ocote, Chiapas offers incredible opportunities for outdoor adventures. But a rich trove of natural resources also makes it a contentious prize in a struggle for its water, lumber, and oil and gas reserves.

Dangers & Annoyances

There have been no Zapatista-related incidents affecting travelers for some time. If you plan to travel off the main roads in the Chiapas highlands, the Ocosingo area and far eastern Chiapas, take local advice about where to avoid going. Numerous military checkpoints have increased security for travelers, though it's best to be off the Carretera Fronteriza or across the Guatemalan border before dark. Indigenous villages are often extremely close-knit, and their people can be suspicious of outsiders and particularly sensitive about having their photos taken. If in any doubt at all, ask first.

SAN CRISTÓBAL DE LAS CASAS

☎ 967 / pop 142,000 / elev 2160m

Set in a gorgeous highland valley surrounded by pine forest, the colonial city of San Cristóbal (cris-*toh*-bal) has been a popular travelers' destination for decades. It's a pleasure to explore San Cristóbal's cobbled streets and markets, soaking up the unique ambience and the wonderfully clear highland light. This medium-sized city also boasts a comfortable blend of city and countryside, with restored century-old houses giving way to grazing animals and fields of corn.

Surrounded by dozens of traditional Tzotzil and Tzeltal villages, San Cristóbal is at the heart of one of the most deeply rooted indigenous areas in Mexico. A great base for local and regional exploration, it's a place where ancient customs coexist with modern luxuries.

Orientation

San Cristóbal is very walkable, with straight streets rambling up and down several gentle hills. The Pan-American Hwy (Hwy 190, Blvd Juan Sabines, 'El Bulevar') runs through the southern part of town, and nearly all transportation terminals are on it or nearby. From

TABASCO & CHIAPAS

SAN CRISTÓBAL DE LAS CASAS

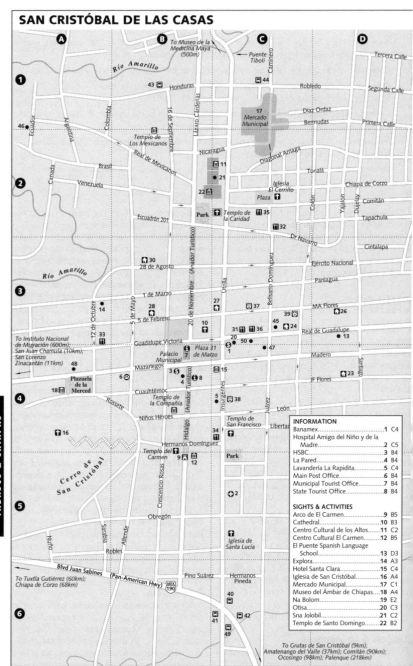

To Grutas de San Cristóbal (9km);
Amatenango del Valle (37km); Comitán (90km);
Ocosingo (98km); Palenque (218km)

TABASCO & CHIAPAS

SLEEPING 🛏
Casa Felipe Flores.........................**23** D4
Casa Margarita.............................**24** C3
Hostal Rincón de los Camellos...**25** E3
Hotel Casavieja............................**26** D3
Hotel Diego de Mazariegos.......**27** C3
Hotel El Paraíso...........................**28** B3
Na Bolom....................................(see 19)
Parador San Juan de Dios...........**29** E1
Posada Ganesha...........................**30** B3

EATING 🍴
El Gato Gordo..............................**31** C3
La Casa del Pan Papalotl **32** C2
L'Eden...(see 28)
Los Barrios...................................**33** A3
Madre Tierra................................**34** C4
Pizzeria El Punto..........................**35** C2
TierrAdentro.................................**36** C3

ENTERTAINMENT 🎭
Café Museo Café..........................**37** C3
DaDa Club....................................**38** C4
La Pera...**39** C3

TRANSPORT
ADO Bus Terminal........................**40** C6
AEXA Bus Terminal.......................**41** C6
Colectivos to Tuxtla Gutiérrez....**42** C6
Combis to San Juan Chamula.......**43** B1
Combis to Zinacantán.................**44** C1
Croozy Scooters...........................**45** C3
Los Pingüinos..............................**46** A1
Mexicana de Aviación..................**47** C4
OCC Bus Terminal.......................(see 40)
Optima..**48** A4
Suburbans to Comitán.................**49** C6
Ticket Bus...................................**50** C3
UNO Transportes Bus Terminal...(see 40)

the OCC bus terminal, it's six blocks north up Avenida Insurgentes to the central square, Plaza 31 de Marzo. Calle Real de Guadalupe, heading east from the plaza, has a concentration of places to stay and eat. A long pedestrian mall, the Andador Turístico (or Andador Eclesiástico), runs up Avenidas Hidalgo and 20 de Noviembre from the Arco de El Carmen in the south to the Templo de Santo Domingo in the north, crossing Plaza 31 de Marzo en route. The Cerro San Cristóbal and Cerro de Guadalupe lord over the town from the west and east, respectively.

Information
San Cristóbal has dozens of inexpensive cybercafés.

Banamex (Plaza 31 de Marzo; ⏰ 9am-4pm Mon-Fri, 10am-2pm Sat) Has an ATM.

Hospital Amigo del Niño y de la Madre (☎ 678-0770; Av Insurgentes) General hospital with emergency facilities.

La Pared (☎ /fax 678-6367; lapared9@yahoo.com; Av Hidalgo 2; ⏰ 10am-2pm & 4-8pm Mon-Sat, 3-7:30pm Sun) Stocks a great choice of new and used books in English.

Lavandería La Rapidita (☎ 678-8059; Av Insurgentes 9; self-service per 5kg M$25, service wash per 3kg M$45; ⏰ 9am-8pm Mon-Sat)

Main post office (☎ 678-0765; Av Allende 3; ⏰ 8:30am-7pm Mon-Fri, 8:30am-1pm Sat)

Municipal tourist office (☎ 678-0665; Palacio Municipal, Plaza 31 de Marzo; ⏰ 8:30am-7pm Mon-Fri, 8am-8.30pm Sat & Sun)

State tourist office (☎ 678-1467; Av Hidalgo 1B; ⏰ 8am-9pm Mon-Fri, 9am-8pm Sat, 9am-2pm Sun) Has English-speaking staff and plenty of leaflets; located one floor up but no signs. It may be moving to the Centro Cultural El Carmen (p235).

Sights
PLAZA 31 DE MARZO
The leafy main plaza is a fine place to take in San Cristóbal's unhurried atmosphere. On the north side of the plaza, the **cathedral** was begun in 1528 but wasn't completed till 1815 because of several natural disasters. Sure enough, new earthquakes struck in 1816 and 1847, causing considerable damage, but it was restored again in 1920–22. The gold-leaf interior has five gilded altarpieces featuring 18th-century paintings by Miguel Cabrera. The **Hotel Santa Clara**, on the plaza's southeast corner, was built by Diego de Mazariegos, the Spanish conqueror of Chiapas. His coat of arms is engraved above the main portal. The house is a rare secular example of plateresque style in Mexico.

TABASCO & CHIAPAS

THE ZAPATISTAS

On January 1, 1994, the obscure day of the North American Free Trade Agreement's (NAFTA) initiation, a previously unknown leftist guerrilla army emerged from the forests to occupy San Cristóbal de Las Casas and other towns in Chiapas. The Ejército Zapatista de Liberación Nacional (EZLN; Zapatista National Liberation Army) linked antiglobalization rhetoric with Mexican revolutionary slogans, declaring that they aimed to overturn the oligarchy's centuries-old hold on land, resources and power and to improve the wretched living standards of Mexico's indigenous people.

The Mexican army evicted the Zapatistas within days, and the rebels retreated to the fringes of the Selva Lacandona (Lacandon Jungle) to wage a propaganda war, mainly fought via the internet. The Zapatistas' balaclava-clad, pipe-puffing Subcomandante Marcos (actually a former university professor named Rafael Guillén) rapidly became a cult figure. High-profile conventions against neoliberalism were held and international supporters flocked to Zapatista headquarters at La Realidad, 80km southeast of Comitán, and Zapatista-aligned peasants took over hundreds of farms and ranches in Chiapas.

In 1996 Zapatista and Mexican government negotiators agreed to a set of accords on indigenous rights and autonomy. However, the governing Institutional Revolutionary Party (PRI) never ratified these agreements, and through 1997 and 1998 tension and killings escalated in Chiapas. A PRI-linked paramilitary group massacred 45 people in the village of Acteal, north of San Cristóbal, in 1997. By 1999 an estimated 21,000 villagers had fled their homes after the Mexican army, aided and abetted by paramilitaries, launched a campaign of intimidation.

After Vicente Fox was elected Mexico's president in 2000, two attempts to make the necessary constitutional changes failed. The Zapatistas refused to participate in further talks, concentrating instead on consolidating their revolution and their autonomy in the villages of highland and eastern Chiapas, where they had the most support.

More recently the Zapatista leadership held three large international gatherings (Encuentros) during 2007. Pockets of the Chiapas countryside remain tense, and occasional incidents bubble up over control of land.

It's interesting to note that the Zapatistas have loudly denounced the concept of ecotourism. They see the expansion of government tourism infrastructure as a nonmilitary means to make inroads into autonomous EZLN communities.

CERRO DE SAN CRISTÓBAL & CERRO DE GUADALUPE

Want to take in the best views in town? Well, you'll have to work for them, because at this altitude the stairs up these hills can be punishing. Churches crown both lookouts, and the Iglesia de Guadalupe becomes a hot spot for religious devotees around the **Día de la Virgen de Guadalupe** (December 12).

TEMPLO & EX-CONVENTO DE SANTO DOMINGO

Located just north of the city center, the 16th-century **Templo de Santo Domingo** (Avenida 20 de Noviembre; admission free; 🕑 6:30am-2pm & 4-8pm) is San Cristóbal's most beautiful church, especially when its façade catches the late-afternoon sun. This baroque frontage, with its outstanding filigree stucco work, was added in the 17th century and includes the double-headed Hapsburg eagle, symbol of the Spanish monarchy in those days. The interior is lavishly gilded, especially the ornate pulpit.

Around Santo Domingo and the neighboring **Templo de La Caridad** (built in 1712), Chamulan women and bohemian types from around Mexico conduct a colorful daily **crafts market**. The ex-monastery attached to Santo Domingo contains two interesting exhibits: one is the weavers' showroom of **Sna Jolobil**; the other is the **Centro Cultural de los Altos** (☎ 678-1609; Calz Lázaro Cárdenas s/n; admission M$33, free Sun & holidays; 🕑 10am-5pm Tue-Sun), with a reasonable Spanish-language museum on the history of the San Cristóbal region.

NA BOLOM

An atmospheric museum-research center, for many years **Na Bolom** (☎ 678-1418; www.nabolom.org; Guerrero 33; view house only M$35, 1½hr tour in English or Spanish regular/student M$45/20; ☺ 10am-6pm, Spanish tour 11:30am, English tour 4:30pm, no tours Mon) was the home of Swiss anthropologist and photographer Gertrude Duby-Blom (Trudy Blom; 1901–93) and her Danish archaeologist husband Frans Blom (1893–1963).

Na Bolom means 'Jaguar House' in the Tzotzil language (as well as being a play on its former owners' name). It's full of photographs, archaeological and anthropological relics, and books.

MERCADO MUNICIPAL

For a closer look at local life – and an assault on the senses – visit San Cristóbal's busy **Mercado Municipal** (Municipal Market; ☺ approx 7am-5pm), eight blocks north of Plaza 31 de Marzo between Avenidas Utrilla and Belisario Domínguez.

MUSEO DE LA MEDICINA MAYA

The award-winning **Museo de la Medicina Maya** (Maya Medicine Museum; ☎ 678-5438; www.medicinamaya .org; Salomón González Blanco 10; admission M$20; ☺ 10am-6pm Mon-Fri, 10am-5pm Sat & Sun) introduces the system of traditional medicine used by many indigenous people in the Chiapas highlands. It's a 15-minute walk north from Calle Real de Guadalupe or M$18 by taxi.

ARCO, TEMPLO & CENTRO CULTURAL EL CARMEN

The **Arco de El Carmen**, at the southern end of the Andador Turístico on Avenida Hidalgo, dates from the late 17th century and was once the city's gateway. The ex-convent just east is a wonderful colonial building, with a large peaceful garden. It's now the **Centro Cultural El Carmen** (Hermanos Domínguez s/n; admission free; ☺ 9am-6pm Tue-Sun), hosting art and photography exhibitions and the occasional musical event.

MUSEO DEL ÁMBAR DE CHIAPAS

Chiapas amber – fossilized pine resin, around 30 million years old – is known for its clarity and diverse colors. Most is mined around Simojovel, north of San Cristóbal. The **Museo del Ámbar de Chiapas** (Chiapas Amber Museum; www .museodelambar.com.mx; Plazuela de la Merced; admission M$2; ☺ 10am-2pm & 4-7pm Tue-Sun) explains all things amber (with information sheets in English and other languages) and displays and sells some exquisitely carved items and insect-embedded pieces.

Courses

For language classes, contact **El Puente Spanish Language School** (☎ 678-3723; www.elpuenteweb.com; Calle Real de Guadalupe 55), which offers individual/group lessons per week for M$2300/1900.

Tours

Recommended tour agencies include the following:

Explora (☎ 678-4295; www.ecochiapas.com; 1 de Marzo 30; ☺ 9:30am-2pm & 4-8pm Mon-Fri, 9:30am-2pm Sat) Adventure trips to the Selva Lacandona (Lacandon Jungle; four/five days M$3600/4540, minimum four people) and more.

Otisa (☎ 678-1933; www.otisatravel.com; Calle Real de Guadalupe 3; ☺ 8am-9pm)

Festivals & Events

Semana Santa The crucifixion is acted out on Good Friday in the Barrio de Mexicanos in the northwest of town.

Feria de la Primavera y de la Paz (Spring and Peace Fair) Easter Sunday is the start of the weeklong town fair, with parades, musical events, bullfights and so on.

Festival Cervantino Barroco In late October and early November, this is a lively cultural program with music, dance and theater.

Sleeping

BUDGET

Camping Rancho San Nicolás (☎ 678-0057; Prolongación León s/n; camping per person M$50; r with shared bathroom per person M$60, rustic cabana per person M$60, villa d M$350) Past cornfields and grazing horses, this grassy spot on the edge of town is a tranquil dose of el campo in the city. Bring a tent or trailer, or choose from a spectrum of options, including basic rooms and modern apartments with kitchens and fireplaces.

ourpick Posada Ganesha (☎ 678-0212; www .ganeshaposada.com; 28 de Agosto 23; s/d/tr/q with shared bathroom M$100/160/240/320; 💻) A new incense-infused posada (inn) trimmed in Indian fabrics, it's a friendly and vibrant place to rest your head, with yoga and papier-mâché classes and a guest kitchen. The freestanding cabana is especially nice.

Hostal Rincón de los Camellos (☎ 967-116-0097; loscamellos@hotmail.com; Calle Real de Guadalupe 110; dm M$60, s/d/tr/q with shared bathroom M$140/180/230/270, with private bathroom M$200/220/270/330) 'Camels' Corner' is a clean, tranquil little spot run by welcoming French folk. The brightly painted rooms are set round two patios, with a grassy little garden out back. A small purple kitchen has free drinking water and coffee, and a *shisha* (waterpipe) café clad in psychedelic fabrics is a pleasant low-key hangout.

MIDRANGE

Casa Margarita (☎ 678-0957; agchincultik@hotmail.com; Calle Real de Guadalupe 34; s/d/tr/q M$350/450/550/650; 🖳) This popular and well-run travelers' haunt offers tastefully presented, impeccably clean rooms with reading lights, and a pretty courtyard at the center of things. Rates can go down by M$50 to M$100 in low season. There's free internet, an in-house travel agency and a good restaurant.

Hotel El Paraíso (☎ 678-0085; www.hotelposada paraiso.com; 5 de Febrero 19; s/d/tr M$450/650/850) Combining colonial style with a boutique-hotel feel, El Paraíso has a bright, wood-pillared patio and courtyard garden, and loads of character. The high-ceilinged rooms are not huge, and some have limited natural light, but several are bi-level with an extra bed upstairs. The in-house restaurant, L'Eden (opposite), is excellent.

Hotel Diego de Mazariegos (☎ 678-0833; www.diegodemazariegos.com; 5 de Febrero 1; s/d/tr/q M$730/780/850/920, ste M$1250-1500; 🅿) This classy, long-established hotel occupies two 18th-century mansions built around beautiful, wide courtyards. The 76 rooms are large and decked out with traditional fabrics and fittings, but also have modern comforts, including cable TV. Some have fireplaces (M$15 per load of wood), and suites have spa tubs. The hotel has a lively tequila-and-mariachi-theme bar.

Hotel Casavieja (☎ /fax 678-6868; www.casavieja .com.mx; MA Flores 27; s/d/tr M$800/850/900, ste M$950-1000; 🅿 🖳) Set in a beautifully renovated 18th-century house with lots of wooden pillars, balustrades and old-world atmosphere, Casavieja also boasts modern comforts. The large comfortable rooms, arranged around flowery courtyards, all have two double beds, heater, cable TV and phone.

Na Bolom (☎ 678-1418; www.nabolom.org; Guerrero 33; s/d/tr/q incl breakfast M$660/880/1045/1100, ste M$1210; 🅿 🖳) This famous museum/research institute (p234), about 1km from the plaza, has 16 stylish guestrooms, all loaded with character and all but one with log fires. Meals are served in the house's stately dining room. Room rates include a house tour and wireless internet.

TOP END

Casa Felipe Flores (☎ 678-3996; www.felipeflores.com; JF Flores 36; r incl full breakfast US$92-118; ✖) A dreamy colonial guesthouse decorated with outstanding Mexican and Guatemalan art, crafts and furnishings, the 200-year-old building contains five rooms with fireplace located off two flowery courtyards. The lounge is a wonderful place to sit by the fire, have a glass of wine and leaf through some of its terrific library. Room 5 is a cozy rooftop hideaway, with a private terrace looking out over tiled rooftops and clusters of bougainvillea.

Parador San Juan de Dios (☎ /fax 678-1167; www .sanjuandios.com; Calz Roberta 16; ste M$1400-3700; 🅿) A stunning boutique hotel on the northern edge of town, the Parador San Juan de Dios offers voluminous and luxurious suites furnished with fascinating antique and modern art. The hotel occupies the former Rancho Harvard, which dates from the 17th century and has lodged many anthropologists and archaeologists. It has beautiful gardens, vast lawns, and a top-class restaurant with an inventive, expensive Chiapas/Mediterranean menu using herbs and vegetables grown in the on-site organic garden.

Eating

CALLE REAL DE GUADALUPE AREA

El Gato Gordo (☎ 678-8313; Calle Real de Guadalupe 20; mains M$25-49; 🕑 1-11pm Wed-Mon; 🆅) El Gato Gordo attracts hungry travelers in droves for its excellent, well-prepared food at terrific prices. There's an unbeatable set lunch (M$28), and excellent pastas, crêpes, Mexican snacks and meat dishes, plus a great choice of drinks.

TierrAdentro (☎ 674-6766; www.tierradentro.org.mx; Calle Real de Guadalupe 24; menús M$30-70; 🕑 8am-11pm) A popular gathering center for political progressives and coffee-swigging, laptop-toting locals (not that they're mutually exclusive), this large indoor courtyard restaurant and café is a comfortable place to while away the hours. It's run by Zapatista supporters, who hold frequent cultural events and conferences on local issues. A simple *menú compa* (fixed-price meal named for the Zapatistas; M$30), with rice and beans and handmade tortillas, is hearty and delicious. Also inside are a good (Spanish-only) bookstore and an indigenous women's weaving co-op.

PLAZA 31 DE MARZO

Madre Tierra (☎ 678-4297; Av Insurgentes 19; mains M$30-65; 🕑 8am-10pm; **V**) A long-time travelers' favorite, Madre Tierra serves an eclectic and mainly vegetarian menu on a tranquil patio or in an atmospheric dining room. Breakfasts are superb, but perhaps sliding by on its reputation; other meals can be hit-or-miss.

L'Eden (☎ 678-0085; Hotel El Paraíso, 5 de Febrero 19; mains M$45-110; 🕑 7am-noon & 1-11pm) This quality restaurant's tempting European and Mexican menu includes *fondue suiza* (Swiss fondue), *sopa azteca* (tortilla soup) and succulent meat dishes. There's a lengthy wine list, too, including French and Spanish vintages.

Pizzería El Punto (☎ 678-7979; Comitán 13; pizzas M$60-100; 🕑 2-11pm Tue-Sun) Forget the cardboard crap that passes for pizzas in some parts, these crispy pies are the best in town, bar none.

Drinking & Entertainment

Check out **Café Museo Café** (☎ 678-7876; MA Flores 10; 🕑 7am-10pm), **DaDa Club** (☎ 631-3293; www.dadajazz.com; Av Insurgentes 16A; 🕑 1pm-midnight Mon-Sat) or **La Pera** (☎ 678-1209; MA Flores 23; 🕑 1-11pm Mon-Sat) for live music.

Getting There & Away

On the corner of the Pan-American Hwy, the **Instituto Nacional de Migración** (☎ 678-0292; Diagonal El Centenario 30) is 1.2km west of the OCC bus terminal.

From Tuxtla Gutiérrez you'll most likely travel here on the fast new toll highway (M$33 for cars). See p243 for a warning about Hwy 199 from San Cristóbal to Palenque.

AIR

San Cristóbal's airport, about 15km from town on the Palenque road, has no regular passenger flights; the main airport serving town is in Tuxtla Gutiérrez. To get there, take a Tuxtla-bound *colectivo* to Soriana (M$35, 1¼ hours) in Tuxtla's eastern suburbs; from the stand at the *colectivo* stop, hire a taxi to the airport (M$150, 30 minutes). A number of tour agencies, including Viajes Chincultik and **Otisa** (☎ 678-1933; www.otisatravel.com; Calle Real de Guadalupe 3), run shuttles to the Tuxtla airport for M$150 to M$160 per person, but scheduled service is generally at 9am only. Reserve in advance, especially if you want to leave at another time.

Mexicana de Aviación (☎ 678-9309; Belisario Domínguez 2B) sells direct flights from Tuxtla Gutiérrez to Mexico City, and connecting flights to Villahermosa, Mérida and Cancún.

BUS, COLECTIVO & VAN

San Cristóbal has around a dozen bus terminals, mostly on or just off the Pan-American Hwy. Most important for travelers is the 1st-class **OCC bus terminal** (☎ 678-0291; cnr Pan-American Hwy & Av Insurgentes), also used by ADO and UNO 1st-class and deluxe buses, and 2nd-class Transportes Dr Rodulfo Figueroa (TRF) and Rápidos del Sur. Tickets for all of these lines are sold at **Ticket Bus** (☎ 678-8503; Calle Real de Guadalupe 5A; 🕑 7am-10pm) in the city center.

First-class **AEXA** (☎ 678-6178) and 2nd-class Ómnibus de Chiapas share a bus terminal on the south side of the highway; and various Suburban-type vans and *colectivo* services have depots on the highway in the same area. Daily departures are listed in the table (below).

For Guatemala, most agencies offer daily van service to Quetzaltenango (M$260, eight hours), Panajachel (M$260, 10 hours), Antigua (M$360, 12 hours) and Flores (via Palenque, M$400).

BUS SERVICES FROM SAN CRISTÓBAL DE LAS CASAS

Destination	Fare ($M)	Duration (hr)	Departures
Campeche	314	11	1 OCC bus
Cancún	606-724	16-18	4 OCC buses
Ciudad Cuauhtémoc (Guatemalan border)	100	3½	4 OCC buses
Mérida	448	13	1 OCC bus
Palenque	75-134	5	9 OCC buses & 3 AEXA buses
Villahermosa	194	7-8	2 OCC buses

TABASCO & CHIAPAS

CAR

For car rental, **Optima** (☎ 674-5409; optimacar1 @hotmail.com; Mazariegos 39) has VW Beetles for M$400/2400 per day/week.

Getting Around

Combis go up Cresencio Rosas from the Pan-American Hwy to the city center. Taxis cost M$18 within the city.

Friendly **Los Pingüinos** (☎ 678-0202; www.bike mexico.com/pinguinos; Ecuador 4B; bike hire per 4/6/9hr M$100/ 130/150; ☑ phone 8am-8pm, office 10am-2:30pm & 3:30-7pm Mon-Sat) rents good-quality mountain bikes.

Croozy Scooters (☎ 631-4329; www.prodigyweb .net.mx/croozyscooters; Belisario Domínguez 7; scooter hire per 1/5/9/24hr M$75/200/250/350; ☑ 9am-7pm), under new ownership, rents well-maintained 80cc scooters.

AROUND SAN CRISTÓBAL

The inhabitants of the beautiful Chiapas highlands are descended from the ancient Maya and maintain some unique customs, costumes and beliefs. It's particularly important to be respectful of local customs in this part of Mexico.

While walking or riding by horse or bicycle by day along the main roads to San Juan Chamula and San Lorenzo Zinacantán should not be risky, it's not wise to wander into unfrequented areas or down isolated tracks.

Transportation to most villages goes from points around the Mercado Municipal in San Cristóbal. Combis to San Juan Chamula (M$8) leave from Calle Honduras frequently from 4am to about 6pm; for Zinacantán, *combis* (M$10) and *colectivos* (M$12) go at least hourly from 5am to 7pm, from a yard off Robledo.

San Juan Chamula

pop 3000 / elev 2200m

The Chamulans are a fiercely independent Tzotzil group, about 80,000 strong. Their main village, San Juan Chamula, is 10km northwest of San Cristóbal.

Outsiders can visit San Juan Chamula, but a big sign at the entrance to the village strictly forbids photography in the village church or at rituals. Do *not* ignore these restrictions; the community takes them very seriously. Nearby, around the shell of an older church, is the village **graveyard**, with black crosses for people who died old, white for the young and blue for others.

On Sunday the weekly **market** is held, when people from the hills stream into the village to shop, trade and visit the main church. Standing beside the main plaza, Chamula's main church, the **Templo de San Juan**, is a ghostly white, with a vividly painted arch of green and blue. A sign tells visitors to obtain tickets (M$15) at the **tourist office** (☑ 9am-6pm), beside the plaza, before entering the church. Inside the darkened sanctuary, hundreds of flickering candles, clouds of incense and worshippers kneeling with their faces to the pine-needle-carpeted floor make a powerful impression.

San Lorenzo Zinacantán

pop 3700 / elev 2558m

The orderly village of San Lorenzo Zinacantán, about 11km northwest of San Cristóbal, is the main village of the Zinacantán municipality (population 45,000). Zinacantán people, like Chamulans, are Tzotzil.

A small **market** is held on Sunday until noon, and during fiesta times. The huge central **Iglesia de San Lorenzo** (admission M$20) was rebuilt following a fire in 1975. Photography is banned in the church and churchyard. The small thatched-roof **Museo Jsotz' Levetik** (admission by donation; ☑ 9am-5pm), three blocks below the central basketball court, covers local culture and has some fine textiles and musical instruments.

PALENQUE

☎ 916 / pop 37,000 / elev 80m

Deservedly one of the top destinations of Chiapas, the soaring jungle-swathed temples of Palenque are a national treasure and one of the best examples of Maya architecture in Mexico. Modern Palenque town, a few kilometers to the east, is a sweaty, humdrum place without much appeal except as a jumping-off point for the ruins. Many prefer to base themselves at one of the forest hideouts along the road between the town and the ruins, including the funky travelers' hangout of El Panchán.

The name Palenque (Palisade) is Spanish and has no relation to the city's ancient name, which may have been Lakamha (Big Water). Palenque was first occupied around 100 BC, and flourished from around AD 630 to 740. The city rose to prominence under the ruler Pakal, who reigned from AD 615–83.

Pakal's son Kan B'alam II (684–702), who is represented in hieroglyphics by the jaguar and the serpent (and also called Jaguar

PALENQUE

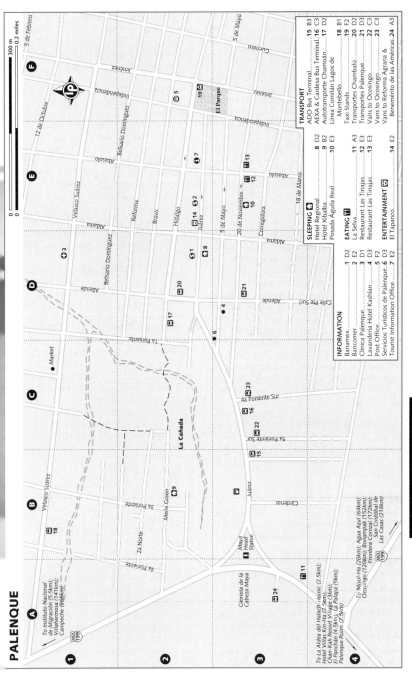

INFORMATION
Banamex..............................1 D2
Bancomer.............................2 E2
Clínica Palenque....................3 D1
Lavandería Hotel Kashlan.....4 D3
Post Office............................5 F2
Servicios Turísticos de Palenque..6 D3
Tourist Information Office.......7 E2

SLEEPING
Hotel Regional......................8 D2
Hotel Xibalba........................9 B2
Posada Aguila Real...............10 E3

EATING
La Selva.............................11 A3
Restaurant Las Tinajas.........12 E3
Restaurant Las Tinajas.........13 E3

ENTERTAINMENT
El Tapanco.........................14 E2

TRANSPORT
ADO Bus Terminal................15 B3
AEXA & Cardesa Bus Terminal..16 C3
Autotransporte Chamoán......17 D2
Línea Comitán Lagos de
 Montebello.......................18 B1
Taxi Stands........................19 F2
Transportes Chambalú..........20 D2
Transportes Palenque...........21 D3
Vans to Ocosingo.................22 C3
Vans to Ocosingo.................23 C3
Vans to Reforma Agraria &
 Benemérito de las Américas..24 A3

Serpent II), continued Palenque's expansion and artistic development. He presided over the construction of the Grupo de las Cruces temples, placing sizable narrative stone stelae within each.

During Kan B'alam II's reign, Palenque extended its zone of control to Río Usumacinta, but was challenged by the rival Maya city of Toniná, 65km south. Kan B'alam's brother and successor, K'an Joy Chitam II (Precious Peccary), was captured by forces from Toniná in 711, and probably executed there. Palenque enjoyed a resurgence between 722 and 736 under Ahkal Mo' Nahb' III (Turtle Macaw Lake), who added many substantial buildings.

Orientation

Hwy 199 meets Palenque's main street, Avenida Juárez, at the Glorieta de la Cabeza Maya, an intersection with a large statue of a Maya chieftain's head, at the west end of the town. From here Avenida Juárez heads 1km east to the central square, El Parque. The main bus terminals are on Avenida Juárez just east of the Maya head statue.

A few hundred meters south from the Maya head statue, the paved road to the Palenque ruins, 7.5km away, diverges west off Hwy 199. This road passes the Museo de Sitio (Site Museum) after about 6.5km, then winds about 1km further to the main entrance of the ruins.

Accommodations are scattered around the central part of town and along the road to the ruins. The commercial heart of town, where you'll hardly ever see another tourist, is north of the center along Avenida Velasco Suárez.

Information

There are over a dozen cybercafés; rates cost M$50 to M$80 per hour.

Banamex (Av Juárez 62; ☽ 9am-4pm Mon-Fri) Has an ATM.

Clínica Palenque (☎ 345-0273; Av Velasco Suárez 33; ☽ 7am-11pm) Dr Alfonso Martínez speaks English.

Lavandería Hotel Kashlan (5 de Mayo 105; per 1-3kg M$50)

Maya Exploration Center (www.mayaexploration.org) Provides lectures, slide shows and documentary films on weekends in the main tourism seasons.

Post office (Independencia s/n; ☽ 9am-6pm Mon-Fri, 9am-1pm Sat)

Servicios Turísticos de Palenque (☎ 345-1340; www.stpalenque.com; cnr Av Juárez & 5 de Mayo) A tour agency.

Tourist information office (cnr Av Juárez & Abasolo; ☽ 9am-9pm Mon-Sat, 9am-1pm Sun)

Palenque Ruins

Ancient **Palenque** (admission M$45, 2hr guided tour M$650-700; ☽ 8am-5pm, last entry 4:30pm) stands at the precise point where the first hills rise out of the Gulf Coast plain, and the dense jungle covering these hills forms an evocative backdrop to Palenque's exquisite Maya architecture. Hundreds of ruined buildings are spread over 15 sq km, but only a fairly compact central area has been excavated. The ruins and surrounding forests form a national park, the Parque Nacional Palenque, for which you must pay a separate M$20 admission fee at Km 4.5 on the road to the ruins.

Palenque's **Museo de Sitio** (Site Museum; ☎ 348-9331; Carretera Palenque-Ruinas Km 7; admission free; ☽ 9am-4:30pm Tue-Sun) is worth a wander, displaying finds from the site and interpreting, in English and Spanish, Palenque's history.

Transportes Chambalú (☎ 345-2849; Allende s/n) and **Transportes Palenque** (☎ 345-2430; cnr Allende & 20 de Noviembre) run *combis* from Palenque town to the ruins about every 15 minutes from 6am to 7pm daily (M$10 each way). They will pick you up or drop you anywhere along the town-to-ruins road.

Note that the mushrooms sold by locals along the road to the ruins from about May to November are of the hallucinogenic variety.

EXPLORING THE SITE

As you enter the site, a line of temples rises in front of the jungle on your right, culminating about 100m ahead at the **Templo de las Inscripciones** (Temple of the Inscriptions), the tallest and most stately of Palenque's buildings. From the top, interior stairs lead down into the tomb of Pakal (closed indefinitely to avoid further damage from the humidity exuded by visitors). Pakal's jewel-bedecked skeleton and jade mosaic death mask were moved from the tomb to Mexico City, and the tomb was re-created in the Museo Nacional de Antropología (from where the priceless death mask was stolen in 1985), but the carved stone sarcophagus lid remains at the Museo de Sitio.

Diagonally opposite the Templo de las Inscripciones is **El Palacio** (The Palace), a large structure divided into four main courtyards, with a maze of corridors and rooms. Soon after the death of his father, Pakal's son Kan B'alam II (684-702) started designing the temples of the **Grupo de las Cruces** (Group of the Crosses). All three main pyramid-

shaped structures surround a plaza southeast of the Templo de las Inscripciones. The **Templo del Sol** (Temple of the Sun), on the west side of the plaza, has the best-preserved roofcomb at Palenque. Steep steps climb to the **Templo de la Cruz** (Temple of the Cross), the largest and most elegantly proportioned in this group.

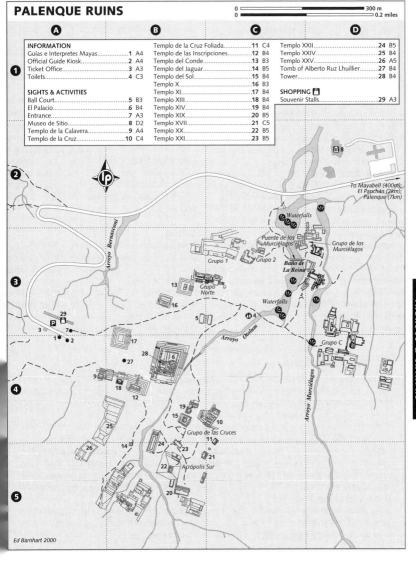

PALENQUE RUINS

0 — 300 m
0 — 0.2 miles

TABASCO & CHIAPAS

Ed Barnhart 2000

South of the Grupo de las Cruces is the **Acrópolis Sur**, where archaeologists have recovered some terrific finds in recent excavations. It appears to have been constructed as an extension of the Grupo de las Cruces, with both groups set around what was probably a single long, open space.

Sleeping

The first choice to make is whether you want to stay in or out of Palenque town. Most out-of-town places, including **El Panchán** (www.elpanchan.com; Carretera Palenque-Ruinas Km 4.5), are along the road to the ruins.

IN TOWN

Hotel Regional (☎ /fax 345-0183; www.regionalpalenque.com; Av Juárez 119; s/d/tr/q with fan M$180/230/320/420, tr/q with air-con M$400/500; ☒) Something slightly different from the run of the Avenida Juárez mill: bright paintwork and extremely bright murals enliven two floors of rooms set around a courtyard with a turtle pond.

Posada Águila Real (☎ 345-0004; Av 20 de Noviembre s/n; s/d M$350/400, tr M$450-500; ☒ ☐) Seventeen spotless, well-kept, blue-and-yellow rooms are arranged on three floors based around an open-air patio. There's a small café-restaurant, too.

Hotel Xibalba (☎ 345-0411; www.hotelxibalba.com; Merle Green 9; r M$550, tr/q M$600/700; ☒ ☒ ☐) Preened to perfection by a loving owner, the Xibalba enjoys a tranquil location in two buildings (one in an imitation of the ancient Maya corbel roof style, the other with a full-size replica of the lid from Pakal's sarcophagus).

OUTSIDE TOWN

Margarita & Ed Cabañas (☎ 348-4205; El Panchán; cabanas r M$170, r with fan M$250-300, r with air-con M$350, tr/q with air-con M$500; ☒ ☒ ☒) Teeming with local information, Margarita has welcomed travelers to her exceptionally homey place in the jungle for more than 10 years. Bright, clean and cheerful rooms have good mosquito netting, and the more rustic screened cabanas are well kept, too.

Hotel Villas Kin-Ha (☎ 345-0533; www.villaskinha.com; Carretera Palenque-Ruinas Km 2.7; r M$660-800, ste M$1320; ☒ ☒ ☒) Most accommodations are palm-thatched and wood-beamed, and all have air-con. The grounds hold two good pools, an open-sided *palapa* (thatched-roof shelter) restaurant and a theater.

Chan-Kah Resort Village (☎ 345-1100; www.chan-kah.com.mx; Carretera Palenque-Ruinas Km 3; r/ste US$120/330; ☒ ☒ ☒) Swimmers will go woozy contemplating the Chan-Kah's stupendous 70m stone-lined swimming pool in lush jungle gardens. A quality resort on the road to the ruins, 3km from town, it has handsome, well-spaced, wood-and-stone cottages with generous bathrooms, ceiling fans, terrace and air-con.

Eating

Cafetería Motiepa (Carretera Palenque-Ruinas Km 6; snacks M$20-40; ☺ 8am-3pm) Next to the Museo de Sitio near the Palenque ruins, this is a good stop for a snack or drink.

Restaurant Las Tinajas (☎ 345-4970; cnr 20 de Noviembre & Abasolo; mains M$50-100; ☺ 7am-11pm) It doesn't take long to figure out why this place is always busy. It slings enormous portions of

---

THE SELVA LACANDONA

The Selva Lacandona (Lacandon Jungle), in eastern Chiapas, occupies just one quarter of 1% of Mexico. Yet it contains more than 4300 plant species, 450 types of butterfly, at least 340 birds and 163 mammals. Among these are such emblematic creatures as the jaguar, red macaw, white turtle, tapir and harpy eagle.

This great fund of natural resources and genetic diversity is the southwest end of the Selva Maya, a 30,000-sq-km corridor of tropical rainforest stretching from Chiapas across northern Guatemala into Belize and the southern Yucatán. But the Selva Lacandona is shrinking fast, under pressure from ranchers, loggers, oil prospectors and farmers desperate for land. From around 15,000 sq km in the 1950s, an estimated 3000 to 4500 sq km of jungle remains today. Most of what's left is in the Reserva de la Biósfera Montes Azules and the neighboring Reserva de la Biósfera Lacan-tun.

The Mexican government deeded a large section of the land to a small number of Lacandón families in the 1970s, creating tensions with other indigenous communities whose claims were put aside. Land within the region remains incredibly contested.

BUS SERVICES FROM PALENQUE

Destination	Fare ($M)	Duration (hr)	Departures
Campeche	226-230	4½-5½	4 ADO buses
Cancún	498-584	13-14	5 ADO buses
Mérida	316-346	8	4 ADO buses
San Cristóbal de Las Casas	75-142	5¼	10 ADO buses & 5 AEXA buses
Villahermosa	50-98	2	12 ADO buses & 11 AEXA buses

excellent homestyle food, enough to keep you (and possibly another person) fueled up for hours. Note: there is another branch on the opposite side of the intersection.

La Selva (☎ 345-0363; Hwy 199; mains M$50-160; ◷ 11:30am-11:30pm) Palenque's most upscale restaurant serves up well-prepared steaks, seafood, salads and *antojitos* ('little whims,' corn- and tortilla-based snacks) under an enormous *palapa* roof.

Don Mucho's (☎ 341-8209; El Panchán; mains M$55-110) The hot spot of El Panchán, popular Don Mucho's provides great-value meals in a jungly setting with a candlelit atmosphere at night.

Entertainment

Palenque doesn't have much of a nightlife scene. But you can try **El Tapanco** (☎ 345-0415; Av Juárez 65C) or **La Palapa** (Carretera Palenque-Ruinas Km 5; ◷ until 4am) for dancing and live music.

Getting There & Away

Palenque's airport, 3km north of town along Hwy 199, has been closed to regular passenger flights for several years.

Highway holdups were once weekly occurrences on Hwy 199 between Ocosingo and Palenque, but an increased military and police presence has made this route pretty safe now. Still, most people consider daytime travel to be best.

The main **ADO bus terminal** (☎ 345-1344; Av Juárez s/n) has deluxe and 1st-class services; it's also used by OCC (1st-class) and TRF (2nd-class) bus lines. The **AEXA bus terminal** (☎ 345-2630; Av Juárez 159), with 1st-class buses, and Cardesa (2nd class), is located 1½ blocks east, with an on-site internet café. Vans to Ocosingo wait on 4a Poniente Sur and 5a Poniente Sur, near the bus terminals, and leave when full. **Transportes Palenque** (☎ 345-2430; cnr Allende & 20 de Noviembre) runs vans to Tenosique.

For a sample of daily departures, see the table (above).

Getting Around

Taxis wait at the northeast corner of El Parque and at the ADO bus terminal; they charge M$40 to El Panchán or Mayabell, and M$50 to the ruins.

BONAMPAK & YAXCHILÁN

The ancient Maya cities of Bonampak and Yaxchilán, southeast of Palenque, are easily accessible thanks to the Carretera Fronteriza, a good paved road running parallel to the Mexico–Guatemala border, all the way from Palenque to the Parque Nacional Lagunas de Montebello (Lagos de Montebello), around the fringe of the Selva Lacandona. Bonampak, famous for its frescoes, is 148km by road from Palenque; the bigger and more important Yaxchilán, with a peerless jungle setting beside the broad and swift Río Usumacinta, is 173km by road, then about 22km by boat.

Tours

While independent travel is certainly possible in this region, most choose to take an organized tour from Palenque (p240).

Getting There & Away

From Palenque, Autotransporte Chamoán runs vans to Frontera Corozal (M$60, 2½ to three hours, 13 times daily), and vans to Benemérito de las Américas (M$60, 3½ hours, every 40 minutes from 4am to 5:30pm) depart from a terminus on Hwy 199 just south of the Maya head statue.

Línea Comitán Lagos de Montebello (☎ 916-345-1260; Av Velasco Suárez s/n), two blocks west of the Palenque market, runs vans to Benemérito (M$60, 10 times daily from 4am to 2:45pm), with the first five services (4am, 5:30am, 7:15am, 8:45am and 10:15am) continuing round the Carretera Fronteriza to the Lagos de Montebello (M$160, seven hours to Tziscao) and Comitán (M$170, eight hours).

All these services stop at San Javier (M$45, two hours), the turnoff for Lacanjá

Chansayab and Bonampak, 140km from Palenque; and at Crucero Corozal (M\$50, 2½ hours), the intersection for Frontera Corozal.

There are no gas stations on the Carretera Fronteriza, but plenty of entrepreneurial locals sell reasonably priced gasoline from large plastic containers.

Bonampak

The site of **Bonampak** (admission M\$37; 🕗 8am-4:45pm) spreads over 2.4 sq km, but all the main ruins stand around the rectangular Gran Plaza. Never a major city, Bonampak spent most of the Classic period under Yaxchilán's sphere of influence. The most impressive surviving monuments were built under Chan Muwan II, a nephew of the Yaxchilán's Itzamnaaj B'alam II, who acceded to Bonampak's throne in AD 776. The 6m-high **Stela 1** in the Gran Plaza depicts Chan Muwan holding a ceremonial staff at the height of his reign. He also features in **Stela 2** and **Stela 3** on the Acrópolis, which rises from the south end of the plaza.

However, it's the vivid frescoes inside the modest-looking **Templo de las Pinturas** (Edificio 1) that have given Bonampak its fame – and its name, which means 'Painted Walls' in Yucatecan Maya.

The Bonampak site abuts the Reserva de la Biósfera Montes Azules, and is rich in wildlife. Drinks and snacks are sold at the entrance to the Monumento Natural Bonampak protected zone, 8km before the ruins, and by the archaeological site entrance.

Visitors to Bonampak can stay in the neighboring village of Frontera Corozál. **Escudo Jaguar** (☎ 502-5353-5637; http://mx.geocities .com/hotel_escudojaguar; camping per person M\$70, cabana with shared bathroom d/tr M\$200/258, cabana with 1/2/3 d beds M\$380/572/760; **P**) has solidly built, pink, thatched cabanas, which are all kept spotless and come equipped with fans and mosquito nets.

GETTING THERE & AWAY

Bonampak is 12km from San Javier on the Carretera Fronteriza. The first 3km, to the Lacanjá Chansayab turnoff, is paved, and the rest is good gravel/dirt road through the forest. Taxis will take you from San Javier or the Lacanjá turnoff to the ruins and back for M\$70 per person, including waiting time. Private vehicles cannot pass the Monumento Natural Bonampak entrance, 1km past the Lacanjá turnoff, but you can rent bicycles there for M\$60 for three hours, or take a *combi* to the ruins for M\$70 round-trip.

Yaxchilán

Jungle-shrouded **Yaxchilán** (admission M\$45; 🕗 8am-4:30pm, last entry 3:30pm) has a terrific setting above a horseshoe loop in the Río Usumacinta. The control this location gave it over river commerce, and a series of successful alliances and conquests, made Yaxchilán one of the most important Classic Maya cities in the Usumacinta region. Archaeologically, Yaxchilán is famed for its ornamented façades and roofcombs, and its impressive stone

---

INDIGENOUS PEOPLES OF CHIAPAS

Of the 4.2 million people of Chiapas, approximately 1.25 million are indigenous, with language being the key ethnic identifier. Each of the eight principal groups has its own language, beliefs and customs. Travelers to the area around San Cristóbal are most likely to encounter the Tzotziles and the Tzeltales. Their traditional religious life is nominally Catholic, but integrates pre-Hispanic elements. Most people live in the hills outside the villages, which are primarily market and ceremonial centers.

Tzotzil and Tzeltal clothing is among the most varied, colorful and elaborately worked in Mexico. It not only identifies wearers' villages but also carries on ancient Maya traditions. Many of the seemingly abstract designs on these costumes are, in fact, stylized snakes, frogs, butterflies, birds, saints and other beings.

The Lacandones dwelt deep in the Selva Lacandona and largely avoided contact with the outside world until the 1950s. They now number 800 or so and live in three main settlements in that same region, with low-key tourism being one of their major means of support. Lacandones are readily recognizable in their white tunics and long black hair cut in a fringe. Most Lacandones have now abandoned their traditional animist religion in favor of Presbyterian or evangelical forms of Christianity.

EXPLORE MORE OF CHIAPAS

This short chapter only touches the surface. For more information, check out our comprehensive coverage in *Mexico* or download a pdf copy at www.shop.lonelyplanet.com. Or better yet, leave the guidebook behind and try out some of these DIY adventures:

- **Agua Azul & Misol-Ha** These spectacular water attractions – the thundering cascades of Agua Azul and the 35m jungle waterfall of Misol-Ha (www.misol-ha.com) – are both short detours off the Ocosingo–Palenque road.

- **Amatenango del Valle** The women of this Tzeltal village by the Pan-American Hwy, 37km southeast of San Cristóbal, are renowned potters.

- **Chiapa de Corzo** Set 12km east of Tuxtla Gutiérrez on the way to San Cristóbal, Chiapa de Corzo is a small and attractive colonial town with an easygoing, provincial air. Set on the north bank of the broad Río Grijalva, it's the main starting point for trips into the **Cañón del Sumidero**.

- **Grutas de San Cristóbal** The entrance to this long cavern is among pine woods 9km southeast of San Cristóbal, a five-minute walk south of the Pan-American Hwy.

- **Lacanjá Chansayab** The largest Lacandón Maya village is 12km from Bonampak. Its family compounds are scattered around a wide area, many of them with creeks or even the Río Lacanjá flowing past their grassy grounds. The website www.ecochiapas.com/lacanja (in Spanish) offers information on visiting the region.

- **Lagos de Montebello** The temperate pine and oak forest along the Guatemalan border east of Chinkultic is dotted with over 50 small lakes of varied hues. The nearby **Chinkultic ruins** add to the mystery.

- **Laguna Miramar** Ringed by rainforest 140km southeast of Ocosingo in the Reserva de la Biósfera Montes Azules, this is one of Mexico's most remote and exquisite lakes.

- **Ocosingo** A respite from both the steamy lowland jungle and the chilly highlands, the bustling regional market town of Ocosingo sits in a gorgeous and broad temperate valley midway between San Cristóbal and Palenque. The impressive Maya ruins of **Toniná** are just a few kilometers away.

- **Reserva de la Biósfera El Triunfo** The luxuriant cloud forests high in the remote Sierra Madre de Chiapas are a bird-lover's paradise.

- **Reserva de la Biósfera La Encrucijada** This large biosphere reserve protects a 1448-sq-km strip of coastal lagoons, sand bars and wetlands.

- **Sima de Las Cotorras** This is a dramatic sinkhole (☎ 968-689-0289; simacotorras@hotmail .com) punching 160m wide and 140m deep into the earth. It's about 1½ hours from Tuxtla Gutiérrez.

TABASCO & CHIAPAS

lintels carved with conquest and ceremonial scenes. A flashlight (torch) is helpful for exploring some parts of the site.

Yaxchilán peaked in power and splendor between AD 681 and 800 under the rulers Itzamnaaj B'alam II (Shield Jaguar II, 681–742), Pájaro Jaguar IV (Bird Jaguar IV, 752–68) and Itzamnaaj B'alam III (Shield Jaguar III, 769–800). The city was abandoned around 810.

As you walk toward the ruins, a signed path to the right leads up to the **Pequeña Acrópolis**, a group of ruins on a small hilltop – you can visit this later. Staying on the main path, you soon reach the mazy passages of **El Laberinto** (Edificio 19), built between 742–52, during the interregnum between Itzamnaaj B'alam II and Pájaro Jaguar IV. Dozens of bats shelter under the structure's roof today. From this complicated two level building you emerge at the northwest end of the extensive **Gran Plaza**.

Though it's hard to imagine anyone here ever wanting to be hotter than they already were, **Edificio 17** was apparently a sweat house. About halfway along the plaza, **Stela 1**, flanked by weathered sculptures of a crocodile and a jaguar, shows Pájaro Jaguar IV in a ceremony that took place in 761. **Edificio 20**, from the time of Itzamnaaj B'alam III, was the last significant structure built at Yaxchilán; its lintels are now in Mexico City. **Stela 11**, at the northeast corner of the Gran Plaza, was originally found in front of Edificio 40. The bigger of the two figures visible on it is Pájaro Jaguar IV.

An imposing stairway climbs from Stela 1 to **Edificio 33**, the best-preserved temple at Yaxchilán, with about half of its roofcomb intact. The final step in front of the building is carved with ball-game scenes, and splendid relief carvings embellish the undersides of the lintels. Inside is a statue of Pájaro Jaguar IV, minus his head, which he lost to treasure-seeking 19th-century timber cutters.

From the clearing behind Edificio 33, a path leads into the trees. About 20m along this, fork left uphill; go left at another fork after about 80m, and in some 10 minutes, mostly going uphill, you'll reach three buildings on a hilltop: **Edificio 39**, **Edificio 40** and **Edificio 41**. Climb to the top of Edificio 41 for great views across the top of the jungle to the distant mountains of Guatemala.

Visitors can stay in the village of Lacanjá Chansayab. At **Campamento Río Lacanjá** (www .ecochiapas.com/lacanja; bunk M$120, d M$290, Ya'ax Can r/tr/q M$480/580/650; **P**), 2km south of the central intersection, rustic semi-open-air wood-frame cabanas, with mosquito nets, stand close to the jungle-shrouded Río Lacanjá. A separate group of large rooms with fan, called Cabañas Ya'ax Can, have two solid wooden double beds, tiled floors and hot-water bathroom.

GETTING THERE & AWAY

River *lanchas* (motorboats) take 40 minutes running downstream from Frontera Corozal and one hour to return. *Lancha* outfits, with desks in a thatched-roof building near the Frontera Corozal embarcadero, all charge the same price for trips (return journey with 2½ hours at the ruins for three/four/seven/ 10 people M$650/780/950/1300). *Lanchas* normally depart frequently until 1:30pm or so, and it's sometimes possible to hook up with other travelers or a tour group to share costs.

Directory

CONTENTS

ACCOMMODATIONS

Two storms in 2007 hit the region hard, devastating tourist infrastructure in Tabasco, parts of Chiapas and southern Quintana Roo. Hurricane Dean (see boxed text, p133) wiped out the southern Quintana Roo town of Mahahual, destroying the port and leveling most hotels. We were on the ground just weeks after the disaster and were unable to complete our research, so we did the next best thing and arranged for American expat Kevin Graham to update as much as possible closer to press time. Dean also affected some hotels and restaurants around Laguna Bacalar and Chetumal, but all were up and

> **BOOK ACCOMMODATIONS ONLINE**
>
> For more accommodations reviews and recommendations by Lonely Planet authors, check out the online booking service at www.lonelyplanet.com. You'll find the true, insider lowdown on the best places to stay. Reviews are thorough and independent. Best of all, you can book online.

running – though a bit windswept – by the time we passed through. The other big storm of the year (see boxed text, p228) buried 80% of Tabasco under water, and caused several landslides in Chiapas. In order to get the most up-to-date info, we did a phone update of our Tabasco material after the flooding subsided.

The good news is that the Yucatán Peninsula has finally recovered (for the most part) from 2005's Hurricane Wilma (see boxed text, p59), which wiped out many Caribbean coastal destinations, including Cancún, Isla Cozumel, Isla Holbox, Puerto Morelos and, to a lesser extent, Playa del Carmen.

Accommodations in the Yucatán range from hammocks and cabanas to hotels of every imaginable standard to world-class luxury resorts. This book divides accommodations into three price ranges: budget (where a typical room for two people costs under M$400), midrange (M$400 to M$900) and top end (above M$900).

Budget accommodations include camping grounds, hammocks, palm-thatched cabanas, backpacker hostels, guesthouses and economical hotels. Recommended accommodations will be without frills but generally clean. Hotel rooms, even in the budget range, usually have a private bathroom containing hot shower, toilet and washbasin. (In this book rooms are assumed to have private bathroom unless otherwise stated.)

Midrange accommodations are chiefly hotels. In some areas of the Yucatán M$400 can get you a cozy, attractively decorated room in a friendly small hotel. Many of the region's most appealing and memorable lodgings are in the midrange bracket – small or medium-sized hotels, well cared for, with a friendly

PRACTICALITIES

- All international visitors (including US and Canadian citizens) need a valid passport to enter Mexico.

- Mexico's only English-language daily is the *Herald,* an international edition of the *Miami Herald,* with a Mexico insert. It's available in some upmarket hotels in Mérida and Cancún and at some Sanborns stores.

- Mérida's *El Diario de Yucatán* (www.yucatan.com.mx, in Spanish) is one of the country's most respected newspapers. *Yucatán Today* (www.yucatantoday.com) offers good English-language info on Yucatán state.

- Local TV is dominated by Televisa, which runs four of the six national channels; TV Azteca has the other two. A growing number of viewers have multichannel cable or satellite systems, such as Cablevision or Sky TV.

- Electrical current is 110V, 60Hz, and most plugs have two flat prongs, just like in the USA and Canada.

- Mexicans use the metric system for weights and measures.

- DVDs are encoded for Zone 4, the same as for Australia and New Zealand, though most use the NTSC image registration system, which makes them incompatible with the PAL system used in most of Western Europe and Australia. Many DVDs sold in Mexico are illegal copies.

- As a rule, don't drink the tap water. Cancún has potable tap water.

atmosphere and personal attention from staff. In some areas you'll also find apartments, bungalows and more comfortable cabanas in this price range.

Top-end hotels run from classy international hotels in cities to deluxe coastal resorts and luxurious smaller establishments catering to travelers with a taste for comfort and beautiful design, and the funds to pay for them.

Room prices given in this book are high-season rates unless otherwise stated. In the Yucatán, high season runs from Christmas right through to Easter, plus most of July and August. Outside the high season, many midrange and top-end establishments in tourist destinations cut their room prices by 10% to 40%. They may also have special offers and low weekend rates. Budget accommodations are more likely to keep the same rates year-round.

In this book we use 'single' (abbreviated 's') to mean a room for one person, and 'double' ('d') to mean a room for two people. Mexicans sometimes use the phrase *cuarto sencillo* (literally, single room) to mean a room with one bed, which is often a *cama matrimonial* (double bed). Sometimes one person can occupy such a room for a lower price than two people. A *cuarto doble* often means a room with two beds, which may both be *camas matrimoniales.*

In popular destinations, at busy times it's best to reserve a room in advance, or seek a room early in the day. Many places take reservations via their websites or by email. If a place is not booked out, a simple phone call earlier in the day, saying what time you'll arrive, is usually sufficient. A few places are reluctant to take reservations, but don't worry: you should end up with a room somewhere.

Accommodations prices are subject to two taxes: *impuesto de valor agregado* (IVA, or value-added tax; 15%) and *impuesto sobre hospedaje* (ISH, or lodging tax; 2% in most states). Many budget and some midrange establishments only charge these taxes if you require a receipt. Generally, though, IVA and ISH are included in quoted prices. In top-end hotels a price may often be given as, say, 'M$1000 *más impuestos*' (M$1000 plus taxes), in which case you must add 17% to the figure. When in doubt, you can ask '¿*Están incluidos los impuestos?*' (Are taxes included?). Prices given in this book are those you are most likely to be charged at each place, around high season unless stated otherwise, with or without the taxes according to the establishment's policy.

Apartments & B&Bs

In some places you can find *departamentos* (apartments) for tourists with fully equipped kitchens. Some are very comfortable and they can be good value for three or four people. Tourist offices and advertisements in local newspapers (especially English-language newspapers) are good sources of information.

In Yucatán B&Bs are generally upmarket guesthouses, often aimed at foreign tourists; they are usually comfortable and enjoyable places to stay.

Camping & Trailer Parks

Most organized campgrounds are actually trailer parks set up for people with camper vans and trailers (caravans) but are open to tent campers at lower rates. They're most common along the coast. Some are very basic, others quite luxurious. Expect to pay about M$50 to pitch a tent for two people, and M$100 to M$200 for two people with a vehicle, using full facilities.

The beach is public property in Mexico, and you can basically pitch a tent anywhere you can access. Of course, you'll need to make sure your luggage is secure and that you're well above the high-tide line. Some restaurants and guesthouses in beach spots or country areas will let you pitch a tent on their patch for a couple of dollars per person.

Casas de Huéspedes & Posadas

Inexpensive and congenial accommodations are often to be found at a *casa de huéspedes,* a home converted into simple guest lodgings. Good *casas de huéspedes* are usually family-run, with a relaxed, friendly atmosphere.

Many *posadas* (inns) are like *casas de huéspedes;* others are small hotels.

Hammocks & Cabanas

You'll find hammocks and cabanas available mainly in low-key beach spots, such as Tulum. A hammock can be a very comfortable place to sleep in hot areas (but mosquito repellent or a net often comes in handy). You can rent a hammock and a place to hang it – usually under a palm roof outside a small guesthouse or beach restaurant – for M$60 to M$130. With your own hammock, the cost comes down a bit. It's easy enough to buy hammocks in the Yucatán (see boxed text, p163); Mérida specializes in them, and you'll find hammocks for sale all along the Riviera Maya.

Cabanas are usually huts – of wood, brick, adobe and stone – with a palm-thatched roof. Some have dirt floors and nothing inside but a bed; others are deluxe, with electric light, mosquito net, fan, fridge, bar and decorations. Prices for simple cabanas cost M$100 to M$350. On the Caribbean some luxury cabanas can cost over M$1000.

Hostels

Hostels exist in many of the towns and cities where backpackers congregate. They provide dorm accommodations (for M$80 to M$120 per person), plus communal kitchens, bathrooms, living space and sometimes some private rooms. Standards of hygiene and security vary, but aside from being cheap, hostels are generally relaxed and good places to meet other travelers. **HostelWorld** (www.hostelworld.com) has listings.

There are a handful of hostels affiliated with Mexico's HI, **Hostelling International Mexico** (www.hostellingmexico.com). If you're an HI member, you get a dollar or two off the nightly rates at these places.

Hotels

Yucatán specializes in good midrange hotels where two people can get a comfortable room with private bathroom, TV and often air-con for M$400 to M$900. Often the hotel also has a restaurant and bar. Among the most charming lodgings, in both the midrange and top-end brackets, are the many old mansions, inns and even convents turned into hotels. These can be wonderfully atmospheric, with fountains gurgling in flower-bedecked stone courtyards. Some are a bit spartan; others have modern comforts and, consequently, are more expensive.

Nearly every town has its cheap hotels, though substantially fewer are found on the Yucatán Peninsula than in other regions of Mexico. There are clean, friendly, secure ones, and there are dark, dirty, smelly ones where you may not feel your belongings are safe. Expect to pay up to M$400 for a decent double room with private shower and hot water, more in Cancún, Cozumel or Playa del Carmen, and perhaps if you arrive during a popular time.

Yucatán has plenty of large, modern luxury hotels, too, particularly in the coastal resorts and in some former haciendas south of Mérida. They offer the expected levels of luxury – with pools, gyms, bars, restaurants and so on – at prices that are sometimes agreeably modest (and sometimes not!). If you like to stay in luxury but also enjoy saving some money, look for a locally owned hotel.

Fortunately for families and small groups of travelers, many hotels in all price ranges have rooms for three, four or five people that cost not much more than a double.

ACTIVITIES

There's absolutely no shortage of things to do on the Yucatán Peninsula: some of the best scuba diving and snorkeling in the world is available here, beach lovers will find plenty of powdery white sand on which to sunbathe, and the ancient Maya cities that dot the landscape of the Yucatán are a thrill to explore.

Good sources on active tourism in Mexico include **Amtave** (Mexican Association of Adventure Travel & Ecotourism; ☎ 55-5688-3883, 800-654-4452; www.amtave .org), based in Mexico City with 60 member organizations and companies around the country, and **Ecoturismo Yucatan** (www.ecoyuc.com.mx), **GORP** (www.gorp.com), **Planeta.com** (www.planeta.com) and **Mexonline.com** (www.mexonline.com).

For more details on the major activities, check the page references below and also the destination chapters of this book.

- bird- and wildlife-watching (p68)
- cycling (p68)
- diving and snorkeling (p64)
- fishing (p69)
- hiking (p67)
- kayaking (p66)
- kiteboarding and windsurfing (p67)
- ziplining (p69)

BUSINESS HOURS

The siesta tradition wisely lives on in this hot climate, with shops generally open from 9am to 2pm, then reopening from 4pm to 7pm Monday to Saturday. Some may not be open on Saturday afternoon. Shops in malls and coastal resort towns often open on Sunday. Supermarkets and department stores usually open from 9am or 10am to 10pm daily.

Government offices have similar Monday-to-Friday hours to shops, with a greater likelihood of having the 2pm to 4pm lunch break. Tourism-related offices usually open on Saturday, too, from at least 9am to 1pm.

Banks are normally open 9am to 5pm Monday to Friday, and some from 9am to 1pm Saturday. In smaller towns they may close earlier or not open on Saturday. *Casas de cambio* (money-exchange offices) are usually open from 9am to 7pm daily, often with even

longer hours in coastal resorts. Post offices typically open from 8am to 6pm Monday to Friday, and 9am to 1pm Saturday.

In this book we only spell out opening hours where they do not fit the above parameters. See the Quick Reference inside this book's front cover for further typical opening hours.

Most museums have one closing day a week, typically Monday. On Sunday nearly all archaeological sites and museums offer free admission for Mexican nationals, and the major ones can get very crowded.

CHILDREN

Snorkeling in caves, playing on the beach, hiking in the jungle...kids will find plenty of ways to keep busy in the Yucatán. And as elsewhere in Mexico, children take center stage – with few exceptions, children are welcome at all kinds of hotels and in virtually every café and restaurant. In this book you'll find especially child-friendly places identified with the 🏃 icon.

Lonely Planet's *Travel with Children* has lots of practical advice on the subject, drawn from firsthand experience.

For details on documents required for under-18 travelers, see p263.

Practicalities

Cots for hotel rooms and high chairs for restaurants are available mainly in midrange and top-end establishments. If you want a rental car with a child safety seat, the major international car-rental firms are the most reliable providers. You will probably have to pay a few dollars extra per day.

It's usually not hard to find an inexpensive babysitter – ask at your hotel. Diapers (nappies) are widely available, but if you depend on some particular cream, lotion, baby food or medicine, bring it with you. Public breastfeeding is not common and, when done, is done discreetly.

Sights & Activities

Apart from the ruins, beaches and swimming pools, you'll find excellent special attractions, such as amusement parks, water parks, zoos, aquariums and other fun places on the peninsula.

Kids can also enjoy activities such as snorkeling, riding bicycles and boats, and watching wildlife (see the Yucatán Outdoors chapter, p64). Archaeological sites can be fun if your kids are into climbing pyramids and exploring tunnels.

CLIMATE CHARTS

Hot, sunny and humid days are the norm for much of the year in the Yucatán, although the season of *nortes* (storms bringing wind and rain from the north) lowers temperatures a bit from November through February or March. During the rainy season, which runs from May through October, you can expect heavy rains for an hour or two most afternoons, but generally clear weather otherwise. The hurricane season lasts from June to November, with most of the activity from mid-August to mid-September. For tips on the best seasons to travel, see p20.

COURSES

Taking classes can be a great way to meet people and get an inside angle on local life as well as study the language or culture. Mexican universities and colleges often offer classes. For long-term study in Mexico you'll need a student visa; contact a Mexican consulate for details. You can also arrange informal Spanish tutoring through most hostels. A good US source on study possibilities in Mexico is the **Council on International Educational Exchange** (www .ciee.org). There are also helpful links on the website of **Lonely Planet** (www.lonelyplanet.com).

Mérida, with its abundance of cultural activities and central location, makes a great place to study Spanish. Among the schools there, **Centro de Idiomas del Sureste** (CIS; ☎ 923-0954; www.cisyucatan.com.mx; Calle 52 No 455 btwn Calles 49 & 51) stands out. Thirty hours of instruction, including a two-week homestay in a local household and three meals a day, costs about M$7300. Other plans are available.

In Campeche, the **Universidad Autónoma de Campeche Centro de Español y Maya** (CEM; etzna.uacam .mx/cem/principal.htm; Av Agustin Melgar) offers four- to eight-week summer language courses, and homestays can be arranged.

In Playa del Carmen, **Playa Lingua del Caribe** (☎ 873-3876; www.playalingua.com; Calle 20) has 20-hour-per-week classes for around M$1850. **International House** (☎ 803-3388; www .ihrivieramaya.com; Calle 14) offers homestays, a small residence hall and Spanish lessons. Twenty hours of instruction per week costs M$2000.

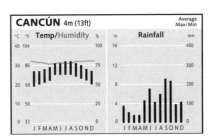

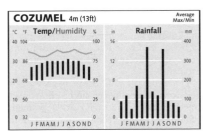

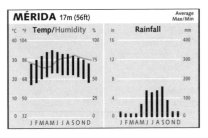

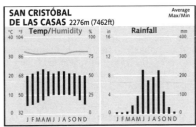

CUSTOMS

Visitors are allowed to bring duty-free items for personal use, such as clothing; a camera and video camera; up to 12 rolls of film or videotapes; a cellular phone; a laptop computer; a portable radio or CD player; medicine for personal use, with prescription in the case of psychotropic drugs; 3L of wine, beer or liquor (adults only); 400 cigarettes (adults);

and M$3000 worth of other goods (M$500 if arriving by land).

The normal routine when you enter Mexico is to complete a customs declaration form (which lists duty-free allowances) and then place it in a machine. If the machine shows a green light, you pass without inspection. If a red light shows, your baggage will be searched.

DANGERS & ANNOYANCES

Despite often alarming media reports and official warnings for Mexico in general, the Yucatán Peninsula remains a safe place to travel, and with just a few precautions you can minimize the risk of encountering problems.

Enjoy yourself in the ocean, but beware of undertows and riptides on any beach. Women traveling alone, and even pairs of women, should be cautious about going to remote beach and jungle spots. Cocaine and marijuana are prevalent in Mexico. They are both illegal. The easiest way to avoid the problems related with these drugs is by avoiding them. If you get busted using or transporting illegal drugs, your consulate will not help you.

Foreign affairs departments can supply a variety of useful data about travel to Mexico:

Australia (☎ 61-2-6261-1111; www.dfat.gov.au)
Canada (☎ in Canada 800-267-8376, outside Canada 613-944-4000; www.dfait-maeci.gc.ca)
UK (☎ 020-7008-1500; www.fco.gov.uk)
USA (☎ 888-407-4747; www.travel.state.gov)

Theft & Robbery

As a rule, Mexicans are extremely honest and are unlikely to steal anything from you. However, the rare individual may target tourists likely to be carrying cash or valuables. Thus, pickpocketing and bag-snatching remain minor risks in crowded buses and bus stations, airports, markets or anywhere frequented by large numbers of tourists.

Mugging is less common than purse-snatching, but more serious: resistance may be met with violence (do *not* resist). Usually these robbers will not harm you: they just want your money, fast.

To minimize the chances of being a victim, think about the following:

- Don't go where there are few other people in the vicinity; this includes camping in secluded places. A simple rule: if there are women and children around, you're probably safe.
- Don't leave any valuables unattended while you swim. Run-and-grab thefts by people lurking in the woods are a common occurrence on the Caribbean coast.
- Leave most of your money, important documents and smaller valuables in a sealed, signed envelope in your hotel's safe, unless you have immediate need of these items. Virtually all hotels, except the very cheapest, provide safekeeping for guests' valuables.
- Leave valuables in a locked suitcase or backpack in your hotel room, or a locker in a hostel dorm, rather than carry them on the street.
- Carry only a small amount of money – enough for an outing – in a pocket. If you do have to carry valuables, keep them hidden (preferably in a money belt, shoulder wallet or pouch underneath your clothing.
- Don't keep money, credit or debit cards, wallets or bags in open view any longer than you have to. At ticket counters, keep a hand or foot on your bag at all times.

HIGHWAY ROBBERY

Though it's rare on the Yucatán Peninsula, bandits occasionally hold up buses and other vehicles on intercity routes, especially at night, taking luggage or valuables. Sometimes buses are robbed by people who board as passengers. Roads linking the peninsula with Chiapas state are sometimes the scene of such robberies. These routes are also notorious for frequent thefts from luggage on 2nd-class buses, whose many stops and sometimes-crowded conditions (and sleepy passengers) afford miscreants the opportunity to unzip or slash open bags. Highway holdups were once weekly occurrences on Hwy 199 between Ocosingo and Palenque, but an increased military and police presence has made this route pretty safe now.

The best way to avoid highway robbery is to travel by day, preferably by toll highway. Deluxe and 1st-class buses use toll highways, where they exist; 2nd-class buses do not.

- Use ATMs only during working hours and choose ones in secure locations, not those open to the street.
- Do not leave anything valuable-looking in a parked vehicle.
- Be careful about accepting drinks from overly social characters in bars, especially in tourist-heavy zones; there have been cases of drugging followed by robbery and assault.
- Be wary of attempts at credit-card fraud. One method is when the cashier swipes your card twice (once for the transaction and once for nefarious purposes). Keep your card in sight at all times.

DISCOUNT CARDS
The ISIC student card, IYTC card for travelers under 26 years, and ITIC card for teachers can help you obtain discounted air tickets to/from Mexico at student- and youth-oriented travel agencies. Reduced prices for buses, museums, archaeological sites and so on are usually only for those with Mexican education credentials, but the aforementioned cards will sometimes get you a reduction. The ISIC card may also get you discounts in a few hostels.

The HI card will save you about M$10 in affiliated hostels in the Yucatán.

EMBASSIES & CONSULATES
It's important to understand what your own embassy – the embassy of the country of which you are a citizen – can and can't do to help you if you get into trouble. Generally speaking, it won't be much help in emergencies if the trouble you're in is remotely your own fault. Remember that you are bound by the laws of the country you are in.

In genuine emergencies you might get some assistance, such as a list of lawyers, but only if other channels have been exhausted.

Mexican Embassies & Consulates
Updated details can be found at **Secretaría Relaciones Exteriores** (www.sre.gob.mx, in Spanish) and **Embassyworld.com** (www.embassyworld.com).

Embassies & Consulates in Mexico
Many embassies or their consular sections are in Mexico City; Cancún is home to several consulates, and there are some diplomatic outposts in Mérida as well.
Australia Mexico City (☎ 55-1101-2200; www.mexico .embassy.gov.au; Rubén Darío 55, Polanco)

Belize Mexico City (☎ 55-5520-1274; embelize@prodigy .net.mx; Bernardo de Gálvez 215, Lomas de Chapultepec)
Canada Mexico City (☎ 55-5724-7900; www.canada.org .mx; Schiller 529, Polanco); Cancún (Map p75; ☎ 998-883-3360; Plaza Caracol II, 3rd fl, Local 330, Blvd Kukulcán Km 8.5, Zona Hotelera)
Cuba Mexico City (☎ 55-5280-8093; www.embacuba .com.mx; Av Presidente Masaryk 554, Polanco); Cancún (Map p77; ☎ 998-884-3423; Pecari 17); Mérida (☎ 999-944-4215; Calle 1-D No 32, Colonia Campestre)
France Mexico City (☎ 55-9171-9700; www.francia .org.mx; Campos Elíseos 339, Polanco); Cancún (Map p77; ☎ 998-883-9816; Calle Pargo 24 SM3); Mérida (☎ 999-930-1500; Calle 60 No 385)
Germany Mexico City (☎ 55-5283-2200; www.mexiko .diplo.de; Horacio 1506, Losw Morales); Cancún (Map p77; ☎ 998-884-1898; Punta Conoco 36, SM24)
Guatemala Mexico City (☎ 55-5540-7520; emba guatemx@minex.gob.gt; Av Explanada 1025, Lomas de Chapultepec)
Ireland Mexico City (☎ 55-5520-5803; embajada @irlanda.org.mx; Cerrada Blvd Ávila Camacho 76, 3rd fl, Lomas de Chapultepec)
Italy Mexico City (☎ 55-5596-3655; www.ambcitta delmessico.esteri.it/Ambasciata_Cittadelmessico; Paseo de las Palmas 1994, Lomas de Chapultepec); Cancún (Map p77; ☎ 998-884-1261; Alcatraces 39, SM22)
Japan Mexico City (☎ 55-5211-0028; www.mx .emb-japan.go.jp; Paseo de la Reforma 395, Lomas de Chapultepec)
Netherlands Mexico City (☎ 55-5258-9921; www .paisesbajos.com.mx; Av Vasco de Quiroga 3000, 7th fl, Santa Fe); Cancún (off Map p77; ☎ 998-886-0070; Marti-nair, Planta Alta, Terminal 2, Aeropuerto Internacional de Cancún); Mérida (☎ 999-924-3122; Calle 64 No 418)
New Zealand Mexico City (☎ 55-5283-9460; kiwimexico @prodigy.net.mx; Jaime Balmes 8, Level 4, Los Morales)
Spain Mexico City (☎ 55-5282-2974; www.mae .es/embajadas/mexico/es/home; Galileo 114, Polanco)
UK Mexico City (☎ 55-5242-8500; www.embajada britanica.com.mx; Río Lerma 71, Colonia Cuauhtémoc); Cancún (Map p75; ☎ 998-881-0100; The Royal Sands, Blvd Kukulcán Km 13.5, Zona Hotelera)
USA Mexico City (☎ 55-5080-2000; mexico.usembassy.gov; Paseo de la Reforma 305); Cancún (Map p75; ☎ 998-883-0272; 2o Nivel No 320-323, Plaza Caracol Dos, Blvd Kukulcán, Zona Hotelera); Mérida (☎ 999-942-5700; Calle 60 No 338-K, btwn Calles 29 & 31)

FESTIVALS & EVENTS
Mexico's frequent fiestas are highly colorful affairs that often go on for several days and add a great deal of spice to everyday life. In addition to the major national festivals listed below, each town has many local saint's days,

DIRECTORY

LOCAL FIESTAS

In addition to national celebrations, every town and city on the Yucatán Peninsula holds its own fiestas, often in honor of its patron saint. Street parades of holy images, special costumes, fireworks, dancing, lots of music and plenty of drinking are all part of the colorful scene. Sometimes bloodless bullfights are on the program as well, or the Danza de la Cabeza de Cochino. This dance, rooted in Maya tradition, takes place around an altar holding a pig's head decorated with offerings of flowers, ribbons, bread, liquor and cigarettes. A likely time to catch it is at the Fiesta de la Inmaculada Concepción. Though Yucatecans also celebrate the Festival of the Immaculate Conception on December 8, with the rest of the Catholic world, many towns on the peninsula hold nine days of devotions leading up to the last Sunday in January when the pig is ritually slaughtered and put to cooking.

Other lively patron-saint festivals and Yucatán-specific celebrations are mentioned in the destination chapters.

---

regional festivals and so on (see destination chapters for information on these). There's also a national public holiday just about every month (see opposite), often the occasion for yet further merriment.

January

Día de los Reyes Magos (Three Kings' Day or Epiphany) On January 6, this is the day when Mexican children traditionally receive gifts, rather than at Christmas (but some get two loads of presents!). A good place to be at this time is Tizimín (p197).

February/March

Día de la Candelaría (Candlemas) Held on February 2, and commemorates the presentation of Jesus in the temple 40 days after his birth; celebrated with processions, bullfights and dancing in many towns.

Carnaval A big bash preceding the 40-day penance of Lent, Carnaval takes place during the week or so before Ash Wednesday (which falls 46 days before Easter Sunday; late February or early March). It's festively celebrated in Mérida, Campeche, Ciudad del Carmen and Chetumal with parades, music, food, drink, dancing, fireworks and fun.

March/April

Semana Santa Held throughout Holy Week (starting on Palm Sunday – Domingo de Ramos), solemn processions move through the streets. On Good Friday (Viernes Santo) there are dramatic re-enactments of the Passion Play, with locals taking the role of penitents following their savior through the Stations of the Cross.

September

Día de la Independencia (Independence Day) On September 16, the anniversary of the start of Mexico's War of Independence in 1810 provokes an upsurge of patriotic feeling every year: on the evening of the 15th, the words of Padre Miguel Hidalgo's famous call to rebellion, the Grito de Dolores, are repeated from the balcony of every town hall in the land, usually followed by fireworks.

November

Día de Todos los Santos (All Saints' Day) & **Día de los Muertos** (Day of the Dead) On November 1 and 2, in Mexico's most characteristic fiesta, the souls of the dead are believed to return to earth. Families build altars in their homes and visit graveyards to commune with their dead, taking garlands and gifts. A happy atmosphere prevails.

Festival Cervantino Barroco (Cultural fair) San Cristóbal de Las Casas (p235) puts on a great art and culture fair, with music, dance, theater and more. Held late October or early November.

December

Día de Nuestra Señora de Guadalupe (Day of Our Lady of Guadalupe) A week or more of celebrations throughout Mexico leads up to the day in honor of the Virgin who appeared to an indigenous Mexican, Juan Diego, in 1531, and has since become Mexico's religious patron. Children are taken to church dressed as little Juan Diegos or indigenous girls. Held on December 12.

Posadas From December 16 to 24, nine nights of candlelit parades re-enact the journey of Mary and Joseph to Bethlehem. More important in small towns than cities.

Día de Navidad Christmas is traditionally celebrated with a feast in the early hours of December 25, after midnight Mass.

FOOD

Some Eating sections of this book are divided into budget, midrange and top-end categories. We define a midrange restaurant as one where a main dish at lunch or dinner costs M$60 to M$120. Budget and top-end places are, respectively, less than M$60 and over M$120.

Typical restaurant hours are 7am to between 10pm and midnight. If a restaurant has a closing day, it's usually Sunday, Monday or Tuesday. Cafés typically open from 8am to 10pm daily. Bars, too, are normally open daily, but each seems to have its own hours. Travelers should be careful of unpeeled fruit and uncooked vegetables. While visitors with iron stomachs shouldn't have much trouble, those with a delicate constitution will only want to eat uncooked veggies in higher-end restaurants. For a full introduction to Yucatán's distinctive cuisine, see the Food & Drink chapter, p50.

GAY & LESBIAN TRAVELERS

Mexico is more broad-minded about sexuality than you might expect. Gays and lesbians rarely attract open discrimination or violence. Discrimination based on sexual orientation has been illegal since 1999 and can be punished with up to three years in prison. Gay men have a more public profile than lesbians. Cancún has a fairly active gay scene, and there are a number of gay-friendly locals in Mérida.

The **International Gay and Lesbian Travel Association** (www.travelglta.com) provides information on the major travel providers in the gay sector. US-based **Arco Iris Tours** (☎ in the USA 800-765-4370; www.arcoiristours.com) specializes in gay travel to Mexico and organizes an annual International Gay Festival in Cancún.

A detailed Mexico gay travel guide and articles are available at **Out&About** (www.gay .com/travel/outandabout). Another good source of information is the **Gay Mexico Network** (www .gaymexico.net). It offers information on gay-friendly hotels and tours in Mexico, and publishes a newsletter offering discounted rooms in gay-friendly accommodations.

HOLIDAYS

The chief holiday periods are Christmas to New Year, Semana Santa (the week leading up to Easter and up to a week afterwards), and mid-July to mid-August. Transportation and tourist accommodations are heavily booked at these times.

Banks, post offices, government offices and many shops throughout Mexico are closed on the following national holidays:

Año Nuevo (New Year's Day) January 1
Día de la Constitución (Constitution Day) February 5
Día de la Bandera (Day of the National Flag) February 24

Día de Nacimiento de Benito Juárez (Anniversary of Benito Juárez' birth) March 21
Día del Trabajo (Labor Day) May 1
Cinco de Mayo (Anniversary of Mexico's victory over the French at Puebla) May 5
Día de la Independencia (Independence Day) September 16
Día de la Raza (Columbus' discovery of the New World) October 12
Día de la Revolución (Revolution Day) November 20
Día de Navidad (Christmas Day) December 25

At Easter businesses usually close from Good Friday (Viernes Santo) to Easter Sunday (Domingo de Resurrección). Many offices and businesses close during major national festivals (see p253).

INSURANCE

A travel insurance policy to cover theft, loss and medical problems is a good idea. Some policies specifically exclude dangerous activities, such as scuba diving, motorcycling and even trekking.

For further information on medical insurance, see p276. Worldwide cover to travelers from over 44 countries is available online at www.lonelyplanet.com/travel_services.

For information on motor insurance, see p270.

INTERNET ACCESS

Cybercafés (which charge about M$10 to M$15 per hour) and web-based email are common in the Yucatán. A number of cybercafés are equipped with CD burners, webcams, headphones and so on. Few have card readers, so bring your own or the camera-to-USB cable if you plan on burning photos to CD along the way.

Quite a few accommodations provide internet access of some kind (shown as 🖳 in this book). Facilities vary from a couple of computers in the lobby, for which you may or may not have to pay, to well-equipped business centers or wi-fi access (internet inalámbrico).

You may also be able to connect your own laptop or hand-held device to the internet through the telephone socket in your room. Be aware that your modem may not work once you leave your home country. The safest option is to buy a reputable 'global' modem before you leave home. For lots of useful stuff on connecting to the internet while traveling,

DIRECTORY

visit **Steve Kropla's Help for World Travellers** (www.kropla.com).

LEGAL MATTERS
Mexican Law

Mexican law presumes an accused person is guilty until proven innocent.

The minimum jail sentence for possession of more than a token amount of any narcotic, including marijuana and amphetamines, is 10 months – trafficking gets you a minimum of 10 years. As in most other countries, the purchase of controlled medication requires a doctor's prescription.

Road travelers should expect occasional police or military checkpoints. They are normally looking for drugs, weapons or illegal migrants.

See p270 for information on the legal aspects of road accidents.

Federal law establishes the minimum age of consent at 12 years, but state laws often override these laws, varying from 14 to 18 years old. For more information on the age of consent and sex tourism, see boxed text, p85.

Useful warnings on Mexican law are found on the website of **US Department of State** (www.travel.state.gov).

MAPS

Free city and regional maps of varying quality are given away by tourist offices around the peninsula.

Quality regional maps include the highly detailed **ITMB** (www.itmb.com) 1:500,000 *Yucatán Peninsula Travel Map* and the sketchier **Guía Roji** (www.guiaroji.com.mx) 1:1,000,000 scale *Maya World* (M$60) showing all of the peninsula and parts of Tabasco and Chiapas.

Guía Roji also publishes maps of each Mexican state (M$50) and an annually updated national road atlas called *Mapa Turístico Carreteras de Mexico* (M$80). It's widely available throughout Mexico and can be bought from online booksellers. Also useful are Quimera publisher's regional road maps.

Riviera Maya, Cancún, Cozumel, Isla Mujeres, Chichén Itzá and *Playa del Carmen* foldout maps are published by the American couple behind **Can-Do Maps** (www.cancunmap.com). In addition to containing multiple insert maps, they also have a useful index for restaurants, hotels and attractions.

A good internet source is **Maps of Mexico** (www.maps-of-mexico.com), with detailed maps of all the states.

Inegi (Instituto Nacional de Estadística, Geografía e Informática; ☎ 800-490-4200; www.inegi.gob.mx) publishes a large-scale map series covering all of Mexico at 1:50,000 and 1:250,000, plus state maps at 1:700,000. Most of these maps have been updated within the past decade, and they are well worth having if you plan to do any hiking or back-country exploring. Inegi's Centros de Información in the peninsula's principal cities sell these maps for M$40 to M$60 each. Its addresses:

Campeche (☎ 981-127-3150; Calles 8 & 63, Planta Baja, Edificio Lavalle)

Cancún (Map p77; ☎ 998-884-4099, ext 7943; Av Tankah 70)

Chetumal (☎ 983-832-2733; cnr Avs Carmen Ochoa de Merino & Independencia)

Mérida (☎ 999-942-1740; Calle 60 No 378 btwn Calles 39 & 41)

GETTING LEGAL HELP

If arrested, you have the right to notify your embassy or consulate. However, what consular staff can do for you is limited; see p253 for details. The longest a person can be detained by police without a specific accusation is 72 hours.

Tourist offices, especially state-run branches, can often help you with legal problems, such as complaints or reporting crimes, police seeking bribes (see p275) or lost articles. The national tourism ministry, **Sectur** (☎ 078, 800-987-8224), offers 24-hour phone advice.

If you are the victim of a crime, you may feel there is little to gain by going to the police, unless you need a statement to present to your insurance company. If you go to the police and your Spanish is poor, take a more fluent speaker. Also take your passport and tourist card, if you still have them. If you just want to report a theft for the purposes of an insurance claim, say you want to '*poner una acta de un robo*' (make a record of a robbery). This should make it clear that you merely want a piece of paper and you should get it without too much trouble.

MONEY

Mexico's currency is the peso, usually denoted by the 'M$' sign. Prices are quoted in Mexican pesos in this book. The peso is divided into 100 centavos. Coins come in denominations of 20 and 50 centavos and one, two, five and 10 pesos; notes in 20, 50, 100, 200 and 500 (and occasionally 1000) pesos.

For exchange rates, see the Quick Reference inside this book's front cover. For information on costs, see p20.

The most convenient form of money is a major international credit or debit card – preferably two if you've got them. Visa, MasterCard and American Express cards can be used to obtain cash easily from ATMs in Mexico, and are accepted for payment by most airlines, car-rental companies, travel agents, many upmarket hotels, and some restaurants and shops. Occasionally there's a surcharge for paying by card. Making a purchase by credit card normally gives you a more favorable rate than exchanging money at a bank, but you'll normally have to pay your card issuer a 'foreign exchange' transaction fee of around 2.5%. (They always figure out a way to get you in the end!)

As a backup to credit or debit cards, it's a good idea to take some traveler's checks *(cheques de viajero)* and a little cash. US dollars are by far the most easily exchangeable foreign currency in Mexico (and indeed are common for payment in Cancún and other heavily touristed zones, though the exchange rate is rarely favorable). Euros, British pounds and Canadian dollars, in cash or traveler's checks, are accepted by most banks and some *casas de cambio* (money-exchange bureaus), but acceptance is less certain outside the main cities and tourist centers. American Express traveler's checks are recognized by banks, *casas de cambio* and top-end hotels, but are not accepted in most mom-and-pop establishments.

For tips on keeping your money safe, see p252.

ATMs

ATMs (*caja permanente* or *cajero automático* in Spanish) are plentiful in Yucatán, and are the easiest source of cash. You can use major credit cards and some bank cards, such as those on the Cirrus and Plus systems, to withdraw pesos (or dollars) from ATMs. The exchange rate that banks use for ATM withdrawals is normally better than the 'tourist rate' – though that advantage may be negated by handling fees, interest charges and other methods that banks have of taking your money.

Banks & Casas de Cambio

You can exchange currency in banks or at *casas de cambio*, which are often single-window kiosks. Banks go through a more time-consuming procedure than *casas de cambio* and usually have shorter hours. *Casas de cambio* can easily be found in just about every large or medium-size town and in many smaller ones. They're quick and often open on evenings or weekends, but be aware that some don't accept traveler's checks.

Currency-exchange rates vary from one bank or *casa de cambio* to another; and there is often a better rate offered for *efectivo* (cash) than for traveler's checks. After hours or on weekends, hotels may exchange currency, though their rates tend to be unfavorable.

International Transfers

Should you need money wired to you in Mexico, an easy and quick method is the 'Dinero en Minutos' (Money in Minutes) service of **Western Union** (☎ in the USA 800-325-6000; www.westernunion.com). The service is offered by thousands of bank branches and other businesses around Mexico, identified by black-and-yellow signs proclaiming 'Western Union Dinero en Minutos.' Your sender pays the money online or at a Western Union branch, along with a fee, and gives the details on who is to receive it and where. When you pick it up, take along photo identification. Western Union has offices worldwide.

US post offices (☎ 888-368-4669; www.usps.com) offer reasonably cheap money transfers to branches of Bancomer bank in Mexico. The service is called Dinero Seguro.

Taxes

Mexico's value-added tax (IVA) is levied at 15%. By law the tax must be included in prices quoted to you and should not be added afterward. Signs in shops and notices on restaurant menus often state '*IVA incluido.*' Occasionally they state instead that IVA must be added to the quoted prices. In Quintana Roo, IVA is 10%.

Hotel rooms are also subject to the lodging tax (ISH). Each Mexican state sets its own rate, but in most it's 2%.

Tipping & Bargaining

In general, employees of small, cheap restaurants don't expect much in the way of tips – though they like to receive them – while those in resorts frequented by foreigners (such as in Cancún and Cozumel) expect you to be lavish in your largesse. At the latter, tipping is up to US levels of 15% or 20%; elsewhere 10% is usually plenty. If you stay a few days in one place, you should leave up to 10% of your room costs for the people who have kept your room clean (assuming they have). A porter in a midrange hotel would be happy with M$10 per bag. Car-parking attendants expect a tip of M$3 to M$5, and the same is standard for gas station attendants. Baggers in supermarkets are usually tipped a peso or two.

Room rates are pretty inflexible, though it can be worth asking if any discounts are available, especially if it's low season or you are going to stay a few nights. In markets bargaining is the rule. You can also sometimes bargain with drivers of unmetered taxis.

PHOTOGRAPHY & VIDEO
Film & Equipment

Camera and film-processing shops, pharmacies and hotels sell film. Most types of film are available in larger cities and resorts, though slide film tends to be rarer outside Cancún (where several varieties of Fuji slide film are sold downtown at decent prices), and usually limited to Agfachrome and Kodak's Ektachrome.

Film on sale at low prices may be outdated. If the date on the box is obscured by a price sticker, look under the sticker. Avoid film from sun-exposed shop windows. Print processing (*revelando*) costs under M$2 per photo; it's almost always done in one hour and quality is usually good.

Most cybercafés can burn your images onto a CD for M$20 or so.

Video cameras and tapes are widely available at photo supply stores in the largest cities and in towns that receive many tourists. Prices are significantly higher than you may be used to in North America or Europe. Videotapes on sale in Mexico (like the rest of the Americas and Japan) nearly all use the NTSC image registration system. This is incompatible with the PAL system common to most of Western Europe and Australia, and the Secam system used in France.

If your camera breaks down, you'll be able to find a repair shop in most sizable towns, and prices will be agreeably low.

For more information on taking travel photographs, check out Lonely Planet's *Travel Photography*.

Photographing People & Places

It is illegal to take pictures in Mexican airports and of police stations and penal institutions. Use of a tripod at most ruins sites requires a special (expensive) permit obtainable only in Mexico City.

Be forewarned that a fee for use of video cameras is charged at many ruins and other attractions. At most Maya sites charging an entry fee, you need to pay an extra M$35 at the first site visited, which gives you a slip you can use all day, at any site you visit.

In general, Yucatecans enjoy having their pictures taken and will be happy to pose for your camera – if you ask. Increasingly, you may be asked to pay for the photo. This is especially true in areas that see heavy tourist traffic.

If local people make any sign of being offended by your desire to photograph them, you should put your camera away and apologize immediately, both out of decency and for your own safety. This is especially so in Chiapas state (see Dangers & Annoyances, p231). Also, many police officers and soldiers do not like having their photos taken.

POST

An airmail letter or postcard weighing up to 20g costs M$10.50 to send to the USA or Canada, M$13 to Europe or South America, and M$14.50 to the rest of the world. Items weighing between 20g and 50g cost M$17.50 to M$24.50 (depending on where you are sending them). *Registrado* (registered) service costs an extra M$5. Mark airmail items '*Vía Aérea.*'

Delivery times are elastic (inbound and outbound). An airmail letter from Mexico to the USA or Canada (or vice-versa) should take between four and 14 days. Mail to or from Europe may take between one and three weeks, to Australasia two to three weeks.

Post offices (oficinas de correos) are typically open from 8am to 6pm Monday to Friday, and 9am to 1pm Saturday.

You can receive letters and packages care of a post office if they're addressed to the post office's lista de correos (mail list), as follows:

Kate REID (last name in capitals and underlined)
Lista de Correos
Cozumel
Quintana Roo 77609 (postcode)
MEXICO

When the letter reaches the post office, the name of the addressee is placed on an alphabetical list, which is updated daily and often pinned up on the wall. To claim your mail, present your passport or other identification. There's no charge, but many post offices only hold lista mail for 10 days before returning it to the sender. If you think you're going to pick mail up more than 10 days after it has arrived, have it sent to Poste Restante, instead of Lista de Correos. Poste restante may hold mail for up to a month, though no list of what has been received is posted up.

You can also have packages sent to most hotels (but you should ask beforehand).

If you're sending a package internationally from Mexico, be prepared to open it for customs inspection; take packing materials with you to the post office and don't seal it till you get there.

For assured and speedy delivery, you can use one of the more expensive international courier services, such as **UPS** (☎ 800-902-9200; www.ups.com), **FedEx** (☎ 800-900-1100; www.fedex.com) or Mexico's **Estafeta** (☎ 800-903-3500; www.estafeta .com). Packages up to 500g cost about M$300 to the USA or Canada, and M$400 to Europe.

SHOPPING

Yucatán travelers will find plenty of wonderful regional handicrafts made predominantly by indigenous people, including hats, hammocks, embroidered clothing and textiles, jewelry and ceramic items. You can buy these artesanías in the villages where they are produced, or in stores and markets in larger cities. Artesanías stores in cities will give you a good overview of what's available and a basis for price comparisons. Traveling out to craft-making villages gives you a chance to see artisans at work, and if you buy there, you'll know that more of

your money is likely to go to the artisans themselves and less to entrepreneurs.

Prices for handicrafts sold in shops are generally nonnegotiable, while in markets bargaining is the rule.

Refunds of the 10% to 15% IVA tax on some purchases are available for tourists who arrived in Mexico by plane or cruise ship. Under the scheme, goods worth at least M$1200 (approximately US$110) from any one store would qualify for the refund, on presentation of receipts with the shop's tax number (Registro Federal de Causantes) when the tourist leaves Mexico.

Guayaberas
Guayaberas – light, elegant shirts with four square pockets that are standard businesswear for men in southeast Mexico – originally hail from Yucatán. The best guayaberas can be purchased in Mérida; see p164 for details.

Hammocks
Yucatecan hammocks are renowned for their quality and durability. There are many hammock stores in Mérida, or bargain with sellers ready to do so in the plazas and along the beach, particularly along the Riviera Maya and Isla Holbox, where many residents weave and sell them. For more on hammocks, see boxed text, p163.

Hats
Attractive and comfortable panama hats, called jipijapas, are woven from locally grown palm fibers in Bécal (p214) in Campeche state. For more about the hats, see boxed text, p214.

Huipiles
Proudly sported by Yucatecan women across the social spectrum, the huipil is an instantly recognizable white tunic with brightly colored flower embroidery around the yoke and near the bottom of the dress. For more information about huipiles, see p46.

Pottery & Other Items
Earthenware pots of varying quality can be found across the peninsula. Among the most interesting are those crafted in Ticul (p176), in Yucatán state, where pottery-making predates the Spanish conquest by hundreds of years. Ticul is equally noted for its fine reproductions of archaeological pieces.

DIRECTORY

Also widely available in the region are handmade blankets, leather goods, decorative cloth, wicker baskets, brilliantly painted gourds and lots of amber jewelry. Filigreed silver baubles are often a good buy in the Yucatán as well.

Edible and drinkable products worth taking back with you include honey, a substance that has been produced by Maya beekeepers for centuries, and a special kind of tequila made from the henequen plant that is produced near Izamal.

SOLO TRAVELERS

A single room normally costs a little less than a double room, but budget travelers can cut accommodation costs by staying in Mexico's increasing number of hostels. Hostels have the additional advantage of providing ready-made company, and often a lot of fun and helpful travel tips. It's often easy to pair up with others at a hostel as there's a steady stream of people following much similar routes. In well-touristed places, notice boards advertise for traveling companions, flatmates, volunteer workers and so on.

Solo travelers should be especially watchful of their luggage when on the road and should stay in places with good security for their valuables. One big drag of traveling alone can be when you want to take a quick dip in the ocean – you're stuck with your possessions and there's no one to watch out for them.

Traveling alone, though, can be a very good way of getting into the local culture and it definitely improves your Spanish skills as Mexicans are very sociable. Single women can also check out the advice on p264.

TELEPHONE & FAX

Local calls are cheap; international calls can be expensive, but needn't be if you call from the right place at the right time. Mexico is well provided with fairly easy-to-use public card phones. *Locutorios* and *casetas de teléfono* (call offices where an on-the-spot operator connects the call for you) are quite widespread and can be cheaper than card phones. Voice Over Internet Protocol (VOIP) calling is available from many internet cafés and is a great money-saver. A final option is to call from your hotel, but hotels charge what they like for this service. It's nearly always cheaper to go elsewhere.

Calling (Phone) Cards

Some phone (or calling) cards from other countries can be used for making phone calls from Mexico by dialing special access numbers:

AT&T (☎ 01-800-288-2872, 001-800-462-4240)
Bell Canada (☎ 01-800-123-0200, 01-800-021-1994)
BT Chargecard (☎ 01-800-123-02-44)
MCI (☎ 001-800-674-7000)
Sprint (☎ 001-800-877-8000)

Warning: if you get an operator who asks for your credit card instead of your calling-card number, or says the service is unavailable, hang up. There have been scams in which calls are rerouted to super-expensive credit-card phone services.

Cell Phones

Like other Mexican phone numbers, every cell (cellular, mobile) phone number has an area code (usually the code of the city where the phone was bought). When calling a cell phone from that same city, you usually need to dial ☎ 044, followed by the area code and number. When calling from other cities, dial ☎ 01 (the normal long-distance prefix), followed by the area code and number. The owner of the phone receiving the call has to pay a small amount as well as the caller.

If you want to use a cell phone in Mexico, one option for short visits is to get an international plan for your own phone, which will enable you to call home. You can also buy a Mexican cell phone for as little as M$300 to M$600, including some air time. The most widespread cellular phone system in Mexico is **Telcel** (www.telcel.com), with coverage almost everywhere that has a significant population. Amigo cards, for recharging Telcel phones, are widely available from newsstands and minimarts. Other companies are **Unefon** (www.unefon.com.mx), with coverage mainly in the major cities; **Iusacell** (www.iusacell.com.mx); and **Movistar** (www.telefonicamovistar.mx). If you already have a Movistar phone from another country, you can insert a Mexican Movistar SIM card into it.

For further information, contact your service provider or visit **Steve Kropla's Help for World Travellers** (www.kropla.com), or www.gsmcoverage.co.uk, which has coverage maps, lists of roaming partners and links to phone companies' websites.

Collect Calls

Una llamada por cobrar (collect call) can cost the receiving party much more than if they call you, so you may prefer to pay for a quick call to the other party to ask them to call you back. If you do need to make a collect call, you can do so from card phones without a card. Call an operator at ☎ 020 for domestic calls, or ☎ 090 for international calls, or use a 'home country direct' service through which you make an international collect call via an operator in the country you're calling. The Mexican term for 'home country direct' is *país directo*: but don't count on Mexican international operators knowing the access codes for all countries.

Some *casetas* and hotels will make collect calls for you, but they usually charge for the service.

Fax

Public fax service is offered in many Mexican towns by the public *telégrafos* (telegraph) office or the companies Telecomm and Computel. Also look for 'Fax' or 'Fax Público' signs on shops, businesses and *casetas,* and in bus stations and airports. Typically you will pay around M$10 per page to the USA or Canada.

Locutorios & Casetas de Teléfono

Costs in *casetas de teléfono* and *locutorios* are often lower than those for Telmex card phones, and their advantages are that they eliminate street noise and you don't need a phone card to use them. They often have a phone symbol outside, or signs saying '*teléfono,' 'Lada'* or '*Larga Distancia.'*

Prefixes & Codes

To call a town or city in Mexico other than the one you're in, you need to dial the long-distance prefix (☎ 01), followed by the area code (two digits for Mexico City, Guadalajara and Monterrey; three digits for everywhere else) and then the local number. For example, to make a call from Cancún to Mérida, dial ☎ 01, then the Mérida area code ☎ 999, then the seven-digit local number. You'll find area codes listed under city and town headings throughout this book.

To make international calls, you need to dial the international prefix ☎ 00, followed by the country code, area code and local number. For example, to call New York City, dial ☎ 00, then the US country code ☎ 1, the New York City area code ☎ 212, then the local number.

To call a number in Mexico from another country, dial your international access code, then the Mexico country code ☎ 52, then the area code and number.

Public Card Phones

These are common in towns and cities: you'll usually find some at airports, bus stations and around the main plazas. Easily the most common, and most reliable on costs, are those marked with the name of the country's biggest phone company, Telmex. To use a Telmex card phone you need a phone card known as a *tarjeta Ladatel.* These are sold at kiosks and shops everywhere – look for the blue-and-yellow signs that read '*De venta aquí Ladatel.*' The cards come in denominations of M$30, M$50 and M$100.

Calls from Telmex card phones cost M$1 per minute for local calls; M$4 per minute long-distance within Mexico; M$5 per minute to the USA or Canada; M$10 per minute to Central America; M$20 per minute to Europe, Alaska or South America; and M$25 per minute to Hawaii, Australia, New Zealand or Asia.

In some parts of Mexico frequented by foreign tourists, you may notice a variety of phones that advertise that they accept credit cards or that you can make easy collect calls to the USA on them. While some of these phones may be a fair value, there are others on which very high rates are charged. Be 100% sure about what you'll pay before making a call on a non-Telmex phone.

Toll-Free & Operator Numbers

Mexican toll-free numbers (☎ 800 followed by seven digits) always require the ☎ 01 prefix. You can call most of these and the ☎ 060 and ☎ 080 emergency numbers from Telmex pay phones without inserting a phone card.

Most US and Canadian toll-free numbers are ☎ 800 or ☎ 888 followed by seven digits. These can be reached from Mexico, by dialing ☎ 001 then replacing the prefix with ☎ 880, but there is a charge for the call.

For a Mexican domestic operator, dial ☎ 020; for an international operator, dial ☎ 090. For Mexican directory information, dial ☎ 040.

To access the Mexican yellow pages online, go to www.seccionamarilla.com.mx.

VOIP

Many internet cafés offer Voice Over Internet Protocol (VOIP) calling. Using services like **Skype** (www.skype.com), travelers can call internationally to and from Mexico at a fraction of the price.

TIME

The entire Yucatán Peninsula observes the Hora del Centro, which is the same as US Central Time – GMT minus six hours in winter, and GMT minus five hours during daylight saving time. Daylight saving time (*horario de verano*, summer time) runs from the first Sunday in April to the last Sunday in October. Clocks go forward one hour in April and back one hour in October.

The fabled relaxed Mexican attitude toward time and urgency – *mañana, mañana* – is still practiced, especially outside the big cities. Most Mexicans value *simpatía* (congeniality) over promptness. But if something is really worth doing, it gets done.

TOILETS

Public toilets are rare, so take advantage of facilities in places such as hotels, restaurants, bus terminals and museums; a fee of about M$2 may be charged. It's fairly common for toilets in budget hotels and restaurants to lack seats. When out and about, carry some toilet paper with you because it often won't be provided. If there's a bin beside the toilet, put soiled paper in it because the drains can't cope otherwise.

TOURIST INFORMATION

Just about every town of interest to tourists in the Yucatán has a state or municipal tourist office. They are generally helpful with maps, brochures and questions, and often some staff members speak English.

You can call the Mexico City office of the national tourism ministry **Sectur** (☎ 55-5250-0123/51, 800-903-9200, in the USA & Canada 800-446-3942, 800-482-9832, in Europe 800-1111-2266; www.visitmexico.com) at any time – 24 hours a day, seven days a week – for information or help in English or Spanish.

Here are the contact details for the head tourism offices of each state covered in this book:

Campeche (☎ 981-811-9229, 800-900-2267; www.campechetravel.com)
Chiapas (☎ 961-617-0550, 800-280-3500; www.turismochiapas.gob.mx)
Quintana Roo (☎ 983-835-0860; sedetur.qroo.gob.mx, in Spanish)
Tabasco (☎ 993-316-3633, 800-216-0842; www.visitetabasco.com)
Yucatán (☎ 999-930-3760; www.mayayucatan.com)

TRAVELERS WITH DISABILITIES

Lodgings on the Yucatán Peninsula are generally not disabled-friendly, though some hotels and restaurants (mostly towards the top end of the market) and some public buildings now provide wheelchair access. The absence of institutionalized facilities is largely compensated for, however, by Mexicans' accommodating attitudes toward others, and special arrangements are gladly improvised.

Mobility is easiest in the major tourist resorts and the more expensive hotels. Bus transportation can be difficult; flying or taking a taxi is easier.

Mobility International USA (☎ in the USA 541-343-1284; www.miusa.org) advises disabled travelers on mobility issues. Its website includes international databases of exchange programs and disability organizations with several Mexican organizations listed.

In the UK, **Radar** (☎ 020-7250-3222; www.radar.org.uk) is run by and for disabled people. Its excellent website has links to good travel-specific sites.

Two further sources for disabled travelers are **MossRehab ResourceNet** (www.mossresourcenet.org) and **Access-able Travel Source** (www.access-able.com).

VISAS

Every tourist must have an easily obtainable Mexican government tourist card (opposite). Some nationalities also need to obtain visas. Because the regulations sometimes change, it's wise to confirm them with a Mexican embassy or consulate before you go (see p253). **Lonely Planet** (www.lonelyplanet.com) has links to updated visa information.

Citizens of the USA, Canada, EU countries, Australia, New Zealand, Iceland, Israel, Japan, Norway and Switzerland are among those who do not require visas to enter Mexico as tourists. The list changes from time to time; check well ahead of travel. Visa procedures, for those who need them, can take several weeks and you may be required to apply in your country of residence or citizenship.

For information on passport requirements, see p266. Non-US citizens passing (even in transit) through the USA on the way to or from Mexico, or visiting Mexico from the USA, should also check the passport and visa requirements for the USA.

Tourist Card & Tourist Fee

The Mexican tourist card – officially the *forma migratoria para turista* (FMT) – is a brief card document that you must fill out and get stamped by Mexican immigration when you enter Mexico and keep till you leave. It's available at official border crossings, international airports and ports, and often from airlines, travel agencies and Mexican consulates. At the US–Mexico border you won't usually be given one automatically – you have to ask for it.

At many US–Mexico border crossings you don't have to get the card stamped at the border itself, as Mexico's Instituto Nacional de Migración (INM; National Immigration Institute) has control points on the highways where it's also possible to do it. But it's preferable to get it done at the border itself, in case there are complications elsewhere.

A tourist card only permits you to engage in what are considered to be tourist activities (including sports, health, artistic and cultural activities). If the purpose of your visit is to work (even as a volunteer), to report or to study, or to participate in humanitarian aid or human-rights observation, you may well need a visa. Check with a Mexican embassy or consulate (p253).

The maximum possible stay is 180 days for most nationalities (90 days for Australians, Austrians, Israelis and Italians, among others), but immigration officers will often put a much lower number (as little as 15 or 30 days in some cases) unless you tell them specifically that you need, say, 90 or 180 days. It's advisable to ask for more days than you think you'll need.

Though the tourist card itself is issued free of charge, a tourist fee of about M$200, called the *derecho para no inmigrante* (DNI; nonimmigrant fee), will need to be paid before you leave the country. If you enter Mexico by air, however, the fee is included in your airfare. If you enter by land, you must pay the fee at a bank in Mexico at any time before you re-enter the frontier zone

on your way out of Mexico (or before you check in at an airport to fly out of Mexico). Most Mexican border posts have on-the-spot bank offices where you can pay the DNI fee. When you pay at a bank, your tourist card will be stamped to prove that you have paid.

Look after your tourist card because it may be checked when you leave the country. You can be fined M$420 for not having it.

EXTENSIONS & LOST CARDS

If the number of days given on your tourist card is less than the maximum for your nationality (90 or 180 days in most cases), its validity may be extended one or more times, up to the maximum. To get a card extended you have to apply to the INM, which has offices in many towns and cities (see www.inm.gob.mx for a list, under Servicios Migratorios/Oficinas y horarios de atención). The procedure costs around M$200 and takes up to three hours. You'll need your passport, tourist card, photocopies of the important pages of these documents and, at some offices, evidence of 'sufficient funds.' A major credit card is usually OK for the latter, or an amount in traveler's checks anywhere from M$1000 to M$10,000 depending on the office.

Most INM offices will not extend a card until a few days before it is due to expire; don't bother trying earlier.

If you lose your card or need further information, contact your nearest tourist office, or the **Sectur tourist office** (☎ 55-5250-0123, 800-903-9200) in Mexico City, or your embassy or consulate. Any of these should be able to give you an official note to take to your local INM office, which will issue a duplicate for M$420.

Under-18 Travelers

To conform with regulations aimed at preventing international child abduction, minors (people aged under 18) traveling to Mexico without one or both of their parents may need to carry a notarized consent form signed by the absent parent or parents, giving permission for the young traveler to make the international journey. Though Mexico does not specifically require this documentation, airlines flying to Mexico may refuse to board passengers without it. In the case of divorced parents, a custody document may be required. If one or both parents are dead, or the traveler has only one legal parent, a death certificate or notarized statement of the situation may be required.

These rules are aimed primarily at visitors from the USA and Canada but may also apply to people from elsewhere. Procedures vary from country to country; contact your country's foreign affairs department and/or a Mexican consulate to find out exactly what you need to do. Forms for the purposes required are usually available from these authorities.

WOMEN TRAVELERS

Women can have a great time in Mexico, traveling with companions or traveling solo, but in this land that invented machismo, some concessions have to be made to local custom. Gender equalization has come a long way in a few decades, and Mexicans are generally a very polite people, but they remain, by and large, great believers in the difference (rather than the equality) between the sexes.

Women traveling alone can expect a few catcalls and attempts to chat them up. Often you can discourage unwanted attention by avoiding eye contact (wear sunglasses), dressing modestly, moving confidently and speaking coolly but politely if you feel that you must respond. Wearing a wedding ring can prove helpful, too. Don't put yourself in peril by doing things that Mexican women would not do, such as challenging a man's masculinity, drinking alone in a cantina, hitchhiking or going alone to isolated places. Keep a clear head. Lone women, and even pairs of women, should be cautious about going to remote beach spots.

In beach resorts many Mexican women dress in shorts, skimpy tops or dresses, and swimsuits of all sizes, though others bow to modesty and swim in shorts and a T-shirt. On the streets of cities and towns you'll notice that women cover up and don't display too much leg or even their shoulders.

On local transportation, especially long journeys, it's best to don long or mid-calf-length trousers and a top that meets the top of your pants, with sleeves of some sort. That way you'll feel most comfortable, and you also have the benefit of keeping your valuables out of sight with ease.

Most of all, appear self-assured.

VOLUNTEER YOUR TIME

Many opportunities exist for short- or longer-term unpaid work (or work that you pay to do) in Mexico. Projects range from sea-turtle conservation to human-rights observation to work with abused children.

- **Alliance of European Voluntary Service Organisations** (www.alliance-network.org) A good service for Europeans.
- **AmeriSpan** (www.amerispan.com) Offers volunteer opportunities in environmental education and other areas.
- **Coordinating Committee for International Voluntary Service** (www.unesco.org/ccivs) UNESCO's volunteer service wing.
- **Council on International Educational Exchange** (www.ciee.org) Arranges volunteer trips.
- **Global Exchange** (www.globalexchange.org) Needs Spanish-speaking volunteer human-rights observers to live for six to eight weeks in peace camps in Chiapas villages threatened by violence.
- **Pronatura** (http://english.pronatura-ppy.org.mx) An environmental NGO that seeks volunteers to work with sea-turtle nesting areas in the Yucatán and in other projects.
- **Sipaz** (www.sipaz.org) An international peace group, Sipaz needs Spanish-speaking volunteers to work for a year or more in Chiapas.
- **Vive Mexico** (www.vivemexico.org) NGO that coordinates international social, ecological and cultural work camps in Mexico.
- **Volunteer Abroad** (www.volunteerabroad.com) Has a very wide range of volunteer openings in Mexico.

WORK

Mexicans themselves need jobs, and people who enter Mexico as tourists are not legally allowed to take employment. The many expats working in Mexico have usually been posted there by their companies or organizations with all the necessary papers.

English speakers (and a few German or French speakers) may find teaching jobs in language schools, *preparatorias* (high schools) or universities, or can offer personal tutoring. The pay is low, but you can live on it.

A foreigner working in Mexico normally needs a permit or government license, but a school will often pay a foreign teacher in the form of a *beca* (scholarship), and thus circumvent the law, or the school's administration will procure the appropriate papers.

Apart from teaching, you might find a little bar or restaurant work in tourist areas. It's likely to be part-time and short-term.

Jobs Abroad (www.jobsabroad.com) posts paid and unpaid job openings in Mexico. **Lonely Planet** (www.lonelyplanet.com) has several useful links.

Transportation

GETTING THERE & AWAY

ENTERING THE COUNTRY

Mexican immigration officers usually won't keep you waiting any longer than it takes to flick through your passport and enter your length of stay on your tourist card. Stay patient and polite, even if the procedure takes some time to complete. Anyone traveling to Mexico via the USA should be sure to check US visa and passport requirements.

Flights, tours and train tickets can all be booked online at www.lonelyplanet.com/travel_services.

Passport

All international travelers – including Canadian and US nationals – will need a valid passport to enter the country, whether they enter by land, air or sea. These passport requirements were recently implemented. For full details, visit the **US State Department website** (www.travel.state.gov).

In Mexico you will often need your passport if you change money or you may be asked to show it when you check into a hotel. Make sure it is valid for at least six months after arriving in Mexico. Before you leave, get photocopies of the main page of your passport as well as your visa and airline tickets in the event the originals are lost or stolen.

For information on Mexican visa requirements and the tourist card, see p262. Travelers under 18 who are not accompanied by both their parents may need special documentation (see p263).

AIR

Most visitors to the Yucatán arrive by air. Air routes are structured so that virtually all international flights into the region pass through a handful of 'hub' cities: Dallas/Fort Worth, Houston, Los Angeles, Mexico City, Miami or New York.

Airports & Airlines

The majority of flights into the peninsula arrive at busy **Aeropuerto Internacional de Cancún** (CUN; ☎ 998-886-0047; www.cancun-airport.com). The region's other gateways are **Cozumel airport** (CZM; ☎ 987-872-2081; www.asur.com.mx); **Chetumal** (CTM; ☎ 983-832-0898), **Mérida** (MID; ☎ 999-946-1530; www.asur.com.mx) and Campeche (CPE).

Mexico's two flag airlines are Mexicana and Aeroméxico. Formerly state-controlled, Mexicana was bought by Grupo Posadas, Mexico's biggest hotel company, in 2005, and Aeroméxico was sold to Banamex in 2007. Their safety records are comparable to major US and European airlines.

AIRLINES FLYING TO/FROM THE YUCATÁN
Aeroméxico (code AM; ☎ 800-021-4010; www.aero mexico.com; hub Mexico City); Campeche (☎ 981-823-4044); Cancún (☎ 998-287-1868); Mérida (☎ 999-920-1293)

> **THINGS CHANGE...**
> The information in this chapter is particularly vulnerable to change. Check directly with the airline or a travel agent to make sure you understand how a fare (and ticket you may buy) works, and be aware of the security requirements for international travel, especially if traveling via the USA. Shop carefully. The details given in this chapter should be regarded as pointers and are not a substitute for your own careful, up-to-date research.

Alaska Airlines (code AS; ☎ 800-252-7522;
www.alaskaair.com; hub Seattle)
America West (code HP; ☎ 800-428-4322;
www.americawest.com; hub Phoenix)
American Airlines (code AA; ☎ 800-904-6000;
www.aa.com; hub Dallas)
ATA (code ATA; ☎ 800-435-9282; www.ata.com;
hub Chicago)
Aviacsa (code 6A; ☎ 800-284-2272; www.aviacsa.com;
hub Mexico City)
Click Mexicana (code QA; ☎ 800-122-5425;
www.clickmx.com; hubs Cancún & Mexico City)
Continental Airlines (code CO; ☎ 800-900-5000;
www.continental.com; hub Houston)
Cubana (code CU; ☎ 52-5250-6355; www.cubana.co.cu;
hub Havana)
Delta Airlines (code DL; ☎ 800-123-4710; www.delta
.com; hub Atlanta)
Frontier Airlines (code F9; ☎ in the USA 800-432-
1359; www.frontierairlines.com; hub Denver)
LTU (code LT; ☎ in Germany 211-9418-333; www.ltu.de;
hub Dusseldorf)
Mexicana de Aviación (code MX; ☎ 800-801-2010;
www.mexicana.com; hub Mexico City)
TACA Airlines (code TA; ☎ 800-400-8222; www.taca.com;
hub San Salvador)
US Airways (code US; ☎ 800-428-4322; www.usairways
.com; hub Philadelphia)

Tickets

The cost of flying to the Yucatán is usually
higher around Christmas and New Year, and
during July and August. Also, weekends can
be more costly than weekdays. During US
spring break (roughly mid-March to mid-
April) Cancún attracts swarms of college students and inexpensive fares vanish months in
advance. In addition to websites and ticket
agents such as those recommended following, it's often worth checking the airlines'
own websites for special deals. Newspapers,
magazines and websites serving Mexican
communities in other countries are also good
sources. **Lonely Planet** (www.lonelyplanet.com) has
good links, too.

On flights to and within Mexico, children
under two generally travel for 10% of the
adult fare, as long as they do not occupy
a seat, and those aged two to 11 normally
pay 67%.

If the Yucatán is part of a trip encompassing other countries, the best ticket for
you may be an open jaw (where you fly
into one place and out of another, covering the intervening distance by land), or a

round-the-world ticket (these can cost as
little as UK£900, A$2100 or US$1700), or
a Circle Pacific ticket, which uses a combination of airlines to circle the Pacific.
Airtreks (www.airtreks.com) is one good source
for multistop tickets.

International online booking agencies worth
a look include **CheapTickets** (www.cheaptickets
.com) and, for students and travelers under the
age of 26, **STA Travel** (www.statravel.com).

Asia

From Asia you normally have to make a
connection in the USA or Canada (often Los
Angeles, San Francisco or Vancouver), and
maybe one in Asia as well. From more west-
erly Asian points such as Bangkok, routes
via Europe are also an option.
No 1 Travel (☎ 03-3205-6073; www.no1-travel.com)
Good Japanese option.
STA Travel Bangkok (☎ 2236-0262; www.statravel
.co.th); Hong Kong (☎ 2736-1618; www.statravel.com.hk);
Singapore (☎ 6737-7188; www.statravel.com.sg);
Tokyo (☎ 03-5391-2922; www.statravel.co.jp) STA
proliferates in Asia.

Australia & New Zealand

The cheapest routes are usually via the USA
(normally Los Angeles). You're normally
looking at A$2300 or NZ$2300 or more,
round-trip (plus several hundred dollars
extra at high season).

The following are well-known agents
for cheap fares, with branches throughout
both countries:
Flight Centre Australia (☎ 133-133; www.flightcentre
.com.au); New Zealand (☎ 0800-243-544; www.flight
centre.co.nz)
STA Travel Australia (☎ 134-782; www.statravel.com.au);
New Zealand (☎ 0800-474-400; www.statravel.co.nz)

For online fares try www.travel.com.au or www
.zuji.com from Australia, and www.travel.co.nz
or www.zuji.co.nz from New Zealand.

Canada

Montreal, Toronto and Vancouver all have
direct flights to Mexico, though better deals
are often available with a change of flight in
the US. Round-trip fares from Toronto start
around C$900 to Cancún. **Travel Cuts** (☎ 866-
246-9762; www.travelcuts.com) is Canada's national
student-travel agency. For online bookings
try www.kayak.com, www.expedia.ca and
www.travelocity.ca.

Central & South America and Cuba

There are direct flights to Cancún from Guatemala City and Flores (Guatemala), Havana, Panama City and São Paulo. The Havana–Cancún flights continue to Mérida. Round-trip fares start around M$5000 from Guatemala City and M$8000 to M$10,000 from South America.

It is illegal for US nationals to visit Cuba, in most circumstances. However, many US visitors visit Cuba through Cancún. If you chose to do this, ensure you get an entry stamp on a piece of paper (and not in your passport); otherwise the US authorities will not be impressed.

Recommended ticket agencies include the following:

Asatej (☎ 011-4114-7595; www.asatej.com) In Argentina.

IVI Tours (☎ 0212-993-6082; www.ividivenezuela.com) In Venezuela.

Student Travel Bureau (☎ 11-3038-1555; www.stb .com.br) In Brazil.

Viajo.com (www.viajo.com) Online and phone bookings from several countries.

Europe

There are few direct flights to Cancún; airlines that do so include Aeroméxico and LTU. One alternative is to fly to Mexico City; another is to change planes in the USA or Canada.

Round-trip fares to Cancún start around €600 to €700. The two budget airlines (LTU from Dusseldorf and Jetair from Brussels) can save you a couple of hundred euros if you chose your dates carefully.

For online bookings throughout Europe, try www.opodo.com or www.ebookers.com.

CONTINENTAL EUROPE

France

Nouvelles Frontières (☎ 08-25-00-07-47; www.nouvelles-frontieres.fr)

OTU Voyages (☎ 01-55-82-32-33; www.otu.fr) A student and youth travel specialist.

Voyageurs du Monde (☎ 08-92-234-834; www.vdm.com)

Germany

Expedia (www.expedia.de)

Just Travel (☎ 089-747-3330; www.justtravel.de)

STA Travel (☎ 069-743-032-92; www.statravel.de) For travelers aged under 26.

Other Countries

Airfair (☎ 0900-771-7717; www.airfair.nl) Dutch.

CTS Viaggi (☎ 199-501-150; www.cts.it) Italian specialist in student and youth travel.

eDreams (☎ 902-422-433; www.edreams.es) Spanish.

CLIMATE CHANGE & TRAVEL

Climate change is a serious threat to the ecosystems that humans rely upon, and air travel is the fastest-growing contributor to the problem. Lonely Planet regards travel, overall, as a global benefit, but believes we all have a responsibility to limit our personal impact on global warming.

Flying & Climate Change

Pretty much every form of motorized travel generates CO2 (the main cause of human-induced climate change) but planes are far and away the worst offenders, not just because of the sheer distances they allow us to travel, but because they release greenhouse gases high into the atmosphere. The statistics are frightening: two people taking a return flight between Europe and the US will contribute as much to climate change as an average household's gas and electricity consumption over a whole year.

Carbon Offset Schemes

Climatecare.org and other websites use 'carbon calculators' that allow travelers to offset the level of greenhouse gases they are responsible for with financial contributions to sustainable travel schemes that reduce global warming – including projects in India, Honduras, Kazakhstan and Uganda.

Lonely Planet, together with Rough Guides and other concerned partners in the travel industry, supports the carbon offset scheme run by climatecare.org. Lonely Planet offsets all of its staff and author travel.

For more information check out our website: www.lonelyplanet.com

---

DEPARTURE TAX

A departure tax equivalent to about M$250 is levied on international flights from Mexico. It's usually included in the price of your ticket, but if it isn't, you must pay in cash during airport check-in. Ask your travel agent in advance.

Kilroy Travels (www.kilroytravels.com) Covers Scandinavia.
Rumbo (☎ 902-123-999; www.rumbo.es) Spanish.

UK

Flight advertisements appear in the travel pages of the weekend broadsheet newspapers, in *Time Out,* the *Evening Standard* and free online magazine *TNT* (www.tntmagazine.com).

An excellent place to start your inquiries is **Journey Latin America** (☎ 020-8747-3108; www.journeylatinamerica.co.uk), which offers a variety of tours as well as flights. Other recommended agencies include the following:

Flight Centre (☎ 0870-499-0040; www.flightcentre.co.uk)
Flightbookers (☎ 0871-223-5000; www.ebookers.com)
STA Travel (☎ 0871-230-0040; www.statravel.co.uk) For travelers under the age of 26.
Travelbag (☎ 0800-804-8911; www.travelbag.co.uk)

USA

From the USA you can fly to airports on the Yucatán Peninsula nonstop or with just one stop from several US cities. If you're lucky you can get round-trip fares to Cancún for as low as US$250. If you're not so lucky, 'budget' operators can cost as much as other airlines. For current bargain offers, check **Airfare Watchdog** (www.airfarewatchdog.com). Some typical discounted low-season fares to Cancún include: Chicago (US$350), Los Angeles (US$400), Miami (US$350) and New York (US$450). In high season you may have to pay an additional US$100 to US$200.

San Francisco is the ticket consolidator (discounter) capital of the USA, but good deals can also be found in other big cities. The following agencies are recommended for online bookings. They offer competitive fares year-round, if you book ahead.

- www.cheaptickets.com
- www.expedia.com
- www.kayak.com
- www.lowestfare.com
- www.orbitz.com
- www.sta.com (for students and travelers under 26)
- www.travelocity.com

LAND
Border Crossings

Mexico can be entered from the USA at around 40 official road-crossing points.

Crossing the Mexico–Belize border at the southern tip of Quintana Roo is easy for most tourists. Although there have been isolated reports of authorities requiring a minimum 72-hour stay in Belize, official word is that day visitors are welcome, and there are no special fees for such a visit; see boxed text, p146.

An old bridge on the Río Hondo at the town of Subteniente López, 8km southwest of Chetumal, marks the official crossing point.

At the time of writing, each person leaving Belize for Mexico needed to pay a departure tax of M$100 and an 'environment tax' of M$37.50 at the border. An additional M$42.50 is charged for fumigation of private vehicles. All fees must be paid in cash (in Belizean or US currency), and officials usually won't have change for US currency. For Mexican entry requirements, see p262.

Bus

Buses run between Chetumal (Quintana Roo) and Belize City (M$100, four hours). **Novelo's Bus Line** (☎ in Belize City 227-2025) runs around 20 buses a day on this route passing through the Belizean towns of Corozal and Orange Walk.

There are a few daily buses between Flores, Guatemala, and Chetumal (M$290, seven to eight hours), via Belize City, run by **Línea Dorada** (☎ in Flores 7926-0070) and **San Juan Travel** (☎ in Flores 7926-0041).

Car & Motorcycle

Driving a car into Mexico is most useful for travelers who:

- like to get off the beaten track;
- have surfboards, kayaks, diving equipment or other cumbersome luggage;
- will be traveling with other companions.

You can check the full requirements for bringing a vehicle into Mexico with the **American Automobile Association** (AAA; www.aaa.com),

TRANSPORTATION

Sanborn's (☎ 800-222-0158; www.sanbornsinsurance .com), a Mexican consulate or Mexican tourist information (in the USA and Canada ☎ 800-446-3942, ☎ 800-482-9832).

For information on driving and motorcycling around the Yucatán, see p272.

INSURANCE

It is very foolish to drive in Mexico without Mexican liability insurance. If you are involved in an accident, you can be jailed and have your vehicle impounded while responsibility and restitution is assessed.

RIVER

From Flores, Guatemala you can take the Río Usumacinta route to Palenque or Yaxchilán, in Chiapas, Mexico. Several daily 2nd-class buses run from Flores to Bethel (M$40, four hours), on the Guatemalan bank of the Usumacinta. The 40-minute boat trip from Bethel to Frontera Corozal, Mexico, costs M$75 to M$133 per person; an alternative is to take a bus from Flores that continues through Bethel to La Técnica (M$50, five to six hours), from where it's only a M$15, five-minute river crossing to Frontera Corozal. Vans run from Frontera Corozal to Palenque (M$60, three hours, 10 daily). From Frontera Corozal, it's well worth first detouring to the outstanding Maya ruins at Yaxchilán. Travel agencies in Palenque and Flores offer bus-boat-bus packages between the two places from around M$300.

SEA

The cruise ship–vehicle ferry between Tampa (Florida) and Progreso, in Yucatán state, is no longer operating.

There are several ports-of-call in the region, including Puerto Morelos, Calica (south of Playa del Carmen) and Progreso. The Costa Maya port in Mahahual was destroyed by Hurricane Dean, but there are plans to rebuild it.

Following are some of the cruise lines visiting Mexico, with US phone numbers:

Carnival Cruise Lines (☎ 888-227-6482; www.carnival.com)

Crystal Cruises (☎ 800-804-1500; www.crystal cruises.com)

Holland America Line (☎ 877-724-5425; www.hollandamerica.com)

Norwegian Cruise Lines (☎ 800-327-7030; www.ncl.com)

P&O Cruises (☎ 415-382-8900; www.pocruises.com)

Princess Cruises (☎ 800-774-6237; www.princess.com)

Royal Caribbean International (☎ 800-398-9813; www.royalcaribbean.com)

GETTING AROUND

AIR

Airlines in the Yucatán

Flights from other parts of Mexico arrive at the airports of Campeche, Mérida, Cancún, Cozumel, Playa del Carmen, Ciudad del Carmen and Chetumal. Another useful gateway for the region is Tuxtla Gutiérrez, which services San Cristóbal de Las Casas in Chiapas. For details, see the Getting There & Away sections of those cities.

Aeroméxico and Mexicana are the country's two major airlines. There are also numerous smaller ones, often cheaper and providing service between provincial cities. The US Federal Aviation Administration considers Mexico to be in compliance with international aviation safety standards.

Each of the following has domestic flights within the Yucatán.

Aeromar (code BQ; ☎ 800-237-6627; www.aeromar .com.mx) Also services central Mexico, west, northeast and the Gulf Coast.

Aeroméxico (code AM; ☎ 800-021-4010; www.aeromexico.com) More than 50 cities nationwide.

Aviacsa (code 6A; ☎ 800-284-2272; www.aviacsa.com) Services 20 cities around the country.

Click Mexicana (code QA; ☎ 800-122-5425; www.clickmx.com) Connections to Veracruz, Guadalajara, Toluca and other cities around the country.

Interjet (☎ 800-011-2345; www.interjet.com.mx) Services to Toluca, Guadalajara and Monterrey.

Magnicharters (☎ in Cancún 800-201-1404; www.magnicharters.com.mx) Mexico City, Guadalajara, Monterrey, León and San Luis Potosí.

Mexicana de Aviación (code MX; ☎ 800-400-8222; www.mexicana.com) More than 50 cities nationwide.

Volaris (☎ 800-786-5274; www.volaris.com.mx) Toluca, Guadalajara, León and Monterrey.

BICYCLE

Cycling on the peninsula's highways can be hair-raising because of the narrow shoulders and speeding traffic. Many routes see a lot of local bicycle traffic, but on some of them you'll often see cyclists, pedestrians and even dogs step off the pavement and wait by the side of the road until traffic passes

The tropical sun can be brutal, but at least the roads are mostly flat. If you're bringing your own bike to tour, be prepared to handle your own repairs.

For details on bike rental, see p68.

Purchase

Of course it's possible to purchase a bicycle in the Yucatán. Indeed, if you plan on staying on the peninsula for months and want to get around by bike or at least exercise on one, purchasing isn't a bad option, as there are many inexpensive models available in the big cities. A good place to pick up a cheap bike is the duty-free Zona Libre between Belize and Mexico; see p147.

BOAT

Ferries run from the mainland to Isla Mujeres (p95), Isla Cozumel (p117) and Isla Holbox (p98).

BUS & COLECTIVO

The Yucatán Peninsula has a good road and bus network, and comfortable, frequent, reasonably priced bus services connect all cities. Most cities and towns have one main bus terminal where all long-distance buses arrive and depart. It may be called the Terminal de Autobuses, Central de Autobuses, Central Camionera or simply La Central (not to be confused with *el centro,* the city center!). If there is no single main terminal, different bus companies will have separate terminals scattered around town.

Baggage is safe if stowed in the bus's baggage hold, but get a receipt for it when you hand it over. Keep your valuables (passport, money etc) on you, and keep them closely protected.

Highway robbery happens very occasionally, usually at night, on isolated stretches of highway. See p252 for details.

Classes
DELUXE

De lujo (deluxe) services, sometimes termed *ejecutivo* (executive), run mainly on the busy routes. They are swift, modern and comfortable, with reclining seats, adequate legroom, air-con, few or no stops, toilets on board (but not necessarily toilet paper), and sometimes drinks or snacks. Deluxe buses usually show movies on video screens, and may offer headphones.

DOMESTIC DEPARTURE TAX

There are two taxes on domestic flights: IVA, the value-added tax (15%), and TUA, an airport tax of about M$85. In Mexico, the taxes are normally included in quoted fares and paid when you buy the ticket. If you bought the ticket outside of Mexico, though, you will have to pay the TUA when you check-in in Mexico.

1ST CLASS

On *primera (1a) clase* (1st-class) buses, standards of comfort are adequate at the very least. The buses usually have air-con and a toilet and they stop infrequently. They always show movies (often bad ones, unless Jean Claude Van Damme is your idea of cinematic glory) for most of the trip.

Bring a sweater or jacket to combat overzealous air-conditioning. As with deluxe buses, you buy your ticket in the bus station before boarding.

2ND CLASS

Segunda (2a) clase (2nd-class) buses serve small towns and villages, and provide cheaper, slower travel on some intercity routes. A few are almost as quick, comfortable and direct as 1st-class buses. Others are old, slow and shabby.

Many 2nd-class services have no ticket office; you just pay your fare to the conductor. These buses tend to take slow, nontoll roads in and out of big cities and will stop anywhere to pick up passengers: if you board midroute you might make some of the trip standing. The small amount of money you save by traveling 2nd class is not usually worth the discomfort or extra journey time entailed, though traveling on these buses is a great way to meet locals and see less-traveled parts of the countryside.

Second-class buses can also be less safe than 1st-class or deluxe buses, for reasons of maintenance, driver standards, or because they are more vulnerable to being boarded by bandits on quiet roads. Out in the remoter areas, however, you'll often find that 2nd-class buses are the only buses available.

Microbuses or '*micros*' are small, usually fairly new, 2nd-class buses with around 25 seats, often running short routes between nearby towns.

TRANSPORTATION

Costs

First-class buses typically cost around M$40 per hour of travel (70km to 80km). Deluxe buses may cost just 10% or 20% more than 1st class, or about 60% more for superdeluxe services such as UNO. Second-class buses cost 10% or 20% less than 1st class. Children under 13 pay half-price on many Mexican long-distance buses, and, if they're small enough to sit on your lap, they will usually go for free.

Reservations

For trips of up to four or five hours on busy routes, you can usually just go to the bus terminal, buy a ticket and head out without much delay. For longer trips, or routes with infrequent service, buy a ticket a day or more in advance. Deluxe and 1st-class bus companies have computerized ticket systems that allow you to select your seat when you buy your ticket.

Seats on deluxe and 1st-class lines such as UNO, ADO and OCC can be booked through **Ticket Bus** (☎ 800-702-8000; www.ticketbus.com.mx), a reservations service with offices in Mérida, Cancún, Cozumel, Campeche and Ciudad del Carmen.

If you pay for a bus ticket in cash, cash refunds of 80% to 100% are available from many bus companies if you return your ticket more than an hour or two before the departure time.

Combi, Colectivo & Truck

On much of the peninsula, a variety of other vehicles, often Volkswagen, Ford or Chevrolet vans, operates shuttle services between some towns, especially on short-haul routes and those linking rural settlements. These vehicles usually leave whenever they are full. Fares are typically a little less than 1st-class buses. *Combi* is often used as a catch-all term for these services regardless of van type, as is *taxi colectivo* (shared taxi) or simply *colectivo*.

More basic than the *combis* are passenger-carrying *camiones* (trucks) and *camionetas* (pickups), usually with benches lining the sides. Standing in the back of a lurching truck with a couple of dozen *campesinos* (farm workers) and their machetes and animals is at least an experience to remember. Fares are similar to 2nd-class bus fares.

CAR & MOTORCYCLE

Driving in Mexico is not as easy as it is north of the border, and rentals are more expensive, but having your own vehicle gives you extra flexibility and freedom.

Drivers should know some Spanish and have basic mechanical knowledge, reserves of patience and access to extra cash for emergencies. Good makes of car to drive in Mexico are Volkswagen, Nissan, General Motors, Chrysler and Ford, which have plants in Mexico and dealers in most big towns. Very big cars are unwieldy on narrow roads. A sedan with a trunk (boot) provides safer storage than a station wagon or hatchback. Mexican mechanics are resourceful, and most repairs can be done quickly and inexpensively, but it still pays to take some spare parts (spare fuel filters are very useful). Tires (including a spare), shock absorbers and suspension should be in good condition. For security, have something to immobilize the steering wheel.

Motorcycling in Mexico is not for the fainthearted. Roads and traffic can be rough, and parts and mechanics hard to come by. The parts you'll most easily find will be for Kawasaki, Honda and Suzuki bikes. Helmets are required by Mexican law.

Fuel

All *gasolina* (gasoline) and diesel fuel in Mexico is sold by the government-owned Pemex (Petróleos Mexicanos). Most towns, even small ones, have a Pemex gas station, and the stations are pretty common on most major roads. In remote areas you should fill up whenever you can.

The gasoline on sale is all *sin plomo* (unleaded). There are two varieties: *magna sin*, roughly equivalent to US regular unleaded, and premium, roughly equivalent to US super unleaded. At the time of research, *magna sin* cost about M$6.70 per liter, and premium about M$7.50. Diesel fuel is widely available at around M$5 per liter. Regular Mexican diesel has a higher sulfur content than US diesel, but there is a *'diesel sin'* with less sulfur.

Pump attendants at gas stations appreciate a tip of M$2 to M$5.

Maps

Mexican signposting can be poor and decent road maps are essential. See p256 for more information on maps.

DRIVING DISTANCES

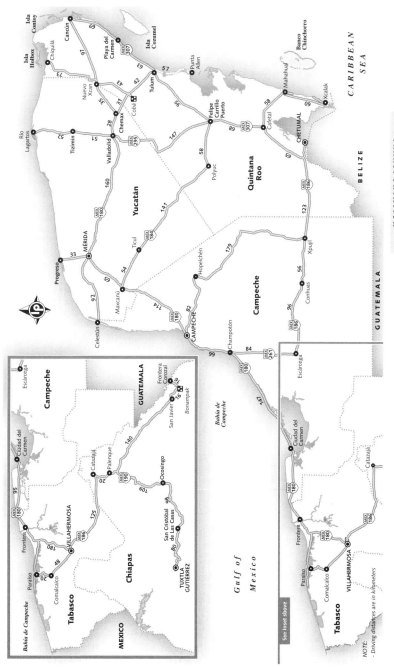

NOTE:
· Driving distances are in kilometers

See inset above

TRANSPORTATION

Rental

Auto rental in the Yucatán is expensive by US or European standards, but is not hard to organize. You can book by internet, phone or in person and pick up cars at city offices, airports and many of the big hotels. You'll save money by booking ahead of time over the internet.

Renters must provide a valid driver's license (your home license is OK), passport and major credit card, and are usually required to be at least 21 (sometimes 25, or if you're aged 21 to 24 you may have to pay a surcharge). Read the small print of the rental agreement. In addition to the basic rental rate, you pay tax and insurance to the rental company, and the full insurance that rental companies encourage can almost double the basic cost. You'll usually have the option of taking liability-only insurance at a lower rate, about M$100 per day. Ask exactly what the insurance options cover: theft and damage insurance may only cover a percentage of costs. It's best to have plenty of liability coverage: Mexican law permits the jailing of drivers after an accident until they have met their obligations to third parties. The complimentary car-rental insurance offered with some US credit cards does not always cover Mexico. Call your card company ahead of time.

Most rental agencies offer a choice between a per-kilometer deal or unlimited kilometers. Local firms may or may not be cheaper than the big international ones. In most places the cheapest car available (often a Volkswagen Beetle) costs M$250 to M$500 a day including unlimited kilometers, insurance and tax. If you rent by the week or month, the per-day cost can come down by 20% to 40%. You can also cut costs by avoiding airport pickups and drop-offs, for which 10% can be added to your total check. The extra charge for drop-off in another city, when available, is usually about M$4 per kilometer.

Some major firms in Mexico:

Alamo (☎ 800-849-8001; www.alamo.com)
Avis (☎ 800-288-8888; www.avis.com.mx)
Budget (☎ 800-700-1700; www.budget.com.mx)
Dollar (☎ 998-886-0222; www.dollar.com)
Europcar (☎ 800-201-2084; www.europcar.com.mx)
Hertz (☎ 800-709-5000; www.hertz.com)
National (☎ 800-716-6625; www.nationalcar.com.mx)
Thrifty (☎ 55-5786-8268; www.thrifty.com.mx)

Motorcycles or scooters are available for rent in a few tourist centers. You're usually required to have a driver's license and credit card. It's advisable to look particularly carefully into insurance arrangements here: some renters do not offer any insurance at all. Note that a locally acquired motorcycle license is not valid under some travel insurance policies.

Road Conditions

Many Mexican highways, even some toll highways, are not up to the standards of US, Canadian or European ones. Still, the main roads are serviceable and fairly fast when traffic is not heavy. Mexicans are not such reckless drivers as they are often supposed to be, and are certainly no worse than their counterparts in southern Europe. Traffic density, poor surfaces and frequent hazards (potholes, speed bumps, animals, bicycles and children) all help to keep speeds down.

Driving on a dark night is best avoided since unlit vehicles, rocks, pedestrians and animals on the roads are common. Also, hijacks and robberies do occur.

In towns and cities and on rural roads, be especially wary of *Alto* (Stop) signs, *topes* (speed bumps) and holes in the road. They are often not where you'd expect, and missing one can cost you a traffic fine or car damage. Speed bumps are also used to slow traffic on highways that pass through built-up areas: they are not always signed, and some of them are severe!

BREAKDOWN ASSISTANCE

The Mexican tourism ministry, Sectur, maintains a network of Ángeles Verdes (Green Angels) – bilingual mechanics in green uniforms and green trucks, who patrol 60,000km of major highways throughout the country daily during daylight hours looking for tourists in trouble. They make minor repairs, change tires, provide fuel and oil, and arrange towing and other assistance if necessary. Service is free; parts, gasoline and oil are provided at cost. If you are near a telephone when your car has problems, you can call its **24-hour hotline** (☎ 078) or contact the network through the national **24-hour tourist-assistance service** (☎ 800-903-9200) in Mexico City. There's a map of the roads it patrols at www.sectur.gob .mx/wb2/sectur/sect_9454_rutas_carretera (in Spanish).

CITY PARKING

It's not usually a good idea to park on the street overnight. If your hotel doesn't have parking, it's best to find a commercial *estacionamiento* (parking lot). These usually cost around M$50 overnight and M$10 per hour during the day.

TOLL ROADS

There are three major toll roads, mostly four-lane, in the Yucatán that connect the major cities. They are generally in much better condition and a lot quicker than the alternative free roads. *Cuotas* (tolls) average about M$10 per 10km.

Road Rules

Drive on the right-hand side of the road.

One-way streets are the rule in cities. Priority at street intersections is indicated by thin black and red rectangles containing white arrows. A black rectangle facing you means you have priority; a red one means you don't. The white arrows indicate the direction of traffic on the cross street; if the arrow points both ways, it's a two-way street.

Speed limits range between 80km/h and 120km/h on open highways (less when highways pass through built-up areas), and between 30km/h and 50km/h in towns and cities. Seat belts are obligatory for all occupants of a car, and children under five must be strapped into safety seats in the rear. Traffic laws and speed limits rarely seem to be enforced on the highways. Obey the rules in the cities so you don't give the police an excuse to demand a 'fine' payable on the spot.

Although less frequent in the Yucatán, there is always the chance that you will be pulled over by traffic police for an imaginary infraction. If this happens, stay calm and polite and don't be in a hurry. You don't have to pay a bribe, and corrupt cops would rather not work too hard to obtain one. You can also ask to see documentation about the law you have supposedly broken, ask for the officer's identification, ask to speak to a superior, and/or note the officer's name, badge number, vehicle number and department (federal, state or municipal). Pay any traffic fines at a police station

and get a receipt, then if you wish to make a complaint head for a state tourist office.

HITCHHIKING

Hitchhiking is never entirely safe in any country in the world, and is not recommended. Travelers who decide to hitch should understand that they are taking a small but potentially serious risk. People who do choose to hitch will be safer if they travel in pairs and let someone know where they are planning to go. A woman traveling alone certainly should not hitchhike in Mexico, and even two women together is not advisable.

However, some people do choose to hitchhike, and it's not an uncommon way of getting to some of the off-the-beaten-track archaeological sites and other places that tend to be poorly served by bus. Keep your wits about you and don't accept a lift if you have any misgivings.

In Mexico it's customary for the hitchhiker to offer to pay for the ride, especially if the ride is in a work or commercial vehicle. As a general rule, offer about M$10 per person for every 30 minutes of the ride but not less than M$20 total and never more than M$100.

TOURS

For details on tours offered by locally based operators, check the destination chapters. Big international operations also offer trips in the region.

Gap Adventures (☎ in the US & Canada 800-708-7761; www.gapadventures.com)

Intrepid Travel (☎ in the US 800-970-7299; www.intrepidtravel.com)

Journey Latin America (☎ in the UK 020-8747-8315; www.journeylatinamerica.co.uk)

TRAINS

Espreso Maya (☎ 999-944-9393; www.expresomaya.com) was the last train service operating in the region, but it is not currently offering service as the rails are being repaired. The high-end trips ran from Palenque to Dzitás (near Chichén Itzá) and to various stops in Yucatán state.

TRANSPORTATION

Health Dr David Goldberg

Travelers to the Yucatán need to be careful chiefly about food- and water-borne diseases, though mosquito-borne infections can also be a problem. Most of these illnesses are not life threatening, but they can certainly impact on your trip. Besides getting the proper vaccinations, it's important that you bring a good insect repellent.

BEFORE YOU GO

Since most vaccines don't produce immunity until at least two weeks after they're given, visit a physician four to eight weeks before departure. Ask your doctor for an International Certificate of Vaccination, which will list vaccinations you've received.

Bring medications in their original containers, clearly labeled. A signed, dated letter from your physician describing all medical conditions and medications, including generic names, is also a good idea. If carrying syringes or needles, be sure to have a physician's letter documenting their necessity.

INSURANCE

Mexican medical treatment is generally inexpensive for common diseases and minor treatment, but if you suffer some serious medical problem, you may want to find a private hospital or fly out for treatment. Travel insurance typically covers the costs but make sure the policy includes such things as ambulances and emergency flights home. Some US health insurance policies stay in effect (at least for a limited time) if you travel abroad, but it's worth checking exactly what you'll be covered for in Mexico. For people whose medical insurance or national health systems don't extend to Mexico (which includes most non-Americans) a travel policy is advisable. Check the website of **Lonely Planet** (www.lonelyplanet.com/travel _services) for more information.

You may prefer a policy that pays medical costs directly rather than requiring you to pay on the spot and claim later. If you have to claim later, keep all documentation. Some policies ask you to call collect to a center in your home country, where an immediate assessment of your problem is made. Some policies offer lower and higher medical-expense options; the higher ones are chiefly for countries such as the USA, which have extremely high medical costs. There is a wide variety of policies; check the small print.

VACCINATIONS

The only required vaccination for Mexico is yellow fever, and that's only if you're arriving from a yellow fever–infected country in Africa or South America (including Guatemala). However, a number of vaccines are recommended: see table below. Rabies injections are only recommended for those who may have contact with animals and won't have access to immediate health care.

Vaccine	Dosage
hepatitis A	1 dose before trip; booster 6-12 months later
typhoid	4 capsules by mouth, 1 taken every other day
hepatitis B	long-term travelers in close contact with the local population; 3 doses over 6-month period
rabies	3 doses over 3-4 week period
tetanus-diphtheria	1 dose lasts 10 years
measles	1 dose

MEDICAL CHECKLIST

- Antibiotics
- Antidiarrheal drugs (eg loperamide)
- Acetaminophen/paracetamol (Tylenol) or aspirin
- Anti-inflammatory drugs (eg ibuprofen)
- Antihistamines (for hay fever and allergic reactions)
- Antibacterial ointment (eg Bactroban) for cuts and abrasions
- Adhesive or paper tape
- Bandages, gauze, gauze rolls
- DEET-containing insect repellent for the skin
- Iodine tablets (for water purification)
- Oral rehydration salts
- Permethrin-containing insect spray for clothing, tents and bed nets
- Pocket knife
- Scissors, safety pins, tweezers
- Steroid cream or cortisone (for poison ivy and other allergic rashes)
- Sunscreen
- Syringes and sterile needles (with doctor's letter)
- Thermometer

INTERNET RESOURCES

There is a wealth of travel health advice on the internet. For further information, the website of **Lonely Planet** (www.lonelyplanet.com) is a good place to start. The World Health Organization publishes a superb book called *International Travel and Health,* which is revised annually and is available online at no cost at www.who.int/ith. Another website of general interest is **MD Travel Health** (www.mdtravelhealth.com), which provides complete travel health recommendations for every country, updated daily, also at no cost.

FURTHER READING

For further information, see *Healthy Travel Central & South America,* also from Lonely Planet. If you're traveling with children, Lonely Planet's *Travel with Children* may be useful. The *ABC of Healthy Travel,* by E Walker et al, and *Medicine for the Outdoors,* by Paul S Auerbach, are other valuable resources.

IN TRANSIT

DEEP VEIN THROMBOSIS (DVT)

Blood clots may form in the legs (deep vein thrombosis) during plane flights, chiefly because of prolonged immobility. The longer the flight, the greater the risk. Though most blood clots are reabsorbed uneventfully, some may break off and travel through the blood vessels to the lungs, where they could cause complications that are life-threatening.

The chief symptom of DVT is swelling or pain of the foot, ankle or calf, usually but not always on just one side. When a blood clot travels to the lungs, it may cause chest pain and difficulty breathing. Travelers with any of these symptoms should immediately seek medical attention.

To prevent the development of DVT on long flights you should walk about the cabin, perform isometric compressions of the leg muscles (ie contract the leg muscles while sitting), drink plenty of fluids, and avoid alcohol and tobacco.

JET LAG & MOTION SICKNESS

Jet lag is common when crossing more than five time zones, resulting in insomnia, fatigue, malaise or nausea. To avoid jet lag try drinking plenty of nonalcoholic fluids and eating light meals. Upon arrival, get exposure to natural sunlight and readjust your schedule (for meals, sleep etc) as soon as possible.

Antihistamines such as dimenhydrinate (Dramamine) and meclizine (Antivert, Bonine) are usually the first choice for treating motion sickness. Their main side effect is drowsiness. A herbal alternative is ginger, which works like a charm for some people.

IN MEXICO

AVAILABILITY & COST OF HEALTH CARE

There are a number of first-rate clinics in Cancún (p74). In general, private facilities offer better health care, though at greater cost, than public hospitals. Adequate medical care is available in other major cities of the region, but facilities in rural areas may be limited.

Many doctors and hospitals expect payment in cash, regardless of whether you have travel health insurance. If you develop a life-threatening medical problem, you'll probably want to be evacuated to a country with state-of-the-art medical care. Be sure you have insurance to cover this (see opposite).

HEALTH

CHILDREN & PREGNANT WOMEN

In general, it's safe for children and pregnant women to go to Mexico. However, because some of the vaccines listed earlier are not approved for children and pregnant women, these travelers should be particularly careful not to drink tap water or consume any questionable food or beverage. Also, when traveling with children, make sure they're up to date on all routine immunizations. It's sometimes appropriate to give children some of their vaccines a little early before visiting a developing nation. You should discuss this with your pediatrician. If pregnant, bear in mind that should a complication such as premature labor develop while abroad, the quality of medical care may not be comparable to that in your home country.

Since yellow-fever vaccine is not recommended for pregnant women or children less than nine months old, if you are arriving from a country with yellow fever, obtain a waiver letter, preferably written on letterhead stationery and bearing the stamp used by official immunization centers to validate the International Certificate of Vaccination.

Mexican pharmacies are identified by a green cross and a 'Farmacia' sign. Most are well stocked and the pharmacists well trained. Reliable pharmacy chains include Sanborns, Farmacia Guadalajara, Benavides and Farmacia Fenix. To find an after-hours pharmacy, look in the local newspaper, ask your hotel concierge, or check the front door of a local pharmacy, which will often post the name of a nearby pharmacy that is open after hours.

INFECTIOUS DISEASES
Malaria
Malaria occurs in every country in Central America, including parts of Mexico. It's transmitted by mosquito bites, usually between dusk and dawn. The main symptom is high spiking fevers, which may be accompanied by chills, sweats, headache, body aches, general weakness, vomiting or diarrhea. Severe cases may involve the central nervous system and lead to seizures, confusion, coma and death.

Taking malaria pills is strongly recommended when visiting rural areas. For Mexico, the first-choice malaria pill is chloroquine, taken once weekly in a dosage of 500mg, starting one to two weeks before arrival and continuing through the trip and for four weeks after departure. Chloroquine is safe, inexpensive and highly effective. Side effects are typically mild. Severe reactions are uncommon.

Protecting yourself against mosquito bites is just as important as taking malaria pills (see p280), as no pills are 100% effective.

If you develop a fever after returning home, see a physician, as malaria symptoms may not occur for months. It can be diagnosed by a simple blood test.

Dengue Fever
Dengue fever is a viral infection found throughout Central America. In Mexico, th risk is greatest along the Gulf Coast, especiall from July to September. Dengue is transmitte by Aedes mosquitoes, which bite preferen tially during the day and are usually found close to human habitations, often indoors They breed primarily in artificial water con tainers, such as barrels, cans, cisterns, meta drums, plastic containers and discarded tires As a result, dengue is especially common i urban environments.

Dengue usually causes flu-like symptoms including fever, muscle aches, joint pains headaches, nausea and vomiting, often fol lowed by a rash. The body aches may b quite uncomfortable, but most cases resolv uneventfully in a few days. Severe cases usu ally occur in children under 15 years who ar experiencing their second dengue infection.

There is no specific treatment for den gue fever, except to take analgesics such a acetaminophen/paracetamol (Tylenol) an drink plenty of fluids. Severe cases may re quire hospitalization. There is no vaccine. Th cornerstone of prevention is insect protectio measures (see p280).

Hepatitis A
Hepatitis A occurs throughout Centra America. It's a viral infection of the live usually acquired by ingestion of contami nated water, food or ice, though it may als be acquired by direct contact with infecte persons. The illness occurs worldwide, bu the incidence is higher in developing nations Symptoms may include fever, malaise, jaun dice, nausea, vomiting and abdominal pain

Most cases resolve uneventfully, though hepatitis A occasionally causes severe liver damage. There is no treatment.

The vaccine for hepatitis A is extremely safe and highly effective. If you get a booster six to 12 months later, it lasts for at least 10 years. You should get it before you go to Mexico. Because the safety of hepatitis A vaccine has not been established for pregnant women or children aged under two, they should instead be given a gammaglobulin injection.

Hepatitis B

Like hepatitis A, hepatitis B is a liver infection that occurs worldwide but is more common in developing nations. Unlike hepatitis A, the disease is usually acquired by sexual contact or by exposure to infected blood, generally through blood transfusions or contaminated needles. The vaccine is recommended only for long-term travelers (on the road more than six months) who expect to live in rural areas or have close physical contact with the local population. Additionally, the vaccine is recommended for anyone who anticipates sexual contact with locals or a possible need for medical, dental or other treatments while abroad, especially if a need for transfusions or injections is expected.

Hepatitis B vaccine is safe and highly effective. However, a total of three injections is necessary to establish full immunity. Several countries added hepatitis B vaccine to the list of routine childhood immunizations in the 1980s, so many young adults are already protected.

Typhoid Fever

Typhoid fever is caused by ingestion of food or water contaminated by *Salmonella typhi*. Fever occurs in virtually all cases. Other symptoms may include headache, malaise, muscle aches, dizziness, loss of appetite, nausea and abdominal pain. Either diarrhea or constipation may occur. Possible complications include intestinal perforation, intestinal bleeding, confusion, delirium or (rarely) coma.

Unless you expect to take all your meals in major hotels and restaurants, the typhoid vaccine is a good idea. It's usually given orally, but is also available as an injection. Neither vaccine is approved for use for children aged under two.

The drug of choice for typhoid fever is usually a quinolone antibiotic, such as ciprofloxacin (Cipro) or levofloxacin (Levaquin), which many travelers carry for treatment of travelers' diarrhea.

Rabies

Rabies is a viral infection of the brain and spinal cord that is almost always fatal without treatment. The rabies virus is carried in the saliva of infected animals and is typically transmitted through an animal bite, though contamination of any break in the skin with infected saliva may result in rabies. Rabies occurs in all Central American countries. Most cases in Mexico are related to dog bites, but bats and other wild species remain sources of infection.

The rabies vaccine is safe, but a full series requires three injections and is quite expensive. Those at high risk of rabies, such as animal handlers and spelunkers (cave explorers), should certainly get the vaccine, as well as people traveling to remote areas away from appropriate medical care. The treatment for a possibly rabid bite consists of rabies vaccine with rabies immune globulin. It's effective, but must be given promptly.

See p281 for what to do if bitten or scratched by an animal.

Cholera

Cholera is an intestinal infection acquired through ingestion of contaminated food or water. The main symptom is profuse, watery diarrhea, which may be so severe that it causes life-threatening dehydration. The key treatment is drinking oral rehydration solution. Antibiotics are also given, usually tetracycline or doxycycline, though quinolone antibiotics, such as ciprofloxacin and levofloxacin are also effective.

Only a handful of cases have been reported in Mexico over the last few years. The cholera vaccine is no longer recommended.

Other Infections

Gnathostomiasis is a parasite acquired by eating raw or undercooked freshwater fish, including ceviche, a popular lime-marinated fish salad. The chief symptom is intermittent, migratory swellings under the skin, sometimes associated with joint pains, muscle pains or gastrointestinal problems. The symptoms may not begin until many months after exposure.

Leishmaniasis occurs in the mountains and jungles of all Central American countries.

HEALTH

The infection is transmitted by sand flies. Leishmaniasis may be limited to the skin, causing slowly growing ulcers over exposed parts of the body. The disease may be particularly severe in those with HIV. There is no vaccine for leishmaniasis. To protect yourself from sand flies, follow the same precautions as for mosquitoes (below), except that netting must be finer mesh (at least 18 holes to the linear inch).

Brucellosis is an infection occurring in domestic and wild animals that may be transmitted to humans through direct animal contact or by consumption of unpasteurized dairy products from infected animals. Symptoms may include fever, malaise, depression, loss of appetite, headache, muscle aches and back pain. Complications can include arthritis, hepatitis, meningitis and endocarditis (heart valve infection).

Typhus may be transmitted by lice in scattered pockets of the country.

HIV/AIDS has been reported in all Central American countries. Be sure to use condoms for all sexual encounters.

TRAVELERS' DIARRHEA

To prevent diarrhea, avoid tap water unless it has been boiled, filtered or chemically disinfected (eg by iodine tablets); only eat fresh fruits or vegetables if cooked or peeled; be wary of dairy products that might contain unpasteurized milk; and be very selective when eating food from street vendors.

If you develop diarrhea, be sure to drink plenty of fluids, preferably an oral rehydration solution containing lots of salt and sugar. A few loose stools don't require treatment, but if you start having more than four or five stools a day, you should start taking an antibiotic (usually a quinolone drug) and an antidiarrheal agent (eg loperamide). If diarrhea is bloody or persists for more than 72 hours or is accompanied by fever, shaking chills or severe abdominal pain, you should seek medical attention.

ENVIRONMENTAL HAZARDS & TREATMENT
Mosquito Bites

To prevent mosquito bites, wear long sleeves, long pants, hats and shoes (rather than sandals). Bring along a good insect repellent, preferably one containing DEET, which should be applied to exposed skin and clothing, but not to the eyes, mouth, cuts, wounds or irritated skin. Products containing lower concentrations of DEET are as effective, but for shorter periods of time. In general, adults and children over 12 years should use preparations containing 25% to 35% DEET, which usually last about six hours. Children between two and 12 years should use preparations containing no more than 10% DEET, applied sparingly, which will usually last about three hours. Neurological toxicity has been reported from DEET, especially in children, but appears to be extremely uncommon and generally related to overuse. Don't use DEET-containing compounds on children under two years.

Insect repellents containing certain botanical products, including eucalyptus oil and soybean oil, are effective but last only 1½ to two hours. Where there is a high risk of malaria, use DEET-containing repellents. Products based on citronella are not effective.

For additional protection, apply permethrin to clothing, shoes, tents and bed nets. Permethrin treatments are safe and remain effective for at least two weeks, even when items are laundered. Permethrin should not be applied directly to the skin.

Don't sleep with the window open unless there is a screen. If sleeping outdoors or in accommodations that allows entry of mosquitoes, use a bed net treated with permethrin, with edges tucked in under the mattress. The mesh size should be less than 1.5mm. Alternatively, use a mosquito coil, which will fill the room with insecticide through the night. Repellent-impregnated wristbands are not effective.

Tick Bites

To protect yourself from tick bites, follow the same precautions as for mosquitoes, except that boots are preferable to shoes, with pants tucked in. Be sure to perform a thorough tick check at the end of each day. You'll generally need the assistance of a friend or mirror for a full examination. Remove ticks with tweezers, grasping them firmly by the head. Insect repellents based on botanical products (see left) have not been adequately studied for insects other than mosquitoes and cannot be recommended to prevent tick bites.

Water

Tap water is generally not safe to drink. Vigorous boiling for one minute is the most effective means of water purification.

Another option is to disinfect water with iodine pills. Instructions are usually provided and should be carefully followed. Or you can add 2% tincture of iodine to one quart or liter of water (five drops to clear water, 10 drops to cloudy water) and let stand for 30 minutes. If the water is cold, a longer time may be required. The taste of iodinated water can be improved by adding vitamin C (ascorbic acid). Don't drink iodinated water for more than a few weeks. Pregnant women, those with a history of thyroid disease and those allergic to iodine should not drink iodinated water.

Numerous water filters are on the market. Those with smaller pores (reverse osmosis filters) provide the best protection, but they are relatively large and are readily plugged by debris. Those with somewhat larger pores (microstrainer filters) are ineffective against viruses, although they do remove other organisms. Manufacturers' instructions must be carefully followed.

Sun & Heat

To protect yourself from excessive sun exposure, you should stay out of the midday sun, wear sunglasses and a wide-brimmed hat, and apply sunscreen with SPF 15 or higher, providing both UVA and UVB protection. Sunscreen should be applied to all exposed parts of the body approximately 30 minutes before sun exposure and be reapplied after swimming or vigorous activity.

Drink plenty of fluids and avoid strenuous exercise when the temperature is high. Heat exhaustion is characterized by dizziness, weakness, headache, nausea or profuse sweating. Salt tablets or rehydration salts may help, but fluids, rest and shade are essential.

Animal Bites

Do not attempt to pet, handle or feed any animal, with the exception of domestic animals known to be free of any infectious disease. Most animal injuries are directly related to a person's attempt to touch or feed the animal.

Any bite or scratch by a mammal, including bats, should be promptly and thoroughly cleansed with large amounts of soap and water, followed by application of an antiseptic, such as iodine or alcohol. Contact the local health authorities immediately for possible postexposure treatment, whether or not you've been immunized against rabies. It may also be advisable to start an antibiotic, since wounds caused by animal bites and scratches frequently become infected. One of the newer quinolones, such as levofloxacin (Levaquin), which many travelers carry in case of diarrhea, would be an appropriate choice.

SNAKE & SCORPION BITES

Venomous snakes in the Yucatán generally do not attack without provocation, but may bite humans who accidentally come too close. Coral snakes are somewhat retiring and tend not to bite humans unless considerably provoked.

In the event of a venomous snake bite, place the victim at rest, keep the bitten area immobilized and move them immediately to the nearest medical facility. Avoid using tourniquets, which are no longer recommended.

Scorpions are a problem in many states. If stung, you should immediately apply ice or cold packs, immobilize the affected body part and go to the nearest emergency room. To prevent stings, be sure to inspect and shake out clothing, shoes and sleeping bags before use, and wear gloves and protective clothing when working around piles of wood or leaves.

HEALTH

Language

The predominant language of Mexico is Spanish. Mexican Spanish is unlike Castilian Spanish (the language of much of Spain) in a few respects: in Mexico the Castilian lisp has more or less disappeared, the *vosotros* form (informal plural 'you') isn't used and numerous indigenous words have been adopted.

There are more than 30 Maya dialects still spoken today. Chiapas has eight dialects, with Tzeltal, Tzotzil and Chol being the most widely spoken. Yucatec Maya is the predominant indigenous language of the Yucatán. For some background information and a few handy words and phrases in the language, see p288.

Travelers in cities, towns and larger villages can almost always find someone who speaks at least some English. All the same, it is advantageous and courteous to know at least a few words and phrases in Spanish. Mexicans will generally respond much more positively if you attempt to speak to them in their own language.

It's easy enough to pick up some basic Spanish, and for those who want to learn the language in greater depth, courses are available in the Yucatán itself (p251). You can also study using books, records and tapes before you leave home. These resources are often available for loan from public libraries. Evening or college courses are also an excellent way to get things started.

For a more comprehensive guide to the Spanish of Mexico, get a copy of Lonely Planet's *Mexican Spanish Phrasebook*. For words and phrases that will come in handy when dining, see p55.

SPANISH

PRONUNCIATION
Vowels

a	as in 'father'
e	as in 'met'
i	as in 'marine'
o	as in 'or' (without the 'r' sound)
u	as in 'rule'; the 'u' is not pronounced after **q** and in the letter combinations **gue** and **gui**, unless it's marked with a diaeresis (eg *argüir*), in which case it's pronounced as English 'w'
y	at the end of a word or when it stands alone, it's pronounced as the Spanish **i** (eg *ley*); between vowels within a word it's as the 'y' in 'yonder'

Consonants

As a rule, Spanish consonants resemble their English counterparts. The exceptions are listed below.

While the consonants **ch**, **ll** and **ñ** are generally considered distinct letters, **ch** and **ll** are now often listed alphabetically under **c** and **l** respectively. The letter **ñ** is still treated as a separate letter and comes after **n** in dictionaries.

b	similar to English 'b,' but softer; referred to as 'b larga'
c	as in 'celery' before **e** and **i**; otherwise as English 'k'
ch	as in 'church'
d	as in 'dog,' but between vowels and after **l** or **n**, the sound is closer to the 'th' in 'this'
g	as the 'ch' in the Scottish *loch* before **e** and **i** ('kh' in our guides to pronunciation); elsewhere, as in 'go'

h	invariably silent. If your name begins with this letter, listen carefully if you're waiting for public officials to call you.
j	harsh and breathy, as the 'ch' in 'loch' (written as 'kh' in our guides to pronunciation)
ll	varies between the 'y' in 'yes' and the 'lli' in 'million'
ñ	as the 'ni' in 'onion'
r	a short **r** except at the beginning of a word, and after **l**, **n** or **s**, when it's often rolled
rr	very strongly rolled (not reflected in the pronunciation guides)
v	similar to English 'b,' but softer; referred to as 'b corta'
x	as in 'taxi,' and sometimes as 'sh,' especially by indigenous people
z	as the 's' in 'sun'

Word Stress

In general, words ending in vowels or the letters **n** or **s** have stress on the next-to-last syllable, while those with other endings have stress on the last syllable. Thus *vaca* (cow) and *caballos* (horses) both carry stress on the next-to-last syllable, while *ciudad* (city) and *infeliz* (unhappy) are both stressed on the last syllable.

Written accents will almost always appear in words that don't follow the rules above, eg *sótano* (basement), *porción* (portion).

GENDER & PLURALS

In Spanish, nouns are either masculine or feminine, and there are a few rules to help determine gender (with the mandatory exceptions, of course). Feminine nouns generally end with -**a** or with the groups -**ción**, -**sión** or -**dad**. Other endings typically signify a masculine noun. Endings for adjectives also change to agree with the gender of the noun they modify (masculine/feminine -**o**/-**a**). Where both masculine and feminine forms are included in this language guide, they are separated by a slash, with the masculine form first, eg *perdido/a*.

If a noun or adjective ends in a vowel, the plural is formed by adding **s** to the end. If it ends in a consonant, the plural is formed by adding **es** to the end.

ACCOMMODATIONS

I'm looking for ...
Estoy buscando ...   e·*stoy* boos·*kan*·do ...

Where is ...?
¿Dónde hay ...?   don·de ai ...
  a cabin/cabana
  una cabaña   oo·na ca·*ba*·nya
  a camping ground
  un área para acampar oon *a*·re·a *pa*·ra a·kam·*par*
  a guesthouse
  una pensión   oo·na pen·*syon*
  a hotel
  un hotel   oon o·*tel*
  a lodging house
  una casa de huéspedes oo·na ka·sa de wes·pe·des
  a posada
  una posada   oo·na po·sa·da
  a youth hostel
  un albergue juvenil oon al·*ber*·ge khoo·ve·*neel*

MAKING A RESERVATION

To ...	*A ...*
From ...	*De ...*
Date	*Fecha*
I'd like to book ...	*Quisiera reservar ...* (see under 'Accommodations' for bed and room options)
in the name of ...	*en nombre de ...*
for the nights of ...	*para las noches del ...*
credit card ...	*tarjeta de crédito ...*
number	*número*
expiry date	*fecha de vencimiento*
Please confirm ...	*Puede confirmar ...*
availability	*la disponibilidad*
price	*el precio*

Are there any rooms available?
¿Hay habitaciones libres?
ay a·bee·ta·syon·es *lee*·bres

| **I'd like a ...** | *Quisiera una* | kee·*sye*·ra oo·na |
room.	*habitación ...*	a·bee·ta·*syon* ...
double	*doble*	do·ble
single	*individual*	een·dee·vee·*dwal*
twin	*con dos camas*	kon dos ka·mas

| **How much is it** | *¿Cuánto cuesta* | kwan·to kwes·ta |
per ...?	*por ...?*	por ...
night	*noche*	no·che
person	*persona*	per·so·na
week	*semana*	se·ma·na

full board	*pensión completa*	pen·*syon* kom·*ple*·ta
private/shared bathroom	*baño privado/ compartido*	ba·nyo pree·*va*·do/ kom·par·*tee*·do

too expensive	*demasiado caro*	de·ma·*sya*·do *ka*·ro
cheaper	*más económico*	mas e·ko·*no*·mee·ko
discount	*descuento*	des·*kwen*·to

Does it include breakfast?
¿Incluye el desayuno? een·*kloo*·ye el de·sa·*yoo*·no
May I see the room?
¿Puedo ver la *pwe*·do ver la
habitación? a·bee·ta·*syon*
I don't like it.
No me gusta. no me *goos*·ta
It's fine. I'll take it.
Está bien. La tomo. es·ta byen la *to*·mo
I'm leaving now.
Me voy ahora. me voy a·*o*·ra

CONVERSATION & ESSENTIALS

When approaching a stranger for information you should always extend a greeting, and use only the polite form of address, especially with the police and public officials. Young people may be less likely to expect this, but it's best to stick to the polite form unless you're quite sure you won't offend by using the informal mode. The polite form is used in all cases in this guide; where options are given, the form is indicated by the abbreviations 'pol' and 'inf.'

The use of *por favor* (please) and *gracias* (thank you) are second nature to most Mexicans and a recommended tool in your travel kit.

Hi.	*Hola.*	*o*·la (inf)
Hello.	*Buen día.*	bwe·n *dee*·a
Good morning.	*Buenos días.*	bwe·nos *dee*·as
Good afternoon.	*Buenas tardes.*	bwe·nas *tar*·des
Good evening/ night.	*Buenas noches.*	bwe·nas *no*·ches
Goodbye.	*Adiós.*	a·*dyos*
See you soon.	*Hasta luego.*	as·ta *lwe*·go
Yes.	*Sí.*	see
No.	*No.*	no
Please.	*Por favor.*	por fa·*vor*
Thank you.	*Gracias.*	*gra*·syas
Many thanks.	*Muchas gracias.*	moo·chas *gra*·syas
You're welcome.	*De nada.*	de *na*·da
Apologies.	*Perdón.*	per·*don*
May I?	*Permiso.*	per·*mee*·so
Excuse me.	*Disculpe.*	dees·*kool*·pe

(used before a request or when apologizing)

What's your name?
¿Cómo se llama usted? *ko*·mo se *ya*·ma oo·*sted* (pol)
¿Cómo te llamas? *ko*·mo te *ya*·mas (inf)

How are things?
¿Qué tal? ke tal
My name is ...
Me llamo ... me *ya*·mo ...
It's a pleasure to meet you.
Mucho gusto. *moo*·cho *goos*·to
The pleasure is mine.
El gusto es mío. el *goos*·to es *mee*·o
Where are you from?
¿De dónde es/eres? de *don*·de es/*er*·es (pol/inf)
I'm from ...
Soy de ... soy de ...
Where are you staying?
¿Dónde está alojado? *don*·de es·ta a·lo·*kha*·do (pol)
¿Dónde estás alojado? *don*·de es·tas a·lo·*kha*·do (inf)
May I take a photo?
¿Puedo sacar una foto? *pwe*·do sa·*kar* oo·na *fo*·to

SIGNS

Entrada	Entrance
Salida	Exit
Información	Information
Abierto	Open
Cerrado	Closed
Prohibido	Prohibited
Comisaria	Police Station
Servicios/Baños	Toilets
Hombres/Varones	Men
Mujeres/Damas	Women

DIRECTIONS
How do I get to ...?
¿Cómo llego a ...? *ko*·mo *ye*·go a ...
Is it far?
¿Está lejos? es·*ta le*·khos
Go straight ahead.
Siga/Vaya derecho. see·ga/va·ya de·*re*·cho
Turn left.
De vuelta a la izquierda. de *vwel*·ta a la ees·*kyer*·da
Turn right.
De vuelta a la derecha. de *vwel*·ta a la de·*re*·cha
Can you show me (on the map)?
¿Me lo podría señalar me lo po·*dree*·a se·nya·*lar*
(en el mapa)? (en el *ma*·pa)

north	*norte*	*nor*·te
south	*sur*	soor
east	*este*	*es*·te
west	*oeste*	o·*es*·te
here	*aquí*	a·*kee*
there	*ahí*	a·*ee*
avenue	*avenida*	a·ve·*nee*·da
block	*cuadra*	*kwa*·dra
street	*calle/paseo*	*ka*·lye/pa·*se*·o

EMERGENCIES

Help!	¡Socorro!	so-ko-ro
Fire!	¡Fuego!	fwe-go
I've been robbed.	Me han robado.	me an ro-ba-do
Go away!	¡Déjeme!	de-khe-me
Get lost!	¡Váyase!	va-ya-se

Call ...!	¡Llame a ...!	ya-me a
the police	la policía	la po-lee-see-a
a doctor	un médico	oon me-dee-ko
an ambulance	una ambulancia	oo-na am-boo-lan-sya

It's an emergency.
Es una emergencia.   es oo-na e-mer-khen-sya
Could you help me, please?
¿Me puede ayudar,   me pwe-de a-yoo-dar
por favor?   por fa-vor
I'm lost.
Estoy perdido/a.   es-toy per-dee-do/a
Where are the toilets?
¿Dónde están los baños?   don-de stan los ba-nyos

HEALTH

I'm sick.
Estoy enfermo/a.   es-toy en-fer-mo/a
I need a doctor.
Necesito un doctor.   ne-se-see-to oon dok-tor
Where's the hospital?
¿Dónde está el hospital?   don-de es-ta el os-pee-tal
I'm pregnant.
Estoy embarazada.   es-toy em-ba-ra-sa-da
I've been vaccinated.
Estoy vacunado/a.   es-toy va-koo-na-do/a

I have ...	Tengo ...	ten-go ...
diarrhea	diarrea	dya-re-a
nausea	náusea	now-se-a
a headache	un dolor de cabeza	oon do-lor de ka-be-sa
a cough	tos	tos

I'm allergic to ...	Soy alérgico/a a ...	soy a-ler-khee-ko/a a ...
antibiotics	los antibióticos	los an-tee-byo-tee-kos
nuts	las nueces	las nwe-ses
peanuts	los cacahuates	los ka-ka-khwa-tes

I'm ...	Soy ...	soy ...
asthmatic	asmático/a	as-ma-tee-ko/a
diabetic	diabético/a	dya-be-tee-ko/a
epileptic	epiléptico/a	e-pee-lep-tee-ko/a

LANGUAGE DIFFICULTIES

Do you speak (English)?
¿Habla/Hablas (inglés)?   a-bla/a-blas (een-gles) (pol/inf)
Does anyone here speak English?
¿Hay alguien que hable   ai al-gyen ke a-ble
inglés?   een-gles
I (don't) understand.
(No) Entiendo.   (no) en-tyen-do
How do you say ...?
¿Cómo se dice ...?   ko-mo se dee-se ...
What does ...mean?
¿Qué significa ...?   ke seeg-nee-fee-ka ...

Could you please ...?
¿Puede ..., por favor?   pwe-de ... por fa-vor
repeat that
repetirlo   re-pe-teer-lo
speak more slowly
hablar más despacio   a-blar mas des-pa-syo
write it down
escribirlo   es-kree-beer-lo

NUMBERS

1	uno	oo-no
2	dos	dos
3	tres	tres
4	cuatro	kwa-tro
5	cinco	seen-ko
6	seis	says
7	siete	sye-te
8	ocho	o-cho
9	nueve	nwe-ve
10	diez	dyes
11	once	on-se
12	doce	do-se
13	trece	tre-se
14	catorce	ka-tor-se
15	quince	keen-se
16	dieciséis	dye-see-says
17	diecisiete	dye-see-sye-te
18	dieciocho	dye-see-o-cho
19	diecinueve	dye-see-nwe-ve
20	veinte	vayn-te
21	veintiuno	vayn-tee-oo-no
30	treinta	trayn-ta
31	treinta y uno	trayn-ta ee oo-no
40	cuarenta	kwa-ren-ta
50	cincuenta	seen-kwen-ta
60	sesenta	se-sen-ta
70	setenta	se-ten-ta
80	ochenta	o-chen-ta
90	noventa	no-ven-ta
100	cien	syen
101	ciento uno	syen-to oo-no
200	doscientos	do-syen-tos

LANGUAGE

1000	*mil*	meel
5000	*cinco mil*	seen·ko meel

SHOPPING & SERVICES
I'd like to buy ...
Quisiera comprar ...   kee·*sye*·ra kom·*prar* ...
I'm just looking.
Sólo estoy mirando.   so·lo es·*toy* mee·*ran*·do
May I look at it?
¿Puedo verlo/la?   *pwe*·do *ver*·lo/la
How much is it?
¿Cuánto cuesta?   *kwan*·to *kwes*·ta
That's too expensive for me.
Es demasiado caro   es de·ma·*sya*·do *ka*·ro
   para mí.   *pa*·ra mee
Could you lower the price?
¿Podría bajar un poco   po·*dree*·a ba·*khar* oon *po*·ko
   el precio?   el *pre*·syo
I don't like it.
No me gusta.   no me *goos*·ta
I'll take it.
Lo llevo.   lo *ye*·vo

Do you accept ...?
¿Aceptan ...?   a·*sep*·tan ...
   American dollars
   dólares americanos   do·la·res a·me·ree·*ka*·nos
   credit cards
   tarjetas de crédito   tar·*khe*·tas de *kre*·dee·to
   traveler's checks
   cheques de viajero   che·kes de vya·*khe*·ro

less	*menos*	me·nos
more	*más*	mas
large	*grande*	gran·de
small	*pequeño/a*	pe·*ke*·nyo/a

I'm looking	*Estoy buscando ...*	es·toy boos·*kan*·do
for (the) ...		
ATM	*el cajero*	el ka·*khe*·ro
	automático	ow·to·to·*ma*·tee·ko
bank	*el banco*	el *ban*·ko
bookstore	*la librería*	la lee·bre·*ree*·a
exchange office	*la casa de*	la *ka*·sa de
	cambio	*kam*·byo
general store	*la tienda*	la *tyen*·da
laundry	*la lavandería*	la la·van·de·*ree*·a
market	*el mercado*	el mer·*ka*·do
pharmacy/	*la farmacia*	la far·*ma*·sya
chemist		
post office	*la oficina*	la o·fee·*see*·na
	de correos	de ko·*re*·os
supermarket	*el supermercado*	el soo·per· mer·*ka*·do
tourist office	*la oficina de*	la o·fee·*see*·na de
	turismo	too·rees·mo

What time does it open/close?
¿A qué hora abre/cierra?
a ke o·ra a·bre/sye·ra
I want to change some money/traveler's checks.
Quisiera cambiar dinero/cheques de viajero.
kee·sye·ra kam·byar dee·ne·ro/che·kes de vya·khe·ro
What is the exchange rate?
¿Cuál es el tipo de cambio?
kwal es el *tee*·po de *kam*·byo
I want to call ...
Quisiera llamar a ...
kee·*sye*·ra lya·*mar* a ...

airmail	*correo aéreo*	ko·*re*·o a·*e*·re·o
letter	*carta*	*kar*·ta
registered (mail)	*certificado*	ser·tee·fee·*ka*·do
stamps	*timbres*	*teem*·bres

TIME & DATES
What time is it?
¿Qué hora es?   ke *o*·ra es
It's one o'clock.
Es la una.   es la *oo*·na
It's seven o'clock.
Son las siete.   son las *sye*·te
Half past two.
Dos y media.   dos ee *me*·dya

midnight	*medianoche*	me·dya·*no*·che
noon	*mediodía*	me·dyo·*dee*·a
now	*ahora*	a·*o*·ra
today	*hoy*	oy
tonight	*esta noche*	es·ta *no*·che
tomorrow	*mañana*	ma·*nya*·na
yesterday	*ayer*	a·*yer*

Monday	*lunes*	*loo*·nes
Tuesday	*martes*	*mar*·tes
Wednesday	*miércoles*	*myer*·ko·les
Thursday	*jueves*	*khwe*·ves
Friday	*viernes*	*vyer*·nes
Saturday	*sábado*	*sa*·ba·do
Sunday	*domingo*	do·*meen*·go

January	*enero*	e·*ne*·ro
February	*febrero*	fe·*bre*·ro
March	*marzo*	*mar*·so
April	*abril*	a·*breel*
May	*mayo*	*ma*·yo
June	*junio*	*khoo*·nyo
July	*julio*	*khoo*·lyo
August	*agosto*	a·*gos*·to
September	*septiembre*	sep·*tyem*·bre
October	*octubre*	ok·*too*·bre
November	*noviembre*	no·*vyem*·bre
December	*diciembre*	dee·*syem*·bre

TRANSPORTATION
Public Transportation

What time does	¿A qué hora ...	a ke o·ra ...
... leave/arrive?	sale/llega?	sa·le/ye·ga
the boat	el barco	el bar·ko
the bus (city)	el camión	el ka·myon
the bus (intercity)	el autobús	el ow·to·boos
the minibus	el combi/	el kom·bee/
	minibús	mee·nee·boos
the plane	el avión	el a·vyon
the airport	el aeropuerto	el a·e·ro·pwer·to
the bus station	la estación de	la es·ta·syon de
	autobuses	ow·to·boo·ses
the bus stop	la parada de	la pa·ra·da de
	autobuses	ow·to·boo·ses
a luggage locker	un casillero	oon ka·see·ye·ro
the ticket office	la taquilla	la ta·kee·ya
A ticket to ...,	Un boleto a ...,	oon bo·le·to a ...
please.	por favor.	por fa·vor
What's the fare	¿Cuánto cuesta	kwan·to kwes·ta
to ...?	hasta ...?	a·sta ...
student's	de estudiante	de es·too·dyan·te
1st class	primera clase	pree·me·ra kla·se
2nd class	segunda clase	se·goon·da kla·se
single/one way	viaje sencillo	vee·a·khe sen·see·yo
round-trip	redondo	re·don·do
taxi	taxi	tak·see

Private Transportation

I'd like to	Quisiera	kee·sye·ra
hire a/an ...	rentar ...	ren·tar ...
4WD	un cuatro por	oon kwa·tro por
	cuatro	kwa·tro
car	un coche	oon ko·che
motorbike	una moto	oo·na mo·to
bicycle	bicicleta	bee·see·kle·ta
hitchhike	pedir aventón	pe·deer a·ven·ton
pickup (ute)	pickup	pee·kop
truck	camión	ka·myon

Where's a gas/petrol station?
¿Dónde hay una   don·de ai oo·na
gasolinera?   ga·so·lee·ne·ra
How much is a liter of gasoline/petrol?
¿Cuánto cuesta el litro   kwan·to kwes·ta el lee·tro
de gasolina?   de ga·so·lee·na

Please fill it up.
Lleno, por favor.   ye·no por fa·vor

I'd like (100) pesos worth.
Quiero (cien) pesos.   kye·ro (syen) pe·sos

diesel	diesel	dee·sel
gas/petrol	gasolina	ga·so·lee·na
unleaded	gasolina sin	ga·so·lee·na seen
	plomo	plo·mo
oil	aceite	a·say·te

> **ROAD SIGNS**
> Though Mexico mostly uses the familiar international road signs, you should be prepared to encounter these others as well:
>
> | Acceso | Entrance |
> | Estacionamiento | Parking |
> | Ceda el Paso | Give Way |
> | Curva Peligrosa | Dangerous Curve |
> | Despacio | Slow |
> | Desviación | Detour |
> | Dirección Única | One-Way |
> | No Adelantar | No Overtaking |
> | No Hay Paso | Road Closed |
> | Peligro | Danger |
> | Prepare Su Cuota | Have Toll Ready |
> | Prohibido Aparcar/ | No Parking |
> | No Estacionar | |
> | Prohibido el Paso | No Entry |
> | Topes | Speed Bumps |

Is this the road to (...)?
¿Por aquí se va a (...)?
por a·kee se va a (...)
Where do I pay?
¿Dónde se paga?
don·de se pa·ga
I need a mechanic/tow truck.
Necesito un mecánico/remolque.
ne·se·see·to oon me·ka·nee·ko/re·mol·ke
Is there a garage near here?
¿Hay un garaje cerca de aquí?
ai oon ga·ra·khe ser·ka de a·kee
The car has broken down (in ...).
El coche se se descompuso (en ...).
el ko·che se des·kom·poo·so (en ...)
I have a flat tire.
Tengo una llanta ponchada.
ten·go oo·na yan·ta pon·cha·da
I've run out of gas/petrol.
Me quedé sin gasolina.
me ke·de seen ga·so·lee·na
I've had an accident.
Tuve un accidente.
too·ve oon ak·see·den·te

YUCATEC MAYA

Yucatec Maya, spoken primarily in Yucatán, Campeche and Quintana Roo, and in the northern and western parts of Belize, is part of the Amerind family of Native American languages. This means that Yucatec Maya (commonly called 'Yucatec' by scholars and 'Maya' by local speakers) is related to many languages spoken in the southeastern United States, as well as many of the indigenous languages of far-off California and Oregon (eg Costanoan, Klamath and Tsimshian). Yucatec is just one of 28 modern Mayan languages but it probably has the largest number of speakers, estimated at 900,000 people.

You can hear Yucatec spoken in the markets and occasionally by hotel staff in cities throughout the peninsula. If you really want to hear Yucatec spoken by monolingual Maya (and learn a lot about Maya culture besides!), you must travel to some of the peninsula's more remote villages. Maya speakers will not assume that you know any of their language. If you attempt to say something in Maya, people will usually respond quite favorably. A useful learning resource is the online Maya dictionary (www.famsi.org/mayawriting/dictionary .htm). So give it a try!

PRONUNCIATION

Mayan vowels are similar to English vowels but the consonants can be a bit tricky.

c	always hard, as the 'k' in 'kick'
j	always an aspirated 'h' sound. So *abaj* is pronounced ah·*bahh*; to get the '*hh*' sound, take the 'h' sound from 'half' and put it at the end of ah·*bahh*.
u	as 'oo' except at the start or end of a word, in which case it's like English 'w.' Thus *baktun* is 'bak·*toon*,' but *Uaxactún* is 'wa·shak·*toon*' and *ahau* is is 'a·*haw*'.
x	as the 'sh' in 'she'; a shushing sound

Mayan glottalized consonants (ie those followed by an apostrophe: **b'**, **ch'**, **k'**, **p'**, **t'**) are similar to normal consonants, but are pronounced more forcefully and 'explosively.' However, an apostrophe following a vowel

> **VILLAGE GREETINGS**
>
> The most polite thing to do in a village setting is to greet the male head of the household first. If you have trouble figuring out who this is, simply try to greet the oldest man present. Men should try to speak to other men or possibly older women. Approaching young women might give people a mistaken idea of your intentions. Women should try to greet the eldest man (as above), and any of the women you think are your age or older.

signifies a glottal stop (the sound between the two syllables in 'uh-oh') – it doesn't signify a more forceful vowel. See 'Tongue Twisters – A Difficult Decision' (p41) for more information on the glottal stop.

Maya is a tone language, which means that some words take on different meanings when pronounced with a high tone or a low tone. For example, *aak* said with a high tone means 'turtle,' but 'grass' or 'vine' when said with a low tone.

In many Mayan place names the stress falls on the last syllable. When these names are written out, Spanish rules for indicating stress are often followed (see p283). This practice varies; in this book we have tried to include accents as much as possible. Here are some pronunciation examples:

Abaj Takalik	a·*bah* ta·ka·*leek*
Acance	a·kan·*ke*
Dzibilchaltún	dzee·beel·chal·*toon*
Hopelchén	ho·pel·*chen*
Oxcutzkab	osh·kootz·*kab*
Pacal	pa·*kal*
Pop	pope
Tikal	tee·*kal*
Uaxactún	wa·shak·*toon*
Xcaret	shka·*ret*
Yaxchilán	yash·chee·*lan*

USEFUL WORDS & PHRASES

Spanish borrowings tend to be stressed differently in Yucatec Maya, eg *amigo* (Spanish for 'friend') is pronounced 'a·*mee*·go' in Spanish and '*aa*·mee·go' in Yucatec.

Hello.
   Hola.   *o*·la

Good day.
  Buenos días.   bwe·nos dee·as
Good afternoon.
  Buenas tardes.   bwe·nos tar·des
Good evening.
  Buenas noches.   bwe·nos no·ches

You might also hear someone saying simply *buenos* to stand in for the full greeting; this isn't considered as improper to Maya speakers as it is for many Spanish speakers.

How are you?
  Bix a beel?   beesh a bail?
  Bix yanikech?   beesh yaw·nee·*kech* (less
                          formal)
OK/Well.
  Maalob.   ma·lobe
Bye/See you tomorrow.
  Hasta saamal.   as·ta sa·mal
Goodbye.
  Pa'atik kin bin.   pa'a·teek keen been
Thank you.
  Gracias/Dios Bo'otik.   gra·see·as/dyose boe'o·teek
Yes.
  Haa/He'ele.   haa/he'e·le
    (Maya speakers often reiterate what is said to them,
    instead of saying 'yes'; eg 'Are you going to the store?'
    'I'm going.')
No.
  Ma'.   ma'
What's your name?
  Bix a k'aaba?   beesh a k'aa·ba?
My name is ...
  In kaabae' ...   een ka·ba·e'
I understand English.
  Kin na'atik ingles.   keen na·'a·teek een·gles

I don't speak Maya.
  Ma tin na'atik mayat'aani.
  ma' teen na·'a·teek ma·ya·taa·nee

Also available from Lonely Planet:
Mexican Spanish Phrasebook

Do you speak Spanish?
  Teche', ka t'aanik wa castellano t'aan?
  te·che' ka t'a·neek wa ca·stay·ya·no t'an?
Who is the head of the house?
  Maax u pool u nail?
  mash oo pole oo na·heel?

Where is the ...?
  Tu'ux yaan le ...   too·'oosh yan le ...
  bathroom
  baño   ba'·nyo
  road to ...
  u be ti' ...   u be tee ...
  hotel
  hotel   o·tel
  doctor
  médico   me·dee·ko
  Comisario
  Comis   ko·mees

How much is ...?
  Baux ...?   ba·hoosh ...?
  this one
  lela'   le·la'
  that one
  lelo'   le·lo'

  expensive
  ko'o   ko·'o
  not expensive
  mix ko'oi   meesh ko·'o·hi
  pretty
  ki'ichpam   kee·'eech·pam
I'm hungry.
  Wiihen.   wee·hen
It's (very) tasty.
  (Hach) Ki'.   (hach) kee'
I want to drink water.
  Tak in wukik ha'.   tak een woo·keek ha'

1	un peel	oom pail
2	ka peel	ka pail
3	ox peel	osh pail

When counting animate objects, like people, replace *peel* with *tuul* (pronounced 'tool'). Beyond three, use Spanish numbers.

Glossary

Words specific to food, restaurants and eating are listed on p55. See also the Language chapter, p288.

Ah Tz'ib – Maya scribes. They penned the Chilam Balam and still practice their craft today.

alux (s), **aluxes** (pl) – Maya 'leprechauns,' benevolent 'little people'

Ángeles Verdes – 'Green Angels'; bilingual mechanics in green trucks who patrol major highways, offering breakdown assistance

ayuntamiento – municipal government; commonly seen as H Ayuntamiento (Honorable Ayuntamiento)

baluartes – bastions or bulwarks

barrio – district, neighborhood

billete – bank note (unlike in Spain, where it's a ticket)

boleto – ticket (bus, train, museum etc)

cacique – indigenous chief; also used to describe a provincial warlord or strongman

cafetería – literally 'coffee-shop,' it refers to any informal restaurant with waiter service; it is not usually a self-service restaurant

cajero automático – Automated Teller Machine (ATM)

camión (s), **camiones** (pl) – truck; bus

camioneta – pickup

campechanos – citizens of Campeche

campesinos – countryfolk, farm workers

casa de cambio – currency-exchange office

casetas de teléfono – call offices where an on-the-spot operator connects the call for you; often shortened to *casetas*

cenote – a deep limestone sinkhole containing water

cerveza – beer

Chac – Maya god of rain

chac-mool – Maya sacrificial stone sculpture

chenes – name for cenotes (limestone sinkholes) in the Chenes region

chilangos – natives of Mexico City

chultún (s), **chultunes** (pl) – Maya cistern found at Puuc archaeological sites south of Mérida

cocina – cookshop (literally 'kitchen'), a small, basic restaurant usually run by one woman, often located in or near a municipal market; also seen as *cocina económica* (economical kitchen) or *cocina familiar* (family kitchen); see also *lonchería*

colectivo – literally, 'shared,' a car, van (VW combi, Ford or Chevrolet) or minibus that picks up and drops off passengers along its set route; also known as *taxi colectivo*

combi – a catch-all term used for taxi, van and minibus services regardless of vehicle type

comida corrida – set meal, meal of the day

conquistador – explorer-conqueror of Latin America from Spain

correo, correos – post office

costera – waterfront avenue

criollo – a person of pure Spanish descent born in Spanish America

cuota – toll road

daños a terceros – third-party car insurance

de lujo – deluxe class of bus service

DNI – Derecho para No Inmigrante; nonimmigrant fee charged to all foreign tourists and business travelers visiting Mexico

ejido – communal landholding, though laws now allow sale of *ejido* land to outside individuals

encomenderos – owners of Maya lands divided into large estates

encomienda – a grant made to a conquistador, consisting of labor by or tribute from a group of indigenous people; the conquistador was supposed to protect and convert them, but usually treated them as little more than slaves

feria – fair or carnival, typically occurring during a religious holiday

gala terno – women's straight, white, square-necked dress with an embroidered overyoke and hem, worn over an underskirt, which sports an embroidered strip near the bottom; fancier than a *huipil* and often accompanied by a hand-knitted shawl

gringo/a – male/female US or Canadian visitor to Latin America (sometimes applied to any visitor of European heritage); can be used derogatorily but more often is a mere statement of fact

gruta – cave, grotto

guardaequipaje – room for storing luggage (eg in a bus terminal)

guayabera – man's thin fabric shirt with pockets and appliquéd designs on the front, over the shoulders and down the back; often worn in place of a jacket and tie

hacendado – landowner

hacienda – estate; Hacienda (capitalized) is the Treasury Department

henequen – agave fiber used to make rope, grown particularly around Mérida

h-menob – Maya shaman still practicing their trade in the Yucatán today.

huipil (s), **huipiles** (pl) – indigenous women's sleeveless white tunic, usually intricately and colorfully embroidered

iglesia – church

INAH – Instituto Nacional de Arqueología e Historia; the body in charge of most ancient sites and some museums

INM – Instituto Nacional de Migración (National Immigration Institute)

Itzamná – lord of the heavens; a popular figure on the wooden panels of contemporary architecture

IVA – *impuesto al valor agregado* or 'ee-bah,' a 15% value-added tax added to many items in Mexico

Ixchel – Maya goddess of the moon and fertility

jarana – a folkloric dance that has been performed by Yucatecans for centuries

jipijapa – an alternative name for panama hats (which are made from *jipijapa* palm fronds)

Kukulcán – Maya name for the Aztec-Toltec plumed serpent Quetzalcóatl

ladino – also known as *mestizo*, a person of mixed indigenous and European blood'

lagunas – small lakes, lagoons

larga distancia – long-distance; usually refers to telephones, often seen on signs outside *casetas* as 'Lada'

lavandería – laundry; a *lavandería automática* is a coin-operated laundry

lista de correos – general delivery in Mexico; literally 'mail list,' the list of addressees for whom mail is being held, displayed in the post office

lonchería – from English 'lunch'; a simple restaurant that may in fact serve meals all day (not just lunch), often seen near municipal markets. See also *cocina*.

lotería – Mexico's version of bingo

machismo – maleness, masculine virility or bravura

malecón – waterfront boulevard

manzana – apple; also a city block. A *supermanzana* is a large group of city blocks bounded by major avenues. Cancún uses *manzana* and *supermanzana* numbers as addresses.

maquiladora – export-only factory paying workers around M$40 per day

mariachi – small ensemble of Mexican street musicians; strolling mariachi bands often perform in restaurants

más o menos – more or less, somewhat

méridanos – citizens of Mérida

mestizo – also known as *ladino*, a person of mixed indigenous and European blood; the word now more commonly means 'Mexican'

metate – flattish stone on which corn is ground with a cylindrical stone roller

Montezuma's revenge – Mexican version of 'Delhi-belly' or travelers' diarrhea

mudéjar – Moorish architectural style

mul – mound in Maya. Often used to describe pyramid sites.

mulatto – a person of mixed white and black ancestry

municipios – townships

na – thatched Maya hut

nohoch – 'big' in Maya. The word is used by everybody around the peninsula to describe large men.

nortes – relatively cold storms bringing wind and rain from the north

Nte – abbreviation for *norte* (north), used in street names

oficina de correos – post office; also called *correo* or *correos*

Ote – abbreviation for *oriente* (east), used in street names

palacio de gobierno – building housing the executive offices of a state or regional government

palacio municipal – town or city hall; municipal government

palapa – thatched, palm-leaf-roofed shelter usually with open sides

Pemex – government-owned petroleum extraction, refining and retailing monopoly

pisto – colloquial Maya term for money

plateresque – 'silversmith-like'; the architectural style of the Spanish renaissance (16th century), rich in decoration

Popol Vuh – painted Maya book containing sacred legends and stories; equivalent to the Bible

porfiriato – the name given to the era of Porfirio Diaz's 35-year rule as president-dictator (1876–1911), preceding the Mexican Revolution

PRI – Partido Revolucionario Institucional (Institutional Revolutionary Party); the controlling force in Mexican politics for much of the 20th century

primera (1a) clase – 1st class of bus service

Quetzalcóatl – plumed serpent god of the Aztecs and Toltecs

retablo – altarpiece (usually an ornate gilded, carved wooden decoration in a church)

ría – estuary

río – river

roofcomb – a decorative stonework lattice atop a Maya pyramid or temple

sacbé (s), **sacbeob** (pl) – ceremonial limestone avenue or path between great Maya cities

segunda (2a) clase – 2nd class of bus service
Semana Santa – Holy Week, the week from Palm Sunday to Easter Sunday; Mexico's major holiday period
stela (s), **stelae** (pl) – standing stone monument, usually carved
supermercado – supermarket, ranging from a corner store to a large, US-style supermarket
sur – south; often seen in street names
temescal – bathhouse, sweat lodge
templo – in Mexico, a church; anything from a wayside chapel to a cathedral
tequila – clear, distilled liquor produced, like pulque and mezcal, from the maguey cactus
Tex-Mex – Americanized version of Mexican food
típico – typical or characteristic of a region; particularly used to describe food
topes – speed bumps, sometimes indicated by a highway sign depicting a row of little bumps

torito – a vivacious song that evokes the fervor of a bullfight
tranvía – tram or motorized trolley

vaquería – a traditional Yucatecan party where couples dance in unison to a series of songs; the parties are often held in town halls or on haciendas

viajero/a – male/female traveler
vulcanizadora – automobile tire repair shop

War of the Castes – bloody 19th-century Maya uprising in the Yucatán

Xibalbá – in Maya religious belief, the secret world or underworld

xtabentún – a traditional Maya spirit in the Yucatán; an anise-flavored liqueur made by fermenting honey

The Authors

GREG BENCHWICK

A former commissioning editor at Lonely Planet, Greg turned down a life of high-walled cubicle insanity to get back to his writing and rambling roots. He's rumbled in the jungles of Peru and Costa Rica, walked across Spain on the Camino de Santiago, and challenged the peaks of Alaska and his native Colorado. He specializes in Latin American travel, sustainable travel and new media, and has written more than a dozen guidebooks on travel in Latin America. When he's not on the road, he develops his new-media companies www.monjomedia.com and www.soundtraveler.com. Someday he dreams of being a media magnate or a philosopher warrior poet, whichever comes first.

CONTRIBUTING AUTHORS

Beth Kohn is someday going to make her San Francisco neighbors revolt. Why must she blast those *ranchera* and *norteño* songs while cooking dinner? And is it really necessary for her to sing along? But after spending time in Mexico for more than 20 years, she has a fine appreciation for green jungles with sopping waterfalls and noisy animals, as well as all the soulful songs the *combi* drivers play. A freelance writer and photographer, her last trip south was to check in on the world's tallest falls for Lonely Planet's *Venezuela*. You can see more of her work at www.bethkohn.com. Beth wrote the Tabasco & Chiapas chapter for Lonely Planet's *Mexico* guide, which Greg condensed for this book.

Eduardo Douglas reviewed our history section, adding his unique historic insight to our coverage. He received his PhD (2000) in the History of Art from the University of Texas, Austin, and is currently an assistant professor in the Department of Art History, University of Wisconsin, Milwaukee. Professor Douglas is currently at work on a study of mid-16th-century indigenous pictorial history manuscripts from Tetzcoco, Mexico.

Kevin Graham updated our Mahahual section in the Quintana Roo chapter months after Hurricane Dean razed the town, ensuring we had the most up-to-date information. Kevin fell in love with the Costa Maya in 2003. Scuba diving is a passion, and he lives just a few kilometers south of Mahahual now. He owns and operates www.costamayaliving.com.

David Goldberg, MD wrote the Health chapter. David completed his training in internal medicine and infectious diseases at Columbia-Presbyterian Medical Center in New York City, where he has also served as voluntary faculty. At present he is an infectious diseases specialist in Scarsdale, New York, and the editor-in-chief of the website MDTravelHealth.com.

LONELY PLANET AUTHORS

Why is our travel information the best in the world? It's simple: our authors are independent, dedicated travelers. They don't research using just the internet or phone, and they don't take freebies, so you can rely on their advice being well researched and impartial. They travel widely, to all the popular spots and off the beaten track. They personally visit thousands of hotels, restaurants, cafés, bars, galleries, palaces, museums and more – and they take great pride in getting all the details right, and telling it how it is. Think you can do it? Find out how at lonelyplanet.com.

Mauricio Velázquez de León was born in Mexico City, where he was given boiled chicken feet and toasted corn tortillas to sooth his teething pains. Since then he has developed an enormous curiosity for food. As a journalist, he has worked for the Mexican newspaper *Reforma, Críticas* magazine, the New York daily *El Diario/La Prensa,* and the magazines *Escala, Viceversa, Cinemania* and *Travel Guide*. His food writing has been published in *Saveur* and *Gourmet* magazines, the website Leite's Culinaria and Lonely Planet guidebooks. Like anybody else with a heartbeat, Mauricio has a blog: Josefina's Kitchen (http://josefina -food.blogspot.com/). He currently lives in New York City, working as an editor, writer and full-time father of twin toddlers, whose teething pains have been soothed using toasted corn tortillas. According to the internet, his favorite *taquería* (taco shop) is 3370km (2094 miles) from his current home. Mauricio wrote the Food & Drink chapter for this book.

Behind the Scenes

THIS BOOK

The 4th edition of this guidebook was written by Greg Benchwick. The previous edition, known simply as *Yucatán*, was written by Daniel C Schechter and Ray Bartlett. This book was commissioned in Lonely Planet's Oakland office, and produced in Melbourne by the following:

Commissioning Editors Greg Benchwick, Catherine Craddock

Coordinating Editors Chris Girdler, Kristin Odijk, Carolyn Bain

Coordinating Cartographer Jolyon Philcox

Coordinating Layout Designer Katherine Marsh

Senior Editors Katie Lynch, Helen Christinis

Managing Cartographer Alison Lyall

Managing Layout Designers Adam McCrow, Celia Wood

Assisting Editor Kate Evans

Assisting Cartographer Sam Sayer

Assisting Layout Designer Jim Hsu

Cover Designer Pepi Bluck

Language Content Coordinator Quentin Frayne

Project Manager Chris Love

Thanks to Sin Choo, Andrea Dobbin, Eoin Dunlevy, Mark Griffiths, Stacey Kersting, Lisa Knights, Malcolm O'Brien

THANKS
GREG BENCHWICK

My unending love and appreciation goes to my lovely, intelligent and spirited girlfriend, Alejandra Castañeda. Not only was she a great support and travel companion through much of this book's research, she also played a huge role in looking up obscure statistics, correcting my 'gringo-fied' Spanish and keeping things on an even keel. Of course, I'd also like to thank my family – Mom, Dad, George, Cara and Bryan – for all their support over these years.

The people of the Yucatán Peninsula are amazing, and I wish to thank each and every person I met along my way. And I especially want to thank: Beth Kohn (who penned the Tabasco & Chiapas chapter), Vanessa Trava (who showed me around Cancún and penned the feature on her favorite restaurants); Laura Alonzo (who wrote about her Mérida picks, and gave me the grand tour of Mérida at about 100 miles an hour in her car); Dr Eduardo Douglas (a Mexican art historian from the University of Wisconsin, who reviewed the History section); Kevin Graham (who runs www.costamayaliving.com and was

THE LONELY PLANET STORY

Fresh from an epic journey across Europe, Asia and Australia in 1972, Tony and Maureen Wheeler sat at their kitchen table stapling together notes. The first Lonely Planet guidebook, *Across Asia on the Cheap,* was born.

Travelers snapped up the guides. Inspired by their success, the Wheelers began publishing books to Southeast Asia, India and beyond. Demand was prodigious, and the Wheelers expanded the business rapidly to keep up. Over the years, Lonely Planet extended its coverage to every country and into the virtual world via lonelyplanet.com and the Thorn Tree message board.

As Lonely Planet became a globally loved brand, Tony and Maureen received several offers for the company. But it wasn't until 2007 that they found a partner whom they trusted to remain true to the company's principles of traveling widely, treading lightly and giving sustainably. In October of that year, BBC Worldwide acquired a 75% share in the company, pledging to uphold Lonely Planet's commitment to independent travel, trustworthy advice and editorial independence.

Today, Lonely Planet has offices in Melbourne, London and Oakland, with over 500 staff members and 300 authors. Tony and Maureen are still actively involved with Lonely Planet. They're traveling more often than ever, and they're devoting their spare time to charitable projects. And the company is still driven by the philosophy of *Across Asia on the Cheap*: 'All you've got to do is decide to go and the hardest part is over. So go!'

kind enough to update the Mahahual section months after Hurricane Dean passed through town); Lucy Gallagher (Marine Projects Director from Mexiconservación, who penned a short boxed text for our Environment chapter); and Raul from Nómadas Youth Hostel in Mérida (for being an invaluable source of information).

The editors, cartographers and everybody that works behind the scenes at Lonely Planet are amazing – especially Catherine Craddock-Carrillo, my ever-patient, ever-incisive commissioning editor. And, a big shout out goes to the great writers that penned the previous editions of this book.

OUR READERS

Many thanks to the travelers who used the last edition and wrote to us with helpful hints, useful advice and interesting anecdotes:

Audrey Bélanger, Sharon Berardino, Luis Cabrera, Patricia Catchpole, George Dinkelmeyer, Pat Dixon, Bob Feidler, Ribca Fisher, Justin Fried, Alison Gill, Betsy Husband, John Ives, Zoe Jones, Eunice Kim, Eliane Menghetti, James Mitchell, Alfieri Morales, Alexandra Papineau, Samantha Peterson, E R, Andrew Robinson, Lisa Ros, Piotr Sobczak, Diego Sotelo, Venita De Souza, Colleen Suche, Jack Walsh, Audrey Wittenburg

ACKNOWLEDGMENTS

Many thanks to the following for the use of their content:

Globe on title page ©Mountain High Maps 1993 Digital Wisdom, Inc.

Internal photographs: p5 Joe McBride/Corbis; p9 (#7) blickwinkel/Alamy; p9 (#4) Danita Delimont/Alamy; p8 (#3) Stock Connection Blue/Alamy; p8 (#1), p10 (#1) Eric Nathan/Alamy; p12 (#1) Sami Sarkis Underwater/Alamy; p13 (#5) Bob Krist/Corbis; p11 (#3) Diana Bier San Cristobal Native/Alamy; p10 (#4) David Sanger Photography/Alamy; p10 Emmanuel LATTES/Alamy; p7 (#5) Diana Bier Valladolid Cenote Dzitnup/Alamy; p7 (#1) Chris A Crumley/Alamy; p6, p15 (#6) M Timothy O'Keefe/Alamy; p15 (#1) Martin Norris/Alamy. All other photographs by Lonely Planet Images, and by Pascale Beroujon p8 (#8); Witold Skrypczak p13 (#4), p14 (#5); Uros Ravbar p12 (#3); Greg Elms p11; Jon Davison p14 (#4); Greg Johnston p15 (#7), p16.

All images are the copyright of the photographers unless otherwise indicated. Many of the images in this guide are available for licensing from Lonely Planet Images: www.lonelyplanetimages.com.

BEHIND THE SCENES

Index

GreenDex

GOING GREEN

The following listings have been selected by the authors because they demonstrate an active sustainable-tourism policy. Some are involved in conservation or environmental education, while others are owned and operated by local and indigenous operators, thereby maintaining and preserving the regional identity and culture.

We have also included several DIY listings. We believe this style of content fits wholly within the sustainable-tourism model. Rather than further perpetuate the 'Lonely Planet trail,' we are increasingly encouraging our readers to go beyond the pages of our guidebooks. By heading to places far off the Lonely Planet trail, you are supporting grass-roots tourism development, encouraging local communities to retain their culture and language, and of course, providing locals with a viable alternative from fleeing to Cancún and the other tourist megadraws to eke out a hard-won living.

We want to keep developing our sustainable-tourism content. If you think we've omitted somewhere that should be listed here, or if you disagree with our choices, email us at talk2us @lonelyplanet.com.au. For more information about sustainable tourism and Lonely Planet, see www.lonelyplanet.com/responsibletravel.

12am	1am	2am	3am	4am	5am	6am	7am	8am	9am	10am	11am	12pm

ARCTIC OCEAN

International Date Line
Mon | Sun

CHUKCHI SEA

Russia

Alaska (US)
3am

BEAUFORT SEA

Banks Is (Can)
Victoria Is (Can)

Queen Elizabeth Is (Can)

Ellesmere Is (Can)

BAFFIN BAY

9am Greenland (Denmark)

11am

GREENLAND SEA

NORWEGIAN SEA

Iceland

NORTH SEA

United Kingdom

Ireland

BERING SEA

GULF OF ALASKA

2am

4am

5am

Baffin I. (Can)

HUDSON BAY

Canada

6am

LABRADOR SEA

8am

7am

8.30am

NORTH ATLANTIC OCEAN

Azores (Port)

Portugal

Spain

Morocco

Canary Is (Sp)

NORTH PACIFIC OCEAN

1am
Midway Is (US)

Hawaii (US)

Mexico

GULF OF MEXICO

Cuba

The Bahamas

Haiti

CARIBBEAN SEA

Eastern Caribbean Islands

Bermuda (UK)

Cape Verde

Mauritania

Mali

Senegal

Burkina Faso

Guinea

Liberia

Ghana

GULF OF GUINEA

Guatemala
Nicaragua

Panama

Venezuela

Guyana

Suriname

Colombia

EQUATOR

Kiribati

Samoa

2.30am

Tahiti (Fr)
French Polynesia (Fr)

Cook Is (NZ)

2am

Pitcairn Is (UK)

Easter Is (Chile)

Galapagos Is (Ecuador)

Ecuador

Peru

7am

8am

Brazil

9am

Bolivia

Paraguay

Ascension (UK)

SOUTH ATLANTIC OCEAN

Tonga

12am

1am

Chile

Uruguay

Argentina

SOUTH PACIFIC OCEAN

New Zealand

12.45am
Chatham Is (NZ)

Falkland Is (UK)

Tristan da Cunha (UK)

Gough Is (UK)

South Georgia & South Sandwich Is (UK)

Bouvet Is (Norway)

12am	1am	2am	3am	4am	5am	6am	7am	8am	9am	10am	11am	12pm

| 12pm | 1pm | 2pm | 3pm | 4pm | 5pm | 6pm | 7pm | 8pm | 9pm | 10pm | 11pm | 12am |

Mon | Sun

International Date Line

Svalbird (Norway)

Zemlya Frantsa-Josifa (Russia)

Severnaya Zemlya (Russia)

Novaya Zemlya (Russia)

KARA SEA

Novosibirskie Ostrovo (Russia)

LAPTEV SEA

EAST SIBERIAN SEA

BARENTS SEA

Sweden 1pm

2pm Finland

Norway

3pm

Estonia

Denmark

Latvia
Lithuania

Germany

Poland Belarus

France Austria

Ukraine

4pm

5pm

6pm

7pm

9pm

11pm

12am

10pm

SEA OF OKHOTSK

BERING SEA

3am

2am

Italy

Romania

Bulgaria

Kazakhstan

Russia

Mongolia

NORTH PACIFIC OCEAN

Greece Turkey

4pm

Uzbekistan

Kyrgyzstan

North Korea

Tunisia MEDITERRANEAN SEA

Syria

Turkmenistan

China

South Korea Japan

Algeria

2pm

Iran 3.30pm

Iraq

Afghanistan 4.30pm

Tibet (China)

8pm

EAST CHINA SEA

Libya

Egypt

Pakistan

5pm

Nepal 5.45 pm

Taiwan

1pm

Niger

Saudi Arabia

UAE

India

6.30 pm Myanmar

Laos

Northern Mariana Is (US)

9pm

Marshall Is (US)

12am

Chad

Oman

4pm

5.30 pm

Thailand

Eritrea Yemen

Vietnam

Philippines

Nigeria

Sudan

ARABIAN SEA

BAY OF BENGAL

Federated States of Micronesia 11am

Kiribati

Central African Republic

Ethiopia

3pm

6pm

Sri Lanka

5.30pm

Malaysia

Palau

Congo

Somalia

Maldives

Nauru EQUATOR

Gabon 1pm

Congo (Zaire)

Kenya

Indonesia

Papua New Guinea

Solomon Is

SOUTH PACIFIC OCEAN

Tanzania

Seychelles 4pm

6.30 pm Cocos (Keeling) Is (Aust)

East Timor

Vanuatu

Angola

Zambia

Malawi

Madagascar

Mauritius

New Caledonia (Fr)

Fiji

Namibia

Zimbabwe

Botswana Mozambique

Reunion (Fr)

INDIAN OCEAN

9.30 pm

Australia

11.30 pm

10.30 pm Norfolk Is (Aust)

Lord Howe Is (Aust)

South Africa

New Zealand

Prince Edward Is (S. Africa)

French Southern & Antarctic Territories (Fr) thu

TASMAN SEA

SOUTHERN OCEAN

Heard & McDonald Is (Aust)

| 12pm | 1pm | 2pm | 3pm | 4pm | 5pm | 6pm | 7pm | 8pm | 9pm | 10pm | 11pm | 12am |

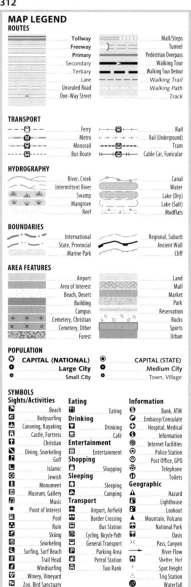

LONELY PLANET OFFICES

Australia
Head Office
Locked Bag 1, Footscray, Victoria 3011
☎ 03 8379 8000, fax 03 8379 8111
talk2us@lonelyplanet.com.au

USA
150 Linden St, Oakland, CA 94607
☎ 510 250 6400, toll free 800 275 8555
fax 510 893 8572
info@lonelyplanet.com

UK
2nd fl, 186 City Rd,
London EC1V 2NT
☎ 020 7106 2100, fax 020 7106 2101
go@lonelyplanet.co.uk

Published by Lonely Planet Publications Pty Ltd
ABN 36 005 607 983

© Lonely Planet Publications Pty Ltd 2008

© photographers as indicated 2008

Cover photograph: Parque Chankanaab, Isla Cozumel, Yucatán Peninsula, Mexico, Michael Friedel/Austral Press. Many of the images in this guide are available for licensing from Lonely Planet Images: www.lonelyplanetimages.com.